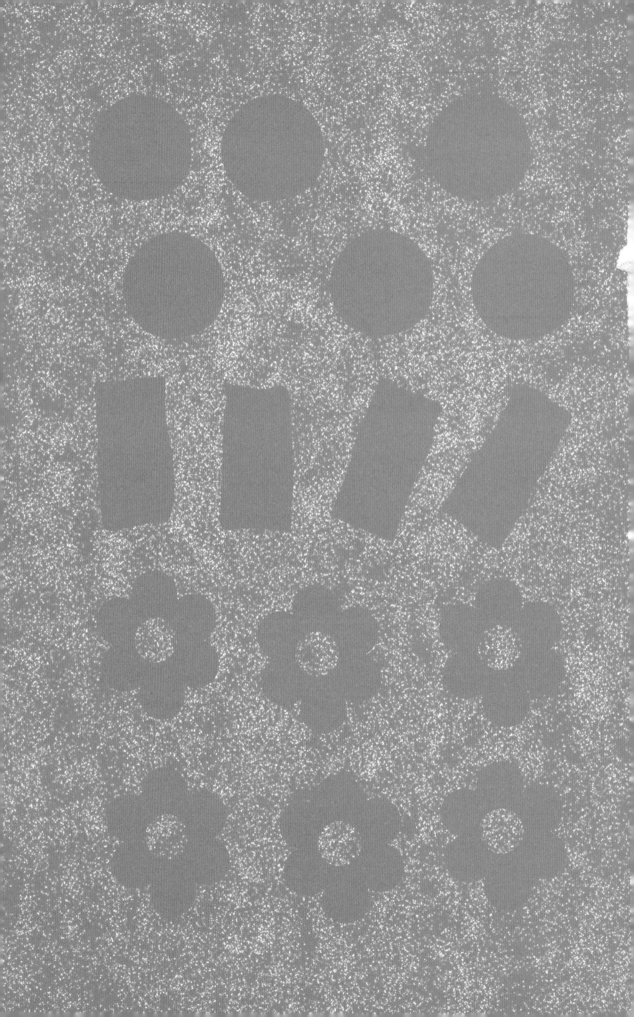

crumbs

crumbs

Cookies and Sweets from Around the World

Ben Mims

Introduction

I have been baking cookies my whole life. They were the first things I learned to make growing up in Mississippi and were what I always reached for when I wanted to chew on a little something sweet after dinner. I never thought about them beyond that.

After studying journalism in college in my home state, I moved to New York City for culinary school. While there, I had the opportunity for a months-long stint at the Jean-Georges Vongerichten restaurants Jean-Georges and Perry St as an intern. I later saw an opening for an editorial internship at *Saveur* magazine—it seemed like the perfect fit.

My first three months at *Saveur*, I spent a lot of time in libraries, both the extensive one in the office, but also the iconic main branch of the New York Public Library at Bryant Park. I remember many research assignments, whether esoteric dishes or ingredients or pondering seventeenth-century illustrative drawings of butchery in the archives of the Rare Book Division.

That type of love for culinary research stayed with me when I transitioned into the *Saveur* test kitchen as an assistant. Some of my first tasks were to shop across the five boroughs of New York City to find the best dried pasta, types of ricotta, or every store-bought butter for a taste test. I learned so much from those excursions: what was available and where (and to whom), the cost of basic ingredients at neighborhood grocery stores versus those at markets, and the minute differences in seemingly identical ingredients.

When I first developed my own recipe at the magazine, it was a dessert and it was carrot cake. I researched two dozen recipes and recorded their similarities and differences on a chart written across six pages of taped paper. I was proud of that research, and though the resulting cake maybe had one too many things in it, I learned what people consider essential to carrot cake, what actually is essential carrot cake, and then my opinions on how to make it—and any recipe—my own.

My love affair with cookies (biscuits) developed further when I was tasked with rounding up Christmas cookies for an issue. Every cookie had to be "real," that is, existing in the world from a real tradition, not a new creation. There were some I had never heard of before: *speculaas* from the Netherlands with their wooden molds used for shaping the dough, *krumkake* from Norway made in intricately designed waffle irons, and Ginger Crunch from New Zealand, which were so delicious—I'll eat the whole batch if I make them (and so I rarely do). Many of those cookies have made it into this book. Realizing that something like cookies had complex histories that reached back millennia was an eye-opener, and I relished digging deeper into researching cookies and every dish I developed thereafter.

As I continued to work at magazines and recipe sites, I continued to work on desserts and cookies.

At Food Network, we brainstormed different flavors in relation to cookies like American classic Snickerdoodles ("would a peppermint version work?") and different flavor styles in relation to various forms ("how about a fruitcake biscotti?"). I first learned of Welsh cakes and the fact that, even though they were cooked on a griddle and tasted more like chewy pancakes, they could be considered a cookie, and that our definitions didn't need to adhere to strict American-centric ideas. I loved coming up with new cookies each holiday season.

When I arrived at my job as the cooking columnist for the *Los Angeles Times*, I knew I wanted to bring that tradition with me. I polled colleagues and friends to see what types of cookies, flavors, and ideas people expected out of holiday cookies, particularly when thinking about them in Los Angeles, a city that cooks and thinks about food in a fresher, simpler, and more seasonal way than New York City. I drew sketches of the cookies to ensure I had a variety of flavors and styles, but also colors and shapes to make them visually interesting, too. I then set about researching, learning ways to improve them by adding a pinch of this or that to make the fillings, glazes, or powdered (icing) sugar coatings more interesting.

So when I was commissioned to write this book a few years later, it felt like such a natural fit. I always thought about cookies obsessively, anyway, so why not finally be able to put all that energy into researching hundreds of cookies around the world to figure out their origins and why we eat them. It has given me an opportunity to also return to the library and poll friends who are experts in their respective heritages' cuisines, tapping into source material that set me on my path in the first place to becoming the biggest, and proudest, cookie nerd in history.

The first cookie I ever learned to make as a child was a tea cake. They were small pillows of dough made of flour, sugar, eggs, vegetable oil, and almond extract. I remember being beguiled by the almond extract since it was never used in my mom's kitchen for anything but those tea cakes. (Why was it used instead of the more familiar vanilla extract? Why weren't real almonds mixed in instead? I never asked those questions then, but now I have a clue.) I would stir together the dough with a spoon, then use that spoon to drop rough mounds onto an ungreased cookie sheet. They'd bake in about 12 minutes, and I'd eat two or three, each one getting to cool a little longer than the one before, so the textures were all different. Soft, cakey, and sweet, they were my perfect after-school snack.

The second and third cookies I ever made were Christmas cookies. As an American, this holiday in particular is strongly associated with cookies meant to share, gift, and feed a crowd.

I still make those same Christmas cookies I made as a child. One was a buttery shortbread, shaped into a disc, ringed with salted nuts, and baked. Once cooled, the nut crown is filled with melted chocolate. The second was a softer, cocoa-tinged thumbprint cookie, filled with melted caramels and drizzled with a zigzag of melted chocolate. Each cookie held its shape well and stood up to layers of stacking in giant decorative metal tins used to hold them throughout the week or two leading up to Christmas. I would eat the shortbreads for a snack throughout the day—the salty nuts, sweet chocolate, and buttery cookie base were my idea of a granola bar. When everyone else reached for pecan pie and coconut cake for Christmas dessert, I ate the caramel-filled thumbprints for a less filling but equally decadent holiday finisher.

So many of the American cookies I grew up with didn't originate within its borders, but instead traveled around the world and through centuries of cross-cultural influences to end up as we know

them today. It is my goal in this book to highlight all of these cookies, both the ones familiar to us and those we would never have thought of before as cookies. Think of it as a Greatest Hits of the world's cookies that, when viewed and packaged together in this way, shows better how the phenomenon of baking tiny little sweet things came about. I shed light on their origin stories in order to understand the cultures they come from. Along this journey, you will see that the story of cookies around the world is largely a story of societal movement throughout history, from the sugar trade and colonialism to the digital global spread of ideas today.

The why and when of a cookie gives you a peek into how certain ingredients wound up included and how baking traditions were formed that may seem like anomalies today. Like that almond extract in my mom's tea cakes, there's a world of information and intrigue that lives within two bites of a sweet snack we all turn to for the simplest pleasure.

What Is a Cookie?

At first, I thought the answer would be easy to manifest. Flat, circular, crisp or chewy, and made with flour, sugar, and fat! Though actually many things that are decidedly not cookies can fit in that definition—and many cookies don't fit in it at all.

Thinking about cookies so much quickly became an abstract exercise. When are cookies eaten? Celebrations, sure, but also any time of day for a treat. And are they really thought of as "special" in that context anymore? We do eat cookies during holidays, at birthdays, and as treats after dinner. But we also eat them on a Wednesday afternoon, while traveling, and at bake sales and other events. The list goes on and on.

So I came up with my own criteria by which I would judge all possible cookies to see if they fit. For the physical properties, it is a cookie if it can sit upright on its own, be shaped and baked, be held by your fingers, be eaten in a couple or few bites, and be made without yeast. But quickly, even those general categorizations yield exceptions. Many cookies contain yeast, even though it is not the chief raising agent and only contributes nominal flavor and softness to the dough—think of it more as a vestigial ingredient where the original purpose is no longer relevant. Some treats that are considered cookies are not baked but rather deep-fried and soaked in syrup.

Instead of trying to define a cookie physically, I decided instead to look at the sweet treats that so many countries and cultures around the world eat to see what makes sense or what feels natural to include, within the context of those cultures and borders. Foods have morphed and adapted so much throughout history that one country's baklava is a dessert eaten with a fork while another's is a two-bite treat held in your fingers. These types of variances can cause debate about what

is technically a cookie versus a pastry, sweet, candy, fritter, or even snack cake (such as madeleines).

I found it helpful when judging whether a cookie is a cookie to not just trust those who've had them but also my gut, intuiting what I know makes a cookie, even if I couldn't verbalize it at the time. And just when I think I landed on a quality that had an airtight argument for any alternatives, there was always an exception, a loophole. So instead of trying to build parameters around what is a cookie, I decided whether it had the soul of a cookie, if not the outright appearance.

It's these differences in how cookies have evolved separately around the world that I find so fascinating. As much as we are connected globally, we all also hold fast to our individual and cultural traditions that have stood the test of time. These traditions show off our heritages and homelands, and the ingredients, foods, and recipes that represent them.

So when it came time to "define" a cookie (a process that took the entire duration of writing this book), I had to get a bit tedious. First, in my definition, cookies must contain at least three of the following four ingredients to count as a cookie:

- **Dry matter:** This is what I like to call any powdered "solid" that bulks up the cookie and gives it substance. Most people would call it "flour," and that encapsulates flour from any grain (like wheat) or nuts (like almonds or hazelnuts). This is typically the ingredient that comprises the largest amount, proportionately, of any cookie.
- **Sweetener:** Typically, especially in modern times, this is granulated white sugar, but it can also include other granulated sugars like brown sugars, superfine (caster) sugar, and powdered (icing) sugar, as well as liquids like honey, maple syrup, brown sugar syrup, or molasses.

- **Fat:** This is typically butter, but due to dietary or traditional customs, this also includes ghee or clarified butter, vegetable oil, coconut oil, vegetable shortening, or in many Iberian and Latin American recipes, pork lard. It can also include egg yolks, which contain all the fat of an egg, or melted chocolate, which is mostly cocoa butter.
- **Eggs:** Whole eggs are used quite often to emulsify fat and sugar together and give the cookie structure, as well as its chew. But cookies like macaroons use only egg whites, while some shortbread-type cookies just use egg yolks. Any of the three counts in my book.

If something has just flour and sugar, what is it? Texturally it would be very hard and very flat, so I would call that a candy, because anytime sugar or honey is mixed with "dry matter," usually nuts, it becomes a candy that you can't really chew like a cookie. If it's mostly flour, I would be generous and call it a sweetened cracker, but a cookie it is not.

If you just have flour and eggs, that's called pasta. Flour and fat? Those two ingredients produce flaky layers, so you have pie crusts, puff pastry, and other cracker-like pastry doughs. Sugar and eggs? Meringue or sabayon. Sugar and fat? At best, a rich syrup, and at worst, I'd call it a greasy, gritty mess.

When you add a third ingredient to any of those pairings, then cookies start to take shape. Add eggs to the flour-and-sugar cracker, and the little bit of fat in the yolk and texture provided by the white will make it chewable, like Italian *cantucci* (recipe, page 112). Add some chocolate to beaten egg whites and sugar, and you have chocolate meringues, or Icelandic *lakkristoppar* (recipe, page 292). Add sugar to your fat and flour? That's shortbread (recipe, page 274) and countless other crumbly types.

For the cookies in this book, most have all four, but they at least had to have three or they didn't make the cut. They also had to, for the most part, contain no yeast. There are a few exceptions that keep yeast in the mix out of tradition, or because yeast was used before modern conveniences made it easier to use chemical leaveners. But if any foodstuff actually uses yeast to provide leavening, that's where you start venturing into doughnut, fritter, and, if baked, bun territory. So, while fried "bowtie" cookies like Polish *chrusciki* (which go by many other names depending on where you are in the world) are considered cookies and often called that, they actually felt more like fritters or small, thin beignets to me. So those are not in this book.

Another criterion, and probably the most important, was all about texture. After developing and thinking about cookies my whole career, textural through lines emerge. Cookies and biscuits are often, if not always, crumbly, crunchy, or chewy—meaning they have a discernible texture that must be chewed. When cookies are "cakey," they are usually labeled as such and made to be an exception. I found that as long as a cookie has a crumbly/crunchy/chewy, or otherwise dense texture, it can be virtually any shape and size and still be considered a cookie. But if the texture becomes cakey, then the cookie must actually look like a stereotypical cookie: that is, round and flat. Because, if the cakey cookie isn't round and flat, then it starts to feel like a "snack cake," a petit four, or another sweet/dessert altogether. For this reason, things like French madeleines didn't make the cut, though they are often served as part of a cookie tray in France. Neither did American-style brownies, because, though there are bar cookies in this book, brownies are a uniform cakey or fudgy texture and seem like a completely separate category of sweet thing.

One of the biggest determining factors of whether a cookie made it into this book was if it was one that was made at home or had a tradition of being, specifically, homemade. I was happy to see this sentiment echoed by Richard Sax in his indispensable cookbook, *Classic Home Desserts*, when he wrote, "cookies are the province of home bakers." Factory-made or industrial cookies are delicious, but they have more to say about individual businesses or corporations than they do about the ingenuity of cooks and bakers throughout centuries making magic out of a few ingredients. And in parts of the world where maybe a tradition of home baking isn't that old or wasn't commonplace, I made exceptions for cookies that came from revered local bakeries, since oftentimes those bakeries were the only outlet for sweets in a particular area, or they were the domain of the communal oven that people in that region used to bake everything. So the cookies I include in this book are, for the most part, those that people have made at home, not store-bought treats. Restaurants are the domain of fancy cakes, tarts, ice creams, and the like; cookies belong at home, where their shareable nature fits in with the idea of fellowship with friends, family, and community.

A last, and perhaps controversial, criterion for modern times pertains to size. Historically, and ideally, cookies should be small treats that can be eaten in two bites and held in the fingers; no plates and silverware, because that's a dessert. If a cookie gets any larger, it might as well be a cake or pie or some other similar dessert, because at a certain size, it gets too unwieldy to be handheld. Today, especially in the United States, cookies based on the classics—like chocolate chip cookies and sugar cookies—have grown bigger and thicker in the quest to sate social media. Chocolate chip cookies are the main offenders, as people try to pack in as much browned butter, chopped chocolate, and nuts as possible, then underbake it in mounds to make a sort of lightly stable raw cookie dough confection. I subscribe to the Scandinavian approach to cookies in their *fika* (coffee break) culture, which is to make them small so that you can sample as many different types as you want without getting a stomachache.

A Brief History of Cookies

Grasping the history of cookies is an overwhelming prospect. Whether made as edible tokens to be placed in tombs or small lumps of dough tossed in an oven to test temperature, small grain-based things have—like their cousin bread—been "invented" several times over throughout the history of civilization. There is no neat timeline. This book, and the recipes within it, chronicle hundreds of little individual histories that, when taken together, paint a better picture of the breadth and reach of cookies throughout modern history than any linear catalog of dates.

Thinking about cookies as both a separate and global phenomenon, there are some general turning points and a few milestones, spanning a thousand-plus years and several hundred styles of cookie-like things, that give a general sense of how we arrived at, and think about, cookies today.

It's generally held that Persia—the region where modern-day Iran exists—is credited with the invention of cookies, mostly because the production of granulated sugar from sugarcane originated there in the seventh century, which led to things being made with it, commonly biscuits and cookies. (That is why this book starts with that area's cookies.) Throughout my research into the *ghorayeba*-style cookie (recipe, page 49), I also infer that cookies from this region, which used processed sugar and flour, were likely the first of the most modern-looking cookies that fit our definition today. Before sugar production was the norm, many cookie-like things were sweetened with honey, particularly in Europe and around the Mediterranean. But once spices and sugar were traded with Europe, the use of granulated cane sugar then spread throughout the continent and made a lasting impression on the culture of cookie-making.

Before these types of sugar and flour cookies came to be, things like "hardtack" and other sweetened crackers were popular because they traveled and stored well, particularly on ships. But there were also early unrisen or enriched bread-like rounds that would eventually, through the increased taste for soft and sweet things, become more cookie-like, similar to shortbread (recipe, page 274) in the UK.

Many small and sweet things were once the domain of the wealthy, who employed chefs to create them or had the skill set. Wealthy families had the money and resources to pay for butter, granulated white sugar, and spices from faraway lands. It wasn't until the Industrial Revolution that factory-made treats became accessible to the masses, as they became easier to make, and they became sweeter when sugar became cheaper and more common.

Cookies in many "Western" countries became part of households due to product marketing during the early part of the twentieth century, when manufacturers selling items from vegetable shortening to baking powders were educating their consumers on how to use their products via small recipe pamphlets. Cookbooks, often produced by these manufacturers, were printed as guides for the emerging post–World War home cooks, mostly women. This set about a cultural reset in the way many people thought about cookies; no longer something for the wealthy or even an industrially produced sweet from the store, but a humble treat to make at home that contributed to the general family- and community-oriented sentiment of the time.

While cookies became simpler and more commonplace in certain parts of the world, in others, they maintained their reputation as celebratory or religious treats that used costly ingredients and the type of labor that one could only muster once a year and with a group of family members present to help. Many cookies made for Ramadan or Eid, important religious times for Muslims, fit this mold. And in other parts of the world, like Southeast Asia or Sub-Saharan Africa, where home ovens weren't so common, many cookies evolved to be made by street vendors as street snacks, often adapting from oven baking to deep-fat frying.

Part of the wonderment of cookies is seeing the expansive array of shapes, textures, and flavors that can come out of a simple mix of flour, fat, sugar, and some pinches of spices or dashes of potent aromatic elixirs. No matter where they come from in the world—there are over one hundred countries represented by cookies in this book—they all served the purpose of representing a culture—whether at a certain time in history or with timeless significance—in edible form.

How Cookies Fit in Our World

When is the best time for a cookie? Why do we eat cookies for certain occasions—and even non-occasions? These are the questions I pondered almost daily while writing this book. And let me confess: The answer never really manifested.

Most foods we know of come from a certain place, are generally served at a certain time, and serve a particular purpose—pancakes and toast for breakfast, sandwiches at lunchtime, or a bowl of spiced nuts with drinks at a bar.

Cookies, on the other hand, don't really have any of that. Culturally, they serve a vague purpose that can be described with such adjectives as "fun," "celebratory," or "snacky." Their indefinability is what makes them so universal. I love a cookie after lunch as a sort of smaller, lighter, handheld dessert. But I also love a cookie in the afternoon with a cup of coffee. But I would never eat one in the morning with a cup of coffee. What's the difference here?

You could argue that cookies are too sweet for breakfast, but then what about our global penchant for fried dough covered in sugar glazes, pastries, or even lots of sugar in our coffee? A case could be made for cookies in the afternoon, something to have around when you need a pick-me-up. The British have "high tea" as a custom that sets aside time for cookies to be enjoyed alongside other small nibbles like scones and tea sandwiches. But not every culture in the world snacks on sweet things in the afternoon. Cookies do feel out of place as desserts in restaurants for dinner. There's something about the playful casualness of cookies that makes them feel incongruous with the formality of a nighttime meal, no matter if you're in a fine-dining restaurant or eating takeout. But then again, fortune cookies are served as the dessert with Chinese American take-out meals.

The point is that there are no broad rules or generalizations to be made about cookies for when they're appropriate to eat or even why they exist.

However, when it comes to our human need to gather and celebrate occasions, the cookie's meaning narrows into focus. Whether it's at a birthday party, a retirement office potluck, a holiday get-together, or even a funeral, we need foods that bring us joy to mark special occasions or soothe the sadder parts of life. Cookies, even more so than cake, are fitting for such occasions. They serve lots of people, are cheap and (most) are easy to make, and they're crowd-pleasers that everyone can find joy in. Sure, a cake can and does do that as well, but it feels a little more formal, whereas cookies are for the people. You can take a bite or two of a cookie or try several different ones; you don't have to commit to a whole slice of cake.

Cookies fulfill the sweet need that chips (crisps) do on the savory side: Something bite-size and crunchy (or with a texture) that quells hunger and offers a respite from the usual. This manifests more commonly during holidays, but it can also be an everyday thing. It's a little something sweet that everyone craves when they're up or down to mark their change in emotions. When we're really happy and excited, we want to share that feeling. Sometimes we need comfort to help pick us back up. All food serves one of those purposes, but it's the rare one that does both, and cookies are that.

And they fit so well in home celebrations precisely because of their simplicity. They're mostly easy enough that anyone can make them.

They're treats to make at home so that anyone, no matter how rich or poor, can enjoy something sweet that brings them joy. They take basic ingredients—flour, fat, sugar—and turn them into delicious round pucks that you can't help but smile about. They represent all the ways cultures around the world have formed happiness from the humblest of ingredients.

From dark winters to midday pick-me-ups, being shared is inherent in a cookie's nature. A cookie recipe usually yields a lot of pieces, which are portable and so are meant to be brought to gatherings and shared with everyone. In that way, cookies are almost community building, a way to express love and affection across borders and between languages. And that's what I think their greatest purpose is and why I wanted to write a book about them. Their history is fascinating, yes, but it's their commonality in cultures around the world—acting as small ambassadors of a culture's most prized resources, flavors, or ingredients—that is so special.

Cookie Equipment

Whether you're baking in Dublin or Dallas, there are some core pieces of equipment that you will want to make cookies. I tried my best in the recipes to only use equipment that you absolutely needed and that most novice home bakers would already have (or could purchase inexpensively). Aside from the specialty equipment that literally shapes many

culturally significant cookies around the world, their doughs and batters are brought together with typically just a bowl and spoon. Arm yourself with the basics to get started, then branch out from there as you get more comfortable using them and explore more cookies outside your comfort zone.

THE BASICS

Baking Sheets
I suggest metal half-sheet pans (baking trays) that measure roughly 13 × 18 inches (33 × 46 cm). Buy two or four, but you won't need more or any others. They're affordable, durable, and get the job done. You will use these every time you make cookies and perhaps for everyday cooking, too. If you have multiples, keep at least two for baking cookies only, so they never venture into a 500°F (260°C) oven with a giant roast on top, which might cause them to warp or dull over time.

Bowls
Though you might never guess, bowls will be the most used item in your kitchen to make cookies. You need a big one for mixing most doughs, and you need small and medium ones to hold premixed ingredients (like dry ingredients or chopped nuts) and chocolate, before they go into the big bowl. They sit atop saucepans to make double boilers, hold small amounts of icings or beds of sanding sugars, and work as storage containers for overnight doughs. I own both metal and glass graduated sets of seven to ten bowls. That may seem like a lot of bowls, but I guarantee that as you make cookies

over and over again, you'll be glad to have them. And you'll even find that certain sizes are deep enough for dipping biscotti in chocolate or wide enough for folding batter for macarons. Those will become your bowls that make the whole process more fun.

Cutting Boards

The type of tasks you'll be doing the most on cutting boards for making cookies is chopping nuts or chocolate or slicing rolls of dough.

For that reason, I love the flimsy plastic cutting boards that come in different colors because they're lightweight, and you can mold and bend them, to act as chutes for getting nuts and chocolate into the mixing bowl with no mess. Or use any smaller, lightweight cutting board that you prefer.

Digital Kitchen Scale

Though I hear complaints about having to buy what might seem to the novice an unnecessary piece of equipment, let me state its importance this way: No other piece of equipment will improve your baking like a kitchen scale. The precision it offers all but guarantees your baking never comes out too dry again, as is often the problem with non-metric volume measurements. It also means you won't be dirtying all those measuring cups; instead, it allows you to add ingredients one by one to the mixing bowl. I prefer an 11-pound (5 kg) capacity digital kitchen scale, which can toggle between ounces and grams, so in addition to using the grams for baking, you can also use the ounces for measuring amounts of meat, fruit, or vegetables for meal planning and other dietary needs.

Food Processor

If you had to choose between buying a stand mixer or food processor, I'd suggest going with the latter. You can do many more things with it that I think are indispensable, like grinding down nuts to make very finely ground flour (which I call for often in this book) and mixing fillings to ensure they're evenly textured, thus easier to work with. I have an 11-cup (2.6-liter) model that I think is the perfect size for nearly every purpose that a home cook would need. But if you want to go the extra mile, also buy a mini 4-cup (900 ml) model for grinding smaller amounts of nuts or for other smaller jobs.

Hand Mixer

Almost every recipe in this book calls for it to be made with a hand mixer. They are affordable, and you will use them for creaming butter and sugar together to start most cookie recipes, plus whip cream for garnishes. I like my standard 5-speed model just fine because it has never let me down. The best perk to seek out is the "slow start" feature, so when you turn on the mixer, it doesn't move the beaters with such a force that butter and sugar are flung all over you and your counter.

Knives

I have no special knives for making cookies and think the standard combination of large chef's knife, serrated knife, and small paring knife is plenty. The serrated knife is great for gripping nuts and chocolate and chopping them into fine pieces, while the paring knife is great for cleanly slicing logs of dough or halving garnishes like maraschino cherries or whole pistachios. The chef's knife can be used for anything else.

Offset Spatulas

These are the ultimate cookie lifters. Like whisks, offset spatulas are extensions of my hand, and I'd be lost without them. I don't even use large ones, but instead I keep about six of the small 4½-inch (11.5 cm) ones. They're perfect for lifting cut shapes of dough onto baking sheets, lifting those same baked cookies onto racks, and for spreading glazes and icings and chocolate. I even use the tips of them for raking out small teaspoons of jam into divots when making thumbprint cookies.

Piping Bags

Aside from making French macarons (recipe, page 262), dedicated piping bags aren't necessary for the cookies in this book. However, if you're any sort of curious baker, you'll want to have them for piping icings for cakes or for having an easier time piping meringues or filling cupcakes. A large zip-top plastic bag can be used for most things in a pinch, but if you're so inclined, get an 18-inch (46 cm) canvas piping bag with a set of tips (nozzles). As long as you clean and dry the bag properly after each use, it will last a lifetime.

Precut Parchment Paper Sheets

This is another indispensable piece of equipment that I use so often. These precut sheets fit perfectly within the dimensions of baking sheets without trying to curl back in on themselves like torn sheets from a roll. Buy precut sheets and keep them with your baking sheets.

Rolling Pins

For rolled-out cookies, you need a solid rolling pin. While many prefer tapered pins or those with handles, I feel they leave inconsistencies in the dough or are difficult to manipulate—and that's the last thing I need when trying to roll out already fragile dough to cut shapes. I have three rolling pins of the exact same type: the "dowel" rolling pin, so-named because it is all one even thickness its full length and has no handles. They're typically 19 inches (48 cm) long and 2 inches (5 cm) in diameter. You only need one, but I like to keep more, to dedicate one for dry rolling with lots of flour and one that I don't mind getting messy with sticky dough or oil.

Ruler

The measurements in these recipes are all necessary. The difference between a cookie that is 2 inches (5 cm) wide and one that is 2¼ inches (5.5 cm) wide can be the difference between perfectly baked and burnt. A cheap school ruler is fine to accurately measure lengths and widths of your cookies.

Sifters and Sieves

Most dry ingredients in these recipes only require a whisking to lighten them up and mix with other ingredients. Though sometimes you want the extra lightness that a sieve or sifter provides, like when mixing ground almonds or flour into meringues. Also, powdered (icing) sugar and cocoa powder are two ingredients that are notoriously clumpy, so you'll always want to sift them as well to ensure no lumps make it into your baking. I employ a 6¼-inch (16 cm) stainless steel sieve for 99 percent of my baking tasks and then keep a tiny, cheap 3-inch (7.5 cm) one for dusting cookies with powdered (icing) sugar.

Silicone Spatulas

These things are an extension of my fingers and arms. No matter what cookie you're making, you'll need to scrape something, whether the sides and bottom of a bowl to ensure the butter and sugar have creamed properly or to get that last bit of jam out of the measuring cup so you have an accurate amount. I keep a set of silicone spatulas that I find to be the perfect shape and rigidity for scraping the sides of bowls, the corners of saucepans, and getting in between the paddle attachment of my stand mixer or the blades of my food processor. Get a small 8-inch (20 cm) spatula, a longer one, a larger flat 11-inch (28 cm) one and, if you want, a large spoonula (spoon-shaped spatula). You'll find unlimited uses for each of them and will always be glad they're in reach.

Spring-loaded Ice Cream Scoops

These are now sold and labeled as "cookie scoops" in many US markets and online, but their original purpose was for scooping ice cream. They ensure that each portion of dough is the exact same, leading to even baking times for each cookie and more uniform results. I keep many sizes—small (½-ounce/ 1 tablespoon), medium (1 ounce/2 tablespoons), and large (1½-ounces/3 tablespoons). Yes, for decades cookies were made with just a spoon, but these scoops ensure all the cookies are as uniform as possible, which makes them all bake at the same rate, keeping the process tidy.

Stand Mixer

I have a stand mixer, and I use it often because I leave it out on my counter. It allows me to mix batters and doughs while leaving my hands free to crack eggs, mix dry ingredients, or melt chocolate to later pour into the mixer bowl. That said, only one or two recipes in this book call for it—the rest are made with a hand mixer or spoon—so if you really don't want to make the investment, borrow it from a friend to make those cookies.

Wire Cooling Racks

When I was growing up, a sheet of freshly baked cookies was placed on the stove as a "cooling rack." But times have changed and not everyone has raised metal grates on their stove, nor is leaving the cookies to cool on the sheets good for all cookies. Buy a couple standard wire cooling racks that fit the same dimensions as your baking sheets. You can efficiently cool your cookies on them and use them when glazing or dusting cookies with icings and sugars, allowing the cookies to sit on a flat surface, ensuring they have clean edges all around.

Whisks

Like silicone spatulas, I keep several sizes of these around for all sorts of uses, from mixing teaspoons of spices to whipping cups of cream. Sturdy wire whisks are my choice for lightening flour and mixing it evenly with chemical leaveners, which eliminates the need for sifting. It's helpful to find a brand where the wires don't bend or warp and the handles are comfortable. I keep a set of the 9-inch (23 cm) and 11-inch (28 cm) sizes.

Wooden Spoon

If mixing cookie dough without an electric hand mixer, you want a sturdy spoon that can hold up to the intense pressure needed to beat the fat and sugar together, a process that starts nearly every cookie in this book. I like to have several spoons of varying lengths and widths to fit the amount of ingredients I'm mixing and the size of my bowls. The most common one I use is 10 inches (25 cm) long and the bowl of the spoon is about 2 inches (5 cm) wide. Make sure to keep any wooden spoons for baking separate from those you'd use for savory cooking, so you don't accidentally end up with a batch of shortbread that tastes like curry powder.

SPECIALTY TOOLS

Cookie Cutters

These are used in most cookie recipes in this book. Though many of the gingerbread-like cookies benefit from, and have history based in, whimsical, holiday-themed shapes, all you really need is a graduated set of round cutters. A cutter 2 inches (5 cm) in diameter will be the most common, but I have smaller and larger sizes to switch up the size based on my personal preference. You can even use a drinking glass turned upside down to cut out rounds.

Cookie Press

Sometimes called a "dough gun" or "cookie gun," these presses are ideal for making tiny cookies out of basic butter-and-sugar dough that would be difficult to press into shapes with a piping bag or by hand. The pressure exerted by pressing the handle extrudes the dough like pasta through a die, leaving behind a clean shape that bakes up neat and tidy. I have a 14-piece model that comes with several discs to switch up shapes.

Speculaas Molds

Like *Springerle* molds (see below), these are made to imprint designs onto dough to make *speculaas* (recipe, page 232) cookies. Unlike *Springerle* molds, though, *speculaas* molds are typically large wooden planks with engravings, onto which you press dough, then tap out onto the work surface. Vintage molds can be pricey, but newer, smaller molds are available for less. The most important aspect of using the molds, as with any equipment, is to clean them well after each use, so no excess food particles rot or grow mold in the crevices of the designs. Using enough rice flour to dust the molds helps get the dough out in the first place, then if there are any pieces that accidentally stick, use a toothpick to pry them out. Wipe the molds dry with paper towels as best you can, and store them so plenty of air flows around them.

Springerle Molds

Though German *Springerle* (recipe, page 246) can be made with other molds or cookie cutters, they're commonly made now with molded rolling pins named for their intended use. You roll out the dough flat with a regular rolling pin and then roll the *Springerle* pin over the dough to imprint the design. Clearly, unless you plan to make them, you don't need to own one. But if you do want to make them, it's worth shopping for vintage pins. However, newer models are affordable and can be used on other types of cookies, too, like any type of gingerbread or even plain shortbread.

Waffle Irons

If you want to make all the waffle-like cookies in this book, you'll need a few different models of waffle iron. The most common one that can be used for most of the waffle cookies is a Norwegian *krumkake* (recipe, page 303) iron or Italian *pizzelle* (recipe, page 130) iron. They're intended to form thin, crisp cookies. Some have intricate designs, while others have a simple close stitch, but shallow grid pattern. I use electric models of both for convenience, but like *Springerle* and *speculaas* molds, there are vintage models made of cast iron that are intended to be used over an open fire. Specialty irons for other cookies like Norwegian *goro* (recipe, page 304) and Russian *oreshki* (recipe, page 212) are typically going to be of the cast-iron style, as those cookies are not popular enough to have warranted creating a convenient electric version. If you choose to buy these molds, simply take care of them per the manufacturer's instructions, and they'll be worth the investment.

Cookie Techniques

To give more detail than is possible in each recipe, here is a breakdown of common cookie-making techniques and why they're important to the outcome of the cookie, starting from those you encounter at the beginning of a recipe, when you are preparing the cookie dough, and moving toward those concerned with shaping and baking cookies at the end.

PREPARING COOKIE DOUGH

Measuring

Though weighing in grams is the most accurate way to measure ingredients for making cookies—and all baking—if you must use ounces or volume measuring cups, stick to one method to ensure there's no confusion, and thus, no mistakes when preparing your ingredients. I like to measure out all the dry ingredients first, combining those called for in separate bowls, so that when I need them, they're all ready to go and there's no need to stop the process to measure, sift, and whisk, which can add minutes to your prep time, and in some cases, affect the combined ingredients already in the mixer bowl.

Creaming

In this book, almost every recipe starts with combining fat and sugar that I then instruct you to "beat" together. That process, or beating the two together with a mixer, is also called "creaming." It refers to the act of scraping and mushing together the fat and sugar in a way that partially dissolves the sugar and makes the butter softer and smoother, allowing the rest of the ingredients to be more readily absorbed and make the dough. It's the foundation upon which most baking rests. While 1 minute of mixing would likely be serviceable, I call for 2–3 minutes minimum, to ensure you've adequately mixed the two ingredients together.

Sifting

This is not something absolutely necessary for most cookies, but nonetheless it is important at certain times. Powdered (icing) sugar and cocoa powder tend to clump together, and you don't want lumps in your cookie dough, so sifting them removes those lumps and allows them to incorporate into the dough more smoothly. Sifting flour also lightens it, which is a boon in certain instances when all the leavening is coming from air beaten into eggs, and you want extra insurance that the dough doesn't inadvertently get weighed down.

Softened Butter

After the fat ingredient in most recipes, you'll see the word "softened." This means you want the butter to be soft and moldable like clay. If the butter is stiff and cold from the refrigerator, it won't be able to mix with the other ingredients. Using soft butter means the sugar, and then the rest of the ingredients, incorporates more easily, which leads to a smooth dough that's easy to work with. The night before I plan to make cookies, I always leave out the amount of butter I need on the counter, to ensure it's at the right temperature and texture. But in a pinch, microwave the butter in a heatproof bowl in 5-second bursts, pressing it all over with your finger after each round, until the butter can just hold the imprint of your finger.

"One Egg at a Time"

Making cookie dough or cake batter is similar to creating mayonnaise in that you're creating an emulsion between the fat and sugar with eggs. If you add a couple eggs at once to a well-creamed mixture of butter and sugar, the liquid from the eggs would overwhelm them and cause the mixture to look "curdled," although really, it's just bits of fat that are suspended in liquid. To avoid that, you add eggs one at a time and wait until each is fully absorbed into the butter and sugar before adding the next one.

Chilling Shapes

Once cookies have been rolled flat and cut out with cutters and placed on baking sheets, they've been through a lot. All that flattening, no matter how careful you are, can toughen the gluten in the dough and also warm it up. Chilling the cut-out shapes on their baking sheets afterward does two things: First, it gives the gluten time to relax, and second, it firms up the dough to help produce cleaner lines for the shapes you cut them into. It also, practically, gives you a break from the task of making cookies, so you can clean up—or store the unbaked cookies overnight until you're ready to bake and enjoy them the next day.

Rolling in Sugar

Some cookies get rolled in sugar before they're baked to add extra sweetness to the outside, while providing more texture via their crunchy crystals. Sugar crystals, whether plain granulated or more coarser sanding sugar, stick best to soft dough, so you'll see that most dough balls are rolled in sugar first, before being chilled. If rolling in sugar after being baked, as is the case with most cookies covered with powdered (icing) sugar, you want to do this gently, since a freshly baked cookie will be hot and fragile. Work gently, one or two at a time, so they stay looking pristine.

Thumbprinting

Ironically, the best way to actually make a "thumbprint" for such cookies is to use your index finger or the narrow end of a wooden spoon. But instead of going at it from an angle, position your finger vertically, pointing directly at the cookie ball on the sheet, and press straight down. This gives you an evenly centered well with an even diameter for filling.

Making Dough Logs

Many recipes in this book call for shaping pieces of dough into logs that then get chilled and sliced. This is best achieved when the dough is freshly mixed and soft. I shape the dough into a vague cylinder first, then I place it in the middle of a large sheet of parchment paper. Fold one end of the paper over the log, then take something wide and flat-edged like a ruler or a bench scraper and press the ruler or scraper on the top of the paper just under the cylinder. While holding steady the end of the paper laying against the counter, use the ruler to push the dough away from you, creating a uniformly thick and smooth log of dough. Then roll up the log fully in the paper and twist the open ends together like a candy wrapper. Place the log in the refrigerator until it's firm enough to slice.

SHAPING COOKIES

Cookies are generally shaped one of three ways: scooping, rolling, or slicing.

Scooping

This refers to using an ice cream/cookie scoop or spoon to literally scoop up a nugget of dough from a bowl. Typically, you would then take this dough in your hand and roll it into a ball before placing it on the baking sheet. This allows the ball to either be baked as is or flattened first; either way, it produces a slightly raised mound. This method is used for cookies where you want some chewiness or lightness and thickness to the cookie.

Rolling

This refers to flattening the dough into a uniformly thick sheet using a rolling pin. Once the dough is rolled flat, you can use cookie cutters, a knife, or a pizza cutter to cut out shapes. This technique is usually used for thin, crisp, or brittle cookies.

Slicing

This refers to slicing discs of dough from a preformed log. Often referred to as "slice-and-bake" cookies, you shape the dough into an evenly thick log, chill it in the refrigerator to firm it up, then cut across the log with a knife to produce clean pucks of dough. This shaping technique is often used for shortbreads and other crumbly dense doughs that bake up crunchy and snappy.

BAKING COOKIES

Rack Position

Almost all of the recipes in the book will have you bake two baking sheets at once. Because two half-sheet pans cannot fit side by side in a typical home oven, this means that you have to bake on two racks. So, before you preheat the oven, position the racks in the top and bottom thirds of the oven.

Rotating Pans

In order for the cookies to bake evenly, because all ovens will have hot spots, it's best to rotate the baking sheets from front to back halfway through the baking time. At the same time, switch the baking sheets from one rack to the other. This, too, helps with the evenness of the bake.

Batch Cooking
A number of the recipes will make more cookies than you can fit on two baking sheets. When this happens, keep the remaining dough chilled, if it is a dough that is meant to be chilled. Then when the first batch is done, let the baking sheets cool

completely before lining them with fresh parchment and putting more cookies on them. Keep in mind that the cook time listed for a recipe allows for a single batch.

Cooling Cookies
Some cookies need to sit on the baking sheet for a brief amount of time before you can move them to wire cooling racks. And other cookies can (or should) cool completely on the pans. Each recipe will give you the appropriate instructions.

Cookie Ingredients

The ingredients for the recipes in this book are fairly standard, but there are minute differences that you'll encounter when shopping for and using them that can sometimes make a huge difference in the outcome of the baked cookie. Add to that the cultural and country-specific differences in

ingredients that come with providing recipes for cookies from all over the world and you'll soon see that not all ingredients we take for granted are created the same. Here's a breakdown of everything you'll come across in the recipes to follow.

FATS

Butter
The cookies for this book were developed and tested with regular store-bought American unsalted butter. Using unsalted butter levels the playing field and allows you to control the amount of salt in the recipes. If you use salted butter, because of the differences in the amount of salt used by the manufacturer, you would have no idea how much salt is in your actual recipe. For that reason, always use unsalted.

Unless specifically called for, don't use high-fat, often labeled "European-style," butters because they, as the name suggests, have a higher fat-to-water ratio. (Look on the package and it will usually say; high-fat butters have 82%–85% butterfat while a typical US grocery store butter has 80%.) The high-fat butters are great for spreading on warm bread, but can sometimes affect the texture of baked goods that have been crafted to be a balance of lower-fat butter with the other ingredients. However, if you only have access to higher-fat butters, you can bake with them, but just be aware that the cookies will be slightly softer and/or greasier after baking because of the extra fat present in the dough.

Other Fats
In some parts of the world, butter is not used because of dietary restrictions, or it simply contributes the wrong texture and flavor to the cookie. Ghee and clarified butter are, for the intents and purposes of this book, the same thing and are pure fat, no water. Vegetable oil is a neutral oil that is kosher and suitable for vegan and vegetarian diets. Lard is rendered pork fat that when used in this book is always cold-rendered, which leaves it with as neutral a taste as possible, so your cookies don't

taste like meat. Vegetable shortening is often given as an alternative to lard in cases where you'd rather not use lard or are vegan/vegetarian.

SWEETENERS

Sugars
Most cookies are sweet, so sugar is the most important ingredient. For the most part, regular white sugar is used in the cookies in this book because it is the most common now and has been for centuries. However, the fineness of the granulation does vary between countries, with American granulated sugar being a bit finer than UK granulated. So, for all recipes that just call for sugar, US cooks should use granulated and UK cooks should use caster sugar. When superfine sugar is called for, it's because you want a finer-grained sugar that dissolves faster and produces tinier, and thus crumblier, crumbs in the cookie. In that instance, British cooks should also use caster sugar. Powdered (icing) sugar is even finer than superfine and gives the crumb of a cookie a delicate crumble; it also coats many cookies in a fine, sweet down-like coating. Brown sugars are used rarely in this book, but if so, are referred to in their American designations as either "light" or "dark" to denote the amount of molasses used in each. Turbinado sugar (sold as demerara in the UK) is used to add crunch and sparkle to certain cookies. To learn more about the various "raw sugars" used in cookies around the world, see page 164.

Vanilla and Vanilla Sugar
In many European cookies, vanilla sugar adds the spice's signature flavor to the dough. In other parts of the world, vanilla extract is used and more common. In most of the recipes in this book, vanilla extract is used because it's more commonly available and can be swapped for other liquid

extracts. However, in certain instances, the texture and flavor of vanilla sugar is desired. If making vanilla sugar the old-fashioned way, vanilla beans are nestled in a large amount of sugar and left for months to allow the aroma time to permeate the sugar granules. If a recipe calls for either regular vanilla sugar or powdered vanilla sugar, here's how to make them quickly:

Recipe: *Vanilla Sugar*
Scrape the seeds from 1 large vanilla bean and place them in a bowl with about ¼ cup (50 g) white US granulated (UK caster) sugar. Use your fingers to rub the vanilla seeds in the sugar until they're evenly dispersed. Add another 1¾ cups (350 g) sugar and mix until the vanilla seeds are evenly incorporated. Store in an airtight container.

Recipe: *Vanilla Powdered Sugar*
In a food processor, combine 1 large vanilla bean, chopped, with ½ cup (100 g) white US granulated (UK caster) sugar and pulse repeatedly until the sugar is powdered and the vanilla very finely ground. Add 2 cups (270 g) powdered (icing) sugar and pulse until evenly combined. Store in an airtight container.

Liquid Sweeteners and Syrups
Before white granulated sugar was the de facto choice of sweetener for cookies, there was honey. It's still often used in many European cookie recipes to add its distinct flavor that pairs so well with spices and lends a specific snappy texture to many gingerbread-like cookies. British golden syrup is sometimes given as an alternative to honey, but they are not quite the same, as golden syrup has a completely different flavor—almost butterscotch-y—and is thicker than honey. Molasses, the by-product of sugarcane refining, has a bitter flavor that works in some cookies but is undesirable in others. It is often called for in many European gingerbread-like cookies, but it's a mistranslation, as those cookies were originally made with caramelized sugar syrups. These syrups are made by caramelizing sugar and then mixing it with water to create a brown syrup that has the color of light molasses but none of its characteristic mineral-y bitterness. These syrups often go by the names *mørk sirup*, *tumma siirappi*, or *schenkstroop*, depending on the country. For this book, *mørk sirup* (see page 307) is the most referenced, and while you can find it online most anywhere, substitutes are given in the form of dark corn syrup or golden syrup, which have the closest approximation of its flavor available globally.

EGGS

All eggs used in this book are US large (the equivalent of UK medium or Australian large). For ease of measuring, these recipes don't call for the weight of eggs, but if needing to adjust based on availability of other egg sizes, know that 1 standard American large or UK medium egg, out of the shell, should weigh about 2 ounces or 58 grams.

FLOURS

Wheat Flours
White all-purpose (plain) flour is used more than any other ingredient in this book. It is the standard American variety that contains around 12% protein (versus cake/soft flour, which has around 10%, and bread/strong flour, which is around 14%). Though there can be a range of protein percentages in all-purpose or plain flour, depending on the brand, those differences will not significantly impact the outcome. All-purpose flour used in this book is unbleached (which is the default for plain flour in the UK). For other wheat flours, store leftovers in the freezer to keep them from spoiling.

Nut and Other Grain Flours
Nut flours like almond flour (ground almonds) and hazelnut flour aren't called for much in this book, because I prefer to grind fresh nuts down into the flour needed to make these cookies. But they are used in some recipes, so store leftovers in the freezer to keep them from spoiling.

FLAVORINGS

Spices
Most spices are preground these days, and they're fine to use in these recipes. However, many of these cookies exist as conduits for spices, so in the interest of honoring their history and purpose, I like to freshly grind all my spices before making a batch of cookies. Cinnamon is the one spice where I usually buy preground, but in some recipes even that is called to be freshly ground.

I suggest buying an affordable coffee or spice grinder and using it exclusively to grind spices; it will make everything you bake taste better and more alive. You can also use a small mortar and pestle to grind spices like cardamom seeds, cloves, and anise seeds, which I often do if the amount is less than a teaspoon.

Extracts and Flower Waters
Vanilla and almond extract are the only extracts called for in this book because they're the most common to find and use. They should always be pure and not imitation. Rose water and orange blossom water are also used prodigiously throughout the book, so find a brand you love. Specific amounts are called for in these recipes, but in many instances the amounts can be adjusted to suit your personal preference.

LEAVENERS

Baking Powder and Baking Soda
Your standard baking powder and baking soda (bicarbonate of soda) are represented well in this book. But they can't be used interchangeably. Think of baking soda as a leavener that spreads, while baking powder lifts. If you want a flatter and crisper cookie, baking soda is typically the leavener to use; if you want something lighter or slightly cakey, go with baking powder. And for something in the middle use a mix.

Baker's Ammonia

Most older cookie recipes have been updated through history, and especially in this book, to now use baking soda (bicarb) and powder. But baker's ammonia, or ammonium bicarbonate, is a leavener that was once made from the distillation of oil from deer antlers (known as hartshorn). It was and is still used as a leavening agent in many European baked goods, particularly in Scandinavia, where the exceedingly crisp texture it provides is desirable. And it is in more than a few recipes in this book. Once commonly found in pharmacies, now you can find it in specialty baking and craft stores or online. The chief ingredient in old-fashioned smelling salts, it has a distinct odor that's not for the faint of heart. Thankfully, when heated, it decomposes into two chemicals: carbon dioxide, which leavens the dough, and ammonia, which dissipates, leaving no aroma behind in the finished product. Baker's ammonia works best in cookies where there's plenty of surface area for the ammonia to dissipate and where you want a snappy texture, like in Swedish *drömmar* (recipe, page 313) and many Northern European gingerbreads. Simply open your windows in your kitchen while working with it and try not to inhale it directly. The odor will linger while the cookies bake, but by the time they're done, the smell will be, too. If you don't want to go through the trouble of buying it, you can easily swap it out for baking powder; however, the texture of the finished cookie will be crisp outside and slightly chewy inside, as opposed to meltingly brittle and crisp throughout with the baker's ammonia.

Potash

Potassium bicarbonate—a leavener akin to baking soda (bicarb) that releases carbon dioxide to raise dough—is still used today, but not in this book as baking soda is so common and easier to use.

Yeast

Yeast isn't commonly used in cookies anymore, but it still shows up in a few recipes that likely descended from sweetened, enriched breads. For the recipes in this book, active dry or instant yeast is used and either can be substituted, since the yeast is added for a small amount of flavor or novelty and not for substantial raising properties.

MIX-INS

Chocolate and Cocoa Powders

Though not used often, where they are, the specific percentages of cacao solids in bar chocolate are given. As for cocoa powder, either "natural" or "Dutch-process" is specified. Natural cocoa powder is slightly sour/acidic and produces a lighter brown color, while Dutch-process cocoa powder is treated with alkali, so it is richer and darker in color.

Nuts

Of all the nuts used in cookies, almonds are the most common. Many older recipes call for blanched almonds, which are whole almonds that have had their skins removed, producing a pure white color and no bitterness from the skins. While you can blanch and remove the almond skins yourself, it's a time-consuming process I wouldn't ask anyone to take on. So if you can't find blanched almonds, use the same weight of slivered almonds, which are simply blanched almonds that have been cut into sticks or slivers. Hazelnuts, pistachios, pine nuts, and walnuts are also used in many recipes throughout this book. Store nuts in the freezer to preserve their freshness, then let them thaw before using.

DECORATIONS AND FILLINGS

Pearl Sugars, Nonpareils, Sprinkles, and Sanding Sugars

Various decorating sugars are utilized through the book to add colors and textures to the outsides of cookies. Pearl sugar is matte white and stays that way during baking; it's a favorite of Scandinavian bakers. Nonpareils (also known as hundreds & thousands) are tiny little multicolored balls of sugar that are a favorite decoration in Italian cookies; they are not the same as sprinkles, which are larger and rod-shaped. Sanding sugars are large-grained sugars that add loads of crunch and glass-like shimmer to the outsides of many cookies. They're often dyed in various colors.

Oblaten Wafers

This niche ingredient is only used in one cookie in this book—German *Elisenlebkuchen* (recipe, page 244)—but it's an important one. The dough for these German cookies is a loose mix of ground nuts and sugar, so the *Oblaten* wafers provide structure and allow you to easily shape the mounds on top of them. Made of flour or "starch," they are likely descended from Eucharist wafers that were common in monasteries and convents centuries ago, when monks and nuns produced many of the European baked goods, cookies, and candies we know today.

Jams and Preserves

Many cookies in this book utilize jams and fruit preserves to add a fresh pop of fruit flavor and color to otherwise beige balls of dough. In Eastern Europe, jam is spread over various doughs and used as a filling for rolled-up or dumpling-like cookies. The most common among them is apricot or raspberry jam because those fruits are tart, which is great for balancing the sweetness of the cookies or adding a jolt of acidity to wake up the rich, butter-heavy dough.

While you can buy great preserves, if you want to make your own at home, use the Homemade (Any) Fruit Jam and Plum Butter recipes that I have provided on page 18.

Recipe: *Homemade (Any) Fruit Jam*
Makes 2½ cups (800 g)

-

1¾ lb (795 g) chopped stone fruit
  (such as apricots, peaches, nectarines,
  or plums), berries, or figs
9 oz (255 g) white US granulated
  (UK caster) sugar
⅓ cup (2½ fl oz/80 ml) fresh lemon juice
Pinch of fine sea salt

-

In a large Dutch oven (casserole dish) or heavy-bottomed saucepan, combine the fruit, sugar, lemon juice, and salt. Stir everything together and let the mix macerate at room temperature, stirring occasionally, to allow the sugar to draw out the moisture from the fruit, for at least 1 hour or up to 4 hours.

Place the pot over high heat and bring to a boil, stirring to ensure all the sugar is dissolved. Once the mixture begins boiling, continue cooking, stirring often, especially toward the end, until the jam is thickened and glossy and no longer watery. At the beginning of cooking, use a spoon to skim off any foam or scum from the surface of the jam, rinsing it off in a bowl of cold water in between uses; this will give the jam a clearer appearance. You'll know the jam is ready when you stir and it feels like it is sticking to the bottom of the pot, is bubbling like lava, and there is no longer separation between the fruit and the liquid, rather it moves as one mass. You can also monitor the temperature of the jam with an instant-read thermometer; when the temperature of the jam reaches between 218° and 221°F (103° and 105°C), it is done.

Remove the pot from the heat and let the jam cool to room temperature in the pot before transferring to sterilized containers. Store the jam in the refrigerator for up to 3 months. If you need the jam to be completely smooth, purée it in a food processor.

Recipe: *Plum Butter*
Makes 2 cups (590 g)

Another fruit preserve that's used often in Eastern European sweets is called lekvar or *magiun de prune*, or more commonly, plum butter. Different from regular fruit jam made with sugar, it is made with fresh plums and traditionally has no sugar at all. The fruit is cooked down in water slowly until the water evaporates and the fruit pulp naturally breaks down into a smooth mass that is sweetened only by the sugar present in the fruit. While some recipes call for cooking the plums in water, letting the water evaporate before puréeing them, others I found cut out the step and simply purée soft, high-quality dried prunes with lemon juice in a food processor until the mixture is smooth. I like that approach much better.

-

1 lb (450 g) soft prunes
⅓ cup (2½ fl oz/80 ml) fresh lemon juice
Small pinch of fine sea salt
2–4 tablespoons honey or white
  US granulated (UK caster) sugar

-

In a food processor, combine the prunes, lemon juice, and salt. Blend the mixture together until smooth. Taste the plum butter; it should not be too sweet but assertively tart and inky from the caramelized sugar-y nature of the prunes. To sweeten it slightly, add some honey or sugar and purée again until smooth. Transfer the plum butter to an airtight sterilized container and refrigerate for up to 1 month.

Dairy-free   DF

Gluten-free   GF

Vegetarian   V

Vegan   VE

5 ingredients or fewer   -5

30 minutes or less   -30

southwest asia
& southern asia

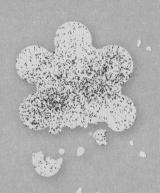

The so-called "birthplace of cookies," this area is dominated by the former Persian empire. It shows its influence in the many small and crumbly shortbread-like cookies that started there, then moved east toward India, with immigrants (now called Parsis) who made their way from Iran to India in the seventh century and influenced many cookies that are still beloved today. Shortbread-like cookies made with rice flour, split chickpea (gram) flour, and ground almonds proliferated in the region showing how they mastered the art of creating crunchy cookies before processed wheat flour became the norm.

Almond Cookies
Ghorabieh / Ghorabiye / Qurabiya

Preparation time: 35 minutes
Cooking time: 25 minutes
Makes: About 12 cookies

2⅔ cups (300 g) slivered almonds
½ cup (105 g) superfine (caster) sugar
2 egg whites
1 teaspoon fine sea salt
1 teaspoon rose water or
  pure vanilla extract
Chopped pistachios and/or
  slivered almonds, for decorating

This group of cookies—spelled variously as *ghorabieh, ghorabiye, qurabiya*, or *qarabieh* (see "Wedding" Cookies, opposite)—is a specialty of the city of Tabriz in the East Azerbaijan province of Iran. Here they are macaroon-type cookies made most popularly with almonds and called *badami ghorabieh*. (When made with walnuts, they're called *gerdui ghorabieh*, and when made with coconut, they're called *nargili ghorabieh*; both are given as variations below.) Somewhat confusingly, the names to describe these sweets are sometimes used interchangeably with cookies that contain flour and/or butter and are translated to English as "shortbreads." To add to the confusion, the suffix *nan-e*, which means "bread" in Persian, is often added to the names of these cookies even though they're not bread-like at all.

Though most recipes vary and the naming conventions make it difficult to be certain, it seems the almond versions are made with egg whites; the walnut versions are made with egg yolks and are less sweet; and the coconut versions are made with whole eggs, and sometimes, a small amount of flour.

Position racks in the top and bottom thirds of the oven and preheat the oven to 350°F (180°C/Gas Mark 4). Line two large baking sheets with parchment paper.

Spread the almonds out in a single layer on one of the baking sheets and bake until lightly toasted and fragrant, about 6 minutes.

Transfer the nuts to a cutting board and let cool. Reserve the baking sheet. In a food processor, process the nuts until very finely ground, about 25 pulses. Add the sugar and pulse to combine, then add the egg whites, salt, and rose water and pulse until the mixture forms a solid dough.

Using a 1-ounce (2-tablespoon) ice cream scoop, drop mounds of the dough onto the prepared baking sheets, spaced 2 inches (5 cm) apart, and flatten slightly with the palm of your hand. Sprinkle the top of each dough mound with a pinch of chopped pistachios and/or slivered almonds.

Bake until light golden brown on the bottom and dry to the touch in the center, 15–20 minutes.

Transfer the baking sheets to wire racks. Let the cookies cool on the pans for 1 minute, then transfer them to the racks to cool completely.

Variations
Walnut Cookies
Use 3 cups (350 g) walnuts in place of the almonds. Reduce the amount of sugar to ⅓ cup (65 g). Omit the egg whites and use 4 egg yolks. Shape as directed. Bake as directed.
Coconut Cookies
Use 3 cups (300 g) unsweetened shredded (desiccated) coconut in place of the ground nuts (do not toast). Omit the egg whites and use 1 whole egg. Add ⅓ cup (45 g) all-purpose (plain) flour along with the coconut. Shape as directed, but use only chopped pistachios to decorate. Bake as directed.

"Wedding" Cookies

The first reference to cookies made with white sugar and flour comes from a tenth-century Arabic cookbook—translated in the *Annals of the Caliphs' Kitchens*—that named them *"gharib khushkananaj"* or "exotic cookies," which was likely a reference to their Persian roots, as the region was the first to use processed cane sugar to make sweets like what we know today as cookies. That first recipe contained approximately 3 pounds (1.4 kg) granulated sugar, 1½ pounds (680 g) wheat flour, and ½ cup (4 fl oz/120 ml) untoasted sesame oil. Everything was mixed together and you were instructed to "press into small dome shapes, then bake in a slow oven until golden brown."

Those first cookies had a huge influence on how the idea of a cookie came to be and would continue to influence others after it. In Turkish, they named their version of that cookie *un kurabiyesi* (recipe, page 60), or "the little extraordinary thing." Clearly, they were impressed. They saved it for special occasions, like religious ceremonies and weddings.

The labor it takes to make such a cookie—that can easily crumble and needs to be tossed in powdered (icing) sugar while hot—is no small task, so that's also why such a labor was reserved for important events. With time, the cookies came to be called "wedding" cookies, possibly because their dusting in pure white powdered sugar resembles a bride's white wedding gown and carries other meanings of purity.

Early versions of cookies similar to Persian *nan-e berenji* (recipe, page 30) and *nan-e nokhodchi* (recipe, page 26) are likely the "wedding" cookies referenced in all these texts. They then went on to be filtered through innumerable references, spelled variously as *ghorabieh, ghorabiye, qurabiye* (recipe, opposite); *ghorayeba, ghurayiba, raybeh* (recipe, page 49), or *ghoriba* (recipe, page 136), depending on where in the world and which cookie you're referring to. From there, similar cookies show up throughout history variously as Turkish *kurabiye* (recipe, page 60) and Greek *kourabiedes* (recipe, page 83), which then made the jump to Europe with Austrian *Vanillekipferl* (recipe, page 195). This created a gateway to Russia and elsewhere in Eastern Europe. From there, European and Western versions of the "wedding" cookie proliferated.

At the same time, that first cookie may have influenced early versions of other crumbly, sugar-coated cookies like Spanish *polvorones* (recipe, page 97), which then veered in a slightly different shape direction and influenced Portuguese *areias de Cascais* (recipe, page 96), Filipino *polvorón* (recipe, page 376), and Mexican *polvorones de canela* (recipe, page 156), which in turn begat even more crumbly cookies that then ended up being called "Mexican wedding cookies" in the United States.

In the US, these cookies are largely known by two names: Russian tea cakes and Mexican wedding cookies/cakes. The late Lynne Olver, a reference librarian who created the web-based Food Timeline during her time at Virginia Tech, posits a fascinating theory: "Why the name? [. . .] Perhaps timing is everything? Culinary evidence confirms Mexican wedding cakes are almost identical to Russian Tea Cakes. During the 1950s and 1960s relations between Russia and the United States were strained. It is possible the Cold War provided the impetus for renaming this popular cookie. Coincidentally? This period saw the mainstreaming of Tex-Mex cuisine into American culture."

Egg Yolk Thumbprint Cookies

Sheker Chorek / Səkərçörəyi

Preparation time: 35 minutes
Cooking time: 20 minutes
Makes: About 24 cookies

3½ cups (490 g) all-purpose (plain) flour
1 teaspoon baking powder
¾ teaspoon fine sea salt
2 sticks (8 oz/225 g) plus 2 tablespoons (30 g) unsalted butter, softened
1½ cups (205 g) powdered (icing) sugar
2 teaspoons pure vanilla extract
1 egg, separated

Though their name means "sweet bread" or "bun," these Azerbaijani sweets are cookies and different from the braided egg-enriched loaf bread that often goes by the same name. They have few ingredients, but the way they're brought together gives them a meltingly tender, unique texture. The butter and sugar are whipped—first by themselves, then with an egg white—for several minutes (some recipes suggest as long as 30 minutes). This process incorporates lots of air into the dough, both helping the dough to absorb more flour and helping the baked cookies to dissolve in your mouth when you take a bite. The leftover egg yolk is drizzled into a tiny divot pressed into the dough balls, thumbprint cookie–style, which bakes up like a golden jewel in the center of these crumbly, buttery treats.

Position racks in the top and bottom thirds of the oven and preheat the oven to 350°F (180°C/Gas Mark 4). Line two large baking sheets with parchment paper.

In a medium bowl, whisk together the flour, baking powder, and salt.

In a large bowl, with a hand mixer, beat the butter and sugar on medium speed until very light with a whipped cream-like texture, 6–8 minutes. Add the vanilla and egg white and continue beating for 4 minutes more. Add the dry ingredients and stir until a dough forms and there are no dry patches of flour remaining.

Using a 1-ounce (2-tablespoon) ice cream scoop, portion the dough and roll into balls. Arrange them on the prepared baking sheets, spaced at least 2 inches (5 cm) apart. Using your index finger, lightly press the center of each dough ball to make a tiny divot.

Place the egg yolk in a small bowl and break it open, stirring until it's uniformly liquid. Using the tip of a table knife or a tiny paint brush, fill each divot with about ⅛ teaspoon of the liquid egg yolk.

Bake until very lightly golden brown on the bottom and dry to the touch all over, 15–20 minutes, switching racks and rotating the baking sheets front to back halfway through.

Transfer the baking sheets to wire racks. Let the cookies cool on the pans for 1 minute, then transfer them to the racks to cool completely.

Egg Yolk Thumbprint Cookies

Chickpea Shortbreads
Nan-e Nokhodchi

Preparation time: 1 hour 10 minutes,
  plus 30 minutes chilling time
Cooking time: 20 minutes
Makes: About 24 cookies

1 cup (135 g) powdered (icing) sugar
½ cup (115 g) clarified butter or ghee
2 teaspoons ground cardamom
1½ teaspoons rose water
½ teaspoon fine sea salt
2 cups (185 g) besan or chickpea
  (gram) flour (see headnote)
Slivered or chopped pistachios,
  for decorating

These classic shortbread cookies are served for Nowruz, Persian new year. They are made of flour from split chickpeas or chana dal (often labeled as besan or gram flour). Though technically not the same as flour made from the common chickpeas we usually eat—like Italian-style chickpea flour—they can be used interchangeably in these cookies. Like *nan-e berenji* (recipe, page 30), these cookies are crumbly and dissolve in your mouth, thanks to the fine texture of the besan.

They are typically rolled thick and cut into the shapes of a four- or five-leaf flower, but many bakers cut them into squares, diamonds, or circles, too. The cut cookies are studded with a single pistachio sliver; though slivered pistachios can be difficult to find outside of Persian, Indian, or specialty grocery stores, chopped pistachios are a fine substitute. The besan is typically roasted before making these cookies, but this recipe skips that step in favor of a less savory cookie. However, if you would like to roast the flour, spread it out on a baking sheet and bake at 350°F (180°C/Gas Mark 4), stirring occasionally, until a shade darker and fragrant, about 8 minutes.

In a large bowl, with a hand mixer, beat the sugar and clarified butter on medium speed until light and fluffy, 2–3 minutes. Add the cardamom, rose water, and salt and beat until smooth. Add the besan and beat on low speed until a dough forms and there are no dry patches of flour remaining.

Scrape the dough onto a large sheet of parchment paper and cover with another sheet of parchment. Use a rolling pin to flatten the dough between the sheets to a round 7 to 8 inches (18 to 20 cm) across and ¾ inch (2 cm) thick. Slide the dough, still between the paper, onto a baking sheet and refrigerate until firm, about 30 minutes.

Position racks in the top and bottom thirds of the oven and preheat the oven to 325°F (160°C/Gas Mark 3). Line two large baking sheets with parchment paper.

Remove the dough from the refrigerator and slide the dough onto a work surface. Remove the top sheet of parchment paper and, using a 1¼-inch (3 cm) flower or similar-shaped cutter dusted in more besan, cut out shapes of dough. Arrange the shapes on the prepared baking sheets, spaced 1 inch (2.5 cm) apart. Stud the center of each shape with a sliver of pistachio or sprinkle it with a pinch of chopped pistachios.

Bake until barely light golden brown on the bottom and dry to the touch in the center, 15–20 minutes (err on the side of underbaking the cookies because they should have hardly any color at all).

Transfer the baking sheets to wire racks. Let the cookies cool on the pans for 1 minute, then transfer them to the racks to cool completely.

Southwest Asia & Southern Asia

Chickpea Shortbreads

Persian Raisin Cookies

Shirini Keshmeshi

Preparation time: 45 minutes
Cooking time: 15 minutes
Makes: About 24 cookies

1½ sticks (6 oz/170 g) unsalted
   butter, softened
1 cup (200 g) white US granulated
   (UK caster) sugar
3 eggs
2 tablespoons boiling water
   mixed with ½ teaspoon crushed
   saffron and cooled (optional) or
   2 tablespoons rose water
1 teaspoon pure vanilla extract
¾ teaspoon fine sea salt
2 cups (280 g) all-purpose (plain) flour
1 cup (165 g) raisins

Raisins are an important ingredient in Persian cuisine, adding sweetness to yogurt, rice, and braised meat dishes. They also add sweetness to desserts and these cookies, which are as common in Iran as chocolate chip cookies (recipe, page 346) are to Americans. Because of the added sugar in the cookies, the raisins here are added more for their chewy, fruity flavor than to add sweetness—like in Romanian *fursecuri cu stafide* (recipe, page 207).

Some recipes for these cookies call for saffron, while others use rose water or keep the dough unflavored—save some vanilla extract—to let the flavor of the raisins shine. The saffron is an optional ingredient in this recipe; add it if you like, it will also give the cookies a beautiful golden yellow hue.

Position racks in the top and bottom thirds of the oven and preheat the oven to 350°F (180°C/Gas Mark 4). Line two large baking sheets with parchment paper.

In a large bowl, with a hand mixer, beat the butter and sugar on medium speed until light and fluffy, 2–3 minutes. Add the eggs, one at a time, beating well after each addition. Beat in the saffron water (if using) or rose water, vanilla, and salt. Add the flour and raisins, and beat on low speed until a dough forms and there are no dry patches of flour remaining.

Using a 1-ounce (2-tablespoon) ice cream scoop, drop mounds of the dough onto the prepared baking sheets, spaced 2 inches (5 cm) apart.

Bake until golden brown at the edges and dry to the touch in the center, 12–15 minutes, switching racks and rotating the baking sheets front to back halfway through.

Transfer the baking sheets to wire racks and let the cookies cool completely on the pans.

Persian Raisin Cookies

Persian Rice Shortbreads
Nan-e Berenji

Preparation time: 40 minutes,
 plus 15 minutes chilling time
Cooking time: 20 minutes
Makes: About 24 cookies

1 cup (225 g) clarified butter or ghee
1½ cups (205 g) powdered
 (icing) sugar
1 teaspoon ground cardamom
¾ teaspoon fine sea salt
3 egg yolks
¼ cup (2 fl oz/60 ml) rose water
3 cups (480 g) white rice flour
Poppy seeds, for sprinkling

These crumbly Persian shortbread cookies get their fragile texture from the use of rice flour and whipped clarified butter, which enhances the brittle, melt-in-the-mouth texture of the baked cookies. Traditional recipes call for making a rose water-flavored simple syrup, though modern recipes typically mix the sugar and rose water into the dough.

While poppy seeds seem to be the throughline decoration for the top of these cookies—often made to celebrate the Persian new year, Nowruz—many bakers also add chopped pistachios or dried rose petals. This recipe is for rustic drop-style cookies, but you can flatten the mounds of dough with a cookie stamp, as many Persian bakers do.

In a large bowl, with a hand mixer, beat the clarified butter on medium speed until light and fluffy, about 3 minutes. Add the sugar, cardamom, and salt and beat until extremely light and whipped, about 3 minutes more. With the mixer on low speed, add the egg yolks, followed by the rose water, beating until incorporated. Add the rice flour and beat on low speed until a dough forms and there are no dry patches of flour remaining. Place the bowl of dough in the refrigerator for 15 minutes to firm up slightly.

Position racks in the top and bottom thirds of the oven and preheat the oven to 350°F (180°C/Gas Mark 4). Line two large baking sheets with parchment paper.

Using a 1-ounce (2-tablespoon) ice cream scoop, drop mounds of the dough onto the prepared baking sheets, spaced 2 inches (5 cm) apart, then flatten each slightly with the palm of your hand or use a cookie stamp. Sprinkle the top of each dough mound with a pinch of poppy seeds.

Bake until light golden brown on the bottom and dry to the touch in the center, 15–18 minutes (err on the side of underbaking the cookies because they should hardly have any color at all).

Transfer the baking sheets to wire racks and let the cookies cool completely on the pans.

Cardamom Biscuits
Kulche-e Khetaye / Khatae / Khatai

Preparation time: 45 minutes
Cooking time: 15 minutes
Makes: About 24 cookies

2 cups (280 g) all-purpose (plain) flour
1 cup (135 g) powdered (icing) sugar
½ cup (115 g) instant nonfat dry milk
1 teaspoon baking powder
1 teaspoon ground cardamom
½ teaspoon fine sea salt
1 cup (8 fl oz/250 ml) vegetable oil
Very finely ground pistachios,
 for decorating

Almost identical to Indian *nankhatai* (recipe, page 37), this version uses all wheat-based flour. Another name for these cookies is more poetic: *awb-e dandaan*, meaning "water from the teeth"—a whimsical translation of the oft used "melt in the mouth" descriptor for these rich shortbread cookies. Vegetable oil is often mixed with milk powder, which approximates the qualities of butter, an unused and expensive ingredient in Afghanistan.

Position racks in the top and bottom thirds of the oven and preheat the oven to 325°F (160°C/Gas Mark 3). Line two large baking sheets with parchment paper.

In a large bowl, whisk together the flour, sugar, milk powder, baking powder, cardamom, and salt.

In a small saucepan, warm the oil until just warm to the touch. Pour the warm oil into the bowl and stir with a fork, until a dough forms and there are no dry patches of flour remaining.

Using a 1-ounce (2-tablespoon) ice cream scoop, portion the dough and roll into balls. Arrange them on the prepared baking sheets, spaced 2 inches (5 cm) apart. Flatten each mound slightly with the palm of your hand, then use your finger to press a shallow indentation in the center of each. Fill the indentation with a pinch of finely ground pistachios.

Bake until light golden brown on the bottom and dry to the touch, 8–10 minutes, switching racks and rotating the baking sheets front to back halfway through.

Transfer the baking sheets to wire racks. Let the cookies cool on the pans for 1 minute, then transfer them to the racks to cool completely.

Afghani Rice Cookies

Kolcheh Nowrozi / Birinjee

Preparation time: 30 minutes
Cooking time: 15 minutes
Makes: About 24 cookies

¾ cup (170 g) clarified butter or ghee
¾ cup (150 g) white US granulated
  (UK caster) sugar
2 egg whites
1 teaspoon ground cardamom
¾ teaspoon fine sea salt
2 cups (320 g) white rice flour
½ cup (65 g) pistachios,
  finely chopped, plus more
  for sprinkling

The name for these treats translates roughly to "Nowruz cookie," which points to them being closely related to Iranian *nan-e berenji* (recipe, page 30). While the Iranian versions are crumbly and dense and typically made only with egg yolks, many recipes for this version use only egg whites, which gives these cookies a firmer snap.

Recipes for these cookies call for cardamom to flavor the dough, while the Iranian cookie is heady with rose water. Afghani versions are decorated with pistachios, rather than the ubiquitous poppy seeds found in Iranian versions, and they might also include pistachios in the dough.

Position racks in the top and bottom thirds of the oven and preheat the oven to 350°F (180°C/Gas Mark 4). Line two large baking sheets with parchment paper.

In a large bowl, with a hand mixer, beat the clarified butter and sugar on medium speed until light and fluffy, 2–3 minutes. Add the egg whites, one at a time, beating well after each addition, then beat in the cardamom and salt. Add the rice flour and pistachios and beat on low speed until a dough forms and there are no dry patches of flour remaining.

Using a 1-ounce (2-tablespoon) ice cream scoop, drop mounds of the dough onto the prepared baking sheets, spaced 2 inches (5 cm) apart. Flatten each slightly with the palm of your hand. Sprinkle the top of each dough mound with a pinch of chopped pistachios.

Bake until light golden brown on the bottom and dry to the touch in the center, about 15 minutes, switching racks and rotating the baking sheets front to back halfway through.

Transfer the baking sheets to wire racks and let the cookies cool completely on the pans.

Khalifa-Style Almond Shortbread Cookies

Khalifa Nankhatai

Preparation time: 40 minutes
Cooking time: 20 minutes
Makes: About 9 cookies

1½ cups (210 g) all-purpose (plain) flour
½ cup (50 g) besan or chickpea
  (gram) flour
1 teaspoon ground cardamom
½ teaspoon baking soda
  (bicarbonate of soda)
½ teaspoon fine sea salt
¾ cup (170 g) ghee, softened
¾ cup (160 g) superfine (caster) sugar
4 oz (115 g) almonds, roughly chopped
1 tablespoon whole milk
1 egg yolk

This riff on the classic Indian *nankhatai* (recipe, page 37) is credited as the invention of Khalifa Bakers in Lahore, Pakistan. There, they make their biscuits much bigger and thicker than the Indian version. This Pakistani style also typically uses a higher proportion of all-purpose (plain) wheat flour to besan, which makes the cookies sturdier. Large chunks of chopped almonds are dotted throughout the cookies, which are brushed with a thick egg wash to give them a golden glaze on top.

Position racks in the top and bottom thirds of the oven and preheat the oven to 350°F (180°C/Gas Mark 4). Line two large baking sheets with parchment paper.

In a medium bowl, whisk together the flour, besan, cardamom, baking soda (bicarb), and salt.

In a large bowl, with a hand mixer, beat the ghee and sugar on medium speed until light and fluffy, 2–3 minutes. Add the flour mixture and almonds and beat on low speed until a dough forms and there are no dry patches of flour remaining.

Using a 2-ounce (4-tablespoon) ice cream scoop, portion the dough and roll into balls. Place each ball on the prepared baking sheets, spaced 2 inches (5 cm) apart. Flatten into a disc ½ inch (13 mm) thick with the palm of your hand. In a small bowl, whisk together the milk and egg yolk to make an egg wash. Brush some of the egg wash liberally over the top of each dough disc.

Bake until golden brown all over and dry to the touch in the center, 15–20 minutes, switching racks and rotating the baking sheets front to back halfway through.

Transfer the baking sheets to wire racks and let the cookies cool completely on the pans.

Atta Biscuits

Preparation time: 40 minutes
Cooking time: 15 minutes
Makes: About 24 cookies

½ teaspoon cardamom seeds
1⅓ cups (200 g) atta (whole wheat
  durum wheat flour; see headnote)
½ teaspoon baking soda
  (bicarbonate of soda)
½ teaspoon fine sea salt
½ cup (105 g) superfine (caster) sugar
⅓ cup (75 g) ghee, at room
  temperature
¼ cup (2 fl oz/60 ml) whole milk

These thin and crisp whole wheat cardamom cookies are beloved in India to have with a glass of milk, tea, or chai. They get their signature dark color and hearty flavor from using *atta*, a type of whole-grain durum wheat flour that's sometimes sold as a blend of refined durum flour and wheat bran. (It is not technically the same as the common whole wheat/wholemeal flour that is widely available in US and UK grocery stores, but the latter can be substituted for the former in a pinch.) Like *nankhatai* (recipe, page 37), freshly ground cardamom seeds flavor these simple cookies, with some recipes adding nutmeg to the mix as well.

Traditionally, these cookies are piped into lengths using a cookie press, but you can also roll them out thinly and cut them into whatever shapes you like. Typically, they are cut into squares or rectangles if done this way and docked with a fork to keep them from puffing up while baking. They also use superfine (caster) sugar—often sold in US grocery stores as baker's sugar—which gives the cookie's crumb a finer texture. These cookies are also eggless, which, in addition to the superfine sugar, *atta*, and ghee, further helps them achieve a crisp, shortbread-like texture.

- -

Position racks in the top and bottom thirds of the oven and preheat the oven to 350°F (180°C/Gas Mark 4). Line two large baking sheets with parchment paper.

Using a spice grinder or mortar and pestle, process the cardamom seeds until very finely ground and set aside.

In a medium bowl, whisk together the atta flour, baking soda (bicarb), and salt.

In a large bowl, with a hand mixer, beat the sugar, ghee, and ground cardamom on medium speed until light and fluffy, 2–3 minutes. Add half the dry ingredients and the milk and stir until almost combined. Add the remaining dry ingredients and stir until a dough forms and there are no dry patches of flour remaining.

Working in batches, scrape the dough into a cookie press fitted with a ridged line disc, sometimes called the "biscuit" disc, to pipe 3-inch (7.5 cm) lengths of dough, arranging them 1 inch (2.5 cm) apart on the baking sheets. (Alternatively, flatten the dough with a rolling pin until ¼ inch (6 mm) thick and cut into 1½ × 3-inch (4 × 7.5 cm) rectangles. Pierce each dough rectangle with the tines of a fork a few times.)

Bake until a shade darker on the bottom and dry to the touch all over, 14–16 minutes, switching racks and rotating the baking sheets front to back halfway through.

Transfer the baking sheets to wire racks. Let the cookies cool on the pans for 1 minute, then transfer them to the racks to cool completely.

Atta Biscuits

Split Chickpea Flour Shortbread Balls

Besan Ke Laddu / Besan Ke Ladoo

Preparation time: 15 minutes
Cooking time: 15 minutes
Makes: About 12 cookies

¼ teaspoon cardamom seeds
½ cup (105 g) ghee
¾ cup (75 g) besan or chickpea
  (gram) flour
¼ cup (25 g) unsweetened shredded
  (desiccated) coconut or ¼ cup (35 g)
  very finely chopped almonds
⅔ cup (140 g) superfine (caster) sugar
Halved pistachios, for
  decorating (optional)

The prototype of these tiny, sweet orbs that are beloved all over Northern India and Nepal were originally made with sesame seeds, peanuts, and jaggery (a type of raw sugar), coated in honey and used as an antiseptic and as a way to deliver medicine. They can be made with any kind of flour or nuts. Today, the most popular version is made with besan—a flour made from split chickpeas (chana dal) that is sometimes labeled gram flour. Look for besan at Indian grocery stores or online.

The besan is roasted in ghee in a frying pan and flavored with cardamom before getting mixed with sugar and nuts, often coconut. Once the mixture cools slightly, you form tiny balls with your hands.

Using a spice grinder or mortar and pestle, process the cardamom seeds until very finely ground and set aside.

In a large nonstick frying pan, melt the ghee over medium-high heat. Add the besan to the ghee, one spoonful at a time, stirring constantly with a silicone spatula or wooden spoon until it is all added. Continue cooking the besan, stirring often, until it smells fragrant and toasted and is golden brown. Stir in the coconut and cardamom and stir until warmed through, about 30 seconds more.

Remove the pan from the heat and stir in the sugar until evenly incorporated. Let stand until cool enough to handle with your hands.

Line a large baking sheet with parchment paper. Using a ½-ounce (1-tablespoon) ice cream scoop, portion the dough and roll into balls. If you like, stud the top of each ball with half a pistachio. Arrange the laddu on the prepared baking sheet and let cool completely.

Split Chickpea Flour Shortbread Balls

Cumin Seed Cookies

Khasta Jeera

Preparation time: 25 minutes
Cooking time: 20 minutes
Makes: About 30 cookies

1½ teaspoons cumin seeds
1¼ cups (175 g) all-purpose (plain) flour
½ teaspoon baking powder
¾ teaspoon fine sea salt
1 stick (4 oz/115 g) unsalted
  butter, softened
⅓ cup (65 g) white US granulated
  (UK caster) sugar
1 egg

The British custom of making teatime biscuits has influenced many of these cookie-like treats in India and Pakistan. One of the most popular is made with a spice typically only used in savory cooking: cumin. Since India is one of the world's largest producers of cumin seeds, it is not a surprise that they made their way into a cookie there—the spice lending the cookies a floral essence that walks a line between savory and sweet. The cumin seeds here are toasted to enhance their flavor and soften them before mixing into the dough.

Position racks in the top and bottom thirds of the oven and preheat the oven to 350°F (180°C/Gas Mark 4). Line two large baking sheets with parchment paper.

In a small frying pan, toast the cumin seeds over medium heat until fragrant, about 2 minutes.

Transfer the seeds to a mortar and pestle or cutting board and grind or chop them roughly. Transfer the chopped seeds to a medium bowl and whisk in the flour, baking powder, and salt to combine.

In a large bowl, with a hand mixer, beat the butter and sugar on medium speed until light and fluffy, 2–3 minutes. Add the egg and beat until smooth. Add the dry ingredients and beat on low speed until a dough forms and there are no dry patches of flour remaining.

Working on a lightly floured work surface, roll out the dough with a rolling pin to ¼ inch (6 mm) thick. Using a 1½-inch (4 cm) round cutter, cut out rounds of dough and transfer them to the prepared baking sheets spaced 1 inch (2.5 cm) apart.

Bake until golden brown at the edges and dry to the touch in the center, 10–15 minutes, switching racks and rotating the baking sheets front to back halfway through.

Transfer the baking sheets to wire racks. Let the cookies cool on the pans for 1 minute, then transfer them to the racks to cool completely.

Cardamom Shortbread Cookies

Nankhatai

Preparation time: 35 minutes
Cooking time: 25 minutes
Makes: About 12 cookies

¼ teaspoon cardamom seeds
½ cup (70 g) all-purpose (plain) flour
½ cup (80 g) semolina flour
⅓ cup (30 g) besan or chickpea (gram) flour
½ teaspoon fine sea salt
¼ teaspoon baking soda (bicarbonate of soda)
⅛ teaspoon cream of tartar
½ cup (100 g) ghee, softened
½ cup (105 g) superfine (caster) sugar
2 tablespoons full-fat yogurt
Slivered almonds or chopped pistachios, for decorating

Popular lore has it that a couple Dutch settlers in Mumbai (then Bombay) set up a bakery to sell their cookies made with butter, sugar, flour, eggs, and palm wine. When they left, they sold their bakery to a Persian man who changed the recipe (omitting eggs and wine) to suit locals' tastes, and this crumbly shortbread-like cookie was born. Whether true or not, these cardamom-scented cookies have been a part of the cooking of Parsis— an ethnoreligious group of people who emigrated from Persia to India to preserve their Zoroastrian religion—for generations in Gujarat and the western states of India. Because of India's influence on Eastern Africa over the past couple centuries, these cookies are popular in Kenya as well.

Ghee is traditionally used along with a mix of all-purpose (plain) and semolina flours as well as besan, a flour made from split chickpeas (chana dal), also called gram flour, which can be found in some supermarkets (especially in the UK), at Indian grocery stores, or online. All of these ingredients contribute qualities that make for a crumbly dry cookie that's often served with tea. Freshly ground cardamom seeds perfume the dough and decorate the tops of the cookies, though most home cooks now use slivered almonds or chopped pistachios as a decoration.

Position racks in the top and bottom thirds of the oven and preheat the oven to 325°F (160°C/Gas Mark 3). Line two large baking sheets with parchment paper.

Using a spice grinder or mortar and pestle, process the cardamom seeds until very finely ground and set aside.

In a medium bowl, whisk together the all-purpose (plain) flour, semolina flour, besan, salt, baking soda (bicarb), and cream of tartar.

In a large bowl, with a hand mixer, combine the ghee, sugar, yogurt, and ground cardamom and beat on medium speed until light and fluffy, 2–3 minutes. Add the dry ingredients and stir until a dough forms and there are no dry patches of flour remaining.

Using a 1-ounce (2-tablespoon) ice cream scoop, portion the dough and roll into balls. Place a piece of slivered almond or a few pieces of chopped pistachio in the palm of one hand, then place a dough ball on top of the nuts and flatten the ball with your other hand into a disc. Invert the disc and place it on a prepared baking sheet. Repeat with the remaining dough balls and nuts, arrange the discs 1 inch (2.5 cm) apart on the sheets.

Bake until barely browned on the bottom and dry to the touch all over, 20–25 minutes, switching racks and rotating the baking sheets front to back halfway through.

Transfer the baking sheets to wire racks. Let the cookies cool on the pans for 1 minute, then transfer them to the racks to cool completely.

Fried Whole Wheat Biscuits
Thekua

Preparation time: 30 minutes,
 plus chilling time
Cooking time: 45 minutes
Makes: About 18 cookies

8 oz (225 g) jaggery, or piloncillo, or
 1 cup packed dark muscovado sugar
½ cup (4 fl oz/120 ml) water
1½ teaspoons fennel seeds
2¼ cups (338 g) whole wheat
 (wholemeal) flour
¼ cup (25 g) unsweetened shredded
 (desiccated) coconut
1 teaspoon ground cardamom
½ teaspoon fine sea salt
¼ cup (50 g) ghee, clarified butter,
 or refined coconut oil, chilled
Vegetable oil, for deep-frying

In Northern India and Southern Nepal these cookies are traditionally made for Chhath Puja, a Hindu holiday celebrating their sun god, Surya, hence they are typically stamped with ornate designs mimicking sun rays or stars. The cookies—flavored with fennel seeds, cardamom, and sometimes coconut—are also deep-fried, as is customary with many sweets in India. Deep-frying the cookies allows them to achieve an extra-crispy texture and use less fat in the dough. While modern recipes are often adapted to baking cookies in the oven, this recipe calls for deep-frying in the traditional method. Take care when frying the cookies as they are delicate and should be handled more gently than a deep-fried bread or pastry.

Similar to many cookies in Central America, these are sweetened with a syrup made from a raw cane sugar (see page 164), in this case, jaggery; if you can't find jaggery at an Indian grocery store, you can use *piloncillo* or another raw brown sugar. Instead of buying a special stamp to imprint a design on each cookie, this recipe calls for creating a star pattern with a toothpick or simply pressing the cookies flat with the tines of a fork.

- -

Using a serrated knife, roughly chop the jaggery (or grate on the large holes of box grater).

In a small saucepan, combine the jaggery and water and bring to a boil over high heat, stirring to dissolve the sugar completely. Once the syrup boils, remove the pan from the heat and let the syrup cool completely.

Working in a mortar and pestle, or on a cutting board and using the bottom of a heavy pot, lightly crush the fennel seeds so none of the seeds are still whole.

Line a large baking sheet with parchment paper. Transfer the crushed seeds to a large bowl and add the flour, coconut, cardamom, and salt and whisk to combine. Add the ghee and use your hands to rub the ghee into the flour mixture until the fat breaks down into crumbles the size of peas. Pour in the cooled syrup and stir with a fork until a dough forms and there are no dry patches of flour remaining.

Using a 1-ounce (2-tablespoon) ice cream scoop, portion the dough and roll into balls. Arrange them on the parchment-lined baking sheet, flattening them with your hand as you work so they're about ¼ inch (6 mm) thick. Using a toothpick or the tines of a fork, lay the toothpick across each flattened dough "bowl" in repeating positions—like you're mimicking the hours on the face of a clock—to create a radiating star pattern. Place the sheet of cookies in the refrigerator for at least 30 minutes or up to 1 day.

Line a large baking sheet with paper towels. Pour enough oil into a medium saucepan to come 2 inches (5 cm) up the sides of the pan. Attach a candy/deep-fry thermometer to the side of the pan. Heat the oil until it reaches 325°F (160°C) on the thermometer.

Working in batches of 1 or 2, and maintaining the oil temperature, fry the cookies, flipping them with a slotted spoon occasionally, until golden brown and cooked through, 2–4 minutes. Using a slotted spoon, lift the cookies from the oil and transfer them to the paper towels to drain.

Let the cookies cool completely—they will firm up when cooled—before serving.

Fried Whole Wheat Biscuits

Karachi Biscuits

Preparation time: 1 hour, plus
  chilling time
Cooking time: 30 minutes
Makes: About 36 cookies

4 oz (115 g) cashews
1½ cups (210 g) all-purpose
  (plain) flour
½ cup (60 g) custard powder
1 teaspoon baking powder
¾ teaspoon fine sea salt
2 sticks (8 oz/225 g) unsalted
  butter, softened
½ cup (100 g) white US granulated
  (UK caster) sugar
2 tablespoons whole milk
1 teaspoon rose water
  or ground cardamom
¾ cup (150 g) tutti frutti mix or finely
  diced candied papaya

Also known as Karachi "fried biscuits" or tutti frutti biscuits, these mosaic slice-and-bake cookies are a specialty of Karachi Bakery, a chain that started in the city of Hyderabad, India, in 1953. Though not all vegetarians in India typically abstain from eating eggs, these cookies may have been developed to be eggless so they could appeal to the largest swath of the population. They are now a popular homemade cookie for bakers wanting to re-create their favorite bakery treat.

The cookies get their signature look from pieces of candied papaya mottling the dough. In India, you can buy something called "tutti frutti mix," which is candied papaya that's been dyed—typically, red, green, and orange—scented with rose water, and chopped. The mix is sold in Indian grocery stores, but if you can't find it or don't want to use dyed fruit, use regular candied papaya and chop it into ¼-inch (6 mm) pieces before mixing into the dough.

Preheat the oven to 350°F (180°C/Gas Mark 4). Line a large baking sheet with parchment paper.

Spread the cashews out in a single layer on the baking sheet and bake until lightly toasted and fragrant, 8–10 minutes.

Transfer the nuts to a cutting board and let cool. Reserve the baking sheet. Using a food processor or a knife, process or chop the cashews until finely ground.

In a medium bowl, whisk together the flour, custard powder, baking powder, and salt.

In a large bowl, with a hand mixer, beat the butter and sugar on medium speed until light and fluffy, 2–3 minutes. Add the milk and rose water and beat until smooth. Add the flour mixture, cashews, and tutti frutti mix and stir until a dough forms and there are no dry patches of flour remaining.

Divide the dough in half. Form each half into a vague cylinder and place on separate sheets of parchment paper. Shape the dough into logs 2 inches (5 cm) in diameter and wrap tightly (see page 14). Lightly press on each log to give it four flat edges and a rectangular shape. Transfer the dough logs to the refrigerator to firm up for at least 30 minutes or up to 2 days.

When ready to bake, position racks in the top and bottom third of the oven and preheat the oven to 350°F (180°C/Gas Mark 4). Line two large baking sheets with parchment paper.

Unwrap the dough log and cut into slices ¼ inch (6 mm) thick. Transfer the slices to the prepared baking sheets, arranging them at least 2 inches (5 cm) apart.

Bake until golden brown and dry to the touch in the center, 15–20 minutes, switching racks and rotating the baking sheets front to back halfway through.

Transfer the baking sheets to wire racks. Let the cookies cool on the pans for 1 minute, then transfer them to the racks to cool completely.

Karachi Biscuits

the levant & arabian peninsula

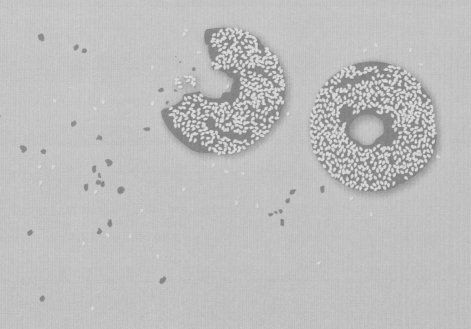

The area including and surrounding the Fertile Crescent (an historical area in the Middle East arching over the top of Arabia and stretching from Egypt down to Kuwait) shows a penchant for cookies stuffed with dried fruits, like dates, or ground nuts sweetened with honey or perfumed with flower waters or sesame seeds. Countless shortbread-like *ghorayeba* cookies proliferate and show up in as many forms as there are households that make them. Often perfumed with cardamom or enriched with ground nuts, the cookies show just how beloved the crumbly, buttery texture is in the region.

Nut-Filled Shortbread Cookies
Maamoul

Preparation time: 1 hour,
  plus overnight standing
Cooking time: 15 minutes
Makes: About 12 cookies

For the nut filling:
1 cup (115 g) walnuts or pistachios
2 tablespoons white US granulated
  (UK caster) sugar
1½ teaspoons orange blossom
  water (for walnuts) or rose water
  (for pistachios)
⅛ teaspoon ground cinnamon
  (for walnuts)

For the cookies:
1⅔ cups (255 g) semolina flour
1 stick (4 oz/115 g) unsalted
  butter, melted
¼ cup (2 fl oz/60 ml) vegetable oil
½ cup (70 g) all-purpose (plain) flour
¼ cup (50 g) white US granulated
  (UK caster) sugar
¾ teaspoon fine sea salt
½ teaspoon instant or active dry yeast
½ teaspoon ground mahleb
2 tablespoons water
1 tablespoon orange blossom water
1 tablespoon rose water
Powdered (icing) sugar, for dusting

Arguably the most well-known Middle Eastern cookie, these filled shortbreads are descended from the Egyptian *kahk* (recipe, page 50), but are now considered a separate cookie with special shapes to denote three distinct fillings. Only semolina is traditionally used in the dough, though many recipes now add all-purpose (plain) flour to create a softer texture. *Mahleb* (a spice made of ground cherry kernels) and flower waters give these cookies a distinct, intensely aromatic flavor.

According to Anissa Helou's *Feast: Food of the Islamic World*, when the cookies are filled with nuts they are called *maamoul*, while the date-filled cookie goes by the name *qrass bil-tamr* (see the variation that follows). When walnuts are used, the cookies are shaped in a round, domed mold, while a pistachio filling gets a domed oval shape. Both nut versions get dusted with powdered (icing) sugar, whereas the date version is molded flat and left plain. The cookies are traditional for breaking the fast during Ramadan, but are now so widespread that they are eaten year-round. In Iran, *kolucheh* or *koloocheh* refers to a version made of spiced dough filled with spiced date paste and nuts—usually walnuts or walnuts combined with pistachios. They are either imprinted with a mold or simply left as mounds and topped with more ground nuts.

- -

Make the nut filling: In a food processor, combine the walnuts or pistachios, the white US granulated (UK caster) sugar, orange blossom water (if making walnut filling) or rose water (for pistachio), and cinnamon (for walnuts) and pulse until finely ground, 6–8 pulses. Transfer to a bowl and keep covered in plastic wrap (cling film) until ready to use.

Make the cookies: In a large bowl, combine the semolina, melted butter, and oil and mix with your fingers until the mixture resembles coarse sand or couscous. Cover the bowl with plastic wrap (cling film) and let stand overnight (at least 8 hours) to allow the semolina to soften.

In a medium bowl, whisk together the all-purpose (plain) flour, white US granulated (UK caster) sugar, salt, yeast, and mahleb. Uncover the bowl and add the flour/sugar mixture to the semolina mixture along with the water, orange blossom water, and rose water. Stir with your hands until a dough forms, kneading to form a smooth dough.

Line two large baking sheets with parchment paper. Using a 1-ounce (2-tablespoon) ice cream scoop, portion the dough and roll into balls. Flatten each ball in your hand and place 1 heaping teaspoon of walnut or pistachio filling in the center. Gather the dough around the filling to encase it and then reroll the dough into a smooth ball.

Lightly press the cookie ball into a maamoul mold to imprint its design, using a 2-inch (5 cm) round domed mold for the walnut-filled balls and 3 × 2-inch (7.5 × 5 cm) oval domed mold for the pistachio-filled balls. (Alternatively, slightly flatten the balls on the baking sheets and imprint a crisscross design on top with the tines of a fork.)

Arrange the shaped dough balls on the prepared baking sheets, spaced 1 inch (2.5 cm) apart. Chill the cookies for 10 minutes.

Meanwhile, position racks in the top and bottom thirds of the oven and preheat the oven to 400°F (200°C/Gas Mark 6).

Bake until light golden brown, 12–15 minutes, switching racks and rotating the baking sheets front to back halfway through.

Transfer the baking sheets to wire racks and let the cookies rest on the pans for 1 minute. While the cookies are still warm, dust each with powdered (icing) sugar on top, then let cool completely on the pans.

Dust with more powdered sugar again before serving.

Variation
Date-Filled Maamoul (Qrass bil-Tamr)
Replace the nut filling with the date filling from the Date-Filled "Bracelet" Cookies (recipe, page 48), using half the amount of dates, 1 tablespoon melted unsalted butter instead of the oil, ¼ teaspoon ground cinnamon and omitting the cardamom. Make as above, flattening by hand rather than using a maamoul mold. Do not dust with powdered (icing) sugar.

Sesame and Pistachio Cookies

Barazek

Preparation time: 30 minutes,
 plus 1 hour resting time
Cooking time: 15 minutes
Makes: About 30 cookies

2⅔ cups (375 g) all-purpose
 (plain) flour
1 teaspoon ground mahleb
1 teaspoon baking powder
1 teaspoon fine sea salt
½ teaspoon instant or active dry yeast
2 sticks (8 oz/225 g) unsalted
 butter, softened
½ cup (100 g) white US granulated
 (UK caster) sugar
2 eggs
½ cup (170 g) mild honey
1 cup (150 g) sesame seeds
1 cup (130 g) pistachios,
 roughly chopped

Popularly thought to be the creation of bakeries in Damascus, these distinct cookies are also eaten in Lebanon, Palestine, Jordan, and all over the Middle East. Though made with yeast and semolina in the past, many recipes call for a simple butter cookie flavored with *mahleb* (the kernels of a type of cherry, sold whole or ground). This recipe still incorporates the yeast for flavoring though it doesn't give rise to the cookies.

The shaped discs of dough are pressed into chopped pistachios on one side and then brushed or dipped in honey and crusted in sesame seeds on the other side. This contrast of nuts and seeds makes for a beautiful cookie that's often eaten for Eid at the end of Ramadan.

In a medium bowl, whisk together the flour, mahleb, baking powder, salt, and yeast.

In a large bowl, with a hand mixer, beat the butter and sugar on medium speed until light and fluffy, 2–3 minutes. Add the eggs, one at a time, beating until smooth after each addition. Add the dry ingredients and beat on low speed until a dough forms and there are no dry patches of flour remaining. Cover the bowl with plastic wrap (cling film) and let the dough rest for 1 hour at room temperature.

Meanwhile, pour the honey into a frying pan or saucepan and warm over low heat until loose. (Alternatively, microwave in a heatproof bowl until loose.) Spread the sesame seeds on one plate and spread the pistachios on another.

Position racks in the top and bottom thirds of the oven and preheat the oven to 350°F (180°C/Gas Mark 4). Line two large baking sheets with parchment paper.

Using a 1-ounce (2-tablespoon) ice cream scoop, portion the dough and roll into balls. Flatten one ball into a disc ¼ inch (6 mm) thick in the palm of your hand, then place one side in the pistachios. Lightly brush the plain side with some of the honey, then place the honey side in the sesame seeds. Transfer the disc to the prepared baking sheets, sesame seed side-up; repeat with the remaining dough balls, pistachios, honey, and sesame seeds to form more cookies, arranging the discs 2 inches (5 cm) apart on the sheets.

Bake until golden brown all over and dry to the touch in the center, 12–15 minutes, switching racks and rotating the baking sheets front to back halfway through.

Transfer the baking sheets to wire racks and let the cookies cool completely on the pans.

Twice-Baked Almond Cookies

Mandelbrot

Preparation time: 25 minutes
Cooking time: 45 minutes
Makes: About 72 cookies

3 cups (420 g) all-purpose (plain) flour
2 teaspoons baking powder
¾ teaspoon fine sea salt
1½ cups (300 g) white US granulated
 (UK caster) sugar
1 cup (8 fl oz/250 ml) vegetable oil
1 teaspoon pure vanilla extract
½ teaspoon pure almond extract
4 eggs
8 oz (225 g) blanched whole almonds,
 roughly chopped, or slivered almonds
1 teaspoon ground cinnamon (optional)

Yiddish for "almond bread," the dough for *mandelbrot* is formed into logs, parbaked, and then sliced and baked again to crisp up, just like Italian biscotti or *cantucci* (recipe, page 112). It's also possible that these twice-baked cookies are related to German *Zwieback*, a double-baked bread rusk popular throughout Europe. Because of the almond in this Jewish cookie's name, *mandelbrot* are traditionally made with almonds and almond extract, though many modern versions have other nuts, dried fruits, and even chocolate mixed in.

Mandelbrot is often made with neutral vegetable oil to keep the cookies pareve, a term in Jewish dietary laws denoting something that is made without meat or dairy products. This also gives the cookies a more tender crumb that doesn't bake up as crisp as biscotti. Though not seen in all recipes, many call to coat the parbaked slices in cinnamon-sugar, to give the cookies a sweet sheen when they go in the oven for their second bake.

Position racks in the top and bottom thirds of the oven and preheat the oven to 350°F (180°C/Gas Mark 4). Line two large baking sheets with parchment paper.

In a medium bowl, whisk together the flour, baking powder, and salt.

In a large bowl, combine 1 cup (200 g) of the sugar, the oil, vanilla, almond extract, and eggs and whisk until smooth. Add the flour mixture and almonds and stir until a dough forms and there are no more dry patches of flour in the bowl. Shape the dough into a ball, then divide into 4 portions.

Working on a lightly floured work surface, shape each portion of dough into a 10-inch (25 cm) log. Transfer 2 dough logs to each prepared baking sheet, spaced at least 4 inches (10 cm) apart. Flatten and shape each log into a rectangle ½ inch (13 mm) thick.

Bake until the rectangles are lightly browned on the bottom and dry to the touch, 20–25 minutes, switching racks and rotating the baking sheets front to back halfway through.

Transfer the baking sheets to wire racks and let the rectangles rest for 10 minutes. Leave the oven on.

While the rectangles cool, in a small bowl, combine the remaining ½ cup (100 g) sugar with the cinnamon, if using.

Carefully transfer each rectangle to a cutting board and use a sharp knife to cut the rectangles every ½ inch (13 mm) into slices. Return the slices to the baking sheets, spaced evenly apart, and sprinkle them with half of the cinnamon-sugar. Bake for 10 minutes.

Flip each cookie over and sprinkle with the remaining cinnamon-sugar. Return to the oven and bake until the cookies are golden brown all over and dry to the touch, about 10 minutes more.

Transfer the baking sheets to wire racks. Let the cookies cool on the pans for 1 minute, then transfer them to the racks to cool completely.

Date-Filled "Bracelet" Cookies
Ka'ak Asawer / Ka'ak bi Ajwa / Ka'ak Tita

Preparation time: 1 hour 40 minutes
Cooking time: 20 minutes
Makes: About 30 cookies

For the dough:
½ cup (4 fl oz/120 ml) barely warm
   tap water
1 tablespoon white US granulated
   (UK caster) sugar
1 teaspoon instant or active dry yeast
1½ cups (230 g) semolina flour
1¼ cups (180 g) all-purpose
   (plain) flour
2 tablespoons whole anise seeds
   or chopped fennel seeds
1 teaspoon ground cardamom
1 teaspoon fine sea salt
1 stick (4 oz/115 g) unsalted butter,
   at room temperature
⅓ cup (2½ fl oz/80 ml) vegetable oil

For the date filling:
10 oz (285 g) pitted Medjool dates
2 teaspoons vegetable oil
1 teaspoon ground cinnamon
½ teaspoon ground cardamom

Ka'ak is an Arabic term for "cookie" or "biscuit" that describes various cookies across the Middle East. But it can also sometimes refer to a bread-based savory ring, as in Lebanon, that more resembles a bagel. This *ka'ak* goes by three different names: *ka'ak asawer* ("bracelet cookies"), *ka'ak bi ajwa* (date-filled cookies), and *ka'ak tita* (grandmother's cookies). Though the cookie may have several different names, it's essentially made the same way. The dough is made often with just oil (though sometimes it's also mixed with butter or ghee, as this recipe does) and flavored with anise seeds or cardamom or orange zest. Typically, all or half of the flour is semolina, the hard durum wheat that adds strength to the dough that might fall apart if made with lower-protein flour. There is also added yeast, to give a softness to the dough, though it's culturally considered a cookie and not a bread. Once cooled, the dough is more akin to a snappy cracker than a soft, toothsome traditional cookie dough.

Strips of the dough encase a log of date paste filling—usually left plain or flavored with orange blossom water or more anise seeds or spices that were used in the dough—before being enclosed with a signature pinch to bond the dough ends together in what looks like a bangle or bracelet. This particular *ka'ak* is known as a Palestinian treat and is often served for Eid or to celebrate other religious holidays.

Make the dough: In a small bowl, stir together the water, sugar, and yeast until the sugar dissolves and set aside.

In a large bowl, whisk together the semolina, all-purpose (plain) flour, anise seeds, cardamom, and salt. Add the butter and oil and use your fingers to rub the flour mixture together with the fats repeatedly until the mixture resembles couscous. Slowly pour in the yeast mixture and stir with a fork until the dough comes together and is smooth, kneading briefly to ensure there are no dry pockets of flour remaining. Cover the dough with a clean tea towel while you make the filling.

Make the filling: In a food processor, pulse the dates until very finely chopped. Add the oil, cinnamon, and cardamom to the date paste and purée or knead everything together until smooth. Divide the date filling into 30 pieces (each approximately 1 teaspoon/12 g). Set aside.

Position racks in the top and bottom thirds of the oven and preheat the oven to 425°F (220°C/Gas Mark 7). Line two large baking sheets with parchment paper.

Uncover the dough and divide it into 30 balls (each approximately 1½ tablespoons/24 g). Working on a lightly floured work surface, with one dough ball, use the heel of your hand, or a rolling pin, to flatten it into a strip 5 × 1½ inches (13 × 4 cm); the corners don't need to be squared off. Place a piece of date filling in the center of the dough strip and use your fingers to distribute it into a rope down the center of the strip. Then encase the rope in the dough, pinching the edges all around to seal it. Bring the ends of the dough rope together to form a ring and pinch where they meet with your fingernail or the end of a chopstick, so it makes an impression. Transfer the dough ring to a prepared baking sheet. Repeat with the remaining dough balls and date filling pieces, spacing them at least 1 inch (2.5 cm) apart.

Bake until the cookies are deep golden brown all over and crisp, 16–20 minutes, switching racks and rotating the baking sheets front to back halfway through.

Transfer the baking sheets to wire racks and let the cookies cool completely on the pans.

Middle Eastern Shortbread Cookies

Ghorayeba / Ghurayiba / Raybeh

Preparation time: 25 minutes,
  plus 15 minutes chilling time
Cooking time: 20 minutes
Makes: About 24 cookies

1 cup (225 g) clarified butter or ghee
1 cup (135 g) powdered (icing) sugar
1 teaspoon fine sea salt
2 cups (280 g) all-purpose (plain) flour
Whole cloves, slivered almonds,
  or whole pistachios, for decorating

These simple shortbread-like cookies are beloved across the Middle East. Traditionally, the Egyptian version is made with only clarified butter, sugar, and flour. In Lebanon, Syria, and other Middle Eastern countries, the cookies are often flavored with orange blossom water, rose water, or a mix of both. In Saudi Arabia, the cookies are typically found flavored with cardamom. And in Palestine, anisette, or arak—an anise-flavored liquor—is often used. The simple Egyptian version comes first, with three variations to follow, letting you decide which you like best.

Though similarly named, these cookies are different from the Iranian *ghorabieh* (recipe, page 22), which are made with almonds, egg whites, and sugar and bake up like macaroons, and also from Moroccan *ghoriba bahla* (recipe, page 136), which are like shortbreads but often contain chemical leavening and ground nuts mixed into the dough. However, though all the aforementioned cookies are likely related in some way, these Arabian *ghorayeba* are most closely related to Turkish *un kurabiyesi* (recipe, page 60), which are shortbread cookies shaped into logs or diamonds and dusted with powdered (icing) sugar.

For these *ghorayeba*, the dough is formed into balls, flattened slightly, and studded with a nut like almonds or pistachios, or with a whole clove, which is usually only found in the Egyptian version. In addition, some recipes shape the dough into a ring and place the nut over the seam where the two ends join. The unique melt-in-the-mouth texture of these cookies comes from beating the clarified butter or ghee for several minutes, so it whips up and produces a smooth texture.

In a large bowl, with a hand mixer, beat the clarified butter on medium speed until light and fluffy, about 5 minutes. Add the sugar and salt and beat until extremely light and whipped, 5 more minutes. Add the flour and beat on low speed until a dough forms and there are no dry patches of flour remaining. Place the bowl of dough in the refrigerator for 15 minutes to firm up slightly.

Meanwhile, position racks in the top and bottom thirds of the oven and preheat the oven to 325°F (160°C/Gas Mark 3). Line two large baking sheets with parchment paper.

Using a 1-ounce (2-tablespoon) ice cream scoop, portion the dough and roll into balls. Arrange them on the prepared baking sheets, spaced 1 inch (2.5 cm) apart. Flatten each slightly with the palm of your hand. Stud the top of each dough disc with a whole clove, sliver of almond, or whole pistachio.

Bake until barely light golden brown on the bottom and dry to the touch in the center, 15–20 minutes (err on the side of underbaking the cookies because they should have hardly any color at all).

Transfer the baking sheets to wire racks. Let the cookies cool on the pans for 1 minute, then transfer them to the racks to cool completely.

Variations
Saudi Arabian Ghorayeba
Add 1 teaspoon ground cardamom to the butter. Decorate each cookie with a whole pistachio.
Lebanese/Syrian Ghorayeba
Add 1 tablespoon orange blossom water or rose water (or a 50/50 mix) to the butter. Decorate each cookie with a whole almond or pistachio.
Palestinian Ghorayeba
Add 1 tablespoon arak or anise liqueur to the butter. Decorate each cookie with a whole pistachio.

Egyptian Stuffed Eid Cookies
Kahk / Ka'ak bel Agameya

Preparation time: 45 minutes
Cooking time: 30 minutes
Makes: About 24 cookies

For the filling:
1½ tablespoons ghee
1 tablespoon all-purpose (plain) flour
½ cup (170 g) mild honey
1½ teaspoons toasted sesame seeds
¼ cup (30 g) finely chopped toasted
   nuts, such as walnuts, almonds,
   pistachios, or hazelnuts (optional)

For the dough:
1 cup (225 g) ghee or unsalted butter
⅓ cup (2½ fl oz/80 ml) whole milk
1 teaspoon active dry or instant
   yeast (optional)
1 tablespoon Reehet el Kahk (recipe
   follows) or rose water (or 2 teaspoons
   pure vanilla extract)
3 cups (420 g) all-purpose (plain) flour
½ cup (65 g) powdered (icing) sugar,
   plus more for dusting
1 teaspoon baking powder
¾ teaspoon fine sea salt

This may be the oldest cookie on earth, at least in terms of how we would describe them today. Images of them can be found in tombs of nobles in Thebes and Memphis dating back to pharaonic times, and historians believe the custom of making them started with the wives of kings who presented them as offerings to ancient priests. These were circular-shaped cookies often filled with dried fruit or honey and, over time, gained various markings on top, often sun rays as a sign of worship for sun gods. These imprinted markings on the top of *kahk* were once a part of their identity, but many recipes today simply leave the cookies plain or smooth.

Kahk, sometimes spelled *ka'ak* or referred to as *kahk el-Eid*, are popular to celebrate the end of Ramadan in Egypt. Their stuffings are various—from dates to Turkish delight to nuts like pistachios, almonds, or walnuts—but the historically traditional filling is one called *agameya* made of honey, sesame seeds, ghee, and sometimes nuts thickened with flour. When stuffed with other fillings, *kahk* takes on different names in other parts of the Middle East and Arab world. The dough is typically flavored with a spice mix called *reehet el kahk*—sometimes referred to as *kahk* "essence" or "seasoning"—made of fennel or anise seeds, cinnamon, cloves, cardamom, and *mahleb*, the dried and ground kernel of a type of cherry.

Some bakers use a *maamoul* mold (see page 44) or serrated *maamoul* tongs to imprint designs and differentiate different types of fillings. There are also special *kahk* stamps (which you can find online) that imprint the cookies with a crosshatch design, but most bakers simply use the tines of a fork to make the cookie's distinct markings. Though the markings once held religious symbolism, now they act as vessels to catch lots of powdered (icing) sugar, which is liberally dusted on top of the cookies while warm from the oven.

- -

Make the filling: In a small saucepan, melt the ghee over medium heat. Add the flour and cook, whisking often, until light golden brown, about 2 minutes. Pour in the honey and bring to a simmer, whisking to mix it evenly with the ghee-flour mixture. Once the honey begins bubbling, reduce the heat to medium-low to maintain a gentle simmer and continue cooking, stirring occasionally, until reduced and thickened, about 5 minutes. Remove the pan from the heat and stir in the sesame seeds and nuts (if using). Let the mixture cool to room temperature.

Using a teaspoon, scoop some of the honey mixture and roll it into a small ball. Place it on a plate and repeat rolling balls of honey filling. Place the plate in the refrigerator to chill the balls of honey filling until ready to use.

Make the dough: In a small saucepan, melt the ghee completely. Remove the pan from the heat and stir in the milk and yeast (if using). If using rose water or vanilla instead of the spice mix, stir it in now.

In a large bowl, whisk together the flour, sugar, baking powder, salt, and spice mix. Form a well in the center of the dry ingredients and pour in the warm ghee mixture. Stir with your hands until a dough forms and there are no dry patches of flour remaining, kneading only as long as needed to form a smooth dough.

Line two large baking sheets with parchment paper. Using a 1-ounce (2-tablespoon) ice cream scoop, portion the dough and roll into balls. Flatten each ball in your hand into about a 3-inch (7.5 cm) round and place 1 ball of honey filling in the center. Gather the dough around the filling to encase it and then reroll the dough into a ball. Arrange the filled dough balls on the prepared baking sheets, spaced 1 inch (2.5 cm) apart.

If using a kahk stamp, press it lightly onto each flattened dough ball. If using a maamoul mold, lightly press the cookie ball into the mold to imprint its design. If using tongs, pinch a design on the top of each flattened dough ball. If using a fork, press its tines on the top of the cookie in a crosshatch pattern. Place the baking sheets in the refrigerator to chill the cookies for 10 minutes.

Meanwhile, position racks in the top and bottom thirds of the oven and preheat the oven to 350°F (180°C/Gas Mark 4).

Bake until golden brown all over, about 20 minutes, switching racks and rotating the baking sheets front to back halfway through.

Transfer the baking sheets to wire racks and let the cookies rest on the pans for 1 minute. While the cookies are still warm, dust each with powdered (icing) sugar on top and let cool completely on the pans.

Once completely cooled, dust the cookies with more powdered sugar before serving.

Reehet el Kahk

Makes 4 tablespoons

2 tablespoons ground mahleb
1 tablespoon ground cinnamon
1 teaspoon ground cardamom
1 teaspoon ground cloves
1 teaspoon ground fennel
  or anise seeds
1 teaspoon freshly grated nutmeg

In a bowl, whisk together all the spices. Transfer to an airtight container and store for up to 6 months.

Phono-Semantics

One phenomenon I came back to over and over again while writing this book is how so many cookies end up with names that are variations of something else they no longer have any relation to. This game of telephone is called "phono-semantics" and refers to how similar-sounding names change over time, especially when passing from one culture and language to another.

This is most evident in the "exotic cookies" (see "Wedding" Cookies, page 23) of the Middle East. The names of those cookies produced countless variations on the same word that, depending on who the speaker or writer was, spelled it differently or pronounced it with a different accent.

Another instance of phono-semantics was for the American Snickerdoodle (recipe, page 350), from the German *Schneckennudel*, a cinnamon roll-like bun that came to the United States with German immigrants. Over time and through repeated filtering and mishearings, it changed to Snickerdoodle, in reference to a cinnamon-laced cookie. In this case in particular, the phenomenon spawned countless articles theorizing on where the name came from, relishing in perpetuating fantastical fairy tales and urban legends.

The best example of this phenomenon is when the name of a particular food leads people to think it's a clue to its origins, as in the case of *Hamantaschen* (recipe, page 250). Though many like to repeat that the tricorn-shaped cookie takes its name from the hat of the biblical figure Haman, there are no records of him wearing such a hat. Instead, the cookie likely got its name from *Mantasch*, the German word for "poppy seed pockets," which is a pastry that German Jews made for Purim. Over time and with the association of Haman with the holiday, it's easy to see how the two similar-sounding words blended and the more enticing and dramatic story of the latter won.

Egyptian Stuffed Eid Cookies (p. 50)

Date-Filled Spiral Cookies (p. 54)

Date-Filled Spiral Cookies
Kleicha / Al-Kelaijah

Preparation time: 50 minutes,
  plus chilling time
Cooking time: 30 minutes
Makes: About 24 cookies

For the filling:
3 tablespoons (45 g) unsalted butter
12 oz (340 g) soft pitted dates,
  finely chopped
¾ teaspoon ground cardamom

For the dough:
3 cups (420 g) all-purpose (plain) flour
2 tablespoons white US granulated
  (UK caster) sugar
1 teaspoon instant or active dry yeast
1 teaspoon ground cardamom
½ teaspoon ground nigella seeds, plus
  whole seeds, for sprinkling (optional)
¾ teaspoon fine sea salt
2 sticks (8 oz/225 g) unsalted
  butter, melted
¼ cup (2 fl oz/60 ml) whole milk
1 egg
Egg wash: 1 egg yolk beaten
  with 1 teaspoon water

In *The Iraqi Cookie, Kleicha, and the Search for Identity*, culinary historian Nawal Nasrallah begins: "All Iraqis, irrespective of region, ethnicity or religion, look to the *kleicha* as our national cookie, and no feast, religious or otherwise, is complete without it." Indeed, the fact that Muslims, Christians, and Jews all have a tradition of making these cookies to celebrate their respective holidays shows how important the sweets are to all Iraqis. With their history of Jews making them for Purim and their spiraled shape and thick date filling, these cookies signal possible influence on the modern rugelach (recipe, page 358).

Though the word *kleicha* now refers to the date-filled, spiral-shaped versions—which are most popular—there are also walnut- and coconut-filled versions as well. When filled with walnuts the cookies are typically shaped like half-moons, while the coconut versions are shaped into rounds that can be imprinted using a *maamoul* mold (see page 44). Some recipes call for flavoring the dough with a mix of over a dozen spices, while most pare it down to cardamom and nigella seeds. The cookie filling is typically made of soft dates fried in butter or oil and perfumed with cardamom.

Make the filling: In a medium saucepan, melt the butter over medium heat. Add the dates and cardamom and cook, stirring occasionally, until the dates break down into a chunky paste, 1–2 minutes. Remove the pan from the heat and scrape the dates into a bowl. Set aside until ready to use.

Make the dough: In a large bowl, whisk together the flour, sugar, yeast, cardamom, nigella, and salt. Form a well in the center of the dry ingredients, add the melted butter, milk, and whole egg to the well and stir with your hands until a dough forms, kneading only as much as needed to no longer see any dry patches of flour in the bowl. Shape the dough into a ball, wrap in plastic wrap (cling film), and refrigerate for at least 1 hour or up to 2 days.

Position racks in the top and bottom thirds of the oven and preheat the oven to 350°F (180°C/Gas Mark 4). Line two large baking sheets with parchment paper.

Remove the dough from the refrigerator and let it rest for 10 minutes. Working on a lightly floured work surface, divide the dough in half. Using a rolling pin, flatten each half into a 6 × 14-inch (15 × 36 cm) rectangle. Spoon half the date filling onto each rectangle and use an offset spatula or table knife to spread the paste evenly over the dough, leaving a ½-inch (13 mm) border along one long side of each rectangle.

Starting from the opposite long side, roll each rectangle, jelly roll (Swiss roll) style, to the plain edge, forming a tight spiral. Trim the ends of each cylinder and then cut crosswise into slices 1 inch (2.5 cm) thick. Transfer the dough spirals, standing up so you can see the spirals on each side, to the prepared baking sheets spaced 2 inches (5 cm) apart. Brush the spirals lightly with egg wash, and, if you like, sprinkle with a pinch of whole nigella seeds.

Bake until golden brown all over and dry to the touch on top, 20–25 minutes, switching racks and rotating the baking sheets front to back halfway through.

Transfer the baking sheets to wire racks. Let the cookies cool on the pans for 1 minute, then transfer them to the racks to cool completely.

Cardamom Almond Cookies

Hadgi Badah

Preparation time: 30 minutes
Cooking time: 30 minutes
Makes: About 12 cookies

8 oz (225 g) blanched whole
  or slivered almonds, plus more
  for decorating
½ cup (100 g) white US granulated
  (UK caster) sugar
½ teaspoon fine sea salt
½ teaspoon ground cardamom
¼ teaspoon pure almond extract
2 egg whites

These chewy almond cookies are Iraq's version of an almond macaroon (recipe, page 99). This variation of what Jews call *marunchinos* contains cardamom and is a popular variety with Iraqi Jews. Typically made for Passover, they are also often flavored with rose water. This recipe omits it to let the cardamom shine on its own, but if you like, add 1 teaspoon to the dough along with the egg whites.

Position racks in the top and bottom thirds of the oven and preheat the oven to 325°F (160°C/Gas Mark 3). Line two large baking sheets with parchment paper.

In a food processor, process the almonds until finely ground, 15–20 seconds. Add the sugar, salt, cardamom, and almond extract and pulse until combined. Add the egg whites and pulse until the mixture forms a stiff dough.

Using a 1-ounce (2-tablespoon) ice cream scoop, drop mounds of the dough onto the prepared baking sheets, spaced 2 inches (5 cm) apart. Flatten each mound slightly with the palm of your hand and place a whole almond or piece of slivered almond in the center.

Bake until light golden brown on the bottom and dry to the touch, 25–30 minutes, switching racks and rotating the baking sheets front to back halfway through.

Transfer the baking sheets to wire racks. Let the cookies cool on the pans for 1 minute, then transfer them to the racks to cool completely.

Arabic Sesame-Anise Ring Cookies

Ka'ak bi-Simsim

Preparation time: 1 hour 20 minutes
Cooking time: 25 minutes
Makes: About 24 cookies

2 tablespoons anise or fennel seeds
3 cups (420 g) all-purpose (plain) flour
⅔ cup (130 g) white US granulated
  (UK caster) sugar
2 teaspoons baking powder
½ teaspoon fine sea salt
1 stick (4 oz/115 g) unsalted
  butter, softened
⅔ cup (5½ fl oz/160 ml) whole milk
Egg wash: 1 egg beaten with
  1 tablespoon water
½ cup (75 g) sesame seeds

The Egyptian *kahk* (recipe, page 50) is one of the oldest cookies on earth, so it is not a surprise that variations of that name have been popularly used to describe any sort of small, bread/pastry/cookie-like foodstuff. Depending on where you are in many Middle Eastern countries, *ka'ak* (the Arabic spelling) can be used to describe a bagel, a savory flat cracker, or a ring-shaped rusk. They can be filled (see *ka'ak asawer* on page 48) or left plain, covered in various seeds, or brushed with egg wash or a floral syrup.

That's how, most likely, these sesame-coated, ring-shaped cookies evolved. The word *ka'ak* is usually included, in various iterations and spellings, in their name, as is the word for "sesame." But the combination of sesame and anise and a mini doughnut-like shape is their calling card, with the anise used to flavor the dough and the sesame seeds used to crust the outside of the rings. Some versions skip the sesame coating and mix the seeds straight into the dough, and sometimes they are shaped like small sausages imprinted with a cratered pattern made by pressing the dough against the fine holes of a box grater. While older recipes lean toward lightly sweetened bread rings, more modern recipes have a higher proportion of sugar, without yeast.

Position racks in the top and bottom thirds of the oven and preheat the oven to 350°F (180°C/Gas Mark 4). Line two large baking sheets with parchment paper.

Place the anise seeds in a mortar and pestle or spice grinder and process or pulse until coarsely ground.

Transfer the ground anise to a large bowl. Add the flour, sugar, baking powder, and salt and whisk to combine. Add the butter and rub the butter into the dry ingredients with your fingers until it breaks down and the mixture resembles couscous. Pour in the milk and stir until a dough forms, kneading only as much as needed to see no more dry patches of flour.

Using a 1-ounce (2-tablespoon) ice cream scoop, portion the dough and roll each into a log 3 inches (7.5 cm) long. Connect the ends of the logs to form a small ring and place the rings on the prepared baking sheets, spaced 2 inches (5 cm) apart. Place the baking sheets in the refrigerator to chill the cookies for 10 minutes.

Meanwhile, make the egg wash and spread the sesame seeds out on a small plate.

Remove the cookies from the refrigerator. Brush or dip the top of a ring in the egg wash and then place in the sesame seeds to coat the top. Return the ring, seed-side up, to its place on the baking sheet. Repeat to coat the rest of the rings.

Bake until light golden brown on the bottom and dry to the touch on top, 20–25 minutes, switching racks and rotating the baking sheets front to back halfway through.

Transfer the baking sheets to wire racks. Let the cookies cool on the pans for 1 minute, then transfer them to the racks to cool completely.

Arabic Sesame-Anise Ring Cookies

the anatolian peninsula, the balkans & caucasia

A penchant for honey and crumbly textures is the overarching theme for many cookies in Greece and Caucasia, which take their influence from the former Ottoman empire, whose center was modern-day Turkey. Floral flavors like orange and grape must, which are typical of the eastern Mediterranean, and the native walnuts dominate the sweets of this area. Their cookies also often make use of local agricultural products, such as native grains, beer, olive oil, fruit butters, and jams. Cookies from this region are often served with tea or wine and enjoyed at weddings and other celebrations.

Turkish Shortbread Cookies

Kurabiye / Un Kurabiyesi

Preparation time: 30 minutes
Cooking time: 30 minutes
Makes: About 24 cookies

1 cup (225 g) clarified butter
or ghee, softened
1 cup (135 g) powdered (icing)
sugar, plus more for dusting
1 teaspoon pure vanilla extract
1 teaspoon fine sea salt
2½ cups (350 g) all-purpose
(plain) flour

Though they may seem like another simple shortbread cookie, it's likely this otherwise plain cookie influenced the dozens of "wedding" cookie names to follow (see page 51), especially given the Ottoman/Turkish influence on its surrounding regions for centuries. Though an Arabic reference is given first, this Turkish cookie—first referenced in the fifteenth century—uses a generous dusting of powdered (icing) sugar on the outside, pointing to it likely being the first "wedding" cookie (see page 23) too. This influence set off the trend for centuries of giving crumbly cookies, with or without nuts, dusted in fine white powdered sugar that "wedding" moniker; the Greek *kourabiedes* (recipe, page 83) chief among them.

These Turkish cookies are, by comparison to their descendants, plainer and consist of a flavoring-free, buttery dough, though many recipes today call for vanilla. They also have a unique shape: Rather than a round mound or disc, the dough is rolled into a log, scraped with a fork to create ridges, and then cut into diamond shapes. Like with most cookies imprinted with a mold or scored lines, the ridges catch plenty of powdered sugar, likely a way to add sweetness to treats before sugar was actually incorporated in the dough (this recipe gives it as an optional step). The cookies are also, like many modern recipes for "wedding cookies," baked at a low temperature to set the dough without browning it, which would toughen the cookie and take away from its melt-in-the-mouth character.

Position racks in the top and bottom thirds of the oven and preheat the oven to 325°F (160°C/Gas Mark 3). Line two large baking sheets with parchment paper.

In a large bowl, with a hand mixer, beat the butter, sugar, vanilla, and salt on medium speed until light and fluffy, 2–3 minutes. Add the flour and beat on low speed until a dough forms and there are no dry patches of flour remaining. Shape the dough into a ball and transfer to a clean work surface.

Divide the dough into 4 equal portions and shape each portion into an even log 1 inch (2.5 cm) thick; gently press on each log with your fingers to give it a slightly flattened top and bottom. Using the tines of a fork, lightly scrape lines along the length of the top of the logs. Cut each log on a slight diagonal every 1 inch (2.5 cm) to create diamond-shaped pieces. Transfer the diamonds to the prepared baking sheets, spaced 1 inch (2.5 cm) apart.

Bake until very lightly golden brown on the bottom and dry to the touch in the center, 25–30 minutes, switching racks and rotating the baking sheets front to back halfway through.

Transfer the baking sheets to wire racks and let the cookies cool completely on the pans. Dust the cookies with sugar before serving, if you like.

Turkish Shortbread Cookies

Turkish Orange Cookies
Portakallı Kurabiye

Preparation time: 45 minutes
Cooking time: 15 minutes
Makes: About 12 cookies

2½ cups (350 g) all-purpose
  (plain) flour
1 teaspoon baking powder
½ teaspoon fine sea salt
¾ cup (150 g) white US granulated
  (UK caster) sugar, plus more
  for coating
1 stick (4 oz/115 g) unsalted
  butter, softened
1 egg
Finely grated zest of 2 oranges
¼ cup (2 fl oz/60 ml) fresh
  orange juice
Egg wash: 1 egg yolk beaten
  with 1 tablespoon water

Oranges feature prominently in many Turkish desserts and sweets, and they imbue these simple soft-textured butter cookies with their heady fragrance. Typically painted with an egg yolk to also appear orange in color, many modern versions roll them in granulated or powdered (icing) sugar to give a cracked appearance and sugary shimmer. Once baked, the cookies even resemble whole oranges thanks to their high-domed shape.

Position racks in the top and bottom thirds of the oven and preheat the oven to 350°F (180°C/Gas Mark 4). Line two large baking sheets with parchment paper.

In a medium bowl, whisk together the flour, baking powder, and salt.

In a large bowl, with a hand mixer, beat the sugar and butter on medium speed until light and fluffy, 2–3 minutes. Add the whole egg and beat until smooth. Beat in the orange zest and orange juice. Add the dry ingredients and stir until a dough forms and there are no dry patches of flour remaining.

Make the egg wash. Fill another bowl with more sugar. Using a 1-ounce (2-tablespoon) ice cream scoop, portion the dough and roll into balls. Dip each ball in the egg wash, shake off any excess, then roll in the sugar to coat. Transfer the balls to the prepared baking sheets, spaced 2 inches (5 cm) apart.

Bake until lightly golden brown, cracked open on top, and dry to the touch in the center, about 15 minutes, switching racks and rotating the baking sheets front to back halfway through.

Transfer the baking sheets to wire racks. Let the cookies cool on the pans for 1 minute, then transfer them to the racks to cool completely.

Honey Spice Cookies
Medenjaci

Preparation time: 45 minutes,
  plus cooling and setting time
Cooking time: 20 minutes
Makes: About 24 cookies

½ cup (170 g) honey
½ cup (110 g) packed dark brown sugar
1 stick (4 oz/115 g) unsalted butter
3 cups (420 g) all-purpose (plain) flour
1 teaspoon baking soda
  (bicarbonate of soda)
2 teaspoons ground ginger
2 teaspoons ground cinnamon
1 teaspoon ground cloves
1 teaspoon freshly grated nutmeg
¾ teaspoon fine sea salt
2 eggs
1½ cups (205 g) powdered
  (icing) sugar, sifted
1 teaspoon fresh lemon juice

These Croatian spiced cookies have a striking similarity to Russian *pryaniki* (recipe, page 214) and German *Pfeffernüsse* (recipe, page 240) because of their squat mound shape and powdered (icing) sugar glaze on top. But the most likely precursor is the fancier, spiceless, and heart-shaped *licitar* cookie, which is typically covered with red icing and decorated elaborately with white icing script and designs. These *medenjaci*—Croatian for "gingerbread men"—are much simpler and fall within the realm of home bakers, while *licitars* are a bakery specialty. What the two cookies have in common, however, is their use of honey as the primary sweetener.

Even though these cookies are named after the typically thinner and cut-out style of cookies referred to as gingerbread men, it seems that the round, cakey balls presented here are reflective of the true *medenjaci* name. *Paprenjaci* (recipe, page 66), on the other hand, are the thinner, printed style of cookie more associated with the "gingerbread man" name. Though not all recipes include them, ginger, cinnamon, nutmeg, and cloves are a common quartet of spices used in these Croatian cookies.

Position racks in the top and bottom thirds of the oven and preheat the oven to 350°F (180°C/Gas Mark 4). Line two large baking sheets with parchment paper.

In a small saucepan, combine the honey, brown sugar, and butter. Stir over medium heat until it begins to simmer and the brown sugar is dissolved. Remove the pan from the heat and let the mixture cool to room temperature.

In a large bowl, whisk together the flour, baking soda (bicarb), ginger, cinnamon, cloves, nutmeg, and salt. Form a well in the center of the dry ingredients and pour in the cooled honey-butter mixture, 1 whole egg, and 1 egg yolk (reserve the white). Stir with a fork until a dough forms and there are no dry patches of flour remaining.

Using a ¾-ounce (1½-tablespoon) ice cream scoop, portion the dough and roll into balls. Arrange the dough balls at least 2 inches (5 cm) apart son the prepared baking sheets.

Bake until golden brown at the edges and dry to the touch in the center, 10–12 minutes, switching racks and rotating the baking sheets front to back halfway through.

Transfer the baking sheets to wire racks. Let the cookies cool on the pans for 1 minute, then transfer them to the racks to cool completely.

In a small bowl, whisk the reserved egg white until loosened and foamy. Add the powdered (icing) sugar and lemon juice and stir to create a thick, pourable icing. Dip the top of each cookie in the icing, letting the excess drip off before returning it to the rack. Let the cookies stand until the icing sets before serving.

CROATIA

Plum Jam-Filled "Shell" Cookies

Skoljkice

(v)

Preparation time: 1 hour 10 minutes, plus chilling time
Cooking time: 20 minutes
Makes: About 30 cookies

2¾ cups (390 g) all-purpose (plain) flour
1 teaspoon baking powder
¾ teaspoon fine sea salt
1½ sticks (6 oz/170 g) unsalted butter, softened
½ cup (120 g) sour cream
¼ cup (50 g) white US granulated (UK caster) sugar
1 teaspoon pure vanilla extract
Finely grated zest of ½ lemon
½ cup (160 g) plum jam, store-bought or homemade (see Homemade [Any] Fruit Jam, page 18)
Powdered (icing) sugar, for coating

Filled, hand-pie-like pastries—whether savory and stuffed with meat or sweet and stuffed with nuts or jam—have been around forever. So it's easy to see how pastry cooks and bakers kept whittling down the size of such pastries until they became what we consider cookies today. Even cookies like rugelach (recipe, page 358) fit this archetype, in spite of their fillings being exposed to the outside. These tiny turnover-style cookies—*skoljkice* is Croatian for "shell" or "clam"—enclose a jam filling, usually plum, with a dough made soft and pliable with butter and sour cream.

In the typical style of Eastern European cookies, they are shaped like half-moons or crescents and coated in powdered (icing) sugar after baking, which helps add sweetness to the largely unsweetened dough. That use of sugar on the outside, plus sweet fillings inside, with an unsweetened dough that's enriched with fat also points to how these cookies evolved from their larger, more savory counterparts. You can make an all-purpose dough and simply fill it with something sweet and toss it with sugar—no need to add sugar to the dough, so you can use it with all kinds of pastries and fillings, savory or sweet.

In a large bowl, whisk together the flour, baking powder, and salt. Form a well in the center of the dry ingredients and add the butter, sour cream, white US granulated (UK caster) sugar, vanilla, and lemon zest. Stir the mixture with a fork until it comes together into a solid dough, lightly kneading only as much as needed to no longer see any dry patches of flour in the bowl. Shape the dough into a ball, wrap in plastic wrap (cling film), and refrigerate for at least 1 hour or up to 2 days.

Position racks in the top and bottom thirds of the oven and preheat the oven to 350°F (180°C/Gas Mark 4). Line two large baking sheets with parchment paper.

Working on a lightly floured work surface, flatten the dough with a rolling pin until ⅛ inch (3 mm) thick. Using a 3-inch (7.5 cm) round cutter, cut out rounds of dough, rerolling the scraps to make more cookies. Spoon 1 teaspoon plum jam into the center of each round, then fold the rounds in half to create half-moons. Use a fork to crimp the edges shut. Transfer the half-moons to the prepared baking sheets, spaced 2 inches (5 cm) apart.

Bake until golden brown on the bottom and dry to the touch on top, 15–18 minutes, switching racks and rotating the baking sheets front to back halfway through.

Transfer the baking sheets to wire racks and let the cookies rest for 1 minute. While the cookies are still warm, toss or dust each in powdered (icing) sugar to coat, returning each cookie to its place on the baking sheet to cool completely.

"Peach" Cookies

Breskvice

Preparation time: 1 hour,
  plus cooling time
Cooking time: 15 minutes
Makes: About 12 cookie sandwiches

For the cookies:
2¼ cups (315 g) all-purpose
  (plain) flour
2 teaspoons baking powder
½ teaspoon fine sea salt
⅔ cup (130 g) white US granulated
  (UK caster) sugar
½ cup (4 fl oz/120 ml) vegetable oil
1 teaspoon pure vanilla extract
1 tablespoon sour cream
  or full-fat yogurt
2 eggs

For the filling:
⅔ cup (75 g) walnuts, very
  finely ground
½ cup (160 g) apricot jam (not jelly)
2 tablespoons gold or dark rum
Fresh orange juice or water, as needed

To decorate:
2 cups (16 fl oz/475 ml) water
Yellow food coloring
Red food coloring
White US granulated (UK caster)
  sugar, for coating cookies

These colorful cookies are a staple at weddings in Croatia. In Serbia and Romania, these cookie sandwiches are also popular and go by the name *fursecuri piersici*, or "peach cookies." The word "peach" is not a reference to a peach flavor but to their shape and coloring; the cookies are dipped in orange and pink food coloring to mimic the blushing exterior of a peach. They're more labor-intensive than most cookies, but they're ideal for serving at special occasions and holidays.

Make the cookies: Position racks in the top and bottom thirds of the oven and preheat the oven to 350°F (180°C/Gas Mark 4). Line two large baking sheets with parchment paper.

In a medium bowl, whisk together the flour, baking powder, and salt.

In a large bowl, vigorously whisk together the sugar, oil, vanilla, sour cream, and eggs until smooth and lightened. Add the dry ingredients and stir until the dough forms and there are no dry patches of flour remaining.

Using a ¼-ounce ice cream scoop or a heaping teaspoon, portion the dough and roll into ½-inch (13 mm) balls. Arrange them on the prepared baking sheets, spaced 1 inch (2.5 cm) apart.

Bake until the cookies are very light golden brown on the bottom and dry to the touch, 10–12 minutes, switching racks and rotating the baking sheets front to back halfway through.

Transfer the baking sheets to wire racks and let the cookies cool completely on the pans.

Flip all the cookies over and use the tip of a small paring knife to hollow the centers of each cookie, letting the crumbs fall into a bowl. Transfer the crumbs to a food processor and pulse until the consistency of breadcrumbs. (Alternatively, place the cookies pieces in a large plastic bag and crush with a rolling pin to make crumbs.)

Make the filling: In a small bowl, stir together the ground walnuts, jam, and rum. Add the cookie crumbs and stir until combined. The filling should be thick but still spreadable. If too thick, thin it out with a teaspoon of orange juice or water until it's the proper consistency.

Fill the cavity of each cookie with about ½ teaspoon of the filling—you can do this with a spoon, or for greater ease, transfer all the filling to a piping bag and pipe the filling into the cookies. Join 2 cookies, filling-to-filling, to create a cookie sandwich. Repeat with the remaining cookies and filling.

Decorate the cookies: Set up two shallow bowls side by side and pour 1 cup (8 fl oz/250 ml) water into each. Stir a few drops of yellow food coloring into one bowl of water and a few drops of red food coloring into the other. Next to them, set up a sheet pan and line it with a double-thick layer of paper towels. Place two small paint brushes or cotton swabs next to the bowls, as well.

Pick up one cookie sandwich and use the paint brush to lightly brush only the "equator" or seam with the yellow-colored water. Then, lightly brush the two "poles" in the pink-colored water. Place the cookie sandwich on its equator, or side, on the paper towels to dry. Repeat coloring the remaining cookie sandwiches.

Spread some sugar in a shallow dish or bowl. Toss each cookie sandwich in the sugar until completely coated before serving.

"Peach" Cookies

Molded Gingerbread Cookies with Pepper

Paprenjaci

Preparation time: 1 hour 5 minutes, plus chilling time
Cooking time: 25 minutes
Makes: About 48 cookies

⅔ cup (135 g) cold-rendered leaf lard or vegetable shortening
½ cup (170 g) honey
⅓ cup (65 g) white US granulated (UK caster) sugar
2 teaspoons ground cinnamon
1 teaspoon freshly ground white or black pepper
1 teaspoon freshly grated nutmeg
¾ teaspoon fine sea salt
½ teaspoon ground cardamom
½ teaspoon ground cloves
Finely grated zest of ½ orange
3½ cups (490 g) all-purpose (plain) flour, plus more for rolling/dusting molds
1¼ cups (145 g) walnuts, very finely ground
1 egg
2 egg yolks

These Croatian gingerbread-style cookies seem to have a relation to German *Springerle* (recipe, page 246) and Belgian/Dutch *speculaas* (recipe, page 232), thanks to their use of an engraved wooden block to imprint pagan designs upon the dough (see Printed Cookies, page 245). Though that block isn't necessary to make the cookies—you can cut them into simple rectangles or use different cutter shapes—it's worth seeking one out to make these cookies, often made for the Christmas holidays.

This particular type of *paprenjak* is supposedly from the Croatian city of Zagreb, where the use of black pepper makes the flavor of these cookies unique. Like the simpler, cakier Croatian spiced cookies *medenjaci* (recipe, page 62), these crisp, printed cookies are sweetened primarily with honey and spices before getting mixed with the rest of the ingredients. The honey is warmed with rendered pork lard, as was traditional before the use of butter became widespread. The name of these cookies alludes to the pepper used in the dough, and though white pepper seems more fitting flavorwise than black pepper, both seem to be used interchangeably, so it's impossible to know which is correct. Therefore, white pepper is offered as the first option here, but use whichever version of the spice you prefer.

In a small saucepan, combine the lard, honey, sugar, cinnamon, pepper, nutmeg, salt, cardamom, cloves, and orange zest. Stir over medium heat until the sugar dissolves and the lard is melted, about 10 minutes. Remove the pan from the heat and let cool to room temperature; the mixture will separate as it cools and that is okay.

In a large bowl, whisk together the flour and walnuts. Form a well in the center of the dry ingredients. Stir together the lard-honey mixture and then add it to the well along with the whole egg and egg yolks, and stir the mixture with a fork until it comes together into a solid dough, lightly kneading only as much as needed to no longer see any dry patches of flour. Shape the dough into a ball, wrap in plastic wrap (cling film), and refrigerate for at least 1 hour or up to 2 days.

Position racks in the top and bottom thirds of the oven and preheat the oven to 350°F (180°C/Gas Mark 4). Line two large baking sheets with parchment paper.

Working on a lightly floured work surface, flatten the dough with a rolling pin until ¼ inch (6 mm) thick. Using a wooden cookie mold with 3-inch (7.5 cm) cells, lightly dust the engravings, tapping out any excess, then press it over the dough to print designs on the dough, Repeat over the rest of the dough. Cut the rectangles free from one another and transfer to the prepared baking sheets, spaced 1 inch (2.5 cm) apart. Brush off any excess flour that remains on the dough pieces. (Alternatively, use various cookie cutters of similar dimension to cut out cookies.) Reroll the scraps as needed to make more cookies.

Bake until golden brown on the bottom and dry to the touch on top, 10–15 minutes, switching racks and rotating the baking sheets front to back halfway through.

Transfer the baking sheets to wire racks. Let the cookies cool on the pans for 1 minute, then transfer them to the racks to cool completely.

Syrup-Soaked Shortbread Cookies

Hurmašice

Preparation time: 35 minutes,
 plus soaking time
Cooking time: 35 minutes
Makes: About 18 cookies

For the syrup:
2½ cups (500 g) white US granulated
 (UK caster) sugar
2 cups (16 fl oz/475 ml) water
2 tablespoons fresh lemon juice
1 teaspoon pure vanilla extract

For the dough:
1½ cups (230 g) semolina flour
1½ cups (210 g) all-purpose
 (plain) flour
1 teaspoon baking powder
¾ teaspoon fine sea salt
1½ sticks (6 oz/170 g) unsalted
 butter, melted
½ cup (100 g) white US granulated
 (UK caster) sugar
¼ cup (60 g) sour cream
1 egg
1 egg yolk

These syrup-soaked cookies have a clear connection to Albanian *sheqerpare* (recipe, page 74). Bosnia and Herzegovina's place in the Balkan peninsula means their cuisine is heavily influenced by Turkish and Greek cooking, which commonly soaks cookies and pastries in syrup to add sweetness and moisture to crumbly shortbread cookies.

Many recipes use all wheat flour for these cookies, or add dried coconut for texture and an obviously different flavor. This recipe uses semolina to add texture to the cookies and also because it absorbs the syrup well. Make these cookies at least a day before you plan to serve them so they have plenty of time to soak up the lemony syrup. And as with all syrup-soaked cookies, it should always be cold syrup poured onto hot cookies; if you pour hot syrup on the hot cookies, they will instead get soggy and fall apart.

Make the syrup: In a small saucepan, combine the sugar, water, and lemon juice and bring to a boil over high heat. Reduce the heat to maintain a steady simmer and cook the syrup, stirring to ensure the sugar is completely dissolved, until reduced slightly, about 5 minutes. Remove the pan from the heat and stir in the vanilla. Let the syrup cool completely to room temperature.

Make the cookies: Position racks in the top and bottom thirds of the oven and preheat the oven to 350°F (180°C/Gas Mark 4). Line two large baking sheets with parchment paper.

In a medium bowl, whisk together the semolina, all-purpose (plain) flour, baking powder, and salt.

In a large bowl, with a hand mixer, beat the melted butter, sugar, sour cream, whole egg, and egg yolk on medium speed until lightened and thick, 1–2 minutes. Add the dry ingredients and stir until a dough forms and there are no dry patches of flour remaining.

Using a 1-ounce (2-tablespoon) ice cream scoop, portion the dough and form each into the shape of an egg. Using the zesting side of a box grater, gently press the dough egg against the grater to imprint its pattern onto the dough. Peel off the dough and transfer it to the prepared baking sheets. Repeat with the remaining dough eggs, arranging them at least 2 inches (5 cm) apart on the sheets.

Bake until golden brown on the bottom and dry to the touch in the center, 20–25 minutes, switching racks and rotating the baking sheets front to back halfway through.

Transfer the baking sheets to wire racks. Let the cookies cool on the pans for 1 minute, then transfer all the cookies to a dish that can hold them all in a single layer (you can also simply transfer them all to one of the baking sheets).

Slowly and gently drizzle or ladle the cooled syrup all over the cookies, letting it pool around them on the pan as well. Let the cookies cool completely, then cover with plastic wrap (cling film) and let stand for at least 6 hours at room temperature or overnight in the refrigerator to allow the syrup time to fully absorb into the cookies before serving.

Walnut "Bear Paw" Shortbread

Šapice / Šape

Preparation time: 40 minutes
Cooking time: 40 minutes
Makes: About 18 cookies

1 cup (115 g) walnuts
1¼ cups (175 g) all-purpose (plain) flour
½ cup (75 g) semolina flour
½ cup (100 g) white US granulated
  (UK caster) sugar
1 teaspoon baking powder
½ teaspoon fine sea salt
1 stick (4 oz/115 g) unsalted
  butter, softened
2 tablespoons sour cream
  or full-fat yogurt
2 teaspoons pure vanilla extract
1 egg, lightly beaten
Cooking spray or melted butter
  and flour, for the molds
Powdered (icing) sugar, for coating

These shortbread cookies from Bosnia are crumbly, packed with finely ground walnuts, and tossed in powdered (icing) sugar after baking, so they're closely related to Austrian *Vanillekipferl* (recipe, page 195). But one of the signature characteristics of these cookies is that their dough is pressed into fluted molds, which imprints the "bear paw"–like impressions on the shortbreads. Though there are special molds for the cookies, most people use madeleine molds or small fluted tart tins of various shapes to make these cookies. You can, of course, also use muffin tins in a pinch.

These cookies are made with eggs and sometimes yogurt, so they're slightly softer and more tender in texture than the traditional dense, snappy shortbread. In the Czech Republic and Slovakia, these same shortbreads baked in fluted molds are called *pracny/medvědí tlapičky* or *medevie labky* respectively, and they are typically spiced with cocoa powder, cinnamon, and cloves. If you'd like to make them, see the variation that follows.

Preheat the oven to 350°F (180°C/Gas Mark 4). Line a large baking sheet with parchment paper.

Spread the walnuts out in a single layer on the pan and bake until lightly toasted and fragrant, 8–10 minutes.

Transfer the nuts to a cutting board and let cool. Reserve the baking sheet and leave the oven on. Using a food processor or a knife, process or chop the walnuts until very finely ground.

In a large bowl, combine the ground walnuts, all-purpose (plain) flour, semolina flour, white US granulated (UK caster) sugar, baking powder, and salt. Add the butter and use your fingers to rub the butter into the dry ingredients until it breaks down and the mixture resembles coarse sand. Form a well in the center of the mixture and add the sour cream, vanilla, and egg and stir until a dough forms and there are no dry patches of flour remaining.

Spray the wells of a 12-cup madeleine pan or twelve 2- to 3-inch (5 to 7.5 cm) egg tart/mini tartlet molds with cooking spray or brush them lightly with melted butter and then coat with flour, knocking out any excess. Using a ¾-ounce (1½-tablespoon) ice cream scoop, portion the dough and roll into balls. Place a dough ball in the well of each mold and press it evenly over the bottom, then indent the center of each with the pad of your thumb (this helps the cookies bake up flat on top). Repeat to fill the rest of the molds and place them on the prepared baking sheet.

Bake until the cookies are light golden brown at the edges and dry to the touch in the center, 14–16 minutes, rotating the baking sheet front to back halfway through.

Transfer the baking sheet to a wire rack and let the cookies rest for 1 minute. Using a tea towel to protect your hands, invert the molds onto a wire rack so the cookies fall out; this works more easily when they're still hot. While the cookies are still warm, toss each cookie in powdered (icing) sugar to coat, brushing off any excess so you can still see the pattern of the mold on the cookie. Return each cookie to its place on the rack to cool completely.

Let the pan or molds cool completely, coat with more cooking spray or melted butter and flour and repeat to bake more cookies.

Once all the cookies are completely cooled, dust liberally with more powdered (icing) sugar, if you like, before serving.

Variation
Czech/Slovak "Bear Paw" Shortbread
Add 2 tablespoons Dutch-process cocoa powder, 2 teaspoons ground cinnamon, and 1 teaspoon ground cloves to the dry ingredients.

Walnut "Bear Paw" Shortbread

Walnut Meringue Crescents

Orasnice

Preparation time: 25 minutes
Cooking time: 35 minutes
Makes: About 18 cookies

2 egg whites
2 cups (270 g) powdered (icing) sugar
1 tablespoon fresh lemon juice
¾ teaspoon fine sea salt
2⅔ cups (310 g) walnuts, very finely
  ground (see headnote)
1¾ cups (200 g) walnuts, finely
  chopped, for rolling

Walnuts factor prominently in most Eastern European and Balkan desserts. The tree grows easily in the climate and the nuts are buttery and rich, so it makes sense to want to pair them with sugar for all sorts of cookies and pastries. These crescent-shaped cookies use them in two different forms. First is very finely ground, where they're folded with a fluffy meringue to form the dough for the cookies, kind of like a French dacquoise batter. Then they're rolled in finely chopped nuts to give extra texture on the outside. Their name—Bosnian for "walnuts"—says it all.

You can shape these crispy meringue cookies, also popular in Serbia and other Balkan countries, into simple balls if you like, but the traditional form is a crescent. And you can also dip or drizzle the cookies in melted chocolate or dust them with powdered (icing) sugar after they're cooled. To get the walnuts to be very finely ground for the cookies, pulse them in a food processor until they're the texture of sand, about 12 pulses.

Position racks in the top and bottom thirds of the oven and preheat the oven to 275°F (140°C/Gas Mark 1). Line two large baking sheets with parchment paper.

In a large bowl, with a hand mixer, beat the egg whites on medium speed until foamy, about 1 minute. Reduce the mixer speed to low and begin adding spoonfuls of the powdered (icing) sugar, one at a time, until all the sugar is added. Increase the mixer speed to medium and continue beating until the meringue forms soft-stiff peaks when you lift the beaters out of the bowl. Beat in the lemon juice and salt. Add the very finely ground walnuts and stir until a dough forms and there are no dry patches of walnuts remaining.

Place the finely chopped walnuts in a large shallow bowl or pie dish. Using a 1-ounce (2-tablespoon) ice cream scoop, portion the dough, dropping each portion into the bowl of chopped walnuts and then rolling it back and forth until it's completely coated in walnuts, shaping it into a log as you go. Bend the log at the middle to form a crescent and then transfer the crescent to the prepared baking sheets; they will be a little sticky and soft. Repeat portioning and rolling more cookies with the remaining dough. Arrange the crescents on the prepared baking sheets, spaced 1 inch (2.5 cm) apart.

Bake until light golden brown on the bottom and dry to the touch in the center, 30–35 minutes, switching racks and rotating the baking sheets front to back halfway through.

Transfer the baking sheets to wire racks. Let the cookies cool on the pans for 1 minute, then transfer them to the racks to cool completely.

Walnut Meringue Crescents

Little Vanilla Cookies

Vanilice

DF

Preparation time: 1 hour 10 minutes,
 plus chilling, cooling, and at least
 1 day standing time (optional)
Cooking time: 20 minutes
Makes: About 24 cookie sandwiches

½ cup (100 g) plus 2 tablespoons
 white US granulated (UK caster) sugar
1 vanilla bean
2 cups (270 g) powdered (icing) sugar
1 cup (115 g) walnuts
2 cups (280 g) all-purpose (plain) flour
½ teaspoon fine sea salt
½ cup (115 g) cold-rendered leaf lard
1 teaspoon pure vanilla extract
2 egg yolks
1 lemon
Apricot or rose hip jam, for filling

Though Serbia lies in the Balkans and much of its cuisine looks similar to its Ottoman/Turkish-influenced neighbors to the south, one cookie seems to be a standout. These "little vanilla cookies" are shortbread cookies made with lard and walnuts—typical of the Balkans—but where they depart is in their use of copious amounts of vanilla and apricot jam to sandwich together the tiny cookies. Though no one really knows where the tradition of these cookies comes from, they look like a disc-shaped version of Austria's famous *Vanillekipferl* (recipe, page 195), which would make the most sense owing to the Austro-Hungarian empire's influence over the country for centuries.

The vanilla is the most important part of these cookies, as both vanilla bean and vanilla extract are used here to intensify the flavor. To make an approximation of vanilla sugar—a powdered mix of the two ingredients commonly found in grocery stores and used in baking in Europe but harder to find outside of specific markets in the US—this recipe calls for blending vanilla bean seeds with powdered (icing) sugar in a food processor. The processor is also used to grind the walnuts to the appropriately fine grain so they meld into the dough smoothly.

Position racks in the top and bottom thirds of the oven and preheat the oven to 325°F (160°C/Gas Mark 3). Line two large baking sheets with parchment paper.

Place 2 tablespoons of the white US granulated (UK caster) sugar in a small bowl. Using a paring knife, split the vanilla bean in half lengthwise. Scrape the vanilla seeds into the bowl of sugar (reserve the spent pod for another use). Rub the vanilla seeds and sugar together with your fingers to disperse the seeds evenly in the sugar.

In a food processor, combine the powdered (icing) sugar with the vanilla sugar mixture and pulse until evenly combined. Pour the vanilla powdered sugar into a large bowl and set aside until ready to use.

Without cleaning the food processor bowl, pulse the walnuts until very finely ground, 12–15 pulses. Add the flour and salt and pulse to combine. Let stand until ready to use.

Place the remaining ½ cup (100 g) white US granulated sugar in a large bowl and add the lard, vanilla extract, and egg yolks. Using a Microplane (fine grater) positioned over the bowl, finely grate the zest from half of the lemon over the lard. Juice the lemon and add enough water, if needed, to make ¼ cup (2 fl oz/60 ml) liquid. Add it to the lard and beat on low speed with a hand mixer until combined. Increase the speed to medium and beat until lightened and smooth, about 3 minutes.

Add the flour and walnut mixture and stir until a dough forms and there are no dry patches of flour remaining. Cover the bowl of dough with plastic wrap (cling film) and refrigerate for at least 20 minutes or up to overnight to firm the dough.

Scrape the dough onto a lightly floured work surface and use a lightly floured rolling pin to flatten the dough until ¼ inch (6 mm) thick. Using a 1½-inch (4 cm) round cutter, cut out rounds from the dough and transfer them to the prepared baking sheets, spacing the rounds 1 inch (2.5 cm) apart. Reroll the scraps to cut out more rounds.

Bake until barely browned where they touch the baking sheet and dry to the touch on top, 15–20 minutes, switching racks and rotating the baking sheets front to back halfway through.

Transfer the baking sheets to wire racks. Let the cookies cool on the pans for 1 minute, then transfer them to the racks to cool completely.

Flip half the cookies over and top each with ½–1 teaspoon jam. Place another cookie on top to create sandwiches. Working one at a time, gently toss or roll the cookie sandwiches in the vanilla powdered sugar until completely coated. Return the cookies to the baking sheets or a serving platter. Ideally, cover the cookies with plastic wrap (cling film) and let stand at room temperature for 1–3 days before serving. If you like, sift the leftover vanilla powdered sugar from the bowl over the cooled cookies before serving.

Little Vanilla Cookies

Syrup-Soaked Shortbread Cookies
Sheqerpare

Preparation time: 45 minutes,
  plus cooling and at least 6 hours
  soaking time
Cooking time: 25 minutes
Makes: 16 cookies

For the syrup:
1 cup (200 g) white US granulated
  (UK caster) sugar
¾ cup (6 fl oz/175 ml) water
1 tablespoon fresh lemon juice
2 whole cloves
1 teaspoon pure vanilla extract

For the cookies:
2 cups (280 g) all-purpose (plain)
  flour, sifted
1½ teaspoons baking powder
½ teaspoon fine sea salt
¼ cup (50 g) white US granulated
  (UK caster) sugar
3 egg yolks
1 egg
1 stick (4 oz/115 g) unsalted butter,
  melted and cooled
Whole almonds, for decorating
  (optional)

In Albania, shortbread cookies are soaked in syrup, which adds moisture and sweetness to the cookies after they are baked instead of using a sweetened dough. This practice of adding a syrup to pastries after baking is common in Turkey, Greece, and other countries that influenced the region over the centuries. In fact, the *seqerpare* in Turkey are syrup-soaked pastries or cakes that clearly influenced the Albanian equivalent.

Whereas the Turkish version feels more like a dessert, Albanian *sheqerpare* evolved to be more explicitly shortbread cookies soaked in a fragrant syrup often flavored with cloves. Instead of creaming butter with sugar, as modern bakers are used to, these cookies are made with melted butter mixed into egg yolks that have been first beaten with sugar, a style reminiscent of genoise, or sponge cakes, which allows the cookies to absorb the syrup more readily. Although there are no nuts in the cookies, traditionally a single almond studs the center of each cookie.

- -

Make the syrup: In a small saucepan, combine the sugar, water, lemon juice, and cloves and bring to a boil over high heat. Reduce the heat to maintain a steady simmer and cook the syrup, stirring to ensure the sugar is completely dissolved, until reduced slightly, about 5 minutes. Remove the pan from the heat and stir in the vanilla. Let the syrup cool completely to room temperature before starting to make the cookies.

Make the cookies: Position racks in the top and bottom thirds of the oven and preheat the oven to 350°F (180°C/Gas Mark 4). Line two large baking sheets with parchment paper.

In a medium bowl, whisk together the flour, baking powder, and salt.

In a large bowl, with a hand mixer, beat the sugar, egg yolks, and whole egg on medium speed until lightened and thick, about 3 minutes. With the mixer on low speed, slowly drizzle in the melted butter and mix until smooth. Add the dry ingredients and stir until a dough forms and there are no dry patches of flour remaining.

Divide the dough into 16 equal portions and shape each into a ball. Divide the dough balls between the prepared baking sheets, arranging them at least 2 inches (5 cm) apart. If using, place a whole almond on top of each cookie and press it gently to flatten the dough ball slightly.

Bake until light golden brown and dry to the touch in the center, about 15 minutes, switching racks and rotating the baking sheets front to back halfway through.

Transfer the baking sheets to wire racks. Let the cookies cool on the pans for 1 minute, then transfer all of the cookies to a dish that can hold them all in a single layer (you can also simply transfer them all to one of the baking sheets).

Slowly and gently drizzle the cooled syrup all over the cookies, letting it pool around them in the dish as well. Let the cookies cool completely, then cover with plastic wrap (cling film). Let stand for at least 6 hours to allow the syrup time to fully absorb into the cookies before serving.

Springtime Corn Butter Cookies

Ballokume

Preparation time: 50 minutes
Cooking time: 25 minutes
Makes: About 16 cookies

2 cups (262 g) corn flour (not
  cornmeal; not cornstarch)
¾ teaspoon fine sea salt
1 stick (4 oz/115 g) unsalted butter
1 cup (200 g) white US granulated
  (UK caster) sugar
2 eggs
2 egg yolks

The town of Elbasan in the center of Albania is famous for these sugar cookies made from local corn (maize). They are traditionally made to celebrate Dita e Verës, the spring new year, which in the Gregorian calendar is March 14. The cookies are traditionally flavored with ashes from a fire lit the night before. The ashes are mixed with water and then strained out and used in the dough (for making at home though, the ashes are omitted or milk is used instead). Typically, the cookies are also baked atop an open fire to add even more smokiness, though a wood-fired oven that's cooling down after making pizzas or flatbreads would make a great substitute.

Another tradition is to make the dough in copper pots that must be stirred for upward of 30 minutes total. Such a laborious practice makes sense in the context of local custom, but when making these cookies at home, a saucepan and some patience will work just fine. The prolonged cooking time allows the sugar to partially dissolve in the butter, which gives the exterior of the cookies a crackly sheen.

Position racks in the top and bottom thirds of the oven and preheat the oven to 300°F (150°C/Gas Mark 2). Line two large baking sheets with parchment paper.

In a medium bowl, whisk together the corn flour and salt.

In a small saucepan, melt the butter over medium heat until starting to sizzle. Add the sugar and cook, stirring occasionally, until the sugar melts mostly in the butter, about 5 minutes. Remove the pan from the heat and scrape the butter-sugar mixture into a bowl. Using a hand mixer, beat the mixture on medium-high speed until cooled to the touch.

Add the whole eggs one at a time, beating well after each addition, at least 1 minute. Add both of the egg yolks and beat for 1 minute. Reduce the speed to low and slowly spoon in the dry ingredients until they're all added. Increase the mixer speed to medium and beat until the dough comes together and is smooth, about 1 minute more.

Divide the dough into 16 equal portions and shape each into a ball. Divide the dough balls between the prepared baking sheets, arranging them at least 2 inches (5 cm) apart.

Bake until light golden brown and dry to the touch in the center, 18–20 minutes, switching racks and rotating the baking sheets front to back halfway through.

Transfer the baking sheets to wire racks. Let the cookies cool on the pans for 1 minute, then transfer them to the racks to cool completely.

Beer Cookies

Pivarki

Preparation time: 35 minutes, plus
  cooling and 6 hours soaking time
Cooking time: 30 minutes
Makes: About 36 cookies

For the cookies:
3½ cups (490 g) all-purpose
  (plain) flour
⅔ cup (100 g) semolina flour
1 tablespoon baking powder
½ teaspoon fine sea salt
1 cup (8 fl oz/250 ml) lager-style beer
½ cup (4 fl oz/120 ml) vegetable oil
6 tablespoons (75 g) white US
  granulated (UK caster) sugar
2 cups (230 g) walnuts,
  very finely chopped

For the syrup:
1⅔ cups (335 g) white US granulated
  (UK caster) sugar
1 cup (8 fl oz/250 ml) water
1 tablespoon fresh lemon juice
1 teaspoon pure vanilla extract

The country of North Macedonia is a part of a larger geographical region—called Macedonia—that comprises a large swath of Greece to its southern border and portions of four other countries that surround it. So it makes sense that much of its cuisine is perhaps more influenced by its neighbors than many other countries. North Macedonia has its *gurabii* and *vanilici*, which are its versions of Greek *kourabiedes* (recipe, page 83) and Serbian *vanilice* (recipe, page 72), respectively.

While *pivarki* are very similar in appearance and construction to Greek *melomakarona* (recipe, page 86) and other Turkish-influenced cookies soaked in syrup like Albanian *sheqerpare* (recipe, page 74), the thing that sets them apart is the use of local beer to flavor the soft, pillowy cookies stuffed with walnuts. The beer—typically the national brand Skopsko—adds a pleasant yeasty bitterness to the cookies and differentiates them distinctly from the more well-known sweets of nearby Greece.

Make the cookies: Position racks in the top and bottom thirds of the oven and preheat the oven to 400°F (220°C/Gas Mark 7). Line two large baking sheets with parchment paper.

In a large bowl, whisk together the flour, semolina, baking powder, and salt. In another large bowl, combine the beer, oil, and 4 tablespoons of the sugar and whisk to combine. Add the dry ingredients and stir until a dough forms and there are no dry patches of flour remaining. In a small bowl, stir together the walnuts with the remaining 2 tablespoons sugar.

Using a ¾-ounce (1½-tablespoon) ice cream scoop, portion the dough and roll into balls. Flatten a dough ball in the palm of your hand, fill with 1 teaspoon of the walnut mixture, then bring the edges together over the walnuts to enclose them. Transfer the stuffed dough ball to the prepared baking sheet. Repeat portioning the remaining dough and filling with the walnut mixture, spacing the cookies 2 inches (5 cm) apart on the baking sheets. Reserve any leftover walnut mixture to use as decoration later.

Bake until golden brown all over, 20–25 minutes, switching racks and rotating the baking sheets front to back halfway through.

Transfer the baking sheets to wire racks. Let the cookies cool on the pans for 1 minute, then transfer them to the racks to cool completely.

Make the syrup: In a small saucepan, combine the sugar, water, and lemon juice. Bring to a boil over high heat, stirring to dissolve the sugar. Reduce the heat to maintain a steady simmer and let the syrup cook for 5 minutes. Remove the pan from the heat and stir in the vanilla.

Meanwhile, place as many cooled cookies as will fit loosely in the bottom of a 9 × 13-inch (23 × 33 cm) or similar baking dish and arrange them upside down. Repeat this with the remaining cookies in another dish or dishes until all the cookies are in a dish.

Ladle the hot syrup gently over the cookies in each dish until completely coated, then flip all the cookies over and quickly sprinkle a pinch of the reserved walnut mixture over the top of each. Let the cookies stand until the syrup has completely cooled, then cover the dishes with plastic wrap (cling film). Let the cookies stand until the syrup has soaked into them fully, about 6 hours, before serving. The cookies can be made up to 3 days in advance; keep the dishes full of cookies covered.

Beer Cookies

Honey and Cinnamon Cookies
Medenki

Preparation time: 50 minutes,
 plus cooling and setting time
Cooking time: 25 minutes
Makes: About 24 cookies

2¼ cups (315 g) all-purpose
 (plain) flour
2 teaspoons ground cinnamon
¾ teaspoon baking soda (bicarbonate
 of soda)
¾ teaspoon fine sea salt
⅔ cup (150 g) packed light
 brown sugar
¼ cup (85 g) honey
2 eggs
½ cup (4 fl oz/120 ml) vegetable oil
1 teaspoon pure vanilla extract
8 oz (225 g) bittersweet chocolate,
 roughly chopped
1 tablespoon vegetable shortening
 or refined coconut oil

Most every country and region in Europe has its version of a gingerbread-style cookie, the kind that are made with spices and honey or some type of "brown" sugar syrup, rolled out and cut into shapes. While Bulgaria's *medenki* cookies most likely started out that way, too, now you can find them as easier-to-portion drop cookies that are dipped in chocolate.

Though honey is where these cookies get their name, the cinnamon in the cookie is the dominant flavor. Some recipes call for as little as 1 teaspoon, while others call for 2 or 3 tablespoons. The honey and trace amount of molasses in the brown sugar give these cookies a wonderful, chewy-tender texture. If you want to keep the focus solely on the honey, substitute white sugar for the brown sugar.

- -

Position racks in the top and bottom thirds of the oven and preheat the oven to 350°F (180°C/Gas Mark 4). Line two large baking sheets with parchment paper.

In a medium bowl, whisk together the flour, cinnamon, baking soda (bicarb), and salt.

In a large bowl, with a hand mixer, beat the brown sugar, honey, and eggs on medium speed until pale and thickened, about 3 minutes. Pour in the oil and vanilla and mix on low until smooth. Add the dry ingredients and stir until a dough forms and there are no dry patches of flour remaining.

Using a ¾-ounce (1½-tablespoon) ice cream scoop, portion the dough and roll into balls. Divide the dough balls between the prepared baking sheets, flattening them slightly on the baking sheets and arranging them at least 2 inches (5 cm) apart.

Bake until light golden brown at the edges and dry to the touch in the center, 20–25 minutes, switching racks and rotating the baking sheets front to back halfway through.

Transfer the baking sheets to wire racks. Let the cookies cool on the pans for 1 minute, then transfer them to the racks to cool completely.

In a small heatproof bowl in the microwave or over a pan of simmering water, melt the chocolate and shortening together, stirring until smooth. Dip the top half of each cookie in the chocolate and then return the cookies to the racks or a sheet of parchment to allow the chocolate to cool and set before serving.

Honey and Cinnamon Cookies

Greek Almond Macaroons
Amygdalota

Preparation time: 25 minutes
Cooking time: 20 minutes
Makes: About 24 cookies

2 cups (240 g) packed superfine
   almond flour (ground almonds)
2 cups (270 g) powdered (icing) sugar,
   plus more for dusting (optional)
½ teaspoon fine sea salt
1 tablespoon orange blossom
   water or pure vanilla extract
1 egg white, lightly beaten

Though macaroon-style cookies—sweets made with beaten egg whites and sugar mixed with ground nuts—are a common treat throughout the Mediterranean, the Greeks take the art of making them to the highest level. *Amygdalota*, which roughly translates to "almond," are almond macaroons that can be found in nearly every part of Greece, but particularly in the islands. There are as many variations as there are Greek isles. Some are piped and some are dropped, while many are molded into various shapes that hold significant meaning in Greek culture, such a s pears, almonds, or eggs. *Amygdalota* are often served at weddings because they represent new beginnings.

While the name is also given to Greek almond sweets that are often not baked and contain no egg white, the baked cookie version with egg white is the one included here to help bind and set the rest of the ingredients more easily. It is shaped like a pear, keeping with one of the regional variations and to separate it from the countless other almond macaroons in that part of the world. Superfine almond flour (ground almonds) is used here so you don't have to grind almonds, but if you prefer to, simply start with the same weight of whole blanched almonds and finely grind them in a food processor to make the flour.

Position racks in the top and bottom thirds of the oven and preheat the oven to 350°F (180°C/Gas Mark 4). Line two large baking sheets with parchment paper.

In a large bowl, whisk together the almond flour (ground almonds), sugar, and salt. Add the orange blossom water and egg white and stir to combine with a spoon, then use your hands to knead the dough until it is evenly moistened and comes together in a smooth mass.

Using a ½-ounce (1-tablespoon) ice cream scoop, portion the dough and roll into balls, slightly tapering the balls at one end to give them a teardrop or pear shape. Divide the shaped dough balls between the prepared baking sheets, arranging them rounded-side down so they sit up on the baking sheets, spaced 1 inch (2.5 cm) apart.

Bake until light golden brown where they touch the baking sheet and at the tips, about 20 minutes, switching racks and rotating the baking sheets front to back halfway through.

Transfer the baking sheets to wire racks and let the cookies cool completely on the pans.

Dust the cookies with more powdered (icing) sugar, if you like, before serving.

Grape Must Cookies
Moustokouloura

Preparation time: 40 minutes,
  plus chilling time
Cooking time: 20 minutes
Makes: About 24 cookies

2 cups (280 g) all-purpose (plain) flour
½ teaspoon baking soda
  (bicarbonate of soda)
½ teaspoon ground cinnamon
¼ teaspoon ground cloves
½ teaspoon fine sea salt
½ cup (160 g) grape must/molasses
¼ cup (2 fl oz/60 ml) olive oil
¼ cup (50 g) white US granulated
  (UK caster) sugar
Finely grated zest of 1 navel orange
⅓ cup (2½ fl oz/80 ml) fresh
  orange juice
1 tablespoon brandy

Many cookies that came about before using refined sugar became the norm used liquid sweeteners to provide the necessary sweetness to transform a bread-like cracker into a cookie or biscuit. Many utilized honey as it was the dominant sweetener for millennia. And while Greece is known for its honey-drenched sweets, these *moustokouloura* eschew honey for a more seasonally available product: grape must.

Grape must or grape molasses, also called *petimezi*, is made just like the more well-known pomegranate molasses or even maple syrup: Grape juice—usually the runoff of wine production, hence its availability in autumn—is boiled down to just a fraction of its starting volume until it's thick, black, and intensely sweet, with a bitter edge. The grape must, easily available online or in Greek markets, plays beautifully with the spices, citrus, and olive oil in these simple ring-shaped cookies.

- -

Position racks in the top and bottom thirds of the oven and preheat the oven to 350°F (180°C/Gas Mark 4). Line two large baking sheets with parchment paper.

In a large bowl, whisk together the flour, baking soda (bicarb), cinnamon, cloves, and salt. In another large bowl, whisk together the grape must, olive oil, sugar, orange zest and juice, and brandy until smooth. Add the dry ingredients and stir until a dough forms and there are no dry patches of flour remaining. Cover the bowl of dough with plastic wrap (cling film) and refrigerate for at least 20 minutes or up to overnight to firm the dough.

Using a 1-ounce (2-tablespoon) ice cream scoop, portion the dough and roll each into a rope, about ½ inch (13 mm) thick. Join the ends of the rope together to create a ring. Divide the dough rings between the prepared baking sheets, spaced 2 inches (5 cm) apart.

Bake until light golden brown where they touch the baking sheet and just dry on the top, 15–18 minutes, switching racks and rotating the baking sheets front to back halfway through.

Transfer the baking sheets to wire racks. Let the cookies cool on the pans for 1 minute, then transfer them to the racks to cool completely. The cookies will seem soft at first but will firm upon cooling.

Crescents

People often want to give meaning to things that exist or occur in this world, and throughout my research for this book, I found that the likely explanation for some things was not so exciting or maybe even had no meaning at all. So many urban legends and tales were born to give meaning to the meaningless.

Case in point: crescent-shaped cookies (see "Wedding" Cookies, page 23). There are various theories that have lasted through centuries. Some historians posit that breads and other proto-cookie foods were shaped into crescents to worship the moon in pagan times. Others say crescents were developed in Eastern Europe after two failed Ottoman invasions prompted bakers to bake crescent-shaped pastries, so the victors could, as historian Gil Marks hypothesizes in his *Encyclopedia of Jewish Food*, eat them in an act of "take that" defiance, similar to why *Hamantaschen* are made to mock the biblical figure Haman (see page 250).

While these stories could be true and are fun to read about, it's also possible that the shape came about as a way to be more aesthetically pleasing than something simpler. It's a shape that anyone can produce and makes for beautiful pastries, cookies, and breads in the same way bread bakers today may slash their loaves on top with unique patterns, or how cupcake-makers create unique swirling patterns with their icing. People love to make up stories to give life to the simple things we create, out of our love for cookies and other foods we bake to share.

Greek Shortbreads

Kourabiedes / Kourambiethes

Preparation time: 1 hour 25 minutes,
  plus chilling time
Cooking time: 25 minutes
Makes: About 24 cookies

1 cup (115 g) slivered almonds
2 cups (280 g) all-purpose (plain) flour
1 teaspoon baking powder
¾ teaspoon fine sea salt
2 sticks (8 oz/225 g) unsalted
  butter, softened
½ cup (65 g) powdered (icing) sugar,
  plus 2 cups (270 g) for coating
2 tablespoons ouzo or brandy
  (or 1 tablespoon rose water or pure
  vanilla extract)
1 egg yolk

This is the Greek version of the Turkish *kurabiye* (recipe, page 60), which is very similar in style but has a few small differences. For one, the dough often includes some type of liquor as a flavoring, whether brandy, anise-flavored ouzo, or just rose water. While the shape of the cookies can take the form of a crescent or ball/button, there is always a heavy coating of powdered (icing) sugar around the outside of the cookies after they are baked. This characteristic, along with the fact that *kourabiedes* are often served at Greek weddings, probably influenced the term "wedding" cookie (see page 23) in several other regions around the globe to become that style of cookie we refer to today.

The most common recipe for this cookie uses ground almonds, but walnuts are also popular. Some recipes use primarily finely ground nuts, while others add coarsely chopped nuts, too, for crunch. The baked cookies should not be browned when done—this helps achieve a texture that is crumbly but melts in your mouth, not one that is too snappy or crunchy. It also avoids producing a toasted flavor that would compete with the pure butter and sugar profile, which makes this style of cookie so special. Tossing the nutty cookies in the powdered sugar while warm allows the sugar to better stick to them and create an even coating.

- -

Position racks in the top and bottom thirds of the oven and preheat the oven to 350°F (180°C/Gas Mark 4). Line two large baking sheets with parchment paper.

Place the slivered almonds on one of the baking sheets and bake in the oven until lightly toasted, 6–8 minutes. Immediately transfer the almonds to a cutting board to cool completely. Reserve the baking sheet and leave the oven on. Finely chop the almonds by hand or pulse them in a food processor until coarsely ground.

In a medium bowl, whisk together the flour, baking powder, and salt.

In a large bowl, with a hand mixer, beat the butter, ½ cup (65 g) sugar, the ouzo, and egg yolk on low speed until combined. Increase the speed to medium and beat until pale and lightened, about 3 minutes. Add the flour mixture and almonds and stir until a dough forms and there are no dry patches of flour remaining. Cover the bowl of dough with plastic wrap (cling film) and refrigerate for at least 20 minutes or up to overnight to firm the dough.

Using a ¾-ounce (1½-tablespoon) ice cream scoop, portion the dough and roll into balls or crescent shapes. Divide the dough balls between the prepared baking sheets, flattening them just enough to keep them from rolling around on the baking sheets. Space the dough balls at least 1 inch (2.5 cm) apart.

Bake until barely browned where they touch the baking sheet and dry to the touch on top, 12–15 minutes, switching racks and rotating the baking sheets front to back halfway through.

Transfer the baking sheets to wire racks and let the cookies rest for 5 minutes to cool only slightly.

Place the remaining 2 cups of sugar in a wide bowl. Working a few at a time, gently toss or roll the cookies in the sugar until completely coated. Return the cookies to the baking sheets and let them cool completely. If you like, sift the leftover sugar from the bowl over the cooled cookies before serving.

Butter Cookie Spirals
Koulourakia

Preparation time: 1 hour 40 minutes,
  plus chilling time
Cooking time: 20 minutes
Makes: About 30 cookies

2½ cups (350 g) all-purpose
  (plain) flour
2 teaspoons baker's ammonia
  (see page 17) or baking powder
¾ teaspoon fine sea salt
1½ sticks (6 oz/170 g) unsalted
  butter, softened
⅔ cup (130 g) white US granulated
  (UK caster) sugar
Finely grated zest of 1 lemon
Finely grated zest of ½ orange
1 teaspoon pure vanilla extract
2 eggs
Egg wash: 1 egg beaten with
  1 tablespoon water
Sesame seeds, for decorating

These citrus-spiked, buttery cookies are traditionally served at Easter time in Greece. They differ from most Greek sweets in that they're made with butter and sugar, not olive oil or honey. Typically, they are shaped like the letter "S" (there are references that suggest this might be due to snake-worshiping gods), though nowadays bakers shape them into coils, twists, or braids. What's best about the cookies are their bright citrus taste. While many recipes use orange or lemon zest, both are used here.

Another distinguishing characteristic of these cookies is the use of baker's ammonia, which gives them a lightness and crispness that pairs well with coffee or tea. They also last longer when made with baker's ammonia, so the cookies stay fresh throughout the holiday season.

Position racks in the top and bottom thirds of the oven and preheat the oven to 325°F (160°C/Gas Mark 3). Line two large baking sheets with parchment paper.

In a medium bowl, whisk together the flour, baker's ammonia, and salt.

In a large bowl, with a hand mixer, beat the butter, sugar, lemon zest, orange zest, and vanilla on medium speed until pale and fluffy, about 3 minutes. Add the eggs, one at a time, beating well after each addition. Add the dry ingredients and stir until a dough forms and there are no dry patches of flour remaining. Cover the bowl of dough with plastic wrap (cling film) and refrigerate for at least 20 minutes or up to overnight to firm the dough.

Using a ¾-ounce (1½-tablespoons) ice cream scoop, portion the dough and roll each into a rope about ½ inch (13 mm) thick. Coil the rope around one end to create a snail shape or fold the rope in half and twist the lengths together to form twists. Divide the shaped dough coils/twists between the prepared baking sheets, spaced 2 inches (5 cm) apart. Make the egg wash and brush the top of each cookie, then sprinkle lightly with sesame seeds.

Bake until light golden brown and dry to the touch, 18–20 minutes, switching racks and rotating the baking sheets front to back halfway through.

Transfer the baking sheets to wire racks. Let the cookies cool on the pans for 1 minute, then transfer them to the racks to cool completely.

Butter Cookie Spirals

Olive Oil and Honey Cookies

Melomakarona

Preparation time: 1 hour 40 minutes,
 plus cooling and soaking time
Cooking time: 35 minutes
Makes: About 48 cookies

For the cookies:
6⅔ cups (935 g) all-purpose
 (plain) flour
2 teaspoons baking powder
1¼ teaspoons fine sea salt
1 teaspoon ground cinnamon
¼ teaspoon ground cloves
1¾ cups (14 fl oz/415 ml) plain olive
 oil (not extra-virgin)
½ cup (100 g) white US granulated
 (UK caster) sugar
2 tablespoons Cognac or other brandy
1 teaspoon pure vanilla extract
Finely grated zest of 1 orange
½ cup (4 fl oz/120 ml) fresh
 orange juice
1 teaspoon baking soda
 (bicarbonate of soda)

For the syrup:
1 cup (200 g) white US granulated
 (UK caster) sugar
1 cup (340 g) honey
1 cup (8 fl oz/250 ml) water
1 cinnamon stick
2–6 whole cloves
½ orange
½ lemon

To finish:
1 cup (115 g) walnuts, finely chopped
2 teaspoons ground cinnamon

These Greek syrup-soaked and spiced Christmas-time cookies, are perfumed with cinnamon, cloves, orange and a liquor such as Cognac or brandy. Instead of using butter and molasses, copious amounts of olive oil add a brightness, and citrus-spiked honey syrup soaks the cookies after baking and lightens them considerably. If you were to include semolina flour in this cookie, many bakers would refer to it as *finikia*, but both names are used somewhat interchangeably for this style of cookie.

While many recipes use only honey for sweetening the syrup, sugar is also used here to lessen the intensity of the honey; if you prefer a more honey-forward profile, use 2 cups (780 g) honey and omit the sugar. The key to the syrup soaking into the cookies is to soak the cooled cookies in it while the syrup is hot. Placing all the cookies in dishes and pouring over the syrup all at once helps prevent the syrup from cooling too much by the time you get to the last cookies. Be sure to sprinkle the cookies with the walnut decoration immediately after soaking them with the syrup, to ensure the nuts stick to the cookies.

Make the cookies: Position racks in the top and bottom thirds of the oven and preheat the oven to 350°F (180°C/Gas Mark 4). Line two large baking sheets with parchment paper.

In a large bowl, whisk together the flour, baking powder, salt, cinnamon, and cloves. Set aside.

In a large bowl, with a hand mixer, beat the olive oil, sugar, Cognac, and vanilla on medium-low speed until smooth and emulsified, about 2 minutes. In a medium bowl, whisk together the orange zest, orange juice, and baking soda (bicarb). Once the foaming subsides, pour the orange juice mixture into the olive oil mixture and beat on low speed until evenly combined, 1 minute more. Add the dry ingredients and stir until a dough forms and there are no dry patches of flour remaining.

Using a ¾-ounce (1½-tablespoon) ice cream scoop, portion the dough and roll them into egg shapes or American football-shaped ovals. Divide the cookies between the prepared baking sheets, flattening them slightly on the baking sheets and spacing them 1 inch (2.5 cm) apart.

Bake until light golden brown at the edges and dry to the touch in the center, 20–25 minutes, switching racks and rotating the baking sheets front to back halfway through.

Transfer the baking sheets to wire racks. Let the cookies cool on the pans for 1 minute, then transfer them to the racks to cool completely.

Make the syrup: In a small saucepan, combine the sugar, honey, water, cinnamon stick, and cloves. Using a vegetable peeler, remove strips of zest from the orange and lemon halves and add to the saucepan, then squeeze the juice from the citrus halves into the saucepan as well. Bring to a boil over high heat, stirring to dissolve the sugar. Reduce the heat to maintain a steady simmer and let the syrup cook for 5 minutes.

Meanwhile, place as many cooled cookies as will fit loosely in the bottom of a 9 × 13-inch (23 × 33 cm) or similar baking dish and arrange them upside down. Repeat this with the remaining cookies in as many dishes as needed.

To finish the cookies: In a small bowl, combine the chopped walnuts and ground cinnamon. Ladle the hot syrup gently over the cookies in each dish until completely coated, then flip all the cookies and quickly sprinkle a pinch of the cinnamon walnut mixture over the top of each. Let the cookies stand until the syrup has completely soaked into them, at least 6 hours or preferably overnight.

The cookies can be made up to 3 days in advance; keep the dishes full of cookies covered with plastic wrap (cling film).

Olive Oil and Honey Cookies

the mediterranean

Italy's influence on this region can't be overstated, as it seemingly produces as many types of cookies as it does shapes of pasta. The Mediterranean's seat as the center of the former Roman empire is evident in the influences from North Africa and Malta to the south as are the similarities to the Iberian cookies from Spain and Portugal to the west. Mediterranean staples like almonds, lemons, and anise monopolize the flavor profile of nearly every cookie not soaked in honey and covered with sesame seeds. It's a region deeply in love with celebrating its agriculture through sweets.

Portuguese Lemon Cookies

Biscoitos

Preparation time: 40 minutes
Cooking time: 20 minutes
Makes: About 12 cookies

2½ cups (355 g) all-purpose
   (plain) flour
2 teaspoons baking powder
½ teaspoon fine sea salt
¾ cup (150 g) white US granulated
   (UK caster) sugar
1 stick (4 oz/115 g) unsalted butter
   or cold-rendered leaf lard, or a mix
   of both, softened
2 eggs
Finely grated zest of 1 lemon
2 tablespoons fresh lemon juice

The dough for these lemony cookies is one of those most basic in Portuguese baking and is used in making many different types of cookies. The most distinctive form is ring shapes called *biscoitos*, which likely morphed from smaller versions of Spanish *bizcocho*, an eggy sponge cake from which the American *bizcochitos* (recipe, page 354) also derives its name. The same lengths of dough used to form those rings are often also simply shaped into twists.

Another iteration are so-called *lavadores* (see the variation that follows), which are balls of dough pressed flat with a fork to make distinctive ridges, or "washboards," on the top of the cookies. Because of those distinctive markings, this cookie likely influenced Brazilian *sequilhos* (recipe, page 176) and other such South American butter cookies during Portuguese colonization. Though they were once made with lard, modern recipes now use butter or a 50/50 mix.

- -

Position racks in the top and bottom thirds of the oven and preheat the oven to 350°F (180°C/Gas Mark 4). Line two large baking sheets with parchment paper.

In a medium bowl, whisk together the flour, baking powder, and salt.

In a large bowl, with a hand mixer, beat the sugar and butter on medium speed until pale and fluffy, 2–3 minutes. Add the eggs, one at a time, beating until smooth after each addition. Beat in the lemon zest and lemon juice. Add the dry ingredients and stir until a dough forms and there are no dry patches of flour remaining. Gather the dough into a ball.

Working on a lightly floured work surface, roll pieces of the dough between your fingers and the work surface into ropes ¾ inch (2 cm) thick. Cut the ropes into 5-inch (13 cm) lengths. Bend each length in the center and form a circle, touching the ends together to connect. (Alternatively, bend the lengths in half and then twist the two "arms" together.) Arrange the dough rings (or twists) on the prepared baking sheets, spaced 2 inches (5 cm) apart.

Bake until the cookies are light golden brown and dry to the touch, 15–20 minutes, switching racks and rotating the baking sheets front to back halfway through.

Transfer the baking sheets to wire racks. Let the cookies cool on the pans for 1 minute, then transfer them to the racks to cool completely.

Variation
Lavadores
Make the dough as directed. Using a 1-ounce (2-tablespoon) ice cream scoop, portion the dough and roll into balls. Arrange on the baking sheet and lay the tines of a fork over each ball, flattening to imprint their ridges on the top. Bake as directed.

Molasses and Spice Cookies
Broas de Mel

Preparation time: 40 minutes,
 plus chilling time
Cooking time: 25 minutes
Makes: About 48 cookies

2 cups (200 g) white US granulated
 (UK caster) sugar
½ cup (115 g) cold-rendered leaf lard,
 softened, or ½ cup (4 fl oz/120 ml)
 olive oil
1 stick (4 oz/115 g) unsalted
 butter, softened
⅓ cup (105 g) unsulphured molasses
 (not blackstrap)
2 tablespoons ground cinnamon
2 teaspoons freshly grated nutmeg
½ teaspoon ground cloves
Finely grated zest of 1 lemon
3½ cups (490 g) all-purpose
 (plain) flour
1 teaspoon baking soda
 (bicarbonate of soda)
1 teaspoon fine sea salt
2 eggs
Whole almonds, for decorating
 (optional)

Though their name translates to "honey bread/cakes," these spiced cookies from Madeira are actually sweetened with molasses. The Portuguese island has produced and processed sugarcane since at least the 1500s, and one of its by-products is *mel de cana*, or literally "honey of sugarcane," which is used in many of its sweets.

These cookies are traditionally made for Christmas, and with their molasses-and-spice flavor profile, they resemble other such European holiday drop cookies like German *Pfeffernüsse* (recipe, page 240), Danish *pebernødder* (recipe, page 330), and Dutch *pepernoten* (recipe, page 223). Many recipes call for shaping the dough balls into ovals and studding them with whole almonds on top, while modern recipes leave them as plain rounds.

In a medium saucepan, combine the sugar, lard, butter, and molasses and heat over medium-high heat, stirring until the sugar dissolves. Remove the pan from the heat and pour it into a large bowl. Whisk in the cinnamon, nutmeg, cloves, and lemon zest and let the mixture cool to room temperature.

Meanwhile, in a medium bowl, whisk together the flour, baking soda (bicarb), and salt.

Add the eggs to the cooled sugar mixture and whisk until smooth. Add the dry ingredients and stir until the dough just comes together and there are no dry patches of flour remaining. Cover the bowl with plastic wrap (cling film) and refrigerate for at least 4 hours or overnight, or up to 1 day.

Position racks in the top and bottom thirds of the oven and preheat the oven to 325°F (160°C/Gas Mark 3). Line two large baking sheets with parchment paper.

Using a ¾-ounce (1½-tablespoon) ice cream scoop, portion the dough and roll into balls. Arrange them on the prepared baking sheets, spaced 2 inches (5 cm) apart. If you like, press a whole almond in the center of each cookie.

Bake until darker brown at the edges and dry to the touch on top, 18–20 minutes, switching racks and rotating the baking sheets front to back halfway through.

Transfer the baking sheets to wire racks. Let the cookies cool on the pans for 1 minute, then transfer them to the racks to cool completely.

Cakey Egg Yolk Cookies

Doce de Gema

DF V

Preparation time: 40 minutes,
 plus cooling and setting time
Cooking time: 15 minutes
Makes: About 24 cookies

For the cookies:
3 eggs
4 egg yolks
1 cup (200 g) white US granulated
 (UK caster) sugar
Finely grated zest of 1 lemon
½ teaspoon fine sea salt
¼ teaspoon ground cinnamon
 (optional)
1¾ cups (245 g) all-purpose
 (plain) flour

For the glaze:
1 egg white
1 cup (135 g) powdered (icing) sugar
1 teaspoon fresh lemon juice
Pinch of fine sea salt

These so-called "egg yolk sweets" are a specialty of Margaride, a town east-northeast of Porto that is known for its sponge cakes. These cookies are a diminutive version of those cakes that were once the dominion of nuns who sold them at convents in northern Portugal. The cookies are soft and bright yellow from the yolks and covered in a white icing with a distinctive pattern created by dragging your fingers through the icing. The pattern resembles the lines of a scallop shell, though it's likely that wasn't the true intention of the design, but simply just the finger marks of the nuns left behind as they spread the icing on by hand. A similar version but without the icing exists in Utrera, in southern Spain, called *mostachones*, and is typically dusted with powdered (icing) sugar or brushed with honey after baking and then left to stick to the parchment paper as a preservative measure.

Make the cookies: Position racks in the top and bottom thirds of the oven and preheat the oven to 350°F (180°C/Gas Mark 4). Line two large baking sheets with parchment paper.

In a large bowl, with a hand mixer, beat the whole eggs, egg yolks, white US granulated (UK caster) sugar, lemon zest, salt, and cinnamon (if using) on medium speed until doubled in volume and the mixture falls back into the bowl in a thick ribbon when the beaters are lifted, 3–4 minutes. Add the flour and fold with a silicone spatula until a thick but loose batter forms and there are no dry patches of flour remaining.

Using a 1-ounce (2-tablespoon) ice cream scoop or a piping bag, scoop or pipe portions of the batter onto the prepared baking sheets, spaced at least 4 inches (10 cm) apart since they will spread. Bake until the cookies are golden brown at the edges and dry to the touch in the center, 10–12 minutes.

Transfer the baking sheets to wire racks. Let the cookies cool on the pans for 5 minutes, then transfer them to the racks to cool completely.

Make the glaze: In a medium bowl, whisk the egg white until frothy. Add the powdered (icing) sugar, lemon juice, and salt and stir until it forms a thin glaze, adding a teaspoon or so of water if needed to get it to a drizzle-able consistency.

Dip the tops of each cookie in the glaze or spoon it over the top, letting the excess drain back into the bowl. While holding the glazed cookie over the bowl, use your index, middle, and rings fingers—held together—to swipe through the icing in a circular pattern. Return the cookies to the racks and let the glaze dry completely and set before serving.

Cakey Egg Yolk Cookies

Cinnamon Shortbread "Rage" Cookies
Raivas de Aveiro

Preparation time: 40 minutes
Cooking time: 20 minutes
Makes: About 12 cookies

2 cups (280 g) all-purpose (plain) flour
2 teaspoons ground cinnamon
¾ teaspoon fine sea salt
⅔ cup (130 g) white US granulated
  (UK caster) sugar
4 tablespoons (2 oz/55 g) unsalted
  butter, softened
3 eggs

A specialty of the coastal town of Aveiro, these cinnamon-flavored sugar cookies have a unique form. Their name translates as "rage" and their shape indeed looks like what a baker, in a frustrated fit, might do to a roll of cookie dough, haphazardly squishing it into squiggles. Likely a variation on *biscoitos* (recipe, page 90) or Spanish *polvorones* (recipe, page 97), the dough for these cookies is typically flavored heavily with cinnamon and is dense like shortbread since they contain no leavening.

Position racks in the top and bottom thirds of the oven and preheat the oven to 350°F (180°C/Gas Mark 4). Line two large baking sheets with parchment paper.

In a medium bowl, whisk together the flour, cinnamon, and salt.

In a large bowl, with a hand mixer, beat the sugar and butter on medium speed until pale and fluffy, 2–3 minutes. Add the eggs, one at a time, beating until smooth after each addition. Add the dry ingredients and stir until a dough forms and there are no dry patches of flour remaining. Gather the dough into a ball.

Working on a lightly floured work surface, roll pieces of the dough between your fingers and the work surface into ropes ½ inch (13 mm) thick. Cut the ropes into 8-inch (20 cm) lengths. Bend each length in the center and form a circle, touching the ends together to connect. Then gather the north, south, east, and west points on the circle and bring them together, adjusting the extending pieces of dough into a squiggle shape. Arrange the dough squiggles on the prepared baking sheets, spaced 2 inches (5 cm) apart.

Bake until the cookies are golden brown on the bottom and dry to the touch on top, 15–18 minutes, switching racks and rotating the baking sheets front to back halfway through.

Transfer the baking sheets to wire racks. Let the cookies cool on the pans for 1 minute, then transfer them to the racks to cool completely.

Cinnamon Shortbread "Rage" Cookies

Portuguese Shortbread Cookies
Areias de Cascais

Preparation time: 45 minutes
Cooking time: 15 minutes
Makes: About 24 cookies

3 cups (405 g) powdered (icing) sugar
1 stick (4 oz/115 g) unsalted butter,
 softened
¼ cup (55 g) cold-rendered leaf lard
 or vegetable shortening, softened
¾ teaspoon fine sea salt
Finely grated zest of 1 lemon or
 1 teaspoon pure vanilla extract
 (optional)
2 cups (280 g) all-purpose (plain) flour
1 teaspoon ground cinnamon

Portugal's answer to the ubiquitous "wedding" cookies, these *areias* or "sand cookies," from the coastal town of Cascais were likely influenced by its neighbor Spain's *polvorones* (recipe, opposite). As with most Iberian cookies, they were originally made with lard, but now butter is common or a mix of the two. It's traditional to leave the cookies unflavored and toss them in powdered (icing) sugar scented with a small amount of cinnamon, but modern recipes add lemon zest or vanilla. Options are given in this recipe for both.

- -

Position racks in the top and bottom thirds of the oven and preheat the oven to 325°F (160°C/Gas Mark 3). Line two large baking sheets with parchment paper.

In a large bowl, combine 1 cup (135 g) of the sugar, the butter, lard, salt, and either lemon zest or vanilla, if using. Beat on medium speed with a hand mixer until pale and fluffy, 2–3 minutes. Add the flour and stir until a crumbly dough forms and there are no dry patches of flour remaining.

Using a 1-ounce (2-tablespoon) ice cream scoop, portion the dough and roll into balls. Arrange them on the prepared baking sheets, spaced 2 inches (5 cm) apart.

Bake until the cookies are lightly golden at the edges on the bottom and dry to the touch all over, 10–12 minutes, switching racks and rotating the baking sheets front to back halfway through.

Meanwhile, in a large bowl, whisk together the remaining 2 cups (270 g) sugar and the cinnamon.

Transfer the baking sheets to wire racks and let the cookies rest for 1 minute. While the cookies are still warm, toss them gently in the cinnamon-powdered sugar until fully coated and then return to their spot on the baking sheets. Let cool completely.

Polvorones

The history of Spain's most popular cookie, the *polvorone*, started long before the Moorish invasion of the Iberian Peninsula in the seventh century brought it to fruition. The traditions of making Levantine and Middle Eastern shortbread biscuits like *ghorayeba* (recipe, page 49), Turkish *kurabiye* (recipe, page 60), and Moroccan *ghoriba bahla* (recipe, page 136) all influenced the *polvorone*. But once the Christians regained control of Spain during the reign of the "Catholic monarchs" Ferdinand II of Aragón and Isabella I of Castile, the church took control of bakeries and forced bakers to use pork lard in the making of cookies, which collectively came to be known as "*mantecadas*." These lard-based cookies were used by the Inquisition to identify Jews and Muslims, by serving the cookies during Christmas celebrations and observing who did not eat them.

That sinister history today dictates the use of lard in crumbly cookies like *polvorones*, which are the most famous of the *mantecadas*, and the practice spread throughout its colonies in Central America, South America, and Southeast Asia. Today in Spain, *mantecados* are confusingly sometimes also the name for a type of butter- or olive oil–based cookie with eggs and/or chemical leavening. The name is often also used interchangeably with the word *galletitas*, to refer to biscuits in the same way Americans use the word "cookie."

Spanish Shortbread Cookies
Polvorones

DF

Preparation time: 40 minutes,
  plus cooling time
Cooking time: 35 minutes
Makes: About 18 cookies

1½ cups (210 g) all-purpose
  (plain) flour
3 oz (85 g) blanched whole
  or slivered almonds
½ cup (105 g) superfine (caster) sugar
½ cup (115 g) cold-rendered
  leaf lard, softened
1 tablespoon anise liqueur, such as
  Anis del Mono dulce or sambuca
½ teaspoon ground cinnamon
½ teaspoon fine sea salt
Powdered (icing) sugar, for dusting

From the Spanish *polvo*, which means "sandy," this cookie's influence shows up in both name and style in Filipino *polvoron* (recipe, page 376), Mexican *polvorones de canela* (recipe, page 156), Cuban *torticas de morón* (recipe, page 148), Salvadoran *salpores de arroz* (recipe, page 163), Puerto Rican *mantecaditos* (recipe, page 150), Venezuelan *polvorosas* (recipe, page 170), and Argentinian *alfajores* (recipe, page 182)—whose cookies resemble the Spanish *polvorón*. While these shortbreads are famous in Spain, they descend from a long line of Levantine and Middle Eastern shortbread biscuits (see Polvorones, opposite).

The town of Estepa, once the center of Moorish Spain, is the capital of *polvorón* production in Spain. The basic recipe uses flour with a small amount of ground almonds, lard, and sugar. The most traditional flavorings are ground cinnamon and anise liqueur, which is also often served along with the cookies at Christmas. A popular variation of the cookie is *polvorones de limón*, which swaps the anise and cinnamon for lemon zest (see the variation that follows).

Preheat the oven to 350°F (180°C/Gas Mark 4). Line a large baking sheet with parchment paper.

Spread the flour out on the parchment paper and bake the flour, stirring occasionally to ensure it toasts evenly, until starting to brown at the edges and it smells nutty, 12–14 minutes. Remove the baking sheet from the oven and let the flour cool completely on the paper. Leave the oven on but reduce the oven temperature to 325°F (160°C/Gas Mark 3).

Using the paper like a sling, lift the flour off the baking sheet and transfer it to a large bowl. Return the paper to the baking sheet and reserve until ready to use.

In a food processor, pulse the almonds until finely chopped. Add the superfine (caster) sugar and pulse until very finely ground. Scrape the almond-sugar mixture into the bowl with the flour and whisk to combine. Add the lard, liqueur, cinnamon, and salt and use your hand to mix everything together until it forms a crumbly dough and there are no dry patches of flour remaining. It is ready when you can pick up a handful, make a fist, and the dough in your hand just holds together.

Scrape the dough out onto a lightly floured work surface and use your hands to pat the dough into a disc that's roughly ½ inch (13 mm) thick; if you like, gently roll a rolling pin over the disc to even out the surface. Using a 1½-inch (4 cm) round cutter, stamp out cookies and use an offset or thin metal spatula to carefully transfer the rounds to the prepared baking sheet, spacing them as close as ½ inch (13 mm) apart (the cookies will not spread). Reroll scraps and continue cutting out rounds.

Bake until light golden brown at the edges and dry to the touch in the center, 18–20 minutes, rotating the baking sheet front to back halfway through.

Transfer the baking sheet to a wire rack and let the cookies cool completely on the pan; if you try to move them while warm, the cookies will fall apart.

Dust the tops of the cookies liberally with powdered (icing) sugar before serving.

Variation
Polvorones de Limón
Omit the anise liqueur and cinnamon. Add the finely grated zest of 3 lemons to the dough along with the lard.

Twice-Baked Almond Cookies

Carquinyolis

Preparation time: 45 minutes,
 plus 1 hour soaking time
Cooking time: 55 minutes
Makes: About 36 cookies

7 oz (200 g) almonds
2 cups (280 g) all-purpose (plain) flour
1 teaspoon baking powder
1 teaspoon ground cinnamon or finely
 ground anise seeds
¾ teaspoon fine sea salt
¾ cup (150 g) white US granulated
 (UK caster) sugar
2 eggs
3 tablespoons whole milk
Finely grated zest of ½ lemon
Egg wash: 1 egg yolk beaten with
 1 tablespoon water

These "Catalonian biscotti" are a specialty of the region, particularly in Caldes de Montbui, outside Barcelona. Filled with whole almonds, they resemble the French *croquants aux amandes* (recipe, page 260) in style but are smaller. They contain anise seeds like Italian *cantucci* (recipe, page 112), but lemon zest, cinnamon, and cumin or caraway seeds are also often added to the mix. A small amount of almonds are ground up and mixed into the dough, but most are left whole, which show up as attractive pieces in the slices. The whole almonds are first soaked in water so they soften, to make for easier slicing and better incorporating into the dough. Like the other twice-baked cookies of the Mediterranean and ring-shaped cookies of Italy like *ciambelline al vino* (recipe, page 122) and *zuccherini* (recipe, page 134), these cookies are traditionally served with a glass of sweet wine, or with coffee for breakfast.

Place 4 ounces (115 g) of the almonds in a small bowl and cover with water. Let stand until softened, about 1 hour. Drain the whole almonds and dry thoroughly on paper towels.

Meanwhile, in a food processor, pulse the remaining 3 ounces (85 g) almonds until very finely ground.

Position racks in the top and bottom thirds of the oven and preheat the oven to 350°F (180°C/Gas Mark 4). Line two large baking sheets with parchment paper.

In a medium bowl, whisk together the ground almonds, flour, baking powder, cinnamon, and salt.

In a large bowl, combine the sugar, eggs, milk, and lemon zest and whisk until smooth. Add the dry ingredients and soaked almonds and stir until a dough forms and there are no more dry patches of flour remaining.

Shape the dough into a ball and divide into 4 equal portions. Working on a lightly floured work surface, shape each portion into a log 1½ inches (4 cm) in diameter. Divide the logs between the prepared baking sheets and lightly brush each with some egg wash.

Bake until the logs are lightly browned and dry to the touch, 30–35 minutes, switching racks and rotating the baking sheets front to back halfway through.

Transfer the baking sheets to wire racks and let the logs rest for 10 minutes. Leave the oven on.

Carefully transfer each log to a cutting board and using a sharp knife, cut every ½ inch (13 mm) into thin slices. Return the slices to the baking sheets, spaced evenly apart, and bake until the cookies are golden brown all over and dry to the touch, 15–20 minutes more.

Transfer the baking sheets to wire racks. Let the cookies cool on the pans for 1 minute, then transfer them to the racks to cool completely.

Spanish Almond Macaroon Cookies

Almendrados

Preparation time: 35 minutes
Cooking time: 35 minutes
Makes: About 30 cookies

1 lb (450 g) blanched whole
  or slivered almonds
1½ cups (300 g) white US granulated
  (UK caster) sugar
1 teaspoon fine sea salt
Finely grated zest of 2 lemons
2 eggs
Blanched whole almonds, for
  decorating (optional)

Both Allariz in Galicia and Granada in Andalucia lay claim to these simple almond macaroon cookies. Almond production exists in southern Spain, so it's more likely that Andalucia is where they first started. They may have been adapted by Jewish bakers from Middle Eastern cookies—like Persian *ghorabieh* (recipe, page 22) and Iraqi *hadgi badah* (recipe, page 55), and North African *makrout el louz* (recipe, page 142). These came with the Moors, who also introduced almonds to Spain. Once Christians arrived, the production of these cookies was taken over by convents, which explains why many older recipes call to bake the dough on large *Oblaten*-like wafers (see page 244), similar to German *Elisenlebkuchen* (recipe, page 244).

Similar in texture to Italian *amaretti morbidi* (recipe, page 109) and other soft macaroons, it's likely that these cookies influenced the coconut versions, like Peruvian *cocadas* (recipe, page 177), made all over Central and South America today. Though these and many macaroon-type cookies are now commonly made with all egg whites, old recipes for these Spanish cookies include at least a little egg yolk. Some recipes today use a whole egg, and this recipe reflects that detail.

Position racks in the top and bottom thirds of the oven and preheat the oven to 300°F (150°C/Gas Mark 2). Line two large baking sheets with parchment paper.

Spread the almonds out on one of the baking sheets and bake until fragrant and lightly toasted, 6–8 minutes. Reserve the baking sheet and leave the oven on.

Transfer the baking sheet to a rack and let the almonds cool completely. Reserve the baking sheet.

In a food processor, pulse the almonds until finely chopped. Add the sugar, salt, and lemon zest and pulse until the almonds are very finely ground. Add the eggs and pulse until the dough just comes together.

Using a ¾-ounce (1½-tablespoon) ice cream scoop, portion the dough and roll into balls, wetting your hands as needed to keep the dough from sticking to them. Arrange the balls on the prepared baking sheets, spaced 1 inch (2.5 cm) apart. If you like, stud the top of each dough ball with a whole almond.

Bake until light golden on the bottom and dry to the touch, 20–25 minutes, switching racks and rotating the baking sheets front to back halfway through.

Transfer the baking sheets to wire racks and let the cookies cool completely on the pans.

Pine Nut-Covered Macaroon Cookies
Panellets

Preparation time: 45 minutes
Cooking time: 15 minutes
Makes: About 24 cookies

8 oz (225 g) blanched whole
  or slivered almonds
¾ cup (150 g) white US granulated
  (UK caster) sugar
½ teaspoon fine sea salt
Finely grated zest of ½ lemon
2 oz (55 g) cooked russet potato
  flesh, cooled and lightly mashed
2 eggs, 1 separated and 1 whole
2 tablespoons water
1¼ cups (190 g) pine nuts,
  preferably Spanish

Similar to other baked marzipan or almond paste cookies like German *Bethmännchen* (recipe, page 252), these almond macaroon-like cookies are coated in nuts. In this case the coating is Spanish pine nuts, although there are versions coated with everything from chopped almonds or pistachios to coconut. Cocoa powder, orange zest, and coffee are popular flavorings. With their pine nut coating, they resemble a firmer Italian *pignoli* (recipe variation, page 109).

These are an important treat for Catalonians in the days leading up to All Saints' Day on November 1. The most unusual detail is that cooked potato is often added to these cookies to give them a softer texture. Boil or bake a potato until tender and then weigh out the amount needed for the recipe.

- -

Position racks in the top and bottom thirds of the oven and preheat the oven to 425°F (220°C/Gas Mark 7). Line two large baking sheets with parchment paper.

In a food processor, pulse the almonds until finely ground. Add the sugar, salt, and lemon zest and pulse until the almonds are very finely ground. Add the cooked potato and 1 egg white and pulse until the dough just comes together.

In a small bowl, whisk together the egg yolk, the whole egg, and water. Spread the pine nuts out on a plate.

Using a ½-ounce (1-tablespoon) ice cream scoop, portion the dough and roll into balls. Working a few at a time, dip the dough balls to coat in the egg wash and then roll to coat in the pine nuts, pressing gently so they adhere. Arrange them on the prepared baking sheets, spaced 1 inch (2.5 cm) apart.

Bake until golden brown all over and dry to the touch on top, 10–12 minutes, switching racks and rotating the baking sheets front to back halfway through.

Transfer the baking sheets to wire racks. Let the cookies cool on the pans for 1 minute, then transfer them to the racks to cool completely.

Pine Nut–Covered Macaroon Cookies

Marzipan-Stuffed Figurine Cookies

Figolli

Preparation time: 2 hours 30 minutes,
plus 1 hour chilling time, 30 minutes
resting time, and cooling and
setting time
Cooking time: 25 minutes
Makes: About 18 cookies

For the dough:
3½ cups (490 g) all-purpose
(plain) flour
¾ cup (150 g) white US granulated
(UK caster) sugar
1 teaspoon baking powder
¾ teaspoon fine sea salt
2 sticks (8 oz/225 g) unsalted
butter, softened
3 egg yolks (save the whites for
the filling and icing, below)
Finely grated zest of 1 orange
⅓ cup (2½ fl oz/80 ml) fresh
orange juice
Finely grated zest of 1 lemon (save
the juice for the icing, below)

For the filling:
1 lb (450 g) blanched whole
or slivered almonds
1½ cups (300 g) white US granulated
(UK caster) sugar
¼ teaspoon fine sea salt
2 egg whites
1 teaspoon orange blossom water

To finish:
1 egg white
2 cups (270 g) powdered (icing) sugar
1 tablespoon fresh lemon juice
Pinch of fine sea salt
Multicolored nonpareils
(hundreds & thousands)
Small chocolate eggs, halved
lengthwise (optional)

In Malta, there is a tradition of making *figolli*, large cookie cut-outs stuffed with marzipan. The word comes from the Sicilian for "figure," so it's likely they were made in neighboring Sicily, too, at one point, but they are now a big part of Easter culture in Malta. The cookies are cut into shapes such as hearts, fish, birds, rabbits, and sheep and are usually large and cut into smaller pieces or slices for eating. Many people now use smaller cutters or egg-shaped cutters and embellish the tops of the cookies with a chocolate egg.

This practice is believed to date back to pagan rituals, when the eggs would be placed on women-shaped sweet breads where their womb would be to promote fertility. The custom was then adopted by Christians on the island for Easter. *Figolli* are now typically decorated with powdered (icing) sugar icing or chocolate glaze and then, like Sicilian holiday sweets such as *cuccidati* (recipe, page 132), decorated with multicolored nonpareils or piped with more icing in ornate decorations and flourishes.

Make the dough: In a large bowl, whisk together the flour, white US granulated (UK caster) sugar, baking powder, and salt. Add the butter and rub it into the flour with your fingers until it breaks down into coarse crumbles. Pour in the egg yolks, orange zest, orange juice, and lemon zest and stir with your fingers until a dough forms and there are no dry patches of flour remaining. Gather the dough into a ball, transfer to a clean work surface, and knead until smooth, about 1 minute. Cover the dough in plastic wrap (cling film) and refrigerate for 1 hour.

Meanwhile, make the filling: In a food processor, pulse the almonds until finely chopped. Add the white US granulated sugar and salt and pulse until the almonds are very finely ground. Add the egg whites and orange blossom water and pulse until the mixture forms a smooth paste. Shape the almond paste into a ball, cover with plastic wrap (cling film), and refrigerate for 30 minutes.

Line two large baking sheets with parchment paper. Working on a lightly floured work surface, flatten the dough with a rolling pin until ⅛ inch (3 mm) thick. Using various 3-inch (7.5 cm) cutters, preferably egg-shaped, cut out shapes from the dough and transfer to the prepared baking sheets. Refrigerate the cookie cut-outs while you roll the almond paste.

Place the almond paste on a large sheet of parchment paper and then cover with another sheet. Flatten the paste until ⅛ inch (3 mm) thick, then use the same cutter to cut out shapes from the paste. Dip the cutter in water after each cut to keep the paste from sticking to it. Transfer each almond paste shape to a dough cut-out. Top with another dough cut-out then use your fingers to pinch the seams closed all the way around each shape so the almond paste is fully enclosed. Place the baking sheets in the refrigerator to rest for 30 minutes.

Position racks in the top and bottom thirds of the oven and preheat the oven to 350°F (180°C/Gas Mark 4).

Bake until golden brown on the bottom and dry to the touch on top, 20–25 minutes, switching racks and rotating the baking sheets front to back halfway through.

Transfer the baking sheets to wire racks. Let the cookies cool on the pans for 1 minute, then transfer them to the wire racks to cool completely.

To finish: In a medium bowl, whisk the egg white until frothy. Add the powdered (icing) sugar, lemon juice, and salt and stir until it forms a smooth icing. Dip the top of each cookie in the icing, letting the excess drip off, or use an offset spatula to spread the icing over the tops of the cookies. While the icing is wet, sprinkle the cookies with nonpareils (hundreds & thousands). If you like, place a chocolate egg half, cut-side down, in the center of each cookie. Let the icing dry completely and set before serving.

Marzipan-Stuffed Figurine Cookies

Spice and Almond Lenten Cookies
Kwareżimal

Preparation time: 35 minutes,
 plus 30 minutes chilling time
Cooking time: 25 minutes
Makes: About 48 cookies

7 oz (200 g) blanched whole
 or slivered almonds
½ cup (100 g) white US granulated
 (UK caster) sugar
1 tablespoon natural cocoa powder
1 teaspoon ground cinnamon
½ teaspoon freshly grated nutmeg
¼ teaspoon ground cloves
½ teaspoon fine sea salt
1⅓ cups (185 g) all-purpose
 (plain) flour
Finely grated zest of 1 lemon
Finely grated zest of 1 orange
½ cup (4 fl oz/120 ml) fresh
 orange juice
3 tablespoons orange blossom water
1 tablespoon pure vanilla extract
Honey, for brushing
Finely chopped almonds, for sprinkling

These egg- and dairy-free cookies are a traditional Lenten time cookie in Malta. In fact, their name comes from the Latin *quaresima*, which refers to the forty days of Lent. A sugary treat may seem the opposite of what many participating in Lent should eat, but when the cookie originated on Malta around the mid-1500s, sugar was considered a spice and not a food that should be abstained from.

The cookies are typically brushed with honey while warm from the oven and sprinkled with chopped nuts. In this way, they resemble Greek *melomakarona* (recipe, page 86), which are identical except the Greek cookies include olive oil. All-purpose (plain) flour and ground almonds comprise the dough, flavored with the typical spices such as cinnamon, nutmeg, and cloves, but also oftentimes cocoa powder. They are shaped into long logs, then cut, biscotti-style, into smaller slices to eat.

In a food processor, pulse the almonds until finely chopped. Add the sugar, cocoa powder, cinnamon, nutmeg, cloves, and salt and pulse until the almonds are very finely ground. Add the flour, lemon zest, orange zest, orange juice, orange blossom water, and vanilla and pulse just until a dough forms. Shape the dough into a ball, cover with plastic wrap (cling film), and refrigerate for 30 minutes.

Position racks in the top and bottom thirds of the oven and preheat the oven to 350°F (180°C/Gas Mark 4). Line two large baking sheets with parchment paper.

Working on a lightly floured work surface, roll pieces of the dough between your fingers and the work surface into ropes 1 inch (2.5 cm) thick. Cut the ropes into 6-inch (15 cm) lengths. Arrange the dough lengths on the prepared baking sheets, spaced 2 inches (5 cm) apart, and flatten slightly.

Bake until dry to the touch on top, 22–25 minutes, switching racks and rotating the baking sheets front to back halfway through.

Transfer the baking sheets to wire racks and let the cookies rest for 1 minute. While still hot, lightly brush the cookies with honey to coat and then sprinkle with chopped almonds. Let the cookies cool completely and then slice crosswise into 1-inch (2.5 cm) pieces to serve.

Spice and Almond Lenten Cookies

Maltese Christening Cookies

Biskuttini tar-Rahal

 DF (V)

Preparation time: 40 minutes,
  plus cooling and setting time
Cooking time: 20 minutes
Makes: About 24 cookies

For the cookies:
2¼ cups (315 g) all-purpose
  (plain) flour
1 teaspoon baking powder
½ teaspoon fine sea salt
1½ cups (300 g) white US granulated
  (UK caster) sugar
3 eggs
Finely grated zest of 1 orange
Finely grated zest of 1 lemon
2 teaspoons anise seeds, finely ground
½ teaspoon caraway seeds,
  finely ground
½ teaspoon ground cinnamon
½ teaspoon ground cloves

For the icing:
1 egg white
2 cups (270 g) powdered (icing) sugar
1 tablespoon fresh lemon juice
Pinch of fine sea salt

These cookies or "village" biscuits are typically served at a baby's christening and decorated with icing: pink for girls, blue for boys. Nowadays the icing can be left plain/white or dyed any color to match a particular celebration. The most characteristic design of icing is a hypnotic swirl, although some bakers also pipe the icing in the shape of letters or other shapes to match the theme of the party. The dough for these cookies is traditionally spiced with anise and cloves, as well as caraway seeds and cinnamon.

Make the cookies: Position racks in the top and bottom thirds of the oven and preheat the oven to 350°F (180°C/Gas Mark 4). Line two large baking sheets with parchment paper.

In a medium bowl, whisk together the flour, baking powder, and salt.

In a large bowl, with a hand mixer, beat the white US granulated (UK caster) sugar, eggs, orange zest, lemon zest, anise, caraway, cinnamon, and cloves on medium speed until smooth and frothy, about 1 minute. Add the dry ingredients and stir until a dough forms and there are no dry patches of flour remaining.

Using a 1-ounce (2-tablespoon) ice cream scoop, portion the dough and roll into balls. Arrange them on the prepared baking sheets, spaced 2 inches (5 cm) apart.

Bake until golden brown at the edges and dry to the touch on top, 15–20 minutes, switching racks and rotating the baking sheets front to back halfway through.

Transfer the baking sheets to wire racks. Let the cookies cool on the pans for 1 minute, then transfer them to the racks to cool completely.

Make the icing: In a medium bowl, whisk the egg white until frothy. Add the powdered (icing) sugar, lemon juice, and salt and stir until it forms a smooth icing. Transfer the icing to a piping bag or a plastic bag with a corner snipped off and pipe swirls on top of each cookie. Let the icing dry completely and set before serving.

Maltese Christening Cookies

Sesame-Coated and Spiced "Eights" Cookies

Ottijiet

Preparation time: 1 hour 10 minutes,
  plus chilling time
Cooking time: 20 minutes
Makes: About 8 large cookies

2 cups (280 g) all-purpose (plain) flour
½ cup (100 g) white US granulated
  (UK caster) sugar
2 teaspoons baking powder
2 teaspoons anise seeds, finely ground
1 teaspoon ground cloves
½ teaspoon fine sea salt
1 stick (4 oz/115 g) unsalted
  butter, softened
1 egg, lightly beaten
1 teaspoon pure vanilla extract
  (optional)
Finely grated zest of 1 lemon
Finely grated zest of 1 orange
2 tablespoons fresh orange juice
Whole milk or water, for brushing
Sesame seeds, for sprinkling

Malta's position in the center of the Mediterranean Sea is seen most clearly in these cookies. With influences from North African cultures and Muslim and Christian customs, the cookies—named "eights" in Maltese after their shape—are spiced with cloves and anise seeds and bright with citrus. They're also crusted in sesame seeds, signaling their resemblance to other similar sesame-strewn cookies like Italian *biscotti regina* (recipe, page 127), Middle Eastern *ka'ak bi-simsim* (recipe, page 56), Syrian *barazek* (recipe, page 46), and Algerian *makroud* (recipe, page 140). The cookies are often eaten for teatime, and though large, they can be broken in half to serve or you can bake the dough in smaller shapes.

In a large bowl, whisk together the flour, sugar, baking powder, anise seeds, cloves, and salt. Add the butter and use your fingers to rub it into the dry ingredients until it breaks down into coarse crumbs. Add the egg, vanilla (if using), lemon zest, orange zest, and orange juice and stir until the dough forms and there are no dry patches of flour remaining. Shape the dough into a ball, wrap in plastic wrap (cling film), and refrigerate for at least 2 hours or overnight.

Line two large baking sheets with parchment paper. Working on a lightly floured work surface, roll pieces of the dough between your fingers and the work surface into ropes ¾ inch (2 cm) thick. Cut the ropes into 8-inch (20 cm) lengths. Bend each length to form a circle, attaching the ends, then twist the circle in the center to create a slightly elongated "figure 8" shape. Arrange the dough twists on the prepared baking sheets, spaced 2 inches (5 cm) apart. Lightly brush with some milk or water and then sprinkle liberally with sesame seeds. Place the baking sheets in the freezer and chill for 20 minutes.

Position racks in the top and bottom thirds of the oven and preheat the oven to 400°F (200°C/Gas Mark 6). Bake until the cookies are golden brown all over and dry to the touch on top, 16–20 minutes, switching racks and rotating the baking sheets front to back halfway through.

Transfer the baking sheets to wire racks. Let the cookies cool on the pans for 1 minute, then transfer them to the racks to cool completely.

Soft Bitter Almond Cookies
Amaretti Morbidi

Preparation time: 25 minutes
Cooking time: 20 minutes
Makes: About 12 cookies

8 oz (225 g) blanched whole
  or slivered almonds
⅓ cup (65 g) white US granulated
  (UK caster) sugar
½ teaspoon fine sea salt
1 cup (135 g) powdered (icing) sugar,
  plus more for coating
2 egg whites, lightly beaten

These cookies are said to have been invented in the late eighteenth century by Francesco Moriondo, a pastry chef at the court of Savoy, a former historical territory overlapping parts of modern-day France and Italy in the western Alps. The classic Italian cookies may have descended from Middle Eastern almond and egg white sweets that flourished in Spain during Moorish rule and that came to Italy via Sephardic Jews fleeing Spain in the 1600s. The name *amaretti* translates to "little bitter ones," and these cookies were once made mostly or completely with so-called "bitter almonds," now known as apricot kernels. They're not much used today because of fear of cyanide poisoning, which occurs when the ground kernels are exposed to moisture, though many recipes still use small amounts of ground kernels, which aren't toxic in those amounts. A little ground bitter almond lends the cookies their authentic flavor, but you can also use almond extract, which is often made from the same kernels.

There are two primary kinds of amaretti: *amaretti morbidi* and *amaretti croccanti* (recipe, page 110). The first, which is the recipe here, is the soft kind, sometimes referred to as *pasta di mandorle*, or "almond paste." *Pasta di mandorle* is also the name for the premade paste often used as a starting point for making these cookies. Typically, they're made by mixing unbeaten egg whites into almond paste or ground almonds and sugar to keep the dough dense and moist. The most famous soft amaretti are from Sassello and typical of southern Piedmont and the province of Savona in Liguria. Similar to German *Bethmännchen* (recipe, page 252), the cookies are chewy and tender. *Pignoli*, a specialty of Sicily that are crusted in pine nuts, are this style. *Ricciarelli*, a specialty of Siena, are also this kind but typically contain honey and orange zest, and are shaped into ovals instead of rounds. The *pignoli* and *ricciarelli* are given as variations following this recipe.

Position racks in the top and bottom thirds of the oven and preheat the oven to 350°F (180°C/Gas Mark 4). Line two large baking sheets with parchment paper.

In a food processor, pulse the almonds until finely ground. Add the white US granulated (UK caster) sugar and salt and pulse until the almonds are very finely ground. Add the powdered (icing) sugar and egg whites and pulse until the dough just comes together.

Using a ¾-ounce (1½-tablespoon) ice cream scoop, portion the dough and roll into balls. Roll each dough ball in powdered sugar to coat and then arrange on the prepared baking sheets, spaced 1 inch (2.5 cm) apart. If you like, use the thumb, forefinger, and middle finger of one hand to gently "pinch" each dough ball to indent it.

Bake until the outside of the cookies is cracked and light golden at the edges and on the bottom, 15–18 minutes, switching racks and rotating the baking sheets front to back halfway through.

Transfer the baking sheets to wire racks and let the cookies cool completely on the pans.

Variations
Pignoli Cookies
Roll the dough balls in pine nuts, instead of powdered (icing) sugar, to coat before baking.
Ricciarelli
Add 2 tablespoons honey and the finely grated zest of ¼ orange along with the powdered (icing) sugar and egg whites. Shape the portions of dough into ovals and roll in powdered sugar, but do not pinch them.

Crunchy Bitter Almond Cookies

Amaretti Croccanti / Secchi / Classici

Preparation time: 25 minutes, plus
at least 4 hours standing time
Cooking time: 35 minutes
Makes: About 12 cookies

8 oz (225 g) blanched whole
or slivered almonds
½ cup (100 g) white US granulated
(UK caster) sugar
½ teaspoon fine sea salt
2 egg whites
¼ teaspoon cream of tartar
1 cup (135 g) powdered (icing) sugar,
plus more for coating
½ teaspoon pure almond extract
Pearl sugar, for decorating (optional)

This is one of two main styles of amaretti, the other being *amaretti morbidi* (recipe, page 109). This style of amaretti is the dry, crunchy kind most people outside of Italy know well. Bought in ornate tins or wrapped in tissue paper, these *amaretti croccanti*—or *secchi* or *classici*—are made by whipping egg whites and sugar into a meringue before mixing in ground almonds, which makes them crispier. The most popular crispy amaretti are from Saronno, a small town in Lombardy. *Amaretti di Saronno* are more apt to use the ground apricot kernels instead of almonds, while the soft *amaretti morbidi* typically are made with all plain almonds. In a variation called *mandorlini del ponte*, the whipped egg whites are cooked and flour is folded into the mix, creating a brittle shell on the outside of the cookies.

In a food processor, pulse the almonds until finely ground. Add the white US granulated (UK caster) sugar and salt and pulse until the almonds are very finely ground.

In a large bowl, with a hand mixer, beat the egg whites and cream of tartar on medium speed until starting to form soft peaks. While mixing, slowly add the powdered (icing) sugar one spoonful at a time, then increase the speed to medium-high and continue beating until stiff peaks form. Add the ground almond mixture and almond extract and use a large silicone spatula to gently fold the mixture together until smooth.

Line two large baking sheets with parchment paper. Transfer the dough to a piping bag, or use 2 tablespoons, and pipe mounds of dough 1½ inches (4 cm) wide on the prepared baking sheets, spaced 2 inches (5 cm) apart. If using, sprinkle the tops with pearl sugar. Let the cookies stand until dry to the touch on top, at least 4 hours.

Position racks in the top and bottom thirds of the oven and preheat the oven to 275°F (140°C/Gas Mark 1).

Bake for 25 minutes, switching racks and rotating the baking sheets front to back halfway through. Increase the oven temperature to 350°F (180°C/Gas Mark 4) and continue baking the cookies until uniformly golden brown and dry to the touch, 3–8 minutes more.

Transfer the baking sheets to wire racks and let the cookies cool completely on the pans.

Crunchy Bitter Almond Cookies

Twice-Baked Almond Cookies

Cantucci

Preparation time: 50 minutes
Cooking time: 50 minutes
Makes: About 24 cookies

4 oz (115 g) skin-on almonds
⅓ cup (50 g) pine nuts
2 cups (280 g) all-purpose (plain) flour
1 teaspoon anise seeds, lightly crushed
1 teaspoon baking powder
¾ teaspoon fine sea salt
¾ cup (150 g) white US granulated (UK
  caster) sugar, plus more for sprinkling
3 eggs, 2 whole and 1 separated
Finely grated zest of ½ orange
  or 1 small lemon
2 tablespoons (30 g) unsalted butter,
  melted (optional)
1 tablespoon vin santo, Marsala,
  or light rum

Outside of Italy, the term "biscotti" has come to describe a specific cookie: a slice cut from a baked loaf that's then toasted further to dry it out, rendering it crunchy. In Italy, though, "biscotti" is a catch-all term for most all cookies, and *cantucci* is the name for the famous twice-baked cookies. In Italian, *cantuccio* translates to "little place," "nook," or "corner" and is often used to describe the heels of bread, which are more toasted and drier than the rest of the loaf. These hard cookies are traditionally enjoyed by dipping them in vin santo wine to soften them. Because of this association, modern recipes now add a couple tablespoons of the wine to the dough, too.

The "original" *cantucci* are said to have also included anise seeds, but Biscottificio Antonio Mattei in the Tuscan town of Prato claims to have the original and best *cantucci*. That recipe—on which the company was founded—uses just flour, sugar, eggs, almonds, and pine nuts, which more resembles the French *croquants aux amandes* (recipe, page 260). Modern recipes add a little butter and baking powder to make cookies with a less brick-hard texture. This recipe reflects that change to make the cookies how they're baked today, though you can easily omit the butter if you want firmer, more traditional *cantucci*. You can omit the anise seeds and use vanilla extract in their place. Some recipes insist on orange zest for flavoring these cookies, while others don't mention it at all or use lemon zest; that flavoring is also up to you.

Position racks in the top and bottom thirds of the oven and preheat the oven to 350°F (180°C/Gas Mark 4). Line two large baking sheets with parchment paper.

Spread the almonds and pine nuts out on one of the baking sheets and bake until light golden and fragrant, 6–8 minutes.

Transfer the nuts to a plate and let cool. Reserve the baking sheet.

In a medium bowl, whisk together the flour, anise seeds, baking powder, and salt.

In a large bowl, with a hand mixer, beat the sugar, 2 whole eggs, 1 egg yolk, and the citrus zest on medium speed until lightened and doubled in volume and when you lift the beaters, the mixture falls back in a thick ribbon, 3–4 minutes.

Add the flour mixture, almonds, and pine nuts and use a large silicone spatula to fold everything together until a dough forms and there are no more dry patches of flour remaining. If using the butter, add it now along with the vin santo, and fold until incorporated. Shape the dough into a ball, then divide into 2 equal portions.

Working on a lightly floured work surface, shape each piece of dough into a log 2½ inches (6.5 cm) wide. Transfer each log to a prepared baking sheet.

In a small bowl, lightly beat the remaining egg white and brush some of it all over both dough logs. Sprinkle the logs with some sugar.

Bake until the logs are lightly browned on the bottom and dry to the touch, 20–25 minutes, switching racks and rotating the baking sheets front to back halfway through.

Transfer the baking sheets to wire racks and let the logs rest for 10 minutes. Leave the oven on.

Carefully transfer each log to a cutting board and use a sharp knife to cut them on the slight diagonal every ¾ inch (2 cm) into slices. Return the slices to the baking sheets, spaced evenly apart. Return to the oven and bake until the cookies are light golden all over and dry to the touch, 10–15 minutes more.

Transfer the baking sheets to wire racks. Let the cookies cool on the pans for 1 minute, then transfer them to the racks to cool completely.

Twice-Baked Almond Cookies

Flower-Shaped Butter Cookies
Canestrelli

Preparation time: 45 minutes
Cooking time: 15 minutes
Makes: About 24 cookies

1 cup (140 g) all-purpose (plain) flour
¾ cup (105 g) potato starch
or cornstarch (cornflour)
¾ teaspoon fine sea salt
2 hard-boiled egg yolks
1 stick (4 oz/115 g) unsalted
butter, softened
½ cup (65 g) powdered (icing) sugar,
plus more for dusting
1 teaspoon pure vanilla extract
or almond extract
Finely grated zest of 1 lemon

Similar to Norwegian *berlinerkranser* (recipe, page 300), these Ligurian cookies are traditionally made with hard-boiled egg yolks. This was a holdover from convent-produced cookies made with leftover yolks—after nuns used the whites for starching their habits—which helped stabilize the dough and make it crumbly. The name of these cookies seems to refer to any type of shortbread-like cookie in Italy, though now it mostly refers to a version made with a flower-shaped cutter. The name *canestrelli* is also the Italian word for "little scallops," which is likely a reference to the "scalloped" edge of the cookies that looks like flower or daisy petals.

The cookies are often made with a smaller proportion of cornstarch (cornflour) or potato starch to all-purpose (plain) flour, which gives the *canestrelli* a softer texture. In Castagna, chestnut flour is used in place of the starch (see the variation that follows). However, the name doesn't universally stand for this cookie. In Piedmont, *canestrelli* is used to describe a thin wafer-like cookie made with hazelnut flour that sandwiches a chocolate filling. In Corsica, the name, locally known as *cujuelle de Calenzana*, describes a diamond-shaped shortbread with olive oil, anise seeds, and white wine that's popularly sold on the island. In other parts of Italy, the name simply describes a ring-shaped butter cookie. Though the cookies are often not flavored at all, many modern versions at least add lemon zest, vanilla or almond extract, and/or rum.

Position racks in the top and bottom thirds of the oven and preheat the oven to 350°F (180°C/Gas Mark 4). Line two large baking sheets with parchment paper.

In a medium bowl, whisk together the flour, potato starch, and salt. Place a fine sieve over a large bowl and use a silicone spatula to press the hard-boiled egg yolks through the sieve, scraping the back of the sieve to ensure you get all the egg yolk. Add the butter and sugar, and beat on medium speed with a hand mixer until pale and fluffy, 2–3 minutes. Beat in the vanilla extract and lemon zest. Add the dry ingredients and stir until the dough forms and there are no dry patches of flour remaining. Gather the dough into a ball.

Working on a lightly floured work surface, roll out the dough with a rolling pin to ⅜ inch (1 cm) thick. Using a 2½-inch (6.5 cm) flower-shaped cutter, cut out shapes of dough. Reroll the scraps to cut out more cookies. Transfer the shapes to the prepared baking sheets, spaced 1 inch (2.5 cm) apart. Using the end of a narrow-handled wooden spoon or a ½-inch (13 mm) round piping tip (nozzle), punch out the center of each dough flower. Reroll the centers to make more cookies or discard them.

Bake until golden brown at the edges and dry to the touch on top, 10–15 minutes, switching racks and rotating the baking sheets front to back halfway through.

Transfer the baking sheets to wire racks and let the cookies rest on the pans for 1 minute. While they are still hot, dust the cookies with sugar and then transfer directly to the racks to cool completely.

Variation
Castagnese
Substitute the same weight of chestnut flour for the potato starch.

Flower-Shaped Butter Cookies

"Ugly but Good" Hazelnut Meringue Cookies

Brutti ma Buoni

Preparation time: 20 minutes
Cooking time: 45 minutes
Makes: About 24 cookies

1 lb (450 g) blanched hazelnuts
8 egg whites, at room temperature
2 cups (400 g) white US granulated
  (UK caster) sugar
2 teaspoons pure vanilla extract
1½ teaspoons fine sea salt

Ironically, the selling point for these beloved cookies is their name. As a showcase for toasted hazelnuts in a lumpy mound, these "ugly but good" meringue cookies are true to their claim. A specialty of northern Italy, particularly the Piedmont, the cookies are a variation of *amaretti morbidi* (recipe, page 109) with one main exception: Characteristically, the dough is cooked in a pan until lumpy and browned, before being baked like a traditional drop cookie. This extra step drives off excess moisture and lightly browns the sugar to give the cookies a crisp, caramelized flavor.

In Tuscany, *brutti ma buoni* are often made with half hazelnuts and half almonds, and sometimes ground coriander is also added. In Venice, cocoa powder is often added to the dough or dusted over the finished cookies, which leans into the classic chocolate-hazelnut flavor profile. If you want to try either option, add 1 teaspoon ground coriander or ⅓ cup (30 g) natural cocoa powder, respectively, along with the hazelnuts.

Position racks in the top and bottom thirds of the oven and preheat the oven to 300°F (150°C/Gas Mark 2). Line two large baking sheets with parchment paper.

In a food processor, pulse the hazelnuts until roughly chopped. Scoop out ⅓ cup (40 g) of the chopped hazelnuts and set aside. Pulse the remaining hazelnuts in the food processor until very finely ground.

In a large bowl, with a hand mixer, beat the egg whites on medium speed until starting to form soft peaks. While mixing, slowly add the sugar one spoonful at a time, then increase the speed to medium-high and continue beating until stiff peaks form. Beat in the vanilla and salt. Add the chopped and finely ground hazelnuts and use a large silicone spatula to fold the mixture together until smooth.

Scrape the mixture into a large saucepan and place over medium-low heat. Cook, stirring constantly, until the mixture starts pulling away from the side of the pan, forms one big lump, and is light golden brown, 18–22 minutes.

Remove the pan from the heat and use two dinner spoons to quickly scoop up a heaping portion of dough with one spoon and then use the second to scrape it off and onto the prepared baking sheets. Space the mounds 2 inches (5 cm) apart. Don't worry about making the mounds neat; they're supposed to be rough and "ugly."

Bake until golden brown and dry to the touch, 18–20 minutes, switching racks and rotating the baking sheets front to back halfway through.

Transfer the baking sheets to wire racks and let the cookies cool completely on the pans.

Polenta and Egg Yolk Butter Cookies

Zaléti

Preparation time: 45 minutes
Cooking time: 15 minutes
Makes: About 24 cookies

½ cup (4 fl oz/120 ml) whole milk
⅓ cup (55 g) raisins or dried currants
1 cup (145 g) fine cornmeal
1 cup (140 g) all-purpose (plain) flour
1 teaspoon baking powder
½ teaspoon fine sea salt
1 stick (4 oz/115 g) unsalted butter, softened
½ cup (100 g) white US granulated (UK caster) sugar, plus more for sprinkling
2 egg yolks
1 teaspoon pure vanilla extract
Finely grated zest of ½ lemon
3 tablespoons pine nuts (optional)

Another diamond-shaped cookie, like *mustacciuoli Napoletani* (recipe, page 118), these Venetian cookies are named for their yellow color, which comes from polenta, cornmeal, egg yolks, or lemon zest. The cookies are typically made with golden raisins (sultanas), or raisins, soaked in milk, and sometimes pine nuts. In Bologna, their version eschews the dried fruit and nuts. These cookies are typically dipped in grappa after dinner or served alongside ice cream or zabaglione.

Despite the use of polenta here, the recipe actually uses what Italians refer to as "polenta flour," which is more finely ground than the polenta used to make a porridge. This recipe calls for finely ground cornmeal, which is easier to find and, essentially, the same product, but use finely ground polenta if you are able to find it.

Position racks in the top and bottom thirds of the oven and preheat the oven to 350°F (180°C/Gas Mark 4). Line two large baking sheets with parchment paper.

In a small microwave-safe bowl, combine the milk and raisins and heat in the microwave until hot. Set aside to cool to room temperature. Drain off the milk into another bowl. Set the milk and raisins aside.

In a medium bowl, whisk together the cornmeal, flour, baking powder, and salt.

In a large bowl, with a hand mixer, beat the butter and sugar on medium speed until pale and fluffy, 2–3 minutes. Add the egg yolks and beat until smooth, then beat in the vanilla and lemon zest. Add the dry ingredients, drained raisins, and pine nuts (if using) and stir until the dough forms and there are no dry patches of flour remaining.

Scrape the dough onto a lightly floured work surface and use a rolling pin to flatten until ¼ inch (6 mm) thick. Using a pizza cutter or chef's knife, cut the dough into strips 2 inches (5 cm) wide, then cut each strip every 2 inches (5 cm) at an angle to make diamonds. Transfer the diamonds to the prepared baking sheets, spaced 2 inches (5 cm) apart. Lightly brush the diamonds with some of the reserved milk and sprinkle with some sugar.

Bake until golden brown at the edges and dry to the touch on top, 10–12 minutes, switching racks and rotating the baking sheets front to back halfway through.

Transfer the baking sheets to wire racks. Let the cookies cool on the pans for 1 minute, then transfer them to the racks to cool completely.

Chocolate and Spice Cookies

Mustacciuoli Napoletani / Mostaccioli / Mustazzoli

Preparation time: 1 hour 25 minutes,
 plus cooling and setting time
Cooking time: 30 minutes
Makes: About 18 cookies

4 oz (115 g) blanched whole
 or slivered almonds
1 cup (200 g) white US granulated
 (UK caster) sugar
½ cup (4 fl oz/120 ml) brewed coffee,
 at room temperature
¼ cup (85 g) honey, grape must,
 or dark corn syrup
2 teaspoons ground cinnamon
1 teaspoon ground cloves
1 teaspoon freshly grated nutmeg
Finely grated zest of 1 orange
2 cups (280 g) all-purpose (plain) flour
¼ cup (25 g) natural cocoa powder
1 teaspoon baking powder
½ teaspoon baking soda
 (bicarbonate of soda)
1 teaspoon fine sea salt
1 lb (450 g) bittersweet chocolate,
 roughly chopped
2 tablespoons vegetable shortening
 or refined coconut oil

Various cookies across Italy go by a similar name that's based in the Latin *mostacea* or *mustum*, which refers to grape must (or musk), the concentrated grape juice that was a primary sweetener of Mediterranean cultures before processed cane sugar became the norm. The most well-known version with the most consistent ingredients is the Neapolitan version, which is a dough spiced with cinnamon, cloves, and nutmeg—a mix often called *pisto*, which is sold in grocery stores—and made with cocoa powder, candied citrus, and honey. Oftentimes coffee or diluted espresso is added to enhance the bitterness and color of the cocoa and spices. The dough is cut into diamonds, baked, and then coated in melted chocolate. It's essentially a "chocolate gingerbread," and because of that, recipes are infinitely varied and most suit more modern palates by using sugar and honey instead of grape must, which is difficult to find outside of vineyards that make it.

Of the seemingly infinite other cookies with a similar name, the two most common are *mustazzoli Salentini* and the *rame di Napoli,* both of which play with the same ingredients in different forms. Both are given as variations here.

- -

Position racks in the top and bottom thirds of the oven and preheat the oven to 350°F (180°C/Gas Mark 4). Line two large baking sheets with parchment paper.

Spread the almonds out on one of the baking sheets and bake until lightly toasted, about 6 minutes. Transfer the nuts to a food processor, let cool, and pulse until finely ground. Reserve the baking sheet.

In a small saucepan, combine the sugar, coffee, and honey and heat over medium-high heat, stirring until the sugar dissolves. Remove the pan from the heat and whisk in the cinnamon, cloves, nutmeg, and orange zest. Let the mixture cool to room temperature.

In a large bowl, whisk together the ground almonds, flour, cocoa powder, baking powder, baking soda (bicarb), and salt. Add the cooled syrup mixture and stir until the dough just comes together and there are no dry patches of flour remaining.

Scrape the dough onto a lightly floured work surface and use a rolling pin to flatten until ⅜ inch (1 cm) thick. Using a pizza cutter or chef's knife, cut the dough into strips 2 inches (5 cm) wide, then cut each strip every 2 inches (5 cm) at an angle to make diamonds. Transfer the diamonds to the prepared baking sheets, spaced 2 inches (5 cm) apart.

Bake until darker brown at the edges and just dry to the touch on top, 15–18 minutes.

Transfer the baking sheets to wire racks. Let the cookies cool on the pans for 1 minute, then transfer them to the racks to cool completely.

In a large heatproof bowl in the microwave or over a pan of simmering water, melt the chocolate and shortening together until smooth.

Line a baking sheet with parchment paper. Working with one cookie at a time, dunk it into the melted chocolate and use two forks to turn it and coat each cookie completely. Lift the cookie with the two forks and let the excess drip off into the bowl, then transfer to the parchment paper.

Place the sheet in the refrigerator to set the chocolate before serving.

Variations
Mustazzoli Salentini
Add ½ cup (4 fl oz/120 ml) vegetable or plain olive oil (not extra-virgin) and 1 teaspoon baker's ammonia to the dough. Using a 1-ounce (2-tablespoon) ice cream scoop, drop mounds of dough on the prepared baking sheets, spaced 2 inches (5 cm) apart. Bake as directed. Do not coat in melted chocolate. Dust the cooled cookies with cocoa powder.
Rame di Napoli
Form and bake the *mustazzoli Salentini* variation (above), but while the cookies are still warm, brush their tops with orange marmalade. Once cooled, cover in melted chocolate, as in the Neapolitan version, then sprinkle with chopped pistachios before the chocolate sets.

Chocolate and Spice Cookies

Hazelnut and Chocolate Cookie Sandwiches

Baci di Dama

Preparation time: 35 minutes,
 plus cooling and setting time
Cooking time: 25 minutes
Makes: About 24 cookie sandwiches

4 oz (115 g) blanched hazelnuts
½ cup (100 g) white US granulated
 (UK caster) sugar
½ teaspoon fine sea salt
¾ cup (105 g) all-purpose (plain) flour
1 stick (4 oz/115 g) unsalted butter,
 softened
4 oz (115 g) bittersweet
 chocolate, melted

Like *brutti ma buoni* (recipe, page 116), these tiny butter cookies come from the hazelnut-rich Piedmont region and are made with equal parts (by weight) of flour, sugar, butter, and hazelnuts. Their name translates to "lady's kiss" and comes from the "kiss" of the cookies when they're sandwiched with chocolate. Melted dark chocolate is the traditional filling, but Nutella is a popular choice since it echoes the flavor of the hazelnuts in the cookies.

Position racks in the top and bottom thirds of the oven and preheat the oven to 350°F (180°C/Gas Mark 4). Line two large baking sheets with parchment paper.

Spread the hazelnuts out on one of the baking sheets and bake until fragrant and lightly toasted, 6–8 minutes.

Transfer the nuts to a food processor and let cool. Reserve the baking sheet.

Pulse the cooled hazelnuts until finely ground. Add the sugar and salt and pulse to combine. Add the flour and butter and pulse just until a dough comes together and there are no dry patches of flour remaining.

Using a teaspoon, portion the dough into small balls. Arrange them on the prepared baking sheets, spaced 2 inches (5 cm) apart.

Bake until golden brown at the edges and dry to the touch on top, 15–18 minutes, switching racks and rotating the baking sheets front to back halfway through.

Transfer the baking sheets to wire racks and let the cookies cool completely on the pans.

Spoon about ½ teaspoon of the melted chocolate on the flat bottom of half the cookies and sandwich them with the other half. Return the cookie sandwiches to the baking sheets and let stand until the chocolate sets before serving.

Hazelnut and Chocolate Cookie Sandwiches

Red Wine and Anise Ring Cookies
Ciambelline al Vino

Preparation time: 20 minutes
Cooking time: 25 minutes
Makes: About 12 cookies

3⅓ cups (475 g) all-purpose
 (plain) flour
1 tablespoon anise or fennel seeds,
 lightly crushed
1 teaspoon baking powder (optional)
1 teaspoon fine sea salt
½ cup (4 fl oz/120 ml) red wine
½ cup (100 g) white US granulated (UK
 caster) sugar, plus more for sprinkling
½ cup (4 fl oz/120 ml) plain olive oil
 (not extra-virgin)

In Abruzzo, cookies aren't just for dessert. Here, these "wine rings" are not only made with wine, but are also served with wine. If not served with wine, the rings of dough, which closely resemble the savory yeast-risen *tarallucci*, are crusted in sugar and eaten as a snack or for breakfast. Some recipes call for baking powder in the dough to provide a lighter, more tender cookie, while others prefer to leave it out for the more traditional dense-and-crumbly texture; the choice is up to you. As to whether to use red or white wine: Red is traditional in Abruzzo and lends the cookies a light purple color, but white wine is used, too.

Position racks in the top and bottom thirds of the oven and preheat the oven to 350°F (180°C/Gas Mark 4). Line two large baking sheets with parchment paper.

In a medium bowl, whisk together the flour, anise seeds, baking powder (if using), and salt.

In a large bowl, stir together the wine and sugar until the sugar dissolves. Stir in the olive oil. Add the dry ingredients and stir until a dough forms and there are no dry patches of flour remaining. Gather the dough into a ball.

Working on a lightly floured work surface, roll pieces of the dough between your fingers and the work surface into ropes ½ inch (13 mm) thick. Cut the ropes into 5-inch (13 cm) lengths. Bend each length in the center and form a circle, touching the ends together to connect. Arrange the dough rings on the prepared baking sheets, spaced 2 inches (5 cm) apart. Brush the rings with some water and sprinkle with some sugar.

Bake until the cookies are golden brown on the bottom and dry to the touch, 20–25 minutes, switching racks and rotating the baking sheets front to back halfway through.

Transfer the baking sheets to wire racks. Let the cookies cool on the pans for 1 minute, then transfer them to the racks to cool completely.

Red Wine and Anise Ring Cookies

Piped Cornmeal and Lemon Cookies
Paste di Meliga / Biscotti Meliga

Preparation time: 40 minutes,
  plus 30 minutes chilling time
Cooking time: 20 minutes
Makes: About 30 cookies

1⅓ cups (195 g) fine cornmeal
1⅓ cups (185 g) all-purpose
  (plain) flour
1 teaspoon baking powder
1 teaspoon fine sea salt
1½ sticks (6 oz/170 g) unsalted
  butter, softened
1 cup (200 g) white US granulated
  (UK caster) sugar
1 egg
2 egg yolks
1½ teaspoons pure vanilla extract
  or vanilla bean paste
Finely grated zest of 1 lemon

Corn (maize) has been popular and a mainstay of the northern Italian diet since it was brought to the country from the New World in the 1500s. Most famously, it's cooked into a porridge called polenta that is a staple of the diet in the region, but it also gets mixed into sweets. *Paste di meliga* are cornmeal-based butter cookies from Piedmont flavored with lemon zest and piped most commonly into the shape of wreaths or circles, but also a variety of other shapes. The cookie's name is a curious one. The word *meliga* is often defined as the word for maize in the northern Italian dialect, but many texts also reference the word in relation to the grain sorghum, which was likely also used to make polenta-like porridges in the area before corn became the norm.

It's customary to serve the cookies with coffee or espresso, or for dessert with zabaglione, or with a glass of sweet Moscato or Dolcetto d'Alba for dipping. A similar cookie called *krumiri* is very similar to *paste di meliga*, but it is more of a store-bought cookie than one made at home. *Krumiri* typically have less butter and little or no leavening, so they're crunchier, and are piped into logs bent in the middle to resemble the mustache of the first king of Italy, Vittorio Emmanuele II. A piping bag fitted with a fluted tip (nozzle) is the best method for extruding the dough for these cookies, but you can also use a cookie press/gun if you like.

In a medium bowl, whisk together the cornmeal, flour, baking powder, and salt.

In a large bowl, with a hand mixer, beat the butter and sugar on medium speed until light and fluffy, 2–3 minutes. Add the whole egg and egg yolks and beat until smooth. Beat in the vanilla and lemon zest. Add the dry ingredients and stir until a dough forms and there are no dry patches of flour remaining.

Line two large baking sheets with parchment paper. Working in batches, scrape the dough into a piping bag fitted with a ½-inch (13 mm) fluted or star tip (nozzle), and pipe rings or spirals 2 inches (5 cm) in diameter, or 3- to 4-inch (7.5 to 10 cm) sticks, or slightly larger "S" shapes, spaced 2 inches (5 cm) apart onto the baking sheets.

Place the baking sheets in the refrigerator to chill the piped dough for 30 minutes.

Meanwhile, position racks in the top and bottom thirds of the oven and preheat the oven to 350°F (180°C/Gas Mark 4).

Bake until light golden brown on the bottom and dry to the touch all over, 15–18 minutes, switching racks and rotating the baking sheets front to back halfway through.

Transfer the baking sheets to wire racks. Let the cookies cool on the pans for 1 minute, then transfer them to the racks to cool completely.

Multicolored Epiphany Cookies
Befanini

Preparation time: 45 minutes
Cooking time: 15 minutes
Makes: About 24 cookies

3¼ cups (455 g) all-purpose
  (plain) flour
1 teaspoon baking powder
½ teaspoon fine sea salt
1 teaspoon anise or fennel seeds,
  lightly crushed (optional)
1 cup (200 g) white US granulated
  (UK caster) sugar
1 stick (4 oz/115 g) unsalted
  butter, softened
2 eggs
2 teaspoons pure vanilla extract
Finely grated zest of 1 orange
  or 1 lemon
¼ cup (2 fl oz/60 ml) whole milk
¼ cup (2 fl oz/60 ml) light or gold rum
Egg wash: 1 egg yolk beaten with
  1 tablespoon water
Multicolored nonpareils (hundreds
  & thousands), for decorating

These festively decorated cookie cut-outs are traditionally baked for Epiphany—the Christian holiday commemorating when the Magi visited the baby Jesus—in Tuscany, particularly in the province of Lucca. Their name comes from the tale of an old woman named Befana who passes out the cookies—typically in shapes of letters, animals, hearts, or stars—to children for the holiday. They're a typical butter cookie dough often enriched with milk and spiked with rum, orange zest, and occasionally, anise seeds. But their most distinct feature is the multicolored tiny nonpareils (hundreds & thousands) that dot the tops or completely encrust them. Seek out nonpareils with a mix of pink, yellow, white, and blue colors, or any colors you like.

- -

Position racks in the top and bottom thirds of the oven and preheat the oven to 350°F (180°C/Gas Mark 4). Line two large baking sheets with parchment paper.

In a medium bowl, whisk together the flour, baking powder, salt, and anise seeds (if using).

In a large bowl, with a hand mixer, beat the sugar and butter on medium speed until pale and fluffy, 2–3 minutes. Add the eggs, one at a time, beating until smooth after each addition. Beat in the vanilla and orange zest. Add the dry ingredients, milk, and rum and stir until the dough forms and there are no dry patches of flour remaining.

Scrape the dough onto a lightly floured work surface and use a rolling pin to flatten until ¼ inch (6 mm) thick. Using various 3-inch (7.5 cm) cutters, cut out shapes of dough. Reroll the scraps to cut out more cookies. Transfer the shapes to the prepared baking sheets, spaced 2 inches (5 cm) apart. Lightly brush the shapes with egg wash, then sprinkle them liberally with nonpareils.

Bake until light golden brown at the edges and dry to the touch on top, 12–15 minutes, switching racks and rotating the baking sheets front to back halfway through.

Transfer the baking sheets to wire racks. Let the cookies cool on the pans for 1 minute, then transfer them to the racks to cool completely.

Iced Raisin and Almond Cookies
Papassini Sardi

Preparation time: 45 minutes,
  plus cooling and setting time
Cooking time: 15 minutes
Makes: About 18 cookies

For the cookies:
⅓ cup (55 g) small raisins or dried
  currants
3 tablespoons whole milk
2 cups (280 g) all-purpose (plain) flour
1 teaspoon baker's ammonia
  (see page 17) or baking powder
½ teaspoon fine sea salt
½ cup (115 g) cold-rendered leaf lard
  or unsalted butter, softened
½ cup (100 g) white US granulated
  (UK caster) sugar
1 egg
¼ teaspoon pure almond extract
2 oz (55 g) blanched whole or slivered
  almonds, finely chopped
2 oz (55 g) walnuts, finely chopped

For the icing:
1 egg white
1 cup (135 g) powdered (icing) sugar
Multicolored nonpareils (hundreds
  & thousands), for decorating

Similar to Venetian *zaléti* (recipe, page 117), these Sardinian diamond-shaped cookies feature raisins, or *papassini*, by-products of the wine grape harvest and associated with regional autumn baking traditions. Other fall ingredients like nuts and candied citrus peel—traditionally made with the first fruits of the season—are also mixed in. Though modern recipes use butter, the traditional fat is lard, as it would have also been available at that time of the year.

Typically baked for All Saints' Day on November 1, some older recipes even include saba or sapa, which is grape must syrup, showing the cookie's relation to *mustacciuoli Napoletani* (recipe, page 118) and other diamond-shaped and dried fruit–studded cookies that share its name and that once used the grape must syrup. Many recipes now use sugar, but if you'd like to use the saba, use the same weight as the sugar. Many older recipes use yeast as a leavener while more recent, but not quite modern, recipes call for baker's ammonia—to give lightness to the dense cookies covered in an egg white icing called *cappa* and decorated with multicolored nonpareils that in Italy are called *tragghera* or "little devils."

Make the cookies: Position racks in the top and bottom thirds of the oven and preheat the oven to 350°F (180°C/Gas Mark 4). Line two large baking sheets with parchment paper.

In a small microwave-safe bowl, combine the raisins and milk and heat in the microwave until hot. Set aside to cool to room temperature.

In a medium bowl, whisk together the flour, baker's ammonia, and salt.

In a large bowl, with a hand mixer, beat the lard and white US granulated (UK caster) sugar on medium speed until pale and fluffy, 2–3 minutes. Add the egg and beat until smooth. Beat in the almond extract. Add the dry ingredients, raisins with milk, almonds, and walnuts and stir until the dough forms and there are no dry patches of flour remaining.

Scrape the dough onto a lightly floured work surface and use a rolling pin to flatten to ⅜ inch (1 cm) thick. Using a pizza cutter or chef's knife, cut the dough into strips 2 inches (5 cm) wide, then cut each strip every 2 inches (5 cm) at an angle to make diamonds. Transfer the diamonds to the prepared baking sheets, spaced 2 inches (5 cm) apart.

Bake until golden brown at the edges and dry to the touch on top, 14–16 minutes, switching racks and rotating the baking sheets front to back halfway through.

Transfer the baking sheets to wire racks. Let the cookies cool on the pans for 1 minute, then transfer them to the racks to cool completely.

Make the icing: In a medium bowl, whisk the egg white until frothy. Add the powdered (icing) sugar and stir until it forms a smooth icing. Dip the top of each cookie in the icing, letting the excess drip off, or use an offset spatula to spread the icing over the tops of the cookies. While the icing is wet, sprinkle the cookies liberally with nonpareils (hundreds & thousands). Let the icing dry completely and set before serving.

Sicilian Sesame-Crusted Cookies
Biscotti Regina

Preparation time: 30 minutes,
  plus 20 minutes chilling time
Cooking time: 25 minutes
Makes: About 18 cookies

2½ cups (350 g) all-purpose
  (plain) flour
1 tablespoon baking powder
½ teaspoon fine sea salt
¼ teaspoon ground cinnamon
  (optional)
½ cup (115 g) cold-rendered leaf lard,
  vegetable shortening, or unsalted
  butter, softened
¾ cup (150 g) white US granulated
  (UK caster) sugar
3 eggs, 1 whole and 2 separated
1 teaspoon pure vanilla extract
  (optional)
Finely grated zest of 1 orange
  or 1 lemon
2 tablespoons water
1 cup (150 g) sesame seeds

Popular in the Sicilian town of Palermo, these crunchy butter cookies crusted in sesame seeds are named "queen's cookies." The reason is unclear, but many think they were to honor the eighteenth-century Queen Margherita of Savoy, or the cookies were her favorite. With their coating of sesame seeds, they have a relation to North African cookies that also heavily use sesame seeds, like Moroccan *fekkas* (recipe, page 138), Algerian *boussou la tmessou* (recipe, page 143), and *makroud* (recipe, page 140). In bakeries in Palermo, the cookies are often sold *tostati* (very toasted), which explains why many recipes have high oven temperatures or bake the cookies for longer than the usual time for cookies of their size. This recipe keeps the temperature at a slightly high level, but it gives a range to allow you to bake the cookies to your desired doneness level.

Like many southern Italian cookies, lard is the traditional fat, though butter is now commonly used instead; take your pick or mix half and half. The flavorings here are also up to the individual baker, as most recipes call for either orange or lemon zest, but fewer call for ground cinnamon and/or vanilla; use all three or pick one to suit your taste. The cookies often have a higher proportion of baking powder than is needed, but it gives them their characteristic "crack" on top, created from the leavening bursting up through the coating of sesame seeds when the cookies hit the hot oven. While most recipes call for dipping the dough ovals in milk to get the sesame seeds to stick, others recommend beaten egg whites, which works better and allows you to use leftover whites from the yolks needed in the dough.

In a medium bowl, whisk together the flour, baking powder, salt, and cinnamon (if using).

In a large bowl, with a hand mixer, beat the lard and sugar on medium speed until pale and fluffy, 2–3 minutes. Add 1 whole egg and 2 egg yolks and beat until smooth. Beat in the vanilla (if using) and orange zest. Add the dry ingredients and stir until the dough forms and there are no dry patches of flour remaining. Cover the bowl with plastic wrap (cling film) and chill the dough for 20 minutes.

Position racks in the top and bottom thirds of the oven and preheat the oven to 400°F (200°C/Gas Mark 6). Line two large baking sheets with parchment paper.

In a shallow bowl, whisk together the remaining 2 egg whites and the water. Place the sesame seeds in another bowl.

Uncover the dough and, using a 1-ounce (2-tablespoon) ice cream scoop or 2 tablespoons, portion the dough and shape into sausages 1½ inches (4 cm) long. Dip each sausage to coat in the egg whites and then roll to coat in the sesame seeds. Arrange the dough sausages on the prepared baking sheets, spaced 2 inches (5 cm) apart.

Bake until cracked on top, golden brown on the outside, and dry to the touch on top, about 25 minutes (depending on how toasted you want the sesame seeds), switching racks and rotating the baking sheets front to back halfway through.

Transfer the baking sheets to wire racks. Let the cookies cool on the pans for 1 minute, then transfer them to the racks to cool completely.

Fava Bean-Shaped Almond Cookies
Fave dei Morti

Preparation time: 30 minutes
Cooking time: 15 minutes
Makes: About 12 cookies

10 oz (285 g) blanched whole
   or slivered almonds
⅓ cup (70 g) white US granulated
   (UK caster) sugar
¾ teaspoon fine sea salt
1 egg
1 tablespoon light rum
1 tablespoon natural cocoa powder
1 tablespoon red alchermes liqueur or
   Campari (or maraschino liqueur such
   as Luxardo, mixed with 4 drops liquid
   red food coloring)

These curiously named cookies—"fava beans of the dead"—are traditionally served for All Souls' Day, which follows All Saints' Day, on November 2. One theory for how the beans got linked to the cookies is that seventeenth-century papists would cook large amounts of fava beans (broad beans) and pass them out to the poor on the holiday, in an attempt to relieve their loved ones' suffering in purgatory. The tradition morphed over time into sweets in the shape of fava beans. Today, in addition to being served for All Souls' Day, the cookies are usually included in the box with a wedding ring, as it's tradition for couples to propose marriage on that holiday.

The cookies are made all over Italy, but there seem to be two distinct styles. In northeastern Italy, particularly Friuli, the cookies are like *amaretti morbidi* (recipe, page 109) and colored three different ways: white (kept plain or flavored with maraschino liqueur), brown (flavored with cocoa powder), and pink (colored with alchermes, a red food coloring that's also an aperitif-like liqueur similar to modern-day Campari). In central and southern Italy, the coloring is omitted, the dough has butter and flour added and is flavored with cinnamon and/or lemon zest. Another variation of the cookies for the holiday is made by simply shaping the same dough into sticks, which are referred to as *ossi dei morti*, or "bones of the dead." This recipe is for the tri-colored northeastern version. The central/southern version made with butter and flour and the *ossi dei morti* are in the variations that follow.

Position racks in the top and bottom thirds of the oven and preheat the oven to 350°F (180°C/Gas Mark 4). Line two large baking sheets with parchment paper.

In a food processor, pulse the almonds until finely chopped. Add the sugar and salt and pulse until the almonds are very finely ground. Add the egg and pulse until the dough just comes together.

Divide the dough equally among three small bowls. To one bowl, add the rum and cocoa powder and knead into the dough until evenly incorporated. To the second bowl, add the red liqueur and knead into the dough until evenly incorporated; the dough should be pink, not red. Leave the third bowl of dough plain.

Using a ¾-ounce (1½-tablespoon) ice cream scoop, portion the dough and roll into ovals. Arrange the ovals on the prepared baking sheets, spaced 1 inch (2.5 cm) apart. Press the pad of your thumb gently on the top of each cookie to leave a shallow indent; this creates the shape of the fava bean (broad bean).

Bake until the outside of the cookies is cracked and light golden on the bottom, 12–15 minutes, switching racks and rotating the baking sheets front to back halfway through.

Transfer the baking sheets to wire racks and let the cookies cool completely on the pans.

Variations
Central/Southern Almond Cookies
After grinding the almonds, sugar, and salt, when adding the egg, add a second egg along with 1 cup (140 g) all-purpose (plain) flour, 2 tablespoons softened unsalted butter, ½ teaspoon ground cinnamon, and the finely grated zest of 1 lemon. Increase the rum to 2 tablespoons and add it to all the dough with the other ingredients. Omit the cocoa powder and alchermes. Pulse until the dough just comes together. Shape and bake the dough as directed.
Ossi dei Morti
If making the northeastern version, leave the dough plain (no rum, cocoa powder, or alchermes). Shape the portioned dough balls into sticks 3 inches (7.5 cm) in length. Bake as directed.

Fava Bean-Shaped Almond Cookies

Italian Waffle Cookies

Pizzelle

Preparation time: 1 hour 15 minutes,
  plus chilling time
Cooking time: 45 minutes
Makes: About 12 cookies

2 teaspoons anise seeds
2¼ cups (315 g) all-purpose
  (plain) flour
2 teaspoons baking powder
¾ teaspoon fine sea salt
¾ cup (150 g) white US granulated
  (UK caster) sugar
3 eggs
2 teaspoons pure vanilla extract
Finely grated zest of 1 lemon (optional)
1 stick (4 oz/115 g) unsalted butter,
  melted and cooled
Powdered (icing) sugar, for dusting

The oft-repeated history of *pizzelle*—also often referenced as "the world's oldest cookie"—is that the cookies were eaten as celebration food in the town of Colcullo, after St. Dominica relieved its citizens of a snake infestation in the eighth century. Today, The Festival of Snakes commemorates this event in the town every May, and thin, iron-pressed waffle cookies are sold. Named from the word *pizze*, or "flat and round"— that also gives the savory pizza its name—there are many theories for how these cookies came to be. One possible scenario dates back to ancient Rome when a treat called *crustulum* was made, likely a round and flat sweetened bread rusk. When Christianity arrived, so did their communion or Eucharist wafers, which could also have been what the citizens of Colcullo ate post-snake infestation.

The tradition of using such wafers shows up in German *Elisenlebkuchen* (recipe, page 244), where a spiced almond batter is scraped atop small rice-paper wafers called *Oblaten*, and in another southern Italian treat called *ostie piene*, which consists of honey-coated almonds sandwiched between two communion wafers. It's likely that, with time, the wafers used for celebrations grew richer in fat and sweeter to differentiate them for such special occasions. Iron plates with patterns started appearing in the 1700s, as blacksmiths commissioned by wealthy noble families made them with the families' engraved coats of arms or initials; the plates were often the dowry women brought to their new husbands. Older irons appear to be larger than modern ones, and they were often engraved with lines that allowed you to break the giant round into smaller quadrants for easier eating.

Pizzelle are now typically made by whipping eggs and sugar first, then mixing in large amounts of butter and/or cream, making them more akin in texture to Norwegian *goro* (recipe, page 304) or Dutch *ijzerkoekjes* (recipe, page 228). They are often served, similar to waffle cones or other crisp cookies, as an accompaniment with gelato or other smooth, cold desserts. The traditional flavor for *pizzelle* seems to be anise seeds, though those averse to the spice's licorice flavor typically swap it for cinnamon, lemon zest, and/or vanilla. There is a substantial tradition among Italian-Americans in the United States for making the cookies for Christmas, where mechanical or electric irons are passed down through families and cherished.

In a small frying pan, toast the anise seeds over medium heat, swirling the pan occasionally, until the seeds are aromatic and lightly toasted, about 2 minutes. Transfer to a cutting board and roughly chop while they're still warm, then let cool. (If you prefer, process the seeds until finely ground after they're cooled.)

Meanwhile, in a medium bowl, whisk together the flour, baking powder, and salt.

In a large bowl, with a hand mixer, combine the chopped anise seeds, white US granulated (UK caster) sugar, eggs, vanilla, and lemon zest (if using) and beat on medium speed until lightened and pale, 2–3 minutes. Beat in the melted butter. Add the flour mixture and beat on low speed until a thick batter forms. Cover the bowl with plastic wrap (cling film) and refrigerate for at least 1 hour or overnight.

Place a pizzelle or krumkake iron over medium heat on your stove or heat an electric version. Using a 1-tablespoon measure, pour heaping tablespoonfuls of batter into the center of the iron. Close the iron and let cook, flipping the iron halfway through, if using the stove, until the batter spreads and sets as a wafer, 2–3 minutes, depending on the heat of your stove (or follow the manufacturer's instructions for the electric maker).

Open the iron and transfer the cookies to a wire rack to cool. Repeat with the remaining batter to cook more cookies.

Dust the cooled cookies with powdered (icing) sugar to serve.

Rich Italian Waffle Cookies

Ferratelle

Preparation time: 1 hour 15 minutes,
  plus chilling time
Cooking time: 45 minutes
Makes: About 12 cookies

6 tablespoons plain olive oil (not
  extra-virgin) or vegetable oil
6 tablespoons (75 g) white US
  granulated (UK caster) sugar
3 tablespoons anise liqueur (such
  as anisette or sambuca) or light rum
½ teaspoon fine sea salt
3 eggs
Finely grated zest of 1 lemon
2¼ cups (315 g) all-purpose
  (plain) flour

These ancestors of *pizzelle* (recipe, opposite) date from the 1700s, when blacksmiths began making cookie irons for wealthy noble families. The cookies went by the name *ferratelle*, after *ferro*, the word for "iron," and they're still called that today in Abruzzo, where they're believed to have been invented. *Ferratelle* differs from *pizzelle* in that the former is usually made from a lightly sweetened egg, flour, and oil dough cooked in a rectangular iron with convex bumps, so the cookies have high raised grooves akin to modern breakfast waffles.

In a large bowl, whisk together the oil, sugar, liqueur, salt, eggs, and lemon zest until smooth. Add the flour and stir until a soft dough forms. Cover the bowl with plastic wrap (cling film) and refrigerate for at least 1 hour or overnight.

Place a square ferratelle iron or pizzelle iron over medium heat on your stove or heat an electric waffle iron. Using a 1-tablespoon measure, pour heaping tablespoonfuls of batter into the center of the iron. Close the iron and let cook, flipping the iron halfway through, if using the stove, until the batter spreads and sets as a wafer, 2–3 minutes, depending on the heat of your stove (or follow the manufacturer's instructions for the electric waffle iron).

Open the iron and transfer the cookies to a wire rack to cool. Repeat with the remaining batter to cook more cookies.

Sicilian Fig-Stuffed Butter Cookies
Cuccidati / Buccellati

Preparation time: 1 hour 50 minutes
 plus cooling and setting time
Cooking time: 25 minutes
Makes: About 24 cookies

For the dough:
2 cups (280 g) all-purpose (plain) flour
1 teaspoon baker's ammonia
 (see page 17) or baking powder
½ teaspoon fine sea salt
1 stick (4 oz/115 g) unsalted butter,
 softened
½ cup (100 g) white US granulated
 (UK caster) sugar
1 egg
1 egg yolk (save the white for the icing)
¼ cup (2 fl oz/60 ml) whole milk
1 teaspoon pure vanilla extract

For the filling:
4 oz (115 g) blanched whole or slivered
 almonds, blanched hazelnuts,
 or walnuts (or pick two and use
 2 oz/55 g of each)
6 oz (170 g) dried figs, stemmed
 and quartered
⅓ cup (55 g) golden raisins (sultanas)
¼ cup (2 fl oz/60 ml) Marsala or white
 wine (or 2 tablespoons light rum
 mixed with 2 tablespoons water)
½ teaspoon ground cinnamon
⅛ teaspoon ground cloves
¼ teaspoon fine sea salt
Finely grated zest of 1 orange
⅓ cup (2½ fl oz/80 ml) fresh
 orange juice

For the icing:
1 egg white
2 cups (270 g) powdered (icing) sugar
2 tablespoons hot tap water
1 tablespoon fresh lemon juice
Pinch of fine sea salt
Multicolored nonpareils (hundreds
 & thousands), for decorating

In Sicily, these cookies are a must-have for Christmas. Made of a simple butter cookie dough stuffed with a line of dried fig filling, they show an Arab influence via North African *makroud* (recipe, page 140) and the use of spices in the filling. They make use of dried fruits—in this case, figs, raisins, and candied citrus—and nuts of the fall harvest to make a rich, celebration sweet. Because they're a holiday cookie, they're topped with icing and multicolored nonpareils (hundreds & thousands), similar to *befanini* (recipe, page 125) and *papassini sardi* (recipe, page 126).

Recipes vary wildly based on personal tastes. Modern ones add chocolate to the mix, while others use only almonds or add hazelnuts, walnuts, and pistachios as well. Baker's ammonia is used in older recipes, with baking powder in modern ones. The cookies are often cut into small pieces from one long log before baking, while others bake the log whole, scoring the top with evenly spaced lines, then cut through the lines to separate the cookies after baking. Some recipes shape narrower logs into 4-inch (10 cm) lengths that are cut on one side and then bent to flare out the notches, like a bear's claw. If shaped into wreaths or bracelets, they're typically called *buccellati*.

Make the dough: In a medium bowl, whisk together the flour, baker's ammonia, and salt.

In a large bowl, with a hand mixer, beat the butter and white US granulated (UK caster) sugar on medium speed until pale and fluffy, 2–3 minutes. Add the whole egg and egg yolk and beat until smooth. Beat in the milk and vanilla. Add the dry ingredients and stir until a dough forms and there are no dry patches of flour remaining. Shape the dough into a ball, then divide into 2 equal portions. Shape each portion into a ball, wrap separately, and refrigerate for 30 minutes.

Meanwhile, make the filling: In a food processor, pulse the almonds until roughly chopped. Add the figs and raisins (sultanas) and pulse until finely chopped. Add the wine, cinnamon, cloves, salt, orange zest, and orange juice and pulse until everything forms a paste that holds together. Divide the filling in half and wrap each half in plastic wrap (cling film).

Position racks in the top and bottom thirds of the oven and preheat the oven to 350°F (180°C/Gas Mark 4). Line two large baking sheets with parchment paper.

On a lightly floured work surface, unwrap one ball of dough and shape it into a log 12 inches (30 cm) long. Using your thumb, press along the top of the log to flatten the middle, creating a narrow trench. Take one-half of the filling and roll it on a clean work surface into a rope the same width and length as the trench, then place it in the trench. Using your fingers, bring the dough on either side of the trench up and over to cover the filling, pinching to seal it shut.

Roll the log back and forth, elongating it to 18 inches (46 cm), while also smoothing its seam. Flatten the log slightly until ¾ inch (2 cm) thick. Using a paring knife, trim and discard the ends, then cut the log crosswise every 1½ inches (4 cm) to create rectangles. Repeat with the remaining dough and filling to make more cookies. Arrange the rectangles on the prepared baking sheets, spaced 2 inches (5 cm) apart.

Bake until golden brown on the outside and dry to the touch, 20–25 minutes, switching racks and rotating the baking sheets front to back halfway through.

Transfer the baking sheets to wire racks. Let the cookies cool on the pans for 1 minute, then transfer them to the racks to cool completely.

Make the icing: In a medium bowl, whisk the egg white until frothy. Add the powdered (icing) sugar, hot water, and lemon juice and stir until it forms a smooth icing. Dip the top of each cookie in the icing, letting the excess drip off, or use an offset spatula to spread the icing over the tops of the cookies. While the icing is wet, sprinkle the cookies with nonpareils (hundreds & thousands). Let the icing dry completely and set before serving.

Sicilian Fig-Stuffed Butter Cookies

Sugar-Coated Anise Ring Cookies
Zuccherini

Preparation time: 1 hour,
 plus cooling time
Cooking time: 30 minutes
Makes: About 36 cookies

For the cookies:
2 cups (280 g) all-purpose (plain) flour
2 teaspoons anise seeds,
 lightly crushed
1 teaspoon baking powder
1 teaspoon fine sea salt
4 tablespoons (2 oz/55 g) unsalted
 butter, softened
¼ cup (50 g) white US granulated
 (UK caster) sugar
2 eggs
1 tablespoon anise liqueur (such as
 anisette or sambuca) or light rum

For the sugar coating:
1 cup (200 g) white US granulated
 (UK caster) sugar
½ cup (4 fl oz/120 ml) water

A specialty of Tuscany, these cookies are sometimes referred to as *zuccherini di Vernio*, for a town outside Florence, and *zuccherini montanari*, or "mountain sugars." This is a small donut-shaped cookie flavored with anise and/or fennel seeds that is very dry but coated in crystallized sugar, which preserves it, gives extra sweetness, and makes it look festive. They are often given as gifts for weddings, confirmations, communions, and other celebrations. Similar to *ciambelline al vino* (recipe, page 122), they're typically served with wine, usually vin santo, or eaten for breakfast with coffee.

Make the cookies: Position racks in the top and bottom thirds of the oven and preheat the oven to 350°F (180°C/Gas Mark 4). Line two large baking sheets with parchment paper.

In a large bowl, whisk together the flour, anise seeds, baking powder, and salt. Form a well in the center and add the butter, sugar, eggs, and liqueur. First stir to combine the wet ingredients, then stir to incorporate the dry ingredients, continuing to stir until a dough forms and there are no dry patches of flour remaining. Gather the dough into a ball.

Working on a lightly floured work surface, pinch off pieces of dough and roll them between your fingers and the work surface into ropes ½ inch (13 mm) thick. Cut the ropes into 2½-inch (6.5 cm) lengths. Bend each length in the center and form a circle or mini donut, touching the ends together to connect. Arrange the dough rings on the prepared baking sheets, spaced 2 inches (5 cm) apart.

Bake until the cookies are golden brown and dry to the touch, 15–18 minutes, switching racks and rotating the baking sheets front to back halfway through.

Transfer the baking sheets to wire racks. Let the cookies cool on the pans for 1 minute, then transfer them to the racks to cool completely.

Once cooled, place all the cookies in a large, wide heatproof bowl.

Make the sugar coating: In a small saucepan, combine the sugar and water and bring to a boil over high heat, stirring to dissolve the sugar. Attach a candy/deep-fry thermometer to the side of the saucepan and let the syrup cook, undisturbed, until it reaches 235°F (113°C) on the thermometer.

When ready, remove the saucepan from the heat and carefully remove the thermometer from the side of the pan. Gently pour the boiling syrup over the baked cookies and immediately use two heatproof spoons to gently toss the cookies repeatedly until the syrup crystallizes and fully coats them in an opaque sugar glaze.

Return the cookies to a wire rack, separating any that have stuck together. Let the cookies stand until completely cooled before serving.

"Gazelle Heel" Almond Paste Cookies
Kaab el-Ghazal

Preparation time: 45 minutes,
plus 1 hour resting time and 30
minutes chilling time
Cooking time: 15 minutes
Makes: About 12 cookies

For the dough:
1⅔ cups (230 g) all-purpose
(plain) flour
½ teaspoon fine sea salt
2 tablespoons clarified butter,
softened
¼ cup (2 fl oz/60 ml) water
2 tablespoons orange blossom
water (or more water)

For the filling:
8 oz (225 g) blanched whole
or slivered almonds
½ cup (75 g) powdered (icing) sugar
2 tablespoons orange blossom water
1 tablespoon clarified butter
1 teaspoon ground cinnamon or ½
teaspoon ground mastic (optional)
¼ teaspoon fine sea salt

Often translated erroneously as gazelle "horns" because of their curved crescent shape, the name for these Moroccan cookies comes from their resemblance to gazelle "heels" or "ankles," thanks to their bulging filling in the center. The cookies always consist of a thin flour-based dough enveloping an almond paste filling scented with orange blossom water and, sometimes, cinnamon or ground mastic. The cookies can be served plain, but they are often brushed with more orange blossom water or syrup. They can also be coated in powdered (icing) sugar, finely ground walnuts, or left *tcherek el-aryan*, which translates to "naked," as this recipe does. Variations for the syrup, sugar, and nut variations follow.

In Tunisia, a similar cookie, shaped into rings and flavored with rose water, is called *kaak warka*, while in Algeria, *arayeche* is the name of a three-pronged version often covered in a powdered (icing) sugar icing and decorated with marzipan flowers.

- -

Make the dough: In a large bowl, whisk together the flour and salt. Add the butter and rub it into the flour with your fingers until it breaks down into coarse crumbles. Pour in the water and orange blossom water and stir with your fingers until a dough forms and there are no dry patches of flour remaining. Gather the dough into a ball, transfer to a clean work surface, and knead just briefly to form a cohesive dough. Cover the dough in plastic wrap (cling film) and let rest at room temperature for 1 hour.

Meanwhile, make the filling: In a food processor, combine the almonds, sugar, orange blossom water, butter, cinnamon, and salt and pulse until the mixture forms a smooth paste. Using a ½-ounce (1-tablespoon) ice cream scoop, portion the filling and roll into balls. Shape each ball into a 3-inch (7.5 cm) log, tapering the ends to a point. Place the shaped filling pieces on a plate and cover with plastic wrap (cling film) until ready to use.

Line two large baking sheets with parchment paper. Working on a clean, unfloured work surface, uncover the dough and cut it into 4 equal portions. Keep 3 pieces covered while you work with one. Using a rolling pin, flatten the dough into a rectangle roughly 4 × 8 inches (10 × 20 cm), preferably 1/16 inch (2 mm) thick. Place one almond filling log next to one short side of the rectangle and then roll the dough rectangle around it. Cut along the seam with a pizza cutter or knife to trim off most of the overlap (there can be some overlap, but not a lot), then smooth the seams of dough and bend the filled dough into a slight crescent.

Place a crescent on the prepared baking sheet seam-side down. Repeat rolling, cutting, and shaping more cookies with the remaining dough and filling logs, re-using the scraps as needed. Once all the crescents are made, prick the top of each a few times with a toothpick (this prevents the dough from puffing during baking), then place the baking sheets in the refrigerator to rest for 30 minutes.

Position racks in the top and bottom thirds of the oven and preheat the oven to 325°F (160°C/Gas Mark 3).

Bake until barely golden brown on the bottom and dry to the touch on top, 12–15 minutes, switching racks and rotating the baking sheets front to back halfway through. Do not bake any longer than directed or the dough will become tough once the cookies cool.

Transfer the baking sheets to wire racks. Let the cookies cool on the pans for 1 minute, then transfer them to the racks to cool completely.

Variations
Syrup-Coated "Gazelle Heels"
Make the syrup from the *makrout el louz* (recipe, page 142) and brush it over the cookies while hot from the oven.
Powdered Sugar or Walnut "Gazelle Heels"
Follow the directions for Syrup-Coated "Gazelle Heels" (above). After brushing the syrup over the cookies, toss them in powdered (icing) sugar or finely ground walnuts to coat.

Almond Shortbread Cookies

Ghoriba Bahla

Preparation time: 40 minutes
Cooking time: 30 minutes
Makes: About 12 cookies

2 oz (55 g) slivered almonds
2 tablespoons sesame seeds
2 cups (280 g) all-purpose (plain) flour
1 teaspoon baking powder
½ teaspoon fine sea salt
10 tablespoons (5 oz/140 g) unsalted
 butter, softened
½ cup (105 g) superfine (caster) sugar
1 egg
1 teaspoon pure vanilla extract
 or rose water

With the prevalence of "wedding" cookies (see page 23) across the Middle East, it's clear that bakers have been experimenting and slightly shifting what that cookie or name represents for centuries. It is typically the shapes and styles that change more than the primary ingredients. For example, the simple Middle Eastern shortbreads that are popular across the Levant and the Arabian Peninsula, variously spelled *ghorayeba*, *ghurayiba*, or *raybeh* (recipe, page 49), take on a slight variation in Morocco. While the former are made with a plain dough and studded with a single whole almond or pistachio on top, these *ghoriba bahla*—which means "silly cookie," a reference to their cracked appearance—show up as cookies with ground almonds and sesame seeds, or sometimes sesame seeds alone, mixed into the dough and their tops left unadorned. One curious detail is that sometimes the names of these cookies are translated as "semolina" cookies, even though none use semolina flour today. It's likely the cookies once did use semolina but replaced it with finer-grained all-purpose (plain) flour in the modern era.

Orange blossom water or rose water is typically added to the dough, which also has egg and/or baking powder, for a less dense and crumbly texture than the Arabian version and to accentuate the desirable cracks. A special *ghoriba* pan with numerous convex humps is traditionally used to shape the cookies, though you can use an upside-down mini muffin tin or simply bake them flat on a regular baking sheet.

Position racks in the top and bottom thirds of the oven and preheat the oven to 325°F (160°C/Gas Mark 3). Line two large baking sheets with parchment paper.

Spread the almonds out on one of the baking sheets and bake until lightly browned and fragrant, 6–8 minutes. Transfer the almonds to a cutting board to cool.

Sprinkle the sesame seeds over the baking sheet and place in the oven until lightly browned and fragrant, 2–4 minutes. Transfer the sesame seeds to a bowl to cool. Reserve the baking sheet.

In a food processor or on a cutting board, process or chop the almonds until finely ground. Add the ground nuts to the bowl with the sesame seeds.

In a medium bowl, whisk together the flour, baking powder, and salt.

In a large bowl, with a hand mixer, beat the butter and sugar on medium speed until light and fluffy, 2–3 minutes. Add the egg and beat until smooth. Beat in the vanilla or rose water. Add the flour mixture and ground nuts/sesame seeds and beat on low speed until a crumbly dough forms and there are no dry patches of flour remaining.

Using a 1-ounce (2-tablespoon) ice cream scoop, portion the dough and roll into balls. Place the balls on the prepared baking sheets, spaced 2 inches (5 cm) apart. With the palm of your hand, flatten each slightly into a disc ½ inch (13 mm) thick. (Alternatively, you can use a ghoriba pan or upside-down mini muffin tin. Spray the humps with cooking spray and dust with flour. Place a dough disc on top of each hump on the pan.)

Bake until golden brown all over, cracked on top, and dry to the touch in the center, 15–20 minutes, switching racks and rotating the baking sheets front to back halfway through.

Transfer the baking sheets to wire racks and let the cookies cool completely on the pans.

Almond Shortbread Cookies

Twice-Baked Anise and Sesame Cookies
Fekkas / Feqqas

Preparation time: 50 minutes,
 plus 20 minutes cooling time
Cooking time: 40 minutes
Makes: About 30 cookies

2 cups (280 g) all-purpose (plain) flour
¼ cup (35 g) sesame seeds
1 tablespoon anise seeds
2 teaspoons baking powder
½ teaspoon fine sea salt
¼ teaspoon ground mastic (optional)
½ cup (100 g) white US granulated
 (UK caster) sugar
⅓ cup (2½ fl oz/80 ml) vegetable oil
2 tablespoons orange blossom water
1 egg
Egg wash: 1 egg yolk stirred with
 1 tablespoon whole milk

Small, crunchy anise and sesame seed cookies appear all over the Middle East in various forms. This Moroccan cookie is often described as "Moroccan biscotti" because it is twice-baked and crisp. Traditional recipes, while described as cookies, were often made with yeast and were more like sweetened bread that was twice-baked. Modern recipes, however, use chemical leavening—similar to Tunisian *boulou* (recipe, page 144)—giving these sweets a more expected cookie-like texture. The classic flavor profile for these cookies is a mix of sesame seeds, anise seeds, and orange blossom water, but another classic variation is called *fekkas msseoues* and is made with almonds and raisins. In some parts of Morocco, leftover fragmented pieces of *fekkas* are collected in a bowl and served with milk to kids like cereal.

Position racks in the top and bottom thirds of the oven and preheat the oven to 350°F (180°C/Gas Mark 4). Line a large baking sheet with parchment paper.

In a medium bowl, whisk together the flour, sesame seeds, anise seeds, baking powder, salt, and mastic (if using).

In a large bowl, whisk together the sugar, oil, orange blossom water, and whole egg until smooth. Add the dry ingredients and stir until a dough forms and there are no dry patches of flour remaining. Shape the dough into a smooth ball, then divide in half.

Working on a lightly floured work surface, roll each dough half into a log roughly 9 inches (23 cm) long and 2 inches (5 cm) wide. Transfer the dough logs to the prepared baking sheet spaced 3 inches (7.5 cm) apart. Brush the logs with some of the egg wash.

Bake until golden brown all over and a toothpick inserted in the center of each loaf comes out with no raw batter attached, about 20 minutes, rotating the baking sheet front to back halfway through.

Transfer the baking sheet to a wire rack and let the loaves cool for 20 minutes. Leave the oven on.

Using a serrated knife, cut each loaf crosswise into slices ½ inch (13 mm) thick. Arrange the slices on the baking sheet, spaced ½ inch (1.3 cm) apart, and return to the oven.

Bake until the cookies are golden brown all over and dry to the touch, 15–20 minutes, rotating the baking sheet front to back halfway through.

Transfer the baking sheet to a wire rack. Let the cookies cool on the pan for 1 minute, then transfer them to the rack to cool completely.

Tiny Anise and Sesame Shortbread Cookies

Krichlate

Preparation time: 15 minutes
Cooking time: 30 minutes
Makes: About 54 cookies

2 cups (285 g) all-purpose (plain) flour
½ cup (75 g) sesame seeds
2 teaspoons anise seeds
1 teaspoon fennel seeds
1 teaspoon baking powder
½ teaspoon fine sea salt
½ cup (100 g) white US granulated
  (UK caster) sugar
¼ cup (2 fl oz/60 ml) vegetable
  oil or clarified butter
¼ cup (2 fl oz/60 ml) orange
  blossom water
1 egg

Another Moroccan cookie-like treat similar to *fekkas* (recipe, page 138*)*, *krichlate* seems to be a cookie version of the sweetened brioche buns called *krichel*. They have the same flavors as *fekkas* and are shaped in a similar fashion, but are much smaller, made of shortbread dough, and are only baked once. They are often served during the Ashura holiday and/or with mint tea. Though the amount of orange blossom water here may seem to be too much, the fragrance cooks off considerably during baking so the resulting cookie has a balanced floral scent.

Position racks in the top and bottom thirds of the oven and preheat the oven to 350°F (180°C/Gas Mark 4). Line two large baking sheets with parchment paper.

In a medium bowl, whisk together the flour, sesame seeds, anise seeds, fennel seeds, baking powder, and salt.

In a large bowl, whisk together the sugar, oil, orange blossom water, and egg until smooth. Add the dry ingredients and stir until a dough forms and there are no dry patches of flour remaining. Shape the dough into a ball and transfer to a clean work surface.

Split the dough ball in half and shape each half into an even log 1 inch (2.5 cm) thick. Cut each log on a slight bias every ½ inch (13 mm) to make small diamonds. Transfer the diamonds, cut-sides down, to the prepared baking sheets, spaced 1 inch (2.5 cm) apart.

Bake until golden brown and dry to the touch, 25–30 minutes, switching racks and rotating the baking sheets front to back halfway through.

Transfer the baking sheets to wire racks and let the cookies cool completely on the pans.

Fried Date-Filled Semolina Cookies

Makroud / Maqrud

Preparation time: 1 hour 10 minutes,
 plus 1 hour standing time
Cooking time: 40 minutes
Makes: About 30 cookies

For the dough:
½ cup (4 fl oz/120 ml) warm water
¼ teaspoon crushed saffron threads
2¾ cups (425 g) fine semolina flour
½ teaspoon fine sea salt
¼ teaspoon baking soda (bicarbonate
 of soda)
½ cup (4 fl oz/120 ml) vegetable oil
 or melted clarified butter or ghee

For the date filling:
8 oz (225 g) pitted soft dates
¼ cup (2 fl oz/60 ml) boiling hot water
3 tablespoons plain olive oil (not
 extra-virgin)
½ teaspoon ground cinnamon
¼ teaspoon ground cloves
¼ teaspoon fine sea salt
Finely grated zest of 1 orange

For the honey syrup:
1 cup (8 fl oz/250 ml) water
⅔ cup (140 g) white US granulated
 (UK caster) sugar
½ cup (170 g) honey
2 tablespoons fresh lemon juice
2 tablespoons orange blossom water
¼ teaspoon fine sea salt

To finish:
Vegetable oil, for frying
Toasted sesame seeds,
 for sprinkling (optional)

Often credited as a specialty of the Tunisian city of Kairouan, this stuffed cookie is popular across the Maghreb countries of North Africa. Filled with a spiced, orange-scented date paste, *makroud* are sometimes referenced as a Berber form of *maamoul* (recipe, page 44), which is also often filled with dates. Unlike *maamoul*, these diamond-shaped cookies are traditionally deep-fried and then coated in a fragrant honey syrup.

The cookies are often eaten, again like *maamoul*, by Muslims throughout Ramadan and for the Eid holidays. For Sephardic Jews, the cookies are often served for Purim and Hanukkah. They are traditionally stamped using a *makrout* mold, but these are difficult to source; using a box grater and cutting the dough into diamonds, as this recipe does, is a common workaround in many recipes. The baking soda (bicarbonate of soda) in the recipe helps to provide a little aeration to the dough, so it's not so dense, but omit it if you like. But don't omit the saffron; it's essential to the flavor, and color, of these rich cookies.

Make the dough: In a small bowl, combine the warm water and saffron and let stand for 5 minutes.

Meanwhile, place the semolina in a large bowl and form a well in the center. Stir the salt and baking soda (bicarb) into the saffron water and then pour the mixture into the well of the semolina along with the oil. Stir until a smooth dough forms and there are no dry patches of semolina remaining. Shape the dough into a ball, divide into 2 equal portions, and shape each piece into a ball. Wrap each ball separately and let them stand at room temperature for 1 hour.

Meanwhile, make the filling: In a food processor, combine the dates, hot water, olive oil, cinnamon, cloves, salt, and orange zest and pulse until it forms a smooth paste. Divide the filling in half and scrape each half into a small plastic piping bag or zip-top food storage bag. Set aside until ready to use; do not snip off the tips yet.

Make the honey syrup: In a small saucepan, combine the water, sugar, honey, lemon juice, orange blossom water, and salt and bring to a simmer over medium-high heat. Reduce the heat to maintain a gentle simmer and cook, stirring occasionally, until slightly reduced, about 20 minutes. Remove the pan from the heat and let the syrup cool completely.

On a lightly floured work surface, unwrap one ball of dough and shape it into a log 12 inches (30 cm) long. Using your thumb, press along the top of the log to flatten the middle, creating a narrow trench. Snip the bottom corner of one bag of filling and pipe it into the trench. Using your fingers, bring the dough on either side of the trench up and over to cover the filling, pinching to seal it shut. Roll the log back and forth, elongating it to 18 inches (46 cm), while also smoothing its seam.

Using the zesting side of a box grater, gently stamp the pattern of the holes on top of the log while flattening it slightly to ¾ inch (2 cm) thick. Using a paring knife, trim and discard the ends, then cut the log on the diagonal every 1 inch (2.5 cm) to create diamonds. Repeat with the remaining dough and filling to make more diamonds.

To finish: Line a large baking sheet with paper towels. Place a serving platter next to it. Place a slotted spoon in the cooled honey syrup.

Pour enough oil into a large frying pan to come ½ inch (13 mm) up the sides of the pan. Heat the oil over medium-high heat until it registers 350°F (177°C) on a deep-fry thermometer.

Working in four batches, fry the diamonds, flipping halfway through, until golden brown all over, 3–4 minutes total.

Using tongs, remove the cookies from the oil and transfer to the paper towels to drain for 10 seconds, then place them directly in the honey syrup, turning to ensure they're fully coated. Lift the cookies from the syrup with the slotted spoon, let the excess drain away, then transfer them to the platter. Repeat frying and coating the remaining cookies.

If you like, sprinkle the top of the cookies with sesame seeds before serving. For storing, pour any remaining syrup around the cookies on the platter and store at room temperature, covered in plastic wrap (cling film).

Fried Date-Filled Semolina Cookies

Sugar-Coated Orange Blossom Almond Cookies

Makrout el Louz

Preparation time: 25 minutes,
 plus cooling time
Cooking time: 35 minutes
Makes: About 36 cookies

½ lemon
1½ cups (300 g) white US granulated
 (UK caster) sugar
1 cup (8 fl oz/250 ml) water
2 tablespoons orange blossom water
1 lb (450 g) blanched whole
 or slivered almonds
1 teaspoon pure vanilla extract
¾ teaspoon fine sea salt
2 eggs
Powdered (icing) sugar, for coating

Many sweets in Algeria are commonly flavored with orange blossom water, whether added to their dough or added to a syrup that coats everything from cakes, cookies, and marzipan-like candies. Recipes for diamond-shaped cookies abound that are dunked in orange blossom syrup after baking, then coated in powdered (icing) sugar. Some are crumbly shortbreads—see *boussou la tmessou* (page 143)—that either have almonds, sesame seeds, or are left plain.

These *makrout el louz* ("almond diamonds") are made of ground almonds mixed with whole eggs to make macaroon-like cookies, similar to the dough for Iraqi *hadgi badah* (recipe, page 55). Shaped like Turkish *kurabiye* (recipe, page 60) crossed with *makroud* (recipe, page 140), these chewy almond cookies are covered in powdered sugar, thanks to a layer of orange blossom syrup on the cookies, caked on thick. They are intentionally sweet, and the lemon zest and juice, while they may not be traditional, help balance the sweetness perfectly.

Finely grate the zest from the lemon half onto a plate; cover with plastic wrap (cling film) and set aside. Juice the lemon half and pour it into a small saucepan. Add 1 cup (200 g) of the white US granulated (UK caster) sugar and the water and bring to a simmer over medium-high heat. Reduce the heat to maintain a gentle simmer and cook, stirring occasionally, until slightly reduced, about 20 minutes.

Remove the pan from the heat, stir in the orange blossom water, and let the syrup cool completely.

Position racks in the top and bottom thirds of the oven and preheat the oven to 325°F (160°C/Gas Mark 3). Line two large baking sheets with parchment paper.

In a food processor, combine the almonds and remaining ½ cup (100 g) sugar and pulse until the mixture has the texture of coarse sand. Add the reserved lemon zest, the vanilla, salt, and eggs and pulse until a dough forms. Shape the dough into a ball and transfer to a clean work surface.

Split the dough ball into 4 equal portions and shape each quarter into an even log 1 inch (2.5 cm) thick. Gently flatten the logs and then cut each on a slight diagonal every 1 inch (2.5 cm) to create diamond-shaped pieces. Transfer the diamonds to the prepared baking sheets, spaced 1 inch (2.5 cm) apart. Using your thumb, very gently press a shallow divot in the center of each diamond.

Bake until very lightly golden brown at the edges and dry to the touch in the center, 12–15 minutes, switching racks and rotating the baking sheets front to back halfway through.

Transfer the baking sheets to wire racks and let the cookies cool completely on the pans.

Fill a large shallow bowl with powdered (icing) sugar. Working in batches, place the cookies directly in the orange blossom syrup, turning to ensure they're fully coated, then lift them from the syrup and let the excess drain away. Toss the cookies in the powdered (icing) sugar until fully coated. Transfer to a plate or platter to serve.

Sugar-Coated Shortbread Diamonds

Boussou la Tmessou

Preparation time: 45 minutes,
 plus cooling time
Cooking time: 35 minutes
Makes: About 36 cookies

½ lemon
1 cup (200 g) white US granulated
 (UK caster) sugar
1 cup (8 fl oz/250 ml) water
2 tablespoons orange blossom water
2 cups (280 g) all-purpose (plain) flour
½ teaspoon baking powder
¾ teaspoon fine sea salt
¾ cup (170 g) clarified butter, softened
½ cup (65 g) powdered (icing) sugar,
 plus more for coating
1 teaspoon pure vanilla extract
½ cup (75 g) toasted sesame seeds
 or finely ground almonds (optional)

In North Africa, these cookies are the crumbly shortbread-like cousins to the chewy almond-based *makrout el louz* (recipe, opposite). The richer, more buttery cookies are baked similar to Turkish *kurabiye* (recipe, page 60), but then soaked in the same fragrant citrus syrup as *makrout el louz* and coated in copious amounts of powdered (icing) sugar. The dough itself is made with only a small amount of sugar, so don't skimp on the powdered sugar coating on the outside; this ensures the cookies have plenty of sweetness.

- -

Finely grate the zest from the lemon half onto a plate; cover with plastic wrap (cling film) and set aside. Juice the lemon half and pour it into a small saucepan. Add the white US granulated (UK caster) sugar and the water and bring to a simmer over medium-high heat. Reduce the heat to maintain a gentle simmer and cook, stirring occasionally, until slightly reduced, about 20 minutes.

Remove the pan from the heat, stir in the orange blossom water, and let the syrup cool completely.

Position racks in the top and bottom thirds of the oven and preheat the oven to 325°F (160°C/Gas Mark 3). Line two large baking sheets with parchment paper.

In a medium bowl, whisk together the flour, baking powder, and salt.

In a large bowl, with a hand mixer, combine the butter, powdered (icing) sugar, vanilla, and reserved lemon zest and beat on medium speed until light and fluffy, 2–3 minutes. Add the flour mixture and, if using, the sesame seeds or ground almonds. Beat on low speed until a dough forms and there are no dry patches of flour remaining.

Split the dough ball into 4 equal portions and shape each quarter into an even log 1 inch (2.5 cm) thick. Gently flatten the logs and then cut each on a slight diagonal every 1 inch (2.5 cm) to create diamond-shaped pieces. Transfer the diamonds to the prepared baking sheets, spaced 1 inch (2.5 cm) apart. Using your thumb, very gently press a shallow divot in the center of each diamond.

Bake until very lightly golden brown at the edges and dry to the touch in the center, 12–15 minutes, switching racks and rotating the baking sheets front to back halfway through.

Transfer the baking sheets to wire racks and let the cookies cool completely on the pans.

Fill a large shallow bowl with powdered sugar. Working in batches, place the cookies directly in the orange blossom syrup, turning to ensure they're fully coated, then lift them from the syrup and let the excess drain away. Toss the cookies in powdered sugar until fully coated and then transfer to a plate or platter to serve.

Stuffed Maghrebi Loaf Cookies with Fruit, Nuts, and Chocolate

Boulou

Preparation time: 25 minutes,
  plus 1 hour chilling time
Cooking time: 35 minutes
Makes: About 60 cookies

3¾ cups (525 g) all-purpose
  (plain) flour
1 tablespoon baking powder
1 tablespoon ground anise seeds
  or fennel seeds
1 tablespoon sesame seeds,
  plus more for sprinkling
¾ teaspoon fine sea salt
1 cup (200 g) white US granulated
  (UK caster) sugar
¾ cup (6 fl oz/175 ml) vegetable oil
2 teaspoons pure vanilla extract
1 teaspoon orange blossom water
  or finely grated orange zest
3 eggs
½ cup (85 g) dark or golden raisins
  (sultanas)
½ cup (60 g) sliced (flaked) almonds,
  pine nuts, pistachios, hazelnuts,
  or a mix of all, roughly chopped
2 oz (55 g) bittersweet chocolate,
  roughly chopped, or chocolate chips
Egg wash: 1 egg yolk stirred with
  1 tablespoon water

Though sometimes erroneously labeled as "Tunisian biscotti," this cookie does not get baked twice. It does, however, get baked as a loaf and is then cut into thin slices to serve. Though it's traditionally been called a sweet bread or cake, modern versions treat it fully like a cookie. Stuffed with dried fruit, nuts, and/or chocolate, these cookies are typically eaten by Maghrebi Jews to break the fast after Yom Kippur. Almonds, raisins, and chocolate are popular mix-in ingredients, either all together or as stand-alone fillings.

This Tunisian version uses chemical leavening like baking powder, while the equally well-known Libyan version is yeast-risen and more bread-like. Because of its close proximity, these cookies are likely related to Moroccan *fekkas* (recipe, page 138), another fruit-stuffed sweet bread now made with chemical leavening, but that like *cantucci* (recipe, page 112), bakes its slices a second time to crisp them up and make the cookies last longer.

In a medium bowl, whisk together the flour, baking powder, ground anise, sesame seeds, and salt.

In a large bowl, whisk together the sugar, oil, vanilla, orange blossom water, and eggs until smooth. Add the dry ingredients and stir until a dough forms and there are no dry patches of flour remaining. Knead the dough briefly to form a smooth ball. Halve the dough, wrap each half in plastic wrap (cling film), and refrigerate for 1 hour.

Position racks in the top and bottom thirds of the oven and preheat the oven to 325°F (160°C/Gas Mark 3). Line two large baking sheets with parchment paper.

In a medium bowl, mix together the raisins, nuts, and chocolate.

Unwrap one piece of dough and, working on a sheet of parchment paper, shape the dough into a rectangle roughly 12 × 5 inches (30 × 13 cm). Sprinkle half the fruit-and-nut mixture over the dough and then, starting from one long side, use the paper to aid in rolling the dough up jelly roll (Swiss roll) style, resting it seam-side down. Transfer the dough log to a prepared baking sheet and flatten it with the palm of your hand until about ½ inch (13 mm) thick. Repeat with the second piece of dough, remaining fruit-and-nut mixture, and second baking sheet.

Brush each loaf with some of the egg wash and then sprinkle with sesame seeds.

Bake until golden brown all over and a toothpick inserted in the center of each loaf comes out with no raw batter attached, 30–35 minutes, switching racks and rotating the baking sheets front to back halfway through.

Transfer the baking sheets to wire racks and let the loaves cool completely on the pans. Cut the loaves into slices ½ inch (13 mm) thick to serve.

Stuffed Maghrebi Loaf Cookies with Fruit, Nuts, and Chocolate

the caribbean, central america & south america

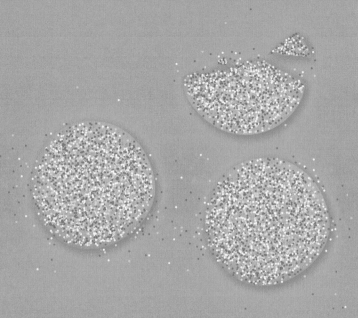

Spain's influence on Latin America is evident in its cookies. Pork lard is the predominant fat used in making the favored crumbly shortbread-like cookies that descend from *polvorones*. But those descendants adapted to native starches and flavors well, utilizing coconut, cornstarch (cornflour), and ground yuca (cassava) to form the base of their sweets, while fruits like lime and guava, and spices like cinnamon, add intense florality. The native raw sugars of the region also add sweetness to cookies where honey or granulated white sugar wasn't traditionally common.

Lime Sugar Cookies
Torticas de Morón

Preparation time: 40 minutes, plus
at least 30 minutes chilling time
Cooking time: 20 minutes
Makes: About 24 cookies

2¼ cups (315 g) all-purpose
(plain) flour
1 teaspoon baking powder
1 teaspoon fine sea salt
1 cup (225 g) cold-rendered leaf lard
or vegetable shortening
1 cup (200 g) white US granulated (UK
caster) sugar, plus more for sprinkling
Finely grated zest of 3 limes
1 egg
1 teaspoon pure vanilla extract

A descendant of Spanish *polvorones* (recipe, page 97), *torticas de morón* are Cuba's answer to that simple buttery cookie. While modern versions use butter or vegetable shortening, which are more widely available, traditional recipes use rendered pork lard. If possible, use pork lard, which is widely available now, to maintain the authenticity of the cookie.

Though these cookies may originally have been shortbread-like, their texture evolved into one with a slightly chewy center and crisp edges. Some Cuban bakers add a piece of guava paste to the center of the dough slices, thumbprint-cookie style, before baking. Lime zest adds tropical freshness and a distinctive Cuban aroma to these simple treats, finished with a sprinkling of sugar on top to add more texture to contrast the rich dough.

In a medium bowl, whisk together the flour, baking powder, and salt.

In a large bowl, with a hand mixer, beat the lard, sugar, and lime zest on medium speed until smooth and fluffy, about 3 minutes. Add the egg and vanilla and beat until incorporated. Add the dry ingredients and beat on low speed until the dough comes together.

Scrape the dough onto a sheet of parchment paper. Form the dough into a vague cylinder, then shape the dough into a log 1¾ inches (4.5 cm) in diameter and wrap tightly (see page 14). Transfer the log to the refrigerator to firm up for at least 30 minutes.

Position racks in the top and bottom thirds of the oven and preheat the oven to 350°F (180°C/Gas Mark 4). Line two large baking sheets with parchment paper.

Unwrap the dough log and cut the dough into slices ½ inch (13 mm) thick. Transfer the slices to the prepared baking sheets, arranging them at least 2 inches (5 cm) apart. Dampen a pastry brush with water and lightly brush the tops of the cookies. Sprinkle each cookie with a pinch of sugar.

Bake until golden brown at the edges and set, about 20 minutes, switching racks and rotating the baking sheets front to back halfway through.

Transfer the baking sheets to wire racks. Let the cookies cool on the pans for 1 minute, then transfer them to the racks to cool completely.

Cassava Shortbread Cookies

Bonbon Amidon

Preparation time: 1 hour 10 minutes
Cooking time: 20 minutes
Makes: About 36 cookies

2 cups (260 g) cassava flour
1 teaspoon baking powder
½ teaspoon fine sea salt
1 stick (4 oz/115 g) unsalted
  butter, softened
1 cup (135 g) powdered (icing) sugar
1 teaspoon pure vanilla extract
½ teaspoon finely grated lemon zest

Though it has a French name, the influences on this Haitian cookie are more likely to be a mix of both French and Spanish, owing to the nation's history of occupation and influences. *Bonbon amidon* are dry shortbread-like cookies that resemble Spanish *polvorones* (recipe, page 97) and French *sablés Breton* (recipe, page 258). Where those two cookies are made with all-purpose (plain) wheat flour and the focus is on their use of pork lard or butter, respectively, the distinguishing factor of *bonbon amidon* is its use of a flour made from the yuca (cassava) root, also called manioc, which is essential to the Haitian diet.

While many recipes list tapioca starch as an ingredient, tapioca starch (or flour) and cassava flour are different. Both are derived from the yuca root, but cassava flour is made from the ground whole pulp of the root, while tapioca is the starch that comes out of the pulp when washed in water (think of the difference between cornmeal and cornstarch/cornflour). Cassava flour has a nuttier flavor when baked and acts differently in the cookie, so do not use tapioca starch as a substitute here. Look for cassava flour online or in Caribbean or Latin grocery stores. Just take care to read the fine print on the label, as some packages are labeled as cassava flour or manioc flour, but they are actually tapioca starch.

Position racks in the top and bottom thirds of the oven and preheat the oven to 350°F (180°C/Gas Mark 4). Line two large baking sheets with parchment paper.

In a medium bowl, whisk together the cassava flour, baking powder, and salt.

In a large bowl, with a hand mixer, combine the butter, sugar, vanilla, and lemon zest and beat on medium speed until light and fluffy, 2–3 minutes. Add the dry ingredients and stir until a dough forms and there are no dry patches of flour remaining.

Scrape the dough onto a lightly floured work surface and use a rolling pin to flatten the dough to ½ inch (13 mm) thick. Using a 2-inch (5 cm) round cutter, cut out cookies and transfer them to the prepared baking sheets, spaced 1 inch (2.5 cm) apart. Reroll the dough and cut out more cookies.

Bake until light golden brown at the edges and dry to the touch in the center, about 20 minutes, switching racks and rotating the baking sheets front to back halfway through.

Transfer the baking sheets to wire racks. Let the cookies cool on the pans for 1 minute, then transfer them to the racks to cool completely.

Guava and Almond Thumbprint Cookies

Mantecaditos

Preparation time: 40 minutes
Cooking time: 20 minutes
Makes: About 24 cookies

⅔ cup (130 g) white US granulated
(UK caster) sugar
1 stick (4 oz/115 g) unsalted butter,
softened
½ cup (115 g) cold-rendered leaf lard
or vegetable shortening, softened
2 egg yolks
1¼ teaspoons pure almond extract
½ teaspoon pure vanilla extract
¾ teaspoon fine sea salt
2¼ cups (315 g) all-purpose
(plain) flour
Decorations/fillings: Guava paste or
jam, maraschino cherries, nonpareils
or sprinkles, powdered (icing) sugar

Popular in Puerto Rico and the Dominican Republic, these simple shortbread cookies are typically made with lard or shortening, either exclusively or mixed with butter, and flavored with almond extract. A descendant of Spanish *mantecados* and *polvorones* (recipe, page 97), they are crumbly shortbread cookies that are typically formed thumbprint-cookie style and filled with guava jam, but they can also be topped with sprinkles, powdered (icing) sugar, or a maraschino cherry.

The lard or shortening in the recipe is traditional for these cookies because their name classifies them as part of a group of cookies—also with the name *mantecados*—that are made with pork lard (read more in Polvorones, page 96). You can substitute the amount with all butter, but you will lose some of the crumbly texture and unique flavor. As to the suggested fillings and decorations here, don't limit yourself to just one: Do as many home bakers do and use all of them to create a diverse assortment of these tiny, rich cookies.

Position racks in the top and bottom thirds of the oven and preheat the oven to 350°F (180°C/Gas Mark 4). Line two large baking sheets with parchment paper.

In a large bowl, with a hand mixer, beat the white US granulated (UK caster) sugar, butter, and lard on medium speed until light and fluffy, 2–3 minutes. Add the egg yolks, almond extract, vanilla, and salt and beat until combined. Add the flour and stir until a dough forms and there are no dry patches of flour remaining.

Using a 1-ounce (2-tablespoon) ice cream scoop, portion the dough and roll into balls. Arrange them on the prepared baking sheets spaced at least 2 inches (5 cm) apart.

If making thumbprint-style cookies, press the center of each dough ball with the tip of your index finger to create a divot and then fill it with a tile of guava paste ½ inch (13 mm) square and ¼ inch (6 mm) thick, or about ½ teaspoon guava jam.

For all other styles, use the palm of your hand to gently flatten each dough ball into a disc. If using maraschino cherries, blot dry ½ cherry on a paper towel before placing it in the center of each disc. If using nonpareils or sprinkles, spread some out on a plate and dip one side of each disc in the sprinkles to coat. Return it to the baking sheet sprinkle-side up.

Bake until golden brown at the edges and dry to the touch in the center, 18–20 minutes, switching racks and rotating the baking sheets front to back halfway through.

Transfer the baking sheets to wire racks. Let the cookies cool on the pans for 1 minute, then transfer them to the racks to cool completely.

If using powdered (icing) sugar, liberally dust the cooled cookies with some sugar before serving.

Guava and Almond Thumbprint Cookies

Coconut and Ginger Cookies

Coconetes / Conconetes Dominicanos

Preparation time: 35 minutes
Cooking time: 25 minutes
Makes: About 24 cookies

3 cups (420 g) all-purpose (plain) flour
1½ teaspoons baking powder
1 teaspoon ground cinnamon
1 teaspoon freshly grated nutmeg
½ teaspoon fine sea salt
¼ teaspoon baking soda
  (bicarbonate of soda)
1 stick (4 oz/115 g) unsalted butter,
  softened
1¼ cups (280 g) packed light
  brown sugar
¼ cup (85 g) honey
1 tablespoon finely grated fresh ginger
2 eggs
3 cups (300 g) finely grated coconut,
  fresh (from 1 mature coconut)
  or thawed frozen

Typically found in grocery and corner stores across the Dominican Republic, these spiced coconut cookies get their characteristic hit of heat not just from spices like cinnamon and nutmeg, but from a grating of fresh ginger. The combination of the fresh ginger and coconut is what makes them so distinct from other coconut-flavored cookies. And though they may seem like coconut macaroons (recipe, page 177), they contain all-purpose (plain) flour, creating a texture between a chewy macaroon and tender American sugar cookie (recipe, page 348).

The coconut used in the cookies is freshly grated, typically right before mixing into the dough. If you don't want to grate your own coconut or cannot find it, buy frozen grated coconut and let it thaw completely before using. Similar to an American-style oatmeal cookie, the large amount of coconut bakes up crisp at the edges and chewy in the center.

Position racks in the top and bottom thirds of the oven and preheat the oven to 350°F (180°C/Gas Mark 4). Line two large baking sheets with parchment paper.

In a medium bowl, whisk together the flour, baking powder, cinnamon, nutmeg, salt, and baking soda (bicarb).

In a large bowl, with a hand mixer, combine the butter, sugar, honey, and ginger and beat on medium speed until light and fluffy, 2–3 minutes. Add the eggs, one at a time, beating well after each addition. Add the flour mixture and grated coconut and stir until a dough forms and there are no dry patches of flour remaining.

Using a 1-ounce (2-tablespoon) ice cream scoop, portion the dough and roll into balls. Arrange them on the prepared baking sheets, spaced at least 2 inches (5 cm) apart.

Bake until golden brown all over and dry to the touch in the center, 20–25 minutes, switching racks and rotating the baking sheets front to back halfway through.

Transfer the baking sheets to wire racks. Let the cookies cool on the pans for 1 minute, then transfer them to the racks to cool completely.

Fried Ginger Spice Cookies

Kurma

Preparation time: 50 minutes,
  plus standing time
Cooking time: 40 minutes
Makes: About 72 cookies

Vegetable oil, for frying

For the dough:
2 cups (280 g) all-purpose (plain) flour
½ teaspoon fine sea salt
½ teaspoon ground ginger
¼ teaspoon ground cinnamon
6 tablespoons (3 oz/85 g) cold
  unsalted butter, diced
⅓ cup (2½ fl oz/80 ml) cold water

For the syrup:
½ cup (4 fl oz/120 ml) water
1 cinnamon stick
2-inch (5 cm) piece fresh ginger,
  peeled and thinly sliced crosswise
1 cup (200 g) white US granulated
  (UK caster) sugar

Though Trinidad and Tobago is a country in the southernmost part of the Caribbean, a majority of its population are descendants of Indians, first brought to the country in the mid-nineteenth century by the British during colonial rule to work as indentured servants in plantations. That legacy is reflected in these cookies, often called "Trini *kurma*," which are descended from Indian *shankarpali*, a sweet served at Diwali, made from fried dough coated in a crystallized sugar syrup. In nearby Guyana, a similar treat is called *mithai*.

The dough is made in the same manner as American pie dough (shortcrust pastry), where butter is cut into flour, then mixed with cold water, to create cold pockets of fat in the flour. Once those pockets expand in the hot oil of the fryer, the layers of dough separate, creating a flaky texture in the *kurma*. The dough strips are then coated in a sugar syrup flavored with cinnamon and fresh ginger that crystallizes around the strips, coating them in an opaque shellac. Cooking the syrup requires the use of a candy/deep-fry thermometer to attain the proper temperature that ensures the crystallization of the sugar.

Line a large baking sheet with paper towels. Pour enough oil into a medium saucepan to come 2 inches (5 cm) up the sides of the pan. Attach a candy/deep-fry thermometer to the side of the pan.

Make the dough: In a medium bowl, whisk together the flour, salt, ground ginger, and ground cinnamon. Add the butter and use your fingers to press and rub the butter into the flour until it breaks down into pea-size crumbles. Pour in the water and stir the mixture with a fork until it comes together into a dough with no dry patches of flour remaining; do not knead the dough any longer than you need to get it to fully come together.

Scrape the dough onto a lightly floured work surface and use a lightly floured rolling pin to flatten to ¼ inch (6 mm) thick. Using a pizza cutter or a chef's knife, cut the dough into strips ½ inch (13 mm) wide. Then cut each strip on the diagonal into diamonds 2 inches (5 cm) long.

Heat the oil in the saucepan until it reaches 350°F (177°C) on the thermometer. Maintaining the oil temperature and working in batches of 12 pieces, fry the dough strips, flipping them with a slotted spoon occasionally, until golden brown and cooked through, about 4 minutes. Using the slotted spoon, lift the strips from the oil and transfer them to the paper towels to drain; repeat frying the remaining dough strips.

Once done, remove the thermometer and let the oil cool to room temperature. Wash and dry the thermometer thoroughly. Gently place all the fried cookies in a large heatproof bowl; discard the paper towels but reserve the baking sheet. Place two large heatproof spoons, such as wood or silicone, next to the bowl.

Make the syrup: In a small saucepan, combine the water, cinnamon stick, and fresh ginger slices. Bring to a boil over high heat, then slowly pour in the sugar and gently swirl the pan until all the sugar dissolves. Attach the candy/deep-fry thermometer to the side of the saucepan and let the syrup cook, undisturbed, until it reaches 235°F (113°C) on the thermometer, which can take 8–15 minutes depending on the power of your stove. Place a tall container of hot water nearby.

When ready, remove the saucepan from the heat. Carefully remove the thermometer from the side of the pan and place it in the container of hot water; this allows the thermometer to cool down safely and dissolves the syrup stuck to it. Gently pour the boiling syrup over the fried cookies and then immediately use the heatproof spoons to toss the cookies repeatedly until the syrup crystallizes and coats the strips in an opaque sugar glaze.

Transfer the cookies to the reserved baking sheet, separating any that have stuck together. Let the cookies cool completely before serving.

Fried Ginger Spice Cookies (p.153)

Cinnamon Shortbreads (p.156)

Cinnamon Shortbreads
Polvorones de Canela

DF

Preparation time: 55 minutes,
 plus cooling time
Cooking time: 30 minutes
Makes: About 36 cookies

2 cups (280 g) all-purpose (plain) flour
2 Mexican cinnamon (canela) sticks
 or 2 teaspoons ground canela
 or cinnamon
1 cup (200 g) white US granulated
 (UK caster) sugar
1 cup (135 g) powdered (icing) sugar
⅔ cup (150 g) cold-rendered leaf lard
 or unsalted butter, softened
1 teaspoon pure vanilla extract,
 preferably Mexican
½ teaspoon fine sea salt

These tiny, crumbly cinnamon-packed cookies may well be the most ubiquitous cookie in Mexico. A clear descendant of Spanish *polvorones* (recipe, page 97) in both name and style, these *polvorones de canela* are a distinct Mexican iteration, swapping the usual nuts (though many modern recipes do include them) for the country's prized, softer form of cinnamon. As with *salpores de arroz* (recipe, page 163), freshly ground *canela* makes a huge difference in these cookies since it is the chief flavoring agent. A well-known offshoot of *polvorones de canela* are cookies called *hojarascas*.

Being a *polvorón* offspring, lard makes an appearance in these cookies, though you can certainly use butter. What's most unique about these *polvorones* is that the flour is first baked in the oven before combining with the lard, sugar, and *canela*. This enhances the final cookie's melt-in-your-mouth quality and adds a little extra toastiness. Note that when bringing the dough together, it is intentionally very crumbly, so be patient and diligent (and very careful) when rolling and cutting the fat discs of dough, to keep them together throughout the rest of the process. And while you could coat these cookies in powdered (icing) sugar, it's more common to find them coated in cinnamon-sugar, as is done here.

Preheat the oven to 350°F (180°C/Gas Mark 4). Line a large baking sheet with parchment paper.

Spread the flour out on the parchment paper and bake the flour, stirring occasionally to ensure it toasts evenly, until starting to brown at the edges and it smells nutty, 5–8 minutes.

Remove the baking sheet from the oven and let the flour cool completely on the paper. Using the paper like a sling, lift the flour off the baking sheet and transfer it to a medium bowl. Return the paper to the baking sheet and set aside until ready to use.

In a spice grinder, process 1 stick of canela until very finely ground. Add the ground canela (1 teaspoon of preground if using) to the toasted flour and whisk to combine. Process the second stick of canela until very finely ground and transfer it to a small bowl. Add the white US granulated (UK caster) sugar to the bowl and stir to combine (or add the remaining 1 teaspoon preground canela). Set this cinnamon-sugar aside until ready to use.

In a large bowl, with a hand mixer, combine the powdered (icing) sugar, lard, vanilla, and salt and beat on medium speed until light and fluffy, 2–3 minutes. Add the toasted flour and stir until a dough forms and there are no dry patches of flour remaining. You may need to switch to your hands and lightly knead the dough; it is ready when you can pick up a handful, make a fist, and the dough in your hand just holds together.

Scrape the dough out onto a lightly floured work surface and use your hands to pat the dough into a disc that's roughly ¾ inch (2 cm) thick; if you like, gently roll a rolling pin over the disc to even out the surface. Using a 1½-inch (4 cm) round cutter, stamp out cookies and use an offset or thin metal spatula to carefully transfer the rounds to the prepared baking sheet, spacing them as close as ½ inch (13 mm) apart (the cookies will not spread). Reroll scraps and continue cutting out rounds.

Bake until golden brown at the edges and just dry to the touch in the center, 18–20 minutes, rotating the baking sheet front to back halfway through.

Transfer the baking sheet to wire racks and let the cookies rest on the pan for 5 minutes. While the cookies are still warm, carefully lift one and gently roll it in the bowl of cinnamon-sugar until completely coated. Return the coated cookie to its place on the baking sheet and continue coating the remaining cookies. Let them cool completely.

Piloncillo-Stuffed Cookies
Coyotas

Preparation time: 55 minutes,
  plus chilling time
Cooking time: 25 minutes
Makes: About 6 large cookies

12 oz (340 g) piloncillo or 1½ cups
  packed dark muscovado sugar
¼ cup (2 fl oz/60 ml) plus 2
  tablespoons water
2½ cups (350 g) plus 1 tablespoon
  all-purpose (plain) flour
1 teaspoon baking powder
1 teaspoon fine sea salt
1 cup (225 g) cold-rendered leaf lard
  or vegetable shortening, chilled
  and cut into ½-inch (13 mm) pieces
Egg wash: 1 egg whisked with 1
  tablespoon water
White US granulated (UK caster)
  sugar, for sprinkling (optional)

The origin of these *piloncillo*-stuffed cookies from Mexico can more or less be pinpointed to one specific area, the neighborhood of Villa de Seris in Hermosillo, a city in the state of Sonora. No one knows why or how the cookies came about, but it's easy to draw comparisons to their empanada-like shape and see how sweet versions of that dish would have evolved. What's special about these cookies is their use of *piloncillo*, the raw brown sugar often used in Mexican sweets. The sugar is first melted into a syrup that flavors the dough, then more is crushed and used as a filling for two very thin, very large rounds of dough.

The name is a nickname for young girls of mixed Indigenous and Spanish heritage who sold the cookies when they first started being made in the 1950s. Although the term can be seen by some as problematic because it came from Spanish colonizers, it is a name that—like the Dutch *jodenkoeken* (recipe, page 335)—is used pridefully in Mexico, which consists of a population largely and proudly mestizo (of mixed Indigenous and European heritages). And although it seems the original *coyotas* sold then were made to be around 6 inches (15 cm) in diameter, this recipe makes cookies that are 4 inches (10 cm) in diameter to be more manageable and in line with modern-day recipes.

Using a serrated knife, or the large holes of box grater, finely chop or grate the piloncillo.

Transfer half the piloncillo (or ¾ cup/170 g of the muscovado) to a small saucepan, add the water, and bring to a boil over high heat, stirring to dissolve the piloncillo completely. Once the syrup boils, remove the pan from the heat and let the syrup cool completely.

Transfer the remaining piloncillo to a small bowl. Add 1 tablespoon of the flour and toss to coat the sugar in the flour (if using muscovado, simply stir to combine). Set the filling aside until ready to use.

In a large bowl, whisk together the remaining 2½ cups (350 g) flour, the baking powder, and salt. Add the lard and use your fingertips to rub the lard into the flour until the fat breaks down into pea-size crumbles. Pour in the cooled sugar syrup and stir the mixture with a fork until it comes together into a solid dough, lightly kneading only as much as needed to no longer see any dry patches of flour in the bowl. Shape the dough into a ball, wrap in plastic wrap (cling film), and refrigerate for at least 1 hour or up to 2 days.

Position racks in the top and bottom thirds of the oven and preheat the oven to 350°F (180°C/Gas Mark 4). Line two large baking sheets with parchment paper.

Using a slightly heaped 1½-ounce (3-tablespoon) ice cream scoop, portion the dough and roll into balls. Using a tortilla press lined with plastic wrap, flatten half the dough balls into 4-inch (10 cm) rounds. Gently peel the round off the plastic wrap and transfer the rounds to the prepared baking sheets, spaced 1 inch (2.5 cm) apart. (Alternatively, working on a lightly floured work surface, roll out the dough with a rolling pin to ⅛ inch/3 mm thick; use a 3- or 4-inch/7.5 or 10 cm round cutter to cut out cookies, rerolling the scraps to make more cookies.)

Spoon 2 tablespoons of the piloncillo filling into the center of each round, spreading it out to within ½ inch (13 mm) of the edge of the dough. Flatten the remaining dough balls in the same manner, placing one on top of each filling-topped dough round. Using a fork, crimp the edges of each filled dough round.

Using a pastry brush, lightly coat the top of each round with some of the egg wash and then sprinkle it with a pinch of white US granulated (UK caster) sugar, if using. Prick the top of each cookie three or four times with the tines of the fork.

Bake until golden brown all over (some of the piloncillo filling may bubble out of the holes in the top of the cookie), 16–18 minutes, switching racks and rotating the baking sheets front to back halfway through.

Transfer the baking sheets to wire racks. Let the cookies cool on the pans for 1 minute, then transfer them to the racks to cool completely.

Rainbow Sprinkle-Covered Cookies
Galletas de Grageas

Preparation time: 15 minutes,
 plus 1 hour chilling time
Cooking time: 15 minutes
Makes: About 36 cookies

2 cups (280 g) all-purpose (plain) flour
1½ teaspoons baking powder
¾ teaspoon fine sea salt
¾ cup (150 g) white US granulated
 (UK caster) sugar
½ cup (115 g) cold-rendered leaf lard
 or vegetable shortening, softened
4 tablespoons (2 oz/55 g) unsalted
 butter, softened
1 teaspoon pure vanilla extract,
 preferably Mexican
2 eggs, 1 whole and 1 separated
1 tablespoon water
½ cup (120 g) rainbow-colored
 nonpareils (hundreds & thousands)
 or small dragées

These festively colored *galletas de grageas* are a party in cookie form. More in the American, chewy sugar cookie vein than the crumbly *polvorón*-style, these cookies are crusted with nonpareils (hundreds & thousands), the smallest kind of sprinkle-type decoration you can find. The use of the nonpareils most likely evolved from the practice of sprinkling powdered (icing) or other sugar on top of cookies for extra sweetness. When nonpareils and sprinkles were invented, the colors they added to the sweetness were a natural next step.

The nonpareils used here are tiny balls that you can find in single colors, but these *galletas* are traditionally made with the "rainbow" mix of all colors, which you can find in any grocery store. You can also use regular sprinkles instead, though the tiny, round nature of the nonpareils sets apart these delightful cookies.

Position racks in the top and bottom thirds of the oven and preheat the oven to 350°F (180°C/Gas Mark 4). Line two large baking sheets with parchment paper.

In a medium bowl, whisk together the flour, baking powder, and salt.

In a large bowl, with a hand mixer, combine the sugar, lard, butter, and vanilla and beat on medium speed until light and fluffy, 2–3 minutes. Add the whole egg, beat until smooth, then add the egg yolk to the bowl, beating until smooth. Add the flour mixture to the bowl and stir until a dough forms and there are no dry patches of flour remaining. Cover the bowl with plastic wrap (cling film) and refrigerate the dough for 30 minutes to firm.

Scrape the dough onto a lightly floured work surface and use a rolling pin to flatten the dough to ¼ inch (6 mm) thick. Using a 2½-inch (6.5 cm) round cutter, cut out cookies and transfer them to the prepared baking sheets, spaced 2 inches (5 cm) apart. Reroll the dough and cut out more cookies. Place the baking sheets in the refrigerator for 30 minutes to firm the dough rounds.

Meanwhile, make an egg wash by whisking the remaining egg white with the water until smooth. Place the nonpareils in a shallow dish or large plate.

Using a pastry brush, brush some of the egg wash over the top of a dough round and place the round, brushed-side down, in the nonpareils to completely encrust that side. Invert the cookie and return it to its spot on the baking sheet. Repeat with the remaining dough rounds.

Bake until light golden brown at the edges and just set in the center, 12–15 minutes, switching racks and rotating the baking sheets front to back halfway through.

Transfer the baking sheets to wire racks. Let the cookies cool on the pans for 1 minute, then transfer them to the racks to cool completely.

Rainbow Sprinkle-Covered Cookies

Pig-Shaped Piloncillo Cookies

Marranitos / Cochinitos / Galletas de Puerquito

 DF (V)

Preparation time: 30 minutes,
 plus chilling time
Cooking time: 40 minutes
Makes: About 18 cookies

For the syrup:
8 oz (225 g) piloncillo or 1 cup
 packed dark muscovado sugar
1 cup (8 fl oz/250 ml) water
½ teaspoon anise seeds
3 whole cloves
1 cinnamon stick, preferably
 Mexican canela

For the dough:
4 cups (560 g) all-purpose (plain) flour
1¼ teaspoons baking powder
1 teaspoon fine sea salt
¾ teaspoon baking soda
 (bicarbonate of soda)
¾ cup (170 g) cold-rendered leaf lard
 or vegetable shortening, chilled
 and cut into ½-inch (13 mm) cubes
2 eggs, lightly beaten
1 teaspoon pure vanilla extract,
 preferably Mexican
Egg wash: 1 egg whisked with
 1 tablespoon water

These gingerbread-style cookies are a classic addition to a group of Mexican baked goods called *pan dulce* ("sweet breads"). And this makes sense because, while they're considered cookies, their texture is more bready and less chewy than you'd expect, placing them closer to Old World European gingerbread (see page 328) than what we consider the modern equivalents. It's not really clear why they are pig-shaped, but with every country's penchant for cutting out their unique gingerbread-style cookies in shapes that are culturally relevant within their borders, it's easy to see how the pig, inarguably one of the most important animals in the country's cuisine, fits into Mexico's cookie-making tradition.

Many European gingerbreads use regionally specific brown sugar syrups to sweeten their cookies, and Mexico is no exception, making a syrup out of *piloncillo* to give bittersweetness and color to these quirky cut-outs. And while European gingerbreads utilize several spices to lend aroma to the dough, these *marranitos* get their aroma from Mexican cinnamon (*canela*), cloves, and sometimes anise seeds. Some recipes steep the whole spices in the *piloncillo* syrup, while others opt for ground spices mixed directly in the dough. This recipe goes the former route, imbuing the syrup base with a heady aroma that perfectly accents the rustic sugar highlighted in these whimsical treats.

Make the syrup: Working with a serrated knife, roughly chop the piloncillo or grate on the large holes of a box grater. Transfer the piloncillo (or muscovado) to a small saucepan. Add the water, anise, cloves, and cinnamon and bring to a boil over high heat, stirring to dissolve the piloncillo completely. Once the syrup boils, reduce the heat to maintain a gentle simmer and cook until the syrup is reduced by half, about 15 minutes. Remove the pan from the heat and let the syrup cool completely.

Make the dough: In a large bowl, whisk together the flour, baking powder, salt, and baking soda (bicarb). Add the lard and use your fingertips to rub the lard into the flour until the fat breaks down into pea-size crumbles. Pour the cooled piloncillo syrup through a fine sieve into the flour and lard mixture (discard the whole spices). Add the eggs and vanilla and stir the mixture with a fork until it comes together into a solid dough, lightly kneading only as much as needed to no longer see any dry patches of flour in the bowl. Shape the dough into a ball, wrap in plastic wrap (cling film), and refrigerate for at least 1 hour or up to 2 days.

Position racks in the top and bottom thirds of the oven and preheat the oven to 350°F (180°C/Gas Mark 4). Line two large baking sheets with parchment paper.

Working on a lightly floured work surface, roll out the dough with a rolling pin to ¼ inch (6 mm) thick. Using a roughly 4-inch (10 cm) pig-shaped cutter, cut out cookies. Reroll the scraps to cut out more. Arrange the cut-outs on the prepared baking sheets, spaced 1 inch (2.5 cm) apart. Using a pastry brush, lightly coat the top of each cut-out with some of the egg wash.

Bake until the edges of each cookie are more deeply browned than the rest of the dough and the cookies are dry to the touch in the center, 15–20 minutes, switching racks and rotating the baking sheets front to back halfway through.

Transfer the baking sheets to wire racks. Let the cookies cool on the pans for 1 minute, then transfer them to the racks to cool completely.

Pig-Shaped Piloncillo Cookies

Sesame-Topped "Tortilla" Cookies
Champurradas

Preparation time: 40 minutes
Cooking time: 20 minutes
Makes: About 12 cookies

2 cups (280 g) all-purpose (plain) flour
1 cup (130 g) masa harina
2 teaspoons baking powder
1¼ teaspoons fine sea salt
8 oz (225 g) piloncillo, finely grated,
  or 1 cup packed dark muscovado sugar
2 sticks (8 oz/225 g) unsalted
  butter, softened
2 eggs
2 tablespoons whole milk
1 tablespoon pure vanilla extract,
  preferably Mexican
Egg wash: 1 egg white beaten
  with 1 tablespoon whole milk
¼ cup (35 g) toasted sesame seeds

These thin cookies the size of a corn tortilla are a specialty of Guatemala and often served with other *pan dulce* ("sweet breads") at breakfast time. Though they could be considered a lightly sweetened flatbread in some contexts, their use of baking powder and a substantial amount of sugar make them cookies. Though modern recipes use all-purpose (plain) flour and sugar, many traditional recipes call for masa harina (nixtamalized corn/maize flour, the same flour used to make tortillas and tamales) and grated *piloncillo*, the raw brown sugar popular in Latin American cooking that adds a pleasant nutty bitterness to the dough.

The cookies can be baked into squat rounds like most other cookies, but flattening them in a tortilla press, as many bakers do, gives them more character and also helps explain how these cookies possibly evolved from tortilla-making to be the large, thin rounds they are today. The tops are brushed with egg white and sprinkled with sesame seeds, which bake up toasty and fragrant, a wonderful complement to the robust corn and *piloncillo* flavors in these unique treats.

Position racks in the top and bottom thirds of the oven and preheat the oven to 350°F (180°C/Gas Mark 4). Line two large baking sheets with parchment paper.

In a medium bowl, whisk together the flour, masa harina, baking powder, and salt.

In a large bowl, with a hand mixer, beat the piloncillo and butter on medium speed until light and fluffy, about 3 minutes. Add the whole eggs, one at a time, beating until smooth after each addition. Add the milk and vanilla and beat until combined. Add the dry ingredients and stir until a dough forms and there are no dry patches of flour remaining.

Using a slightly heaped 2-ounce (4-tablespoon) ice cream scoop, portion the dough and roll into balls. Using a tortilla press lined with plastic wrap (cling film), flatten each dough ball into a 4-inch (10 cm) round. Gently peel the round off the plastic wrap and transfer to the prepared baking sheets, spaced 1 inch (2.5 cm) apart. (Alternatively, working on a lightly floured work surface, roll out the dough with a rolling pin to ¼ inch/6 mm thick; use a 3- to 4-inch (7.5 to 10 cm) round cutter to cut out cookies, rerolling the scraps to make more cookies.)

Using a pastry brush, lightly coat the top of each round with some of the egg wash and then sprinkle it with a pinch of sesame seeds.

Bake until golden brown all over and dry to the touch in the center, 15–20 minutes, switching racks and rotating the baking sheets front to back halfway through.

Transfer the baking sheets to wire racks. Let the cookies cool on the pans for 1 minute, then transfer them to the racks to cool completely.

Cinnamon Rice Flour Cookies

Salpores de Arroz

Preparation time: 40 minutes
Cooking time: 20 minutes
Makes: About 18 cookies

2 cups (320 g) white rice flour
1 teaspoon baking powder
¾ teaspoon fine sea salt
1 Mexican cinnamon (canela)
  stick or 1 teaspoon ground canela
  or cinnamon
½ cup (115 g) cold-rendered leaf
  lard or unsalted butter, softened
½ cup (100 g) white US granulated
  (UK caster) sugar
1 teaspoon pure vanilla extract,
  preferably Mexican
1 egg
Red or pink sanding sugar or more
  white sugar, for sprinkling (optional)

As in most countries in Central America, rice is an important part of the national diet of El Salvador, so much so that a variation of its iconic pupusas (griddled flatbreads) uses dough made from rice flour. It's no surprise then that rice is also used in their desserts: Besides the ubiquitous rice pudding, there is also a cake called *quesadilla Salvadoreña*, which is a *pan dulce*—a lightly sweetened pastry often eaten for breakfast—made with rice flour and a salty, hard cheese. Rice flour is also used in these *salpores de arroz*, El Salvador's answer to Spain's *polvorones* (recipe, page 97) and nearby neighbor Mexico's *polvorones de canela* (recipe, page 156). As such, lard is present in recipes for these crumbly, shortbread-like cookies.

You can use preground cinnamon for this recipe if you like, but traditional recipes call for freshly grinding *canela*, aka Mexican cinnamon, which is softer than the hard sticks more commonly found in grocery stores. *Canela* is easily found in Mexican or Latin grocery stores and online. Many recipes call for decorating the *salpores de arroz* with red or pink sanding sugar, but you can also use more sugar or leave them plain. Use your middle three fingers to indent the top of the cookies, a common marker that sets these cookies apart from their Spanish ancestor.

- -

Position racks in the top and bottom thirds of the oven and preheat the oven to 350°F (180°C/Gas Mark 4). Line two large baking sheets with parchment paper.

In a medium bowl, whisk together the rice flour, baking powder, and salt. Using a spice grinder, process the stick of canela until very finely ground. Add the ground canela to the other dry ingredients and whisk to combine.

In a large bowl, with a hand mixer, combine the lard, white US granulated (UK caster) sugar, and vanilla and beat on medium speed until light and fluffy, 2–3 minutes. Add the egg and beat until smooth. Add the flour mixture and stir until a dough forms and there are no dry patches of flour remaining.

Using a 1-ounce (2-tablespoon) ice cream scoop, portion the dough and shape into egg-shaped ovals. Arrange the ovals on the prepared baking sheets, spaced 1 inch (2.5 cm) apart. Position the tips of your index, middle, and ring finger—slightly spread apart—lengthwise over one oval and gently press down to indent the top. Repeat with the rest of the ovals. If you like, sprinkle the tops of each oval with sanding sugar or more white sugar.

Bake until golden brown at the edges and dry to the touch in the center, about 20 minutes, switching racks and rotating the baking sheets front to back halfway through.

Transfer the baking sheets to wire racks. Let the cookies cool on the pans for 1 minute, then transfer them to the racks to cool completely.

Raw Sugars

Though processed white cane sugar is so commonplace today, that wasn't always the case. Before cane sugar was processed to remove its molasses—via a process called centrifugation, where the molasses is literally spun off the grains of sugar in a large, washing machine-like spinner—the raw cane juice was, and still is, boiled down to drive off excess moisture, much like the maple syrup process. Once the syrup reaches a certain temperature, it can be agitated to make crystals or granules of sugar.

If not separated from the molasses and other minerals, the grains clump together into a rock-hard mass. This is what many countries, particularly in Latin America and India, refer to as *piloncillo, panela, rapadura*, or jaggery, respectively. These "raw" sugars are usually formed into cones, discs, or hemispheres that the user then breaks off into chunks, melts, or grates as needed. In this case, the word "raw" means not processed to remove its molasses.

Even muscovado sugar is this type of sugar, though it is often broken apart and granulated so it can be scooped like sand. American brown sugars, while looking similar, are made by removing the molasses from the sugar and then adding back a prescribed amount to gain "light," "golden," or "dark" shades and levels of molasses flavor.

PANAMA

Raw Sugar and Coconut Cookies
Queques

Preparation time: 35 minutes
Cooking time: 25 minutes
Makes: About 18 cookies

8 oz (225 g) piloncillo or 1 cup
  packed dark muscovado sugar
½ cup (4 fl oz/120 ml) water
2 cups (280 g) all-purpose (plain) flour
1¼ teaspoons ground cinnamon
1 teaspoon baking soda
  (bicarbonate of soda)
¾ teaspoon fine sea salt
1 cup (100 g) finely grated coconut,
  fresh or thawed frozen
2 tablespoons vegetable
  shortening, softened
2 tablespoons (30 g) unsalted
  butter, softened

Panama is a country caught between two continents, and this cookie is an embodiment of that. One of the primary ingredients is freshly grated coconut, making them similar to other Latin American-style coconut macaroons (recipe, page 177) that came from Spanish colonialism. The other primary ingredient is a syrup made from *rapadura*, an unrefined cane sugar that's the same as *piloncillo* in Mexico. *Rapadura*, however, is the Portuguese word for such a sugar, showing Brazil's influence on Panama's cuisine possibly more than other Central American countries.

Since *rapadura* is not readily available around the world, this recipe calls for you to make your own with *piloncillo*, although any unrefined dark brown sugar will work. You can also use cane syrup.

- -

Working with a serrated knife, roughly chop the piloncillo or grate it on the large holes of a box grater. Transfer the piloncillo to a small saucepan, add the water, and place over high heat. Bring the mixture to a boil, stirring to dissolve the piloncillo completely. Once the syrup boils, remove the pan from the heat and let the syrup cool completely.

Position racks in the top and bottom thirds of the oven and preheat the oven to 350°F (180°C/Gas Mark 4). Line two large baking sheets with parchment paper.

In a medium bowl, whisk together the flour, cinnamon, baking soda (bicarb), and salt.

In a large bowl, combine the grated coconut, shortening, and butter. Stir in the cooled syrup and mix until evenly incorporated. Add the flour mixture and stir until a dough forms and there are no dry patches of flour remaining.

Using a 1-ounce (2-tablespoon) ice cream scoop, drop mounds onto the prepared baking sheets, spaced at least 2 inches (5 cm) apart.

Bake until light golden brown at the edges and dry to the touch in the center, 16–18 minutes, switching racks and rotating the baking sheets front to back halfway through.

Transfer the baking sheets to wire racks. Let the cookies cool on the pans for 1 minute, then transfer them to the racks to cool completely.

Raw Sugar and Coconut Cookies

Cakey Spice Cookies

Galletas Cucas

Preparation time: 30 minutes,
 plus chilling time
Cooking time: 30 minutes
Makes: About 12 cookies

For the syrup:
12 oz (340 g) panela or piloncillo or 1½
 cups packed dark muscovado sugar
1 lemon
1 orange
½ cup (4 fl oz/120 ml) water
5 whole cloves
2 cinnamon sticks

For the dough:
3 cups (420 g) all-purpose (plain) flour
1 teaspoon baking soda
 (bicarbonate of soda)
1 teaspoon fine sea salt
1 stick (4 oz/115 g) unsalted butter,
 softened
1 egg

These cookies are sometimes referred to as "Colombian gingerbread," but their soft and cakey texture is the opposite of the thin and crispy European style. These cookies make use of *panela*, the name for the raw cane sugar (see Raw Sugars, page 164) in Colombia, by dissolving it into a syrup perfumed with cloves, cinnamon, and citrus zest, although sometimes other spices like ginger and cardamom are also added. In Venezuela, a similar cookie is called *catalinas*.

Panela, sometimes interchangeably labeled as *piloncillo*, is easily found at most Latin grocery stores, but if you can't find it, use dark muscovado sugar, which is a brown sugar similar to *panela/piloncillo* that has been granulated and can be measured like regular sugar. (If you can't find that, regular dark brown sugar will also work just fine.)

Make the syrup: Working with a serrated knife, roughly chop the panela, or grate it on the large holes of a box grater. Transfer the panela to a small saucepan. Using a Microplane (fine grater), finely grate the zest (no white pith) from the lemon and orange over the sugar in the pan. Add the water, cloves, and cinnamon sticks. Bring the mixture to a boil over high heat, stirring to dissolve the panela completely. Once the syrup boils, reduce the heat to maintain a bare simmer and let the syrup cook until reduced slightly, about 10 minutes. Remove the pan from the heat and let the syrup cool completely.

Make the dough: In a large bowl, whisk together the flour, baking soda (bicarb), and salt. Form a well in the middle of the dry ingredients. Fish out and discard the cloves and cinnamon sticks from the cooled piloncillo syrup and pour it into the dry ingredients. Add the butter and egg to the syrup and stir the mixture with a fork until it comes together into a solid dough, lightly kneading only as much as needed to no longer see any dry patches of flour in the bowl. Shape the dough into a ball, wrap in plastic wrap (cling film), and refrigerate for at least 1 hour or up to 2 days.

Position racks in the top and bottom thirds of the oven and preheat the oven to 350°F (180°C/Gas Mark 4). Line two large baking sheets with parchment paper.

Working on a lightly floured work surface, roll out the dough with a rolling pin to ½ inch (13 mm) thick. Using a 3-inch (7.5 cm) round cutter, cut out rounds of dough, rerolling the scraps to make more cookies. Transfer the rounds to the prepared baking sheets, spaced 2 inches (5 cm) apart.

Bake until light golden brown all over and barely soft in the center (the cookies will continue to cook and firm up when cooled), about 20 minutes, switching racks and rotating the baking sheets front to back halfway through.

Transfer the baking sheets to wire racks. Let the cookies cool on the pans for 1 minute, then transfer them to the racks to cool completely.

Tapioca and Anise Cookies

Panderos

Preparation time: 1 hour 15 minutes
Cooking time: 15 minutes
Makes: About 24 cookies

2 cups (280 g) tapioca starch,
  plus more for dusting
1 teaspoon baking powder
½ teaspoon fine sea salt
4 oz (115 g) panela or piloncillo or ½
  cup packed dark muscovado sugar
¼ cup (50 g) white US granulated
  (UK caster) sugar
4 tablespoons (2 oz/55 g) unsalted
  butter, softened
1 egg
2 tablespoons Aguardiente
  (recipe follows)

These crumbly Colombian cookies most likely were influenced by Brazilian *sequilhos* (recipe, page 176). Whereas *sequilhos* are made with cornstarch (cornflour), these *panderos* are made with tapioca starch and sweetened with *panela*, Colombia's version of raw cane sugar (see Raw Sugars, page 164). While the store-bought versions of the cookie are circular and look like a tambourine, virtually all homemade recipes call for the cookies to be shaped into diamonds or squares.

The other key characteristic of these cookies is the use of *aguardiente*, a light syrup infused with anise seeds or star anise, which perfumes the dough with the spice's characteristic aroma. It's typically made by simmering the spice in syrup to leach out all its flavor. Some recipes call for no sugar—just water and anise—while others substitute brandy for it, or keep the anise and use brandy instead of water. This recipe adds some brandy to the traditional *aguardiente*, to help it enhance the aroma of the anise and complement the warm notes from the *panela*.

Position racks in the top and bottom thirds of the oven and preheat the oven to 350°F (180°C/Gas Mark 4). Line two large baking sheets with parchment paper.

In a medium bowl, whisk together the tapioca starch, baking powder, and salt.

On the large holes of box grater, grate the panela and place it in a large bowl. Add the white US granulated (UK caster) sugar and butter and beat with a hand mixer on medium speed until light and fluffy, 2–3 minutes. Add the egg and aguardiente and beat until smooth. Add half the dry ingredients and stir until almost completely incorporated, then add the remaining dry ingredients and stir until a dough forms and there are no dry patches of tapioca starch remaining. (There's no worry about overmixing this dough because tapioca starch does not contain gluten.)

Shape the dough into a ball, then divide it into 4 equal portions. Dust a work surface lightly with more tapioca starch. Roll each portion into a rope 1 inch (2.5 cm) thick and then flatten the rope slightly. Using the tines of a fork, gently scrape the tips of the tines along the top of each rope to create rough channels along the length of the rope. Using a knife, cut each rope every 1½ inches (4 cm) on the diagonal to create diamonds. Arrange the diamonds on the prepared baking sheets, spaced at least 1 inch (2.5 cm) apart.

Bake until light golden brown on the bottom and dry to the touch in the center, 12–15 minutes, switching racks and rotating the baking sheets front to back halfway through.

Transfer the baking sheets to wire racks. Let the cookies cool on the pans for 10 minutes, then transfer them to the racks to cool completely.

Aguardiente

Makes: ¾ cup (6 fl oz/175 ml)

½ cup (4 fl oz/120 ml) water
¼ cup (50 g) white US granulated
  (UK caster) sugar
2 tablespoons anise seeds
2 tablespoons brandy

In a small saucepan, combine the water, sugar, and anise seeds and bring to a boil over medium-high heat. Cook for 5 minutes, stirring to dissolve the sugar. Remove from the heat, stir in the brandy and let cool completely. Strain the syrup through a fine sieve into an airtight container (discard the anise seeds). Cover and refrigerate the aguardiente for up to 1 month.

Brown Sugar "Little Starch" Cookies
Almidoncitos

Preparation time: 25 minutes,
  plus cooling time
Cooking time: 20 minutes
Makes: About 18 cookies

4 oz (115 g) papelón, panela,
  or piloncillo, or 1 cup packed dark
  muscovado sugar
1 stick (4 oz/115 g) unsalted butter
1¾ cups (245 g) tapioca starch
1 teaspoon baking powder
¾ teaspoon fine sea salt
1 teaspoon ground cinnamon (optional)
½ teaspoon ground anise
  seeds (optional)
½ teaspoon ground cloves (optional)
1 teaspoon pure vanilla extract
2 egg yolks

Similar to many Latin American cookies, tapioca starch forms the base of these Venezuelan treats, which gives them a crumbly, melt-in-the-mouth quality. The dough is made by first dissolving *papelón*—Venezuela's version of raw sugar, like *panela* or *piloncillo* (see Raw Sugars, page 164)—in butter before mixing it with the rest of the ingredients. Sometimes spices like cloves, cinnamon, and/or anise seeds are added to the dough, so they are included in this recipe as optional ingredients. Including them will lend the cookies a gingerbread-like flavor profile, especially in combination with the melted *papelón*.

These cookies have a distinctive shape: that of a mini baguette. The dough is shaped into logs, cut into thumb-length pieces, then scored three times on top. Where the shape came from is unknown—it could either be a precursor to the fork tine-stamped ridges that are common on many tapioca- or cornstarch- (cornflour-) based cookies, or it's a way, as it is in bread baking, to control the splitting of the dough.

- -

Position racks in the top and bottom thirds of the oven and preheat the oven to 350°F (180°C/Gas Mark 4). Line two large baking sheets with parchment paper.

On the large holes of a box grater, grate the papelón, and place it in a small saucepan along with the butter. Set the pan over medium heat and cook, stirring occasionally, until the butter melts and the sugar dissolves. Remove the pan from the heat and let the mixture cool to room temperature.

In a large bowl, combine the tapioca starch, baking powder, and salt. If using, add the cinnamon, anise, and/or cloves. Whisk to combine. Form a well in the center of the dry ingredients and pour in the cooled butter-sugar mixture along with the vanilla and egg yolks. Stir until a dough forms and there are no dry patches of tapioca starch remaining.

Divide the dough into 4 equal portions and shape each into a rope 1 inch (2.5 cm) thick. Flatten the rope slightly with your fingers. Cut each rope on a slight diagonal every 2 inches (5 cm). Using the blade of the knife, gently score the top of each dough length with three equally spaced cuts. Arrange the dough lengths on the prepared baking sheets, spaced at least 2 inches (5 cm) apart.

Bake until golden brown and dry to the touch in the center, 12–15 minutes, switching racks and rotating the baking sheets front to back halfway through.

Transfer the baking sheets to wire racks. Let the cookies cool on the pans for 1 minute, then transfer them to the racks to cool completely.

Brown Sugar "Little Starch" Cookies

Venezuelan Shortbread Cookies
Polvorosas

Preparation time: 30 minutes
Cooking time: 15 minutes
Makes: About 12 cookies

½ cup (115 g) vegetable
  shortening, softened
1 cup (135 g) powdered (icing) sugar,
  plus more for dusting (optional)
½ teaspoon ground cinnamon,
  preferably Mexican canela
¾ teaspoon fine sea salt
2 teaspoons pure vanilla extract
1½ cups (210 g) all-purpose
  (plain) flour

These shortbreads are popular all throughout Latin America, particularly in Venezuela. A descendant in style and name from Spanish *polvorones* (recipe, page 97), these Venezuelan cookies once used rendered pork lard, but many modern recipes use vegetable shortening exclusively. In many Venezuelan bakeries that sell the cookies, a characteristic cross is stamped on the top, though most home bakers just use a fork to stamp the dough balls. Here the cookies are cut out from rolled dough to produce flat discs.

Similar to Mexican *polvorones de canela* (recipe, page 156), a little ground cinnamon is often added to the dough for aroma, but unlike other *polvorón* derivatives, it doesn't seem like a coating of powdered (icing) sugar is essential in the Venezuelan version. The cookies are often presented as plain discs or very lightly dusted with powdered sugar.

Preheat the oven to 350°F (180°C/Gas Mark 4). Line a large baking sheet with parchment paper.

In a large bowl, with a hand mixer, combine the shortening, sugar, cinnamon, salt, and vanilla and beat on medium speed until light and fluffy, 2–3 minutes. Add the flour and stir until a dough forms and there are no dry patches of flour remaining.

Scrape the dough out onto a lightly floured work surface and use a lightly floured rolling pin to flatten the dough into a disc ½ inch (13 mm) thick. Using a 1½-inch (4 cm) round cutter, stamp out cookies and use an offset or thin metal spatula to transfer the rounds to the prepared baking sheet, spacing them as close as 1 inch (2.5 cm) apart. Reroll scraps and continue cutting out rounds.

Bake until golden brown at the edges and dry to the touch in the center, 14–16 minutes, rotating the baking sheet front to back halfway through.

Transfer the baking sheet to a wire rack and let the cookies cool completely on the pan.

If you like, lightly dust them with powdered (icing) sugar before serving.

Brown Sugar and Coconut Cookies

Besitos de Coco

Preparation time: 55 minutes
Cooking time: 20 minutes
Makes: About 12 cookies

12 oz (340 g) papelón, panela,
   or piloncillo, or 1½ cups packed
   dark muscovado sugar
⅓ cup (2½ fl oz/80 ml) water
3 whole cloves
1 cinnamon stick
2 cups (280 g) all-purpose (plain) flour
1 teaspoon baking powder
½ teaspoon baking soda
   (bicarbonate of soda)
¾ teaspoon fine sea salt
1 cup (100 g) finely grated coconut,
   fresh or thawed frozen
2 eggs, lightly beaten

Grated coconut and *papelón*, Venezuela's native raw cane sugar (see Raw Sugars, page 164), are key components of this macaroon-like cookie. Like Colombian *galletas cucas* (recipe, page 166), Mexican *marranitos* (recipe, page 160), and Panamanian *queques* (recipe, page 164), raw sugar is dissolved into a syrup with spices like cinnamon, cloves, and anise or allspice, then blended with grated coconut and wheat flour to make cookies that are crisp at the edges and chewy in the center. Some sugar syrup is reserved for brushing over the cookies after baking, which adds an appealing gloss and reinforces the syrup's unique bittersweetness.

This blend of ingredients nods to various European, African, and native influences—often referred to as *criolla*—on Venezuelan cuisine and particularly these cookies, which share their name with a Puerto Rican cookie that's made with sugar and sometimes sweetened condensed milk. In Venezuela, these cookies are often paired with *queso de mano*, a crumbly salty cheese similar to Mexican *queso fresco* or *queso casero*, as a salty-sweet snack.

Working with a serrated knife, roughly chop the papelón or grate it on the large holes of a box grater. Transfer the papelón to a small saucepan, add the water, cloves, and cinnamon stick. Bring to a boil over high heat, stirring to dissolve the sugar completely. Once the syrup boils, remove the pan from the heat and let the syrup cool completely. Pour one-quarter of the syrup into a small bowl and set aside.

Position racks in the top and bottom thirds of the oven and preheat the oven to 350°F (180°C/Gas Mark 4). Line two large baking sheets with parchment paper.

In a medium bowl, whisk together the flour, baking powder, baking soda (bicarb), and salt.

In a large bowl, stir together the coconut and eggs. Pick out and discard the spices from the syrup in the saucepan and then pour the cooled syrup into the bowl and mix until evenly incorporated. Add the flour mixture and stir just until a dough forms and there are no dry patches of flour remaining.

Using a 1-ounce (2-tablespoon) ice cream scoop, drop mounds onto the prepared baking sheets, spaced at least 2 inches (5 cm) apart.

Bake until dry to the touch in the center, 12–15 minutes, switching racks and rotating the baking sheets front to back halfway through.

Transfer the baking sheets to wire racks and immediately brush the tops of the cookies with some of the reserved syrup. Let the cookies cool completely on the pans.

Cornstarch Cookies with Sprinkles

Gomma Koekjes / Maizena Koekjes / Biskut Gomma

Preparation time: 30 minutes
Cooking time: 15 minutes
Makes: About 18 cookies

1 stick (4 oz/115 g) unsalted
  butter, softened
¾ cup (150 g) white US granulated
  (UK caster) sugar
1 egg
½ teaspoon pure vanilla extract
½ teaspoon fine sea salt
2 cups (280 g) cornstarch (cornflour)
Nonpareils (hundreds & thousands)
  or sprinkles, for decorating

Suriname's proximity to Brazil most likely explains these cornstarch-based cookies, which are very similar to older recipes for the latter country's *sequilhos / biscoitos de Maizena* (recipe, page 176). Instead of using sweetened condensed milk, these *gomma koekjes* use sugar and an egg to add sweetness and bind the dough. The cookies are flattened with a fork several times to create pockets on top of the cookies to catch lots of sprinkles, another distinction of the Surinamese version.

Because Suriname has a history of colonization by the Netherlands, there is no doubt some influence from its baking traditions in these cookies as well. This simple butter cookie closely resembles the Dutch *jodenkoeken* (recipe, page 335) but uses cornstarch (cornflour) instead of regular flour. And the use of sprinkles is also most likely from that European influence since most recipes call for sprinkles made by Oetker, a Germany-based baking ingredient company.

Position racks in the top and bottom thirds of the oven and preheat the oven to 350°F (180°C/Gas Mark 4). Line two large baking sheets with parchment paper.

In a large bowl, with a hand mixer, beat the butter and sugar on medium speed until light and fluffy, 2–3 minutes. Add the egg, vanilla, and salt and beat until smooth. Add half the cornstarch (cornflour) and stir until almost completely incorporated, then add the remaining cornstarch and stir until a dough forms and there are no dry patches of cornstarch remaining. (There's no worry about overmixing this dough because cornstarch does not contain gluten.)

Using a 1-ounce (2-tablespoon) ice cream scoop, portion the dough and roll into balls. Arrange them on the prepared baking sheets, spaced at least 2 inches (5 cm) apart. Use the tines of a fork to press a crosshatch pattern in the dough at the same time flattening the cookie. Top each flattened dough round with some nonpareils or sprinkles.

Bake until very light golden brown on the bottom and dry to the touch in the center, 12–15 minutes, switching racks and rotating the baking sheets front to back halfway through.

Transfer the baking sheets to wire racks. Let the cookies cool on the pans for 1 minute, then transfer them to the racks to cool completely.

Cornstarch Cookies with Sprinkles

Guava-Filled Butter Cookies

Casadinhos de Goiabada

Preparation time: 1 hour 45 minutes,
  plus cooling time
Cooking time: 15 minutes
Makes: About 36 cookie sandwiches

10 tablespoons (5 oz/140 g) unsalted
  butter, softened
½ cup (100 g) white US granulated (UK
  caster) sugar, plus more for coating
½ teaspoon fine sea salt
1¾ cups (245 g) all-purpose
  (plain) flour
4 oz (115 g) guava paste
1 tablespoon boiling water

Brazilians have a thing for sweets at weddings—specifically cookie sandwiches, where two pieces are joined into one, like a couple getting married. There are *bem casados*, which are snack cake rounds sandwiched with dulce de leche. There are *casadinhos*, which are fudge balls—one plain, one chocolate—sandwiched with guava paste or dulce de leche. And then there are these cookies, *casadinhos de goiabada*, which though they share the same name as the fudge balls, are quite different: Tiny, marble-size cookie sandwiches—made usually of just butter, flour, and sugar—held together with guava paste. All of these cookie names contain some riff on the word *casadinho*, which means "married" in Portuguese.

These cookies most resemble Italian *baci di dama* (recipe, page 120) in appearance, and their diminutive size is part of the appeal. You can, of course, fill them with dulce de leche, chocolate-hazelnut spread, or any other fruit jam, but the softness and florality of the classic guava paste works wonderfully to contrast with the crunchy, buttery cookies.

Position racks in the top and bottom thirds of the oven and preheat the oven to 350°F (180°C/Gas Mark 4). Line two large baking sheets with parchment paper.

In a large bowl, with a hand mixer, combine the butter, sugar, and salt and beat on medium speed until pale and fluffy, 2–3 minutes. Add the flour and stir until a dough forms and there are no dry patches of flour remaining.

Using a ¼-ounce ice cream scoop or a heaping teaspoon, portion the dough and roll into ½-inch (13 mm) balls. Arrange the dough balls on the prepared baking sheets, spaced 1 inch (2.5 cm) apart.

Bake until the cookies are light golden brown on the bottom and dry to the touch, 10–12 minutes, switching racks and rotating the baking sheets front to back halfway through.

Transfer the baking sheets to wire racks. Let the cookies cool on the pans for 1 minute, then transfer them to the racks to cool completely.

Place the guava paste in a heatproof bowl and mash with a fork. Warm the paste in the microwave for 20 seconds, then stir in the boiling hot water, to loosen it.

Flip over half of the baked cookies and top each with ½ teaspoon of the warm guava paste. Cover the guava paste with another cookie to create sandwiches. Roll the cookie sandwiches in more sugar before serving.

Guava-Filled Butter Cookies

Cornstarch Butter Cookies

Sequilhos / Biscoitos de Maizena / Sequilhos de Amido de Milho

Preparation time: 30 minutes
Cooking time: 15 minutes
Makes: About 12 cookies

1 stick (4 oz/115 g) unsalted butter, softened
½ cup (4 fl oz/120 ml) plus 2 tablespoons sweetened condensed milk (half of a 14 oz/396 g can)
¾ teaspoon fine sea salt
2 cups (280 g) cornstarch (cornflour)

As with most cookies throughout the world, a definitive timeline is a fool's errand. However, even though it's difficult to say when these beloved cornstarch-based cookies surfaced in Brazil, it is easier to parse together some clues as to how they evolved in their modern form. Portuguese settlers most likely introduced their baking traditions to Brazil during colonization, including *lavadores* (see recipe variation, page 90), which have the same distinctive fork-stamped ridges on top as these Brazilian examples. From there, the cookies most likely evolved into various forms depending on the starch used—tapioca starch begat *sequilhos*, wheat flour begat *tarecos*—while the rest of the ingredients stayed the same.

The cookies today more often go by the name *biscoitos de Maizena* because they are made with cornstarch (cornflour) and Maizena is a popular brand of the ingredient in Brazil—although the name *sequilhos* is still used to refer to this cornstarch-based cookie and sometimes the ring-shaped style. Older recipes combine cornstarch with butter, sugar, and an egg, while many newer ones eschew the sugar and egg in favor of sweetened condensed milk (the version here). For a recipe that doesn't use sweetened condensed milk, make the Surinamese *gomma koekjes* (recipe, page 172).

Position racks in the top and bottom thirds of the oven and preheat the oven to 350°F (180°C/Gas Mark 4). Line two large baking sheets with parchment paper.

In a large bowl, with a hand mixer, combine the butter, sweetened condensed milk, and salt and beat on medium speed until smooth, 1–2 minutes. Add half the cornstarch (cornflour) and stir until almost completely incorporated, then add the remaining cornstarch and stir until a dough forms and there are no dry patches of cornstarch remaining. (There's no worry about overmixing this dough because cornstarch doesn't contain gluten.)

Using a 1-ounce (2-tablespoon) ice cream scoop, portion the dough and roll into balls. Arrange them on the prepared baking sheets, spaced at least 2 inches (5 cm) apart. Using the tines of a fork, press them against each ball once to flatten and create the characteristic ridges on top.

Bake until very light golden brown on the bottom and dry to the touch in the center, 12–15 minutes, switching racks and rotating the baking sheets front to back halfway through.

Transfer the baking sheets to wire racks. Let the cookies cool on the pans for 1 minute, then transfer them to the racks to cool completely.

Fresh Coconut Macaroons

Cocadas

Preparation time: 35 minutes
Cooking time: 25 minutes
Makes: About 18 cookies

2 tablespoons white US granulated
  (UK caster) sugar
2 egg whites
½ cup (4 fl oz/120 ml) sweetened
  condensed milk
1 teaspoon pure vanilla extract
1 teaspoon fine sea salt
3 cups (300 g) finely grated coconut,
  fresh (from 1 mature coconut)
  or thawed frozen

Coconut macaroons are made across the globe where coconuts grow. However, it's generally believed that the use of coconut in macaroon-style cookies—which originated with Italian *amaretti morbidi* (recipe, page 109) and Spanish *almendrados* (recipe, page 99)—most likely occurred during the Spanish colonization of much of Latin America. While coconut macaroons are popular in Mexico, Bolivia, and all of Latin America—where they're referred to as *cocadas*—Peru's version is unique in that it often uses freshly grated coconut, instead of the shredded dried (desiccated) form. You can grate your own using a food processor, or purchase pre-grated fresh coconut in the freezer aisle of most Latin grocery stores or online.

There are recipes for *cocadas* in which the treats are cut out from a slab baked in a pan, but now most recipes preshape them into the recognizable flat mounds. The freshly grated coconut is bound with only egg whites and sugar in many older recipes, while the use of sweetened condensed milk is a modern adaptation to make use of the convenience product and enrich the cookies; this recipe combines both approaches. A popular way to serve these *cocadas* in Peru is to sandwich two of them with a spoonful of *manjarblanco*—Peru's version of dulce de leche.

Position racks in the top and bottom thirds of the oven and preheat the oven to 350°F (180°C/Gas Mark 4). Line two large baking sheets with parchment paper.

In a large bowl, combine the sugar and egg whites and whisk vigorously by hand until lightened and smooth, about 1 minute. Add the sweetened condensed milk, vanilla, and salt and whisk until smooth. Add the coconut and stir until the mixture is well combined and forms a thick batter.

Using a 1-ounce (2-tablespoon) ice cream scoop, portion the dough and roll into balls. Arrange them on the prepared baking sheets, spaced at least 2 inches (5 cm) apart.

Bake until the cookies are golden brown and dry to the touch on top, 20–25 minutes, switching racks and rotating the baking sheets front to back halfway through.

Transfer the baking sheets to wire racks. Let the cookies cool on the pans for 1 minute, then transfer them to the racks to cool completely.

Fresh Coconut Macaroons (p.177)

Meringue-Coated Dulce de Leche Butter Cookies (p. 180)

Meringue-Coated Dulce de Leche Butter Cookies

Chilenitos

Preparation time: 25 minutes,
 plus 20 minutes resting time
 and cooling and drying time
Cooking time: 35 minutes
Makes: About 18 cookie sandwiches

For the cookies:
4 egg yolks (save the whites for
 the meringue, below)
1 egg
2 tablespoons gold or dark rum
1 teaspoon pure vanilla extract
1 cup (140 g) all-purpose (plain)
 flour, plus more for dusting
½ teaspoon fine sea salt
1½ cups (375 g) dulce de leche
 repostero, store-bought or
 homemade (page 182)

For the meringue:
1 cup (200 g) white US granulated
 (UK caster) sugar
4 egg whites
1 teaspoon pure vanilla extract
¼ teaspoon fine sea salt

These cookies are the Chilean answer to the more widely known *alfajores* (recipe, page 182) from neighboring Argentina. Instead of a dense shortbread-like cookie, these cookies have more of a sweetened cracker texture. The dough—mainly flour and eggs flavored with alcohol and other flavorings—is kneaded until smooth, then rolled out, cut into rounds, and docked with a fork to prevent any air bubbles in the dough. This also keeps the cracker-like cookies flat and crisp.

Like Argentinian *alfajores*, *chilenitos* contain a luscious dulce de leche filling, which enriches the relatively lean cookies. Traditionally, the cookie sandwiches are coated in meringue and then baked until dry, which helps preserve them in bakeries. That is the version here, but you can also simply coat the sides of *chilenitos* in unsweetened shredded (desiccated) coconut or crushed cookie crumbs, if you like.

- -

Make the cookies: Position racks in the top and bottom thirds of the oven and preheat the oven to 350°F (180°C/Gas Mark 4). Line two large baking sheets with parchment paper.

In a large bowl, whisk together the egg yolks, whole egg, rum, and vanilla. Add the flour and salt and stir until a loose dough forms. Scrape the dough onto a floured work surface and knead the dough, adding as much extra flour as needed to keep it sticking to the counter, until smooth and elastic, 6–8 minutes. Wrap the dough ball in plastic wrap (cling film) and let rest at room temperature for 20 minutes.

Unwrap and transfer the dough to a lightly floured work surface. Using a lightly floured rolling pin, roll out the dough to ⅛ inch (3 mm) thick. Using a 2-inch (5 cm) round cutter, cut out as many cookies as you can from the dough. Transfer them to the prepared baking sheets, spaced 1 inch (2.5 cm) apart. Use the tines of a fork to dock the cookies all over; make sure the tines go all the way through the dough rounds to the sheet below. Repeat with the remaining dough to cut out more rounds.

Bake until the cookies are light golden brown at the edges and dry to the touch, 12–15 minutes, switching racks and rotating the baking sheets front to back halfway through.

Transfer the baking sheets to wire racks and let the cookies cool completely on the pans. Leave the oven on and reduce the oven temperature to 225°F (105°C/Gas Mark ¼).

Flip over half of the baked cookies and top each with 1 tablespoon dulce de leche. Cover the dulce de leche with another cookie to create sandwiches. Leave the sandwiches on the lined baking sheets.

Make the meringue: Pour 1 inch (2.5 cm) of water into a medium saucepan and bring to a boil, then reduce the heat to maintain a steady simmer. In a large heatproof bowl (that can sit over, not in, the saucepan), whisk together the sugar, egg whites, vanilla, and salt. Place the bowl over the pan of simmering water and stir steadily with a whisk until the whites are just hot to the touch and all the sugar is dissolved. The best way to tell is to dip your index finger into the mixture and rub it between it and your thumb to make sure there are no sugar granules remaining.

Remove the bowl from the pan and use a hand mixer (or transfer the mixture to a stand mixer fitted with the whisk) and beat the meringue until fluffy, it forms stiff peaks, and is cool to the touch.

Using an offset spatula or a dinner knife, spread an even layer of meringue around the sides and top of each cookie sandwich. Place each sandwich, uncoated-side down, back onto the reserved baking sheets.

Once all the cookies are coated, return the baking sheets to the oven and bake until the meringue coating is dry to the touch on all the cookies, about 20 minutes. Close the oven door, turn off the oven, and allow the chilenitos to cool completely in the oven; this allows the meringue coating to dry out appropriately and set.

Serve the cookies at room temperature. Store in an airtight container at room temperature for up to 3 days.

Quince Paste Thumbprint Cookies

Pepas de Membrillo / Pepitas

Preparation time: 45 minutes, plus
at least 30 minutes chilling time
Cooking time: 30 minutes
Makes: About 24 cookies

1½ cups (210 g) all-purpose
  (plain) flour
½ cup (70 g) cornstarch (cornflour)
1½ teaspoons baking powder
½ teaspoon fine sea salt
1 stick (4 oz/115 g) unsalted butter,
  softened
½ cup (100 g) white US granulated
  (UK caster) sugar
1 egg
1 egg yolk
1 tablespoon finely grated lemon zest
1 teaspoon pure vanilla extract
4 oz (115 g) quince paste, cut into
  ½-inch (13 mm) cubes

These simple thumbprint-style cookies are Argentina's version of the Cuban *torticas de morón* (recipe, page 148), both descended from the Spanish *polvorones* (recipe, page 97) but adapted to local ingredients. A variation on Cuba's cookie adds guava paste to the lime-scented dough base, but in Argentina, *membrillo*—a fruit paste made from quince that's very popular—fills these treats scented with lemon, though sometimes orange, zest in the dough. And similar to the dough for *alfajores* (recipe, page 182), cornstarch (cornflour) is added to the flour to give the cookie a crumbly-but-tender texture.

Quince paste is made by cooking down puréed quince with sugar, similar to applesauce, until it condenses into a paste that holds its shape thanks to the high pectin content found in quince. The quince transforms in color from pale yellow to bright pink and then ruby red and produces a heady, floral aroma that pairs beautifully with these buttery cookies. You can roll the dough into balls and indent it with your finger before filling, but many traditional recipes call to slice the dough into thick rounds from a log—as they do in Argentinian bakeries—and then fill the cookies with quince paste.

In a medium bowl, whisk together the flour, cornstarch (cornflour), baking powder, and salt.

In a large bowl, with a hand mixer, beat the butter and sugar on medium speed until smooth and fluffy, 2–3 minutes. Add the whole egg and beat until smooth. Then add the egg yolk, lemon zest, and vanilla and beat until incorporated. Add the dry ingredients and beat on low speed until the dough just comes together and there are no dry patches of flour remaining.

Scrape the dough onto a sheet of parchment paper. Form the dough into a vague cylinder, then shape the dough into a log 2 inches (5 cm) in diameter and wrap tightly (see page 14). Transfer the log to the refrigerator to firm up for at least 30 minutes.

Position racks in the top and bottom thirds of the oven and preheat the oven to 350°F (180°C/Gas Mark 4). Line two large baking sheets with parchment paper.

Unwrap the dough log and cut the dough into slices ½ inch (13 mm) thick. Arrange the slices on the prepared baking sheets, spaced at least 2 inches (5 cm) apart. Using the pad of your thumb, gently press in the center of each slice to create a divot. Place a cube of quince paste in each divot.

Bake until golden brown at the edges and dry to the touch on top, 25–30 minutes, switching racks and rotating the baking sheets front to back halfway through.

Transfer the baking sheets to wire racks. Let the cookies cool on the pans for 1 minute, then transfer them to the racks to cool completely.

Dulce de Leche-Filled Butter Cookies

Alfajores

Preparation time: 1 hour 15 minutes,
plus cooling time
Cooking time: 15 minutes
Makes: About 24 cookie sandwiches

1½ cups (210 g) cornstarch (cornflour)
1¼ cups (178 g) all-purpose (plain) flour
1 teaspoon baking powder
¾ teaspoon fine sea salt
½ teaspoon baking soda (bicarbonate
of soda)
1½ sticks (6 oz/170 g) unsalted
butter, softened
½ cup (100 g) white US granulated
(UK caster) sugar
3 egg yolks
1 tablespoon brandy or Cognac
1 teaspoon finely grated lemon zest
1 teaspoon pure vanilla extract
1½ cups (375 g) dulce de leche
repostero, store-bought or
homemade (recipe follows)
Powdered (icing) sugar, for
dusting (optional)

When you say the name of these cookies to most people, the Argentinian version is the one that comes to mind most commonly (although there are numerous country-specific iterations). Even within Argentina, these dulce de leche-filled cookie sandwiches can be found plain, rolled in coconut, coated in chocolate, or coated in meringue, like the Chilean *chilenitos* (recipe, page 180). The Spanish version from which this cookie takes its name is more like a candy or confection, made with almonds bound by honey and spices and coated in powdered (icing) sugar. A regional variation of Spanish *alfajore* from Medina-Sedonia in southern Spain that stuffs the honey-nut mixture between two wafer cookies provides a possible link to how these sandwiches of dulce de leche-filled cookies gained their name over time.

The basic recipe mixes wheat flour with cornstarch (cornflour) to produce the fine texture of the cookies, while lemon zest and alcohol, usually Cognac or other brandy, spikes the cookies and cuts through their sweetness. The dulce de leche that fills these sandwiches, however, is not the typical kind you drizzle from a squeeze bottle. You need to look for *dulce de leche repostero* online and in Latin markets. It has the consistency of peanut butter and will stay put when sandwiched between the cookies. It's also easy to make your own at home, if you have the time (see the recipe that follows).

Position racks in the top and bottom thirds of the oven and preheat the oven to 350°F (180°C/Gas Mark 4). Line two large baking sheets with parchment paper.

In a medium bowl, whisk together the cornstarch (cornflour), all-purpose (plain) flour, baking powder, salt, and baking soda (bicarb).

In a large bowl, with a hand mixer, beat the butter and white US granulated (UK caster) sugar on medium speed until pale and fluffy, 2–3 minutes. Add the egg yolks and beat until smooth. Beat in the brandy, lemon zest, and vanilla. Add the dry ingredients and stir until the dough forms and there are no dry patches of flour remaining.

Transfer the dough to a lightly floured work surface. Using a lightly floured rolling pin, roll out the dough to ¼ inch (6 mm) thick. Using a 2-inch (5 cm) round cutter, cut out rounds of dough and transfer them to the prepared baking sheets, spaced 1 inch (2.5 cm) apart. Reroll the scraps to cut out more rounds.

Bake until the cookies are light golden brown at the edges and dry to the touch, 12–15 minutes, switching racks and rotating the baking sheets front to back halfway through.

Transfer the baking sheets to wire racks. Let the cookies cool on the pans for 1 minute, then transfer them to the racks to cool completely.

Flip over half of the baked cookies and top each with 1 tablespoon dulce de leche. Cover the dulce de leche with another cookie to create sandwiches. Dust the cookie sandwiches with powdered (icing) sugar, if you like, before serving.

Dulce de Leche Repostero

Makes 1½ cups (375 g)

2 cans (14 oz/396 g each) sweetened
condensed milk

Remove the label from the cans of sweetened condensed milk. Place the cans on their sides in a large deep saucepan and add water to come 2 inches (5 cm) above the cans. Bring the water to a boil over high heat, then reduce the heat to medium-low to maintain a bare simmer. Place the lid on the pot, leaving it slightly ajar, and let the water simmer for 3 hours, making sure the cans are submerged by at least 2 inches (5 cm) of water the entire time and adding more water if needed.

Remove the pot from the heat and let the cans sit, undisturbed and submerged in the water, until they cool completely, at least 4 hours.

Remove the cans from the water, open the cans, and stir the dulce de leche to ensure it's evenly mixed before using. Transfer to an airtight container and store in the refrigerator for up to 2 weeks.

Dulce de Leche-Filled Butter Cookies

eastern europe

In this region, the heady aromas of the Turkish influence start to give way to the richer, sweeter, more buttery cookies of Western Europe. This bridging of styles is evident in the Austrian *Vanillekipferl*, which blends the Mediterranean style of crumbly walnut cookie with the buttery, sugar-coated cookies of colder climates. Chocolate adds richness to other cookies, while European-style gingerbread-like cookies start to make their appearance.

Filled Cream Cookies

Kołaczki

Preparation time: 2 hours,
 plus chilling time
Cooking time: 15 minutes
Makes: About 48 cookies

8 oz (225 g) cream cheese, softened
2 sticks (8 oz/225 g) unsalted
 butter, softened
⅔ cup (90 g) powdered (icing) sugar,
 plus more for dusting
2 teaspoons pure vanilla extract
1 teaspoon fine sea salt
3 cups (420 g) all-purpose (plain) flour
¾ cup (240 g) thick prune or apricot
 jam (see headnote)

Many cookies derive their name and size from simply being diminutive versions of other, larger cakes and desserts. The Polish *kołaczki* is most likely one such cookie, derived from the *kołocz*, a sweetened round bread. Though the name stands for several different types of pastries throughout Poland, the Czech Republic, and Slovakia, this cookie version—made with no yeast in the dough and often shaped into "envelopes" instead of rounds—seems to be mostly associated with Polish baking, while the Czech style of *kolache* denotes a pastry made with yeasted dough. The two often share similar fillings.

The name derives from the Czech word for "wheel" and while these cookies do exist as rounds, they're most commonly shaped as the characteristic "envelopes"—meaning a square with two opposing corners folded over to meet in the center. The yeasted pastry is often found in the "wheel" shape. Apricot jam is the simplest filling for these cookies, but if you want, fill them with prune jam, poppy seeds, sweet cheese, or walnuts (see Eastern European Fillings, page 203). And while the older versions of these cookies were most likely made with sour cream or another thickened dairy, cream cheese is now the standard for the smoothness and stability it lends the dough.

In a large bowl, with a hand mixer, combine the cream cheese, butter, sugar, vanilla, and salt and beat on medium speed until creamy and smooth, 1–2 minutes. Add the flour and beat on low speed until the dough comes together. Stop the mixer and lightly knead with your hands only as much as needed to no longer see any dry patches of flour in the bowl. Shape the dough into a ball, wrap in plastic wrap (cling film), and refrigerate for at least 1 hour or up to 2 days.

Position racks in the top and bottom thirds of the oven and preheat the oven to 350°F (180°C/Gas Mark 4). Line two large baking sheets with parchment paper.

Working on a lightly floured work surface, roll out the dough with a rolling pin to ⅛ inch (3 mm) thick. Using a ruler or 2-inch (5 cm) square cutter, cut out 2-inch (5 cm) squares from the dough, rerolling the scraps as needed to get more squares. Spoon a slightly heaped ½ teaspoon jam into the center of each square, then fold two opposing corners of each square over the filling and pinch to join them. Transfer the envelopes to the prepared baking sheets, spaced 2 inches (5 cm) apart.

Bake until golden brown on the bottom and dry to the touch on top, 14–16 minutes, switching racks and rotating the baking sheets front to back halfway through.

Transfer the baking sheets to wire racks. Let the cookies cool on the pans for 1 minute, then transfer the cookies directly to the racks to cool completely.

Dust the cookies with some sugar before serving.

Filled Cream Cookies

Chocolate-Glazed Polish Gingerbread
Katarzynki

Preparation time: 50 minutes,
  plus cooling and setting time
Cooking time: 20 minutes
Makes: About 30 cookies

For the cookies:
6 tablespoons (125 g) honey
¼ cup (50 g) white US granulated
  (UK caster) sugar
2½ tablespoons (35 g) unsalted butter
1 tablespoon water
1 teaspoon ground cinnamon
¾ teaspoon freshly grated nutmeg
½ teaspoon ground cloves
½ teaspoon ground allspice
½ teaspoon ground cardamom
2 tablespoons sour cream
2¼ cups (315 g) all-purpose (plain)
  flour, plus more for dusting
½ teaspoon baking soda (bicarbonate
  of soda)
¾ teaspoon fine sea salt

For the chocolate glaze:
1½ cups (200 g) powdered (icing)
  sugar
⅓ cup (30 g) natural cocoa powder
1 teaspoon pure vanilla extract
3 tablespoons whole milk, plus
  more if needed

The Polish city of Torun is famous for its gingerbread, or *pierniki toruńskie*, which comes in various shapes, either produced by using a cookie cutter or pressing the dough into wooden molds that form intricate designs and shapes. When produced in factories—the most famous brand being Kopernik, who label their *pierniki* as *katarzynki*—the gingerbread's shape resembles a cartoon dog bone with an extra pair of rounded knobs in the center. An urban legend states that the daughter of a gingerbread baker baked six cookies next to each other one day and as they baked, the cookies spread and formed together to create the characteristic shape.

At home, bakers use simple round or heart cutters for the soft gingerbread, which resembles tender German *Elisenlebkuchen* (recipe, page 244) more than the chewy American-style ginger-molasses cookies or crunchy ginger snaps. *Katarzynki* are also honey-based, so their flavor is milder, particularly because ground ginger is often not included in Polish gingerbread. Instead, cinnamon, nutmeg, cloves, allspice, and cardamom are more commonly used. Though the cookies are often served plain or with a simple sugar glaze, the most popular topping seems to be a coating of chocolate, so that is used here. If you want to omit the chocolate glaze, instead give the cooled cookies a dusting of powdered (icing) sugar before serving.

- -

Make the cookies: Position racks in the top and bottom thirds of the oven and preheat the oven to 350°F (180°C/Gas Mark 4). Line two large baking sheets with parchment paper.

Pour the honey into a small frying pan and place over medium-high heat until the honey starts to bubble around the edges and is loose. Remove the pan from the heat and stir in the white US granulated (UK caster) sugar, butter, water, cinnamon, nutmeg, cloves, allspice, and cardamom until the sugar dissolves. Pour the mixture into a medium bowl and let cool for 10 minutes.

Stir in the sour cream until smooth, then add the flour and sprinkle over the baking soda (bicarb) and salt. Fold the mixture with a silicone spatula or wooden spoon until the dough just comes together and there are no dry pockets of flour remaining.

Scrape the dough onto a lightly floured work surface. Using a lightly floured rolling pin, roll out the dough to ½ inch (13 mm) thick. Using a 2½- to 3-inch (6.5 to 7.5 cm) round or heart-shaped cutter, cut out cookies and transfer them to the prepared baking sheets, spaced 2 inches (5 cm) apart. Reroll the scraps to cut out more cookies.

Bake until the cookies are risen, golden brown at the edges, and give just slightly when pressed on top, 15–20 minutes, switching racks and rotating the baking sheets front to back halfway through. The cookies will firm up considerably upon cooling so err on the side of underbaking them.

Transfer the baking sheets to wire racks. Let the cookies cool on the pans for 1 minute, then transfer them to the racks to cool completely.

Make the chocolate glaze: In a small bowl, whisk together the powdered (icing) sugar and cocoa. Add the vanilla and 2 tablespoons of the milk and stir until a thick paste forms. Add another 1 tablespoon milk and stir until the glaze is pourable and smooth but not too runny. Add more milk if needed to reach the consistency you want.

Balance a cookie on the tines of a fork and position it over the bowl of glaze. Use a spoon in your other hand to spoon glaze over the cookie, allowing the excess to drip back into the bowl. Once the glaze stops dripping, return the cookie to a rack or a baking sheet. Repeat glazing the remaining cookies. Let the glaze dry until set before serving.

Chocolate-Glazed Polish Gingerbread

Soft Spiced Gingerbread Cookies

Perníčky / Pernik na Figurky

Preparation time: 1 hour 30
minutes, plus chilling, cooling,
and setting time
Cooking time: 15 minutes
Makes: About 36 cookies

2½ cups (355 g) all-purpose
  (plain) flour
2 tablespoons Dutch-process
  cocoa powder
1½ teaspoons ground cinnamon
1 teaspoon baking soda
  (bicarbonate of soda)
1 teaspoon ground allspice
1 teaspoon ground anise seeds
1 teaspoon ground star anise
½ teaspoon ground cloves
½ teaspoon fine sea salt
½ cup (100 g) white US granulated
  (UK caster) sugar
4 tablespoons (55 g) vegetable
  shortening or unsalted
  butter, softened
3 tablespoons honey
1 egg
2 tablespoons gold or dark rum
1 teaspoon finely grated lemon zest
Egg wash: 2 egg yolks, beaten

For the icing:
1 egg white
2 cups (270 g) powdered (icing)
  sugar, sifted
1 teaspoon fresh lemon juice

These gingerbread-style cookies from the Czech Republic are known for their chewy, soft texture, as compared to the typical crisp and snappy gingerbread cookies throughout the rest of Europe. Honey and rum spike the dough perfumed primarily with spices like star anise, anise seeds, cloves, and cinnamon. Even more unique is their use of cocoa powder as a kind of spice, with only a small amount to add bitterness and a touch of color to the fragrant dough.

This dough is used primarily to make gingerbread men-style cut-outs that are iced with various designs. Many recipes call for baking the cookies and storing them in a permeable container for three to four weeks, to allow the cookies to achieve their unique soft texture. They will also be soft after just a few days if kept in a tin (not airtight) lined with paper towels. Another unique touch to these gingerbread cookies is that they are glazed with beaten egg yolk fresh out of the oven, which gives them a shiny finish once dried.

In a medium bowl, whisk together the flour, cocoa powder, cinnamon, baking soda (bicarb), allspice, anise, star anise, cloves, and salt.

In a large bowl, with a hand mixer, combine the white US granulated (UK caster) sugar, shortening, and honey and beat on medium speed until light and fluffy, 1–2 minutes. Add the whole egg and beat until smooth. Beat in the rum and lemon zest. Add the dry ingredients and stir until the mixture comes together into a solid dough, lightly kneading only as much as needed to no longer see any dry patches of flour in the bowl. Shape the dough into a ball, wrap in plastic wrap (cling film), and refrigerate for at least 1 hour or up to 2 days.

Position racks in the top and bottom thirds of the oven and preheat the oven to 350°F (180°C/Gas Mark 4). Line two large baking sheets with parchment paper.

Working on a lightly floured work surface, roll out the dough with a rolling pin to ¼ inch (6 mm) thick. Using cookie cutters, cut out as many cookies as you can, transferring them to the prepared baking sheets, spaced 1 inch (2.5 cm) apart. Reroll the scraps as needed to cut out more cookies.

Bake until darker brown at the edges and dry to the touch on top, 10–15 minutes, depending on the size and shape of the cookies.

Meanwhile, prepare the egg wash and keep it covered with a sheet of plastic wrap so it doesn't dry out.

Transfer the baking sheets to wire racks. While the cookies are hot from the oven, brush each lightly with some of the egg wash to glaze. Transfer them to the racks to cool completely.

Make the icing: In a medium bowl, beat the egg white with a fork until frothy. Add the powdered (icing) sugar and lemon juice and stir until the mixture forms a smooth icing. Transfer the icing to a small piping bag and use to decorate the cookies. Let the icing stand until hardened and set before serving.

Soft Spiced Gingerbread Cookies

Hazelnut Butter Cookies

Masarykovo Cukrovi

Preparation time: 45 minutes, plus
 1 hour soaking time and chilling time
Cooking time: 15 minutes
Makes: About 36 cookies

1 cup (145 g) skin-on hazelnuts
⅔ cup (5⅓ oz/150 g) unsalted butter,
 softened
⅔ cup (90 g) powdered (icing) sugar,
 plus more for dusting
2 teaspoons pure vanilla extract
¾ teaspoon fine sea salt
2 egg yolks
1½ tablespoons Dutch-process cocoa
 powder (optional)
2 cups (280 g) all-purpose (plain) flour

These cookies share a distinction with Icelandic *bessastaðakökur* (recipe, page 334) in that they're both named after presidents. These "Masaryk's cookies" were named for the first president of Czechoslovakia, Tomáš Masaryk, who helped the country gain independence from the Austro-Hungarian empire in 1918.

The dough is a simple butter-based one enriched with egg yolks. Whole hazelnuts stud the dough, which gets formed into a log so you can slice rounds of dough off to bake the cookies. The hazelnuts are first soaked in water to soften them so they slice cleanly and don't break apart when cutting the dough log. A common variation includes cocoa powder in the dough, so it is included in this recipe as an optional ingredient.

- -

Position racks in the top and bottom thirds of the oven and preheat the oven to 350°F (180°C/Gas Mark 4). Line two large baking sheets with parchment paper.

Place the hazelnuts in a heatproof bowl and pour over boiling water to cover. Let the hazelnuts soak for 1 hour, then drain and dry on paper towels; do not over-soak the hazelnuts.

In a large bowl, with a hand mixer, combine the butter, sugar, vanilla, and salt and beat on medium speed until smooth and fluffy, 2–3 minutes. Add the egg yolks and beat until incorporated. Beat in the cocoa powder (if using). Add the flour and stir until the dough comes together and there are no dry patches of flour remaining. Stir in the hazelnuts.

Divide the dough in half. Form each half into a vague cylinder and place on separate sheets of parchment paper. Shape the dough into logs 1½ inches (4 cm) in diameter and wrap tightly (see page 14). Transfer the logs to the refrigerator to firm up for at least 30 minutes or up to 2 days.

Unwrap the dough logs and cut the dough into slices ½ inch (13 mm) thick. Arrange the slices on the prepared baking sheets, spaced at least 1 inch (2.5 cm) apart.

Bake until golden brown at the edges and dry to the touch in the center, 14–16 minutes, switching racks and rotating the baking sheets front to back halfway through.

Transfer the baking sheets to wire racks. Let the cookies cool on the pans for 1 minute, then transfer them to the racks to cool completely.

Toss or dust the cookies in sugar before serving.

Crisp Ginger Cookies

Zazvorniky

Preparation time: 30 minutes,
 plus overnight chilling and
 overnight resting
Cooking time: 30 minutes
Makes: About 18 cookies

1 cup (200 g) white US granulated
 (UK caster) sugar
2 eggs
4 tablespoons (2 oz/55 g) unsalted
 butter, melted and cooled
1 tablespoon ground ginger
1 teaspoon baker's ammonia (see
 page 17), baking soda (bicarbonate
 of soda), or baking powder
2¼ cups (315 g) all-purpose
 (plain) flour
¾ teaspoon fine sea salt

Despite the name, most "gingerbread" cookies in Europe don't contain any ginger (read more in the essay on Gingerbread, page 328). But this Slovakian cookie uses the spice as its primary flavoring, and it even shapes the cookie in the form of the rhizome. The traditional cookie cutter for these looks like a stick with three fat knobs on each side to resemble a finger of fresh ginger. Most bakers use snowflake or flower-shaped cookies in lieu of the ginger shape, so if you can't find it, you can use any shape you like.

Another quality of these cookies that makes them unique is their use of ammonium bicarbonate, or baker's ammonia. This leavening agent gives the cookies a lightness and crispness that is their signature. The cut cookies are left uncovered overnight before baking, which dries out the surface so that when baked, they rise like a *macaron* (recipe, page 262) to produce a three-dimensional ginger-shaped cookie.

In a large bowl, with a hand mixer, beat the sugar and eggs on medium-high speed until creamy, pale, and the mixture falls back in a thick ribbon when lifted from the beater, 3–4 minutes. Reduce the mixer speed to low, and slowly drizzle in the melted butter, followed by the ginger and baker's ammonia. Add the flour and salt and stir until a soft dough forms and there are no dry patches of flour remaining. Cover the bowl with plastic wrap (cling film) and let the dough rest for at least 8 hours or overnight in the refrigerator.

Line two large baking sheets with parchment paper.

Scrape the dough onto a lightly floured work surface. Using a lightly floured rolling pin, roll out the dough to ¼ inch (6 mm) thick. Using a 3-inch (7.5 cm) ginger-shaped cutter or other cutter of similar size, cut out cookies and transfer them to the prepared baking sheets, spaced 2 inches (5 cm) apart. Let the cookies rest on the baking sheets for at least 8 hours or up to overnight.

Position racks in the top and bottom thirds of the oven and preheat the oven to 300°F (150°C/Gas Mark 2).

Bake until the cookies are risen, dry to the touch, and golden brown all over, 25–30 minutes, switching racks and rotating the baking sheets front to back halfway through.

Transfer the baking sheets to wire racks. Let the cookies cool on the pans for 1 minute, then transfer them to the racks to cool completely.

Crisp Honey Spice Cookies

Medovníky

Preparation time: 50 minutes,
 plus cooling and chilling time
Cooking time: 20 minutes
Makes: About 36 cookies

1 cup (135 g) powdered (icing) sugar
6 tablespoons (125 g) honey
4 tablespoons (2 oz/55 g)
 unsalted butter
1½ teaspoons ground cinnamon
1 teaspoon ground anise seeds
¼ teaspoon ground cloves
2½ cups (350 g) all-purpose
 (plain) flour
1 teaspoon baking soda
 (bicarbonate of soda)
¾ teaspoon fine sea salt
2 eggs, 1 whole and 1 separated

Though these Slovakian *medovníky* ("honey cookies") are similar to Czech *pernik na figurky* ("spice cookies;" recipe, page 190)—in fact, the names are often used interchangeably—there appear to be small differences between the two gingerbreads from countries that used to be united as one. The Slovakian cookies contain a higher proportion of honey than their Czech cousins, and they typically are thinner and crisper, as opposed to soft and chewy *pernik na figurky*.

While Czech gingerbreads use lots of anise in addition to half a dozen other spices, many recipes for Slovakian *medovníky* call out cinnamon, anise seeds, and cloves as the main three that must be included (and in smaller amounts so the honey flavor is still dominant). Whether these differences are parsed out so minutely in real life, many bakers don't really agree on. Nevertheless, it's an interesting showcase of how the same cookie evolved—even ever so slightly—in two different environments.

In a small saucepan, combine the sugar, honey, butter, cinnamon, anise, and cloves and heat over medium heat, stirring occasionally, until the butter melts and the mixture just begins to simmer at the edges. Remove the pan from the heat and pour the honey mixture into a large bowl to cool completely.

Meanwhile, in a medium bowl, whisk together the flour, baking soda (bicarb), and salt.

Add the whole egg and 1 egg yolk to the cooled honey mixture and whisk until smooth. Add the dry ingredients and stir until the mixture comes together into a solid dough, lightly kneading only as much as needed to no longer see any dry patches of flour in the bowl. Shape the dough into a ball, wrap in plastic wrap (cling film), and refrigerate for at least 1 hour or up to 2 days.

Position racks in the top and bottom thirds of the oven and preheat the oven to 350°F (180°C/Gas Mark 4). Line two large baking sheets with parchment paper.

Working on a lightly floured work surface, roll out the dough with a rolling pin to ⅛ inch (3 mm) thick. Using 2- to 3-inch (5 to 7.5 cm) cookie cutters, cut out shapes of dough. Reroll the scraps to cut out more. Arrange the dough shapes on the prepared baking sheets, spaced 2 inches (5 cm) apart. Lightly beat the remaining egg white to loosen and brush a thin film of egg white over each round of dough.

Bake until the cookies are darker brown at the edges and dry to the touch on top, 8–10 minutes, switching racks and rotating the baking sheets front to back halfway through.

Transfer the baking sheets to wire racks. Let the cookies cool for 1 minute on the pans, then transfer them to the racks to cool completely.

Vanilla Sugar-Coated Crescent Cookies
Vanillekipferl

Preparation time: 50 minutes
Cooking time: 25 minutes
Makes: About 30 cookies

1½ cups (175 g) walnuts
½ cup (100 g) white US granulated
  (UK caster) sugar
2 sticks (8 oz/225 g) unsalted butter,
  softened
2 teaspoons pure vanilla extract
¾ teaspoon fine sea salt
1 egg yolk
2 cups (280 g) all-purpose (plain) flour
Vanilla Powdered Sugar (page 16),
  for coating

Popular lore states that the crescent shape, or *Kipfel*, found in so many Austrian baked goods is because of a culinary tribute to the victory over Ottoman soldiers at the siege of Vienna in 1529 ... or the battle of Vienna in 1683. Either way, crescent-shaped baked goods existed in the Austro-Hungarian empire as early as 1227, and moon-shaped breads date back centuries further, like Swiss *panis lunatis*, a crescent-shaped bread made in the eighth century. But there is a striking similarity between these crescent-shaped cookies and Turkish *ay çöreği*, pastries that are crescent shaped and filled with walnuts, and Moroccan *kaab el-ghazal* (recipe, page 135), cookies stuffed with almond paste.

In these cookies, which are considered more "Viennese" than "Austrian"—a splitting of hairs that nods to Vienna's more intercontinental influences over Austria's strictly Germanic-leaning influences—ground walnuts are mixed directly into the dough, which is shaped into crescents, then coated in copious amounts of vanilla sugar. Though many recipes coat the cookies in vanilla-scented sugar, the version made with powdered (icing) sugar seems to have overtaken the former in popularity.

In the Czech Republic, these cookies are known as *vanilkove rohlicky*, and in Croatia, they're known as *kiflice*. Though any nuts, such as almonds or hazelnuts, can be used in these cookies, the traditional nuts are walnuts, so those are used in this recipe. Make sure the nuts are very finely ground so they blend in seamlessly with the dough.

- -

Position racks in the top and bottom thirds of the oven and preheat the oven to 350°F (180°C/Gas Mark 4). Line two large baking sheets with parchment paper.

Spread the walnuts out in a single layer on one of the baking sheets and bake until lightly toasted and fragrant, 6–8 minutes.

Transfer the nuts to a cutting board and let cool. Reserve the baking sheet. Using a food processor or a knife, process or chop the walnuts until very finely ground.

In a large bowl, with a hand mixer, combine the white US granulated (UK caster) sugar, the butter, vanilla, salt, and egg yolk and beat on medium speed until light and fluffy, 2–3 minutes. Add the ground walnuts and flour and stir until a dough forms and there are no dry patches of flour remaining.

Using a ¾-ounce (1½-tablespoon) ice cream scoop, portion the dough and roll into balls. Shape each ball into a 2½-inch (6.5 cm) cylinder and then bend it in the middle to form a crescent moon shape, slightly tapering the ends. Arrange the crescents on the prepared baking sheets, spaced 1 inch (2.5 cm) apart.

Bake until light golden brown on the bottom and dry to the touch in the center, 14–16 minutes, switching racks and rotating the baking sheets front to back halfway through.

Transfer the baking sheets to wire racks and let the cookies rest for 5 minutes. Fill a bowl with the vanilla powdered sugar. While the cookies are still warm and working a few at a time, place the cookies in the bowl of vanilla sugar and turn them to coat, returning each to their place on the baking sheet to cool completely.

Once completely cooled, dust liberally with more of the vanilla powdered sugar before serving.

Jam-Filled Cookie Cut-Out Sandwiches

Linzer Augen

Preparation time: 45 minutes,
 plus cooling time
Cooking time: 15 minutes
Makes: About 12 cookie sandwiches

2½ cups (350 g) all-purpose
 (plain) flour
1 cup (120 g) almond flour
 (ground almonds)
¾ teaspoon fine sea salt
2 sticks (8 oz/225 g) unsalted
 butter, softened
1 cup (135 g) powdered (icing)
 sugar, plus more for dusting
2 teaspoons pure vanilla extract
1 egg yolk
1 cup (320 g) red currant
 or raspberry jam

While many cookies are influenced by other cookies from around the world, these famous cookie sandwiches are simply the diminutive form of a much more famous dessert. The Linzer torte, named after the town of Linz, Austria, is a large open-faced tart usually made with a short pastry dough packed with ground hazelnuts and covered in red currant or raspberry jam. More dough is latticed over the top of the jam before being baked. How these cookies—called *Linzer augen* or "Linzer eyes"—most likely evolved from that dessert seems pretty straightforward: Switch the hazelnuts for almonds and simply stack cookies on top of each other, making sure the top cookie has a cut out so you can see the jam in the center, similar to how the latticed dough provides a peek at the insides of the torte.

In France, there's a version of these cookies called *lunette du romans*, or "Roman glasses," that are basically *Linzer augen* shaped as ovals and with two holes punched in the top cookie. In Switzerland, these cookies are called *spitzbuben*, while in Bulgaria, they're called *maslenki*. When apricot jam is used instead of red currant jam, these Austrian cookies take on the name *Marillenringe* or "apricot rings." The traditional jam used to sandwich these cookies together is red currant, though raspberry jam can substitute.

Position racks in the top and bottom thirds of the oven and preheat the oven to 325°F (160°C/Gas Mark 3). Line two large baking sheets with parchment paper.

In a medium bowl, whisk together the flour, almond flour, and salt.

In a large bowl, with a hand mixer, beat the butter and sugar on medium speed until pale and fluffy, 2–3 minutes. Add the vanilla and egg yolk and beat until smooth. Add the dry ingredients and stir until the dough forms and there are no dry patches of flour remaining.

Transfer the dough to a lightly floured work surface. Using a lightly floured rolling pin, roll out the dough to ¼ inch (6 mm) thick. Using a 3-inch (7.5 cm) round cutter, preferably fluted, cut out rounds of dough and transfer them to the prepared baking sheets, spaced 1 inch (2.5 cm) apart. Reroll the scraps to cut out more rounds. Using a 1-inch (2.5 cm) round cutter, cut out the centers of half of the dough rounds. Save the centers to bake separately or reroll to cut out a few more cookies.

Bake until the cookies are light golden brown at the edges and dry to the touch, 12–15 minutes, switching racks and rotating the baking sheets front to back halfway through.

Transfer the baking sheets to wire racks. Let the cookies cool on the pans for 1 minute, then transfer them to the racks to cool completely.

Spread a heaping teaspoon of the red currant jam over each of the whole cookies. Using a fine sieve, dust the ring-shaped cookies with sugar. Place each ring-shaped cookie over a jam-coated cookie to create sandwiches to serve.

Jam-Filled Cookie Cut-Out Sandwiches

Railroad Man Cookies

Eisenbahner / Eisenbahnschnitten

(v)

Preparation time: 1 hour 45 minutes
Cooking time: 20 minutes
Makes: About 48 cookies

For the shortbread dough:
2 cups (280 g) all-purpose (plain) flour
¾ teaspoon fine sea salt
½ teaspoon baking powder
1½ sticks (6 oz/170 g) unsalted
  butter, softened
½ cup (100 g) white US granulated
  (UK caster) sugar
1 teaspoon pure vanilla extract
1 egg yolk

For the marzipan dough:
1 log (7 oz/200 g) almond paste
3 tablespoons powdered (icing) sugar
2 tablespoons (30 g) unsalted
  butter, melted
1 egg white

For the filling:
2 cups (640 g) red currant
  or raspberry jam

These quirkily named cookies are a recent evolution of Austrian/German cookie baking since there seem to be no recipes in older cookbooks. Called *Eisenbahnschnitten* in German, these cookies consist of a long strip of thin shortbread, piped on either side with marzipan—to resemble the tracks of a railroad—then filled with red currant jam. The strip is then cut crosswise into small bar cookies.

These cookies are unique in that you parbake the shortbread base, then pipe the marzipan on top and return it to the oven to finish baking and to set the marzipan. Jam is then spooned into the wells between the marzipan "rails" while the cookie base is still hot, so it settles into the well evenly and sets up solid again by the time the cookie base cools. If you like, use raspberry or apricot jam in the center.

Position racks in the top and bottom thirds of the oven and preheat the oven to 350°F (180°C/Gas Mark 4). Line two large baking sheets with parchment paper.

Make the shortbread dough: In a medium bowl, whisk together the flour, salt, and baking powder.

In a large bowl, with a hand mixer, beat the butter and white US granulated (UK caster) sugar on medium speed until pale and fluffy, 2–3 minutes. Add the vanilla and egg yolk and beat until smooth. Add the dry ingredients and stir until the dough forms and there are no dry patches of flour remaining.

Transfer the dough to a lightly floured work surface. Using a lightly floured rolling pin, roll out the dough to a 12-inch (30 cm) square. Cut the square into 4 equal strips and carefully transfer 2 strips to each prepared baking sheet, arranging them lengthwise and spacing them at least 2 inches (5 cm) apart.

Bake until the cookies are half-baked and lightly golden, 10–12 minutes, switching racks and rotating the baking sheets front to back halfway through.

Meanwhile, make the marzipan dough: On the large holes of a box grater, grate the almond paste and place in a medium bowl. Add the powdered (icing) sugar, melted butter, and egg white and beat on medium speed with a hand mixer until the mixture is smooth. Scrape the dough into a piping bag fitted with a ½-inch (13 mm) fluted tip (nozzle).

When the cookies come out of the oven, immediately pipe a row of marzipan dough along both long sides of each cookie strip. Return the baking sheets to the oven and continue baking until the cookies are golden brown and dry to the touch in the center and the marzipan is set, about 10 minutes more.

Fill the cookies: As soon as the baking sheets come out of the oven, spoon the jam evenly over all 4 baked cookie strips, gently spreading it so it fills in the spaces between the marzipan "rails." Let the cookies cool completely on the pans.

To serve, cut each strip crosswise into bars 1 inch (2.5 cm) thick.

Railroad Man Cookies

Chocolate-Glazed Almond and Butter Cookie Sandwiches

Ischler Krapferl

Preparation time: 1 hour 10
 minutes, plus chilling, cooling,
 and setting time
Cooking time: 20 minutes
Makes: About 30 cookie sandwiches

For the dough:
2 cups (230 g) sliced (flaked) almonds
2¼ cups (315 g) all-purpose
 (plain) flour
1½ cups (205 g) powdered
 (icing) sugar
¾ teaspoon fine sea salt
2½ sticks (10 oz/285 g) unsalted
 butter, softened
2 egg yolks
2 teaspoons pure vanilla extract

To finish:
1 cup (320 g) apricot or raspberry jam
½ cup (100 g) white US granulated
 (UK caster) sugar
3 tablespoons light corn syrup
3 tablespoons water
4 oz (115 g) bittersweet chocolate,
 roughly chopped

Popular lore has it that these cookies were a favorite of Emperor Franz Joseph I, when he spent summers in the Austrian town of Bad Ischl. A bakery in the town called Zauner Confectionery even claims to be the birthplace of the Ischler cookies in 1832. The original version was two Linzer-style or shortbread cookies sandwiched with a chocolate pastry cream that is then glazed in more chocolate. Another variation sandwiches the cookies with chocolate ganache and apricot jam inside but leaves them plain outside.

Though these cookies were invented in Austria, they seem to be more popular now in Hungary. Their version eschews the chocolate cream and instead sandwiches two butter cookies—crumbly with ground almonds—with apricot jam, and then glazes the sandwiches with chocolate. Numerous decorations and variations exist based on what type of jam is in the center and the glazes that cover them, either just on top or fully encased. In the Czech Republic, these cookies are called *Išlské dortičky*, and in Germany, almond paste-based shortbread cookies sandwiched with apricot jam, glazed with chocolate, and decorated with walnuts are called *Hausfreunde*. Though they may not be related to these Ischler cookies, it's likely they've influenced each other over the years.

Make the dough: In a food processor, pulse the almonds until the consistency of fine sand, about 12 pulses. Add the flour, powdered (icing) sugar, and salt and pulse to combine. Add the butter, egg yolks, and vanilla and pulse just until a dough forms and there are no dry patches of flour remaining. Scrape the dough onto a clean work surface and shape into a ball. Wrap the dough ball in plastic wrap (cling film) and refrigerate for 1 hour or up to 2 days.

Position racks in the top and bottom thirds of the oven and preheat the oven to 350°F (180°C/Gas Mark 4). Line two large baking sheets with parchment paper.

Unwrap and transfer the dough to a lightly floured work surface. Using a lightly floured rolling pin, roll out the dough to ⅛ inch (3 mm) thick. Using a 2-inch (5 cm) round cutter, cut out as many cookies as you can from the dough. Reroll the dough to cut out more cookies. Arrange them on the prepared baking sheets, spaced 1 inch (2.5 cm) apart.

Bake until the cookies are light golden brown at the edges and dry to the touch, 12–15 minutes, switching racks and rotating the baking sheets front to back halfway through.

Transfer the baking sheets to wire racks and let the cookies cool completely on the pans.

To finish the cookies: Line a baking sheet with parchment paper and set a wire rack on the pan. Flip half the cookies over and spread each with about 2 teaspoons of the jam. Top with another cookie to make sandwiches. Arrange the cookie sandwiches on the wire rack.

In a small saucepan, combine the white US granulated (UK caster) sugar, corn syrup, and water. Bring to a boil over high heat, stirring to dissolve the sugar. Once the syrup boils, remove the pan from the heat, add the chocolate, and swirl the pan to ensure the chocolate is coated in syrup. Let stand for 2 minutes, then stir the mixture until you have a smooth chocolate glaze.

Using a spoon, pour some of the chocolate glaze over each cookie, letting it fall over the sides and through the rack. Lightly rap the baking sheet on the counter to settle and even out the glaze on top of the cookies. Let stand until the glaze sets before serving.

Chocolate-Glazed Almond and Butter Cookie Sandwiches

Walnut-Filled Crescent Cookies

Hókifli

Preparation time: 1 hour 40 minutes
Cooking time: 20 minutes
Makes: About 24 cookies

For the dough:
1 cup (135 g) powdered (icing) sugar
2 sticks (8 oz/225 g) unsalted
 butter, softened
⅓ cup (80 g) sour cream
¾ teaspoon fine sea salt
3 cups (420 g) all-purpose
 (plain) flour

For the filling:
1¾ cups (7 oz/200 g) walnuts,
 very finely ground
½ cup (4 fl oz/120 ml) whole milk
½ cup (65 g) powdered (icing) sugar
½ teaspoon pure vanilla extract
¼ teaspoon fine sea salt
Vanilla Powdered Sugar (page 16),
 for coating

Referred to as "snow crescents," these Hungarian cookies share many similarities with cookies stemming from Eastern Europe like rugelach (recipe, page 358), Croatian *skoljkice* (recipe, page 63), and Polish *kołaczki* (recipe, page 186) because of their similar shape and fillings—usually sour fruit jam, walnuts, or poppy seeds. While these cookies are typically shaped into half-circles or crescents—as in the case of Ukrainian *kiflyky* or *roczki*—they're also often shaped like rectangular pockets, which is the shape in this recipe. Also, many old recipes added yeast, even though it didn't provide rise to the dough, but most modern recipes omit it.

The filling is typically walnuts that have been boiled or softened in milk with sugar and vanilla, though you can swap out any filling (see Eastern European Fillings, opposite). When made with walnut filling, it's easy to see their relation to Turkish *kurabiye* (recipe, page 60) and Austrian *Vanillekipferl* (recipe, page 195), especially the latter in their shared coating of powdered (icing) sugar.

Make the dough: In a large bowl, with a hand mixer, combine the powdered (icing) sugar, butter, sour cream, and salt and beat on medium speed until creamy and smooth, 1–2 minutes. Add the flour and beat on low speed until the dough comes together. Stop the mixer and lightly knead with your hands only as much as needed to no longer see any dry patches of flour in the bowl. Shape the dough into a ball, wrap in plastic wrap (cling film), and refrigerate for at least 1 hour or up to 2 days.

Position racks in the top and bottom thirds of the oven and preheat the oven to 350°F (180°C/Gas Mark 4). Line two large baking sheets with parchment paper.

Make the filling: In a small saucepan, stir together the ground walnuts, milk, powdered sugar, vanilla, and salt. Cook over medium heat, stirring, until the mixture thickens and begins to bubble. Remove the pan from the heat, scrape the filling into a bowl, and let cool completely.

Working on a lightly floured surface, roll out the dough with a rolling pin to ⅛ inch (3 mm) thick. Cut the dough in half. Arrange one half of the dough so the cut side is facing you. Using a teaspoon, drop heaping spoonfuls of the filling along the cut edge, spaced 1 inch (2.5 cm) apart. Lift the cut edge up and roll it and all the filling mounds over twice to completely enclose them. Using a knife, cut the roll of dough free from the rest of the sheet, then cut between the filling mounds to create flat-edged pockets of dough. Transfer the dough pockets to the prepared baking sheets spaced 1 inch (2.5 cm) apart. Repeat with the rest of the filling and dough to make more dough pockets.

Bake until golden brown on the bottom and dry to the touch on top, 14–16 minutes, switching racks and rotating the baking sheets front to back halfway through.

Transfer the baking sheets to wire racks and let the cookies rest for 5 minutes. While the cookies are still warm, toss each cookie in the vanilla powdered sugar to coat, returning each to their place on the baking sheet to cool completely. Dust with more vanilla sugar before serving.

Eastern European Fillings

Have you ever wondered why rugelach (recipe, page 358), *hamantaschen* (recipe, page 250), and other cookies descended from Eastern European traditions all have the same fillings? Whether it's a strudel, torte, or Polish *kołaczki* (recipe, page 186), many of the fillings for these treats are the same, no matter if they're used for cookies or cakes or pastries.

The simplest filling was a jam made from tart apricots or raspberries, often used to fill cookies or sandwich two together. Prunes and plums—with their concentrated, inky sweetness—lent a dark, caramelized edge to buttery pastries. Ground nuts and seeds like walnuts, almonds, or poppy seeds offered a bitter counterpoint to sweet dough, too. Often such nut fillings were sweetened not with all granulated sugar or honey, but with raisins or grated fresh apple, which provided a more wholesome sweetness. And when it came to dairy, fresh farmer cheese or cottage cheese was sweetened with dried fruits or sugar and honey to fill tarts, turnovers, and thumbprint cookies. In time, cream cheese and sour cream offered more stability and tartness.

These fillings, which we see as commonplace now, are all rooted in the agricultural traditions of Eastern Europe, specifically Hungary, Romania, and Poland. Apricots, walnuts, poppy seeds, etc. all grew well and proliferated in the region, and when immigrants—mainly Jews to the United States—left the area, they took their fillings with them. This explains why so many bakeries today use these ingredients, at least in large parts of Europe and the United States where such populations settled.

And though these fillings are delicious and classic now, starting with them as a template and then using more local ingredients is truer to their original intent. It's like Scandinavians using their native lingonberries instead of apricots in baked goods. By using a preserve or jam made from a local tart fruit, or using local nuts or seeds like pecans or sunflower seeds, or a fresh cheese made from your local dairy, you can adapt the fillings for the Eastern European cookies and pastries to match your locality.

Chocolate-Drizzled Tea Cake Cookies
Néro Teasütemény / Keksz

Ⓥ

Preparation time: 45 minutes,
 plus cooling and setting time
Cooking time: 15 minutes
Makes: About 12 cookie sandwiches

1⅓ cups (180 g) powdered
 (icing) sugar
1 stick (4 oz/115 g) unsalted
 butter, softened
1 teaspoon pure vanilla extract
½ teaspoon fine sea salt
Finely grated zest of ½ lemon
4 egg yolks
1½ cups (210 g) all-purpose
 (plain) flour
½ cup (160 g) thick apricot jam
2 oz (55 g) bittersweet
 chocolate, melted

These cookies are a more modern—and, thus, easier—version of *Ischler krapferl* cookies (recipe, page 200). Given the popularity of the Ischler cookies in Hungary, it's no surprise that they have spawned countless variations, each taking on the name of a ruler or influential figure to give the cookies cachet. These "néro tea cakes" are a good example of this, though it's difficult to know if the name is even in reference to the famous Roman emperor. There's a variation of the cookie, filled with pistachio paste, sold at Demel bakery in Vienna named Amadeus. In Romania, these cookies are also popular and go by the name *paleuri cu ciocolată*.

These cookie sandwiches are filled with apricot jam and then drizzled with melted chocolate, a departure from the more formal full coating of the Ischler cookies. In another slight departure, the cookies for these contain no almonds, are eggier, and are piped onto the baking sheets, so they bake up lighter and crisper than shortbread-like dough.

- -

Position racks in the top and bottom thirds of the oven and preheat the oven to 350°F (180°C/Gas Mark 4). Line two large baking sheets with parchment paper.

In a large bowl, with a hand mixer, combine the sugar, butter, vanilla, salt, and lemon zest and beat on medium speed until creamy and smooth, 1–2 minutes. Add the egg yolks, one at a time, beating well after each addition. Add the flour and beat on low speed until the dough comes together and there are no dry patches of flour remaining.

Scrape the dough into a piping bag fitted with a ½-inch (13 mm) round tip (nozzle). Pipe mounds 1 inch (2.5 cm) wide on the prepared baking sheets, spaced 2 inches (5 cm) apart. Wet the tip of your index finger and lightly flatten the tip of dough left behind from the piping bag to ensure the cookies are smooth on top.

Bake until the cookies are light golden brown at the edges and dry to the touch, 10–12 minutes, switching racks and rotating the baking sheets front to back halfway through.

Transfer the baking sheets to wire racks and let the cookies cool completely on the pans.

Line a baking sheet with parchment paper and set a wire rack over it. Flip half the cookies over and spread each with about ½ teaspoon of the jam. Top with another cookie to make sandwiches. Arrange the sandwiches on the wire rack.

Pour the chocolate into a small piping bag and snip off the tip (or use a spoon), then drizzle thin lines of chocolate back and forth over all the cookie sandwiches, creating zigzags or stripes. Let stand until the chocolate sets before serving.

Chocolate-Drizzled Tea Cake Cookies

"Serrated" Butter Cookies
Biscuiți Șprițați

Preparation time: 25 minutes
Cooking time: 15 minutes
Makes: About 24 cookies

2 cups (280 g) all-purpose (plain) flour
1 teaspoon baking powder
¾ teaspoon fine sea salt
1 cup (225 g) cold-rendered leaf lard
  or vegetable shortening, softened
1 cup (135 g) powdered (icing) sugar
1 teaspoon pure vanilla extract
3 egg yolks

This style of cookie, often called "spritz," is pressed through a meat grinder. The fat used for these cookies is pork lard, so it's possible that the cookie came about via industrious cooks using dough to clean their meat grinder (though that's just a theory). German *Spritzgebäck* (recipe, page 241), likely the precursor to these cookies, are softer and more moist than the Romanian version. And though a meat grinder was used in the beginning and still today, most bakers now use a cookie press to pipe the lengths of dough. These cookies, popular in the Republic of Moldova as well, can be dusted with powdered (icing) sugar or dipped in melted chocolate before serving.

Position racks in the top and bottom thirds of the oven and preheat the oven to 350°F (180°C/Gas Mark 4). Set out two large baking sheets and leave them unlined.

In a medium bowl, whisk together the flour, baking powder, and salt.

In a large bowl, with a hand mixer, beat the lard and sugar on medium speed until light and fluffy, 2–3 minutes. Add the vanilla and egg yolks and beat until smooth. Add the dry ingredients and stir until a dough forms and there are no dry patches of flour remaining.

Working in batches, scrape the dough into a cookie press fitted with a ridged line disc, sometimes called the "biscuit" disc, and pipe 3-inch (7.5 cm) lengths of dough, arranging them 1 inch (2.5 cm) apart on the baking sheets.

Bake until golden brown on the bottom and dry to the touch all over, 10–12 minutes, switching racks and rotating the baking sheets front to back halfway through.

Transfer the baking sheets to wire racks. Let the cookies cool on the pans for 1 minute, then transfer them to the racks to cool completely.

Golden Raisin Cookies

Fursecuri cu Stafide

Preparation time: 10 minutes
Cooking time: 20 minutes
Makes: About 12 cookies

1 stick (4 oz/115 g) unsalted
  butter, softened
½ cup (100 g) white US granulated
  (UK caster) sugar
2 egg whites
2 teaspoons golden or dark rum
1 teaspoon pure vanilla extract
1 teaspoon finely grated lemon zest
½ teaspoon fine sea salt
½ cup plus 2 tablespoons (105 g)
  golden raisins (sultanas),
  roughly chopped if large
1 cup (140 g) all-purpose (plain) flour

Raisins often take a back seat to other fruits or punchy flavors in baked goods, offering a gentle sweetness to balance rich cheese or bitter poppy seed fillings (see Eastern European Fillings, page 203). Common in countries with wine-growing cultures, raisins star in these Romanian cookies perfumed with rum and lemon zest.

Using only egg whites in the cookies helps them to spread and get crisp at the edges, rather than bake up with the cakier texture that the fat in yolks provide. You can use regular raisins or dried currants here, too, but the rum and lemon flavors pair particularly well with the lighter sweetness of golden raisins (sultanas). If your golden raisins are larger than regular raisins, as they often are, roughly chop them so the pieces spread evenly throughout the dough.

Position racks in the top and bottom thirds of the oven and preheat the oven to 300°F (150°C/Gas Mark 2). Line two large baking sheets with parchment paper.

In a large bowl, with a hand mixer, beat the butter and sugar on medium speed until creamy and light, 1–2 minutes. Add the egg whites, one at a time, beating well after each addition. Add the rum, vanilla, lemon zest, and salt and beat until evenly incorporated. Beat in the raisins. Add the flour and stir until a dough forms and there are no dry patches of flour remaining.

Using a ½-ounce (1-tablespoon) ice cream scoop, portion and drop mounds of dough on the prepared baking sheets, spaced 2 inches (5 cm) apart.

Bake until golden brown at the edges and dry to the touch in the center, 15–20 minutes, switching racks and rotating the baking sheets front to back halfway through.

Transfer the baking sheets to wire racks. Let the cookies cool on the pans for 1 minute, then transfer them to the racks to cool completely.

Jam-Filled Crescent Cookies

Cornulețe cu Gem

Preparation time: 40 minutes,
 plus chilling time
Cooking time: 20 minutes
Makes: About 30 cookies

2 cups (280 g) all-purpose (plain) flour
1 teaspoon baking powder
¾ teaspoon fine sea salt
1 stick (4 oz/115 g) unsalted
 butter, softened
½ cup (120 g) sour cream,
 at room temperature
1 teaspoon pure vanilla extract
2 egg yolks
2 cups (590 g) Plum Butter
 (page 18) or thick plum jam
2 cups (270 g) Vanilla Powdered
 Sugar (page 16), for coating

Though nothing is definitive, these Romanian crescent-shaped cookies bear more than a striking resemblance to rugelach (recipe, page 358). It's possible that these cookies—with their sour cream–based dough, plum filling, and crescent shape formed by rolling up wedges of dough—are, along with the Polish yeasted pastry *rogaliki*, the precursor to the more famous Jewish cookie, which swaps the sour cream in the dough for cream cheese.

Whereas the dough wedges for rugelach are usually spread with jam before being rolled up, these *cornulețe* are formed by rolling dough around a spoonful of jam, specifically a type of plum jam referred to as *magiun de prune*. This plum jam is unique because it uses no sugar; it's simply plums cooked down until they fall apart to mush and thicken to a jam consistency. You can use any thick jam made with sour fruit like plums or apricots, but the homemade plum butter is worth making for these cookies. The cookies are coated in powdered (icing) sugar after they're baked, so they're plenty sweet.

In a medium bowl, whisk together the flour, baking powder, and salt.

In a large bowl, with a hand mixer, combine the butter, sour cream, vanilla, and egg yolks and beat on medium speed until creamy and smooth, 1–2 minutes. Add the dry ingredients and beat on low speed until the dough comes together. Stop the mixer and lightly knead with your hands only as much as needed to no longer see any dry patches of flour in the bowl. Shape the dough into a ball, wrap in plastic wrap (cling film), and refrigerate for at least 1 hour or up to 2 days.

Position racks in the top and bottom thirds of the oven and preheat the oven to 350°F (180°C/Gas Mark 4). Line two large baking sheets with parchment paper.

Working on a lightly floured work surface, divide the dough into 4 equal portions. Working with one portion at a time, keep the remaining dough covered with plastic wrap and store in the refrigerator until ready to use. Roll out the dough with a rolling pin into an 8-inch (20 cm) round; cut the dough into 8 wedges. Using a 1-tablespoon measure, dollop level spoonfuls of jam at the wide end of each wedge. Starting from the wide end, roll up each wedge so the dough wraps around the jam filling.

Arrange the dough crescents on the prepared baking sheets, spaced 2 inches (5 cm) apart. Repeat with the remaining portions of dough and the jam to make more dough crescents.

Bake until golden brown on the bottom and dry to the touch on top, 18–20 minutes, switching racks and rotating the baking sheets front to back halfway through.

Transfer the baking sheets to wire racks and let the cookies rest for 1 minute. While the cookies are still warm, toss each cookie in vanilla powdered sugar to coat, returning each to their place on the baking sheet to cool completely.

Jam-Filled Crescent Cookies

russia, the baltics & central asia

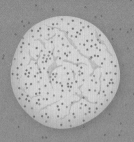
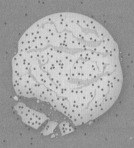

The scarcity of fresh ingredients themes the cookies from this region, with many historical recipes not lasting past the time period when the former USSR dominated the area, resetting the diet and what was available to cook with. Shelf-stable convenience ingredients like sweetened condensed milk, mayonnaise, or margarine are used here to add richness to sweets crafted with other simple ingredients like farmer cheese and fruit jam or native agricultural products like rye or poppy seeds.

Filled Walnut-Shaped Cookies
Oreshki

Preparation time: 1 hour 35 minutes
Cooking time: 25 minutes
Makes: About 30 cookies

1 stick (4 oz/115 g) unsalted
  butter, softened
½ cup (100 g) white US granulated
  (UK caster) sugar
2 eggs
2 tablespoons mayonnaise
1 teaspoon pure vanilla extract
½ teaspoon fine sea salt
1 teaspoon distilled white vinegar
¼ teaspoon baking soda
  (bicarbonate of soda)
2⅔ cups (370 g) all-purpose
  (plain) flour
2 cups (500 g) dulce de leche
  repostero, store-bought or
  homemade (page 182), or Nutella

These whimsical cookies may get their names from the Russian word for "walnuts," but there are no walnuts in them. The name comes from their shape, complete with the ridges and grooves from the nut's exterior shell. These cookies are a twentieth-century invention of industrious home cooks during Soviet-era scarcity who were forced to be more creative with inexpensive, shelf-stable ingredients like vinegar, mayonnaise, and sweetened condensed milk. An eggy, wafer-like dough is cooked in a special waffle iron-like pan to create the two halves of the "walnuts." Then the two are filled and sandwiched together with *sguschonka*, sweetened condensed milk that's boiled until caramelized (also known as dulce de leche). Some recipes now include the cookie's namesake nut in the filling.

The popularity of these cookies extends throughout former Soviet and neighboring countries. They're well known in Georgia, and in Ukraine, they're called *horishky*. In Romania, they go by *nuci umplute* and are typically filled with chocolate ganache instead of dulce de leche. Further afield, they're known in Tunisia as *zouza*—their appearance most likely due to favorable Russia-Tunisia diplomatic relations that began in the late 1950s. *Oreshki* are made with hinged "*oreshnitsa*" pans with walnut-shaped divots that are 1¼ inches (3 cm) long; they can be found online.

In a large bowl, with a hand mixer, beat the butter and sugar on medium speed until creamy and light, 1–2 minutes. Add the eggs, one at a time, beating well after each addition. Add the mayonnaise, vanilla, and salt and beat until evenly incorporated.

In a small bowl, stir together the vinegar and baking soda (bicarb) until it fizzes. Pour into the bowl and beat until smooth. Add the flour and stir until a dough forms and there are no dry patches of flour remaining.

Place an oreshnitsa iron over medium heat on your stove. Using a scant 1-teaspoon measure, portion the dough into small balls. Open the iron and place one dough ball in each divot in the iron. Close the iron and let cook until the dough spreads to fill the divots and sets, 6–8 minutes, depending on the heat of your stove.

Open the iron and invert it over a tea towel so the cookies fall out, using the tip of a table knife to nudge the cookies from the molds, if needed. Repeat filling the iron with dough balls and cooking cookies. As with making waffles or pancakes, the heat will ebb and flow under the iron, so remove the iron from the heat while loading in dough balls and return it to the heat once they're filled, so the iron doesn't overheat.

When all the cookies are done, use your fingers or a paring knife to trim away the excess cooked batter from the shells so they have clean edges. Fill each shell flush with dulce de leche—about 1 teaspoon each—then sandwich two shells together to form the "walnuts."

Process any cooked cookie scraps in a food processor until the consistency of breadcrumbs, then roll the seams of each oreshki in the crumbs to stick to any dulce de leche seeping out before serving.

Filled Walnut-Shaped Cookies

Jam-Filled Russian Honey Tea Cakes

Pryaniki

Preparation time: 1 hour, plus
  cooling, chilling, and setting time
Cooking time: 30 minutes
Makes: About 12 cookies

½ cup (170 g) honey
4 tablespoons (2 oz/55 g)
  unsalted butter
1 teaspoon ground cardamom
1 teaspoon ground cinnamon
1 teaspoon ground ginger
1 teaspoon freshly grated nutmeg
2 cups (280 g) all-purpose (plain) flour
½ teaspoon baking soda
  (bicarbonate of soda)
¾ teaspoon fine sea salt
1 egg
½ cup (160 g) thick plum jam,
  homemade (see Homemade [Any]
  Fruit Jam, page 18) or store-bought
1 cup (135 g) powdered (icing)
  sugar, sifted
2 tablespoons fresh lemon juice

The word for Russia's style of gingerbread is *pryanik*, but within that one word exists limitless variations and styles, both cakes and what we'd call cookies now, all termed *pryaniki*. The word essentially means "spiced," but Russian gingerbread, especially compared to other styles in the rest of Europe, has fewer spices. Over the centuries, and with influence from neighboring regions and trade with Asian countries that had spices, a few spices crept into the mix, but no recipes seem to agree on which ones they are. Even in the *Book of Tasty and Healthy Food*, from the USSR Ministry of the Food Industry in 1939, there's a recipe for *pryanichki* (spice cookies) made simply of egg, sugar, and flour and only flavored with cardamom or vanilla.

The essential ingredient, however, is honey, which harkens back to the original gingerbread made in the country in the ninth century that consisted of rye flour, honey, and fermented berry juice. The recipe below is a modernized version of the most famous style of gingerbread in Russia, from the town of Tula. Their gingerbread consists of two sheets of dough filled with jam, then "printed" or stamped with elaborate designs before being baked and glazed in a white icing. This *Tulskii pryaniki* influences the style of cookie that's most popular now, sandwiching a spoonful of jam between two rounds of soft dough cut-outs that get glazed after baking. Though they resemble German *Elisenlebkuchen* (recipe, page 244), it's more likely they evolved as simply an easier, homemade version of the beloved treat from Tula.

In a medium saucepan, combine the honey, butter, cardamom, cinnamon, ginger, and nutmeg and heat over medium heat, stirring occasionally, until the butter melts and the mixture just begins to simmer at the edges. Remove the pan from the heat and let the honey mixture cool completely.

Meanwhile, in a medium bowl, whisk together the flour, baking soda (bicarb), and salt.

Add the egg to the cooled honey mixture in the pan and whisk until smooth. Add the dry ingredients and stir until the mixture comes together into a solid dough, lightly kneading only as much as needed to no longer see any dry patches of flour in the pan. Shape the dough into a ball, wrap in plastic wrap (cling film), and refrigerate for at least 1 hour or up to 2 days.

Position racks in the top and bottom thirds of the oven and preheat the oven to 350°F (180°C/Gas Mark 4). Line two large baking sheets with parchment paper.

Working on a lightly floured work surface, roll out the dough with a rolling pin to ⅛ inch (3 mm) thick. Using a 2½-inch (6.5 cm) round cutter, cut out rounds of dough. Reroll the scraps as needed to cut out more rounds. Spoon a heaping ½ teaspoon of plum jam in the center of half of the dough rounds. Cover each with a plain dough round, pressing on the edges lightly to seal. Arrange the jam-stuffed dough rounds on the prepared baking sheets, spaced 2 inches (5 cm) apart.

Bake for 10 minutes. Rotating the baking sheets front to back and top to bottom, then reduce the oven temperature to 325°F (160°C/Gas Mark 3) and bake until the cookies are darker brown at the edges and dry to the touch on top, 10–15 minutes more.

Transfer the baking sheets to wire racks. Let the cookies cool on the pans for 1 minute, then transfer them to the racks to cool completely.

In a heatproof medium bowl, stir together the sugar and lemon juice. Place the bowl in the microwave (or over a small pan of simmering water) and heat until hot to the touch. Stir again to form a smooth, loose icing.

Rest a cookie on the tines of a fork and hover it over the bowl of icing. Holding a spoon in the other hand, spoon some of the icing over the cookie to cover it completely. Lightly rap the stem of the fork on the edge of the bowl to settle the icing on the cookie and shake off any excess. Transfer the iced cookie to a sheet of parchment paper. Repeat icing the remaining cookies, rewarming the icing as needed to keep it loose. Let the icing on the cookies stand until set before serving.

Folded Farmer Cheese Cookies

Gusinyye Lapki

Preparation time: 35 minutes,
 plus chilling time
Cooking time: 25 minutes
Makes: About 30 cookies

2 cups (280 g) all-purpose (plain) flour
½ teaspoon baking powder
¾ teaspoon fine sea salt
7½ oz (215 g) farmer cheese
 or drained small-curd cottage
 cheese (see headnote)
1 stick (4 oz/115 g) unsalted butter, cut
 into ½-inch (13 mm) cubes, chilled
1 egg
2 tablespoons cold water
1 teaspoon pure vanilla extract
1 cup (200 g) white US granulated
 (UK caster) sugar

Charting the lineage of many cookies is often simple because the form doesn't change from place to place, usually just the name. But these cookies—popular in Russia and former Soviet states like Ukraine, Turkmenistan, Tajikistan, and Uzbekistan—seemed to evolve, specifically, by being folded. They started as *vatrushki*, small open-faced tart-like pastries with yeasted dough and a sweetened filling of Russian fresh cheese called *tvorog*, sometimes also called farmer cheese. From there, they lost the yeast and were folded in half to make cookies called *sochniki*. In their final form, the farmer cheese filling blended with the dough and was folded one more time to produce these *gusinyye lapki*, or "geese feet," named for their distinctive appearance.

Both *sochniki* and *gusinyye lapki* seem to be more modern cookies that possibly evolved after the USSR dissolution, when many older pastries became simpler and took the form of cookies. Look for *tvorog* in Eastern European markets or online. In the US, you can easily find farmer cheese, which is firmer than *tvorog* and comes in blocks; look for it next to cream cheese. Or you can use small-curd cottage cheese as a substitute, but will need to drain it in a sieve overnight to firm it up.

In a large bowl, whisk together the flour, baking powder, and salt. Grate the farmer cheese on the large holes of a box grater into the dry ingredients. Add the butter and rub the butter and cheese into the dry ingredients until broken down into coarse crumbs the size of peas.

In a small bowl, stir together the egg, water, and vanilla. Add to the bowl and stir until the mixture comes together into a solid dough, lightly kneading only as much as needed to no longer see any dry patches of flour remaining. Shape the dough into a ball, wrap in plastic wrap (cling film), and refrigerate for at least 1 hour or up to 2 days.

Position racks in the top and bottom thirds of the oven and preheat the oven to 375°F (190°C/Gas Mark 5). Line two large baking sheets with parchment paper.

Working on a lightly floured work surface, roll out the dough with a rolling pin to ⅛ inch (3 mm) thick. Using a 3-inch (7.5 cm) round cutter, cut out rounds of dough. Reroll the scraps to cut out more rounds. Spread the sugar out on a large plate. Place one dough round in the sugar and then flip it so both sides are coated in sugar. Fold the round in half to create a half-moon, then fold in half again to form a triangle. Arrange the triangles on the prepared baking sheets, spaced 1 inch (2.5 cm) apart. Repeat with the remaining dough rounds and sugar.

Bake until the cookies are golden brown all over and the sugar on the bottom of the cookies is lightly caramelized, 20–25 minutes, switching racks and rotating the baking sheets front to back halfway through.

Transfer the baking sheets to wire racks. Let the cookies cool on the pans for 1 minute, then transfer them to the racks to cool completely.

ESTONIA

Mayonnaise Cookies

Majoneesiküpsised

Preparation time: 30 minutes
Cooking time: 15 minutes
Makes: About 18 cookies

2 cups (280 g) all-purpose (plain) flour
1 teaspoon baking soda
  (bicarbonate of soda)
¾ teaspoon fine sea salt
1 cup (210 g) mayonnaise
1 cup (200 g) white US granulated
  (UK caster) sugar
1 teaspoon pure vanilla extract

Like many retro recipes from the middle of the twentieth century, industrial convenience food products like canned soup and mayonnaise were often used in various ways to show their adaptability in the home kitchen. In Estonia, mayonnaise found its way into cookies. Like a plain tea cake, these cookies use mayonnaise as a two-in-one ingredient swap for eggs and oil. It's best to use the most neutral-flavored mayonnaise you can find to ensure these cookies stay sweet. Fork tines are often used all over the world to imprint a crisscross design on cookies, except here, they're used to imprint only one half of the dough ball.

Position racks in the top and bottom thirds of the oven and preheat the oven to 350°F (180°C/Gas Mark 4). Line two large baking sheets with parchment paper.

In a large bowl, whisk together the flour, baking soda (bicarb), and salt.

In a medium bowl, whisk together the mayonnaise, sugar, and vanilla until smooth. Add the dry ingredients and stir until a dough forms and there are no dry patches of flour remaining.

Using a 1-ounce (2-tablespoon) ice cream scoop, drop mounds of dough on the prepared baking sheets, spaced 2 inches (5 cm) apart. Dip the outermost half of the tines of a fork in some flour to keep them from sticking to the dough, then barely press them just once along one half of each dough ball to leave their mark rather than to flatten the dough.

Bake until light golden brown at the edges and dry to the touch on top, 14–16 minutes, switching racks and rotating the baking sheets front to back halfway through.

Transfer the baking sheets to wire racks. Let the cookies cool on the pans for 1 minute, then transfer them to the racks to cool completely.

ESTONIA

Rye Butter Cookies

Ruiskatut

Preparation time: 45 minutes
Cooking time: 15 minutes
Makes: About 30 cookies

1 cup (145 g) rye flour
⅔ cup (95 g) all-purpose (plain) flour
1 teaspoon baking powder
¾ teaspoon fine sea salt
1 stick (4 oz/115 g) unsalted
  butter, softened
½ cup (110 g) packed light
  brown sugar
3 tablespoons whole milk

Rye is one of the most prevalent grains in the Baltics and used in their staple bread. It is also put to use in these simple cookies, which are likely an update of an older honey-and-rye flour cookie that resembles older European styles of gingerbread, before fat and eggs were added. This recipe adds some all-purpose (plain) flour to lighten the rye, and it adds milk and butter to give the cookie a modern richness. Brown sugar is used in place of honey, to mimic the earthy flavor of the rye flour and give the cookies a pleasant chew.

Position racks in the top and bottom thirds of the oven and preheat the oven to 350°F (180°C/Gas Mark 4). Line two large baking sheets with parchment paper.

In a large bowl, whisk together the rye flour, all-purpose (plain) flour, baking powder, and salt.

In a medium bowl, with a hand mixer, beat the butter and sugar on medium speed until light and fluffy, 2–3 minutes. Add the dry ingredients and milk and stir until a dough forms and there are no dry patches of flour remaining.

Working on a lightly floured work surface, roll out the dough with a rolling pin to ¼ inch (6 mm) thick. Using a 2-inch (5 cm) round cutter, cut out rounds of dough. Reroll the scraps to cut out more cookies. Arrange the dough rounds on the prepared baking sheets, spaced 1 inch (2.5 cm) apart.

Bake until light golden brown at the edges and dry to the touch on top, 10–12 minutes, switching racks and rotating the baking sheets front to back halfway through.

Transfer the baking sheets to wire racks. Let the cookies cool on the pans for 1 minute, then transfer them to the racks to cool completely.

Russia, The Baltics & Central Asia

Rye Butter Cookies

Sweetened Condensed Milk Cookies
Kondenspiimaküpsised

Preparation time: 35 minutes
Cooking time: 10 minutes
Makes: About 24 cookies

1¾ cups (245 g) all-purpose
  (plain) flour
1 teaspoon baking powder
¾ teaspoon fine sea salt
10 tablespoons (5 oz/140 g)
  unsalted butter, cut into ½-inch
  (13 mm) cubes, chilled
½ cup (4 fl oz/120 ml) canned
  sweetened condensed milk
2 tablespoons water
1 teaspoon pure vanilla extract
1 teaspoon finely grated lemon zest

Shelf-stable convenience foods make their way into many sweets of countries that were part of the former USSR because of that era's fresh food scarcity. These Estonian cookies use sweetened condensed milk to add richness and sweetness in place of butter and sugar, similar to Peruvian *cocadas* (recipe, page 177) and Brazilian *sequilhos* (recipe, page 176). Modern recipes add butter, to make the cookies softer and more appealing. Lemon zest is added to brighten the rich, creamy dough.

Position racks in the top and bottom thirds of the oven and preheat the oven to 400°F (200°C/Gas Mark 6). Line two large baking sheets with parchment paper.

In a large bowl, whisk together the flour, baking powder, and salt. Add the butter and use your fingers to rub it into the dry ingredients until it breaks down into coarse crumbs. Add the sweetened condensed milk, water, vanilla, and lemon zest and stir until a dough forms and there are no dry patches of flour remaining.

Working on a lightly floured work surface, roll out the dough with a rolling pin to ¼ inch (6 mm) thick. Using a pizza cutter or knife, cut the dough into strips 1½ inches (4 cm) wide, then cut each strip every 1 inch (2.5 cm) on a diagonal to make diamonds. Arrange the diamonds on the prepared baking sheets, spaced 2 inches (5 cm) apart.

Bake until light golden brown at the edges and dry to the touch on top, 8–10 minutes, switching racks and rotating the baking sheets front to back halfway through.

Transfer the baking sheets to wire racks. Let the cookies cool on the pans for 1 minute, then transfer them to the racks to cool completely.

Poppy Seed Cookies
Sausainiai su Aguonomis

Preparation time: 45 minutes,
  plus cooling time
Cooking time: 20 minutes
Makes: About 12 cookies

1 stick (4 oz/115 g) unsalted butter
¼ cup (40 g) poppy seeds
1 cup (140 g) all-purpose (plain) flour
½ teaspoon baking soda
  (bicarbonate of soda)
¾ teaspoon fine sea salt
¾ cup (150 g) white US granulated
  (UK caster) sugar
1 egg
1 tablespoon fresh lemon juice
1 teaspoon pure vanilla extract

Poppy seeds grow well in Baltic countries, so they are everywhere, from breads, pastries, and pancakes to cookies, where their slightly bitter, floral flavor contrasts sweetness perfectly. This cookie is popular in all Baltic countries, but many recipes reference Lithuania as being particularly enthralled. Some recipes cut all-purpose (plain) flour with oats or rye, while others have dairy or eggs. Citrus juice, a classic pairing with poppy seeds, is often used, but orange and lemon juice are used interchangeably.

In a small saucepan, combine the butter and poppy seeds and heat over medium heat until the butter fully melts. Scrape the melted butter and poppy seeds into a large bowl and let stand until cooled and resolidified.

Position racks in the top and bottom thirds of the oven and preheat the oven to 350°F (180°C/Gas Mark 4). Line two large baking sheets with parchment paper.

In a medium bowl, whisk together the flour, baking soda (bicarb), and salt.

Add the sugar to the bowl of butter and poppy seeds and beat on medium speed with a hand mixer until light and fluffy, 2–3 minutes. Add the egg and beat until smooth. Beat in the lemon juice and vanilla. Add the dry ingredients and stir until a dough forms and there are no dry patches of flour remaining.

Using a ¾-ounce (1½-tablespoon) ice cream scoop, drop mounds of dough on the prepared baking sheets, spaced 3 inches (7.5 cm) apart; they will spread.

Bake until light golden brown at the edges and dry to the touch on top, 14–16 minutes, switching racks and rotating the baking sheets front to back halfway through.

Transfer the baking sheets to wire racks. Let the cookies cool on the pans for 1 minute, then transfer them to the racks to cool completely.

Poppy Seed Cookies

western europe

The heart of Western European baking traditions lies within this region dominated by the once famous Swabia that encompassed much of southern Germany, with an influence that stretched to parts of present-day Switzerland, Austria, France, and Liechtenstein. Soft spiced cookies, waffle cookies, and other cookies made with a prodigious use of butter cue to a "fattening" of cookies in this region. Toward the end of the Middle Ages, Catholic monks and nuns spent years perfecting sweets and confections that utilized locally grown dairy and honey, and imported spices from Southeast Asia, to great effect.

Crisp Brown Sugar Cookies

Arnhemse Meisjes

Preparation time: 30 minutes,
 plus overnight chilling
Cooking time: 30 minutes
Makes: About 24 cookies

1⅓ cups (185 g) all-purpose
 (plain) flour
⅓ cup (2½ fl oz/80 ml) whole milk
½ teaspoon instant or active dry yeast
½ teaspoon fine sea salt
¼ teaspoon fresh lemon juice
1 stick (4 oz/115 g) unsalted butter, cut
 into ½-inch (13 mm) cubes, softened
Turbinado (demerara) sugar, for rolling
 and coating

While these sugar-coated treats are leavened by yeast, they are considered cookies by the Dutch. Translated as "Arnhem girls," they are large ovals of buttery pastry, rolled and coated in coarse turbinado (demerara) sugar, and then baked. The sugar on top bakes up crunchy and glistening while the sugar on the bottom caramelizes into buttery brown candy. These cookies are traditionally coated with Dutch *kandij suiker*, a rock-like brown sugar, but turbinado sugar here is similar and more accessible.

In a stand mixer fitted with the dough hook, combine the flour, milk, yeast, salt, and lemon juice and mix on low speed until a dough forms. Increase the speed to medium and start adding one piece of butter at a time to the dough, waiting until it mixes in fully before adding the next. Continue mixing the dough until smooth, 6–8 minutes total. Scrape any dough off the hook and form the dough into a ball. Wrap the dough in plastic wrap (cling film) and refrigerate for at least 12 hours or overnight.

Position racks in the top and bottom thirds of the oven and preheat the oven to 300°F (150°C/Gas Mark 2). Line two large baking sheets with parchment paper.

Spread an even coating of sugar over a clean work surface. Set the dough on top and sprinkle the dough with more sugar, then roll out with a rolling pin, stopping to sprinkle the dough with more sugar if needed, until it is ¼ inch (6 mm) thick. Using a 3-inch (7.5 cm) oval or round cutter, cut out shapes from the dough. (You won't be able to reroll scraps here, but you can bake the scraps off as they are and eat as a snack.) Arrange the cookies on the prepared baking sheets, spaced 2 inches (5 cm) apart. Sprinkle any sugar left from the work surface on top of the dough ovals.

Bake until the cookies are golden brown all over and crisp, 25–30 minutes, switching racks and rotating the baking sheets front to back halfway through.

Transfer the baking sheets to wire racks. Let the cookies cool on the pans for 1 minute, then transfer them to the racks to cool completely.

Tiny Honey and Anise Cookies
Pepernoten

Preparation time: 25 minutes,
  plus chilling time
Cooking time: 20 minutes
Makes: About 54 cookies

½ cup (170 g) plus
  2 tablespoons honey
¼ cup (50 g) white US granulated
  (UK caster) sugar or packed light
  brown sugar
1 egg
2 teaspoons ground anise seeds
1 teaspoon baking soda
  (bicarbonate of soda)
½ teaspoon fine sea salt
¼ teaspoon ground allspice (optional)
¼ teaspoon ground
  cardamom (optional)
¼ teaspoon ground cinnamon
  (optional)
¼ teaspoon freshly grated
  nutmeg (optional)
2 cups (295 g) white rye
  or all-purpose (plain) flour
Vegetable oil, for greasing

Similar in size and style to Danish *pebernødder* (recipe, page 330) and German *Pfeffernüsse* (recipe, page 240), these Dutch cookies belong to a group of cookies called *strooigoed*, or "tossing treats," which are tossed to kids at festivals and holidays. These *pepernoten* are typically tossed by St. Nicholas's helper, Black Peter, on Sinterklaas, or St. Nicholas Day. Often made with rye flour, these cookies are typically spiced only with anise and sweetened with honey, so they're chewy. Meanwhile, *kruidnoten* (recipe, page 224) are the same size but have gingerbread-like spices added and are crunchier.

Because the use of the word *pepernoten*—"pepper nuts," a name that refers to their tiny cube- or dice-like shape, not an ingredient—has come to be used as an umbrella term for all spiced *strooigoed*, this particular style is usually referred to as *oud-Hollandsche pepernoten*, or "old Dutch" *pepernoten*, to distinguish the two. For that reason, this recipe hues closely to the older honey-and-anise flavor profile, with extra spices given as optional ingredients. The cookies are also baked in the traditional way: Instead of rounds of dough separated out on baking sheets, the balls of dough are baked near each other, so they join and bake up in a rhombohedron that is then separated into individual pieces to serve.

- -

In a medium bowl, combine the honey, sugar, egg, ground anise, baking soda (bicarb), and salt. If using, add the allspice, cardamom, cinnamon, and/or nutmeg. Whisk until smooth. Add the flour and stir until the dough forms and there are no dry patches of flour remaining. Shape the dough into a ball, wrap in plastic wrap (cling film), and refrigerate for at least 2 hours or overnight.

Preheat the oven to 350°F (180°C/Gas Mark 4). Line a 9 × 13-inch (23 × 33 cm) light metal baking pan with parchment paper and grease generously with oil.

Pinch off marble-size pieces, about 1½ teaspoons each, of the chilled dough, roll them into balls, and toss the dough balls into the prepared baking pan, rolling them around in the oil as you go. There will be some space around the dough balls.

Bake until the dough balls have risen into a single, cobblestone-like cookie that's golden brown on top, 18–22 minutes, rotating the baking pan front to back halfway through.

Transfer the baking pan to a wire rack and let the cookies cool in the pan for 10 minutes. Invert the pan onto the rack and use your fingers to break apart the pepernoten along the seams. Let the cookies cool completely on the rack before serving.

Tiny Mixed Spice Cookies

Kruidnoten

Preparation time: 40 minutes
Cooking time: 20 minutes
Makes: About 36 cookies

2 cups (280 g) all-purpose (plain) flour
2 tablespoons Speculaas Spice Mix (page 233)
1 teaspoon baking powder
½ teaspoon baking soda (bicarbonate of soda)
¾ teaspoon fine sea salt
⅔ cup (150 g) packed dark brown sugar
1 stick (4 oz/115 g) unsalted butter, softened
⅓ cup (2½ fl oz/80 ml) buttermilk (or whole milk mixed with 1 teaspoon fresh lemon juice)

These tiny, crunchy cookies are the spiced-up version of *pepernoten* (recipe, page 223). Typically made with brown sugar and *speculaaskruiden* —a mix of spices used for making *speculaas*—they're baked into tiny rounds and are crunchy, like tiny gingerbread-like tokens. *Speculaaskruiden* is similar to "pumpkin pie spice" in the United States and is usually found premixed in grocery stores. For the spice mix used in this specific recipe, omit the coriander and white pepper.

Position racks in the top and bottom thirds of the oven and preheat the oven to 325°F (160°C/Gas Mark 3). Line two large baking sheets with parchment paper.

In a medium bowl, whisk together the flour, spice mix, baking powder, baking soda (bicarb), and salt.

In a large bowl, with a hand mixer, beat the sugar and butter on medium speed until pale and fluffy, 2–3 minutes. Beat in the buttermilk until smooth. Add the dry ingredients and stir until the dough forms and there are no dry patches of flour remaining.

Using a ¼-ounce (½-tablespoon) ice cream scoop, portion the dough into marble-size balls. Arrange them on the prepared baking sheets, spaced 1 inch (2.5 cm) apart. If you like, flatten the balls slightly with your thumb; otherwise, leave them round.

Bake until darker brown at the edges and dry to the touch on top, 15–20 minutes, switching racks and rotating the baking sheets front to back halfway through.

Transfer the baking sheets to wire racks. Let the cookies cool on the pans for 1 minute, then transfer them to the racks to cool completely.

Almond and Sugar Cookie Bars

Jan Hagel Koekjes

Preparation time: 20 minutes, plus 10 minutes resting time
Cooking time: 25 minutes
Makes: About 24 cookies

2 cups (280 g) all-purpose (plain) flour
1 teaspoon baking powder
1 teaspoon ground cinnamon
¾ teaspoon fine sea salt
1½ sticks (6 oz/170 g) unsalted butter, softened
¾ cup (150 g) white US granulated (UK caster) sugar
1 egg, separated
⅓ cup (40 g) sliced (flaked) almonds
¼ cup (50 g) pearl sugar or roughly crushed sugar cubes

In Dutch, *jan hagel* refers to an unruly mob. Some people have interpreted that as a take on the cookie's jumbled garnishes of sliced (flaked) almonds and crushed pearl sugar. Others have taken it to mean a term for the type of people who'd enjoy such a simple cookie since the term has also been documented as a slang term for sailors, common people, and others on the fringes of society. However the name came about, it is an appealing cookie.

Preheat the oven to 350°F (180°C/Gas Mark 4). Line a 9 × 13-inch (23 × 33 cm) light metal baking pan with parchment paper, leaving the excess hanging over the edges.

In a bowl, whisk together the flour, baking powder, cinnamon, and salt.

In a large bowl, with a hand mixer, beat the butter and white US granulated (UK caster) sugar on medium speed until light and fluffy, 2–3 minutes. Add the egg yolk and beat until smooth. Add the dry ingredients and stir until there are no dry patches of flour remaining.

Press the dough into the bottom of the prepared baking pan to make an even layer. Beat the egg white in a small bowl until frothy, then lightly brush the dough with only enough of the beaten egg white to moisten it fully (you should not use all the egg white). Sprinkle the almonds and pearl sugar evenly over the dough.

Bake until the cookie slab is golden brown all over and dry to the touch in the center, 20–25 minutes, rotating the baking pan front to back halfway through.

Transfer the baking pan to a wire rack and let the cookie slab rest for 10 minutes. Using the overhanging parchment paper, slide the cookie slab out of the pan and onto a cutting board. Cut the cookie slab into 3 × 1½-inch (7.5 × 4 cm) rectangles. Transfer the rectangles to a wire rack to cool completely.

Western Europe

Almond and Sugar Cookie Bars

Almond Paste-Stuffed Butter Cookies

Gevulde Koeken

Preparation time: 1 hour 40 minutes,
 plus chilling time
Cooking time: 20 minutes
Makes: About 8 cookies

For the dough:
2 cups (285 g) all-purpose (plain) flour
¾ cup (150 g) white US granulated
 (UK caster) sugar
1 teaspoon baking powder
¾ teaspoon fine sea salt
1½ sticks (6 oz/170 g) unsalted
 butter, softened

For the filling:
5 oz (140 g) blanched whole
 or slivered almonds
⅔ cup (130 g) white US granulated
 (UK caster) sugar
¼ teaspoon finely grated lemon zest
⅛ teaspoon fine sea salt
1 egg

To finish:
Egg wash: 1 egg yolk beaten with
 1 tablespoon water
Sliced (flaked) or whole blanched
 almonds, for decorating

Stuffing almond paste, called *banket*, into pastries is common in the Netherlands, as it was once fashionable to do so when sugar became cheaper and more available. Similar to *gevulde speculaas* (see page 232) and the popular puff pastry-based *banketstaaf* (or *banketletter* when shaped into an "S"), this cookie has almond paste stuffed between two rounds of butter cookie dough. There's even a common variation where *speculaas* spices are added to this dough, but still baked in rounds. This cookie is a diminutive version of the larger *gevulde boterkoek*, typically baked in a large cake round.

These cookies resemble Mexican *coyotas* (recipe, page 157) in their small size and stuffing sandwiched between a top and bottom round of pastry. Many recipes garnish the top with a single whole almond, while others scatter the top with flaked almonds.

- -

Make the dough: In a large bowl, whisk together the flour, sugar, baking powder, and salt. Add the butter and use your fingertips to rub it into the flour until the fat breaks down and the mixture forms a solid dough, lightly kneading only as much as needed to no longer see any dry patches of flour in the bowl. Shape the dough into a ball, wrap in plastic wrap (cling film), and refrigerate for at least 1 hour or up to 2 days.

Make the filling: In a food processor, pulse the almonds until finely ground. Add the sugar, lemon zest, and salt and pulse until very finely ground and just starting to turn to a paste on the bottom of the bowl. Add the egg and pulse until the mixture is homogeneous. Scrape the filling into a piping bag or bowl, cover with plastic wrap (cling film), and set aside until ready to use.

Position racks in the top and bottom thirds of the oven and preheat the oven to 350°F (180°C/Gas Mark 4). Line two large baking sheets with parchment paper.

Working on a lightly floured work surface, roll out the dough with a rolling pin to ⅛ inch (3 mm) thick. Using a 4-inch (10 cm) round cutter, preferably fluted, cut out rounds of dough. Reroll the scraps to cut out more rounds. Pipe or spoon 1 tablespoon of the almond filling into the center of half the rounds, spreading it out to within ½ inch (13 mm) of the edge of the dough.

To finish: Using a pastry brush, brush the outer edges of the dough lightly with some egg wash and place an unfilled dough round on top of each and press gently at the edges to seal. Arrange the rounds on the prepared baking sheets, spaced 1 inch (2.5 cm) apart. Lightly coat the top of each round with some of the egg wash, then either arrange 1–3 whole almonds in the center or sprinkle the whole top with a pinch of sliced (flaked) almonds.

Bake until golden brown all over, 15–20 minutes, switching racks and rotating the baking sheets front to back halfway through.

Transfer the baking sheets to wire racks. Let the cookies cool on the pans for 1 minute, then transfer them to the racks to cool completely.

"Iron" Waffle Cookies

Ijzerkoekjes

Preparation time: 1 hour 25 minutes,
  plus chilling time
Cooking time: 35 minutes
Makes: About 24 cookies

2½ cups (355 g) all-purpose
  (plain) flour
2 teaspoons ground cinnamon
1 teaspoon fine sea salt
2½ sticks (10 oz/285 g) unsalted
  butter, softened
½ cup (100 g) white US granulated
  (UK caster) sugar
⅔ cup (150 g) packed light
  brown sugar
1 egg yolk

Similar in appearance to *stroopwafels*—which are made with yeast and split and filled with Dutch caramel syrup—these "iron" cookies, so named for the waffle iron they're cooked on, are spiced with cinnamon and cooked open-faced on a grid-marked griddle. Thought to be the invention of a woman named Daatje de Koe in the late 1800s, these cookies are considered a specialty of Vlaardingen, a city that was once part of Rotterdam. De Koe's *ijzerkoekjes* were apparently famous with fishermen because they kept well on long boat rides.

Belgian *lukken* (recipe, page 236) are also similar, but they're formed as rounds and usually contain no cinnamon or brown sugar. These *ijzerkoekjes* are prized for having a crisp, crunchy exterior and soft, almost-underbaked texture on the inside.

In a medium bowl, whisk together the flour, cinnamon, and salt.

In a large bowl, with a hand mixer, combine the butter, white US granulated (UK caster) sugar, and brown sugar and beat on medium speed until light and fluffy, 2–3 minutes. Add the egg yolk and beat until smooth. Add the dry ingredients and stir until the dough forms and there are no dry patches of flour remaining. Shape the dough into a disc, wrap in plastic wrap (cling film), and refrigerate for at least 2 hours or, preferably, overnight.

Line two baking sheets with parchment paper. Working on a lightly floured work surface, roll out the dough with a rolling pin to ¼ inch (6 mm) thick. Using a 3-inch (7.5 cm) oblong or oval cutter, cut out ovals of dough. Reroll the scraps to cut out more cookies. Transfer the ovals to the lined pans and refrigerate until ready to bake.

Place an open-face Dutch waffle iron, krumkake iron, or pizzelle iron over medium heat on your stove or heat an electric version. Place as many dough ovals as will fit on the iron and cook open-faced (do not close the iron), flipping once halfway through, until golden brown on both sides, 4–6 minutes, depending on the heat of your stove or follow the manufacturer's instructions for the electric maker. The cookies should be crisp outside and slightly soft on the inside.

Transfer the cookies to a wire rack to cool until firm. Repeat cooking the remaining waffle cookies.

"Iron" Waffle Cookies

Hazelnut and Anise Bar Cookies

Fryske Dúmkes / Fries Duimpje

Preparation time: 50 minutes
Cooking time: 25 minutes
Makes: About 48 cookies

3 oz (85 g) hazelnuts,
  preferably blanched
1 tablespoon anise seeds
1½ cups (210 g) all-purpose
  (plain) flour
1 teaspoon baking powder
1 teaspoon ground cinnamon
1 teaspoon ground ginger
½ teaspoon fine sea salt
⅔ cup (150 g) packed light
  brown sugar
1 stick (4 oz/115 g) unsalted
  butter, softened
1 egg

Whether a baker in the coastal province of Fryslân invented these bar cookies is unclear, but the name is catchy. The name—literally "Frisian thumbs"—stands for the thumb shape of the cookies, or the practice of a baker who presses their thumb into the cookie while it is still soft from the oven so their signature mark is imprinted on their creation. What's consistent with these cookies, however, is their combination of hazelnuts, whole and ground anise seeds, cinnamon, and ginger. Toasting the nuts beforehand improves their flavor immensely here.

Position racks in the top and bottom thirds of the oven and preheat the oven to 325°F (160°C/Gas Mark 3). Line two large baking sheets with parchment paper.

Spread the hazelnuts on one of the baking sheets and bake until fragrant and lightly toasted, 6–8 minutes.

Transfer the nuts to a cutting board and let cool. Reserve the baking sheet. Finely chop the hazelnuts and place in a medium bowl.

Place half the anise seeds in a spice grinder or mortar and pestle and process until finely ground. Add the ground and whole anise seeds to the hazelnuts along with the flour, baking powder, cinnamon, ginger, and salt and whisk to combine.

In a large bowl, with a hand mixer, beat the sugar and butter on medium speed until light and fluffy, 2–3 minutes. Add the egg and beat until smooth. Add the dry ingredients and stir until the dough forms and there are no dry patches of flour remaining.

Working on a lightly floured work surface, roll out the dough with a rolling pin into a rectangle ½ inch (13 mm) thick. Cut the dough into 2 × ¾-inch (5 × 2 cm) rectangles. Arrange the rectangles on the prepared baking sheets, spaced 2 inches (5 cm) apart.

Bake until golden brown all over and dry to the touch on top, 14–16 minutes, switching racks and rotating the baking sheets front to back halfway through.

Transfer the baking sheets to wire racks and let the cookies rest for 1 minute. If you want, press the tip of your index finger or thumb on one end of each cookie to form a shallow divot. Transfer them to the racks to cool completely.

Lacy Nut Cookies
Brugse Kant / Kletskoppen

Preparation time: 30 minutes
Cooking time: 15 minutes
Makes: About 24 cookies

¾ cup plus 2 tablespoons
  (125 g) all-purpose (plain) flour
1 teaspoon ground cinnamon
½ teaspoon fine sea salt
6 tablespoons (3 oz/85 g)
  unsalted butter
1 cup (225 g) packed dark brown sugar
2 tablespoons water
3 oz (85 g) blanched whole
  or slivered almonds or peanuts,
  roughly chopped

In the Netherlands, these cookies go by the name *kletskoppen*, or "pat on the head," while in Belgium, they're called *Brugse kant* or *Brugse kletskoppen*, or "lace of Bruges," named after the famous textile produced in that Belgian city. Almonds seem to be the traditional nut used, but peanuts are increasingly popular. These lacy cookies—similar to Swedish *havreflarn* (recipe, page 316)—are crisp and full of butterscotch flavor from the brown sugar, butter, and pinch of cinnamon.

Position racks in the top and bottom thirds of the oven and preheat the oven to 375°F (190°C/Gas Mark 5). Line two large baking sheets with parchment paper.

In a medium bowl, whisk together the flour, cinnamon, and salt.

In a medium saucepan, melt the butter over medium heat. Add the sugar and water and stir until the sugar dissolves. Remove the pan from the heat and stir in the nuts. Add the dry ingredients and stir until a smooth batter forms and there are no dry patches of flour remaining.

Using a ½-ounce (1-tablespoon) ice cream scoop, scoop portions of the batter onto the prepared baking sheets, spaced at least 4 inches (10 cm) apart, as the cookies will spread.

Bake until the cookies are light golden brown all over, 8–10 minutes, switching racks and rotating the baking sheets front to back halfway through.

Transfer the baking sheets to wire racks and let the cookies cool completely on the pans.

Spiced Bar Cookies
Dikke Speculaas

Preparation time: 40 minutes
Cooking time: 25 minutes
Makes: About 30 cookies

3¼ cups (455 g) all-purpose
  (plain) flour
¾ teaspoon fine sea salt
½ teaspoon baking soda
  (bicarbonate of soda)
Speculaas Spice Mix (recipe, opposite)
1½ cups (340 g) packed dark
  brown sugar
2 sticks (8 oz/225 g) unsalted butter,
  softened
⅓ cup (2½ fl oz/80 ml) buttermilk
1 egg white, lightly beaten
⅔ cup (75 g) sliced (flaked) almonds

Pressing dough into wooden molds for *speculaas* (recipe, below) can be seen as tedious, so a few popular, less-laborious, variations of the famous cookie developed. *Gevulde speculaas* is a spiced cookie stuffed with almond paste or marzipan and baked in a cake pan or as a freeform loaf that's cut into finger-size pieces. *Hasseltse speculaas* are round drop cookies that have distinct cracks on top. Then there is this cookie, also sometimes called *speculaasbrokken*, the easiest version, which is made of bars cut from a large sheet of baked dough.

Position racks in the top and bottom thirds of the oven and preheat the oven to 400°F (200°C/Gas Mark 6). Line two large baking sheets with parchment paper.

In a medium bowl, whisk together the flour, salt, baking soda (bicarb), and spice mix.

In a large bowl, with a hand mixer, beat the sugar and butter on medium speed until pale and fluffy, 2–3 minutes. Add the buttermilk and beat until smooth. Add the dry ingredients and stir until the dough forms and there are no dry patches of flour remaining.

Shape the dough into a ball, cut in half, then roll out each half into a rectangle ¾ inch (2 cm) thick. Place each rectangle on a prepared baking sheet. Brush with beaten egg white, then sprinkle each rectangle with half the sliced almonds over the top.

Bake until golden brown at the edges and just dry to the touch in the center, 20–25 minutes, switching racks and rotating the baking sheets front to back halfway through.

Transfer the baking sheets to wire racks and let the cookie blocks cool completely on the pans. Transfer the cookie blocks to a cutting board and cut into 2-inch (5 cm) bars to serve.

Molded Spiced Cookies
Speculaas / Spekulatius

Preparation time: 1 hour, plus chilling
  time
Cooking time: 15 minutes
Makes: About 24 cookies

Speculaas Spice Mix (recipe follows)
2 cups (280 g) all-purpose (plain) flour
½ teaspoon fine sea salt
¼ teaspoon baking soda (bicarbonate
  of soda)
1 cup (225 g) packed light brown sugar
1 stick (4 oz/115 g) unsalted butter,
  softened
3 tablespoons buttermilk
Sliced (flaked) almonds, for decorating
Rice flour, for dusting

These spiced cookies are traditionally made in wooden molds with carved designs. Often nicknamed "windmill" cookies after the famous Dutch windmill that's used as their design today, the original designs were that of St. Nicholas, since the cookies are traditionally made to celebrate Sinterklaas, St. Nicholas Day, on December 6. Their name is even believed to come from the word *speculator*, the original name of a bishop, or St. Nicholas. It's also likely that their name comes from Latin *speculum*, meaning mirror-image, as the dough is a relief-copy of the designs in the wooden molds used to create them. *Speculaas* is not to be confused with *speculoos* (recipe, page 237), which is a cookie that gets its flavor and light brown color from caramelized sugar, not spices.

When using the molds to create them, many recipes use less butter to make a stiffer dough that holds its design. *Taai taai*, a Belgian honey-and-flour treat that predates *speculaas*, is much stiffer—its name translates to "tough-tough"—and holds its designs better because of a lack of any fat or eggs. If you choose not to use molds, do as many Dutch and Belgian bakers do and simply use cookie cutters. Rice flour is traditionally used to dust the molds so they release the printed dough easily, but you can also use regular wheat flour or brush the designs lightly with vegetable oil. Chopped almonds are traditionally pressed onto the back of the imprinted cookies, to keep them from spreading and for added flavor. To prevent any bumpy designs, this recipe uses sliced (flaked) almonds.

In a medium bowl, combine the spice mix, flour, salt, and baking soda (bicarb) and whisk to combine.

In a large bowl, with a hand mixer, beat the sugar and butter on medium speed until pale and fluffy, 2–3 minutes. Add the buttermilk and beat until smooth. Add the dry ingredients and stir until the dough forms and there are no dry patches of flour remaining. Shape the dough into a ball, cut in half, and shape each half into a disc. Wrap the discs separately in plastic wrap (cling film) and refrigerate for at least 2 hours or preferably overnight to allow the spices time to permeate and mellow in the dough.

Position racks in the top and bottom thirds of the oven and preheat the oven to 375°F (190°C/Gas Mark 5). Line two large baking sheets with parchment paper and spread an even single layer of sliced (flaked) almonds all over the parchment paper.

Working on a lightly floured work surface, roll out the dough with a rolling pin to ¼ inch (6 mm) thick. Using a wooden cookie mold with 3-inch (7.5 cm) cells, lightly dust the engravings with some rice flour, tapping out any excess, then press it over the dough to print designs on the dough. Lift the mold off the dough, and if the dough sticks to it, gently tap a corner of the wooden mold on the work surface while you hold your hand underneath the dough piece so that it falls into your hand. Transfer the printed dough to the almonds on the prepared baking sheets (collect the uncovered almonds and save them to make more cookies). Repeat forming more cookies with the rest of the dough, brushing off any excess flour that remains on the dough pieces. (Alternatively, use various cookie cutters of similar dimension to cut out cookies. Reroll the scraps to cut out more cookies.)

Bake until golden brown at the edges and just dry to the touch on top, 10–12 minutes, switching racks and rotating the baking sheets front to back halfway through.

Transfer the baking sheets to wire racks. Let the cookies cool on the pans for 1 minute, then transfer them to the racks to cool completely.

Speculaas Spice Mix

Makes a scant 3 tablespoons

2 tablespoons ground cinnamon
1½ teaspoons freshly grated nutmeg or mace
1 teaspoon ground cloves
¾ teaspoon ground ginger
½ teaspoon ground cardamom
½ teaspoon ground coriander
½ teaspoon ground white pepper
¼ teaspoon ground anise seeds

In a medium bowl, whisk together all the spices.

Molded Spiced Cookies (p. 232)

New Year's Waffle Cookies (p. 236)

New Year's Waffle Cookies

Nieuwjaarswafels

Preparation time: 1 hour
Cooking time: 1 hour 30 minutes
Makes: About 30 cookies

1 cup (225 g) packed light
  brown sugar
1 stick (4 oz/115 g) unsalted
  butter, melted
½ teaspoon fine sea salt
½ teaspoon pure vanilla extract
¼ teaspoon ground anise seeds
⅔ cup (5 fl oz/150 ml) whole
  milk, lukewarm
1 egg
1¾ cups (245 g) all-purpose
  (plain) flour
Whipped cream, for serving

Belgium is famous for all sorts of waffles; they even have a waffle cookie made specifically for New Year's Day. These *nieuwjaarswafels* ("New Year's waffles") are thin and typically either left flat or rolled up like cigars and filled with whipped cream; if the latter, they're called *niewjaarsrolletjes*. Typically, they are flavored with ground anise seeds and/or cinnamon and vanilla.

Sometimes called *ijzerkoeken*, or "iron cakes," for the waffle iron used to make them, a similar cookie in the Netherlands called *ijzerkoekje* (recipe, page 228) usually denotes a thicker cookie spiced with cinnamon that's baked on a griddle-like open-faced iron. This Belgian version, on the other hand, is typically left plain and cooked in a sandwich-style closed iron. Another cookie, called *lukken* (recipe, below), is essentially a thicker version of these *nieuwjaarswafels*, made with a thicker batter and left flat.

In a large bowl, whisk together the sugar, melted butter, salt, vanilla, and ground anise until smooth. Whisk in the milk and egg. Add the flour and stir until a batter forms and there are no dry patches of flour remaining.

Place a Dutch waffle iron, krumkake iron, or pizzelle iron over medium heat on your stove or heat an electric version. Using a 1-tablespoon measure, pour tablespoonfuls of batter into the center of the iron. Close the iron and let cook, flipping the iron halfway through, if using the stove, until the batter spreads and sets as a wafer, 2–3 minutes, depending on the heat of your stove (or follow the manufacturer's instructions for the electric maker).

Open the iron and place the end of a narrow wooden spoon at the edge of the iron closest to you. Lift the wafer and then quickly roll it around the spoon handle like a rolled carpet. Slide the rolled wafer off the handle and place on a wire rack to cool.

Repeat with the remaining batter to cook and roll more cookies. Once cooled, fill the cookies with whipped cream just before serving.

Thick Waffle Cookies

Lukken

Preparation time: 1 hour
Cooking time: 1 hour 30 minutes
Makes: About 30 cookies

1 cup (200 g) white US granulated
  (UK caster) sugar
1 stick (4 oz/115 g) unsalted
  butter, melted
1 tablespoons brandy or gold rum
½ teaspoon fine sea salt
½ teaspoon pure vanilla extract
1 egg
1¾ cups (245 g) all-purpose
  (plain) flour
Whipped cream, for serving

These booze-spiked cookies are essentially a thicker version of Belgian *nieuwjaarswafels* (recipe, above). The batter is thicker, too, and often flavored with just vanilla or rum to allow the flavor of caramelized sugar and butter to shine through. You can use the same waffle iron as *pizzelle* (recipe, page 130) and *krumkaker* (recipe, page 303) to make them.

In a large bowl, whisk together the sugar, melted butter, brandy, salt, and vanilla. Whisk in the egg. Add the flour and stir until a soft dough forms and there are no dry patches of flour remaining.

Place a Dutch waffle iron, krumkake iron, or pizzelle iron over medium heat on your stove or heat an electric version. Using a 1-tablespoon measure, portion tablespoonfuls of the dough and flatten each with your hands into discs ⅛ inch (3 mm) thick. Working in batches, place a disc on the iron, but leave the iron open. Cook the cookies, flipping once halfway through, until golden brown on both sides, 2–3 minutes, depending on the heat of your stove (or follow the manufacturer's instructions for the electric maker).

As the cookies are done, slide them onto a wire rack to cool. Serve the cookies with a bowl of whipped cream for dipping.

Brown Sugar Cinnamon Cookies
Bastognekoeken / Speculoos

Preparation time: 25 minutes,
 plus chilling time
Cooking time: 20 minutes
Makes: About 30 cookies

2¼ cups (315 g) all-purpose
 (plain) flour
2 teaspoons ground cinnamon
1 teaspoon baking powder
¼ teaspoon baking soda
 (bicarbonate of soda)
¾ teaspoon fine sea salt
½ teaspoon freshly grated
 nutmeg (optional)
¼ teaspoon ground allspice
 or cloves (optional)
6 oz (170 g) Dutch brown rock candy
 sugar or ¾ cup (150 g) white sugar
½ cup (170 g) Dutch schenkstroop,
 mørk sirup (see page 307), dark
 corn syrup, or British golden syrup
1 stick (4 oz/115 g) unsalted
 butter, softened
1 egg
1 teaspoon pure vanilla
 extract (optional)

According to some historians, these cookies, often referred to as *speculoos,* were created in Belgium as a cheaper, spice-free alternative to Dutch *speculaas* (recipe, page 232). In the seventeenth century, importing spices into Belgium was more expensive than in the Netherlands. So, instead of spices giving the Belgian cookies their color and flavor, caramelized sugar was used, providing the warming notes characteristic of the Dutch cookie. This style of sugar came about because processed sugar at the time in Belgium was made from sugar beets, and the molasses that came from it (which would typically be added back to white sugar to make "brown sugar") was so high in nitrogenous waste, it was considered unfit to consume. So, as a workaround to get a brown sugar, regular white sugar was caramelized and turned into rock candy-like sugar called *kandij suiker.* This caramel sugar gives these cookies their distinctive taste, which is different from the bitter notes provided by the likes of molasses or other brown sugars made from sugarcane.

Another theory for how the cookie came about involves two rival cookie manufacturers. According to the Lotus Biscoff website, a Belgian baker named Jan Boone, Sr., created a caramelized cookie like *speculoos* and named it Lotus, after the flower that symbolizes purity, and in the 1950s started individually wrapping the cookies and selling them. But at the same time, according to LU (another large cookie manufacturer), a baker in Antwerp named Louis Parein created the "Bastogne cookie"— or *Bastognekoeken,* the name of this recipe—to commemorate the Battle of Bastogne in World War II. It is, like Biscoff's Lotus cookie, a caramelized sugar cookie flavored with only cinnamon, but engraved with ridges on the top.

However the cookie came about, it seems the key ingredient is the brown rock candy sugar and the addition of cinnamon, though many other recipes now include a pinch of cloves or nutmeg and some vanilla, too. Modern recipes mix maple syrup or molasses with regular sugar to replicate the specific taste of *speculoos,* but the authentic syrup would be *schenkstroop,* a Dutch caramel syrup, which is available online or in some specialty food stores. Many recipes use the *kandij suiker* and the caramel syrup together; it's listed as an option in this recipe, but if you use regular white sugar, the caramel flavor will be a little less prominent.

- -

Position racks in the top and bottom thirds of the oven and preheat the oven to 350°F (180°C/Gas Mark 4). Line two large baking sheets with parchment paper.

In a medium bowl, whisk together the flour, cinnamon, baking powder, baking soda (bicarb), salt, nutmeg (if using), and allspice/cloves (if using).

In a large bowl, with a hand mixer, combine the sugar, syrup, and butter and beat on medium speed until pale and smooth, 2–3 minutes. Add the egg and vanilla (if using) and beat until smooth. Add the dry ingredients and mix on low speed until a dough forms and there are no dry patches of flour remaining. Cover the bowl with plastic wrap (cling film) and refrigerate the dough for at least 1 hour or overnight.

Divide the dough into 4 equal portions and shape each piece into a log ½ inch (13 mm) in diameter. Flatten each log slightly, then rake the tines of a fork along the length of the log or use your pinched thumb and index finger to create two ridges down the length of the logs. Cut the logs crosswise into 2½-inch (6.5 cm) pieces. Arrange them on the prepared baking sheets, spaced 2 inches (5 cm) apart.

Bake until the cookies are darker brown at the edges and dry to the touch on top, 18–20 minutes, switching racks and rotating the baking sheets front to back halfway through.

Transfer the baking sheets to wire racks. Let the cookies cool on the pans for 1 minute, then transfer them to the racks to cool completely.

Hand-Shaped Butter Cookies

Antwerpse Handjes

Preparation time: 55 minutes
Cooking time: 15 minutes
Makes: About 36 cookies

2½ cups (350 g) all-purpose
  (plain) flour
¾ teaspoon fine sea salt
2 sticks (8 oz/225 g) unsalted
  butter, softened
1 cup (200 g) white US granulated
  (UK caster) sugar
1 egg
1 teaspoon pure vanilla extract
Sliced (flaked) almonds, for decorating

According to local legend, a giant controlled the Scheldt River in Belgium and would extort money from sailors to pass through. One day, a Roman soldier killed the giant and threw his hands into the river. It's a colorful account of how the city of Antwerp got its name, as *hand werpen* ("hand throwing") eventually became Antwerpen.

It also gives context to these cookies, which are shaped like hands. Made of a simple butter and white sugar dough, the cookies typically are either coated on their underside with sliced (flaked) almonds or the nuts are sprinkled on top, like a spice-free version of *speculaas* (recipe, page 232). Look for a hand-shaped cutter to make these cookies worthy of their name, but if you can't find one, any shape will work.

Position racks in the top and bottom thirds of the oven and preheat the oven to 350°F (180°C/Gas Mark 4). Line two large baking sheets with parchment paper.

In a medium bowl, whisk together the flour and salt.

In a large bowl, with a hand mixer, beat the butter and sugar on medium speed until pale and fluffy, 2–3 minutes. Add the egg and vanilla and beat until smooth. Add the dry ingredients and stir until the dough forms and there are no dry patches of flour remaining. Shape the dough into a ball, cut in half, then shape each half into a disc.

Working on a lightly floured work surface, roll out the dough discs with a rolling pin to ¼ inch (6 mm) thick. Using a roughly 2-inch (5 cm) hand-shaped cutter, cut out cookies. Reroll the scraps to cut out more cookies. Arrange the dough hands on the prepared baking sheets, spaced 1 inch (2.5 cm) apart. Moisten the top of the shapes by brushing them very lightly with water, then sprinkle some sliced (flaked) almonds over the top.

Bake until golden brown at the edges and just dry to the touch on top, 12–14 minutes, switching racks and rotating the baking sheets front to back halfway through.

Transfer the baking sheets to wire racks. Let the cookies cool on the pans for 1 minute, then transfer them to the racks to cool completely.

Hand-Shaped Butter Cookies

German Pepper and Spice Cookies
Pfeffernüsse

Preparation time: 45 minutes, plus
  chilling, cooling, and setting time
Cooking time: 15 minutes
Makes: About 24 cookies

For the dough:
¾ cup (170 g) packed light
  brown sugar
¼ cup (50 g) white US granulated
  (UK caster) sugar
3 tablespoons honey
2 tablespoons gold or dark rum
1 egg
Finely grated zest of 1 lemon
¼ cup (30 g) almond flour
  (ground almonds)
2 teaspoons ground cinnamon
1 teaspoon ground allspice
1 teaspoon baker's ammonia
  (see page 17) or baking soda
  (bicarbonate of soda)
¾ teaspoon fine sea salt
½ teaspoon ground cardamom
½ teaspoon ground white pepper
¼ teaspoon ground cloves
2 cups (280 g) all-purpose
  (plain) flour

For the glaze:
1½ cups (205 g) powdered
  (icing) sugar
2 tablespoons hot water
2 tablespoons fresh lemon juice

Whereas most spiced holiday cookies are formed in molds or cut into various shapes, these "pepper nuts" are rolled into small balls that bake up as mounds. Similar in name, size, and ingredients to Danish *pebernødder* (recipe, page 330) and Dutch *pepernoten* (recipe, page 223), these German cookies are typically glazed with a white icing, or at least a heavy dusting of powdered (icing) sugar. Their spices are typically the same as other German Christmas sweets like *Elisenlebkuchen* (recipe, page 244), but pepper, usually white, is added for more potent spice.

Some old recipes reference making "cheap" *Pfeffernüsse* by taking leftover scraps of other honey and gingerbread cakes and mixing in more molasses and spices until you make a new dough. You break off a small bit to test and see if there was already enough leavening in the original doughs, or if you need to add more. Some recipes add ground almonds and candied citrus, treating the cookies like mini versions of *Lebkuchen* (recipe, page 247), while others resemble simply spiced honey cookies, sometimes with cocoa powder or rum. This recipe includes almond flour (ground almonds), but it eschews candied citrus in favor of keeping the focus on the spices that give the cookies their name. While many recipes call for pepper, white pepper seems the most traditional here, playing better with the other warm spices than black pepper. If you like, though, use black pepper instead.

- -

Make the dough: In a large bowl, whisk together the brown sugar, white US granulated (UK caster) sugar, honey, rum, egg, and lemon zest until smooth. Add the almond flour (ground almonds), cinnamon, allspice, baker's ammonia, salt, cardamom, pepper, and cloves and whisk again until smooth. Add the flour and stir until the dough forms and there are no dry patches of flour remaining. Cover the bowl in plastic wrap (cling film) and refrigerate the dough for at least 2 hours or overnight.

Position racks in the top and bottom thirds of the oven and preheat the oven to 375°F (190°C/Gas Mark 5). Line two large baking sheets with parchment paper.

Using a ¾-ounce (1½-tablespoon) ice cream scoop, portion the dough and roll into balls. Arrange them on the prepared baking sheets, spaced 2 inches (5 cm) apart.

Bake until light golden brown at the edges and dry to the touch on top, 12–14 minutes, switching racks and rotating the baking sheets front to back halfway through.

Transfer the baking sheets to wire racks. Let the cookies cool on the pans for 1 minute, then transfer them to the racks to cool completely.

Make the glaze: In a small bowl, combine the powdered (icing) sugar and hot water and stir until the mixture forms a thick paste. Add the lemon juice and stir until the icing is smooth and pourable.

Spoon the glaze over each cookie or dip its top in the glaze to cover. Let the cookies stand until the glaze sets before serving. These cookies are best stored in an airtight container at room temperature for at least 3 days before eating as they soften and become chewier.

Piped Butter Cookies
Spritzgebäck

Preparation time: 30 minutes,
  plus cooling and setting time
Cooking time: 15 minutes
Makes: About 48 cookies

2 sticks (8 oz/225 g) unsalted
  butter, softened
1 cup (135 g) powdered (icing) sugar
1 egg
2 teaspoons pure vanilla extract
¾ teaspoon fine sea salt
Finely grated zest of ½ lemon
2 cups (280 g) all-purpose
  (plain) flour
Bittersweet chocolate, melted,
  for dipping (optional)

In German baking, one way of organizing cookies is by how their ingredients are brought together. *Mürbteig* is when butter is crumbled into flour and sugar, while *Rührteig* describes when butter and sugar are whipped before adding flour, making a softer dough. These piped or extruded cookies are the latter and likely the basis for "spritz" cookies that came after it, whether piped from a pastry bag or extruded via a cookie press or gun. These doughs often use powdered (icing) sugar, producing a smoother dough that can be extruded more easily.

These cookies are typically made into "S" shapes, likely a reference to the former region known as Swabia, but they're also shaped as rings, wreaths, pretzels, rods, and circles. If S-shaped, the cookies are often left plain, while other shapes are dipped halfway in melted chocolate. The Dutch version of these cookies is called *spritsen* or *botersprits*, and the Utrecht version is piped in a characteristic zigzag. In Switzerland, they're called *spitzbuben*.

Position racks in the top and bottom thirds of the oven and preheat the oven to 375°F (190°C/Gas Mark 5). Line two large baking sheets with parchment paper.

In a large bowl, with a hand mixer, beat the butter and sugar on medium speed until pale and fluffy, 2–3 minutes. Add the egg and beat until smooth. Beat in the vanilla, salt, and lemon zest. Add the flour and stir until the dough forms and there are no dry patches of flour remaining.

Scrape the dough into a fabric piping bag fitted with a ¾-inch (2 cm) fluted tip (nozzle) or a cookie gun and pipe shapes, such as 3- to 4-inch (7.5 to 10 cm) "S" shapes, rods, or wreaths, on the prepared baking sheets, spaced 2 inches (5 cm) apart.

Bake until golden brown and dry to the touch on top, 10–15 minutes, switching racks and rotating the baking sheets front to back halfway through.

Transfer the baking sheets to wire racks. Let the cookies cool on the pans for 1 minute, then transfer them to the racks to cool completely.

If dipping in chocolate, dip the cookies halfway in a bowl of melted chocolate, then lift and let the excess drain off. Transfer the cookies to a sheet of parchment paper and let the chocolate set before serving.

Piped Butter Cookies (p. 241)

Small Mounded Spice Cookies and Variation (pp. 244–245)

Small Mounded Spice Cookies
Elisenlebkuchen

Preparation time: 1 hour, plus overnight
  standing and setting time
Cooking time: 30 minutes
Makes: About 24 cookies

For the dough:
1 lb 2 oz (510 g) blanched whole
  or slivered almonds (or 9 oz/255 g
  blanched almonds mixed with
  9 oz/255 g blanched hazelnuts)
7 oz (200 g) almond paste,
  roughly chopped
1 tablespoon ground cinnamon
1 teaspoon ground cloves
½ teaspoon ground cardamom
½ teaspoon freshly grated
  nutmeg or ground mace
¼ teaspoon ground allspice
¼ teaspoon ground ginger
¾ teaspoon fine sea salt
1½ cups (300 g) white US granulated
  (UK caster) sugar
4 eggs
4 oz (115 g) candied citron or lemon
  peel, finely diced
4 oz (115 g) candied orange peel,
  finely diced
Finely grated zest of 1 lemon
12–15 Oblaten (rice paper wafers;
  see headnote), for forming cookies
Whole blanched almonds, for
  decorating (optional)

For the powdered (icing) sugar icing:
2 egg whites
1¼ cups (170 g) powdered (icing) sugar
1 tablespoon fresh lemon juice

By most accounts, when anyone outside of Germany thinks of "lebkuchen," they think of *Elisenlebkuchen*, which is the most famous. It is a spiced cookie that has no wheat flour, is made with ground almonds and candied citrus, and is scraped onto small wafers to form mounds decorated with almonds or glazed. Those wafers, called *Oblaten*, are made of rice starch and are believed to have been Eucharist wafers that nuns in German monasteries repurposed, to give structure to the loose mix of dough. While *Honiglebkuchen* (recipe, page 247) are sweetened with honey, these mounded cookies use sugar.

The dough is typically started by whisking eggs and sugar together, which provides leavening. Spices—predominantly cinnamon, cloves, cardamom, and nutmeg and/or allspice—chopped candied orange and citron peel, and finely ground nuts are then mixed in until the dough is stiff enough to be spread. Some recipes call for a small amount of all-purpose (plain) flour, but it's typically understood that *Elisenlebkuchen* contains none. Almonds are the traditional choice of nuts, but another style made with hazelnuts is also popular; many modern recipes use a 50/50 mix of both.

The mounds of dough can be left plain, though many bakers garnish them with a single blanched almond in the center or three almonds with their points facing the center. If the cookies are topped with almonds, they are typically left plain or glazed with a powdered (icing) sugar icing while hot. If the cookies have no almond on top, they can be coated with a chocolate glaze, which must be done once cooled down (see the variation that follows). You'll need to use 2¾-inch (7 cm) round *Oblaten* wafers (sometimes labeled "*Back Oblaten*"). They can be purchased online or from a bakery supply store and come in packs of 100.

- -

Make the dough: In a food processor, pulse the almonds until finely chopped. Add the almond paste, cinnamon, cloves, cardamom, nutmeg, allspice, ginger, and salt and pulse until the almonds are very finely ground and the spices are evenly incorporated. Leave the mixture in the food processor.

In a large bowl, with a hand mixer, beat the white US granulated (UK caster) sugar and eggs on medium speed until tripled in volume, lightened, and pale; when you lift the beaters, the mixture should fall back in thick ribbons. Scoop ½ cup (4 fl oz/120 ml) of the whipped egg mixture into the food processor and pulse just until the mixture moistens the ground nuts. Scrape the ground nut mixture into the egg mixture and add the candied citron, candied orange, and lemon zest. Fold everything together until evenly combined.

Line two large baking sheets with parchment paper. Using the tip of a table knife or your finger nail, separate the two thin layers of each Oblaten to produce two thinner wafers.

Spoon about 3 tablespoons of dough onto a wafer, and use an offset spatula or the spoon—dipped in warm water as needed to keep the dough from sticking—to spread the dough to the edges while leaving it mounded in the center. Place the dough mound on a prepared baking sheet. Repeat portioning and shaping the rest of the cookies on the wafers, spacing them 1 inch (2.5 cm) apart on the baking sheets. If decorating with almonds, top each mound with 1 almond in the center or 3 in a starburst pattern with the points facing the center. Let stand at room temperature until dry to the touch, at least 8 hours or overnight, or up to 1 day.

Make the powdered (icing) sugar icing: In a large bowl, with a whisk, beat the egg whites until soft peaks begin to form. Add the powdered sugar and lemon juice and whisk vigorously until it forms a smooth glaze. Cover with plastic wrap (cling film) and let stand until ready to use.

Position racks in the top and bottom thirds of the oven and preheat the oven to 300°F (150°C/Gas Mark 2).

Bake until very lightly browned and a toothpick inserted into the center of the cookies comes out clean, 25–30 minutes, switching racks and rotating the baking sheets front to back halfway through.

Western Europe

Transfer the baking sheets to wire racks. While the cookies are hot from the oven, brush or spoon the glaze over the cookies, then let cool completely on the pans. Let the glaze set before serving.

Variation
Chocolate-Glazed Elisenlebkuchen
Omit the almonds on the top of the cookies and the powdered sugar icing. Once the cookies are baked, let them cool completely on the baking sheets. While they cool, make the chocolate glaze: Place 4 ounces (115 g) roughly chopped bittersweet chocolate in a small heatproof bowl. In a small saucepan, bring ⅔ cup (130 g) white US granulated (UK caster) sugar and ⅓ cup (2½ fl oz/80 ml) water to a boil and cook, stirring, for 2 minutes to ensure the sugar is dissolved. Pour the hot syrup over the chocolate and let it stand for 1 minute to melt the chocolate. Stir the mixture to form a smooth glaze. Stir in 1 teaspoon pure vanilla extract. Brush or spoon the glaze over the cooled cookies. Let the glaze set before serving.

Printed Cookies

The act of printing cookies, or stamping them with a design, is not so common anymore, but the practice is likely why cookies, or cookie-like foods, were invented in the first place. Going back to the Egyptian *kahk* (recipe, page 50), which was printed with a design of the sun's rays to present as an offering to the sun god Ra, cookies that followed in that fashion, chiefly Levantine *maamoul* (recipe, page 44), also bore the design of those first cookies. They were seen as edible tokens that held as much significance for their culture as for their taste.

In Europe, the forebears of modern shortbread (recipe, page 274) also took on the visage of the sun, while other cookie-like foods took on the designs of pagan idols, then transitioned to religious and symbolic figures like priests, animals, and other cultural icons. The motifs of pagan times are believed to have come about because poorer people didn't have animals to sacrifice during winter solstice, so they instead made token sacrifices on cookies with images of animals on them. From that point, religious symbols and culturally important symbols made their way onto the cookies over the centuries that followed. Nowadays we call them "Christmas" cookies, but early molds also showed motifs with Easter lambs, rabbits, and other religious iconography. Designed cookies used to be hand-painted in bright colors and some hung them on their Christmas trees. The cookies were then given to children as a treat when the tree came down on Epiphany.

Belgian and Dutch *speculaas* (recipe, page 232) and German *Springerle* (recipe, page 246) are two lasting examples of such printed cookies. The original molds for *Springerle* were like that for *speculaas*—flat boards you pressed dough into to print the design—but today, rolling pins engraved with various motifs are used to roll over a sheet of dough. This practice was a way to give a plain dough some sort of form that's aesthetically pleasing. Before the advent of piped icings, using molds to stamp their designs on cookies was the best option available. While cutters are a valuable part of history passed down through families and are also easy to use, it's also been valuable to pass down other tools that shape the way we interact with cookies across generations.

Printed Anise Cookies
Springerle

Preparation time: 1 hour 35 minutes,
 plus chilling time and at least
 24 hours drying time
Cooking time: 40 minutes
Makes: About 84 cookies

1¼ cups (260 g) superfine
 (caster) sugar
2 eggs
½ teaspoon fine sea salt
Finely grated zest of 1 small lemon
1¾ cups (245 g) all-purpose
 (plain) flour
¼ teaspoon baker's
 ammonia (optional)
2 tablespoons anise seeds
Rice flour or more all-purpose
 flour, for dusting

These stark-white cookies are often referred to as "Swabian prints" because they originated in an area of southern Germany known as Swabia, but they are now popular all over Germany and in Switzerland and Austria, where many descendants of the region live.

The name—"little springer"—is sometimes attributed to a springing deer that was popular on early designs, but the name likely comes from the way the cookies "spring" up when baked. The printed cookies are allowed to dry out, which sets the design in place and allows the cookie to rise—when they're baked, the moisture inside the dough presses the dried top upward, making it "spring." There's disagreement on whether leavening should be added, with many recipes calling for baker's ammonia (see page 17) to give the cookies rise and their characteristic dry-shattering texture. Old recipes for "fine" *Springerle* have no chemical leavening, but they give an alternative for "cheap" *Springerle* that does contain ammonia. Adding the leavening was possibly a faster way to give rise to the cookies without having to wait as long to let them dry. This recipe gives it as an option, if you want to use it.

Some old recipes do not include anise, while many now do. Older recipes advise baking the cookies on top of a bed of anise seeds, rather than mixing them in, which allows their flavor to permeate the dough, while also leaving the designs on top free from the seeds.

In a stand mixer fitted with the whisk, combine the sugar and eggs and beat on medium speed until well mixed and smooth, about 1 minute. Increase the speed to medium-high and continue beating the mixture until extremely light and pale—almost white—and when you lift the whisk, the mixture falls back in a thick rope, about 10 minutes more. Add the salt and lemon zest and beat until evenly incorporated.

Place a sieve over the bowl of whipped egg mixture, add the flour and baker's ammonia (if using) to the sieve, and sift over the egg mixture. Turn the mixer to the lowest speed and mix until a dough forms. Shape the dough into a ball, cut in half, then shape each half into a disc. Wrap the discs separately in plastic wrap (cling film) and refrigerate for at least 2 hours or preferably overnight.

Line four large baking sheets with parchment paper. Using a mortar and pestle or spice grinder, process the anise seeds just enough to break them in half. Spread an even single layer of crushed anise seeds all over the parchment paper on all four sheets.

Working on a lightly floured work surface, roll out a disc of dough with a rolling pin until ½-inch (13 mm) thick. Using a springerle rolling pin or wooden cookie mold with 2-inch (5 cm) cells, lightly dust the engravings with some rice flour, tapping out any excess, then roll or press it over the dough to print designs on the dough. Cut along the edges of each design to separate them and transfer the printed cookies to the prepared baking sheets, spaced 1 inch (2.5 cm) apart. Repeat forming more cookies with the rest of the dough, brushing off any excess flour that remains on the dough pieces. (Alternatively, use various cookie cutters of similar dimension to cut out cookies. Reroll the scraps to cut out more cookies.) Let the cookies stand until dry to the touch, at least 24 hours.

Position racks in the top and bottom thirds of the oven and preheat the oven to 275°F (140°C/Gas Mark 1).

Wet two large tea towels with water and wring them dry, then place on a work surface. Transfer the cookies to the damp towels and let stand for exactly 5 minutes (this helps partially rehydrate the bottoms of the cookies so the steam created when the moisture hits the heat of the oven makes the cookies rise). Return the cookies to the baking sheets.

Bake two baking sheets at a time until barely light golden at the edges of the bottom and risen, 15–20 minutes, switching racks and rotating the baking sheets front to back halfway through.

Transfer the baking sheets to wire racks and let the cookies cool completely on the pans. The cookies are best stored in an airtight container for 2–4 weeks before serving.

Honey-Sweetened Spiced Bars

Nürnberger Lebkuchen / Honiglebkuchen / Honigkuchen

Preparation time: 30 minutes
plus overnight chilling
Cooking time: 20 minutes
Makes: About 72 cookies

For the dough:
1 cup (340 g) honey
¾ cup (150 g) white US granulated
(UK caster) sugar
4 cups (560 g) all-purpose (plain) flour
1 teaspoon baking powder
1 teaspoon baking soda (bicarbonate
of soda)
1 teaspoon fine sea salt
2 teaspoons ground cinnamon
1 teaspoon ground cloves
¼ cup (2 fl oz/60 ml) whole milk
2 tablespoons rum
3 eggs
½ cup (60 g) finely chopped almonds
½ cup (115 g) finely chopped candied
orange, lemon, or citron peel
(or a mix of all three)

For the glaze:
1½ cups (205 g) powdered
(icing) sugar
3 tablespoons hot water
1 teaspoon fresh lemon juice
⅛ teaspoon pure almond extract
or 1 teaspoon rum (optional)

Though *Elisenlebkuchen* (recipe, page 244) may be the most well-known "German gingerbread cookie," this seems to be the original style. Spread as a sheet before being baked, it falls in line with how the name *Lebkuchen* came to be, most likely from the Latin *libum*, which means "pancake." Though the name varies, it's often simply called *Nürnberger Lebkuchen*, even though any *Lebkuchen* baked in Nuremberg can be called that. Nuremberg is the capital of German gingerbread and credited with inventing it, with the first recipe appearing in the fifteenth century (though the name was first mentioned in correspondences in the early 1300s). This makes sense when taking into account Nuremberg's place on spice trade routes and as the center of Bavarian honey production.

The first recipes were likely used to make printed gingerbreads in the vein of Dutch/Belgian *speculaas* (recipe, page 232). But now, *Lebkuchen* in this style—sweetened with honey and spread as a sheet of dough—are often called *Honiglebkuchen* or *Honigkuchen*, though those names are sometimes used for more cake-like sweets, confusing the names further.

Two variations exist in northern Germany, *Braune Kuchen* and *Aachener Printen*, both typically using molasses in place of honey. Old recipes list baker's ammonia (see page 17) and potash as leavening ingredients, but this was when gingerbread sheets were left to sit for weeks or months, which is conducive to those leaveners; today, bakers use baking soda (bicarb) or baking powder. When rolled thinner, this dough can be cut into shapes of St. Nicholas, stars, pigs, trees, and giant hearts called *Lebkuchenherzen*, making it likely the original "gingerbread" dough that was used as the template for countless variations in other countries. That same thinner dough can also be used for making *Hexehäuschen*—witch's or gingerbread houses—believed to have been inspired by the story of Hansel and Gretel.

Make the dough: In a small saucepan, combine the honey and white US granulated (UK caster) sugar and heat over medium-high heat, stirring until the sugar liquefies. Remove the pan from the heat and scrape the honey mixture into a large bowl to cool for 10 minutes.

Meanwhile, in a medium bowl, whisk together the flour, baking powder, baking soda (bicarb), salt, cinnamon, and cloves.

Whisk the milk and rum into the honey mixture, then whisk in the eggs. Add the dry ingredients, nuts, and candied citrus and stir until the dough just comes together and there are no dry patches of flour remaining. Cover the bowl in plastic wrap (cling film) and refrigerate the dough for at least 8 hours or overnight, or up to 1 day.

Position racks in the top and bottom thirds of the oven and preheat the oven to 400°F (200°C/Gas Mark 6). Line two large baking sheets with parchment paper.

Divide the dough in half. Working on a lightly floured work surface, roll out half the dough with a rolling pin into a rectangle ½ inch (13 mm) thick and transfer it to a prepared baking sheet. Repeat with the other half of the dough and the second baking sheet.

Bake until darker brown at the edges and just dry to the touch in the center, 12–15 minutes, switching racks and rotating the baking sheets front to back halfway through.

Meanwhile, make the glaze: In a small bowl, whisk together the powdered (icing) sugar, water, and lemon juice into a smooth glaze. Flavor the glaze with the almond extract or rum, if you like.

Transfer the baking sheets to wire racks and let the cookie rectangles rest for 1 minute. While still warm, brush them evenly with some of the glaze. Let the rectangles cool completely on the pans. Cut into small rectangles or squares to serve.

Variation
Braune Kuchen / Aachener Printen
Substitute unsulphured molasses (not blackstrap) for the honey.
Glaze the cooled rectangles with a chocolate glaze (recipe, page 245).

Cinnamon Star Cookies
Zimtsterne

Preparation time: 55 minutes, plus
 at least 2 hours chilling time, 30
 minutes standing time, and at least
 24 hours drying time
Cooking time: 5 minutes
Makes: About 12 cookies

10 oz (285 g) blanched whole
 or slivered almonds
½ cup (100 g) white US granulated
 (UK caster) sugar
1 tablespoon ground cinnamon
½ teaspoon fine sea salt
Finely grated zest and juice of 1 lemon
3 egg whites
1½ cups (205 g) powdered
 (icing) sugar
¼ cup (2 fl oz/60 ml) chilled kirsch
 (cherry eau-de-vie) or water

One of the simplest and most popular German Christmas cookies are these "cinnamon stars" made from ground almonds, egg whites, and sugar, like *Elisenlebkuchen* (recipe, page 244) and *Springerle* (recipe, page 246). The dough is made by whipping the egg whites and powdered (icing) sugar into a thick meringue glaze, setting aside some for the glaze, and adding almonds and cinnamon to the rest, so you get two components for the work of one. The dough is then rolled thin and cut into stars. Many recipes call for dipping the cutter in cold water between cuts to keep the dough from sticking, but others use kirsch, which has the added benefit of adding flavor to the cookies. Although you can bake the cookies right away, letting them dry overnight before baking is what gives the cookies their desired set-outside/chewy-inside texture.

Older recipes include lemon juice and zest, but modern ones do not. This recipe adds it back but you can omit it if you want. *Zimtpitten*, or "cinnamon pie," is a more casual Swiss version shaped as a rectangle, covered with meringue, almonds, and pearl sugar, then cut into diamonds or bars after baking.

In a food processor, pulse the almonds until finely ground. Add the white US granulated (UK caster) sugar, cinnamon, salt, and lemon zest and pulse until the almonds are ground into a fine meal.

In a stand mixer fitted with the whisk, beat the egg whites on medium speed until foamy and starting to form soft peaks, about 1 minute. Slowly add the powdered (icing) sugar, then increase the speed to medium-high and continue beating the mixture until it holds stiff peaks when the whisk is lifted from the meringue, 2–3 minutes more. Scoop a heaping ½ cup (4 fl oz/120 ml) of the meringue out and place it in a small bowl; cover with plastic wrap (cling film) and set aside until ready to use.

Add the spiced ground almonds to the meringue in the mixer bowl along with the lemon juice, and use a silicone spatula to fold everything together until a dough forms and there are no dry patches of almonds remaining in the bowl. Shape the dough into a ball, cut in half, then shape each half into a disc. Wrap the discs separately in plastic wrap (cling film) and refrigerate for at least 2 hours.

Unwrap one dough disc and place it on a sheet of parchment paper. Cover with another sheet of parchment paper and roll out the dough with a rolling pin to ¼ inch (6 mm) thick. Remove the top sheet of parchment. Use a pastry brush to spread half the reserved meringue over the sheet of dough. Let stand until the meringue is dry, about 30 minutes. Repeat with the other half of the dough and meringue glaze.

Line two large baking sheets with parchment paper. Pour the kirsch or water into a small plate. Using a 1¾- to 2-inch (4.5 to 5 cm) star-shaped cutter, dip the cutter in the kirsch and then cut out stars of dough, re-dipping the cutter in the kirsch between the cuts. Position the cutter as close to the last one as best as possible to avoid any wasted dough since you won't be able to reroll the scraps. Arrange the cut shapes on the prepared baking sheets, spaced 1 inch (2.5 cm) apart. Let the cookies stand until dry to the touch, at least 24 hours.

Position racks in the top and bottom thirds of the oven and preheat the oven to 450°F (230°C/Gas Mark 8).

Bake just until the outside of the cookies are dry but the glaze isn't browned, 4–5 minutes, switching racks and rotating the baking sheets front to back halfway through.

Transfer the baking sheets to wire racks and let the cookies cool completely on the pans.

Cinnamon Star Cookies

Poppy Seed-Filled Tri-Corner Cookies
Hamantaschen

Preparation time: 1 hour 35 minutes,
 plus chilling and cooling time
Cooking time: 25 minutes
Makes: About 30 cookies

For the dough:
2 cups (280 g) all-purpose (plain) flour
1 teaspoon baking powder
½ teaspoon fine sea salt
1 stick (4 oz/115 g) unsalted butter
 or margarine, softened
½ cup (100 g) white US granulated
 (UK caster) sugar
1 egg
Finely grated zest of ½ orange
2 tablespoons fresh orange juice
1 teaspoon pure vanilla extract

For the poppy seed filling:
1 cup (160 g) poppy seeds
3 tablespoons (45 g) unsalted
 butter or margarine
½ cup (4 fl oz/120 ml) fresh
 orange juice
½ cup (100 g) white US granulated
 (UK caster) sugar
⅓ cup (55 g) raisins, finely chopped
½ teaspoon fine sea salt
Finely grated zest of 1 lemon
1 teaspoon pure vanilla extract

The name for these cookies is commonly translated as "Haman's hat" though there's no mention in the Bible of the infamous Persian prime minister wearing a hat, nor any description of its shape. The name likely came from the word *Mantasch*, or "poppy seed pockets," a pastry that German Jews made for the holiday, Purim. Today, though, they're called *oznei Haman*, or "Haman's ears," to deride his—most likely fictitious—pointy ears.

A filling of cooked poppy seeds is most traditional, while, like rugelach (recipe, page 358), you can fill them with virtually any jam-like filling today. Because of their association with a specific Jewish holiday, many recipes eschew the use of dairy to keep the cookies pareve, or free of animal meat and milk. You can also fill them with Plum Butter (recipe, page 18).

- -

Make the dough: In a medium bowl, whisk together the flour, baking powder, and salt.

In a large bowl, with a hand mixer, beat the butter and sugar on medium speed until creamy and smooth, 1–2 minutes. Add the egg and beat until smooth. Beat in the orange zest, orange juice, and vanilla. Add the dry ingredients and stir until a dough forms and there are no dry patches of flour remaining. Shape the dough into a ball, wrap in plastic wrap (cling film), and refrigerate for at least 1 hour or up to 2 days.

Make the poppy seed filling: Using a spice or coffee grinder and working in batches, process the poppy seeds until very finely ground. In a small saucepan, melt the butter over medium heat, then stir in the ground poppy seeds, orange juice, sugar, raisins, salt, and lemon zest. Bring to a simmer, then continue cooking, stirring occasionally, until the mixture thickens like bubbling lava, 5–7 minutes. Remove the pan from the heat and stir in the vanilla. Transfer to a container and let cool before using.

Position racks in the top and bottom thirds of the oven and preheat the oven to 375°F (190°C/Gas Mark 5). Line two large baking sheets with parchment paper.

Working on a lightly floured work surface, roll out the dough with a rolling pin to ¼ inch (6 mm) thick. Using a 3-inch (7.5 cm) round cutter, cut out rounds of dough. Reroll the scraps to cut out more cookies. Spoon 1 tablespoon of poppy seed filling in the center of each round, then lift the edges of each round at three equidistant points to form a triangle at the base of the cookie; gently pinch where the corners form to secure the sides of dough around the filling. Arrange the shaped cookies on the prepared baking sheets, spaced 1 inch (2.5 cm) apart.

Bake until golden brown on the bottom and sides and dry to the touch, about 15 minutes, switching racks and rotating the baking sheets front to back halfway through.

Transfer the baking sheets to wire racks. Let the cookies cool on the pans for 1 minute, then transfer them to the racks to cool completely.

Poppy Seed-Filled Tri-Corner Cookies

Almond-Studded Marzipan Cookies

Bethmännchen

Preparation time: 45 minutes, plus
  overnight standing and chilling time
Cooking time: 30 minutes
Makes: About 24 cookies

8 oz (225 g) blanched whole or
  slivered almonds, plus more whole
  almonds for decorating
1 cup (200 g) plus 3 tablespoons white
  US granulated (UK caster) sugar
¾ teaspoon fine sea salt
4 tablespoons rose water
½ cup (68 g) powdered (icing) sugar
1 tablespoon cornstarch (cornflour)
1 egg, separated
2 tablespoons heavy (double) cream
2 tablespoons water

One of Frankfurt's most popular cookies, these marzipan-based cookies were invented in the 1840s by a baker employed by the Bethmanns, a prominent Frankfurt banking family. The cookies were apparently originally decorated with four pieces of almonds on the outside to represent the four sons of the family, but after one of the sons died, three almonds became the norm. In any case, a cookie made with marzipan—one of the prized foods of the region—was bound to happen there. Another marzipan-based cookie, *Mandelhörnchen*, is popular and is shaped into crescents and dipped in chocolate.

Older recipes make the dough with raw ingredients, so this recipe does the same. Two components of older recipes that seem to have disappeared in popular use are rose water as a flavoring and an egg yolk wash to adhere the almonds to the dough. But this recipe uses both, which gives the cookies a flavor beyond almond and doesn't waste an egg yolk.

In a food processor, pulse the almonds until finely ground. Add 1 cup (200 g) of the white US granulated (UK caster) sugar and the salt and pulse until the almonds are very finely ground. Scrape the almonds into a medium saucepan and add 2 tablespoons of the rose water. Set over medium-low heat and cook, stirring occasionally, until the almond mixture comes together into a sticky dough and is dry; if the dough begins to brown even in the slightest, remove it from the heat. Scrape the almond paste into a large bowl, cover with a clean tea towel, and let stand until cold and dry, at least 8 hours or overnight.

Line two large baking sheets with parchment paper. Uncover the almond paste, and add the powdered (icing) sugar, cornstarch (cornflour), and the egg white. Use your hands to knead everything together into a smooth dough. Using a ½-ounce (1-tablespoon) ice cream scoop (or eyeball it), portion out the dough and roll into balls. Arrange them on the prepared baking sheets, spaced 1 inch (2.5 cm) apart.

In a small bowl, whisk together the egg yolk and cream until smooth. Using a pastry brush, brush the egg yolk wash over all the dough balls. Halve each whole almond lengthwise and place three halves, cut-side down, against each dough ball; press them together in unison so they stick and the dough ball creates a pyramid-like dome shape. Chill the cookies in the refrigerator for at least 1 hour or up to 1 day.

Position racks in the top and bottom thirds of the oven and preheat the oven to 350°F (180°C/Gas Mark 4).

Bake until golden brown on the outside and dry to the touch, about 15 minutes, switching racks and rotating the baking sheets front to back halfway through.

Transfer the baking sheets to wire racks.

While the cookies cool, in a small saucepan, combine the remaining 3 tablespoons white US granulated sugar, 2 tablespoons rose water, and the water and bring to a boil, swirling to dissolve the sugar. Cook until reduced by half, then pour the syrup into a bowl and let cool for 5 minutes.

Using a pastry brush, brush the outside of the cookies with some of the glaze. Let the cookies cool completely.

Almond-Studded Marzipan Cookies

Vanilla Pretzel-Shaped Cookies
Vanillebrezeln

Preparation time: 30 minutes,
 plus chilling time
Cooking time: 15 minutes
Makes: About 18 cookies

1¾ cups (245 g) all-purpose
 (plain) flour
⅔ cup (140 g) Vanilla Sugar
 (page 16), plus more for sprinkling
½ teaspoon fine sea salt
1½ sticks (6 oz/170 g) unsalted
 butter, cut into ½-inch (13 mm)
 cubes, softened
2 eggs, 1 separated and 1 whole
Finely chopped almonds, for
 sprinkling (optional)

There are countless German cookies made of butter, sugar, and flour with vanilla as the highlight flavor, but these pretzel-shaped cookies are the most popular. The name may have come from the Latin *bracellae*, meaning "little arms," likely in reference to the ends of the rope crossing each other like arms to form the shape. The dough is typically made by rubbing cold butter into the dry ingredients, giving it a crumbly short-crust texture, but there are also just as many recipes that beat the butter and sugar together like many modern cookie recipes.

This recipe uses homemade vanilla sugar to flavor the dough and decorate the cookies when they come out of the oven. You can use regular sugar and add vanilla extract (add 1 tablespoon pure vanilla extract to ⅔ cup/140 g sugar), but it makes sense to use the bean-flecked sugar. Some old recipes add lemon zest to the mix. Many recipes today decorate the pretzels with pearl sugar, while older recipes call for sprinkling with vanilla sugar and/or crushed almonds, while still more call for a vanilla-flavored icing. If you want to use an icing, make the icing for *Pfeffernüsse* (recipe, page 240) and use 1 teaspoon pure vanilla extract mixed with 2 teaspoons extra water in place of the lemon juice.

In a large bowl, whisk together the flour, vanilla sugar, and salt. Add the butter and use your fingers to rub it into the dry ingredients until it breaks down into coarse crumbs; add the whole egg and 1 egg yolk and continue mixing and kneading just enough to form a smooth dough. Shape the dough into a ball, wrap in plastic wrap (cling film), and refrigerate for at least 2 hours or overnight.

Position racks in the top and bottom thirds of the oven and preheat the oven to 350°F (180°C/Gas Mark 4). Line two large baking sheets with parchment paper. In a small bowl, beat the remaining egg white with a fork until loosened.

Working on a lightly floured work surface, cut the dough into 4 equal portions. Roll each portion between your fingers and the work surface into a rope ½ inch (13 mm) thick. Cut the ropes into 3-inch (7.5 cm) lengths. Pick up both ends of each length, cross them over each other, and attach them to the center to form thick pretzels. Arrange the dough pretzels on the prepared baking sheets, spaced 2 inches (5 cm) apart. Brush the pretzels with some of the egg white and then sprinkle with chopped almonds (if using).

Bake until the cookies are light golden brown at the edges and dry to the touch on top, 10–12 minutes, switching racks and rotating the baking sheets front to back halfway through.

Transfer the baking sheets to wire racks and immediately sprinkle the cookies liberally with more vanilla sugar. Let the cookies rest for 5 minutes on the pans, then transfer them to the racks to cool completely.

Vanilla Pretzel-Shaped Cookies

Chocolate-Dipped Hazelnut Triangle Cookies

Nussecken

Preparation time: 55 minutes,
  plus cooling and setting time
Cooking time: 35 minutes
Makes: 24 cookies

For the base:
1⅔ cups (230 g) all-purpose
  (plain) flour
1 teaspoon baking powder
¾ teaspoon fine sea salt
1 stick (4 oz/115 g) unsalted
  butter, softened
½ cup (100 g) white US granulated
  (UK caster) sugar
1 egg
1 teaspoon pure vanilla extract
⅔ cup (210 g) apricot or red
  currant jam

For the filling:
12 ounces (340 g) blanched hazelnuts
10 oz (5 oz/140 g) unsalted butter
¾ cup (150 g) white US granulated
  (UK caster) sugar
2 tablespoons water
2 teaspoons pure vanilla extract
¼ teaspoon fine sea salt

To finish:
8 oz (225 g) bittersweet chocolate,
  roughly chopped
1 tablespoon vegetable shortening
  or refined coconut oil

These triangle-shaped cookie bars are a German bakery staple. They're made by topping a pâte brisée base with a syrupy mix of butter, sugar, and chopped nuts. Hazelnuts—in both chopped and ground forms—bulk up the filling, which bakes atop a thin layer of apricot jam that helps to cut the richness of the filling. Typically, the base and filling are baked as one, but this recipe first parbakes the base, to let it develop more color and flavor and attain a crunchy texture. Traditionally, the two acute angles of the triangles are dipped in melted chocolate, but you can also dip one side or just the bottom in the chocolate.

Preheat the oven to 350°F (180°C/Gas Mark 4). Line a 9 × 13-inch (23 × 33 cm) light metal baking pan with parchment paper, letting the excess paper hang over the two long sides.

Make the base: In a medium bowl, whisk together the flour, baking powder, and salt.

In a large bowl, with a hand mixer, beat the butter and sugar on medium speed until pale and fluffy, 2–3 minutes. Add the egg and beat until smooth. Beat in the vanilla. Add the dry ingredients and stir until the dough forms and there are no dry patches of flour remaining.

Scrape the dough into the prepared baking pan and use your fingers to press it into an even layer on the bottom. Prick the dough all over with the tines of a fork.

Bake until light golden brown at the edges, about 15 minutes. Remove from the oven and let the base cool for 15 minutes. Leave the oven on.

Once cooled, spread the jam evenly over the base.

While the base cools, make the filling: In a food processor, pulse half the hazelnuts (6 oz/170 g) until very finely ground. Place the remaining half of the hazelnuts on a cutting board and roughly chop by hand.

In a small saucepan, melt the butter over medium heat. Add the hand-chopped hazelnuts and cook, stirring often, until lightly toasted, 3–4 minutes. Add the sugar, water, vanilla, and salt and stir until the sugar is dissolved and the mixture is reduced slightly, 4–5 minutes. Remove the pan from the heat and stir in the ground hazelnuts. Spoon the filling evenly over the jam and spread to make an even layer.

Return the baking pan to the oven and bake until golden brown all over and caramelized at the edges, 20–25 minutes, rotating the pan front to back halfway through.

Transfer the baking pan to a wire rack, and let cool completely.

Once cooled, use the overhanging parchment to lift the cookie slab out of the pan and onto a cutting board (discard the parchment paper). Cut the slab lengthwise into thirds, then cut it crosswise into quarters. Finally cut each rectangle in half diagonally to make triangles.

Finish the cookies: Melt the chocolate and shortening in a heatproof medium bowl, either in the microwave or over a pan of simmering water. Dip the two acute corners of each triangle in the chocolate or dip one whole side in the chocolate. Place the triangles on a sheet of parchment paper and let stand until the chocolate is fully set before serving.

Chocolate-Dipped Hazelnut Triangle Cookies

French Butter Cookies

Sablés Breton

Preparation time: 1 hour 15 minutes,
  plus chilling time
Cooking time: 15 minutes
Makes: About 30 cookies

8 oz (225 g) salted European-style
  butter, softened
1 cup (210 g) superfine (caster) sugar
3 egg yolks
2 teaspoons pure vanilla extract
¼ teaspoon fine sea salt
2¼ cups (320 g) all-purpose
  (plain) flour
Egg wash: 1 egg yolk beaten
  with 2 tablespoons water

Hailing from the butter-loving region of Brittany, these French butter cookies are basically diminutive versions of the larger *gâteau Breton*. But recipes for this simple cookie run the gamut thanks to its popularity, enabling countless bakers to put their spin on it. One thing that's always agreed upon is that these cookies—like Scottish shortbread (recipe, page 274)—are a showcase for excellent salted butter; this recipe calls for salted European-style butter to preserve that original intent. Egg yolks are also an essential component, and while many older recipes use hard-boiled egg yolks—similar to Norwegian *berlinerkranser* (recipe, page 300) and Italian *canestrelli* (recipe, page 114)—to help the dough keep its shape, most modern recipes now use raw egg yolks for convenience.

Some recipes call to roll the notoriously soft dough out into a sheet and then cut out rounds of dough, while more modern recipes form the dough into a log and then cut off round slices. For the latter, often the dough is brushed with egg wash and rolled in sugar to give the sliced cookies a shimmery edge, extra sweetness, and extra crunch. Many older recipes brush the top of each dough round with egg yolk wash and then drag fork tines across the top in a crisscross pattern to leave their mark. Going further, some recipes call for baking the rounds of dough in individual metal ring molds to preserve their even edges. One variation of this cookie is the *broyé du Poitou*, which is a giant *sablé* flavored with vanilla sugar and topped with the characteristic crisscrossed fork tine marks. After baking, it's typically punched to break it into more manageable pieces for serving. This recipe combines the best of all the techniques, shaping the dough into logs that can be chilled, easily sliced, brushed with egg wash, and marked with fork tines to produce the traditional aesthetic. If you want to coat your cookies in sugar, see the variation that follows.

In a large bowl, with a hand mixer, beat the butter and sugar on medium speed until light and fluffy, 2–3 minutes. Add the egg yolks, one at a time, beating well after each addition. Beat in the vanilla and salt. Add the flour and stir until a dough forms and there are no dry patches of flour remaining.

Divide the dough in half. Form each half into a vague cylinder and place on separate sheets of parchment paper. Shape the dough into logs 2 inches (5 cm) in diameter and wrap tightly (see page 14). Transfer the logs to the refrigerator to firm up for at least 2 hours or up to 2 days.

Position racks in the top and bottom thirds of the oven and preheat the oven to 350°F (180°C/Gas Mark 4). Line two large baking sheets with parchment paper.

Unwrap the dough logs and use a sharp knife to cut the dough into slices ¼ inch (6 mm) thick. Arrange the slices on the prepared baking sheets, spaced at least 2 inches (5 cm) apart. Lightly brush the top of each dough disc with egg wash, then take the tines of a fork and lightly drag them north-to-south and then east-to-west on top of each disc to create a crisscross of lines.

Bake until light golden brown on the bottom and just dry to the touch on top, 12–16 minutes, switching racks and rotating the baking sheets front to back halfway through.

Transfer the baking sheets to wire racks. Let the cookies cool on the pans for 1 minute, then transfer them to the racks to cool completely.

Variation
Sugar-Coated French Butter Cookies
Brush the chilled logs with the egg wash, then roll in granulated or sparkling sugar to coat. Proceed with slicing and baking the cookies, omitting the step where the individual slices are brushed with egg wash and crisscrossed with fork tines.

Crisp "Cat Tongue" Cookies
Langues-de-Chat

Preparation time: 30 minutes,
 plus 20 minutes chilling time
Cooking time: 15 minutes
Makes: About 30 cookies

1 stick (4 oz/115 g) unsalted
 butter, softened
½ cup (105 g) superfine (caster) sugar
3 egg whites
1 teaspoon pure vanilla extract
½ teaspoon fine sea salt
Finely grated zest of 1 lemon
¾ cup (105 g) all-purpose (plain) flour

The quintessential dessert cookie, these thin and crispy oblong wafers are often served with ice cream, mousse, and other smooth rich desserts to add crunchy contrast. Their name comes from their shape and their texture, which is slightly rough on the surface. Typically consisting of just butter, sugar, and flour bound with egg whites, which allows them to spread and become crisp, these cookies are often flavored simply with vanilla and/or lemon to keep them relatively neutral for pairing with so many other desserts. Another thin and brittle French cookie that usually accompanies smooth-textured desserts is the *tuile*, which essentially has the same batter as *langues-de-chat* but is made without butter; see the variation that follows.

Position racks in the top and bottom thirds of the oven and preheat the oven to 350°F (180°C/Gas Mark 4). Line two large baking sheets with parchment paper.

In a large bowl, with a hand mixer, beat the butter and sugar on medium speed until light and fluffy, 2–3 minutes. Add the egg whites, one at a time, beating well after each addition; the mixture will look curdled, which is fine. Beat in the vanilla, salt, and lemon zest. Add the flour and stir until a soft dough forms and there are no dry patches of flour remaining.

Scrape the dough into a piping bag fitted with a ½-inch (13 mm) round tip (nozzle). Pipe lines of batter 3 inches (7.5 cm) long on the prepared baking sheets, spaced at least 2 inches (5 cm) apart. Refrigerate the baking sheets for 20 minutes.

Bake until golden brown at the edges but still pale in the center, and dry to the touch on top, 14–16 minutes, switching racks and rotating the baking sheets front to back halfway through.

Transfer the baking sheets to wire racks. Let the cookies cool on the pans for 1 minute, then transfer them to the racks to cool completely.

Variation
Tuiles
Omit the butter; whisk the sugar directly with all three egg whites until smooth. Add the flavorings and flour and stir until the mixture forms a smooth batter with no dry patches of flour remaining. Drop tablespoonfuls of batter onto the baking sheets, spaced 4 inches (10 cm) apart; bake as directed above. As soon as the cookies come out of the oven, while they are still warm and pliable, use an offset spatula to drape each cookie round over a rolling pin so the cookie forms to its curve. Let cool completely until rigid before serving.

Crunchy Twice-Baked Almond Cookies

Croquants aux Amandes

DF (V)

Preparation time: 25 minutes
Cooking time: 35 minutes
Makes: About 30 cookies

1¾ cups (245 g) all-purpose
 (plain) flour
½ teaspoon baking powder
½ teaspoon fine sea salt
⅔ cup (140 g) superfine (caster) sugar
2 eggs
1 tablespoon orange blossom water
5 oz (140 g) skin-on almonds,
 roughly chopped

These almond-studded cookies are often called "French biscotti," but that's misleading. The cookies are a particular specialty of the region of Provence, with various towns having different, very Mediterranean flavorings. In Carpentras, almonds and olives are used for a sweet-salty mix, while honey is sometimes used in Marseille, and grapes, hazelnuts, and citrus like lemons or oranges are used for a version from Nîmes. The general recipe now includes almonds and is commonly flavored with orange blossom water.

Unlike Italian *cantucci* (recipe, page 112) and Jewish *mandelbrot* (recipe, page 47), these *croquants* contain no dairy fat or oil, so they're incredibly light and crisp. They're also typically shaped into a cylinder and cut thinner than other twice-baked cookies so they're more rounded. Two older names for these cookies—*cacho dènt* and *casse-dent*—translate roughly to "tooth breaker," in reference to what might happen to your teeth if you simply bite into them as is. Like most twice-baked cookies, they are incredibly crunchy and are better suited to dipping in tea or coffee than eating on their own.

Position racks in the top and bottom thirds of the oven and preheat the oven to 350°F (180°C/Gas Mark 4). Line two large baking sheets with parchment paper.

In a medium bowl, whisk together the flour, baking powder, and salt. In a large bowl, combine the sugar, eggs, and orange blossom water and whisk until smooth. Add the dry ingredients and almonds and stir until a dough forms and there are no more dry patches of flour remaining. Shape the dough into a ball and then cut in half.

Working on a lightly floured work surface, shape each half into a log 2 inches (5 cm) in diameter. Transfer each log to a prepared baking sheet.

Bake until the logs are lightly browned on the bottom and dry to the touch, 20–25 minutes, switching racks and rotating the baking sheets front to back halfway through.

Transfer the baking sheets to wire racks and let the logs rest for 10 minutes. Leave the oven on.

Carefully transfer each log to a cutting board and use a sharp knife to cut every ¼-inch (6 mm) into thin slices. Return the slices to the baking sheets, spaced evenly apart.

Return to the oven and bake until the cookies are golden brown all over and dry to the touch, 5–10 minutes more.

Transfer the baking sheets to wire racks. Let the cookies cool on the pans for 1 minute, then transfer them to the racks to cool completely.

Small Cakey Cookies

Palets de Dames

Preparation time: 50 minutes,
  plus cooling and setting time
Cooking time: 10 minutes
Makes: About 24 cookies

½ cup (65 g) dried currants
2 tablespoons gold or dark rum
⅔ cup (130 g) white US granulated
  (UK caster) sugar
1 stick (4 oz/115 g) unsalted
  butter, softened
2 eggs
1 teaspoon pure vanilla extract
½ teaspoon fine sea salt
1 cup (140 g) all-purpose (plain) flour

For the glaze (optional):
1 cup (135 g) powdered (icing) sugar
1–2 tablespoons whole milk
  (or more rum)

A specialty of northern France, the name for these cookies has a curious origin. *Palets* means "pucks," obviously referencing the shape of these round cookies, but the *dames*, or "ladies," is unclear. It's likely their softer texture—as opposed to dense, crunchy *sablés* (recipe, page 258)—lent them that particular reference as the cookies would be more delicate for ladies' palates.

Old recipes show them as being plain cakey cookies or basically round *langues-de-chat* (recipe, page 259), sometimes decorated with chocolate. Somewhere along the way they became cakier, thicker, and incorporated rum-soaked dried currants, which now seems to be the standard flavoring. Even then, some recipes call for a powdered (icing) sugar glaze while others don't. The choice of whether to glaze is up to you.

Position racks in the top and bottom thirds of the oven and preheat the oven to 400°F (200°C/Gas Mark 6). Line two large baking sheets with parchment paper.

In a small heatproof bowl, toss the currants with the rum, cover with plastic wrap (cling film), and microwave for 20 seconds. Let the currants cool completely, then uncover and toss again with the rum in the bowl.

In a large bowl, with a hand mixer, beat the white US granulated (UK caster) sugar and butter on medium speed until light and fluffy, 2–3 minutes. Add the eggs, one at a time, beating well after each addition. Beat in the rum-soaked currants, the vanilla, and salt. Add the flour and stir until a dough forms and there are no dry patches of flour remaining.

Using a ½-ounce (1-tablespoon) ice cream scoop, portion the dough, dropping spoonfuls onto the prepared baking sheets, spaced 2 inches (5 cm) apart.

Bake until golden brown at the edges but still pale in the center and dry to the touch on top, 8–10 minutes, switching racks and rotating the baking sheets front to back halfway through.

Transfer the baking sheets to wire racks. Let the cookies cool on the pans for 1 minute, then transfer them to the racks to cool completely.

Make the glaze (if using): In a small bowl, stir together the powdered (icing) sugar and 1 tablespoon milk, adding more milk by the teaspoon until the glaze is thick but pourable. Dip the top of each cookie in the glaze or spoon a teaspoon of glaze over each cookie. Let the glaze set before serving.

Almond Meringue Cookie Sandwiches
Macaron Parisien

Preparation time: 35 minutes,
  plus 1 hour drying time and
  cooling and standing time
Cooking time: 20 minutes
Makes: About 36 cookie sandwiches

For the cookies:
1¾ cups (235 g) powdered
  (icing) sugar
1 cup (110 g) superfine almond
  flour (ground almonds)
3 tablespoons Dutch-process
  cocoa powder (optional)
3 egg whites, at room temperature
¼ teaspoon cream of tartar
¼ teaspoon fine sea salt
¼ cup (55 g) superfine (caster) sugar
1 teaspoon pure vanilla extract

For the ganache:
8 oz (225 g) bittersweet chocolate,
  preferably 65%–70% cacao,
  finely chopped
⅔ cup (5 fl oz/150 ml) heavy
  (double) cream
2 tablespoons (30 g) unsalted
  butter, softened

What is there to say about the cookie sandwich popularly known as the macaron that many people don't know? For starters, it originally was a more rustic cookie made with almond flour (ground almonds) moistened with rose water or orange blossom water, beaten with egg whites and sugar, and dropped into a rough round, more akin to the coconut macaroons we know today (which themselves descended from this first style). François Pierre de la Varenne, in his 1625 book *The French Chef*, is credited with changing the course of the cookie by removing the flower water and refining the dough's appearance, which was once piped onto wafers a la *Elisenlebkuchen* (recipe, page 244) into one large round.

In the centuries that followed, regional styles developed using this recipe, mostly made in and sold by convents to support themselves. After the French Revolution, those nuns opened bakeries selling their macarons. But in the 1830s, the macaron cookie we know of today is credited with being invented by the baker Pierre Desfontaines, cousin of the tea-shop owner Louis-Ernest Ladurée, who joined two small macaron cookies together with ganache and called it *le macaron parisien*. It's this cookie that everyone today is so familiar with, sandwiched with the original ganache or fruit jam, citrus curd, or buttercream.

Today, more and more home cooks make macarons at home to test their baking skills. This recipe hews closely to Desfontaines's original: two plain macaron cookies sandwiched with ganache. Some historians interpret the cookies themselves as also containing chocolate, so the option to add cocoa powder to the dough is given here as well.

Make the cookies: Stack two large baking sheets on top of each other, then line the top one with a silicone baking mat; if you don't have one, use parchment paper, but a mat will produce more evenly baked cookies.

Place a sieve over a medium bowl and add the powdered (icing) sugar, almond flour, and cocoa powder (if using) and sift them into the bowl.

In a stand mixer fitted with the whisk, combine the egg whites, cream of tartar, and salt and beat on medium speed until frothy, about 1 minute. Increase the speed to medium-high and slowly pour in the superfine (caster) sugar, continuing to beat until the meringue is just stiff and shiny, 2–2½ more minutes. Add the vanilla.

Using a silicone spatula, scrape the meringue into the almond flour mixture and fold the two together, giving the bowl a quarter turn with each fold. Continue folding and turning, scraping down the bowl, until the batter is smooth and falls off the spatula in a thick ribbon, no more than 2 minutes (about 60 strokes).

Transfer the batter to a piping bag fitted with a ¼-inch (6 mm) round tip (nozzle). Holding the bag perpendicular to and ½ inch (13 mm) above the prepared pan, pipe 1¼-inch (3 cm) rounds 1 inch (2.5 cm) apart. Firmly tap the baking sheet twice against the counter to release any air bubbles. Let the meringue rounds stand at room temperature until the tops are no longer sticky to the touch, about 1 hour.

Preheat the oven to 325°F (160°C/Gas Mark 3).

Bake the macarons until the tops of the cookies are shiny and rise ⅛ inch (3 mm) to form a "foot," about 20 minutes, rotating the baking sheet front to back halfway through.

Transfer the top baking sheet to a wire rack and let the cookies cool completely.

While the cookies cool, make the ganache: Place the chocolate in a small heatproof bowl. In a small saucepan, bring the cream to a simmer. Pour it over the chocolate and let stand for 1 minute, then stir with a small silicone spatula, starting in the center and gradually moving to the edges, until the mixture emulsifies into a shiny ganache. Stir in the butter until smooth. Let the ganache stand until cool to the touch.

Turn half the cookies upside down and use a small piping bag or a spoon to top each with about 1 teaspoon of the ganache. Sandwich the cookies with the remaining plain cookies. Ideally, store the cookies in an airtight container for 12–24 hours to allow them to soften before serving.

Almond Meringue Cookie Sandwiches

Chocolate and Almond Macaroon Cookies

Basler Brunsli

Preparation time: 1 hour 10 minutes, plus at least 2 hours chilling time and 4 hours standing time
Cooking time: 15 minutes
Makes: About 48 cookies

8 oz (225 g) blanched whole or slivered almonds
1 cup (200 g) white US granulated (UK caster) sugar, plus more for rolling
4 oz (115 g) bittersweet chocolate, finely chopped
2 oz (55 g) unsweetened chocolate, finely chopped
1 teaspoon ground cinnamon
¼ teaspoon ground cloves
½ teaspoon fine sea salt
2 egg whites
2 tablespoons kirsch (cherry eau-de-vie) or light rum

This cookie, said to have been invented in Basel (hence the name), is a close cousin to the German *Zimtsterne* (recipe, page 248). Both are made with ground almonds and egg whites flavored with cinnamon and rolled thin and cut into stars. This Swiss cookie differentiates itself by also adding chocolate to the mix, usually in the form of bars that are ground with the almonds. Some recipes call for cocoa powder, but most traditional ones use bar chocolate in various amounts, depending on how chocolaty you want your cookies. Semisweet or bittersweet is typical, but this recipe adds a smaller amount of unsweetened chocolate, to balance the sugar used in the cookie and give a deeper flavor.

Cloves are also typically added to the spice mix, playing well off the chocolate. Though many recipes shape the dough into stars, like the *Zimtsterne*, some older recipes reference the dough being used for all sorts of Christmas-themed shapes and even some shape them into simple bars. This recipe cuts them into bars, but if you want shapes, simply follow the directions for rolling and shaping *Zimtsterne*.

In a food processor, pulse the almonds until finely ground to the consistency of fine sand. Add the sugar, both chocolates, the cinnamon, cloves, and salt and pulse until the chocolate is very finely ground. Add the egg whites and kirsch and pulse until the dough just comes together. Shape the dough into a disc, then wrap in plastic wrap (cling film) and refrigerate for at least 2 hours.

Sprinkle some sugar evenly over a large sheet of parchment paper. Unwrap the dough and place it on the parchment paper. Sprinkle the top of the dough with more sugar, then cover with another sheet of parchment paper. Roll out the dough with a rolling pin into a rough rectangle ½ inch (13 mm) thick. Remove the top sheet of parchment and cut the dough into bars 2 × 1 inches (5 × 2.5 cm).

Line two large baking sheets with parchment paper. Arrange the dough bars on the prepared baking sheets, spaced 1 inch (2.5 cm) apart. Let the cookies stand until dry to the touch on top, at least 4 hours.

Position racks in the top and bottom thirds of the oven and preheat the oven to 325°F (160°C/Gas Mark 3).

Bake until the outside of the cookies is dry and slightly darker at the edges, 14–16 minutes, switching racks and rotating the baking sheets front to back halfway through.

Transfer the baking sheets to wire racks and let the cookies cool completely on the pans.

Chewy Honey and Spice Bar Cookies

Basler Läckerli

Preparation time: 1 hour 20 minutes,
  plus overnight chilling, 30 minutes
  chilling time and setting times
Cooking time: 35 minutes
Makes: 48 cookies

For the dough:
¾ cup (255 g) honey
½ cup (100 g) white US granulated
  (UK caster) sugar
¼ cup (2 fl oz/60 ml) kirsch
  (cherry eau-de-vie) or light rum
1½ teaspoons ground cinnamon
1 teaspoon freshly grated nutmeg
¼ teaspoon ground cloves
Finely grated zest of 1 orange
Finely grated zest of 1 lemon
2½ cups (350 g) all-purpose
  (plain) flour
1 teaspoon baking powder
¾ teaspoon fine sea salt
¼ teaspoon baking soda
  (bicarbonate of soda)
2 oz (55 g) candied citron
  or lemon peel, finely chopped
2 oz (55 g) candied orange peel,
  finely chopped
2 oz (55 g) blanched whole or
  slivered almonds, finely chopped
2 oz (55 g) blanched hazelnuts,
  finely chopped

For the glaze:
1½ cups (205 g) powdered (icing)
  sugar, sifted
2 tablespoons kirsch or light rum
1 tablespoon water

Almost identical to *Nürnberger Lebkuchen* (recipe, page 247), these classic Swiss bar cookies are chewier because they don't contain eggs, unlike the German cookie. Recipes for these cookies typically have nutmeg and their glaze is made with kirsch, the cherry eau-de-vie. The cookies are made in much the same way as the flat German honey cakes: Pressed into a rectangle and baked up as a single sheet, then glazed with hot powdered (icing) sugar icing that cools and sets hard.

They're more fruity tasting than *Elisenlebkuchen* (recipe, page 244), thanks to extra fresh citrus zest that brightens the candied citron and orange peels in the mix. The cookies, whose name roughly translates to "little delicious things from Basel," are cut into small narrow bars, befitting their name. They've been made in Basel since the 1300s and are a staple of the city's bakery repertoire leading up to Christmas. In Alsace and western Germany, the cookies are harder and thinner and go by the name *Lapkueche* or *Leckerli*, and are typically cut into shapes for Christmas instead of bars.

- -

Make the dough: In a small saucepan, combine the honey, white US granulated (UK caster) sugar, and kirsch and heat over medium-high heat, stirring until the sugar dissolves. Remove the pan from the heat and stir in the cinnamon, nutmeg, cloves, orange zest, and lemon zest. Scrape the honey mixture into a large bowl to cool for 10 minutes.

Meanwhile, in a medium bowl, whisk together the flour, baking powder, salt, and baking soda (bicarb).

To the cooled honey mixture, add the flour mixture, candied citron, candied orange peel, almonds, and hazelnuts and stir until the dough just comes together and there are no dry patches of flour remaining. Gather the dough into a ball, wrap in plastic wrap (cling film), and refrigerate for at least 8 hours or overnight, or up to 1 day.

Preheat the oven to 325°F (160°C/Gas Mark 3). Line a large baking sheet with parchment paper. Place a 9 × 13-inch (23 × 33 cm) baking pan on the parchment and use a pencil to trace the outline onto the paper. Flip the paper over so the pencil markings are face down.

Unwrap the dough, place it on the paper, and let stand for 20–30 minutes to take the chill off the dough. Use your hands to flatten it into a rectangle ½ inch (13 mm) thick that fits within the dimensions of the pencil markings. Roll a rolling pin gently over the surface to get a smooth top.

Bake the rectangle until darker brown at the edges and just dry to the touch in the center, 25–30 minutes, rotating the sheet front to back halfway through.

About 5 minutes before the cookies are done, make the glaze: In a small saucepan, whisk together the powdered (icing) sugar, kirsch, and water into a smooth glaze. Heat over medium heat until the mixture begins bubbling and thickens. Cover and keep warm until ready to use.

Transfer the baking sheet to a wire rack and immediately pour the warm glaze (rewarm if necessary to loosen) over the hot cookie rectangle, using a brush or small spatula to spread it evenly over the top. Use a paring knife to score the cookie rectangle into 4 lengthwise columns by 12 crosswise rows. Let the cookie slab stand until completely cooled and the glaze has set hard. Cut along the score lines to separate the cookies before serving.

Swiss Anise "Claw" Cookies

Chräbeli / Anisguetzli

Preparation time: 30 minutes,
  plus at least 24 hours drying time
Cooking time: 15 minutes
Makes: About 36 cookies

2 teaspoons anise seeds
1 cup (210 g) superfine (caster) sugar
2 eggs
1 tablespoon kirsch (cherry
  eau-de-vie; optional)
¾ teaspoon fine sea salt
Finely grated zest of 1 lemon
2¼ cups (315 g) all-purpose
  (plain) flour

In the Middle Ages, a "flour marzipan" dough made of egg whites, sugar, and flour developed called *anisbroetli* and was often referred to as "common marzipan" or "peasant marzipan," because almonds were so expensive and wheat-based flour was cheaper. That dough is what makes German *Springerle* (recipe, page 246). These Swiss cookies are basically the same dough but with the anise seeds mixed inside—as opposed to underneath—and flavored with kirsch, then cut into different shapes.

These white, elongated, and curved *chräbeli* are a specialty of the city of Baden, and their name is from the shape, which roughly translates to animal "claws." The dough is rolled into short logs, cut three times on one side and then bent to expose the slits. The cookies are left to dry for 24 hours before baking so they rise like a French macaron (recipe, page 262). Their name in Germany is *Anisplazchen*, while in Alsace, they're called *anis bredele*.

Line two large baking sheets with parchment paper. Using a mortar and pestle or spice grinder, process the anise seeds just enough to break them in half.

In a large bowl, with a hand mixer, beat the sugar and eggs on medium speed until pale and doubled in volume and when the beater is lifted from the bowl, the mixture falls back in a thick ribbon, about 5 minutes. Add the crushed anise seeds, kirsch (if using), salt, and lemon zest and beat until evenly incorporated. Add the flour, and use a large silicone spatula to fold the mixture until a dough forms and there are no dry patches of flour remaining.

Transfer the dough to a clean work surface. Divide the dough into 4 equal portions. Roll each portion into a long rope ¾ inch (2 cm) thick. Cut the rope into 2½-inch (6.5 cm) lengths. With a short end of a cookie facing you, use a paring knife to cut three equidistant slits along the right-hand side, angling the slits at a slight downward diagonal. Arch the dough toward the uncut side to splay open the slits and form a crescent shape. Repeat with the remaining dough lengths to shape more cookies. Arrange the cookies on the prepared baking sheets, spaced 1 inch (2.5 cm) apart. Let the cookies stand until dry to the touch, at least 24 hours.

Position racks in the top and bottom thirds of the oven and preheat the oven to 350°F (180°C/Gas Mark 4).

Bake until very light golden at the edges of the bottom and risen, 12–15 minutes, switching racks and rotating the baking sheets front to back halfway through.

Transfer the baking sheets to wire racks and let the cookies cool completely on the pans.

Swiss Anise "Claw" Cookies

Egg Yolk and Lemon Butter Cookies

Mailänderli / Milanais

Preparation time: 45 minutes,
 plus chilling time
Cooking time: 15 minutes
Makes: About 36 cookies

2 sticks (8 oz/225 g) unsalted
 butter, softened
1 cup (200 g) white US granulated
 (UK caster) sugar
2 eggs
1 egg yolk
Finely grated zest and juice of 1 lemon
1 teaspoon pure vanilla extract
¾ teaspoon fine sea salt
3 cups (420 g) all-purpose (plain) flour
Egg wash: 1 egg yolk beaten with
 2 teaspoons water

How these "little Milano" cookies got their moniker is unclear, but since northern Italy has many egg yolk-rich cookies, like *canestrelli* (recipe, page 114) and *krumiri* (see page 124), it's likely that association led to these Swiss cookies paying homage to their neighbor to the south. Essentially simple butter cookies, they're enriched with eggs and brushed with more egg yolk on top to give them a deep golden yellow warmth. They're often flavored with lemon zest and cut into various shapes for Christmas baking.

In a large bowl, with a hand mixer, beat the butter and sugar on medium speed until pale and fluffy, 2–3 minutes. Add the whole eggs and egg yolk, one at a time, beating well after each addition. Beat in the lemon zest, lemon juice, vanilla, and salt. Add the flour and mix on low speed until the mixture forms a firm dough. Shape the dough into a ball, wrap in plastic wrap (cling film), and refrigerate for at least 2 hours or overnight.

Position racks in the top and bottom thirds of the oven and preheat the oven to 350°F (180°C/Gas Mark 4). Line two large baking sheets with parchment paper.

Working on a lightly floured work surface, roll out the dough with a rolling pin to ¼ inch (6 mm) thick. Using 1½-inch (4 cm) cutters, cut out shapes of dough. Reroll scraps to cut out more cookies. Arrange the cookies on the prepared baking sheets, spaced 2 inches (5 cm) apart. With a pastry brush, lightly brush the tops of all the cookies with the egg wash.

Bake until the cookies are light golden brown and dry to the touch on top, 12–15 minutes, switching racks and rotating the baking sheets front to back halfway through.

Transfer the baking sheets to wire racks. Let the cookies cool on the pans for 1 minute, then transfer them to the racks to cool completely.

Egg Yolk and Lemon Butter Cookies

the british isles, australia & new zealand

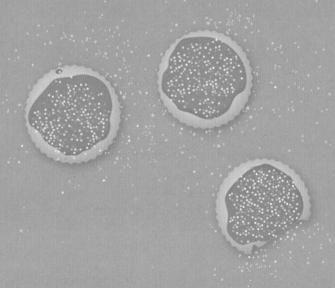

The influence of the British Isles, particularly the famous Scottish shortbread, is felt in this region that extends to the Commonwealth countries of Australia and New Zealand. Other crumbly shortbread-based cookies and those based on oats—which grow well in the wet climates of Ireland and Scotland—are the iconic cookies from this area, although many of them are commercially produced and not typically the province of the home baker.

Oatmeal Biscuits

Preparation time: 1 hour 10 minutes,
  plus chilling time
Cooking time: 20 minutes
Makes: About 36 cookies

2½ cups (240 g) rolled oats
1 cup (140 g) all-purpose (plain) flour
¾ cup (150 g) white US granulated
  (UK caster) sugar
¾ teaspoon fine sea salt
½ teaspoon baking soda
  (bicarbonate of soda; optional)
2 sticks (8 oz/225 g) unsalted
  butter, softened
¼ cup (2 fl oz/60 ml) water

Oats have long been a staple grain for regions around the world, particularly in Ireland, Scotland, and northern Britain where the cold wet climate historically made them easier to grow than wheat. In Ireland, savory, cracker-like oatcakes were made with lard and cooked on an iron griddle to have with everyday meals. Oats are inextricably linked with the national identity of the country, particularly through the association with McCann's, a well-known brand of Irish oatmeal.

The oatcakes gained sugar, as that ingredient got cheaper, and they morphed into a sweet cookie. Today there are innumerable recipes for oatmeal cookies that are soft and chewy or with cinnamon, though the classic Irish oatmeal biscuit resembles a dense shortbread and is typically rolled very thin. Many recipes call for no leavening, while others throw in a pinch of baking soda (bicarb) to allow the dough to expand a bit. The choice is up to you in this recipe.

In a food processor, pulse the oats until they are half the original size. Scrape the oats into a large bowl and add the flour, sugar, salt, and if using, the baking soda (bicarb). Whisk to combine. Add the butter and use your fingers to rub it into the dry ingredients until it breaks down into coarse crumbs. Add the water and stir with your fingers until it comes together into a solid dough, lightly kneading only as much as needed to no longer see any dry patches of flour in the bowl. Shape the dough into a ball, wrap in plastic wrap (cling film), and refrigerate for at least 1 hour or up to 2 days.

Position racks in the top and bottom thirds of the oven and preheat the oven to 350°F (180°C/Gas Mark 4). Line two large baking sheets with parchment paper.

Working on a lightly floured work surface, roll out the dough with a rolling pin to ⅛ inch (3 mm) thick. Using a 2½-inch (6.5 cm) round cutter, cut out rounds of dough. Reroll the scraps to cut out more cookies. Arrange the rounds on the prepared baking sheets, spaced 1 inch (2.5 cm) apart.

Bake until golden brown at the edges and dry to the touch on top, 15–18 minutes, switching racks and rotating the baking sheets front to back halfway through.

Transfer the baking sheets to wire racks. Let the cookies cool on the pans for 1 minute, then transfer them to the racks to cool completely.

Oatmeal Biscuits

Shortbread

Preparation time: 15 minutes
Cooking time: 45 minutes
Makes: 16 cookies

2¼ cups (315 g) all-purpose
  (plain) flour
⅔ cup (105 g) white rice flour (or ¾
  cup/105 g more all-purpose flour)
⅔ cup (140 g) superfine (caster) sugar,
  plus more (optional) for sprinkling
½ teaspoon fine sea salt
10 oz (285 g) salted high-fat European-
  style butter, softened

Scottish shortbread is buttery, dense, and crumbly, and has no leavening. While the shortbread that is exported by manufacturers from Scotland today is very much like that, the original was very much different (read more in the essay on All About Shortbread, see opposite). Today, shortbread is often found in typical petticoat shapes as well as rectangular bars, often referred to as "fingers," and rounds cut from a roll of dough or from a flattened sheet. It's commonly agreed that the classic ratio of ingredients in shortbread is 3:2:1 (3 parts flour, 2 parts butter, 1 part sugar), but modern tastes have adjusted those measurements and added chemical leaveners and other flavorings and spices along the way.

In Wales, shortbread dough is pressed and baked in scallop shells and called Aberffraw biscuits, named for a village in northwestern Wales. Shortbread in Ireland often adds cornstarch (cornflour) and baking powder or other chemical leavening to the Scottish original, and often cuts the cookies into sticks. In Lancashire in northern Britain, Goosnargh cakes are small, round shortbreads flavored with caraway seeds and sometimes ground coriander (see the variation that follows). And in Ayrshire, Scotland, shortbread is made with egg and cream and less butter. All shortbread is intentionally cooked at a lower temperature and for a longer period of time to help achieve its distinctive texture.

Position racks in the top and bottom thirds of the oven and preheat the oven to 275°F (140°C/Gas Mark 1). Using an 8-inch (20 cm) round cake pan as a guide, trace the outline of the pan on two sheets of parchment paper. Flip the paper over and place each sheet on a large baking sheet. (Alternatively, you can bake the shortbread in two 8-inch/20 cm round, fluted tart pans with removable bottoms.)

In a large bowl, whisk together the all-purpose (plain) flour, rice flour, sugar, and salt. Add the butter and use your fingers to rub the butter into the other ingredients until it forms a crumbly, uniform dough. Form the dough into a ball and then cut in half.

Place each half in the center of the 8-inch (20 cm) circle on the parchment paper and use your hands to flatten and shape each into a flat disc that fits within the shape of the circle. You can also press the dough into the 8-inch (20 cm) cake pan, then tap it out onto the parchment paper, if you want. Using your fingers, pinch along the outer edge of each disc similar to crimping a pie. (If using the tart pans, simply press the dough into each pan to an even thickness.)

Using a paring knife, lightly score each round into 8 wedges, then use the tines of a fork to prick the shortbread all over, preferably staying within the score lines.

Bake until the edges are just starting to brown and the top is dry to the touch, 40–45 minutes, switching racks and rotating the baking sheets (or tart pans) front to back halfway through.

Transfer the baking sheets (or tart pans) to wire racks and immediately cut along the score lines through the hot shortbread rounds but do not separate them. If garnishing with sugar, liberally sprinkle it over the top of the hot shortbread. Let the shortbread cool completely before breaking along the lines to serve.

Variations

Softer Shortbread:
Substitute ¾ cup (105 g) cornstarch (cornflour) for the rice flour.

Shortbread Fingers:
Line a 9 × 13-inch (23 × 33 cm) straight-sided light metal baking pan with parchment paper. Press all the dough into the pan. Score the dough into 3 lengthwise columns by 16 crosswise rows. Prick with a fork and bake as directed.

Individual Shortbread Rounds:
Scrape each half of the dough onto a sheet of parchment paper. Form each half into a vague cylinder and shape the dough into logs 2 inches (5 cm) in diameter and wrap tightly (see page 14). Transfer them to the refrigerator to firm up for at least 2 hours or up to 2 days.

Unwrap the dough log and use a sharp knife to cut the dough into slices ¼ inch (6 mm) thick. Arrange the slices on parchment paper-lined baking sheets, spaced at least 2 inches (5 cm) apart. Bake at 300°F (150°C/Gas Mark 2) for 20–25 minutes.

Goosnargh Cakes:
Omit the rice flour and use a total of 3 cups (420 g) all-purpose (plain) flour. Add 1 teaspoon ground coriander to the flour. Mix and shape the dough for Individual Shortbread Rounds (above) and sprinkle each slice of dough before baking with some sugar and a pinch of cracked caraway seeds. Bake as for the Individual Shortbread Rounds (see above).

All About Shortbread

The original Scottish shortbread likely descended from an enriched and sweetened bread/cake that more resembles thick, modern pie pastry. This was eaten for the winter solstice and was called an "oat bannock." The bread was cooked as a round with pinched edges, said to represent the sun's rays, a reference to pagan folklore that believed the shape gave powers during the dark winter. The cake was also scored on top so it could be broken after cooking, which stems from a superstition that to cut this holiday cake would bring bad luck. Though it's now eaten throughout the year, it is still a traditional cookie to have during the holidays, but especially on Hogmanay, or New Year's Eve.

This shape and scoring persisted in modern times when the cake became more buttery and more like the cookies we know today. Along the way, that round, sun-ray shape became known as "petticoat" shortbread, because when the wedges are broken apart, they're said to resemble the panels of fabric in a woman's undergarments, with their "frilly" edge. This folklore is likely also related to the association of shortbread with Mary Queen of Scots, whom many credit with popularizing shortbread when she came to Scotland in 1650. She was a big fan of petites galettes in her native France and brought the tradition of making small buttery cookies with her.

Though many today think of shortbread as only made with all-purpose (plain) or white flour made from wheat, recipes from the 1800s often called for mixing a small amount of rice flour, or "ground rice," into the mix to give the cookies a crunchier, snappier texture. Similarly, recipes from that time also suggested using a small amount of cornstarch (cornflour) to make the cookies softer. In fact, it's common for bakers—then and now—to use ground barley, oats, and even fine semolina in their shortbread to make it grittier, nuttier, or smoother, depending on the texture they're hoping to achieve.

Shortbread (p. 274)

Welsh Griddled Currant Cookies (p. 278)

Welsh Griddled Currant Cookies
Pice Ar y Maen

Preparation time: 25 minutes,
 plus chilling time
Cooking time: 40 minutes
Makes: About 30 cookies

1⅔ cups (230 g) all-purpose
 (plain) flour
½ cup (100 g) white US granulated (UK
 caster) sugar, plus more for sprinkling
½ teaspoon fine sea salt
½ teaspoon freshly grated nutmeg
½ teaspoon ground allspice
¼ teaspoon ground cinnamon
1 stick (4 oz/115 g) unsalted
 butter, softened
1 egg
6 tablespoons buttermilk or whole milk
¾ cup (95 g) dried currants

One of the specialties of Wales in the western United Kingdom are these "cakes on the stone." Descended from Welsh crumpets, which are yeasted pancakes cooked on a griddle in a ring mold, these cookies are cut from a sheet of dough into rounds and then cooked on a griddle until golden and crisp on the outside but still tender inside. Their texture possesses the softness of cake, but the dense firmness of a biscuit or cookie. So while they're often called "Welsh cakes," they're usually referred to as a cookie, since they're eaten out of the hand and sprinkled with sugar while hot like many other cookies.

The dough for these cookies can also be baked and, when candied citrus is added, is sometimes referred to as "Easter biscuits." Older recipes used lard as the primary fat, though today the cookies are a showcase for great butter. Currants are a staple of these cookies as is a mix of spices, typically cinnamon and nutmeg, that scent the dough but don't overwhelm it. While modern recipes use chemical leavening to provide lightness, this recipe doesn't, to keep the cookies crisp and less cakey; if you'd like a cakier cookie, add 1 teaspoon baking powder to the dry ingredients here.

In a large bowl, whisk together the flour, sugar, salt, nutmeg, allspice, and cinnamon. Add the butter and rub it into the dry ingredients with your fingers until it breaks down into crumbles. Add the egg and buttermilk and mix until the dough starts to come together. Add the currants and continue mixing until the mixture forms a dough and there are no dry patches of flour remaining. Shape the dough into a ball, wrap in plastic wrap (cling film), and refrigerate for at least 2 hours or overnight.

Heat a cast-iron skillet or griddle over medium heat. Line a large baking sheet with paper towels.

Working on a lightly floured work surface, roll out the dough with a rolling pin to ⅜ inch (1 cm) thick. Using a 2-inch (5 cm) round cutter, cut out rounds of dough. Reroll the scraps to cut out more rounds of dough.

Working in batches, place a single layer of rounds in the skillet and cook until golden brown and crisp on the bottom, 3–4 minutes. Flip the cookies and cook until golden brown and crisp on the other side, 3–4 minutes more.

Transfer the cookies to the lined baking sheet and sprinkle liberally with more sugar while hot. Let cool completely.

Cornish Fairing

Preparation time: 35 minutes,
  plus chilling time
Cooking time: 10 minutes
Makes: About 12 cookies

1½ cups (210 g) all-purpose
  (plain) flour
½ cup (100 g) white US granulated
  (UK caster) sugar
1 tablespoon ground ginger
1 teaspoon ground cinnamon
1 teaspoon baking powder
1½ teaspoons baking soda
  (bicarbonate of soda)
½ teaspoon ground allspice
½ teaspoon fine sea salt
1 stick (4 oz/115 g) unsalted
  butter, softened
¼ cup British golden syrup,
  such as Lyle's
2 tablespoons whole milk

Popular in Cornwall during Victorian England as a "Cornish Fairing" —an edible souvenir to take home from a fair or festival—these cookies are packed with ground ginger and crisp with a slight chew from the use of golden syrup, a British syrup with a distinct buttery flavor. The dough is slightly thicker than gingerbread-like doughs, and though the cookie likely descended from those doughs, in England it's now more recognizable as a thick round with a characteristically cracked top. Some modern recipes swap white sugar for brown sugar and add syrup-packed ginger or candied ginger to their recipes, giving them even more chew.

Those last two additions make it easy to see the cookies making their way to the United States, getting more syrup (in the form of molasses) and becoming even chewier. It's likely these Cornish Fairings gave us the modern-day, chewy Ginger-Molasses Cookie (recipe, page 343). Cornish Fairings are also closely related to so-called "ginger nuts," which are smaller and crisper (see the variation that follows), and likely influenced what today Americans know as Ginger Snaps (recipe, page 342).

In a large bowl, whisk together the flour, sugar, ginger, cinnamon, baking powder, baking soda (bicarb), allspice, and salt. Add the butter and rub it into the dry ingredients with your fingers until it breaks down into rumbles. In a small bowl, stir together the golden syrup and milk until smooth. Pour into the large bowl and mix until a dough forms and there are no dry patches of flour remaining. Cover the bowl with plastic wrap (cling film) and refrigerate the dough for at least 2 hours or preferably overnight.

Position racks in the top and bottom thirds of the oven and preheat the oven to 375°F (190°C/Gas Mark 5). Line two large baking sheets with parchment paper.

Using a 1½-ounce (3-tablespoon) ice cream scoop, portion the dough and roll into balls. Arrange them on the prepared baking sheets, spaced 3 inches (7.5 cm) apart. Using the palm of your hand, flatten each ball slightly into a thick disc.

Bake until the cookies are slightly darker brown at the edges and cracked all over on top, 8–10 minutes, switching racks and rotating the baking sheets front to back halfway through.

Transfer the baking sheets to wire racks. Let the cookies cool on the pans for 1 minute, then transfer them to the racks to cool completely.

Variation
Ginger Nuts
Substitute ½ cup (110 g) packed light brown sugar for the white sugar. In a small saucepan, heat the brown sugar, butter, and golden syrup together until the sugar dissolves. Remove from the heat and let cool. Omit the cinnamon, baking powder, and allspice. Whisk together the flour, ginger, and salt. Substitute 1 egg yolk for the milk. Add the syrup mixture and egg yolk to form a dough. Using a 1-ounce (2-tablespoon) ice cream scoop, portion the dough and roll into balls. Bake as directed.

Melting Moments

Preparation time: 30 minutes
Cooking time: 15 minutes
Makes: About 18 cookies

2 cups (284 g) self-rising flour
  (or all-purpose/plain flour mixed
  with 2 teaspoons baking powder)
¾ teaspoon fine sea salt
¾ cup (150 g) white US granulated
  (UK caster) sugar
10 tablespoons (5 oz/140 g) unsalted
  butter, softened
6 tablespoons (85 g)
  cold-rendered leaf lard or
  vegetable shortening, softened
1 egg
2 teaspoons pure vanilla extract
Rolled oats or unsweetened shredded
  (desiccated) coconut, for rolling
Halved or quartered glacéed or
  maraschino cherries, for decorating

These are simple buttery cookies rolled in oats or coconut and studded with glacéed cherries. The first recipe for the cookies comes from advertisements by English food manufacturer Be-Ro promoting their "self-raising" flour. The flour, which had baking powder and salt already mixed in, is believed to have been developed by the founder of the company, Thomas Bell, who ran a grocery in Newcastle in the late 1800s.

The original cookies were made with lard and margarine, which would have contributed to the "melt-in-the-mouth" texture in their name, though many recipes today just use butter. The name stuck and influenced other Commonwealth variations for buttery, shortbread-like cookies like the Australian Custard Cookie Sandwiches (recipe, page 284). That first Be-Ro recipe called for crusting the dough balls in oats or shredded (desiccated) coconut, but many also called for crusting the dough balls in cornflakes or chopped nuts. The cherry garnish usually comes in the form of one-quarter of a glacéed, or candied, or maraschino cherry, though more generous recipes call for a half. Some even use the cookie dough as a base for thumbprint cookies and fill them with cherry jam.

Position racks in the top and bottom thirds of the oven and preheat the oven to 375°F (190°C/Gas Mark 5). Line two large baking sheets with parchment paper.

In a medium bowl, whisk together the self-rising flour and salt. (If not using self-rising flour, whisk together the flour, baking powder, and salt.)

In a large bowl, with a hand mixer, combine the sugar, butter, and lard and beat on medium speed until smooth and fluffy, 2–3 minutes. Add the egg and beat until smooth. Beat in the vanilla. Add the dry ingredients and beat on low speed until the dough just comes together and there are no dry patches of flour in the bowl.

Spread out a layer of oats or coconut on a large plate or pie dish. Using a 1-ounce (2-tablespoon) ice cream scoop, portion the dough and roll into balls. Roll each ball in the oats or coconut to coat. Arrange them on the prepared baking sheets, spaced at least 2 inches (5 cm) apart.

Bake until light golden brown at the edges and dry to the touch on top, 12–15 minutes, switching racks and rotating the baking sheets front to back halfway through.

Transfer the baking sheets to wire racks and immediately stud the top of each cookie with a half or quarter of a cherry. Let the cookies rest on the pans for 1 minute, then transfer them to the racks to cool completely.

Melting Moments

Shrewsbury Biscuits

Preparation time: 1 hour 15 minutes
Cooking time: 15 minutes
Makes: 18–24 cookies, depending
  on the size

1¾ cups (245 g) all-purpose
  (plain) flour
⅔ cup (130 g) white US granulated
  (UK caster) sugar
¾ teaspoon fine sea salt
½ teaspoon ground cinnamon
½ teaspoon freshly grated nutmeg
  or ground mace
1 stick (4 oz/115 g) unsalted
  butter, softened
1 egg
1 teaspoon rose water

Named after Shrewsbury, a town in the county of Shropshire, these lightly spiced butter cookies have been made for several centuries, and it seems they acted as a sponge for whatever the fashionable flavors were at a time. Caraway, nutmeg, lemon, cream sherry, and various other spices have often been used, particularly rose water or orange blossom water, which are the most constant. The shortbread-like cookies are arguably more popular in India today than in the UK, where they fit in comfortably with other Parsi-descended crumbly cookies such as *nankhatai* (recipe, page 37). Introduced to India during Britain's rule of the country, the cookies were apparently a favorite of Queen Victoria and other royals.

One of the most useful old recipes is in Peter Brears's *Traditional Food in Shropshire*, which records Madame Susan Avery's "Shropshire cakes" from the seventeenth century, and uses cinnamon, nutmeg, and rose water. The biscuits are marked with a hair comb in a diamond-shaped crosshatch pattern, which likely was done to allow ladies of the time to break the cookie into more manageable pieces at teatime. The Shrewsbury cakes were typically 5 inches (13 cm) in diameter. The crosshatch also contained a hole in the center of each diamond, likely to keep the dough from rising, thus making it crispier. Many more modern, and even older, recipes don't call for the crosshatch pattern at all and even add dried fruit like currants to the mix. This recipe for the traditional British version leans toward Madame Avery's.

Position racks in the top and bottom thirds of the oven and preheat the oven to 350°F (180°C/Gas Mark 4). Line two large baking sheets with parchment paper.

In a large bowl, whisk together the flour, sugar, salt, cinnamon, and nutmeg. Add the butter and use your fingers to rub the butter into the other ingredients until it breaks down into crumbles. Add the egg and rose water and stir until a dough forms and there are no dry patches of flour remaining. Gather the dough into a ball.

Working on a lightly floured work surface, roll out the dough with a rolling pin to ¼ inch (6 mm) thick. Using a 5-inch (13 cm) round cutter (or plate as a guide), cut out rounds of dough. Reroll scraps to cut out more rounds of dough. (You can make smaller, 3-inch/7.5 cm cookies, too, if you prefer.) Arrange the rounds on the prepared baking sheets, spaced 2 inches (5 cm) apart.

Using a clean fine-toothed hair comb, press the teeth of the comb into the cookie to make a dotted line. Move the comb ¾ inch (2 cm) down the cookie and make another line of dots. Continue to mark the whole cookie with these parallel lines, then turn the comb 45 degrees and repeat the lines, forming a diamond-shaped crosshatch pattern on each round. Using a toothpick, wooden skewer, or the tip of a fork tine, prick a hole in the center of each diamond.

Bake until the edges are just starting to brown and the top is dry to the touch, 12–15 minutes, switching racks and rotating the baking sheets front to back halfway through.

Transfer the baking sheets to wire racks. Let the cookies cool on the pans for 1 minute, then transfer them to the racks to cool completely.

ANZAC Biscuits

Preparation time: 15 minutes
Cooking time: 20 minutes
Makes: About 12 biscuits

2 cups (192 g) rolled oats
1 cup (140 g) all-purpose (plain) flour
½ cup (100 g) white US granulated
  (UK caster) sugar
¾ teaspoon fine sea salt
2 tablespoons boiling water
1 teaspoon baking soda
  (bicarbonate of soda)
1 stick (4 oz/115 g) unsalted
  butter, melted
1 tablespoon British golden syrup

Started during World War I when wives baked these for their husbands in the military, ANZAC biscuits (Australian and New Zealand Army Corps) became known as "soldier's biscuits" or "army biscuits." The first recipes that use the acronym more resemble basic hardtack than the crunchy, oat-laden cookies made today. The historical recipes did not include eggs, which helped them last longer in dry storage, but their omission also made the cookies very hard. The cookies were so hard that many colloquialisms of the time warned against breaking a tooth on them. Theoretically, this is why many hardtack biscuits of the wartime were eaten with tea, to moisten them and make them easier to eat.

This recipe—published in *The Capricornian* (Rockhampton, Queensland) in 1926—is based on one of the earliest to include oats and golden syrup together but no eggs, which still seems to be the three main criteria for the popular version of the cookie today.

- -

Position racks in the top and bottom thirds of the oven and preheat the oven to 325°F (160°C/Gas Mark 3). Line two large baking sheets with parchment paper.

In a large bowl, whisk together the oats, flour, sugar, and salt.

In a medium bowl, whisk together the boiling water and baking soda (bicarb) until the soda dissolves. Add the butter and golden syrup and whisk until emulsified and smooth. Pour the liquid ingredients into the dry ingredients and use a spoon to stir together until a dough forms and there are no dry patches of flour remaining.

Using a 2-ounce (4-tablespoon) ice cream scoop, portion the dough and roll into balls. Arrange them on the prepared baking sheets, spaced at least 2 inches (5 cm) apart.

Bake until golden brown and dry to the touch in the center, 15–18 minutes, switching racks and rotating the baking sheets front to back halfway through.

Transfer the baking sheets to wire racks. Let the cookies cool on the pans for 1 minute, then transfer them to the racks to cool completely.

Custard Cookie Sandwiches

Preparation time: 45 minutes,
 plus cooling time
Cooking time: 15 minutes
Makes: About 18 cookie sandwiches

For the cookies:
3 cups (420 g) all-purpose (plain) flour
½ cup (60 g) custard powder
1 teaspoon fine sea salt
3 sticks (12 oz/340 g) unsalted
 butter, softened
½ cup (65 g) powdered (icing) sugar

For the filling:
1 cup (135 g) powdered (icing) sugar
6 tablespoons (3 oz/85 g) unsalted
 butter, softened
¼ cup (30 g) custard powder
4 tablespoons whole milk

First produced in 1932 by Australian confectionery company W. Menz & Co. and now produced by Arnott's, the commercially produced Yo Yo Biscuits were sold primarily in the state of South Australia. They were thin "cream biscuits," so-named because of the addition of milk or milk powder. Despite their shape looking nothing like the toy their moniker suggests, the cookies were named to cash in on the popularity of the yo-yo toy at the time.

Modern homemade recipes resemble the toy in their finished appearance by sandwiching two shortbread cookies with a buttercream filling. The cookies no longer bear resemblance to their industrially produced predecessors—instead of thin and wide, they are thick and narrow and imprinted with the tines of a fork on top. They are made with custard powder (a commonly used and easily available product in Commonwealth countries) instead of fresh eggs to keep the cookies dry and crumbly and to lend a creamy, vanilla flavor. When these same cookie sandwiches are made with cornstarch (cornflour) instead of custard powder, they are referred to as "melting moments," though they bear no resemblance to the British cookie (recipe, page 280) of that same name.

- -

Make the cookies: Position racks in the top and bottom thirds of the oven and preheat the oven to 350°F (180°C/Gas Mark 4). Line two large baking sheets with parchment paper.

In a medium bowl, whisk together the flour, custard powder, and salt.

In a large bowl, with a hand mixer, beat the butter and sugar on medium speed until light and fluffy, 2–3 minutes. Add the dry ingredients and stir until a dough forms and there are no dry patches of flour remaining.

Using a ½-ounce (1-tablespoon) ice cream scoop, portion the dough into ½-inch (13 mm) balls. Arrange them on the prepared baking sheets, spaced at least 2 inches (5 cm) apart. Using the tines of a fork, slightly flatten each ball of dough once, leaving the indentations of the tines on the top.

Bake until light golden brown and dry to the touch in the center, about 15 minutes, switching racks and rotating the baking sheets front to back halfway through.

Transfer the baking sheets to wire racks. Let the cookies cool on the pans for 1 minute, then transfer them to the racks to cool completely.

Make the filling: Sift the sugar into a medium bowl. Add the butter and custard powder and beat with a hand mixer on low speed until smooth. Increase the speed to medium-high and beat until fluffy, about 3 minutes. Add the milk, 1 tablespoon at a time, beating after each addition until smooth. Continue to beat on medium speed until smooth and lightened, about 1 minute more.

Flip over half of the cookies and spread about 1 teaspoon of the buttercream filling over them. Sandwich with the remaining cookies to serve.

Custard Cookie Sandwiches

Hundreds and Thousands Biscuits

Preparation time: 45 minutes,
  plus cooling and setting time
Cooking time: 15 minutes
Makes: About 36 cookies

For the cookies:
2 cups (280 g) all-purpose (plain) flour
1 teaspoon baking powder
½ teaspoon fine sea salt
1 stick (4 oz/115 g) unsalted
  butter, softened
⅔ cup (130 g) white US granulated
  (UK caster) sugar
1 teaspoon pure vanilla extract
1 egg

For the glaze:
1 cup (135 g) powdered (icing)
  sugar, sifted
2–3 tablespoons whole milk
Red or pink gel or liquid food coloring
Multicolored nonpareils (hundreds
  & thousands) or other sprinkles,
  for decorating

Fairy bread, also sometimes called "hundreds and thousands toast," is a beloved New Zealand snack sandwich, made of white sandwich bread spread with soft butter and then crusted in hundreds & thousands, also known as nonpareils (see page 17). This cookie gets its name and appearance from that sandwich.

The cookie is an industrially produced one—Griffin's and Arnott's are the two most popular brands—consisting of a vanilla butter cookie spread with pink icing, similar to iced versions of American animal crackers, and coated in multicolored sprinkles. A 2020 news article credits a woman who claims to have invented the cookie in 1978 in Oxford, New Zealand, after seeing an ad requesting new cookie flavors in her local paper. She loved fairy bread, so she took leftover plain vanilla cookies and then transformed them with icing and sprinkles into the cookie version of her favorite snack. Though the claims she makes can't be verified, it's a fun story, and the cookies are beloved in New Zealand (and Australia) to this day. You can, of course, use any sprinkles you have on hand.

Make the cookies: Position racks in the top and bottom thirds of the oven and preheat the oven to 350°F (180°C/Gas Mark 4). Line two large baking sheets with parchment paper.

In a medium bowl, whisk together the flour, baking powder, and salt.

In a large bowl, with a hand mixer, combine the butter, white US granulated (UK caster) sugar, and vanilla and beat on medium speed until light and fluffy, 2–3 minutes. Add the egg and beat until incorporated and smooth. Add the dry ingredients and stir until a crumbly dough forms and there are no dry patches of flour remaining.

Scrape the dough onto a lightly floured work surface and shape into a disc, then roll out the dough with a rolling pin to ¼ inch (6 mm) thick. Using a 2-inch (5 cm) round or fluted cutter, cut out cookies. Reroll the scraps to cut out more cookies. Arrange the cookies on the prepared baking sheets, spaced 1 inch (2.5 cm) apart.

Bake until light golden brown and dry to the touch in the center, 12–15 minutes, switching racks and rotating the baking sheets front to back halfway through.

Transfer the baking sheets to wire racks. Let the cookies cool on the pans for 1 minute, then transfer them to the racks to cool completely.

Make the glaze: Sift the powdered (icing) sugar into a medium bowl. Add the milk and stir with a whisk until smooth. It should be pourable but not drippy. Add one or two drops of red coloring to tint the glaze pink, or use pink coloring. Stir until the color is evenly distributed in the glaze.

Spoon about ½ teaspoon of the glaze on top of a cookie, using the back of the spoon to spread it just to the edges (if some of the glaze drops over the edge, that's okay). While the glaze is still wet, scatter some nonpareils or sprinkles over the top to completely cover the glaze. Repeat glazing the rest of the cookies, covering with more nonpareils as you work. Let the glaze set on all the cookies before serving.

Hundreds and Thousands Biscuits

Milk Chocolate Roughs

Preparation time: 15 minutes,
  plus cooling time
Cooking time: 15 minutes
Makes: About 18 cookies

For the cookies:
1¼ cups (175 g) all-purpose (plain) flour
¾ cup (150 g) white US granulated
  (UK caster) sugar
¼ cup (24 g) natural cocoa powder
½ teaspoon fine sea salt
2 cups (50 g) unsweetened cornflakes
14 tablespoons (7 oz/200 g) unsalted
  butter, softened

For the icing and decoration:
1 cup (135 g) powdered (icing) sugar
2 tablespoons natural cocoa powder
2–3 tablespoons whole milk
About 18 walnut halves, for decoration

These cocoa-tinged cookies made crunchy with cornflakes, reflect the country's affinity for the popular breakfast cereal. According to the Kellogg's website, one of the first countries they expanded to was Australia and in 1928, the move proved so popular among Australians and New Zealanders, a factory was built in the Botany Bay area of Sydney to cater to the increasing demands from the region.

These cookies are based on one of the earliest available recipes to home cooks and calls for a chocolate icing and walnut half to garnish the center. You can leave the cookies plain, but the icing is traditional in modern recipes, as are sometimes sliced (flaked) almonds in addition to or instead of cornflakes. If using the almonds, they can be in place of a walnut half to decorate. Because the cookies already contain sugar and a frosting, use unsweetened cornflakes so the cookies aren't too sweet.

Make the cookies: Position racks in the top and bottom thirds of the oven and preheat the oven to 350°F (180°C/Gas Mark 4). Line two large baking sheets with parchment paper.

In a large bowl, whisk together the flour, white US granulated (UK caster) sugar, cocoa powder, and salt. Stir in the cornflakes followed by the butter and mix with your hands until a dough forms and there are no dry patches of flour remaining.

Using a 1-ounce (2-tablespoon) ice cream scoop, portion the dough into 1-inch (2.5 cm) balls. Arrange them on the prepared baking sheets, spaced at least 2 inches (5 cm) apart.

Bake until golden brown and dry to the touch in the center, about 15 minutes, switching racks and rotating the baking sheets front to back halfway through.

Transfer the baking sheets to wire racks. Let the cookies cool on the pans for 1 minute, then transfer them to the racks to cool completely.

Make the icing: In a medium bowl, sift together the powdered (icing) sugar and cocoa powder. Add the milk and stir until a smooth, stiff, but spreadable icing forms.

Spread about 1 teaspoon of icing on the top of each cookie and then top it with a walnut half to serve.

Ginger Crunch

Preparation time: 40 minutes,
 plus setting time
Cooking time: 20 minutes
Makes: 64 cookies

For the cookie base:
2 cups (280 g) all-purpose (plain) flour
1½ teaspoons ground ginger
1¼ teaspoons baking powder
¾ teaspoon fine sea salt
1½ sticks (6 oz/170 g) unsalted
 butter, softened
⅔ cup (130 g) white US granulated
 (UK caster) sugar

For the glaze:
7 tablespoons (3½ oz/100 g)
 unsalted butter
1 tablespoon plus 1 teaspoon
 ground ginger
3 tablespoons British golden syrup
1 cup (135 g) powdered (icing) sugar

These ginger-spiced cookies, with a buttery shortbread base covered in a sweet, ginger glaze, are a popular teatime treat in New Zealand. They first appeared in the *Edmonds Cookery Book*, a 1908 collection (first published as *The Sure to Rise Cookery Book*) of recipes by baking powder producer Thomas Edmonds. The baking powder gives the shortbread-like cookies a lightness that leaves them still crisp, but easier to bite into.

The dough itself—and the instruction from the Edmonds company's recipe to score the cookies while hot and then cut or break them along the score lines—means ginger crunch was likely developed from a ginger-spiced shortbread, already popular in Scotland, that then was topped with an extra-spiced syrupy glaze that sets into an icing.

- -

Make the cookie base: Preheat the oven to 375°F (190°C/Gas Mark 5). Line the bottom of a 9 × 13-inch (23 × 33 cm) straight-sided light metal baking pan with parchment paper, leaving the excess hanging over the two long sides.

In a medium bowl, whisk together the flour, ginger, baking powder, and salt.

In a large bowl, with a hand mixer, beat the butter and white US granulated (UK caster) sugar on medium speed until light and fluffy, 2–3 minutes. Add the dry ingredients and stir until a crumbly dough forms and there are no dry patches of flour remaining.

Scrape the dough into the prepared baking pan and press into an even layer in the bottom.

Bake until the edges are just starting to brown and the top is dry to the touch, 15–20 minutes, rotating the baking pan front to back halfway through.

About 5 minutes before the cookie base is done, make the glaze: In a small saucepan, melt the butter over medium heat. Whisk in the ginger, then whisk in the golden syrup, and finally the powdered (icing) sugar. Bring the mixture to a simmer, whisking until smooth, then remove from the heat and cover to keep warm until ready to use.

Transfer the baking pan to a wire rack and immediately pour the hot glaze over the cookie base. Using a paring knife, score the cookies into 4 lengthwise rows by 16 crosswise columns. Let the cookie base cool completely in the pan.

Use the overhanging parchment paper as a sling to lift the cookies out of the baking pan and transfer to a cutting board (discard the parchment paper). Cut along the score lines to separate the cookies before serving.

scandinavia

The isolation of this region led to a largely unique culture of cookies that, though similar to other Eastern and Western European styles, has its own distinct language, full of chewy sliced cookies, buttery shortbreads, vanilla- and cardamom-heavy scents, and an enchantment with spiced gingerbread-like treats. Much of what influenced the cookie culture of the area came from a 1945 book by Märta Holmgren called *Sju Sorters Kakor*, or "Seven Kinds of Cookies." The book popularized the *fika* tradition of serving many small types of cookies with coffee in Sweden, Norway, and beyond.

Licorice and Chocolate Meringue Cookies
Lakkrístoppar

Preparation time: 20 minutes
Cooking time: 25 minutes
Makes: About 27 cookies

3 egg whites
¾ cup (170 g) packed light
  brown sugar
½ teaspoon fine sea salt
5¼ oz (150 g) lakkrís kurl licorice
  candies, preferably chocolate-
  covered, finely chopped
5¼ oz (150 g) semisweet
  chocolate chips

These cookies are a more modern addition to Iceland's Christmas cookie repertoire, consisting of a brown sugar-sweetened meringue teeming with chocolate chips and a type of licorice called *lakkrís kurl* that is milder and softer than other licorice candies. Often the licorice itself is also coated in chocolate, and this preparation is so popular that recipes for these cookies are printed on packaging. If you make them, search online for *lakkrís kurl* to ensure they have the correct texture. Another popular variation is called *marens-kornflexkökur* and swaps the licorice for cornflakes (see the variation that follows).

Position racks in the top and bottom thirds of the oven and preheat the oven to 300°F (150°C/Gas Mark 2). Line two large baking sheets with parchment paper.

In a large bowl, with a hand mixer, beat the egg whites on medium speed until foamy. While continuing to mix, add the sugar 4 tablespoons at a time, beating well after each addition. Once all the sugar is added, add the salt and increase the speed to medium-high and continue beating until stiff peaks form. Add the chocolate chips and licorice and stir to combine.

Using two spoons (one to portion and the other to rake the meringue off the other spoon), spoon the meringue into dollops on the prepared baking sheets, spaced 2 inches (5 cm) apart.

Bake the meringues until light golden brown all over and dry to the touch, about 25 minutes, switching racks and rotating the baking sheets front to back halfway through.

Transfer the baking sheets to wire racks and let the cookies cool completely on the pans. They will feel light and pillowy at first, but will firm up when cooled and be chewy.

Variation
Marens-Kornflexkökur
Substitute ¾ cup (150 g) white sugar for the brown sugar. Omit the licorice and add 3 cups (75 g) cornflakes in its place. Shape and bake as directed. Drizzle the cooled cookies with melted chocolate, if you like.

Ginger and Buttercream Cookie Sandwiches

Mömmukökur

Preparation time: 45 minutes, plus
 overnight chilling and cooling time
Cooking time: 15 minutes
Makes: About 18 cookie sandwiches

For the dough:

¾ cup (250 g) mørk sirup (see page
 307), dark corn syrup, or British
 golden syrup
½ cup (100 g) white US granulated
 (UK caster) sugar
1 stick (4 oz/115 g) unsalted butter
3½ cups (490 g) all-purpose
 (plain) flour
2 teaspoons baking soda
 (bicarbonate of soda)
2 teaspoons ground ginger
¾ teaspoon fine sea salt
1 egg

For the filling:

1½ cups (205 g) powdered
 (icing) sugar
1 stick (4 oz/115 g) unsalted
 butter, softened
1 tablespoon heavy (double) cream
1 teaspoon pure vanilla extract
⅛ teaspoon fine sea salt

A traditional cookie made for Christmas in Iceland, these cookies translate to "mom's cookies." They consist of two gingerbread-like cookies sandwiched with a plain buttercream filling. The cookies are made similar to but spiced differently than *piparkökur* (recipe, page 297) and include egg, so they have a softer texture than the usual gingerbread-like cookies.

Make the dough: In a small saucepan, combine the syrup and white US granulated (UK caster) sugar and heat over medium-high heat, stirring until the sugar dissolves. Remove the pan from the heat and add the butter. Stir until the butter melts, pour the mixture into a large bowl, and let cool to room temperature.

Meanwhile, in a medium bowl, whisk together the flour, baking soda (bicarb), ginger, and salt.

Whisk the egg into the cooled syrup mixture, then add the dry ingredients and stir until the dough just comes together and there are no dry patches of flour remaining. Divide the dough in half and shape each half into a disc. Wrap each disc separately in plastic wrap (cling film) and refrigerate for at least 8 hours or overnight, or up to 1 day.

Position racks in the top and bottom thirds of the oven and preheat the oven to 400°F (200°C/Gas Mark 6). Line two large baking sheets with parchment paper.

Working on a lightly floured work surface, roll out each dough disc with a rolling pin to ¼ inch (6 mm) thick. Using a 3-inch (7.5 cm) round cutter, cut out rounds of dough. Reroll the scraps to cut out more cookies. Transfer the rounds to the prepared baking sheets, spaced 2 inches (5 cm) apart.

Bake until darker brown at the edges and just dry to the touch on top, 8–10 minutes, switching racks and rotating the baking sheets front to back halfway through.

Transfer the baking sheets to wire racks. Let the cookies cool on the pans for 1 minute, then transfer them to the racks to cool completely.

Make the filling: In a large bowl, with a hand mixer, combine the powdered (icing) sugar, butter, cream, vanilla, and salt and beat on medium speed until light and fluffy, 1–2 minutes.

Flip over half of the cookies. Spoon or pipe a heaping tablespoon of the buttercream onto the cookies, then sandwich them with the other half of the cookies to serve.

Ginger and Buttercream Cookie Sandwiches   295

Jam-Filled Half-Moon Cookies

Hálfmánar

Preparation time: 40 minutes,
 plus chilling time
Cooking time: 20 minutes
Makes: About 42 cookies

3½ cups (490 g) all-purpose
 (plain) flour
1 cup (200 g) white US granulated
 (UK caster) sugar
1 teaspoon baker's ammonia
 (see page 17)
1½ teaspoons ground cardamom
¾ teaspoon fine sea salt
2 sticks (8 oz/225 g) unsalted
 butter, softened
⅓ cup (2½ fl oz/80 ml) whole milk
1 egg
½ cup (160 g) tart plum or rhubarb
 jam, preferably homemade (see
 Homemade [Any] Fruit Jam, page 18)
Egg wash: 1 egg yolk beaten with
 1 tablespoon water

These cookies are often filled with either prune or rhubarb jam. The recipes for *hálfmánar* almost exclusively use baker's ammonia, which gives the cookie dough a crumbly texture to contrast the sweet jammy filling. The dough is also scented with cardamom seeds, which helps to brighten the dark-fruit jam. Flavor the plum jam with cinnamon and a splash of brandy, if you like.

In a large bowl, whisk together the flour, sugar, baker's ammonia, cardamom, and salt. Add the butter and rub it into the dry ingredients with your fingers until it breaks down into coarse crumbles. In a small bowl, mix the milk and egg together. Pour into the dry ingredients and stir with a fork until it comes together into a solid dough, lightly kneading only as much as needed to no longer see any dry patches of flour in the bowl. Shape the dough into a ball, cut in half, then wrap each half in plastic wrap (cling film) and refrigerate for at least 1 hour or up to 2 days.

Position racks in the top and bottom thirds of the oven and preheat the oven to 375°F (190°C/Gas Mark 5). Line two large baking sheets with parchment paper.

Working on a lightly floured work surface, roll out one dough ball with a rolling pin to ⅛ inch (3 mm) thick. Using a 3-inch (7.5 cm) round cutter, cut out rounds of dough. Repeat with the second ball of dough, then reroll the scraps to cut out more cookies. Spoon ½ teaspoon jam into the center of each round, brush the border of the dough with the egg wash, then fold the rounds in half to create half-moons. Use a fork to crimp the edges shut. Arrange the half-moons on the prepared baking sheets, spaced 2 inches (5 cm) apart. Refrigerate the baking sheets for 30 minutes.

Bake until golden brown on the bottom and dry to the touch on top, 15–18 minutes, switching racks and rotating the baking sheets front to back halfway through.

Transfer the baking sheets to wire racks. Let the cookies cool on the pans for 1 minute, then transfer them to the racks to cool completely.

Icelandic Gingerbread Cookies

Piparkökur

Preparation time: 2 hours
  15 minutes, plus cooling time
  and overnight chilling
Cooking time: 15 minutes
Makes: About 48 cookies

1 cup (200 g) white US granulated
  (UK caster) sugar
½ cup (170 g) mørk sirup (see page
  307), dark corn syrup, or British
  golden syrup
½ cup (4 fl oz/120 ml) whole milk
1½ sticks (6 oz/170 g) unsalted butter
1 tablespoon ground cinnamon
1 tablespoon ground cloves
1½ teaspoons ground ginger (optional)
1 teaspoon ground black
  pepper (optional)
3½ cups (490 g) all-purpose
  (plain) flour
2 teaspoons baking soda
  (bicarbonate of soda)
¾ teaspoon fine sea salt

This Icelandic version of gingerbread-like cookies resembles Swedish *pepparkakor* (recipe, page 320) more in name than ingredients. Of the recipes that exist, many Icelandic home bakers prefer the combination of cloves and cinnamon above all others (as do Estonian bakers in their *piparkoogid*, which has virtually identical ingredients). This holds true despite the seemingly perfunctory addition of pepper or ginger to many recipes that feels like it was added to make sense of their name: "pepper cookies." Both are listed as optional add-ins in this recipe.

While many recipes call to roll the dough flat and cut out shapes to decorate with an icing once cooled, an equal, if not slightly larger, number advises rolling the dough into balls and flattening them into discs that then bake up in a round shape. These cookies are also slightly chewier in texture than other similar styles of gingerbread cookies.

In a small saucepan, combine the sugar, syrup, and milk and heat over medium-high heat, stirring until the sugar dissolves. Remove the pan from the heat. Add the butter, cinnamon, cloves, ginger (if using), and pepper (if using). Stir until the butter melts and then pour the mixture into a large bowl to cool to room temperature.

Meanwhile, in a medium bowl, whisk together the flour, baking soda (bicarb), and salt.

Add the dry ingredients to the cooled syrup mixture and stir until the dough just comes together and there are no dry patches of flour remaining. Divide the dough in half and shape each half into a disc. Wrap each disc separately in plastic wrap (cling film) and refrigerate for at least 8 hours or overnight, or up to 1 day.

Position racks in the top and bottom thirds of the oven and preheat the oven to 400°F (200°C/Gas Mark 6). Line two large baking sheets with parchment paper.

Using a 1-ounce (2-tablespoon) ice cream scoop, portion the dough and roll into balls. Arrange them on the prepared baking sheets, spaced 2 inches (5 cm) apart, then flatten them with the palm of your hand. (Alternatively, working on a lightly floured work surface, roll out the dough discs with a rolling pin to ⅛ inch/3 mm thick. Using a 2- to 3-inch/5 to 7.5 cm cutter, cut out cookies. Reroll the scraps to cut out more cookies.)

Bake until darker brown at the edges and just dry to the touch on top, 6–10 minutes (the shorter time for the thin cut-out cookies), switching racks and rotating the baking sheets front to back halfway through.

Transfer the baking sheets to wire racks. Let the cookies cool on the pans for 1 minute, then transfer them to the racks to cool completely.

Almond and Meringue Cookies
Bordstabelbakkels

Preparation time: 1 hour 15 minutes
Cooking time: 15 minutes
Makes: About 36 cookies

2 cups (280 g) all-purpose (plain) flour
½ teaspoon fine sea salt
1 stick (4 oz/115 g) unsalted
  butter, softened
½ cup (100 g) white US granulated
  (UK caster) sugar
2 tablespoons heavy (double) cream
2 eggs, separated
1 egg yolk
6 oz (170 g) blanched whole
  or slivered almonds
1 cup (135 g) powdered (icing) sugar

Roughly translated as "board bars," these plank-like cookies consist of a rich buttery base topped with a line of almond meringue. The cookie dough is rolled thin, then cut into long planks, though many modern recipes cut them into diamonds instead of planks. Almond meringue is then piped down the center of the plank so when it bakes up, the meringue spreads and covers most of the cookie base. The meringue is light and crisp and the cookie beneath is crumbly and rich. To serve, bakers often stack them two-by-two.

Position racks in the top and bottom thirds of the oven and preheat the oven to 375°F (190°C/Gas Mark 5). Line two large baking sheets with parchment paper.

In a medium bowl, whisk together the flour and salt.

In a large bowl, with a hand mixer, beat the butter and white US granulated (UK caster) sugar on medium speed until pale and fluffy, 2–3 minutes. Add the cream and 3 egg yolks and beat until smooth. Add the dry ingredients and stir until a dough forms and there are no dry patches of flour remaining. Shape the dough into a ball, cut in half, then shape each half into a disc.

Working on a lightly floured work surface, roll out each disc of dough with a rolling pin to ⅛ inch (3 mm) thick. Using a pizza cutter or knife, cut the dough into strips ¾ inch (2 cm) wide, then cut the strips crosswise into 4-inch (10 cm) lengths. Arrange the lengths on the prepared baking sheets, spaced 1 inch (2.5 cm) apart. Place the baking sheets in the refrigerator while you make the meringue.

In a food processor, pulse the almonds until very finely ground. In a large bowl, whisk the egg whites until soft peaks form. Add the ground almonds and powdered (icing) sugar and stir until they form a smooth batter. Scrape the batter into a piping bag fitted with a ¼-inch (6 mm) round tip (nozzle) or a plastic bag with a ¼-inch (6 mm) hole snipped off one corner. Pipe a line of almond meringue down the center of each cookie plank; don't worry about covering the dough because the meringue will spread as it bakes.

Bake until the cookies are golden brown at the edges and the meringue is puffed and dry to the touch on top, 12–15 minutes, switching racks and rotating the baking sheets front to back halfway through.

Transfer the baking sheets to wire racks. Let the cookies cool on the pans for 1 minute, then transfer them to the racks to cool completely.

Almond and Meringue Cookies

Wreath-Shaped Butter Cookies

Berlinerkranser

Preparation time: 30 minutes,
 plus chilling time
Cooking time: 15 minutes
Makes: About 18 cookies

2 hard-boiled egg yolks
2 raw egg yolks
⅔ cup (140 g) white US granulated
 (UK caster) sugar
¾ teaspoon fine sea salt
1½ sticks (6 oz/170 g) unsalted
 butter, softened
2 cups (280 g) all-purpose (plain) flour
1 egg white, lightly beaten
Pearl sugar, for decorating

These cookies have a shape and decoration similar to *Vanillebrezeln* (recipe, page 254), and some credit a German baker who came to Norway in the seventeenth century as an influence. Around this time Catholic nuns often created egg yolk-based sweets as a way to use up the egg yolks that were left over from using the egg whites to starch their habits, so it's likely a German baker learned of this cookie and brought it to Norway. At the very least, it makes a fun story.

These cookies are unique in that they use both cooked and raw egg yolks in the dough; the cooked yolks help produce a drier dough that holds its shape better than wet/raw yolks. The dough is shaped into thin logs, then formed into wreaths with their ends crossed, and topped with pearl sugar. They are one of the most popular Christmas cookies, or *julekaker*, in Norway.

Place a fine sieve over a large bowl and use a silicone spatula to press the hard-boiled egg yolks through the sieve into the bowl. Scrape the back of the sieve to ensure you get all the egg yolk. Add the raw egg yolks and whisk until smooth. Add the white US granulated (UK caster) sugar and salt and whisk again until smooth and lightened, about 1 minute. Add the butter and beat with a wooden spoon until smooth. Add the flour and stir until the dough forms and there are no dry patches of flour remaining. Shape the dough into a ball, wrap in plastic wrap (cling film), and refrigerate for at least 2 hours or overnight.

Position racks in the top and bottom thirds of the oven and preheat the oven to 350°F (180°C/Gas Mark 4). Line two large baking sheets with parchment paper.

Working on a lightly floured work surface, roll pieces of the dough between your fingers and the work surface into ropes ⅜ inch (1 cm) thick. Cut the ropes crosswise into 4-inch (10 cm) lengths. Bend each length in the center and form a circle, making the ends cross each other by ½ inch (13 mm). Arrange the dough wreaths on the prepared baking sheets, spaced 2 inches (5 cm) apart. Brush the wreaths with some of the egg white and then sprinkle with pearl sugar.

Bake until the cookies are light golden brown at the edges and dry to the touch on top, 10–12 minutes, switching racks and rotating the baking sheets front to back halfway through.

Transfer the baking sheets to wire racks. Let the cookies cool on the pans for 1 minute, then transfer them to the racks to cool completely.

Wreath-Shaped Butter Cookies

NORWAY

Butter Cookies with Pearl Sugar
Serinakaker

Preparation time: 30 minutes
Cooking time: 15 minutes
Makes: About 24 cookies

2 cups (280 g) all-purpose (plain) flour
2 teaspoons baking powder
½ teaspoon fine sea salt
10 tablespoons (5 oz/140 g) unsalted butter, softened
½ cup (100 g) white US granulated (UK caster) sugar
1 egg
2 teaspoons pure vanilla extract
1 egg white, beaten
Pearl sugar and/or chopped almonds, for sprinkling

These are Norway's simplest butter cookies and are often one of the first cookies kids learn to make. Similar to *berlinerkranser* (recipe, page 300), but with more eggs and leavening, they are brushed with egg white and sprinkled with crunchy pearl sugar or chopped almonds before baking.

Position racks in the top and bottom thirds of the oven and preheat the oven to 350°F (180°C/Gas Mark 4). Line two large baking sheets with parchment paper.

In a medium bowl, whisk together the flour, baking powder, and salt.

In a large bowl, with a hand mixer, beat the butter and white US granulated (UK caster) sugar on medium speed until pale and fluffy, 2–3 minutes. Add the egg and beat until smooth. Beat in the vanilla. Add the dry ingredients and stir until the dough forms and there are no dry patches of flour remaining.

Using a ½-ounce (1-tablespoon) ice cream scoop, portion the dough and roll into balls. Arrange them on the prepared baking sheets, spaced 2 inches (5 cm) apart. Using the palm of your hand or the bottom of a glass, flatten each ball slightly into a disc. Brush the discs with some of the egg white and sprinkle with pearl sugar and/or chopped almonds.

Bake until light golden brown at the edges and dry to the touch on top, 10–12 minutes, switching racks and rotating the baking sheets front to back halfway through.

Transfer the baking sheets to wire racks. Let the cookies cool on the pans for 1 minute, then transfer them to the racks to cool completely.

NORWAY

Soft Egg Cookies
Pleskener

Preparation time: 30 minutes
Cooking time: 10 minutes
Makes: About 30 cookies

¾ cup (105 g) all-purpose (plain) flour
½ teaspoon fine sea salt
½ cup (100 g) white US granulated (UK caster) sugar
2 eggs
1 teaspoon pure vanilla extract or ground cardamom (optional)

These simple golden-hued cookies are sometimes called "sponge cake" cookies because their batter is that of a European-style sponge cake or genoise. Eggs are whipped with sugar until thick, then combined with flour to form a loose dough. The air trapped in the eggs from whipping gives rise to the cookies, as it does in a sponge cake. Traditional recipes use only eggs, sugar, and flour, but modern recipes now add vanilla or cardamom to the mix; they are listed here as optional ingredients.

Position racks in the top and bottom thirds of the oven and preheat the oven to 400°F (200°C/Gas Mark 6). Line two large baking sheets with parchment paper.

In a medium bowl, whisk together the flour and salt.

In another medium bowl, with a hand mixer, combine the sugar, eggs, and the vanilla or cardamom (if using) and beat on medium speed until pale and thickened and the mixture falls back in a thick ribbon when lifted from the beaters, 3–4 minutes. Add the dry ingredients and use a small silicone spatula to gently fold the ingredients together until completely smooth and uniform in color.

Scrape the batter into a piping bag fitted with a ¼-inch (6 mm) plain tip (nozzle) or plastic bag with a ¼-inch (6 mm) hole snipped off one corner. Holding the bag perpendicular to the baking sheet, let the batter flow out of the tip until you have a mound 1½ inches (4 cm) in diameter, using your finger to stop the flow of batter after each. Repeat to make more batter mounds, spacing them at least 2 inches (5 cm) apart, as they will spread.

Bake until golden brown at the edges and just dry to the touch on top, 8–10 minutes, switching racks and rotating the baking sheets front to back halfway through.

Transfer the baking sheets to wire racks. Let the cookies cool on the pans for 1 minute, then transfer them to the racks to cool completely.

Cone-Shaped Waffle Cookies

Krumkaker

Preparation time: 30 minutes,
  plus resting time
Cooking time: 1 hour 15 minutes
Makes: About 24 cookies

⅔ cup (130 g) white US granulated
  (UK caster) sugar
½ teaspoon fine sea salt
2 eggs
1 stick (4 oz/115 g) unsalted butter,
  melted, plus more for brushing
¾ cup (105 g) all-purpose (plain) flour
⅓ cup (2½ fl oz/80 ml) water
  or whole milk
1 teaspoon pure vanilla
  extract (optional)

These thin and crispy waffle cookies are perhaps Norway's most famous treat. The cookies are, like *pizzelle* (recipe, page 130), cooked in a special iron. The *krumkake* irons are typically engraved with hearts and floral flourishes like leaves and petals, and many irons are passed down through generations of families. Old-school irons are heated over the flame of a fire or gas stove, while modern irons are electric, like breakfast waffle irons. Once formed, *krumkaker* are traditionally served with cloudberry cream—a mix of cloudberry jam folded into whipped cream—or plain whipped cream.

While some waffle cookies can be left flat or rolled into cigar shapes, *krumkaker* must be shaped into a cone. A special wooden dowel is made specifically for this purpose, and they are typically sold with the irons. *Goro* (recipe, page 304) are another type of Norwegian waffle cookie, but they are made from a solid dough, rather than a liquid batter, pressed in yet a different special iron. Swedish *rullrån* are similar waffle- or tuile-like cookies, but they are typically made without eggs (see the variation that follows). Though many modern recipes use milk to thin the batter, this recipe uses water, which creates a leaner, and thus crisper *krumkaker*. If you prefer a richer-tasting cookie, use milk.

In a large bowl, whisk together the sugar, salt, and eggs until smooth. Whisk in the melted butter. Add the flour and begin whisking until a thick batter forms. While whisking, slowly pour in the water until you have a smooth batter that has the consistency of heavy (double) cream. Stir in the vanilla (if using). Cover the bowl with plastic wrap (cling film) and let rest for at least 1 hour at room temperature, or preferably, overnight in the refrigerator.

Place a krumkake iron over medium heat on your stove or heat an electric krumkake maker. Using a 1-tablespoon measure, pour tablespoonfuls of batter into the center of the iron. Close the iron and let cook, flipping the iron halfway through, if using the stove, until the batter spreads and sets as a wafer, 2–3 minutes, depending on the heat of your stove (or follow the manufacturer's instructions for the electric maker).

Open the iron and place the narrow end of a wooden krumkake cone at the edge of the iron closest to you. Lift the wafer and then quickly roll it around the cone, connecting its edges at the narrow end. Let the wafer cool for 10 seconds on the cone, then slide it off and place the cone on a wire rack to cool. Repeat with the remaining batter to cook and shape more cookies.

Variation
Swedish Rullrån
Omit the eggs. Increase the water to 1 cup (8 fl oz/250 ml). After cooking, open the iron and place the end of a narrow wooden spoon at the edge of the iron closest to you. Lift the wafer and then quickly roll it around the spoon handle like a rolled carpet. Slide the rolled wafer off the handle and place on a wire rack to cool.

Rich Cardamom Waffle Cookies

Goro

Preparation time: 1 hour, plus overnight
  chilling and 30 minutes resting time
Cooking time: 20 minutes
Makes: About 12 cookies

3½ cups (490 g) all-purpose
  (plain) flour
1 teaspoon ground cardamom
¾ teaspoon fine sea salt
3 sticks (12 oz/340 g) unsalted
  butter, cut into ½-inch (13 mm)
  cubes, softened
½ cup (4 fl oz/120 ml) heavy
  (double) cream
½ cup (100 g) white US granulated
  (UK caster) sugar
1 teaspoon pure vanilla extract
1 egg
1 egg yolk

While Norwegian *krumkaker* (recipe, page 303) are thin and delicate Christmas cookies, these are their richer, thicker cousins. Sometimes called "rich man's cookies," these waffle cookies are flavored heavily with cardamom and baked in a special iron, called a *goro*, that is rectangular with flourished details similar to *krumkaker*.

Instead of a batter, these cookies are made from pastry-style dough that is cut into the same dimensions as the iron, then cooked until golden brown. Sometimes the dough is laminated with butter to create layers like croissant dough, while other recipes just call for cutting the butter into the dough, like flaky pie dough (shortcrust pastry), and mixing it together from the start. Many recipes advise wiping away excess butter that seeps out of the iron during cooking. If you have made the Vanilla Sugar (page 16), you can use it instead of plain sugar and omit the vanilla.

In a large bowl, whisk together the flour, cardamom, and salt. Add the butter and use your fingers to rub it into the flour until it breaks down into coarse crumbles.

In a bowl, whisk the cream until it begins to thicken, then whisk in the sugar, vanilla, whole egg, and egg yolk until smooth. Pour into the bowl with the butter and flour and stir until a dough forms and there are no dry patches of flour remaining. Shape the dough into a ball, flatten into a disc, then cover with plastic wrap (cling film) and refrigerate overnight.

Working on a lightly floured work surface, roll out the dough with a rolling pin to ¼ inch (6 mm) thick. Measure the length and width of each cell of the goro iron and cut a piece of cardboard or parchment paper to the same dimensions. Use it to cut out rectangles from the flattened dough. Place all the dough rectangles on a baking sheet and place in the refrigerator and chill for at least 30 minutes for the dough to rest.

Place a goro iron over medium heat on your stove. Place a rectangle of dough on each cell of the goro iron, then close it. Let it cook, flipping the iron halfway through, until the dough sets and is golden brown and crisp, 4–6 minutes, depending on the heat of your stove. Open the iron and use an offset spatula to transfer the cookies to a wire rack to cool. Repeat with the remaining dough to cook more cookies.

Rich Cardamom Waffle Cookies

Soft Butter Cookie Diamonds

Tjukksnipp / Trysilsnipp / Snipper

Preparation time: 45 minutes,
 plus chilling time
Cooking time: 15 minutes
Makes: About 24 cookies

3 cups (420 g) all-purpose (plain) flour
1 teaspoon baker's ammonia
 (see page 17)
1½ teaspoons ground cardamom
¾ teaspoon fine sea salt
1 cup (200 g) plus 2 tablespoons white
 US granulated (UK caster) sugar
1 stick (4 oz/115 g) unsalted
 butter, softened
¾ cup (6 fl oz/175 ml) kefir (see
 headnote), room temperature
1 teaspoon pure vanilla extract
1 teaspoon ground cinnamon

Similar to the gingerbread-like *sirupsnipper* (recipe, page 308), these spice-less cookies are cut into the characteristic *"snipp"* or collar/diamond shape. Flavored with cardamom in the dough and topped with cinnamon-sugar, these fragrant cookies are often eaten at Christmas in Norway. They are typically leavened with baker's ammonia, which gives them an ethereally light, soft texture. Kefir is used to add tanginess to the sweet cookies; if you can't find it, swap the kefir for ½ cup (130 g) yogurt (not Greek) mixed with ½ cup (4 fl oz/120 ml) whole milk.

Position racks in the top and bottom thirds of the oven and preheat the oven to 350°F (180°C/Gas Mark 4). Line two large baking sheets with parchment paper.

In a medium bowl, whisk together the flour, baker's ammonia, cardamom, and salt.

In a large bowl, with a hand mixer, combine 1 cup (200 g) of the sugar and the butter and beat on medium speed until pale and fluffy, 2–3 minutes. Add the kefir and vanilla and mix on low speed until combined. Add the dry ingredients and stir until the dough just comes together and there are no dry patches of flour remaining. Cover the bowl and refrigerate the dough for at least 2 hours or up to 1 day.

Divide the dough in half and shape each half into a disc. Working on a lightly floured work surface, roll out one dough disc with a rolling pin to ½ inch (13 mm) thick. Using a pizza cutter or knife, cut the dough into strips 2 inches (5 cm) wide and then cut the strips on a diagonal every 2 inches (5 cm) to make diamonds. Reroll the scraps to make more cookies. Arrange the diamonds on the prepared baking sheets, spaced 2 inches (5 cm) apart.

In a small bowl, stir together the remaining 2 tablespoons sugar and the cinnamon. Sprinkle a pinch of the cinnamon-sugar over each dough diamond.

Bake until golden brown at the edges and dry to the touch on top, 10–12 minutes, switching racks and rotating the baking sheets front to back halfway through.

Transfer the baking sheets to wire racks. Let the cookies cool on the pans for 1 minute, then transfer them to the racks to cool completely.

Molasses and Sugar Syrups

Today, virtually all cookies are made with granulated sugar, be it white or brown. However, many cookies—or the things that would eventually evolve into cookies—used to be sweetened solely with honey. Its physical properties and viscosity made for firm treats that could be preserved for long ship journeys or extended baking seasons. Many of these honey-made treats came to Western Europe from the Middle East, both having a warm climate that made harvesting honey accessible.

But as those baking traditions moved north, to Scandinavia, honey was less available. To reproduce the texture that honey provided to the various gingerbread (read more in Gingerbread, page 328) and cakes, many Scandinavians developed caramelized sugar syrups made by, as the name suggests, caramelizing white sugar and then dissolving it in hot water to make a syrup, like Norwegian *mørk sirup* (see page 16). The process of making the syrup was often the start of gingerbread recipes, so having the ready-made product on hand cut out that time-consuming step.

And when those same recipes and baking traditions migrated to North America, molasses stepped up to the plate. Molasses is an important ingredient in many North American cookies because, as the by-product of sugar refining, it was much cheaper than refined sugar. In the Atlantic maritime areas of Canada and the US, molasses was the chief sweetener in all foods like bread, baked beans, and especially in cookies, acting as the ideal New World replacement for honey and the caramelized sugar syrups of Europe in the recipes that were brought to the continent by British and French settlers in the 1700s.

Today, though molasses and honey are the chief syrups used in making gingerbreads around the world, both have intense tastes that don't equate to the caramelized sugar syrup that flavors cookies like Danish *brunkager* (recipe, page 329), Finnish *piparkakut* (recipe, page 326), Icelandic *mömmukökur* (recipe, page 294), Norwegian *sirupsnipper* (recipe, page 308), and Swedish *pepparkakor* (recipe, page 320). For that syrup, look for the real thing online or Scandinavian specialty stores. Or make your own (see below).

Homemade Dark Sugar Syrup

Makes 1½ cups (12 oz/350 g)

1 lb (455 g) turbinado (demerara) sugar
1 cup (8 fl oz/250 ml) boiling water

In a heavy-bottomed medium saucepan, heat the sugar until it completely liquefies and turns amber brown, but doesn't bubble or burn. Remove the pan from the heat and pour in the boiling water. Return the pan to the heat and cook for 5 minutes, stirring to dissolve the caramelized sugar.

Remove the pan from the heat and let the syrup cool completely. Store the syrup in an airtight container or bottle, and use as needed for the recipes in the book that call for mørk sirup or dark corn syrup.

Dark Syrup Gingerbread Diamonds
Sirupsnipper

Preparation time: 40 minutes, plus
 cooling time and overnight chilling
Cooking time: 20 minutes
Makes: About 48 cookies

⅔ cup (5 oz/150 g) mørk sirup
 (see page 307), dark corn
 syrup, or British golden syrup
½ cup (100 g) white US granulated
 (UK caster) sugar
½ cup (4 fl oz/120 ml) heavy
 (double) cream
1 stick (4 oz/115 g) unsalted butter
1½ teaspoons freshly ground
 black pepper
1½ teaspoons ground ginger
1½ teaspoons ground cinnamon
1 teaspoon ground cloves
3 cups (420 g) all-purpose (plain) flour
1 teaspoon baking soda (bicarbonate
 of soda)
¾ teaspoon fine sea salt
Blanched whole almonds, halved,
 for decorating

These crispy, thin cookies are Norway's answer to the gingerbread-style cookie (see Gingerbread, page 328). Instead of various shapes (which you can make them into if you want) these cookies are cut into diamonds or a "*snipp*," a shape that looks like a shirt's collar points. They are traditionally topped with a half a blanched almond in the center.

Like other Nordic gingerbreads, these *sirupsnipper* are made with *mørk sirup* (see Molasses and Sugar Syrups, page 307), the caramelized sugar syrup that's like molasses but not as bitter. The two spices consistent across recipes for *sirupsnipper* are black pepper and ginger, with varying amounts of added cinnamon and cloves.

In a small saucepan, combine the syrup, sugar, and cream and heat over medium-high heat, stirring until the sugar dissolves. Remove the pan from the heat and stir in the butter, pepper, ginger, cinnamon, and cloves until the butter melts and the spices are evenly distributed in the mixture. Pour it into a large bowl and let the mixture cool to room temperature.

Meanwhile, in a medium bowl, whisk together the flour, baking soda (bicarb), and salt.

Add the dry ingredients to the cooled syrup mixture and stir until the dough just comes together and there are no dry patches of flour remaining. Divide the dough in half and shape each half into a disc. Wrap each disc separately in plastic wrap (cling film) and refrigerate for at least 8 hours or overnight, or up to 1 day.

Position racks in the top and bottom thirds of the oven and preheat the oven to 350°F (180°C/Gas Mark 4). Line two large baking sheets with parchment paper.

Working on a lightly floured work surface, roll out each dough disc with a rolling pin to ⅛ inch (3 mm) thick. Using a fluted wheel cutter, cut the dough into strips 2 inches (5 cm) wide and then cut the strips on a diagonal every 2 inches (5 cm) to make diamonds. Reroll the scraps to make more cookies. Arrange the diamonds on the prepared baking sheets, spaced 2 inches (5 cm) apart. Place half of a whole blanched almond in the center of each diamond.

Bake until darker brown at the edges and bottom, 14–16 minutes, switching racks and rotating the baking sheets front to back halfway through.

Transfer the baking sheets to wire racks. Let the cookies cool on the pans for 1 minute, then transfer them to the racks to cool completely.

Dark Syrup Gingerbread Diamonds

Chocolate-Dipped Almond Meringue Bars
Kransekakestenger

Preparation time: 50 minutes, plus
  chilling, cooling, and setting time
Cooking time: 10 minutes
Makes: About 42 cookies

8 oz (225 g) skin-on almonds
8 oz (225 g) blanched whole
  almonds or slivered almonds
3 cups (405 g) powdered (icing) sugar
¾ teaspoon fine sea salt
4 egg whites
¼ teaspoon pure almond
  extract (optional)
6 oz (170 g) semisweet chocolate,
  finely chopped
2 tablespoons heavy (double) cream

These cookies are a miniature version of a larger cake made of cookie dough. The *kransekake* is a traditional Norwegian celebration cake made of chewy almond meringue rings stacked on top of each other, with icing drizzled between layers to cement them together. These cookies take the same dough and simply bake it as short bars instead of large rings.

Both blanched and skin-on almonds are used to allow some of the skins to give the cookie plenty of flavor. These cookies typically have either their ends or entire bottom dipped in chocolate, or chocolate is drizzled over the top; the choice is up to you. Similar Dutch treats, called *bokkenpootjes*, use the same cookies, sandwich them with pastry cream, and dip the ends in chocolate, giving the cookies the appearance of their name, which translates to "goat's feet."

In a food processor, combine both types of almonds and pulse until finely ground. Add the sugar and salt and pulse again until the almonds are very finely ground. Add the egg whites and almond extract (if using) and pulse until the mixture forms a firm dough. Shape the dough into a ball, wrap in plastic wrap (cling film), and refrigerate for at least 2 hours or overnight.

Position racks in the top and bottom thirds of the oven and preheat the oven to 400°F (200°C/Gas Mark 6). Line two large baking sheets with parchment paper.

Working on a lightly floured work surface, roll pieces of the dough between your fingers and the work surface into ropes ½ inch (13 mm) thick. Cut the ropes crosswise into 3-inch (7.5 cm) lengths. Arrange the dough bars on the prepared baking sheets, spaced 2 inches (5 cm) apart.

Bake until the cookies are light golden brown on the bottom and dry to the touch on top, 8–10 minutes, switching racks and rotating the baking sheets front to back halfway through.

Transfer the baking sheets to wire racks. Let the cookies cool on the pans for 1 minute, then transfer them to the racks to cool completely.

In a small heatproof bowl set over a pan of simmering water (or in a microwave-safe bowl in the microwave), combine the chocolate and cream and melt together, stirring until smooth.

Dip the bottom or tips of the ends of each cookie in the chocolate and transfer to a sheet of parchment paper. Or drizzle the chocolate in thin lines back and forth over the cookies. Let the cookies stand until the chocolate sets before serving.

Chocolate-Dipped Almond Meringue Bars

Brown Syrup and Ginger Slice Cookies

Kolasnittar / Kolakaker / Brune Pinner

Preparation time: 25 minutes,
  plus chilling time
Cooking time: 20 minutes
Makes: About 18 cookies

1 cup (140 g) all-purpose (plain) flour
2 teaspoons ground ginger
½ teaspoon baking soda
  (bicarbonate of soda)
¾ teaspoon fine sea salt
1 stick (4 oz/115 g) unsalted butter,
  softened
⅓ cup (65 g) white US granulated
  (UK caster) sugar
3 tablespoons mørk sirup (see page
  307), dark corn syrup, or British
  golden syrup
1 teaspoon pure vanilla extract
  (optional)

Cutting slices of chewy cookies from a large baked log is a common style of cookie for *fika*—"coffee break"—in Nordic countries. These *brune pinner* ("brown sticks") are the most common, consisting of a dough made brown and chewy from *mørk sirup* (see Molasses and Sugar Syrups, page 307) and fragrant with ground ginger. The cookie dough is baked in two large logs and then cut into diagonal slices while still warm. A common variation includes cinnamon and nutmeg and is called *muskotsnittar*, or "nutmeg slices" (see the variation that follows).

With their chewy texture, inclusion of a brown sugar syrup and ground ginger, and style of cutting slices from a baked log, it's likely that these cookies influenced what Americans recognize today as the modern Hermit (recipe, page 352) with their molasses-and-spice flavor profiles and identical shape. If you don't have *mørk sirup,* you can omit it and instead of white sugar use ½ cup (110 g) packed dark brown sugar.

- -

Position racks in the top and bottom thirds of the oven and preheat the oven to 350°F (180°C/Gas Mark 4). Line two large baking sheets with parchment paper.

In a medium bowl, whisk together the flour, ginger, baking soda (bicarb), and salt.

In a large bowl, with a hand mixer, combine the butter, sugar, syrup, and vanilla (if using) and beat on medium speed until pale and fluffy, 2–3 minutes. Add the dry ingredients and mix on low speed until a dough forms and there are no dry patches of flour remaining. Cover the bowl in plastic wrap (cling film) and refrigerate for at least 2 hours or up to 1 day.

Divide the dough in half and shape each half into a log 12 inches (30 cm) long. Place one log lengthwise on each baking sheet and flatten slightly with your hand; the logs will spread considerably during baking.

Bake until the cookie logs are flattened and light golden brown on the bottom and dry to the touch on top, 16–20 minutes, switching racks and rotating the baking sheets front to back halfway through.

Transfer the baking sheets to wire racks and let the cookies rest for 5 minutes. While still warm, slide the cookie logs on the parchment paper onto a cutting board and cut at a slight diagonal every 1¼ inches (3 cm) to make slices. Transfer the slices directly to the rack to cool completely.

Variation
Muskotsnittar
Add 2 teaspoons each ground cinnamon and freshly grated nutmeg along with the ginger. Omit the white US granulated (UK caster) sugar and mørk sirup and use in their place ½ cup (110 g) packed dark brown sugar. Flatten the dough logs slightly with the tines of a fork to create lines on their top before baking.

Crisp Oat Cookies

Havrekjeks

Preparation time: 45 minutes,
  plus chilling time
Cooking time: 15 minutes
Makes: About 18 cookies

1 cup (95 g) rolled oats
1 cup (140 g) all-purpose (plain) flour
2 teaspoons baker's ammonia
  (see page 17) or baking powder
½ teaspoon fine sea salt
1 stick (4 oz/115 g) unsalted butter,
  softened
¼ cup (50 g) white US granulated
  (UK caster) sugar
¼ cup (2 fl oz/60 ml) buttermilk,
  at room temperature

These sweetened oat biscuits are a common snack in Norway. They are typically spread with butter and eaten with a slice of *brunost* or *gjetost* cheese. The dough is chilled overnight, giving the oats time to hydrate in the dough, so they cook through evenly when baked.

In a food processor, pulse the oats until half their size. Transfer to a bowl and add the flour, baker's ammonia, and salt and whisk to combine.

In a large bowl, with a hand mixer, beat the butter and sugar on medium speed until pale and fluffy, 2–3 minutes. Add the dry ingredients and the buttermilk and mix on low speed until the mixture forms a firm dough. Shape the dough into a ball, wrap in plastic wrap (cling film), and refrigerate for at least 2 hours or overnight.

Position racks in the top and bottom thirds of the oven and preheat the oven to 350°F (180°C/Gas Mark 4). Line two large baking sheets with parchment paper.

Working on a lightly floured work surface, roll out the dough with a rolling pin to ⅛ inch (3 mm) thick. Using a 2½-inch (6.5 cm) round cutter, cut out rounds of dough. Reroll scraps to cut out more cookies. Arrange the cookies on the prepared baking sheets, spaced 1 inch (2.5 cm) apart.

Bake until the cookies are golden brown, 12–14 minutes, switching racks and rotating the baking sheets front to back halfway through.

Transfer the baking sheets to wire racks. Let the cookies cool on the pans for 1 minute, then transfer them to the racks to cool completely.

Swedish "Dream" Cookies

Drömmar

Preparation time: 15 minutes
Cooking time: 25 minutes
Makes: About 24 cookies

1⅔ cups (230 g) all-purpose
  (plain) flour
1 teaspoon baker's ammonia
  (see page 17)
¾ teaspoon fine sea salt
1 cup (200 g) white US granulated
  (UK caster) sugar
1 stick (4 oz/115 g) unsalted
  butter, softened
⅓ cup (2½ fl oz/80 ml) vegetable oil
1 tablespoon Vanilla Sugar (page 16)
  or 2 teaspoons pure vanilla extract
1 teaspoon ground
  cardamom (optional)

As with many home-baked cookies in Sweden, the recipe for these cookies first appeared in the 1945 book *Sju Sorters Kakor* (see page 291). In it, these cookies were originally called "sugar dreams," and indeed, they are very sweet—though this recipe reduces the amount in the original from 1¼ cups to 1 cup (250 g down to 200 g) of sugar. What made them so special was their lighter-than-air texture that disappeared "like dreams." This was achieved by baker's ammonia. Modern recipes substitute it with baking powder, but it can't replicate the texture correctly here.

That first recipe also called for studding the top of each cookie with a whole blanched almond, though nowadays, many bakers skip it in favor of seeing the desired cracked appearance on top. While modern bakers tend to add cardamom to so many Scandinavian sweets, these cookies are traditionally made with vanilla sugar. This recipe sticks with tradition and uses vanilla, but cardamom is given as an optional flavoring.

Position racks in the top and bottom thirds of the oven and preheat the oven to 300°F (150°C/Gas Mark 2). Line two large baking sheets with parchment paper.

In a medium bowl, whisk together the flour, baker's ammonia, and salt.

In a large bowl, with a hand mixer, combine the white US granulated (UK caster) sugar, butter, oil, vanilla sugar, and cardamom (if using) and beat on medium speed until pale and fluffy, 2–3 minutes. Add the dry ingredients and stir until there are no dry patches of flour remaining.

Using a ½-ounce (1-tablespoon) ice cream scoop, portion the dough and roll into balls. Arrange them on the prepared baking sheets, spaced 2 inches (5 cm) apart.

Bake until barely light golden brown on the bottom and dry to the touch on top, 20–25 minutes, switching racks and rotating the baking sheets front to back halfway through.

Transfer the baking sheets to wire racks and let the cookies cool completely on the pans.

Chocolate Slice Cookies
Chokladsnittar

Preparation time: 40 minutes,
 plus chilling time
Cooking time: 20 minutes
Makes: About 36 cookies

2 cups (280 g) all-purpose
 (plain) flour
⅓ cup (30 g) Dutch-process
 cocoa powder
1 teaspoon baking powder
¾ teaspoon fine sea salt
1¼ cups (250 g) white US
 granulated (UK caster) sugar
2 sticks (8 oz/225 g) unsalted
 butter, softened
1 egg
1 tablespoon Vanilla Sugar (page 16)
 or 2 teaspoons pure vanilla extract
Egg wash: 1 egg yolk beaten
 with 1 tablespoon water
Pearl sugar, for decorating

Around the same time that chocolate made a big splash in the United States in the 1940s with Chocolate Chip Cookies (recipe, page 346), so too did many Swedes get their first taste of a chocolate version of their beloved "slice" cookies, or *snittar*. These "chocolate slices" were published under the name Märta's Chocolate Slices, for the name of the author of the classic book *Sju Sorters Kakor* (see page 291).

Essentially, they're the chocolate version of *kolasnittar* (recipe, page 312), and they have an eye-catching appearance thanks to the deep dark cocoa used in the dough contrasted with bright matte white pearl sugar. The texture of these slices is also very brownie-like and likely played a part in influencing those treats in the United States.

Position racks in the top and bottom thirds of the oven and preheat the oven to 350°F (180°C/Gas Mark 4). Line two large baking sheets with parchment paper.

In a medium bowl, whisk together the flour, cocoa powder, baking powder, and salt.

In a large bowl, with a hand mixer, beat the white US granulated (UK caster) sugar and butter on medium speed until pale and fluffy, 2–3 minutes. Add the egg and beat until smooth. Beat in the vanilla sugar. Add the dry ingredients and mix on low speed until a dough forms and there are no dry patches of flour remaining. Cover the bowl with plastic wrap (cling film) and refrigerate for at least 2 hours or up to 1 day.

Divide the dough into 4 equal portions and shape each piece into a log 12 inches (30 cm) long. Place 2 logs lengthwise on each baking sheet, spaced 4 inches (10 cm) apart, and flatten slightly with your hand. Brush the logs lightly with some egg wash and sprinkle liberally with pearl sugar.

Bake until the cookie logs are flattened and dry to the touch on top, 16–18 minutes, switching racks and rotating the baking sheets front to back halfway through.

Transfer the baking sheets to wire racks and let the cookies rest for 10 minutes. While still warm, slide the cookie logs on the parchment paper onto a cutting board and cut at a slight diagonal every 1¼ inches (3 cm) to make slices. Transfer the slices directly to the rack to cool completely.

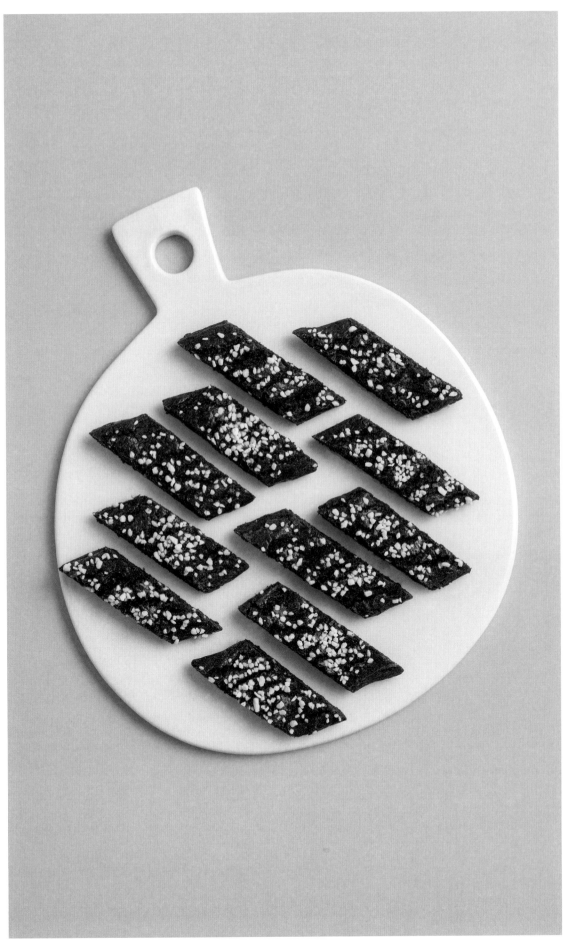

Chocolate Slice Cookies

Thin and Lacy Oat Cookies

Havreflarn

Preparation time: 40 minutes
Cooking time: 20 minutes
Makes: About 24 cookies

1 cup (95 g) rolled oats
1 cup (140 g) all-purpose (plain) flour
1 teaspoon baking powder
½ teaspoon fine sea salt
10 tablespoons (5 oz/140 g) unsalted butter
¾ cup (150 g) white US granulated (UK caster) sugar
¼ cup (85 g) mørk sirup (see page 307), dark corn syrup, or British golden syrup
¼ cup (2 fl oz/60 ml) heavy (double) cream
1 teaspoon pure vanilla extract

So-called "lace cookies" are a popular category in Swedish baking. They consist of a loose, butter-and-syrup-heavy dough that spreads out thin and bakes up almost like candy. The *mørk sirup* typically added to the dough gives the cookies a butterscotch flavor too.

While there are plain ones made with all-purpose (plain) flour and spiced with ginger, or mixed with nuts like almonds and coconut, this version is made with oats and seems to be most popular. Like Norwegian *kransekakestenger* (recipe, page 310), these cookies are often dipped or drizzled with chocolate.

Position racks in the top and bottom thirds of the oven and preheat the oven to 375°F (190°C/Gas Mark 5). Line two large baking sheets with parchment paper.

In a food processor, pulse the oats until half their original size. Scrape the oats into a bowl and whisk in the flour, baking powder, and salt.

In a medium saucepan, melt the butter over medium heat. Add the sugar and syrup and stir until the sugar dissolves. Remove the pan from the heat and stir in the cream and vanilla. Add the dry ingredients and stir until there are no dry patches of flour remaining.

Using a 1-tablespoon measure, scoop portions of the batter onto the prepared baking sheets, spaced at least 4 inches (10 cm) apart, as the cookies will spread.

Bake until the cookies are light golden brown, 6–8 minutes, switching racks and rotating the baking sheets front to back halfway through.

Transfer the baking sheets to wire racks and immediately use a spatula to lift each cookie and place it over a wooden rolling pin or other cylinder. Once the cookies are cool and shaped to the curve of the pin, transfer them to a wire rack.

Raspberry Jam Thumbprint Cookies

Hallongrottor

Preparation time: 40 minutes
Cooking time: 20 minutes
Makes: About 16 cookies

2 cups (280 g) all-purpose (plain) flour
2 teaspoon baking powder
¾ teaspoon fine sea salt
2 sticks (8 oz/225 g) unsalted butter, softened
½ cup (100 g) white US granulated (UK caster) sugar
1 egg yolk
1 teaspoon pure vanilla extract
½ cup (160 g) raspberry jam

Translated as "raspberry caves," these simple Swedish butter cookies filled with raspberry jam likely popularized the idea of a "thumbprint" cookie, as they're called in the United States. In Germany, they're called *Engelsaugen* and filled with red currant jam, while in Austria, they're called *Husaren-Krapferln* or "Calvary puff-balls." In Australia, they're known as "jam drops." This is one of the simplest cookies to make. While the name denotes using raspberry jam, any thick jam can be used here, like apricot, plum, or strawberry.

Position racks in the top and bottom thirds of the oven and preheat the oven to 375°F (190°C/Gas Mark 5). Line two large baking sheets with parchment paper.

In a medium bowl, whisk together the flour, baking powder, and salt.

In a large bowl, with a hand mixer, beat the butter and sugar on medium speed until smooth and fluffy, 2–3 minutes. Add the egg yolk and vanilla and beat until incorporated. Add the dry ingredients and beat on low speed until there are no dry patches of flour remaining.

Using a 1-ounce (2-tablespoon) ice cream scoop, portion the dough and roll into balls. Arrange them on the prepared baking sheets, spaced at least 2 inches (5 cm) apart. Using the tip of your forefinger, gently press in the center of each ball to create a divot. Fill the divot with a heaping ½ teaspoon raspberry jam.

Bake until light golden brown at the edges and dry to the touch on top, 16–18 minutes, switching racks and rotating the baking sheets front to back halfway through.

Transfer the baking sheets to wire racks. Let the cookies cool on the pans for 1 minute, then transfer them to the racks to cool completely.

Raspberry Jam Thumbprint Cookies

Cocoa and Vanilla Checkerboard Cookies

Schackrutor

Preparation time: 30 minutes,
  plus 1 hour chilling time
Cooking time: 15 minutes
Makes: About 48 cookies

1½ sticks (6 oz/170 g) unsalted
  butter, softened
½ cup (100 g) white US granulated
  (UK caster) sugar
2 teaspoons pure vanilla extract
¾ teaspoon fine sea salt
2 cups (280 g) all-purpose (plain) flour
2 tablespoons Dutch-process
  cocoa powder

Cookies of varying colors molded together in swirls, checkerboards, or layers can only come from a culture obsessed with coming up with innumerable ways to make cookies for coffee time. Sweden and Norway's famous *fika* ("coffee break") culture begat such cookies as these checkerboard tiles made with alternating squares of plain and cocoa-tinged dough. Some bakers make elaborate versions with up to eight rows and columns, but the simplest and typical is an easy two-by-two grid.

This dough, without cocoa, is elemental and can also be used to make two other classic Swedish cookies. The first is *brysselkex*, and despite its name—"Brussels biscuits"—the cookie resembles more French *sablés* (recipe, page 258) or Danish *kammerjunker*. *Brysselkex* are simple butter shortbread cookies formed into a log and then rolled in red or pink crystal sugar before being sliced and baked. The second is rye shortbread called *torplyckor* or *ragkåkor* that is typically flattened with a fork. Both variations follow.

In a large bowl, with a hand mixer, combine the butter, sugar, vanilla, and salt and beat on medium speed until pale and fluffy, 2–3 minutes. Add the flour and stir until a dough forms and there are no dry patches of flour remaining. Scrape half the dough onto a clean work surface. Add the cocoa powder to the dough left in the bowl and stir until evenly incorporated.

Divide each half into 2 equal portions (for a total of 4) and shape each piece into a log 12 inches (30 cm) long. Press on the logs so they form square edges. Arrange a vanilla dough log next to a chocolate one, then place a chocolate log over the first vanilla one, and place the second vanilla log over the first chocolate log. Press again to form a large square-shaped log; using the flat side of a ruler helps with this. Wrap in plastic and refrigerate for 1 hour to set.

Position racks in the top and bottom thirds of the oven and preheat the oven to 350°F (180°C/Gas Mark 4). Line two large baking sheets with parchment paper.

Unwrap and cut the log crosswise into slices ¼ inch (6 mm) thick. Arrange the cookies on the prepared baking sheets, spaced 1 inch (2.5 cm) apart.

Bake until light golden brown at the edges and dry to the touch on top, 10–12 minutes, switching racks and rotating the baking sheets front to back halfway through.

Transfer the baking sheets to wire racks. Let the cookies cool on the pans for 1 minute, then transfer them to the racks to cool completely.

Variations
Brysselkex
Omit the cocoa powder. Divide the dough in half. Form each half into a vague cylinder and place on separate sheets of parchment paper. Shape the dough into logs 1½ inches (4 cm) in diameter. Unwrap the logs, brush them lightly with beaten egg white, then roll in pink or red sparkling sugar to cover completely. Rewrap each log in the parchment paper and twist the paper at the ends to close the log. Transfer them to the refrigerator to firm up for at least 30 minutes. After chilling, slice the logs to make cookies and bake as directed above.
Torplyckor or Ragkåkor
Substitute ½ cup (75 g) rye flour for ½ cup (70 g) of the all-purpose (plain) flour. Omit the cocoa powder. Use a 1-ounce (2-tablespoon) ice cream scoop or 2 tablespoons to portion the dough and roll into balls or small logs. Flatten each ball or log on the baking sheet once with the tines of a fork. Bake for 14–16 minutes.

Cocoa and Vanilla Checkerboard Cookies

Swedish Gingerbread Cookies

Pepparkakor

Preparation time: 40 minutes, plus
cooling time and overnight chilling
Cooking time: 20 minutes
Makes: About 42 cookies

⅔ cup (130 g) white US granulated
(UK caster) sugar
½ cup (170 g) mørk sirup (see page
307), dark corn syrup, or British
golden syrup
½ cup (4 fl oz/120 ml) heavy
(double)cream
10 tablespoons (5 oz/140 g)
unsalted butter
2 tablespoons ground cinnamon
4 teaspoons ground ginger
2 teaspoons ground cloves
1 teaspoon ground cardamom
3½ cups (490 g) all-purpose
(plain) flour
2 teaspoons baking soda
(bicarbonate of soda)
1 teaspoon fine sea salt

It's impossible to say whether this version of Sweden's gingerbread-style cookies is the oldest or influenced all other Nordic countries' gingerbreads, but it definitely is the most well known. It's most likely descended from the Dutch and Danish tradition of printed gingerbread-style cookies in molds, like *speculaas* (recipe, page 232), and the German gingerbread tradition of printing and icing cookies—to "freeze" the image—like the *Aachener Printen* (recipe, page 247). One theory is that iced thin gingerbread-style cookies evolved from the more intricate printed and molded styles because they were easier to make and didn't require special molds and rollers. Plus, icing is easy to make and still adds design to the thin spice cookies.

These Swedish cookies are often found cut into shapes like hearts, angels, stars, pigs, and the Dala horse, a wooden toy that's come to represent Swedish culture. You see them left plain more than iced, but they are often decorated with simple designs in thin piped white icing. (For a simple piped icing, see the variation that follows.) Though many modern recipes now feature the favorite spices of each individual baker, the most common recipes seem to have cinnamon, ginger, and cloves. As with other Nordic gingerbread-style cookies, the dark sugar syrup called *mørk sirup* (see Molasses and Sugar Syrups, page 307) is for color and caramel flavor to accent the spices.

In a small saucepan, combine the sugar, syrup, and cream and heat over medium-high heat, stirring until the sugar dissolves. Remove the pan from the heat and add the butter, cinnamon, ginger, cloves, and cardamom. Stir until the butter melts, then pour the mixture into a large bowl to cool to room temperature.

Meanwhile, in a medium bowl, whisk together the flour, baking soda (bicarb), and salt.

Add the dry ingredients to the cooled syrup mixture and stir until the dough just comes together and there are no dry patches of flour remaining. Divide the dough in half and shape each half into a disc. Wrap each disc separately in plastic wrap (cling film) and refrigerate for at least 8 hours or overnight, or up to 1 day.

Position racks in the top and bottom thirds of the oven and preheat the oven to 400°F (200°C/Gas Mark 6). Line two large baking sheets with parchment paper.

Working on a lightly floured work surface, roll out the dough with a rolling pin to ⅛ inch (3 mm) thick. Using a 2- to 3-inch (5 to 7.5 cm) cutter, cut out cookies. Reroll the scraps to cut out more cookies. Arrange the cookies on the prepared baking sheets, spaced 2 inches (5 cm) apart.

Bake until darker brown at the edges and just dry to the touch on top, 8–10 minutes, switching racks and rotating the baking sheets front to back halfway through.

Transfer the baking sheets to wire racks. Let the cookies cool on the pans for 1 minute, then transfer them to the racks to cool completely.

Variation
Iced Pepparkakor
Bake and cool the cookies as directed. In a medium bowl, whisk 1 egg white until frothy. Add 2 cups (270 g) powdered (icing) sugar and whisk until smooth. Whisk in 1 teaspoon fresh lemon juice and a pinch of fine sea salt. Transfer the icing to a small piping bag and use it to decorate the cookies with simple designs or outlines.

Twice-Baked Almond "Rusks"

Mandelskorpor

Preparation time: 25 minutes
Cooking time: 35 minutes
Makes: About 42 cookies

4 oz (115 g) blanched whole or
  slivered almonds
2 cups (280 g) all-purpose (plain) flour
1 teaspoon baking powder
½ teaspoon fine sea salt
¾ cup (150 g) white US granulated
  (UK caster) sugar
1½ sticks (6 oz/170 g) unsalted
  butter, softened
2 eggs

Biscotti-like cookies are often called "rusks" in Sweden because they are dried out like traditional bread rusks. The most classic rusk is *mandelskorpor*, which, like Jewish *mandelbrot* (recipe, page 47), is flavored with almonds that are ground fine and incorporated into the dough. They are usually shaped into narrower logs and cut into wider slices than other biscotti-like cookies.

A popular variation is the *saffransskorpor*, golden and full of saffron, that is often served for Christmas. These saffron cookies typically have larger chunks of almonds in the dough than the plain almond version and are topped with pearl sugar (see the variation that follows).

Position racks in the top and bottom thirds of the oven and preheat the oven to 375°F (190°C/Gas Mark 5). Line two large baking sheets with parchment paper.

In a food processor, pulse the almonds until very finely ground. Scrape the almonds into a medium bowl and whisk in the flour, baking powder, and salt.

In a large bowl, with a hand mixer, beat the sugar and butter on medium speed until pale and fluffy, 2–3 minutes. Add the eggs, one at a time, beating until smooth after each addition. Add the dry ingredients and mix on low speed until a dough forms and there are no dry patches of flour remaining.

Divide the dough into 3 equal portions and shape each piece into a log 12 inches (30 cm) long. Place two logs on one of the baking sheets and place the third log on the second sheet, do not flatten them.

Bake until the cookie logs are lightly browned and dry to the touch, about 15 minutes, switching racks and rotating the baking sheets front to back halfway through.

Transfer the baking sheets to wire racks and let the cookies rest for 10 minutes. Reduce the oven temperature to 300°F (150°C/Gas Mark 2).

While still warm, cut each log crosswise into slices ¾ inch (2 cm) thick. Arrange the slices on the baking sheets, spaced 1 inch (2.5 cm) apart. Return the cookies to the oven and bake again until golden brown all over and dry, 15–20 minutes, again switching racks and rotating the sheets halfway through.

Transfer the baking sheets to wire racks. Let the cookies cool on the pans for 1 minute, then transfer them to the racks to cool completely.

Variation
Saffransskorpor
Do not grind the almonds finely, but instead roughly chop them with a knife. In a small saucepan, melt the butter, then remove from the heat and stir in ½ teaspoon crushed saffron threads. Let the butter cool completely until solidified again and then proceed with the recipe. Brush the formed dough logs lightly with some egg wash and sprinkle liberally with pearl sugar before baking.

Almond Tart-Shell Cookies

Mandelmusslor

Preparation time: 1 hour,
 plus chilling and cooling time
Cooking time: 20 minutes
Makes: About 24 cookies

4 oz (115 g) blanched whole
 or slivered almonds
⅔ cup (130 g) white US granulated
 (UK caster) sugar
¾ teaspoon fine sea salt
½ teaspoon pure almond extract
2 sticks (8 oz/225 g) unsalted
 butter, softened
1 egg
2 cups (280 g) all-purpose (plain) flour
Whipped cream and lingonberry
 or raspberry jam, for serving

These ornate cookies are a staple at most Scandinavian Christmas tables. Ground almonds flavor a basic butter and sugar dough pressed into fluted tart molds in shapes like hearts, diamonds, and long ovals often referred to as "clam shells" (though the cookie's name translates to "almond mussels" so it seems the latter bivalve would be more accurate in describing the shape).

They're almost always served with whipped cream and a bowl of lingonberry jam or other fruit, so you can fill them with the berries and cream. Their "sandy" texture, thanks to the almonds and sugar, explains their name in Norwegian, *sandbakkel*, and also in Finland, called *hiekkahentuset*, both of which translate to "sand cookies" or "sand tarts."

In a food processor, pulse the almonds until finely ground. Add the sugar, salt, and almond extract and pulse again until the almonds are very finely ground. Add the butter and egg and pulse until the butter incorporates into the almonds and sugar. Add the flour and pulse just until the mixture forms a dough and there are no dry patches of flour remaining. Shape the dough into a ball, wrap in plastic wrap (cling film), and refrigerate for at least 2 hours or overnight.

Preheat the oven to 375°F (190°C/Gas Mark 5). Line a large baking sheet with parchment paper.

Grease several 2-ounce 1⅞ × 1⅜-inch (4.7 × 3.5 cm) petit four pans (or tartlet molds) in shapes like clamshells, hearts, or diamonds. Place on the prepared baking sheet.

Using a ½-ounce (1-tablespoon) ice cream scoop, portion the dough and roll into balls. Place one ball in each pan and press into the bottom and up the sides. Trim the edges of each dough mold and refrigerate to firm the dough for at least 20 minutes.

Bake until the cookies are golden brown at the edges and dry to the touch in the center, 14–16 minutes, switching racks and rotating the baking sheets front to back halfway through.

Transfer the baking sheets to wire racks and let the cookies rest for 5 minutes. Using a tea towel to protect your hands, invert the pans over wire racks to let the cookies fall out, tapping on the bottoms of the tins with a spoon, if needed, to help them out. Let the cookies cool completely.

Serve with whipped cream and lingonberry jam on the side.

Browned Butter "Spoon" Cookies
Lusikkaleivät

Preparation time: 1 hour, plus cooling
 time and 2 days standing time
Cooking time: 20 minutes
Makes: About 16 cookie sandwiches

2 sticks (8 oz/225 g) unsalted butter
¾ cup (150 g) white US granulated
 (UK caster) sugar
2 teaspoons pure vanilla extract
1¾ cups (245 g) all-purpose
 (plain) flour
1 teaspoon baking soda
 (bicarbonate of soda)
¾ teaspoon fine sea salt
½ cup (160 g) seedless raspberry
 or strawberry jam
Powdered (icing) sugar, for dusting

These beloved cookie sandwiches get their name from the instrument used to form them: an everyday spoon. Bakers today may use spring-loaded ice cream scoops for portioning dough, but Finland has been using spoons to form mounds of cookie dough for generations. The cookies get their crumbly, nutty flavor from browning the milk solids in butter, which balances the cookie's sweetness wonderfully.

Though it may be difficult, many recipes stress the importance of waiting two days to eat these cookies, as their texture improves during that wait period to a melt-in-the-mouth consistency. Some recipes insist on raspberry jam, while others assert strawberry; use whichever you prefer.

Position racks in the top and bottom thirds of the oven and preheat the oven to 325°F (160°C/Gas Mark 3). Line two large baking sheets with parchment paper.

In a small saucepan, melt the butter over medium heat. Continue cooking, stirring occasionally, until the milk solids begin to brown and smell nutty and fragrant; you'll know the butter is almost there when it ceases bubbling and foaming. Remove the pan from the heat and immediately scrape all the butter into a large bowl.

Add the white US granulated (UK caster) sugar and vanilla to the browned butter, stir to combine, and let the mixture cool for 10 minutes. In a medium bowl, whisk together the flour, baking soda (bicarb), and salt. Add to the large bowl and stir until a dough forms and there are no dry patches of flour remaining.

Using a spoon—the type you'd use for eating soup or cereal—dig into the cookie dough to fill the spoon. Drag the spoon up the side of the bowl and level the dough off by dragging the inverted bowl of the spoon over the edge of the mixing bowl; the spoon should be filled with dough and the surface completely flat. Use your fingers to gently nudge and slide the hump of dough out of the spoon or tap the edge of the spoon lightly on the baking sheet to allow the dough to fall out. Place the dough, flat-side down, on the prepared baking sheet. Repeat to make more humps of dough, spacing them 2 inches (5 cm) apart.

Bake until golden brown at the edges and just dry to the touch on top, 8–12 minutes, switching racks and rotating the baking sheets front to back halfway through.

Transfer the baking sheets to wire racks. Let the cookies cool on the pans for 1 minute, then transfer them to the racks to cool completely.

Once cooled, invert half the cookies and top each with ½ teaspoon raspberry jam. Sandwich them with the remaining plain cookies and transfer the cookie sandwiches to a serving platter. Dust the cookies with powdered (icing) sugar before serving.

Browned Butter "Spoon" Cookies

Finnish Gingerbread

Piparkakut

Preparation time: 1 hour 15 minutes,
  plus overnight chilling
Cooking time: 20 minutes
Makes: About 30 cookies

1 stick (4 oz/115 g) unsalted butter
½ cup (100 g) white US granulated
  (UK caster) sugar
⅓ cup (110 g) mørk sirup
  (see page 307), dark corn
  syrup, or golden syrup
1½ teaspoons bitter orange peel
  powder or 1 tablespoon finely
  grated orange zest
1 teaspoon ground cinnamon
1 teaspoon ground cloves
1 teaspoon ground ginger
2 cups (280 g) all-purpose (plain) flour
1 teaspoon baking soda
  (bicarbonate of soda)
½ teaspoon fine sea salt
1 egg
Powdered (icing) sugar,
  for dusting (optional)

Almost identical to Danish *brunkager* (recipe, page 329) and Swedish *pepparkakor* (recipe, page 320), there are two details that make this Finnish version stand out. The first is that these Finnish gingerbreads are much thinner than the typical gingerbread cookie; rolled to ¹⁄₁₆ inch (1.5 mm) thick, they bake up quickly like crackers. The second is their use of a powdered bitter orange peel—called *pomeranssi* in Finnish or *pomerans* in Swedish—which lends the gingerbread cookies an intense floral note. Furthermore, the rest of the spices vary from the two other styles of Nordic gingerbread with ground cinnamon, cloves, and ginger predominating in roughly equal amounts.

Pomerans is available online but can be difficult to source outside of Scandinavia; modern recipes call for fresh orange zest instead, so use that if you prefer. Like their Danish and Swedish analogs, these Finnish gingerbread cookies get their brown color and caramelized sugar flavor from *mørk sirup* (see Molasses and Sugar Syrups, page 307), which in Finnish is called *tumma siirappi*; if you can't find it or don't want to make it, use dark corn syrup or British golden syrup.

- -

In a small saucepan, combine the butter, white US granulated (UK caster) sugar, and syrup and heat over medium-high heat, stirring until the sugar dissolves. Remove the pan from the heat and pour it into a large bowl. Whisk in the orange peel powder, cinnamon, cloves, and ginger and let the mixture cool to room temperature.

Meanwhile, in a medium bowl, whisk together the flour, baking soda (bicarb), and salt.

Add the egg to the cooled syrup mixture and whisk until smooth. Add the dry ingredients and stir until a dough just comes together and there are no dry patches of flour remaining. Divide the dough in half and shape each half into a disc. Wrap each disc separately in plastic wrap (cling film) and refrigerate for at least 8 hours or overnight, or up to 1 day.

Position racks in the top and bottom thirds of the oven and preheat the oven to 400°F (200°C/Gas Mark 6). Line two large baking sheets with parchment paper.

Working on a lightly floured work surface, roll out the dough discs with a rolling pin to ¹⁄₁₆ inch (1.5 mm) thick. Using a 2- to 3-inch (5 to 7.5 cm) cutter, cut out cookies. Reroll the scraps to cut out more cookies. Arrange the dough shapes on the prepared baking sheets, spaced 2 inches (5 cm) apart.

Bake until darker brown at the edges and just dry to the touch on top, 6–8 minutes, switching racks and rotating the baking sheets front to back halfway through.

Transfer the baking sheets to wire racks. Let the cookies cool on the pans for 1 minute, then transfer them to the racks to cool completely. Dust with powdered (icing) sugar before serving (if using).

Finnish Gingerbread

Gingerbread

The term "gingerbread" is used in several different ways. For example, in the UK, gingerbread usually refers to a cake sweetened with honey or golden syrup and flavored with spices. In the US, on the other hand, gingerbread refers to the thin cookie form, colored dark brown with molasses and spiced heavily with cinnamon, ginger, and cloves. This conflation gets more confusing when you dive into the various textures—"chewy" vs. "snaps"—and the origins of such treats, their various forms, and how they came to have those shapes. That said, throughout this book, when I refer to "gingerbread" it's the flat cookies, whether cut-out or printed, that I'm talking about.

The forebear of modern gingerbread is likely the honey-and-flour cakes of the late Middle Ages in Europe. In her book *Dark Rye and Honey Cake*, historian Regula Ysewijn documents the most plausible sequence of events.

First, these honey cakes evolved from a "natural and logical evolution" of having honey be the primary sweetener and having flour to make bread. The two ingredients combine to make a pliable dough that's easy to work with, so it was used in all sorts of ways. It was mostly used to make printed cookies (see page 245) that stood in for various cultural iconography. At one point it was used to convey local news—bakers would print news on the cookies that would then get disseminated to people around town.

The dough was also used in "free form" ways like rolling into balls or spreading as a sheet that was then broken up after baking. Then the dough was used to bake loaf cakes. The craft of making these honey cakes was largely done in monasteries where bees were kept and their honey and comb used in various ways. Some of those earliest honey cakes were likely similar to the German *Honigkuchen* (recipe, page 247) and *Elisenlebkuchen* (recipe, page 244), because it's documented in the late 1400s, as a guild of *Lebkuchen* bakers was established in Nuremberg.

Spices enter the picture next because the spice trade had emerged at the time, and bakers were looking for ways to use the cinnamon, cloves and other spices coming from Southeast Asia or other parts around the globe during colonization. In Europe, those spiced breads were typically named some variation of "pepper cake"—although back then "pepper" referred more to a mix of spices (as in to "pepper" something up with spices), rather than specifically the black pepper used to season savory food.

Ginger was also a spice that worked well with the popular and available spices of the time—cinnamon, cloves, nutmeg and mace, anise seeds—so it got blended into the mix and its name also eventually came to stand for a "spiced cake." In the same way that many pepper cakes in Europe didn't include pepper in the original recipes, many first gingerbreads didn't contain ginger either. But when names stick around like that, people eventually assume the namesake ingredients must be included and so, form follows function.

Those elaborate printed cookies of Europe eventually gained butter and sugar and became more tender—good for the eater, not so much for holding a shape—and then fell out of fashion. As baking ventured into the kitchens of home bakers, so did preferences for easier methods of creating treats that wereimportant parts of the culture. This is likely where the use of what we call cookie cutters came from. The more complicated printed designs lost their details in favor of softer, more buttery cookies that could easily be cut into figurine, animal, or religiously significant shapes.

When these same flat, spiced "cakes" came to the Americas with the Dutch, the honey was swapped out in favor of sugarcane molasses—the dominant sweetener of the early colonial Americas—and thus a different style of gingerbread was born.

Crisp Danish Gingerbread
Brunkager

Preparation time: 40 minutes,
  plus 30 minutes soaking time
  and overnight chilling
Cooking time: 20 minutes
Makes: About 72 cookies

6 oz (170 g) blanched whole
  or slivered almonds
½ cup (65 g) pistachios
1 cup (200 g) white US granulated
  (UK caster) sugar
½ cup (170 g) plus 2 tablespoons
  mørk sirup (see page 307), dark
  corn syrup, or British golden syrup
⅓ cup (2½ fl oz/80 ml) whole milk
1½ teaspoons potassium carbonate
  (potash) or baking soda
  (bicarbonate of soda)
4 teaspoons ground cinnamon
1½ teaspoons ground cloves
1½ teaspoons ground ginger
1 teaspoon ground allspice
1 teaspoon ground cardamom
1 teaspoon fine sea salt
2 sticks (8 oz/225 g) unsalted butter
3½ cups (490 g) all-purpose
  (plain) flour

Literally "brown cakes," these crisp gingerbread-like cookies are a specialty of Denmark, though they're very similar to Swedish *pepparkakor* (recipe, page 320) and the Norwegian version spelled *pepperkaker*. What sets these Danish cookies apart is their addition of allspice to the dough and use of potash (potassium carbonate), a chemical leavening used before baking soda (bicarb) and powder (see Leaveners, pages 16–17). It gives the cookies a particular crispness, but you can use baking soda as a substitute. While *mørk sirup* (see Molasses and Sugar Syrups, page 307) is used in these cookies, many modern recipes substitute it with British golden syrup or American dark corn syrup. Do not use molasses, however, since it would be too bitter here.

These cookies are typically rolled into logs and cut into round or square slices. The dough is studded with whole almonds and pistachios so when the slices are cut, the nuts contribute a stained-glass effect. The nuts are first soaked in water to make them soft enough to cut through. If you're worried about the nuts making the task difficult, before baking, you can top each sliced dough round with sliced (flaked) almonds and chopped pistachios instead.

- -

In a medium bowl, combine the almonds and pistachios and cover with hot tap water. Let stand for 30 minutes; do not allow the nuts to soak any longer. Drain and spread out on paper towels to fully dry.

In a small saucepan, combine the sugar, syrup, and milk and heat over medium-high heat, stirring until the sugar dissolves. Remove the pan from the heat and pour it into a large bowl. Whisk in the potassium carbonate, cinnamon, cloves, ginger, allspice, cardamom, and salt. Add the butter and stir until the butter melts and the syrup is cooled.

Stir in the almonds and pistachios. Add the flour and stir until a dough just comes together and there are no dry patches of flour remaining.

Divide the dough in half. Form each half into a vague cylinder and place on separate sheets of parchment paper. Shape the dough into logs 2 inches (5 cm) in diameter and wrap tightly (see page 14). Transfer them to the refrigerator to firm up for at least 8 hours or overnight, or up to 2 days.

Position racks in the top and bottom thirds of the oven and preheat the oven to 350°F (180°C/Gas Mark 4). Line two large baking sheets with parchment paper.

Unwrap the dough logs and use a sharp knife to cut the dough into slices ⅛ inch (3 mm) thick. Arrange the slices on the prepared baking sheets, spaced at least 2 inches (5 cm) apart.

Bake until golden brown at the edges and just dry to the touch on top, 12–14 minutes, switching racks and rotating the baking sheets front to back halfway through.

Transfer the baking sheets to wire racks. Let the cookies cool on the pans for 1 minute, then transfer them to the racks to cool completely.

Danish Pepper and Spice Cookies

Pebernødder

Preparation time: 30 minutes
Cooking time: 15 minutes
Makes: About 36 cookies

1⅔ cups (230 g) all-purpose
  (plain) flour
2 teaspoons ground cardamom
1 teaspoon ground cinnamon
½ teaspoon ground cloves
½ teaspoon ground ginger
½ teaspoon ground white or
  black pepper
½ teaspoon baking soda
  (bicarbonate of soda)
½ teaspoon fine sea salt
¾ cup (170 g) packed light
  brown sugar
1 stick (4 oz/115 g) unsalted
  butter, softened
¼ cup (2 fl oz/60 ml) heavy (double)
  cream, at room temperature

Typically made for Christmas as a sweet snack or as tokens or toys for children to play with, these tiny, marble-size cookies are like balls of crunchy, gingerbread-like shortbread. The cookies usually contain pepper, more often white pepper than black, though either can be used. Other spices vary wildly from recipe to recipe, but cardamom and ginger are mainstays. Eggs make an appearance in some modern recipes, but they make the dough softer; to preserve the original denseness of these cookies, this recipe instead uses cream, which was used in older recipes.

Position racks in the top and bottom thirds of the oven and preheat the oven to 350°F (180°C/Gas Mark 4). Line two large baking sheets with parchment paper.

In a medium bowl, whisk together the flour, cardamom, cinnamon, cloves, ginger, pepper, baking soda (bicarb), and salt.

In a large bowl, with a hand mixer, beat the sugar and butter on medium speed until pale and fluffy, 2–3 minutes. Add the cream and beat until smooth. Add the dry ingredients and stir until a dough forms and there are no dry patches of flour remaining.

Using a ½-ounce (1-tablespoon) ice cream scoop, portion the dough and roll into balls. Arrange them on the prepared baking sheets, spaced 1 inch (2.5 cm) apart.

Bake until golden brown on the bottom and just dry to the touch on top, 12–14 minutes, switching racks and rotating the baking sheets front to back halfway through.

Transfer the baking sheets to wire racks. Let the cookies cool on the pans for 1 minute, then transfer them to the racks to cool completely.

Vanilla Butter Cookies

Vaniljekranse

Preparation time: 15 minutes,
  plus 30 minutes freezing
Cooking time: 15 minutes
Makes: About 24 cookies

2 oz (55 g) blanched whole
  almonds or slivered almonds
2 sticks (8 oz/225 g) unsalted
  butter, softened
1 cup (200 g) Vanilla Sugar (page 16)
1 egg
¾ teaspoon fine sea salt
1¾ cups (245 g) all-purpose
  (plain) flour

These simple butter cookies are most famous for their inclusion in Royal Dansk's iconic blue tins. Meaning "vanilla wreaths," *vaniljekranse* are usually piped into rings, but they can also be formed with a cookie press or shaped by rolling the dough into a rope by hand. Because of the dough's versatility, you'll often see recipes for other Danish vanilla cookies in the shape of a horn, crescent, or flat circle. In Norway, these cookies are called *smørkranser*.

Line two large baking sheets with parchment paper. In a food processor, pulse the almonds until finely ground.

In a large bowl, with a hand mixer, beat the butter and vanilla sugar on medium speed until pale and fluffy, 2–3 minutes. Add the egg and beat until smooth. Beat in the ground almonds and salt. Add the flour and stir until a dough forms and there are no dry patches of flour remaining.

Working in batches, scrape the dough into a cookie press or a fabric piping bag fitted with a ½-inch (13 mm) fluted tip (nozzle) and pipe 2-inch (5 cm) diameter rings onto the prepared baking sheets, spaced 2 inches (5 cm) apart. (Alternatively shape pieces of the dough into ropes ½ inch/13 mm thick, cut the ropes into 3-inch/7.5 cm lengths, and form the lengths into rings on the baking sheets.) Freeze the baking sheets for 30 minutes to help the dough rings retain the ridges.

Position racks in the top and bottom thirds of the oven and preheat the oven to 350°F (180°C/Gas Mark 4).

Bake until golden brown at the edges and just dry to the touch on top, 10–12 minutes, switching racks and rotating the baking sheets front to back halfway through.

Transfer the baking sheets to wire racks. Let the cookies cool on the pans for 1 minute, then transfer them to the racks to cool completely.

Vanilla Butter Cookies

Twice-Baked Lemon and Cardamom Cookies
Kammarjunkere

Preparation time: 40 minutes
Cooking time: 35 minutes
Makes: About 24 cookies

1¾ cups (245 g) all-purpose (plain) flour
½ cup (100 g) white US granulated (UK caster) sugar
2 teaspoons baking powder
¾ teaspoon ground cardamom
½ teaspoon fine sea salt
1 stick (4 oz/115 g) unsalted butter, softened
¼ cup (2 fl oz/60 ml) whole milk
1 teaspoon pure vanilla extract
1 egg, lightly beaten
Finely grated zest of 1 small lemon

These cookies are traditionally broken or crumbled over various Danish dessert soups, particularly one made with buttermilk called *koldskål*. Sometimes referred to as "sweet rusks," the cookies are baked once, split in half like a hamburger bun, then baked again to dry out, similar to *cantucci* (recipe, page 112).

Some recipes treat them like traditional cookies and form the dough into logs 2 inches (5 cm) in diameter that are then sliced into rounds ¼ inch (6 mm) thick and baked. If you do this, bake the rounds at 350°F (180°C/Gas Mark 4) until golden brown at the edges, 12–15 minutes.

Position racks in the top and bottom thirds of the oven and preheat the oven to 400°F (200°C/Gas Mark 6). Line two large baking sheets with parchment paper.

In a large bowl, whisk together the flour, sugar, baking powder, cardamom, and salt. Add the butter and mix with your fingers until it breaks down into coarse crumbles. Add the milk, vanilla, egg, and lemon zest and stir until a dough forms and there are no dry patches of flour remaining.

Using a 1-ounce (2-tablespoon) ice cream scoop, portion the dough and roll into balls. Arrange them on the prepared baking sheets, spaced 2 inches (5 cm) apart.

Bake until dry to the touch and cracked on top, 12–14 minutes, switching racks and rotating the baking sheets front to back halfway through.

Remove the baking sheets from the oven and let the cookies cool for 10 minutes. Reduce the oven temperature to 300°F (150°C/Gas Mark 2).

Using a fork, pierce the side of each cookie a few times—as you would for an English muffin or hamburger bun—to split it into a top half and bottom half. Lay the halves cut-side up next to each other on the baking sheet.

Return the cookies to the oven and bake until golden brown at the edges and dry to the touch on top, 15–20 minutes, switching racks and rotating the baking sheets front to back halfway through.

Transfer the baking sheets to wire racks. Let the cookies cool on the pans for 1 minute, then transfer them to the racks to cool completely.

Twice-Baked Lemon and Cardamom Cookies

Almond Shortbread Bars

Finskbrød / Finska Pinnar

Preparation time: 45 minutes
Cooking time: 15 minutes
Makes: About 48 cookies

2½ sticks (10 oz/285 g)
  unsalted butter, softened
⅔ cup (130 g) white US granulated
  (UK caster) sugar
¾ teaspoon fine sea salt
1 teaspoon pure almond
  extract (optional)
3 cups (420 g) all-purpose (plain) flour
Egg wash: 1 egg yolk beaten with
  1 tablespoon water
½ cup (70 g) skin-on almonds,
  roughly chopped
Pearl sugar or turbinado (demerara)
  sugar, for sprinkling

It's not clear why exactly these popular Danish and Swedish cookies are named after their Scandinavian neighbor, Finland. One possible theory is that cookies from Finland are often cut into sticks or bars from a large sheet of dough before baking. The name of these cookies, literally "Finnish bread" or "sticks," could simply be a tribute to that shape. A simple buttery shortbread, these bar cookies are always sprinkled with chopped almonds and pearl sugar or turbinado (demerara) sugar.

While traditional recipes call for no flavoring, some modern recipes add almond extract to play off the flavor of the decoration. You can also swap the almonds for hazelnuts. In Iceland, a similar cookie is shaped as a round and goes by the name *Bessastaðakökur*, as it was popularly believed to be served at Bessastaðir, the official residence of the first female democratically elected president of Iceland, Vigdís Finnbogadóttir (see the variation that follows).

Position racks in the top and bottom thirds of the oven and preheat the oven to 375°F (190°C/Gas Mark 5). Line two large baking sheets with parchment paper.

In a large bowl, with a hand mixer, combine the butter, white US granulated (UK caster) sugar, salt, and almond extract (if using) and beat on medium speed until pale and fluffy, 2–3 minutes. Add the flour and stir until a dough forms and there are no dry patches of flour remaining.

Scrape the dough onto a clean work surface and roll it out with a rolling pin to ½ inch (13 mm) thick. Using a knife or pizza cutter, cut the dough into strips ¾ inch (2 cm) wide and then cut the strips into rectangles 2 inches (5 cm) long. Arrange the dough rectangles on the prepared baking sheets, spaced 1 inch (2.5 cm) apart. Lightly brush the top of each rectangle with egg wash and sprinkle liberally with some chopped almonds and pearl sugar.

Bake until golden brown at the edges and just dry to the touch on top, 10–12 minutes, switching racks and rotating the baking sheets front to back halfway through.

Transfer the baking sheets to wire racks and let the cookies cool completely on the pans.

Variation
Bessastaðakökur
Omit the almond extract. Use a 2-inch (5 cm) round cutter to cut out rounds of dough. Decorate and bake as above.

Jewish Butter Cookies

Jødekager / Jodenkoeken

Preparation time: 30 minutes,
 plus chilling time
Cooking time: 15 minutes
Makes: About 30 cookies

2⅔ cups (370 g) all-purpose
 (plain) flour
1 teaspoon baker's ammonia
 (see page 17) or baking powder
¾ teaspoon fine sea salt
2 sticks (8 oz/225 g) unsalted
 butter, softened
1 cup (225 g) packed light brown
 sugar or 1 cup (200 g) white
 US granulated (UK caster) sugar
2 eggs
Ground cinnamon, for sprinkling

The likely theory about the origin of these cookies is that Sephardic Jews fleeing the Iberian Peninsula in the 1700s brought their bread-baking traditions to the Netherlands, swapping olive oil and honey for the local butter and sugar, and created these shortbread-like cookies.

In the Netherlands, these cookies are typically cut out of rolled dough and left plain or sprinkled with cinnamon only, while the Danish version, called *jødekager*, cuts discs of dough from logs and tops the cookies with cinnamon-sugar and chopped almonds. In Iceland, their "Jewish cookie," called *gyðingakökur*, is flavored with cardamom instead of cinnamon, and topped with just sugar and almonds. This recipe uses the Dutch dough, though for ease the cookies are cut from logs rather than being cut out of rolled dough. The Danish and Finnish versions are provided in the variations that follow.

- -

In a medium bowl, whisk together the flour, baker's ammonia, and salt.

In a large bowl, with a hand mixer, beat the butter and sugar on medium speed until pale and fluffy, 2–3 minutes. Add the eggs, one at a time, beating well after each addition. Add the dry ingredients and mix on low speed until a dough forms and there are no dry patches of flour remaining.

Divide the dough in half. Form each half into a vague cylinder and place on separate sheets of parchment paper. Shape the dough into logs 2 inches (5 cm) in diameter and wrap tightly (see page 14). Transfer them to the refrigerator to firm up for at least 2 hours and up to 2 days.

Position racks in the top and bottom thirds of the oven and preheat the oven to 350°F (180°C/Gas Mark 4). Line two large baking sheets with parchment paper.

Unwrap the logs and cut into slices ¼ inch (6 mm) thick. Arrange the slices on the prepared baking sheets, spaced 2 inches (5 cm) apart. Sprinkle each round with a small pinch of cinnamon.

Bake until the cookies are light brown at the edges and dry to the touch on top, 10–12 minutes, switching racks and rotating the baking sheets front to back halfway through.

Transfer the baking sheets to wire racks. Let the cookies cool on the pans for 1 minute, then transfer them to the racks to cool completely.

Variations
Danish Jødekager
Lightly brush the dough discs with beaten egg white and sprinkle with chopped almonds. Mix together 2 tablespoons sugar and 1 teaspoon ground cinnamon and sprinkle over each cookie. Bake as directed.
Icelandic Gyðingakökur
Add 2 teaspoons ground cardamom to the dry ingredients. Omit the cinnamon; sprinkle the cookies with chopped almonds and more sugar. Bake as directed.

north america

Many North American cookies descend from the traditions of Dutch, German, and English immigrants who brought them over during the colonial days into the early 1800s. On this side of the Atlantic Ocean, they were morphed by chemical leaveners and a high taste for sugar into soft and chewy treats that have been heavily influenced by mass-produced industrial food products post-World War II, such as chocolate chips, peanut butter, and rolled oats. Today, in name and general texture, these cookies are in a league of their own, opting to be large and chewy cookies rather than the largely smaller and crisper/crumblier "biscuits" eaten throughout the rest of the world.

Fat Archies

Preparation time: 30 minutes,
  plus chilling time
Cooking time: 15 minutes
Makes: About 18 cookies

2½ cups (350 g) all-purpose
  (plain) flour
1½ teaspoons ground ginger
1 teaspoon ground cinnamon
1 teaspoon ground cloves
1 teaspoon baking soda
  (bicarbonate of soda)
¾ teaspoon fine sea salt
½ cup (100 g) white US granulated
  (UK caster) sugar
½ cup (160 g) unsulphured molasses
  (not blackstrap)
1 stick (4 oz/115 g) unsalted butter
  or ½ cup (115 g) vegetable
  shortening, softened
1 egg
¼ cup (2 fl oz/60 ml) buttermilk

One of the first styles of cookie that came from colonial times in North America was this "soft" molasses cookie (see Molasses and Suga Syrups, page 307) that was cakey in texture and chewy, a contrast to the harder, snappier gingerbread-style "biscuits" of Europe. The town of Pubnico on the southwestern tip of Nova Scotia claims ownership of this style of cookie and sells them at the Historic Acadian Village of Nova Scotia. They also go by other whimsical names like Long Johns and Moose Hunters. The cookies get their characteristic soft texture from the addition of milk, usually a soured dairy like buttermilk or sour cream. They are rolled out and cut into thick rounds.

Another popular variation of this style of soft molasses cookie is called a Lassy Mog—"lass" being slang for molasses and "mog" a colloquialism for cake. Seen as a separate cookie, it's essentially the same dough as Fat Archies but usually does not contain dairy, adds nuts and dried fruit, and is formed as a drop cookie (not rolled and cut). Also, the Fat Archie style tends to favor cinnamon, cloves, and ginger, while Lassy Mogs tend to swap out the ginger for nutmeg or mace. (See the Lassy Mog variation that follows.)

In a medium bowl, whisk together the flour, ginger, cinnamon, cloves, baking soda (bicarb), and salt.

In a large bowl, with a hand mixer, combine the sugar, molasses, and butter and beat on medium speed until light and fluffy, 2–3 minutes. Add the egg and beat until smooth. Add the buttermilk and beat on low speed until smooth. Add the dry ingredients and stir until a dough forms and there are no dry patches of flour remaining. Scrape the dough onto a clean work surface, shape into a ball, wrap in plastic wrap (cling film), and refrigerate for at least 1 hour or up to 2 days.

Position racks in the top and bottom thirds of the oven and preheat the oven to 350°F (180°C/Gas Mark 4). Line two large baking sheets with parchment paper.

Transfer the dough to a lightly floured work surface. Using a lightly floured rolling pin, roll out the dough to ¼ inch (6 mm) thick. Using a 2½-inch (6.5 cm) round cutter, cut out rounds of dough. Reroll the scraps to cut out more cookies. Arrange them on the prepared baking sheets, spaced 2 inches (5 cm) apart.

Bake until the cookies are a shade darker at the edges and just dry to the touch in the center, 10–14 minutes, switching racks and rotating the baking sheets front to back halfway through.

Transfer the baking sheets to wire racks. Let the cookies cool on the pans for 1 minute, then transfer them to the racks to cool completely.

Variation
Lassy Mogs
Substitute freshly grated nutmeg for the ground cloves. Do not mix the baking soda (bicarb) with the dry ingredients, but instead dissolve it in ¼ cup (2 fl oz/60 ml) water, then add the mixture to the dough after adding the egg; omit the buttermilk. When adding the dry ingredients, add 1 cup (120 g) toasted chopped nuts, such as pecans or walnuts, and 1 cup (145 g) chopped dried fruit, such as raisins or chopped dates or a mix of both. Use a 1-ounce (2-tablespoon) ice cream scoop or 2 tablespoons to drop mounds of dough on the prepared baking sheets, spaced 2 inches (5 cm) apart. Bake as directed.

Fat Archies

Joe Froggers

Preparation time: 45 minutes,
 plus chilling time
Cooking time: 15 minutes
Makes: About 12 cookies

4 cups (560 g) all-purpose (plain) flour
2 teaspoons ground ginger
1 teaspoon ground cloves
1 teaspoon freshly grated nutmeg
1 teaspoon baking soda (bicarbonate
 of soda)
1 teaspoon fine sea salt
½ teaspoon ground allspice
1 cup (320 g) unsulphured molasses
 (not blackstrap)
¼ cup (2 fl oz/60 ml) hot tap water
3 tablespoons dark rum
1 cup (200 g) white US granulated
 (UK caster) sugar
1 stick (4 oz/115 g) unsalted butter
 or ½ cup (115 g) vegetable
 shortening, softened

These giant, disc-shaped molasses cookies—colloquially called Joe Froggers—are generally believed to be named after Joseph Brown, a free Black man who served in the American Revolutionary War and opened a tavern in Marblehead, Massachusetts. His wife, Lucretia, made these cookies—almost identical to Canadian Fat Archies (recipe, page 338) in ingredients and form—named for Joe. Depending on which legend you believe, the "froggers" part of the name may have come from the shape the cookies made when fried in a skillet, their form resembling the frogs in a nearby pond. Since the cookies were a popular treat for fishermen, the most likely source is that "floggers"—slang for a pancake stuffed with dried fruit that was part of a ship's provisions on Atlantic voyages—evolved into froggers over time because it sounded better.

Their popularity with fishermen on long fishing trips also had a lot to do with the fact that the cookies contained no eggs or dairy, so they kept for weeks, and they used rum, arguably the most popular drink among fishermen of the time. Though details of the original recipe cite the cookies as being made in a skillet, the original recipe doesn't exist, so it has morphed into a baked cookie. To preserve the large size of the originals, these cookies are cut into 5-inch (13 cm) rounds—according to one cookbook, if you don't have a cutter that size, you can use a coffee can. Though these cookies are cut out from rolled dough, one detail in many old recipes—forming the dough into balls and rolling it in sugar before baking—point to these possibly starting that exterior decorating practice, which dominates modern chewy Ginger-Molasses Cookies (recipe, page 343).

- -

In a medium bowl, whisk together the flour, ginger, cloves, nutmeg, baking soda (bicarb), salt, and allspice. In a glass measuring cup (jug), stir together the molasses, water, and rum.

In a large bowl, with a hand mixer, beat the sugar and butter on medium speed until pale and fluffy, 2–3 minutes. Add one-third of the dry ingredients and half the molasses mixture and beat on the lowest speed until almost combined. Repeat with another third of the dry ingredients and the remaining molasses mixture. Add the remaining dry ingredients and stir until a dough forms and there are no dry patches of flour remaining. Scrape the dough onto a work surface, shape into a ball, wrap in plastic wrap (cling film), and refrigerate for at least 1 hour or up to 2 days.

Position racks in the top and bottom thirds of the oven and preheat the oven to 375°F (190°C/Gas Mark 5). Line two large baking sheets with parchment paper.

Transfer the dough to a lightly floured work surface. Using a lightly floured rolling pin, roll out the dough to ¼ inch (6 mm) thick. Using a 5-inch (13 cm) round cutter, cut out rounds of dough. Reroll the scraps to cut out more cookies. Arrange them on the prepared baking sheets, spaced 2 inches (5 cm) apart.

Bake until the cookies are a shade darker at the edges and just dry to the touch in the center, 12–16 minutes, switching racks and rotating the baking sheets front to back halfway through.

Transfer the baking sheets to wire racks. Let the cookies cool on the pans for 1 minute, then transfer them to the racks to cool completely.

Moravian Spice Cookies

Preparation time: 1 hour 50 minutes,
  plus chilling time
Cooking time: 10 minutes
Makes: About 48 cookies

2 cups (280 g) all-purpose (plain) flour
2 teaspoons ground ginger
1 teaspoon ground cinnamon
1 teaspoon baking soda
  (bicarbonate of soda)
½ teaspoon ground cloves
½ teaspoon fine sea salt
½ cup (160 g) unsulphured molasses
  (not blackstrap)
½ cup (115 g) vegetable
  shortening, softened
⅓ cup (75 g) packed light brown sugar
1 tablespoon brandy
1 teaspoon finely grated lemon zest

The origin of these super-thin and crisp spice cookies is in the name. The followers of the Moravian church brought their baking traditions with them to the US, specifically to their settlements in Winston-Salem, North Carolina, and Bethlehem, Pennsylvania. One of those traditions was making these thin cookies, swapping in the New World's molasses for the Old World's honey.

Though many credit Germany's *Lebkuchen* (recipe, page 247) as the predecessor for this cookie, it's more likely to be the Czechoslovakian *štramberské uši,* a wafer-like honey-and-spice cookie that was as thin and formed into the shape of a cone. This is especially true since the Moravians came from the Kingdom of Bohemia, in the modern-day Czech Republic and Slovakia. For these Moravian spice cookies, the key to their success is in rolling them very thin; they should be crisp and brittle, not thick or crunchy.

In a medium bowl, whisk together the flour, ginger, cinnamon, baking soda (bicarb), cloves, and salt.

In a large bowl, with a hand mixer, combine the molasses, shortening, and sugar and beat on medium speed until light and fluffy, 2–3 minutes. Add the brandy and lemon zest and beat until smooth. Add the dry ingredients and stir until a dough forms and there are no dry patches of flour remaining. Scrape the dough onto a work surface, shape into a ball, wrap in plastic wrap (cling film), and refrigerate for at least 1 hour or up to 2 days.

Position racks in the top and bottom thirds of the oven and preheat the oven to 375°F (190°C/Gas Mark 5). Line two large baking sheets with parchment paper.

Transfer the dough to a lightly floured work surface. Using a lightly floured rolling pin, roll out the dough to ¹⁄₁₆ inch (2 mm) thick. Using a 2½-inch (6.5 cm) round cutter, preferably fluted, cut out rounds of dough. Reroll the scraps to cut out more cookies. Arrange them on the prepared baking sheets, spaced 2 inches (5 cm) apart.

Bake until the cookies are a shade darker at the edges and just dry to the touch in the center, 8–10 minutes, switching racks and rotating the baking sheets front to back halfway through.

Transfer the baking sheets to wire racks. Let the cookies cool on the pans for 1 minute, then transfer them to the racks to cool completely.

Ginger Snaps

Preparation time: 1 hour,
  plus chilling time
Cooking time: 20 minutes
Makes: About 96 cookies

1 cup (320 g) unsulphured
  molasses (not blackstrap)
½ cup (115 g) vegetable
  shortening, softened
1½ tablespoons ground ginger
¾ teaspoon fine sea salt
½ teaspoon ground cinnamon
  (optional)
2 teaspoons pure vanilla
  extract (optional)
1 teaspoon baking soda
  (bicarbonate of soda)
3 cups (420 g) all-purpose
  (plain) flour
Granulated sugar, for
  coating (optional)

These thin, crisp cookies, with their dominant ginger flavor profile, most likely morphed in the US from the similarly textured Moravian Spice Cookies (recipe, page 341) into this "snap" style of cookie we know today. Many of the first recipes for American-style ginger snaps look very similar to those of Moravian spice cookies, save the extra spices. Another likely influence on these cookies was the Slovakian *zazvorniky* (recipe, page 193)—from the same region in Europe as the Moravians—which are made with only ground ginger, and have a distinctive snappy texture from the rising action of baker's ammonia (see page 17), whereas the American cookies get theirs from baking soda (bicarb).

The cookies are thin and crisp, but not brittle like Moravian Spice Cookies, so they shouldn't be rolled quite as thin. The ginger and molasses are the focus of the flavorings here, so this recipe reflects many earlier ones that included no granulated sugar. The lack of sweetness showcases the intensity of the ginger and molasses in these small cookies that makes them worthy of their name. However, there is an option to coat the cookies in sugar before baking, to provide extra sweetness and enhance their characteristic cracked appearance. (Also, vanilla extract and ground cinnamon are sometimes added to help round out the flavor of the ginger, though they are optional.) Many older recipes for ginger snaps use vegetable shortening as the fat for the cookies, and it aids in giving the cookies their characteristic snappy texture. If you use butter, the water content of that fat will make the cookies chewier.

In a small saucepan, combine the molasses, shortening, ginger, salt, and cinnamon (if using). Set over medium heat and cook, stirring, until the shortening melts and the mixture is loose. Remove the pan from the heat and stir in the vanilla (if using) and the baking soda (bicarb). Pour the molasses mixture into a large bowl and let cool for 5 minutes.

Add the flour and stir until a dough forms and there are no dry patches of flour remaining. Scrape the dough onto a clean work surface, shape into a ball, wrap in plastic wrap (cling film), and refrigerate for at least 1 hour or up to 2 days.

Position racks in the top and bottom thirds of the oven and preheat the oven to 375°F (190°C/Gas Mark 5). Line two large baking sheets with parchment paper.

Transfer the dough to a lightly floured work surface. Using a lightly floured rolling pin, roll out the dough to ⅛ inch (3 mm) thick. Using a 2-inch (5 cm) round cutter, cut out rounds of dough. Reroll the scraps to cut out more cookies. Arrange them on the prepared baking sheets, spaced 2 inches (5 cm) apart. If you like, spread some sugar out on a plate and place each dough round in the sugar, flipping to coat on both sides, before baking.

Bake until the cookies are a shade darker at the edges and dry to the touch in the center, 8–10 minutes, switching racks and rotating the baking sheets front to back halfway through.

Transfer the baking sheets to wire racks. Let the cookies cool on the pans for 1 minute, then transfer them to the racks to cool completely.

Ginger-Molasses Cookies

Preparation time: 40 minutes,
  plus chilling time
Cooking time: 10 minutes
Makes: About 12 cookies

1½ cups (210 g) all-purpose
  (plain) flour
1½ teaspoons baking soda
  (bicarbonate of soda)
1 teaspoon baking powder
4 tablespoons finely chopped
  candied ginger
1 tablespoon ground ginger
1 teaspoon ground cinnamon
½ teaspoon ground allspice
½ teaspoon fine sea salt
1 stick (4 oz/113 g) unsalted butter,
  at room temperature
½ cup (110 g) packed dark brown sugar
¼ cup (80 g) unsulphured molasses
  (not blackstrap)
1 large egg
Turbinado (demerara) sugar,
  for coating

With its thick, chewy texture and crunchy sugar coating, this has become the ideal cookie of fall and the holidays in the US. But like many American cookies, its origins are in the UK. It was likely descended from the Cornish Fairing (recipe, page 279)—many modern recipes for that cookie swap white sugar for brown sugar and add syrup-packed ginger or candied ginger to their recipes, giving them even more chew.

When the cookie came to the US, British golden syrup was swapped for Yankee molasses, which made them even chewier, as does, today, the addition of chopped candied ginger. This cookie takes the gingerbread idea (read more in the essay on Gingerbread, page 328) and applies it to American-style sugar cookies that descended from the baking customs of Dutch and Scandinavian immigrants. Nowadays, the simple granulated sugar coating on the outside is often replaced by a crunchy crackling of the coarser turbinado (demerara) sugar.

In a large bowl, whisk together the flour, baking soda (bicarb), baking powder, candied ginger, ground ginger, cinnamon, allspice, and salt.

In a medium bowl, with a hand mixer, beat the butter, brown sugar, and molasses on medium speed until smooth and fluffy, 2–3 minutes. Add the egg and beat until smooth. Add the dry ingredients and mix until a dough forms and there are no dry patches of flour remaining. Cover the bowl with plastic wrap and refrigerate the dough for at least 2 hours or preferably overnight.

Position racks in the top and bottom thirds of the oven and preheat the oven to 375°F (190°C/Gas Mark 5). Line two large baking sheets with parchment paper.

Spread out a layer of turbinado (demerara) sugar on a large plate or pie dish. Using a 1½-ounce (3-tablespoon) ice cream scoop, portion the dough and roll into balls. Roll each ball in the turbinado sugar to coat. Arrange the balls on the prepared baking sheets, spaced 3 inches (7.5 cm) apart. Using the palm of your hand, flatten each ball slightly into a thick disc.

Bake until the cookies are slightly darker brown at the edges and cracked all over on top, 8–10 minutes, switching racks and rotating the baking sheets front to back halfway through.

Transfer the baking sheets to wire racks. Let the cookies cool on the pans for 1 minute, then transfer them to the racks to cool completely.

Peanut Butter Cookies

Preparation time: 1 hour
Cooking time: 15 minutes
Makes: About 24 cookies

1 stick (4 oz/115 g) unsalted
 butter, softened
½ cup (130 g) smooth peanut
 butter (see headnote)
½ cup (100 g) white US granulated
 (UK caster) sugar
½ cup (110 g) packed light
 brown sugar
1 egg
¾ teaspoon baking soda
 (bicarbonate of soda)
½ teaspoon fine sea salt
1 teaspoon pure vanilla extract
1½ cups (210 g) all-purpose
 (plain) flour
½ cup (75 g) salted roasted peanuts,
 finely chopped (optional)

Many recipes at the beginning of the twentieth century reference "peanut cookies" thanks to George Washington Carver's 1925 text *How to Grow the Peanut and 105 Ways of Preparing It for Human Consumption*. These resembled simple drop cookies containing chopped peanuts only and the curious addition of lemon juice (see the variation for this "first" peanut butter cookie that follows). It wasn't until commercially made peanut butter was developed in the 1930s that cookies using the product began appearing. Using these creamy peanut butters was popularized because of the sweetness and smooth, chewy texture they lent to the cookies.

Since the recipes were actually developed using industrially processed peanut butters—which don't separate into oil and solids—those peanut butters perform best here. If you use a peanut butter that must be stirred beforehand, it will affect the texture and make the finished cookies slightly greasy. Though forks had historically been used to press cookies flat, the crosshatch fork pattern gave the peanut butter cookie a distinctive appearance that remains instantly recognizable today. Adding chopped peanuts to these cookies is a matter of taste, so they are included here as an optional ingredient.

Position racks in the top and bottom thirds of the oven and preheat the oven to 375°F (190°C/Gas Mark 5). Line two large baking sheets with parchment paper.

In a large bowl, with a hand mixer, combine the butter, peanut butter, white US granulated (UK caster) sugar, and brown sugar and beat on medium speed until light and fluffy, 2–3 minutes. Add the egg and beat until smooth. Beat in the baking soda (bicarb), salt, and vanilla. Add the flour and peanuts (if using) and stir until a dough forms and there are no dry patches of flour remaining.

Using a 1-ounce (2-tablespoon) ice cream scoop, portion the dough and roll into balls. Arrange them on the prepared baking sheets, spaced at least 2 inches (5 cm) apart. Use the tines of a fork to press each dough ball in a north-south direction, then turn 90 degrees and press in an east-west direction, flattening each ball into a disc ½ inch (13 mm) thick and creating a crosshatch pattern on top.

Bake until golden brown at the edges and dry to the touch in the center, 10–12 minutes, switching racks and rotating the baking sheets front to back halfway through.

Transfer the baking sheets to wire racks. Let the cookies cool on the pans for 1 minute, then transfer them to the racks to cool completely.

Variation
Old-Fashioned Peanut Cookies
In a medium bowl, beat together 2 tablespoons (30 g) softened unsalted butter with ¼ cup (50 g) white US granulated (UK caster) sugar until smooth. Beat in 1 egg and ½ teaspoon fresh lemon juice. Add ½ cup (70 g) all-purpose (plain) flour, ½ teaspoon baking powder, and ¼ teaspoon fine sea salt. Stir in ½ cup (60 g) finely chopped roasted peanuts. Drop by the tablespoon onto parchment paper-lined baking sheets, spaced 2 inches (5 cm) apart. Bake at 350°F (180°C/Gas Mark 4) until golden brown, 8–10 minutes. Transfer to racks to cool completely.

Peanut Butter Cookies

Chocolate Chip Cookies

Preparation time: 45 minutes
Cooking time: 15 minutes
Makes: About 24 cookies

2 sticks (8 oz/225 g) unsalted
 butter, softened
¾ cup (170 g) packed light
 brown sugar
¾ cup (150 g) white US granulated
 (UK caster) sugar
2 eggs, lightly beaten
1 teaspoon baking soda
 (bicarbonate of soda)
1 teaspoon hot tap water
1 teaspoon fine sea salt
1 teaspoon pure vanilla extract
14 oz (395 g) semisweet
 chocolate candy bars
2¼ cups (315 g) all-purpose
 (plain) flour, sifted
1 cup (120 g) finely chopped walnuts

Though she may not have been the first person to mix chopped chocolate into a drop cookie batter, Ruth Wakefield—who ran the Toll House Inn in Whitman, Massachusetts, in the 1930s—made the practice popular. The batter for the chocolate chip cookie looks like that of a standard Hermit drop cookie (recipe, page 352) from the era without spices. Brown sugar, a convenience mix of the oft-used molasses/white sugar combo in cookie recipes, is used and the cookie's leavening comes from baking soda (bicarb), here dissolved in water instead of getting mixed with the flour. The inclusion of walnuts in the original chocolate chip cookie also points to the cookies likely descending from Hermits, as another legend states Wakefield found herself out of raisins—often mixed with walnuts in hermits—so she chopped up a chocolate bar as a substitute. In fact, early names of this cookie were "chocolate chip drop cookies" and "Toll House chocolate crunch cookies."

Countless chocolate chip cookie recipes have since materialized, many playing with the oven temperature, doneness of the dough, and/or proportions of sugar, salt, chocolate, and flour—all in pursuit of some new texture or flavor enhancer to make the "best" of this iconic cookie. Cookies made with other chocolate-like mix-ins—chocolate candies, white chocolate chips (often with macadamia nuts), chopped peanut butter cups—have all based themselves on this same basic cookie dough. The recipe here reflects Wakefield's first, which is slightly cakier than modern tastes go for and doesn't call for chocolate chips, but rather chocolate bars chopped into "pieces the size of a pea." You can use the same weight of chocolate chips, though, if you prefer. The popularity of using their bars in these cookies caused Nestlé to manufacture morsels of chocolate for the express use of making the cookies. Nestlé placed Wakefield's recipe on the back of the bag, and the rest is history.

Position racks in the top and bottom thirds of the oven and preheat the oven to 375°F (190°C/Gas Mark 5). Line two large baking sheets with parchment paper.

In a large bowl, with a hand mixer, combine the butter, brown sugar, and white US granulated (UK caster) sugar and beat on medium speed until light and fluffy, 2–3 minutes. Add the eggs and beat until smooth. In a small bowl, dissolve the baking soda (bicarb) in the water, then pour into the bowl along with the salt and vanilla and beat to combine.

Roughly chop the chocolate until it forms pieces roughly between ¼ and ½ inch (6 and 13 mm); if you like, place the chocolate in a medium sieve or colander and shake to get rid of the chocolate "dust" that occurs when chopping it. Add the chocolate pieces to the bowl along with the flour and walnuts and stir until a dough forms and there are no dry patches of flour remaining.

Using a 1-ounce (2-tablespoon) ice cream scoop, portion the dough and roll into balls. Arrange them on the prepared baking sheets, spaced 2 inches (5 cm) apart.

Bake until golden brown at the edges and dry to the touch in the center, 10–12 minutes, switching racks and rotating the baking sheets front to back halfway through.

Transfer the baking sheets to wire racks. Let the cookies cool on the pans for 1 minute, then transfer them to the racks to cool completely.

Chocolate Chip Cookies

Sugar Cookies

Preparation time: 45 minutes
Cooking time: 15 minutes
Makes: About 12 cookies

2 cups (280 g) all-purpose (plain) flour
1 teaspoon baking powder
1 teaspoon fine sea salt
2 cups (400 g) white US granulated
  (UK caster) sugar, plus more for rolling
2 sticks (8 oz/225 g) unsalted
  butter, softened
2 eggs
2 teaspoons pure vanilla extract

Though it may seem plain to the naked eye, the sugar cookie has a deep history (see Cookie Texture Transformations, opposite). This recipe is meant to reflect the modern American sugar cookie that evolved through centuries to attain all the characteristics many bakers in the US and around the world now expect of a cookie. The dough is formed into balls and then rolled in granulated sugar, so that when the dough bakes up, it creates light cracks on the surface and the sugar adds a delicate crunch. The cookies are also slightly underbaked, so they achieve that chewy-on-the-edges, soft-in-the-center quality everyone is after today.

Position racks in the top and bottom thirds of the oven and preheat the oven to 375°F (190°C/Gas Mark 5). Line two large baking sheets with parchment paper.

In a medium bowl, whisk together the flour, baking powder, and salt.

In a large bowl, with a hand mixer, beat the sugar and butter on medium speed until light and fluffy, 2–3 minutes. Add the eggs, one at a time, beating until smooth after each addition. Beat in the vanilla. Add the dry ingredients and stir until a dough forms and there are no dry patches of flour remaining.

Spread out more sugar on a large plate. Using a 2-ounce (4-tablespoon) ice cream scoop, portion the dough and drop each piece of dough in the sugar, rolling it to coat and form into a ball. Arrange the sugar-coated dough balls at least 3 inches (7.5 cm) apart on the prepared baking sheets. Using the palm of your hand or the bottom of a drinking glass, flatten each dough ball into a disc ½ inch (13 mm) thick; they will spread out.

Bake until lightly golden brown at the edges and just dry to the touch in the center, 12–16 minutes, depending on your preference for either slightly underbaked centers or more crispy edges.

Transfer the baking sheets to wire racks. Let the cookies cool on the pans for 1 minute, then transfer them to the racks to cool completely.

Cookie Texture Transformations

For the greater part of history, cookies and biscuits were dry and crumbly by design. Cookies that were dry stayed fresh longer and could easily be reinvigorated with a sip of coffee, tea, or wine. The primary ingredients were flour and sugar, then butter, which made things richer. Once eggs were added, they made cookies fluffier and more tender. Many cookies of Europe, if they weren't crumbly and dry, were cakey and dry.

Once those European cookies crossed over the Atlantic Ocean to the United States, things in the cookie world got a lot chewier. This coincided with chemical leaveners like baking soda (bicarb) and baking powder replacing older leaveners like baker's ammonia and potassium carbonate (see page 17), the latter of which often dried out dough and made it crisp. It also coincided with the rise in processed granulated white sugar being cheaper and more available to home cooks. At the same time, America's sweet tooth started to rise and cookies got sweeter. This was likely brought on by the popularity of chocolate chip cookies (recipe, page 346), which switched people's association with cookies from nut-, candied fruit- and spice-based morsels to more confection-based (chocolate chips, candies, etc.) treats. As the sugar levels rose, so did the effect it had on other ingredients in cookies, namely the eggs, combining to make a chewy texture.

This evolution of cookies plays out most evidently in the modern American "sugar" cookie (recipe, opposite). It marked a moment where bakers in the US firmly broke away from European traditions and made a cookie of their own. It had a chewy texture and a relatively "plain" flavor profile of just butter, vanilla, and the pure sweetness of white sugar—though it didn't start that way.

The first instance of what could be called a sugar cookie started with what would come to be called "jumbles," tiny cookie-like cakes made in the late seventeenth and early eighteenth centuries. The very first recipes documented a dough made of butter, sugar, flour, and eggs that was kneaded for several minutes, shaped into ropes, and then twisted into knots, sometimes boiled, then baked until hard. Many theorize the name comes from the jumble of dough that made it easier for people to break apart and soften a bite at a time in tea. These jumbles were often flavored with caraway seeds, rose water, or lemon juice.

Moravian immigrants who settled the town of Nazareth, Pennsylvania, in 1740 came with their Central European baking traditions. They most likely adapted cookies similar to German *Vanillebrezeln* (recipe, page 254), along with the jumbles, into what looks like the more modern sugar cookie, doing away with the spices and long kneading that made the jumbles tough. Separately, "sand tarts" (see page 322) descended from Scandinavian butter cookies that were more like gingerbread without molasses or spices. (Nowadays, that similar dough is used to make "sugar cookie cut-outs" for decorating with icing.)

Once chemical leaveners became widely used in the late 1800s, the final form of the sugar cookie began to take shape. The use of baking powder specifically made it possible to not have to use acidic ingredients like molasses, cream of tartar, and lemon juice reacting with baking soda, so white sugar could be used alone. For decades, the proportions of sugar to butter or shortening in many cookie recipes were one-to-one. When sugar became a larger proportion (typically double that of the fat) and with more eggs being used, American cookies became denser and chewier and that is their defining characteristic today. Exactly when that detail happened is difficult to pinpoint, but it brought about a renaissance in American cookie-making that changed the way these treats are made to this day in the US.

Snickerdoodles

Preparation time: 45 minutes
Cooking time: 15 minutes
Makes: About 30 cookies

2¾ cups (390 g) all-purpose
  (plain) flour
2 teaspoons cream of tartar
1 teaspoon baking soda
  (bicarbonate of soda)
¾ teaspoon fine sea salt
1¾ cups (350 g) white US granulated
  (UK caster) sugar
2 sticks (8 oz/225 g) unsalted
  butter, softened
2 eggs
1 teaspoon pure vanilla extract
1 tablespoon ground cinnamon

These chewy cinnamon-sugar cookies are likely an evolution of a number of baking trends from the late 1800s. For example, the Moravian settlers of Nazareth, Pennsylvania—who had a hand in giving us the American sugar cookie (see page 349)—made what they called "Nazareth sugar cakes." These resembled an American cinnamon bun dough that was pressed into a pan and topped with a cinnamon-sugar filling, instead of being rolled up. Then there were, *Schneckennudel,* or "snail buns," which are German yeasted sweet breads that resemble modern cinnamon rolls and were often made with raisins and nuts laced with cinnamon. Some old references to the name "Snickerdoodles" describe a "sweet biscuit" made with raisins that was a specialty of the Pennsylvania Dutch, pointing to the likely naming quagmire that caused bakers, over many decades of playing the telephone game, to mishear *schneckennudel* as "snickerdoodle." At the same time, Scandinavian "sand tarts" (see page 322) were also being made with their topping of cinnamon-sugar (though they were distinctly crispy, brittle cookies).

It's most likely that all of these baked goods combined and evolved in the slow march of time over the decades to become the Snickerdoodle cookie of today. Whereas modern sugar cookies took on a new life with baking powder, the Snickerdoodle retained its vintage detail of mixing cream of tartar with baking soda (bicarb), to give the cookies their spread-out, cracked top that has become their defining characteristic in appearance and flavor (with the cinnamon-sugar coating).

Position racks in the top and bottom thirds of the oven and preheat the oven to 400°F (200°C/Gas Mark 6). Line two large baking sheets with parchment paper.

In a medium bowl, whisk together the flour, cream of tartar, baking soda (bicarb), and salt.

In a large bowl, with a hand mixer, combine 1½ cups (300 g) sugar and the butter and beat on medium speed until light and fluffy, 2–3 minutes. Add the eggs, one at a time, beating until smooth after each addition. Beat in the vanilla. Add the dry ingredients and stir until a dough forms and there are no dry patches of flour remaining.

In a small bowl, mix together the remaining ¼ cup (50 g) sugar with the cinnamon to make cinnamon-sugar. Using a 1-ounce (2-tablespoon) ice cream scoop, portion the dough and roll into balls. Roll the dough balls in the cinnamon-sugar to coat and then arrange them on the prepared baking sheets, spaced at least 3 inches (7.5 cm) apart. Using the palm of your hand or the bottom of a drinking glass, flatten each dough ball into a disc ½ inch (13 mm) thick.

Bake until lightly golden brown at the edges and just dry to the touch in the center, 10–12 minutes, switching racks and rotating the baking sheets front to back halfway through.

Transfer the baking sheets to wire racks. Let the cookies cool on the pans for 1 minute, then transfer them to the racks to cool completely.

Snickerdoodles

Hermits

Preparation time: 15 minutes
Cooking time: 15 minutes
Makes: About 18 cookies

2 cups (280 g) all-purpose (plain) flour
1 teaspoon ground cinnamon
½ teaspoon freshly grated nutmeg
¾ teaspoon fine sea salt
¼ teaspoon ground allspice (optional)
¼ teaspoon ground cloves (optional)
1¼ cups (280 g) packed light
 brown sugar
1 stick (4 oz/115 g) unsalted
 butter, softened
1 egg
½ teaspoon baking soda
 (bicarbonate of soda)
2 tablespoons milk or water
1 cup (115 g) walnuts or pecans,
 finely chopped
¾ cup (125 g) raisins

So ingrained in the modern American psyche is the combination of molasses and spices like ginger, cinnamon, and cloves that if presented with a cookie that had one but not the other, American bakers would feel like something is missing. That's the theory for how modern Hermit cookies ended up looking nothing like their predecessor. Early recipes for Hermit cookies consisted of a brown sugar drop cookie dough teeming with chopped nuts and raisins. The cookies had spices though, often cinnamon and nutmeg with various levels of allspice and cloves added. The dough was dropped onto baking sheets and baked as a round mound. But as is the modern American baker's want with spiced cookies, molasses somehow made its way into the mix.

Hermits are popular in the northeastern US where molasses has long been used in savory and sweet dishes (see Molasses and Sugar Syrups, page 307), so it makes sense that somewhere along the way, home bakers added some to the batter to accentuate what was already in the brown sugar. But more curious is how the dough got shaped into logs, baked, then sliced into bars. Scandinavian cookies like *kolasnittar* (recipe, page 312) and *muskotsnittar* (recipe, page 312) are formed in a similar fashion and have comparable ingredients, so the modern version could have also been influenced by American bakers from those regions during the evolution of the cookie over time.

In *Maida Heatter's Cookies*, American cookbook author Heatter gives two recipes for slice-/"strip"-style cookies—Connecticut Date Slices and Connecticut Strippers—that resemble the European *snittar* cookies and the modern Hermits. Whatever the case, both cookies, as distinct as they are, highlight how a single cookie can change over time, adapting to different ingredients, in different regions, and with different cooks, so both the original and the modern bar variation are given here.

Position racks in the top and bottom thirds of the oven and preheat the oven to 375°F (190°C/Gas Mark 5). Line two large baking sheets with parchment paper.

In a medium bowl, whisk together the flour, cinnamon, nutmeg, salt, allspice (if using), and cloves (if using).

In a large bowl, with a hand mixer, beat the sugar and butter on medium speed until light and fluffy, 2–3 minutes. Add the egg and beat until smooth. In a small bowl, dissolve the baking soda (bicarb) in the milk or water, then pour into the bowl. Beat to combine. Add the flour mixture, nuts, and raisins and stir until a dough forms and there are no dry patches of flour remaining.

Using a 1-ounce (2-tablespoon) ice cream scoop, drop the dough on the prepared baking sheets, spaced at least 2 inches (5 cm) apart.

Bake until golden brown at the edges and dry to the touch in the center, 12–14 minutes, switching racks and rotating the baking sheets front to back halfway through.

Transfer the baking sheets to wire racks. Let the cookies cool on the pans for 1 minute, then transfer them to the racks to cool completely.

Variation
Modern Hermit Bar
Double the spices (including the optional ones) and baking soda (bicarb), add 1 teaspoon ground ginger, and whisk them all with the flour and salt. Omit the milk or water and add ¼ cup (80 g) unsulphured molasses (not blackstrap) in its place. Omit the nuts, if you like, and substitute the same amount of finely chopped candied ginger for the raisins. Divide the dough in half and shape each half into a log 12 inches (30 cm) long. Bake the logs on separate baking sheets until a shade darker at the edges and just dry to the touch in the center, 20–24 minutes (they should be slightly underdone in the center). Make a glaze by mixing 1 cup (135 g) powdered (icing) sugar and 2 tablespoons rum, milk, or lemon juice until smooth. Pour over the cooled cookie logs. Let the glaze set and then cut the logs into bars 1½ inches (4 cm) wide to serve.

Oatmeal-Raisin Cookies

Preparation time: 25 minutes,
  plus 30 minutes chilling time
Cooking time: 20 minutes
Makes: About 26 cookies

1½ cups (145 g) rolled oats
2 cups (280 g) all-purpose (plain) flour
1½ teaspoons ground cinnamon
1 teaspoon baking soda
  (bicarbonate of soda)
¾ teaspoon fine sea salt
½ teaspoon baking powder
2 sticks (8 oz/225 g) unsalted
  butter, softened
1 cup (200 g) white US granulated
  (UK caster) sugar
1 cup (225 g) packed light brown sugar
2 eggs
2 teaspoons pure vanilla extract
1 cup (165 g) raisins

These cookies are a clear descendant of Scottish, Irish, and English oatcakes or Oatmeal Biscuits (recipe, page 272). On American shores though, the dense cakes cooked on a griddle transformed into the chewy cookies most people expect today. The addition of chemical leavening also made them lighter. The marketing of oats as a convenient, fiber-filled "health food" by the Quaker Oats Company around the beginning of the twentieth century sparked the popularity of oats in numerous American food items, particularly cookies.

Many of the first recipes for these new oatmeal cookies didn't include raisins—in fact some called for grated coconut, dates, or chopped chocolate as mix-ins—but because of the "health" connotation of oats and also raisins, it's easy to see how the raisins made their way into these cinnamon-laced cookies, becoming inextricably linked today.

Position racks in the top and bottom thirds of the oven and preheat the oven to 350°F (180°C/Gas Mark 4). Line two large baking sheets with parchment paper.

In a food processor, pulse the oats until roughly ground, about 6 pulses. Pour the oats into a medium bowl and add the flour, cinnamon, baking soda (bicarb), salt, and baking powder and whisk to combine.

In a large bowl, with a hand mixer, combine the butter, white US granulated (UK caster) sugar, and brown sugar and beat on medium speed until light and fluffy, 2–3 minutes. Add the eggs, one at a time, beating until smooth after each addition. Beat in the vanilla. Add the flour mixture and raisins and stir until a dough forms and there are no dry patches of flour remaining.

Using a 1-ounce (2-tablespoon) ice cream scoop, portion the dough and roll into balls. Arrange them on the prepared baking sheets, spaced at least 2 inches (5 cm) apart. Refrigerate the baking sheets for 30 minutes.

Bake until golden brown at the edges and dry to the touch in the center, 16–18 minutes, switching racks and rotating the baking sheets front to back halfway through.

Transfer the baking sheets to wire racks. Let the cookies cool on the pans for 1 minute, then transfer them to the racks to cool completely.

Small Anise and Cinnamon Cookies

Bizcochitos

Preparation time: 1 hour 10 minutes,
  plus chilling time
Cooking time: 20 minutes
Makes: About 36 cookies

1½ teaspoons anise seeds
2 cups (300 g) whole wheat
  (wholemeal) flour
1 cup (140 g) all-purpose (plain) flour
1 teaspoon baking powder
¾ teaspoon fine sea salt
1 cup (225 g) cold-rendered leaf lard
1 cup (200 g) white US granulated
  (UK caster) sugar
¼ cup (2 fl oz/60 ml) brandy or water
1 teaspoon ground cinnamon

In 1989, these distinctive New Mexican cookies became the first official state cookie in the US. A descendant of Spanish *polvorones* (recipe, page 97) and *bizcochos*, a classification of sweet breads and cakes in Spain, these cookies have a long history in the state. Similar to crisp gingerbread-style cookies, they are made with pork lard, flavored with anise seeds, and sometimes dipped in cinnamon-sugar. Water is added to bring the dough together, though many modern recipes call for brandy or sweet wine (such as Marsala or Moscato) to complement the rest of the flavors.

In *Classic Home Desserts*, author Richard Sax includes an account from Fabiola Cabeza de Baca Gilbert's *The Good Life: New Mexico Traditions and Food* in which the cook Seña Martina makes these anise cookies with only whole wheat (wholemeal) flour. Many recipes substitute all-purpose (plain) flour for a portion of the whole wheat flour, so the cookies retain a pleasant texture. This recipe keeps a larger proportion of whole wheat flour to preserve the intention of Martina's recipe.

Using a spice grinder or small blender, process the anise seeds until finely ground and set aside. In a medium bowl, whisk together the whole wheat (wholemeal) flour, all-purpose (plain) flour, baking powder, and salt.

In a large bowl, with a hand mixer, combine the lard, ¾ cup (150 g) of the sugar, and the ground anise seeds and beat on medium speed until very light and fluffy, 4–6 minutes. Add half the dry ingredients and the brandy and beat on low speed until almost combined. Add the remaining dry ingredients and stir until a dough forms and there are no dry patches of flour remaining. Scrape the dough onto a clean work surface, shape into a disc, wrap in plastic wrap (cling film), and refrigerate for at least 1 hour or up to 2 days.

Position racks in the top and bottom thirds of the oven and preheat the oven to 350°F (180°C/Gas Mark 4). Line two large baking sheets with parchment paper.

Transfer the dough to a lightly floured work surface and let it stand for about 5 minutes to take the chill off the dough. Using a lightly floured rolling pin, roll out the dough to ⅛ inch (3 mm) thick. Using a 2½-inch (6.5 cm) square, star, or round cutter, cut out shapes of dough. Arrange them on the prepared baking sheets, spaced 2 inches (5 cm) apart. Reroll the scraps to cut out more shapes.

Bake until the cookies are golden brown at the edges and dry to the touch in the center, 18–20 minutes, switching racks and rotating the baking sheets front to back halfway through.

Meanwhile, on a small plate, combine the remaining ¼ cup sugar with the cinnamon.

Transfer the baking sheets to wire racks and let the cookies cool on the pans for 1 minute. While the cookies are still hot, dip the top of each in the cinnamon-sugar and transfer the cookies, right-side up, to the racks to cool completely.

Benne Wafers

Preparation time: 45 minutes
Cooking time: 15 minutes
Makes: About 36 cookies

1 cup (150 g) sesame seeds, toasted
1 cup (140 g) all-purpose (plain) flour
½ teaspoon baking soda
  (bicarbonate of soda)
½ teaspoon fine sea salt
½ cup (100 g) white US granulated
  (UK caster) sugar
⅓ cup (75 g) packed light brown sugar
4 tablespoons (2 oz/55 g) unsalted
  butter, softened
4 tablespoons (55 g) vegetable
  shortening, softened
1 egg
1 teaspoon pure vanilla extract

These crisp sesame seed cookies have a long history. Sesame seeds came to the US with enslaved Africans, who called them benne, and their use proliferated in the South. Black cooks mixed sesame seeds into all sorts of dishes, particularly these cookies, which are a specialty of the Gullah Geechee people in South Carolina. The sesame seeds provide a nuttiness to the otherwise simple brown sugar drop cookies that bake into a crisp disc.

The word *benne* comes from the Bantu word for "sesame," and you can find savory benne wafers, which are a popular appetizer cracker in Charleston used for serving with dips, cheese, and relishes. Those small savory crackers, about 1¼ inches (3 cm) across, are made in the style of pie dough (shortcrust pastry)—cold fat cut into flour, then mixed to create flaky layers—while these sweet versions are made slightly larger and with soft fat mixed with sugar, to produce light and airy, crisp-edged cookies.

- -

Position racks in the top and bottom thirds of the oven and preheat the oven to 350°F (180°C/Gas Mark 4). Line two large baking sheets with parchment paper.

In a medium bowl, whisk together the sesame seeds, flour, baking soda (bicarb), and salt.

In a large bowl, with a hand mixer, combine the white US granulated (UK caster) sugar, brown sugar, butter, and shortening and beat on medium speed until light and fluffy, 2–3 minutes. Add the egg and vanilla and beat until smooth. Add the dry ingredients and stir until a dough forms and there are no dry patches of flour remaining.

Using a ½-ounce (1-tablespoon) ice cream scoop, portion the dough and roll into balls. Arrange them on the prepared baking sheets, spaced at least 2 inches (5 cm) apart.

Bake until golden brown at the edges and dry to the touch in the center, 10–12 minutes, switching racks and rotating the baking sheets front to back halfway through.

Transfer the baking sheets to wire racks. Let the cookies cool on the pans for 1 minute, then transfer them to the racks to cool completely.

Chinese Almond Cookies

Preparation time: 45 minutes
Cooking time: 15 minutes
Makes: About 18 cookies

1¼ cups (175 g) all-purpose (plain) flour
½ teaspoon baking soda
  (bicarbonate of soda)
½ teaspoon fine sea salt
1 stick (4 oz/115 g) unsalted
  butter, softened
½ cup (100 g) white US granulated
  (UK caster) sugar
1 egg
¾ teaspoon pure almond extract
Egg wash: 1 egg yolk beaten with
  1 tablespoon water
Sliced (flaked) almonds, for decorating

Because of the omnipresence of Chinese-American take-out restaurants in the United States, many people consider the fortune cookie as the quintessential Chinese American cookie. Those cookies, however, aren't made at home, while these almond cookies are. Almond cookies in China exist in the form of Macau-style cookies, which are typically factory-made and stamped ornately like moon cakes and made with mung bean flour. They were once formed in the shape of an almond, but not flavored with it, though now the Macau-style almond cookies do incorporate almonds.

When Chinese immigrants came to the United States, they brought the Macau-style cookie and adapted it to the recipe for Chinese cookies called *hup toh soh* (recipe, page 393). The result was these simple butter cookies flavored with almonds that are served at Chinese take-out restaurants. Some bakers now add some almonds to the dough or make them fully out of ground almonds. But the "traditional" recipe typically only uses almond extract, which has a more pronounced almond flavor than even the fresh ones, and uses sliced (flaked) almonds to decorate the tops.

Position racks in the top and bottom thirds of the oven and preheat the oven to 350°F (180°C/Gas Mark 4). Line two large baking sheets with parchment paper.

In a medium bowl, whisk together the flour, baking soda (bicarb), and salt.

In a large bowl, with a hand mixer, beat the butter and sugar on medium speed until light and fluffy, 2–3 minutes. Add the egg and beat until smooth. Beat in the almond extract. Add the dry ingredients and stir until a dough forms and there are no dry patches of flour remaining.

Using a ¾-ounce (1½-tablespoon) ice cream scoop, portion the dough and roll into balls. Arrange them on the prepared baking sheets, spaced at least 2 inches (5 cm) apart. Lightly brush the top of each cookie with some of the egg wash and place a slice of almond on the top in the center of each dough ball.

Bake until golden brown and dry to the touch in the center, 12–14 minutes, switching racks and rotating the baking sheets front to back halfway through.

Transfer the baking sheets to wire racks. Let the cookies cool on the pans for 1 minute, then transfer them to the racks to cool completely.

Rugelach

Preparation time: 30 minutes,
  plus chilling time
Cooking time: 30 minutes
Makes: 48 cookies

For the dough:
8 oz (225 g) full-fat cream cheese
2 sticks (8 oz/225 g) unsalted
  butter, softened
½ teaspoon fine sea salt
2 cups (280 g) all-purpose
  (plain) flour, sifted

For the filling:
½ cup (100 g) plus 2 tablespoons
  white US granulated
  (UK caster) sugar
1 tablespoon ground cinnamon
3 tablespoons (45 g) unsalted
  butter, melted
¾ cup (95 g) dried currants
1¼ cups (140 g) walnuts,
  finely chopped

To finish:
Egg wash: 1 egg yolk beaten with
  1 teaspoon water
Sanding sugar, pearl sugar, or more
  sugar, for decorating

Depending on the translation, the name of these world-famous Jewish crescent-shaped cookies comes from Yiddish for "little corners," "little royals," or "little horns." They are an iconic staple of Jewish cuisine. Popularly baked and served for Hanukkah and other Jewish holidays, these rolled crescent-shaped cookies are traditionally filled with walnuts and cinnamon-sugar, though apricot or raspberry jam, dried fruit like raisins or currants, poppy seeds, and prune butter are also used; chocolate is also a popular filling today. Rugelach descend from the same crescent-shaped, sweet, bread-like cookie- or pastry-like foodstuffs of Eastern Europe (see Crescents, page 82)—typically and collectively referred to as *Kipfel*, owing to their Austro-Hungarian origins. Other cookies like Polish *kołaczki* (recipe, page 186), Hungarian *hókifli* (recipe, page 202), Romanian *cornulețe cu gem* (recipe, page 208), and the yeasted Ukrainian *rohalyky* seemed to develop in conjunction with as well as influencing these Jewish cookies.

The tradition of making these rolled pastries came to America with Jewish immigrants, and that is when the cookies became what we know them as today. They lost their yeast, became sweeter, and swapped the sour cream for cream cheese, the latter of which marks them as uniquely American—or New York City Jewish American. The cookie first appeared in its cream cheese form in Mildred O. Knopf's 1950 book *The Perfect Hostess.* Twenty-seven years later, American cookbook author Maida Heatter published the recipe in her 1977 book *Maida Heatter's Book of Great Cookies,* and so is widely credited with popularizing the cookie outside of Jewish immigrant circles. Heatter's grandmother's recipe set a standard used by professional and home bakers alike; this recipe is an adaptation of her original.

Make the dough: In a large bowl, with a hand mixer, combine the cream cheese, butter, and salt and beat on medium speed until creamy and smooth, 1–2 minutes. Add half the flour and beat on low speed until a dough starts to come together. Add the remaining flour and mix with your hands, lightly kneading only as much as needed to no longer see any dry patches of flour in the bowl. Shape the dough into a log, cut the log into thirds, then roll each piece into a ball. Wrap each dough ball in plastic wrap (cling film) and refrigerate for at least 1 hour or up to 2 days.

Position racks in the top and bottom thirds of the oven and preheat the oven to 350°F (180°C/Gas Mark 4). Line two large baking sheets with parchment paper.

Make the filling: In a small bowl, stir together the white US granulated (UK caster) sugar and cinnamon. Working on a lightly floured work surface, place one dough ball on the surface and use a floured rolling pin to roll out the dough into a 12-inch (30 cm) round. Spread 1 tablespoon melted butter over the round and then sprinkle with 3 tablespoons of the cinnamon-sugar. Sprinkle over one-third of the currants followed by one-third of the chopped walnuts. Roll the rolling pin gently over the filling ingredients so they adhere to the dough.

Cut the round into 16 equal wedges. Starting from a wide end, roll up each wedge toward its point. Transfer the crescents, point-side down, to the prepared baking sheets, spaced 2 inches (5 cm) apart. Repeat with the other two balls of dough, butter, cinnamon-sugar, currants, and walnuts to make more crescents.

To finish: Lightly brush all the crescents with some of the egg wash and sprinkle them with sugar.

Bake until golden brown all over, 25–30 minutes, switching racks and rotating the baking sheets front to back halfway through.

Transfer the baking sheets to wire racks. Let the cookies cool on the pans for 1 minute, then transfer them to the racks to cool completely.

Rugelach

Kichel

Preparation time: 1 hour 45 minutes,
 plus 1 hour resting time
Cooking time: 25 minutes
Makes: About 48 cookies

½ cup (4 fl oz/120 ml) vegetable oil
1 teaspoon pure vanilla extract
¾ teaspoon fine sea salt
4 egg yolks
2 eggs
2 cups (400 g) plus 2 teaspoons white
 US granulated (UK caster) sugar
2 cups (280 g) all-purpose (plain) flour

Crusted in sugar and shaped like bow ties or twists, these cookies, known as *kichel*, are a sweet staple of American Jewish bakeries that are often served with pickled herring and schnapps as part of the *kiddush* table in synagogues to begin Shabbat (the sabbath) each week. Their simple name—Yiddish for "cookies"—is likely related to the Austro-Hungarian *Kipfel* (see page 195), which was typically the name ascribed to any pastry that was bent or twisted into a crescent. Though their texture is more akin to sweetened crackers, they are considered cookies.

That snappy, cracker-y characteristic comes from mixing the dough for several minutes to develop the gluten in the flour, giving it a sticky texture akin to challah or brioche dough, which then bakes up light and crisp. The copious amounts of sugar used to roll out the dough and keep it from sticking to the work surface gives the cookies a mottled, sugary shimmer.

In a stand mixer fitted with the paddle, combine the oil, vanilla, salt, egg yolks, whole eggs, and 2 teaspoons of the sugar and beat on low speed to combine. While the mixer is on, slowly add the flour by the spoonful until all of it is added. Continue mixing the dough until it's stretchy and smooth, at least 10 minutes. Remove the bowl from the mixer, cover the bowl with plastic wrap (cling film), and let rest for 1 hour.

Position racks in the top and bottom thirds of the oven and preheat the oven to 350°F (180°C/Gas Mark 4). Line two large baking sheets with parchment paper.

Sprinkle a clean work surface with 1 cup (200 g) of the sugar, keeping it roughly ⅛ inch (3 mm) deep. Scrape the dough onto the sugar (it will be sticky) and then sprinkle the dough with another ½ cup (100 g) sugar. Using your hands, gently press the dough into a rough rectangle, then switch to a rolling pin to roll the dough to ¼ inch (6 mm) thick. Sprinkle the rectangle evenly with the remaining ½ cup (100 g) sugar.

Using a knife or pizza cutter, cut the dough crosswise into strips 1 inch (2.5 cm) wide. Then cut the strips into 2-inch (5 cm) lengths. Pick up each length by its two ends and twist once in the middle. Arrange the lengths on the prepared baking sheets, spaced 1 inch (2.5 cm) apart. Gently press down on each cookie where it twists to keep the cookies from unfurling in the oven.

Bake until the cookies are golden brown and dry to the touch, 20–25 minutes, switching racks and rotating the baking sheets front to back halfway through.

Transfer the baking sheets to wire racks. Let the cookies cool on the pans for 1 minute, then transfer them to the racks to cool completely.

Kichel

southeast asia, east asia & oceania

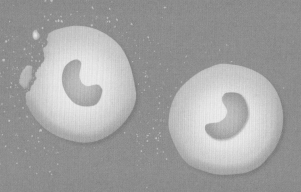

Many cookies in this region are marked distinctly by colonialism: for example, the Dutch in Indonesia and the Spanish in the Philippines. Waffle cookies and sugar-covered shortbreads manifest in the former, while more riffs on shortbread-like *polvorones* dominate in the latter. Native starches and ingredients like sago, tapioca, and coconut are used in place of wheat flour, and other cookies are adapted to deep-frying in street stalls versus baking in home ovens.

Crunchy Sugar Cookies
Gnanakatha

Preparation time: 30 minutes
Cooking time: 15 minutes
Makes: About 12 cookies

1½ cups (215 g) all-purpose
 (plain) flour
1 teaspoon baking powder
½ teaspoon fine sea salt
½ cup (100 g) plus 1 tablespoon white
 US granulated (UK caster) sugar
8 tablespoons (4 oz/115 g) unsalted
 butter, softened
1 egg
1 teaspoon pure vanilla extract
½ cup (100 g) sanding sugar
 or turbinado (demerara) sugar,
 for coating

A specialty of Colombo bakeries, these simple butter cookies—sometimes called "rock sugar cookies"—were historically a store-bought or bakery-made treat in Sri Lanka, but they now are made in home kitchens. Popularly served for Eid, the basic recipe that home bakers use seems to be universal with only the granulation of sugar changing from recipe to recipe.

These cookies, in both name and style, are a cousin to Indian *nankhatai* (recipe, page 37) and their name suggests Portuguese influence in the form of *areias de Cascais* (recipe, page 96). The texture of the cookies is tender but crumbly, emphasized by a coating of sanding sugar on the outside. Some bakers simply use more sugar, but the large grains of sanding sugar produce a sparkling exterior and give the cookies extra crunch and sweetness.

Position racks in the top and bottom thirds of the oven and preheat the oven to 350°F (180°C/Gas Mark 4). Line two large baking sheets with parchment paper.

In a medium bowl, whisk together the flour, baking powder, and salt.

In a large bowl, with a hand mixer, beat the white US granulated (UK caster) sugar and butter on medium speed until light and fluffy, 2–3 minutes. Add the egg and beat until smooth. Beat in the vanilla. Add the dry ingredients and stir until a dough forms and there are no dry patches of flour remaining.

Meanwhile, spread the sanding sugar out on a plate and pour some water in a small bowl. Using a 1-ounce (2-tablespoon) ice cream scoop, portion the dough and roll into balls. Flatten 1 ball in your hand into a disc and dip one side in water, letting the excess drip off before dipping the wet side in the sanding sugar to coat evenly. Invert the dough disc, sugar-side up, and place on the prepared baking sheets. Repeat flattening and dipping the remaining dough balls in the water and sugar. Arrange them on the baking sheets, spaced at least 2 inches (5 cm) apart.

Bake until light golden brown on the bottom and cracked and dry to the touch on top, 12–15 minutes, switching racks and rotating the baking sheets front to back halfway through.

Transfer the baking sheets to wire racks. Let the cookies cool on the pans for 1 minute, then transfer them to the racks to cool completely.

Coconut and Sago Biscuits

Savboro

Preparation time: 30 minutes
Cooking time: 30 minutes
Makes: About 24 cookies

1½ cups (150 g) finely grated coconut,
 fresh or thawed frozen
1¼ cups (160 g) plain dried
 breadcrumbs
1 cup (160 g) small sago pearls
¾ cup (150 g) white US granulated
 (UK caster) sugar
1 teaspoon fennels seeds,
 lightly crushed
½ teaspoon fine sea salt
6–8 tablespoons water

These modern cookies seem to be a riff on the Indonesian/Papuan rusk-type cracker called *sagu lempeng*, once a popular staple with fishermen because it stayed dry for long boat trips. Over time, it seems that sugar was added to the original mix, and bakers have adapted the cracker to be more of a cookie-like baked treat. The sago pearls are mixed with dried breadcrumbs, freshly grated coconut, sugar, and fennel seeds, then moistened with a small amount of water until it forms a cohesive dough.

Like Filipino *polvorón* (recipe, page 376), the dough is pressed into shapes, typically inside a round cookie cutter mold. The cookies are then baked to give them their characteristic crunchy texture akin to the Mexican popped amaranth candy called *alegría*. It makes them the ideal treat to have with tea or coffee. Sago pearls, sometimes labeled "sabudana," are not the same as tapioca pearls, but the latter can be used if you can't find the former; look for sago pearls online or in specialty grocery stores.

- -

Position racks in the top and bottom thirds of the oven and preheat the oven to 325°F (160°C/Gas Mark 3). Line two large baking sheets with parchment paper.

In a large bowl, combine the coconut, breadcrumbs, sago pearls, sugar, fennel seeds, and salt and mix with your hands until evenly incorporated. Add 6 tablespoons of water and massage the mixture until evenly moistened, being sure to scrape the bottom and sides of the bowl with your fingers, too. Pick up a handful of the mixture, make a fist, and if the mixture holds its shape and stays as a clump, it's ready. If it's still too dry, add the remaining 1–2 tablespoons water.

Place a 3-inch (7.5 cm) round cookie cutter on a baking sheet and fill it with 3 tablespoons of the dough. Use a cocktail muddler or the back of a spoon to compress the dough in the mold until it creates a puck ½ inch (13 mm) thick. Gently lift the cutter and continue making more pucks, spaced 1 inch (2.5 cm) apart.

Bake until golden brown and dry to the touch all over, 25–30 minutes, switching racks and rotating the baking sheets front to back halfway through.

Transfer the baking sheets to wire racks. Let the cookies cool on the pans for 1 minute, then transfer them to the racks to cool completely.

Rolled Wafer Cookies

Thong Muan

Preparation time: 30 minutes
Cooking time: 2 hours
Makes: About 36 cookies

3 oz (85 g) Thai coconut palm
  sugar or generous ⅓ cup
  packed dark muscovado sugar
1 teaspoon pure vanilla
  extract (optional)
½ teaspoon fine sea salt
1 egg
1¼ cups (175 g) tapioca starch
½ cup (70 g) all-purpose (plain) flour
¼ cup (40 g) white rice flour
1 can (14 fl oz/400 ml) unsweetened
  full-fat coconut milk
2 tablespoons black sesame seeds

Similar to Indonesian *kue semprong* (recipe, page 384) and Malaysian *kuih kapit* (see page 384), these rolled wafer cookies are a popular street snack in Thailand. Though their recipes are similar, those for these Thai and Laotian cookies typically use less egg, which makes them crispier, and are made with coconut palm sugar, a raw sugar akin to Mexican *piloncillo* and Indian jaggery (see Raw Sugars, page 164) in texture and taste, but made out of coconut, not sugarcane.

There are special molds for making these *thong muan* that have unique prints and markings, but if you can't find one online, a *krumkake* maker or waffle cone iron will work just as well.

- -

Using the small holes of a box grater or a serrated knife, finely grate the palm sugar.

In a large bowl, with a hand mixer, combine the sugar, vanilla (if using), salt, and egg. Beat on medium speed until pale, thickened, and foamy, about 2 minutes.

In a medium bowl, whisk together the tapioca starch, flour, and rice flour. Add the dry ingredients to the wet ingredients and beat on low speed until incorporated. With the mixer on low speed, slowly pour in the coconut milk and continue beating until a smooth batter forms. Stir in the sesame seeds.

Place a krumkake iron over medium heat on your stove or heat an electric krumkake maker. Using a 1-tablespoon measure, pour tablespoonfuls of the batter into the center of the iron. Close the iron and let cook, flipping the iron halfway through, if using the stove, until the batter spreads and sets as a wafer, 2–3 minutes, depending on the heat of your stove (or follow the manufacturer's instructions for the electric maker).

Open the iron and place the end of a narrow wooden spoon at the edge of the iron closest to you. Lift the wafer and then quickly roll it around the spoon handle like a rolled carpet. Slide the rolled wafer off the handle and place on a wire rack to cool. Repeat with the remaining batter to cook and roll more cookies.

Rolled Wafer Cookies

Flower-Shaped Shortbread Cookies

Khanom Kleeb Lamduan

Preparation time: 1 hour 40 minutes,
  plus cooling time and infusing
  time (optional)
Cooking time: 20 minutes
Makes: About 12 cookies

1 cup (140 g) all-purpose (plain) flour
⅓ cup (65 g) white US granulated
  (UK caster) sugar
½ teaspoon fine sea salt
½ cup (115 g) cold-rendered leaf
  lard or vegetable shortening, melted
  and cooled (or vegetable oil)
½ teaspoon rose water or pure
  vanilla extract (optional)
1 tian op (Thai scented
  candle; optional)

These beautiful cookies are named for the flower they mimic, the blossom of the white cheesewood tree, known as *lamduan* in Thailand. Part of a repertoire of classic Thai palace sweets, these cookies traditionally were made with rendered pork lard, sugar, and flour, but modern recipes now swap the lard for vegetable oil. This recipe preserves the original by using lard, but you can use oil or vegetable shortening in its place.

Another unique trait of these cookies is their flavor, which isn't traditionally obtained from an extract or ingredient, but rather the smoke of a Thai scented U-shaped candle called *tian op*. The baked cookies are placed in a large dish and the incense-like candle is lit and placed in a smaller dish in the center. Then, the larger dish is covered to snuff out the flames and trap the aromatic smoke so it can infuse its floral aroma into the cookies. These candles are available online, but if you can't find one, you can add rose water or vanilla extract to the dough of the cookies, as many bakers today do.

Position racks in the top and bottom thirds of the oven and preheat the oven to 325°F (160°C/Gas Mark 3). Line two large baking sheets with parchment paper.

In a large bowl, whisk together the flour, sugar, and salt. Pour in the melted lard and rose water or vanilla (if using) and stir with your hands until a dough forms and there are no dry patches of flour remaining, kneading only as much as needed to produce a smooth ball of dough.

Using a ½-ounce (1-tablespoon) ice cream scoop, portion the dough and roll into balls. Arrange them on the prepared baking sheets, spaced 2 inches (5 cm) apart. Using a paring knife, cut a dough ball into quarters. Remove one quarter and arrange the three remaining quarters equidistant and touching at one end like the petals of a flower. Roll the removed quarter of dough into a tiny ball and place the ball in the center where the "petals" meet, pressing lightly so it adheres to them. Using the back of the tip of the knife, mark the center dough ball three times, each in the direction of a petal. Repeat with the remaining dough balls to shape them into flowers.

Bake until light golden brown on the bottom and dry to the touch all over, 15–20 minutes, switching racks and rotating the baking sheets front to back halfway through.

Transfer the baking sheets to wire racks and let the cookies cool completely on the pans.

If using the scented candle, place it upright in a small bowl and place the bowl in a larger, taller dish or large Dutch oven (casserole dish). Gently arrange the cookies in the dish or pot around the candle. Light the two ends of the candle and let them burn for 10 seconds. Cover the dish with a large plate or cover the pot with its lid and let the cookies stand until suffused with the candle's smoke, at least 30 minutes or up to 1 hour, before serving the cookies.

Flower-Shaped Shortbread Cookies

Mini Coconut Milk and Tapioca Cookies

Kanom Ping

Preparation time: 40 minutes, plus
 cooling time and 30 minutes chilling
 time
Cooking time: 40 minutes
Makes: About 18 cookies

1½ cups (12 fl oz/350 ml) canned
 unsweetened full-fat coconut milk
¾ cup (150 g) white US granulated
 (UK caster) sugar
1 pandan leaf (12 inches/30 cm) long
1¾ cups (245 g) tapioca starch
½ teaspoon fine sea salt
1 egg yolk

These marble-size cookies are a popular store-bought sweet snack in Thailand. But as has been the trend in recent years, many bakers now make them at home to re-create this nostalgic cookie. Once made with soybean or mung bean flour, they are often made with tapioca starch today, which produces a fine-textured, powdery/crumbly cookie.

The cookies can be tinted with food colorings like yellow, pink, and green, but you can leave them plain as this recipe does. A pandan leaf is used to flavor these cookies by boiling it with the coconut milk and sugar to make a fragrant syrup. Search for pandan leaves in the frozen section of Asian markets, but if unavailable, you can use 1 teaspoon of pandan extract in its place, which will also color the cookies pastel green.

In a small saucepan, combine the coconut milk and sugar. Cut the pandan leaf into thumb-size pieces and add to the pan. Bring to a boil over medium-high heat, stirring to dissolve the sugar. Reduce the heat to maintain a steady simmer and cook, stirring occasionally, until the syrup is a shade darker and reduced to the consistency of heavy cream, 20–22 minutes. Remove the pan from the heat and let cool completely to allow the pandan leaves to steep in the syrup and infuse it with their flavor.

Set a fine-mesh sieve over a glass measuring cup (jug) and pour the cooled coconut syrup through the sieve, pressing on the pandan leaves to extract as much syrup as possible; discard the leaves. You should have ¾ cup (6 fl oz/175 ml) syrup. If the syrup has reduced too much, stir in enough water to return the syrup amount to ¾ cup (6 fl oz/175 ml). If the syrup hasn't reduced enough, return it to the pan and simmer until reduced to ¾ cup (6 fl oz/175 ml). Let the syrup cool completely once again. If using the pandan extract, stir it into the cooled syrup.

Place the tapioca starch in a large bowl, form a well in the center and pour in the cooled coconut syrup. Add the salt and egg yolk to the syrup and stir with a fork to combine, then start incorporating the tapioca starch little by little until the mixture begins to clump together. Use your hands to begin kneading the dough until it forms a smooth ball with no dry patches of starch remaining. Cover the bowl with plastic wrap (cling film) and refrigerate for 30 minutes just to firm the dough slightly.

Position racks in the top and bottom thirds of the oven and preheat the oven to 325°F (160°C/Gas Mark 3). Line two large baking sheets with parchment paper.

Using a ½-ounce (1-tablespoon) ice cream scoop, portion the dough and roll into balls. Arrange them on the baking sheets, spaced 1 inch (2.5 cm) apart. Flatten slightly with the palm of your hand.

Bake until light golden brown on the bottom and dry to the touch all over, 15–20 minutes, switching racks and rotating the baking sheets front to back halfway through.

Transfer the baking sheets to wire racks and let the cookies cool completely on the pans (if you try to move them while hot, their bottoms may stick and rip off).

Buttery Almond Cookies

Bánh Hạnh Nhân

Preparation time: 45 minutes,
  plus chilling time
Cooking time: 25 minutes
Makes: About 12 cookies

1 cup (115 g) slivered almonds
1⅓ cups (185 g) all-purpose
  (plain) flour
½ teaspoon baking soda
  (bicarbonate of soda)
½ teaspoon fine sea salt
1 stick (4 oz/115 g) unsalted
  butter, softened
½ cup (100 g) white US granulated
  (UK caster) sugar
1 egg
½ teaspoon pure almond extract
Egg wash: 1 egg yolk beaten
  with 1 tablespoon water
Sliced (flaked) almonds, for decorating

These simple butter cookies are a staple in bakeries in Vietnam. Descended from an almond variation of the *hup toh soh* (recipe, page 393) style of cookies, they are flavored with almonds in three forms. Ground almonds add texture to the dough, which is perfumed with almond extract, and then the cookies are decorated with more almonds on top. Older recipes used an egg wash glaze and a single almond on top, though many modern recipes eschew the glaze and cover the dough balls with sliced (flaked) or slivered almonds before baking.

Position racks in the top and bottom thirds of the oven and preheat the oven to 350°F (180°C/Gas Mark 4). Line two large baking sheets with parchment paper.

Spread the slivered almonds out in a single layer on one of the baking sheets and bake until lightly toasted and fragrant, 6–8 minutes.

Transfer the nuts to a cutting board and let cool. Reserve the baking sheet. Using a food processor, process the almonds until very finely ground.

In a medium bowl, whisk together the flour, baking soda (bicarb), and salt.

In a large bowl, with a hand mixer, beat the butter and sugar on medium speed until light and fluffy, 2–3 minutes. Add the egg and almond extract and beat until smooth. Add the flour mixture and ground almonds and stir until a dough forms and there are no dry patches of flour remaining.

Using a 1-ounce (2-tablespoon) ice cream scoop, portion the dough and roll into balls. Arrange them on the prepared baking sheets, spaced at least 2 inches (5 cm) apart. Using the pad of your thumb, lightly press down on each dough ball to make a depression. Place the sheets of dough balls in the refrigerator to chill for at least 30 minutes or up to 1 day.

When ready to bake, position racks in the top and bottom thirds of the oven and preheat the oven to 350°F (180°C/Gas Mark 4).

Lightly brush the top of each cookie with some of the egg wash and sprinkle the center with a pinch of sliced (flaked) almonds.

Bake until golden brown and dry to the touch in the center, 14–16 minutes, switching racks and rotating the baking sheets front to back halfway through.

Transfer the baking sheets to wire racks. Let the cookies cool on the pans for 1 minute, then transfer them to the racks to cool completely.

Swirled "Pig's Ears" Cookies

Bánh Tai Heo

Preparation time: 30 minutes,
  plus 1 hour chilling time and
  30 minutes freezing time
Cooking time: 15 minutes
Makes: About 30 cookies

2 tablespoons (30 g) unsalted
  butter, softened
2 tablespoons white US granulated
  (UK caster) sugar
1 teaspoon fresh lemon juice
½ teaspoon fine sea salt
2 egg yolks
⅓ cup (2½ fl oz/80 ml) canned
  unsweetened full-fat coconut milk
⅔ cup (95 g) plus ½ cup (70 g)
  all-purpose (plain) flour
2 tablespoons natural cocoa powder
Vegetable oil, for shallow-frying

Another popular street snack in Vietnam that home bakers are starting to make at home, these swirled treats are called "pig's ears" cookies because of their distinct buckled, wavy shape. They get this shape from a shallow fry in oil until crisp and golden brown. The swirled pattern is made by incorporating cocoa powder into half of the dough, rolling each in a sheet, then stacking and rolling the two doughs up together, similar to American pinwheel cookies.

In a medium bowl, combine the butter, sugar, lemon juice, and salt and stir with a small wooden spoon or silicone spatula until smooth and creamy, about 1 minute. Beat in the egg yolks, one at a time, until smooth. Stir in the coconut milk until smooth. Scrape all the batter to the bottom of the bowl, then eyeball half of it and spoon this amount into another medium bowl.

Add the ⅔ cup (95 g) flour to one bowl and stir until it forms a dough and there are no dry patches of flour remaining. Add the remaining ½ cup (70 g) flour and the cocoa powder to the second bowl and stir until it forms a dough. Shape each dough into a disc, wrap in plastic wrap (cling film), and refrigerate for 1 hour.

Working on a lightly floured work surface, roll out the plain dough with a rolling pin into a rough rectangle ¼ inch (6 mm) thick. Roll the chocolate dough in the same manner. Brush the plain dough with water and place the chocolate dough on top of it. Gently roll the rolling pin over the stacked doughs to press them together. Starting from one long side of the stacked dough, roll them up together as you would a jelly roll (Swiss roll). Wrap the log of dough in plastic wrap (cling film) and place in the freezer for 30 minutes.

Meanwhile, line a large baking sheet with paper towels. Place a wire rack nearby. Pour enough oil into a large skillet to come ½ inch (13 mm) up the side of the pan.

When ready to cook, unwrap the dough and trim one end so it's even. Submerge a trimmed piece of dough in the oil in the skillet. Place the skillet over medium-high heat and heat until the dough piece floats to the surface and begins frying. If using a deep-fry thermometer, the temperature should read 350°F (177°C).

Using a sharp, thin-bladed knife, cut off about 6 slices of dough ⅛ inch (3 mm) thick. Wrap the rest of the log and keep it cold in the refrigerator while you fry the first cookies. Remove the test piece of dough, then immediately slide the 6 slices of dough into the oil and fry, flipping once, until golden brown and slightly curled, 1–2 minutes.

Using a slotted spoon or tongs, lift the cookies from the oil and transfer them to the paper towels to drain. As the cookies dry, move them to a wire rack. Repeat frying the remaining cookies, working 6 at a time and maintaining the temperature of the oil as evenly as possible. Let the cookies cool completely—they will firm up when cooled.

Swirled "Pig's Ears" Cookies

Printed Arrowroot Cookies

Panecillos de San Nicolas

Preparation time: 30 minutes
Cooking time: 15 minutes
Makes: About 24 cookies

1 can (14 fl oz/400 ml) unsweetened
  full-fat coconut milk, chilled
  and unshaken
1 cup plus 1 tablespoon (150 g)
  arrowroot powder
1 cup plus 1 tablespoon (150 g)
  all-purpose (plain) flour
2 teaspoons baking powder
¾ teaspoon fine sea salt
1 cup (210 g) superfine (caster) sugar
4 tablespoons (2 oz/55 g) unsalted
  butter, softened
¼ cup (2 fl oz/60 ml) vegetable oil
3 egg yolks
Finely grated zest of 1 lemon

The arrowroot plant has been cultivated in the Philippines for centuries, and the starch from its rhizomes is used extensively in Filipino cuisine. The starch plays an important part in two cookies that are likely related.

The first are the so-called *Sanikulas* cookies—named after the Spanish San Nicolas de Tolentino, the patron saint of bakers—the specialty of culinary historian Atching Lillian Borromeo from Pampanga. Borromeo uses a 300-year-old recipe to make her cookies and special wooden molds to shape them, harkening back to the European gingerbread tradition (see Gingerbread, page 328). According to Borromeo, the recipe came from Spanish nuns who devised the recipe as a means of using leftover egg yolks during a period when Spanish colonists used egg whites in the mortar for constructing churches in the Philippines; this is an adaptation of her recipe. Another simpler, more modern cookie is called *uraró* (recipe, page 375).

Open the can of coconut milk and carefully scoop off ¼ cup (50 g) of the cream on top. Set this aside to come to room temperature; save the rest of the cream and milk in the can for another use.

Position racks in the top and bottom thirds of the oven and preheat the oven to 350°F (180°C/Gas Mark 4). Line two large baking sheets with parchment paper.

In a medium bowl, whisk together the arrowroot powder, flour, baking powder, and salt.

In a large bowl, with a hand mixer, combine the coconut cream, sugar, butter, and oil and beat on medium speed until light and fluffy, 2–3 minutes. Add the egg yolks, one at a time, beating until smooth after each addition. Beat in the lemon zest. Add the dry ingredients and stir until a dough forms and there are no dry patches of flour remaining.

Working on a lightly floured work surface, roll out the dough with a rolling pin to ¼ inch (6 mm) thick. Using a wooden cookie mold with 3-inch (7.5 cm) cells, lightly dust the engravings with flour, tapping out any excess, then press it over the dough to print designs on the dough; repeat over the rest of the dough. Cut the cookies free from each other and transfer to the prepared baking sheets, spaced 1 inch (2.5 cm) apart. Brush off any excess flour that remains on the dough pieces. (Alternatively, use various cookie cutters of similar dimension to cut out cookies.) Reroll the scraps to make more cookies.

Bake until golden brown at the edges and dry to the touch in the center, 12–15 minutes, switching racks and rotating the baking sheets front to back halfway through.

Transfer the baking sheets to wire racks. Let the cookies cool on the pans for 1 minute, then transfer to the racks to cool completely.

Simple Arrowroot Cookies

Uraró / Araró

Preparation time: 45 minutes
Cooking time: 15 minutes
Makes: About 36 cookies

2½ cups (350 g) arrowroot powder
1 cup (140 g) all-purpose (plain) flour
2 teaspoons baking powder
1 teaspoon fine sea salt
2 sticks (8 oz/225 g) unsalted
  butter, softened
1 cup (200 g) white US granulated
  (UK caster) sugar
2 eggs
2 teaspoons pure vanilla extract

These cookies are a simpler, more modern version of the *panecillos de San Nicolas* (recipe, opposite). The name *uraró* is Tagalog for "arrowroot." Their ingredients are nearly the same as the *Sanikulas* cookies, save a few flavoring and fat switches, and they are usually shaped using a cookie press/gun or flattened with a fork to impress a pattern. It's likely that the *Sanikulas* cookies were baked commonly at one point, but then the recipe and technique simplified to become the *uraró* cookies that are baked today.

- -

Position racks in the top and bottom thirds of the oven and preheat the oven to 375°F (190°C/Gas Mark 5). Line two large baking sheets with parchment paper. (If using a cookie press/gun to form the cookies, leave the baking sheets unlined.)

In a medium bowl, whisk together the arrowroot powder, flour, baking powder, and salt.

In a large bowl, with a hand mixer, beat the butter and sugar on medium speed until light and fluffy, about 5 minutes. Add the eggs, one at a time, beating until smooth after each addition. Beat in the vanilla. Add the dry ingredients and beat on low speed until a dough forms and there are no dry patches of flour remaining.

Using a ¾-ounce (1½-tablespoon) ice cream scoop, portion the dough and roll into balls. Arrange them on the prepared baking sheets, spaced at least 2 inches (5 cm) apart and flatten each with the palm of your hand. Use the tines of a fork to press each dough ball in a north-south direction, then turn 90 degrees and press in an east-west direction, creating a crosshatch pattern on top. (If using a cookie press/gun: Working in batches, scrape the dough into a cookie press/gun fitted with a wreath or flower disc and press shapes 1 inch (2.5 cm) apart on the unlined baking sheets.)

Bake until very lightly golden brown on the bottom and dry to the touch all over, 10–12 minutes, switching racks and rotating the baking sheets front to back halfway through.

Transfer the baking sheets to wire racks. Let the cookies cool on the pans for 1 minute, then transfer them to the racks to cool completely.

Filipino Powdered Milk Shortbreads

Polvorón / Pulburon / Polboron

Preparation time: 50 minutes, plus
  at least 30 minutes chilling time
Cooking time: 15 minutes
Makes: About 12 cookies

1 cup (140 g) all-purpose (plain) flour
⅔ cup (140 g) superfine (caster) sugar
½ cup (60 g) instant nonfat dry milk
½ teaspoon fine sea salt
1½ sticks (6 oz/170 g) unsalted butter
1 teaspoon pure vanilla extract

There may be no stronger emblem of Spanish colonial rule in the Philippines than these cookies. Similar to Spanish *polvorones* (recipe, page 97) in both name and ingredients, Filipino *polvorón*, also often spelled *pulburon* or *polboron*, are made with butter and sugar, but their flour is roasted until nutty and lightly browned, like in Mexican *polvorones de canela* (recipe, page 156). They also include milk powder to add richness to the taste of the cookies, which are often sold in many different flavors and colors.

The key distinction in these *polvorón* is that they aren't baked. The ingredients are instead packed into special oval molds, then chilled until firm and wrapped in cellophane. Their unbaked nature and candy-like wrapping leads to them often being referred to as "milk candies." This recipe adds salt and vanilla extract to the base recipe to give them flavor, but feel free to omit both, if you like.

Preheat the oven to 350°F (180°C/Gas Mark 4). Line a large baking sheet with parchment paper.

Spread the flour out on the parchment paper and bake the flour, stirring occasionally to ensure it toasts evenly, until light golden brown throughout and it smells nutty, 10–12 minutes. Remove the baking sheet from the oven and let the flour cool for 1 minute.

Place a fine-mesh sieve over a large bowl. Using the parchment paper like a sling, lift the flour off the baking sheet and transfer it to the sieve. Return the paper to the baking sheet and reserve until ready to use (but turn off the oven). Sift the flour into the bowl and then immediately stir in the sugar, milk powder, and salt.

In a small saucepan, melt the butter. Remove from the heat and stir in the vanilla. Pour the butter over the dry ingredients and stir with a fork until a crumbly, sandy dough forms.

Using a spring-loaded polvorón molder, pack the dough mixture into the press, then release the puck of dough onto the prepared baking sheet. Repeat with the remaining dough mixture, spacing the cookies 1 inch (2.5 cm) apart. (Alternatively, place a 2-inch/5 cm oval, oblong, or round cookie cutter on the baking sheet and fill it with dough. Press with a cocktail muddler to pack it into a puck ½ inch/13 mm thick. Carefully lift the cutter up and repeat to make more cookies. Another option is to line a muffin pan with liners and press the dough into the cups in the same manner.)

Refrigerate the cookies until firm, at least 30 minutes. Individually wrap the cookies in cellophane or wax paper. Store in the refrigerator.

Filipino Powdered Milk Shortbreads

Dry Rice Flour Shortbreads
Puto Seko

Preparation time: 45 minutes
Cooking time: 15 minutes
Makes: About 48 cookies

2 cups (320 g) glutinous (sweet)
  rice flour
½ cup (70 g) cornstarch (cornflour)
½ cup (60 g) instant nonfat dry milk
½ teaspoon baking powder
¾ teaspoon fine sea salt
1 stick (4 oz/115 g) unsalted butter,
  softened
½ cup (100 g) white US granulated
  (UK caster) sugar
2 egg whites
1 teaspoon pure vanilla extract

The name for these cookies comes from the word *puto*, which is a Filipino rice cake, and *seko* or *seco*, Spanish for "dry." These cookies are very dry and crumbly, similar to Filipino *polvorón* (recipe, page 376). They are a cousin of the *uraró* (recipe, page 375), which uses arrowroot powder—whereas *puto seko* uses a mix of glutinous (sweet) rice flour and cornstarch (cornflour). Many modern recipes use all cornstarch or a mix of cornstarch and wheat flour. To preserve the traditional intention of these cookies, this recipe uses a mix of rice flour and cornstarch. The cookies are made with a fragile dough and shaped into thick pucks. Handle them gently because they have a tendency to fall apart.

- -

Position racks in the top and bottom thirds of the oven and preheat the oven to 325°F (160°C/Gas Mark 3). Line two large baking sheets with parchment paper.

In a medium bowl, whisk together the glutinous rice flour, cornstarch (cornflour), milk powder, baking powder, and salt.

In a large bowl, with a hand mixer, beat the butter and sugar on medium speed until light and fluffy, 2–3 minutes. Add the egg whites, one at a time, beating until smooth after each addition. Beat in the vanilla. Add the dry ingredients and stir until a crumbly dough forms and there are no dry patches of flour remaining.

Use your hands to combine the dough into a disc and then roll out the dough with a rolling pin to ¼ inch (6 mm) thick. Using a 1½-inch (4 cm) round cutter, cut out rounds of dough. Reroll the scraps to cut out more cookies. Arrange on the prepared baking sheets, spaced 1 inch (2.5 cm) apart.

Bake until very lightly golden brown on the bottom and dry to the touch all over, 12–15 minutes, switching racks and rotating the baking sheets front to back halfway through.

Transfer the baking sheets to wire racks. Let the cookies cool on the pans for 1 minute, then transfer them to the racks to cool completely.

Milky Shortbread Cookies

Biskut Arab Susu

Preparation time: 35 minutes
Cooking time: 40 minutes
Makes: About 24 cookies

2 cups (280 g) all-purpose (plain) flour
1 cup (225 g) ghee, softened
1 cup (135 g) powdered (icing) sugar
¾ cup (90 g) instant nonfat dry milk
½ teaspoon fine sea salt

Like many cookies made in Malaysia, Singapore, and Indonesia, these "Arab biscuits" are a popular treat for Eid. It's clear, from both the millennia of trade and influence between Arab Muslims and Maritime Southeast Asians and the Malay name for these cookies—*biskut Arab susu*—that they have numerous Middle Eastern influences, such as Afghani *khetaye* (recipe, page 30), Lebanese/Syrian *maamoul* (recipe, page 44), and/or Turkish *kurabiye* (recipe, page 60).

The defining factor of these cookies is their use of milk powder, which along with ghee, enriches the cookies with a creamy dairy flavor but crumbly texture. Their use of copious amounts of powdered (icing) sugar on the outside and spherical shape point to them being part of the tradition of "wedding" cookies (see page 23) like the Indonesian *kue putri salju* (recipe, page 382) and Austrian *Vanillekipferl* (recipe, page 195). *Kuih makmur* (recipe, page 388) are related to these cookies but contain peanuts in the filling.

Position racks in the top and bottom thirds of the oven and preheat the oven to 350°F (180°C/Gas Mark 4). Line two large baking sheets with parchment paper.

Spread the flour out on one of the baking sheets and bake, stirring occasionally to ensure it toasts evenly, until the flour starts to brown at the edges and smells nutty, 10–12 minutes.

Remove the baking sheet from the oven and let the flour cool completely on the paper. Reduce the oven temperature to 300°F (150°C/Gas Mark 2).

Place a fine-mesh sieve over a medium bowl and, using the parchment paper like a sling, lift the flour off the baking sheet and transfer it to the sieve. Sift the flour into the bowl. Return the paper to the baking sheet and reserve until ready to use.

In a large bowl, with a hand mixer, combine the ghee, ½ cup (65 g) of the sugar, ½ cup (60 g) of the milk powder, and the salt and beat on medium speed until light and fluffy, 2–3 minutes. Add the toasted flour and stir until a dough forms and there are no dry patches of flour remaining.

Using a ½-ounce (1-tablespoon) ice cream scoop, portion the dough and roll into balls. Arrange them on the prepared baking sheets, spaced 1 inch (2.5 cm) apart.

Bake until lightly golden brown and dry to the touch all over, 20–25 minutes, switching racks and rotating the baking sheets front to back halfway through.

Meanwhile, in a medium bowl, combine the remaining ½ cup (65 g) sugar and ¼ cup (30 g) milk powder.

Transfer the baking sheets to wire racks and let the cookies rest for 1 minute. While the cookies are still warm, toss each cookie in the bowl of sugar/milk powder mixture to coat, returning each to their place on the baking sheet to cool completely.

Once completely cooled, dust liberally with more of the sugar/milk powder mixture before serving.

Milky Cashew Cookies
Biskut Gajus

Preparation time: 1 hour 5 minutes
Cooking time: 25 minutes
Makes: About 48 cookies

½ cup (70 g) cashews, plus about
  48 cashews for decorating
1½ cups (210 g) all-purpose
  (plain) flour
½ cup (60 g) nonfat dry milk powder
¾ teaspoon fine sea salt
½ teaspoon baking powder
2 sticks (8 oz/225 g) unsalted
  butter, softened
¾ cup (150 g) white US granulated
  (UK caster) sugar
1 teaspoon pure vanilla extract
1 egg yolk
Egg wash: 1 egg yolk beaten
  with 1 tablespoon water

These whimsical cookies are a more modern treat and part of the trend of shaping simple cookies into culturally significant shapes within a country. Brought to Southeast Asia by Portuguese colonists in the fifteenth century, the cashew tree grows well in the maritime environment. This cookie makes use of the nuts both ground finely to mix into the dough and as whole pieces to garnish and signal what's inside. In that way, they are similar to the Chinese *hup toh soh* (recipe, page 393) from where they likely descended.

Bakers in Malaysia use a special cutter shaped like a cashew apple—the pear-shaped fruit on which the cashew nut grows—for these cookies, but that shape is difficult to find elsewhere in the world. Instead, you can use a strawberry-shaped or elongated heart-shaped cutter if you can find them, or a round cutter. As with the *biskut Arab susu* (recipe, page 379), this recipe uses milk powder to enrich these crumbly cookies.

- -

Position racks in the top and bottom thirds of the oven and preheat the oven to 350°F (180°C/Gas Mark 4). Line two large baking sheets with parchment paper.

Spread the ½ cup (70 g) cashews out in a single layer on one of the baking sheets and bake until lightly toasted and fragrant, 6–8 minutes.

Transfer the nuts to a cutting board and let cool. Reserve the baking sheet. Using a food processor, process the baked cashews until very finely ground.

In a medium bowl, whisk together the flour, milk powder, salt, and baking powder.

In a large bowl, with a hand mixer, beat the butter and sugar on medium speed until pale and fluffy, 2–3 minutes. Add the vanilla and egg yolk and beat until smooth. Add the flour mixture and ground cashews and stir until a dough forms and there are no dry patches of flour remaining.

Transfer the dough to a lightly floured work surface. Using a lightly floured rolling pin, roll out the dough to ⅜ inch (1 cm) thick. Using a 2-inch (5 cm) round or cashew apple-shaped cutter, cut out rounds of dough. Reroll the scraps to cut out more rounds. Arrange the cookies on the prepared baking sheets, spaced 1 inch (2.5 cm) apart.

Lightly brush the tops of each dough round with the egg wash and gently press a whole cashew in the center of each round.

Bake until the cookies are golden brown all over and dry to the touch, 12–15 minutes, switching racks and rotating the baking sheets front to back halfway through.

Transfer the baking sheets to wire racks. Let the cookies cool on the pans for 1 minute, then transfer them to the racks to cool completely.

Milky Cashew Cookies

"Snow White" Crescent Cookies

Kue Putri Salju

(v)

Preparation time: 45 minutes
Cooking time: 25 minutes
Makes: About 24 cookies

2 cups (280 g) all-purpose (plain) flour
⅓ cup (40 g) nonfat dry milk powder
3 tablespoons cornstarch (cornflour)
½ teaspoon baking powder
½ teaspoon fine sea salt
1½ sticks (6 oz/170 g) unsalted
  butter, softened
½ cup (65 g) powdered (icing)
  sugar, plus more for coating
2 egg yolks
½ cup (100 g) very finely ground
  almonds, cashews, or walnuts

Covered in powdered (icing) sugar and shaped like crescents, these cookies are Indonesia's version of the ubiquitous "wedding"-style cookie (see page 23) descended from the Austrian *Vanillekipferl* (recipe, page 195). These cookies are typically made for celebratory occasions like Eid and have many variations, including one that mixes grated Dutch Edam cheese into the sweet dough.

One of the defining features of this cookie is its use of milk powder to add richness and a crumbly texture, along with cornstarch (cornflour). Both ingredients make the texture of the baked cookie almost dissolve in the mouth, especially with the powdered sugar coating. The Edam can also be mixed into this dough so if you want to use it, simply substitute ½ cup (100 g) of grated cheese for the ground nuts.

Position racks in the top and bottom thirds of the oven and preheat the oven to 300°F (150°C/Gas Mark 2). Line two large baking sheets with parchment paper.

In a medium bowl, whisk together the flour, milk powder, cornstarch (cornflour), baking powder, and salt.

In a large bowl, with a hand mixer, combine the butter, sugar, and egg yolks and beat on medium speed until light and fluffy, 2–3 minutes. Beat in the ground nuts. Add the dry ingredients and stir until a dough forms and there are no dry patches of flour remaining.

Using a ½-ounce (1-tablespoon) ice cream scoop, portion the dough and roll into balls. Roll each ball into a small log and then bend it in the middle to form a half-moon shape, slightly tapering the ends. Arrange the crescents on the prepared baking sheets, spaced 1 inch (2.5 cm) apart.

Bake until light golden brown on the bottom and dry to the touch in the center, 20–25 minutes, switching racks and rotating the baking sheets front to back halfway through.

Transfer the baking sheets to wire racks and let the cookies rest for 1 minute. While the cookies are still warm, toss each cookie in sugar to coat, returning each to their place on the baking sheet to cool completely.

Once completely cooled, dust liberally with more powdered sugar before serving.

"Snow White" Crescent Cookies

Crisp Rice-Flour Wafers
Kue Semprong

Preparation time: 30 minutes
Cooking time: 2 hours
Makes: About 36 cookies

½ cup (100 g) white US granulated
  (UK caster) sugar
½ teaspoon ground cinnamon
½ teaspoon fine sea salt
½ teaspoon pure vanilla extract
2 eggs
1 cup (160 g) plus 2 tablespoons
  white rice flour (see headnote)
1 cup (8 fl oz/250 ml) plus 2
  tablespoons canned unsweetened
  full-fat coconut milk
2 tablespoons black sesame
  seeds (optional)

The Netherland's influence on Indonesian baking is apparent in these cookies. Made with a waffle iron, the batter of these is similar to the Belgian *nieuwjaarswafels* (recipe, page 236), like a rolled-up *stroopwafel* without the filling. These crisp wafer-like cookies are formed by rolling them into a cylinder while hot, to resemble the smokestacks they're named after. They're also popular in Malaysia and Singapore, and when shaped into folded triangles, go by the name *kuih kapit*.

These rolled cookies are made primarily with rice flour so they're very crisp. Look for plain white rice flour to use here, not glutinous (sweet) rice flour, which would make the cookies chewy. *Kue semprong* are flavored simply with cinnamon, vanilla, and black sesame seeds, but many cooks also flavor them with extracts made from pandan (a tropical leaf used for flavoring) or ube (purple yam).

- -

In a large bowl, with a hand mixer, combine the sugar, cinnamon, salt, vanilla, and eggs and beat on medium speed until pale, thickened, and foamy, about 2 minutes. Add the rice flour and beat on low speed until incorporated. With the mixer on low speed, slowly pour in the coconut milk and continue beating until a smooth batter forms. Beat in the sesame seeds, if using.

Place a krumkake iron over medium heat on your stove or heat an electric krumkake maker. Using a 1-tablespoon measure, pour tablespoonfuls of batter into the center of the iron. Close the iron and let cook, flipping the iron halfway through, if using the stove, until the batter spreads and sets as a light golden wafer, 2–3 minutes, depending on the heat of your stove (or follow the manufacturer's instructions for the electric maker).

Open the iron and place the end of a narrow wooden spoon at the edge of the iron closest to you. Lift the wafer and then quickly roll it around the spoon handle like a rolled carpet. Slide the rolled wafer off the handle and place on a wire rack to cool. If you want to make folded wafers, simply fold the wafer in half while on the iron, then fold it in half once more to create a four-fold triangle. Repeat with the remaining batter to cook and roll/fold more cookies.

Pineapple Jam-Stuffed Cookies

Nastar

Preparation time: 20 minutes
Cooking time: 40 minutes
Makes: About 12 cookies

1¼ cups (175 g) all-purpose (plain) flour
⅓ cup (45 g) powdered (icing) sugar
3 tablespoons cornstarch (cornflour)
3 tablespoons instant nonfat dry milk
½ teaspoon fine sea salt
1 stick (4 oz/115 g) unsalted
  butter, softened
2 egg yolks
1 cup (320 g) pineapple jam,
  store-bought or homemade
  (see Homemade [Any] Fruit
  Jam, page 18)

Egg wash: 1 egg yolk beaten
  with 1 tablespoon water

The name for these cookies comes from an abbreviated portmanteau of the Dutch *ananas taart*, or "pineapple tart." The tarts were based on European pies filled with fruit preserves, but made with pineapples, which the Portuguese brought to Asia from South America. This tart was made smaller and smaller until it became this cookie today.

The cookie dough is made similar to pie dough (shortcrust pastry), so it is flaky, not crumbly. It is filled with pineapple jam; you can use store-bought or make your own. The key to baking the cookies with a clean sheen on the outside is to parbake them before brushing with egg wash, so when they go back in the oven the wash sets into a smooth, crack-free glaze.

- -

Position racks in the top and bottom thirds of the oven and preheat the oven to 300°F (150°C/Gas Mark 2). Line two large baking sheets with parchment paper.

In a large bowl, whisk together the flour, sugar, cornstarch (cornflour), milk powder, and salt. Add the butter and egg yolks and mix with a pastry blender, fork, or your hands until a dough forms and there are no dry patches of flour remaining, kneading only as long as needed to form a smooth dough.

Using a 1-ounce (2-tablespoon) ice cream scoop, portion the dough and roll into balls. Flatten each ball in your hand and place 1 heaping teaspoon pineapple jam in the center. Gather the dough around the jam to encase it and then reroll the dough into a smooth ball. Arrange the jam-filled dough balls on the prepared baking sheets, spaced 1 inch (2.5 cm) apart.

Bake until half-cooked, about 20 minutes.

Remove the cookies from the oven and brush the egg wash over the tops. Return the cookies to the oven and bake until golden brown all over, 15–20 minutes more.

Transfer the baking sheets to wire racks. Let the cookies cool on the pans for 1 minute, then transfer them to the racks to cool completely.

Roasted Sago and Cheese Cookies

Kue Sagu Keju

Preparation time: 40 minutes
Cooking time: 35 minutes
Makes: About 48 cookies

1 can (14 fl oz/400 ml) unsweetened
 full-fat coconut milk, chilled
 and unshaken
1⅔ cups (235 g) sago flour
 (see headnote)
2 pandan leaves, cut into 2-inch
 (5 cm) strips, ½ inch (13 mm) wide
1 stick (4 oz/115 g) unsalted
 butter, softened
1⅓ cups (180 g) powdered
 (icing) sugar
½ teaspoon fine sea salt
1 egg yolk
3 oz (85 g) Edam or mild cheddar
 cheese, finely grated

Popularly served at Hari Raya, the Indonesian name for the Eid holiday, these piped cookies are buttery, flavored with Edam or cheddar cheese—a clear influence from Dutch colonization—and sweet, though there are also savory versions. The sago flour used in these cookies is roasted (and also perfumed with pandan leaves), which, similar to *polvorones de canela* (recipe, page 156), allows the starch to dissolve more easily into the dough and produce a melt-in-the-mouth texture in the baked cookie.

Sago flour is often labeled mistakenly and interchangeably as tapioca starch around the world because both are commonly sold in "pearl" form, but they are not the same. Sago is made from the insides of a type of palm tree, and tapioca is made from yuca (cassava) roots. Look for sago flour in Indian markets where it's often labeled "sabudana." If you can only find sago in pearl form, pulverize the pearls in a blender or food processor until powdery before measuring.

There is a similar cookie called *kue bangkit,* which is shaped with wooden molds. The dough has no butter or cheese so it has the texture of a crumbly shortbread. To make them, see the variation that follows. Look for *kue bangkit* molds online.

Open the can of coconut milk and carefully scoop off ¼ cup (50 g) of the cream on top. Set this aside to come to room temperature; save the rest of the cream and milk in the can for another use.

Position racks in the top and bottom thirds of the oven and preheat the oven to 350°F (180°C/Gas Mark 4). Line two large baking sheets with parchment paper.

Spread the sago flour out on one of the baking sheets and tuck the pieces of pandan leaves evenly throughout the flour. Bake the flour and leaves, stirring occasionally to ensure it toasts evenly, until the flour starts to brown at the edges and it smells nutty, 8–10 minutes.

Remove the baking sheet from the oven and let the flour cool completely on the paper. Reduce the oven temperature to 300°F (150°C/Gas Mark 2).

Place a fine-mesh sieve over a medium bowl. Using the parchment paper like a sling, lift the flour off the baking sheet and transfer it to the sieve. Sift the flour into the bowl (discard the pieces of pandan leaves). Return the paper to the baking sheet and reserve until ready to use.

In a large bowl, with a hand mixer, combine the butter, sugar, salt, and egg yolk and beat on medium speed until light and fluffy, 2–3 minutes. Add half the toasted flour and all the reserved coconut cream and stir until almost combined. Add the remaining flour and the Edam and stir until a dough forms and there are no dry patches of flour remaining.

Working in batches, scrape the dough into a piping bag fitted with a ¾-inch (2 cm) fluted tip (nozzle) and pipe rings or wreaths 1½ inches (4 cm) in diameter, arranging them 2 inches (5 cm) apart on the baking sheets.

Bake until lightly golden brown and dry to the touch all over, 20–25 minutes, switching racks and rotating the baking sheets front to back halfway through.

Transfer the baking sheets to wire racks. Let the cookies cool on the pans for 1 minute, then transfer them to the racks to cool completely.

Variation
Kue Bangkit
Increase the coconut cream to ½ cup (100 g). Reduce the powdered (icing) sugar to ⅔ cup (90 g). Omit the butter and cheese. Combine all the ingredients in a bowl and stir together into a crumbly dough. Press small balls of dough into divots in a kue bangkit cookie mold to form flower and bird shapes. Tap out the shapes from the mold and arrange on baking sheets. Bake as directed.

Roasted Sago and Cheese Cookies

Peanut-Filled Shortbread Cookies

Kuih Makmur

Preparation time: 25 minutes
Cooking time: 35 minutes
Makes: About 12 cookies

¼ cup (35 g) unroasted peanuts
2 tablespoons white US granulated
  (UK caster) sugar
2 cups (280 g) all-purpose (plain) flour
½ teaspoon fine sea salt
¾ cup (170 g) ghee or unsalted
  butter, softened
¼ cup (2 fl oz/60 ml) ice-cold water
Powdered (icing) sugar, for dusting

As with *biskut Arab susu* (recipe, page 379), these beloved Eid cookies show the Muslim influence on the sweets of Indonesia, Singapore, and Malaysia. The dough is made with ghee and wheat flour and stuffed with a mix of finely chopped peanuts and sugar. The nut filling points to these being a descendant of the Lebanese/Syrian *maamoul* (recipe, page 44), while its crimped design mimics that of the Moroccan *kaab el-ghazal* (recipe, page 135) and East Timor Ladder Biscuit (recipe, page 390).

Though it's often mistaken for *biskut Arab susu*, the *kuih makmur*'s dough doesn't contain milk powder and has the distinct peanut filling (though some recipes for *biskut Arab susu* do mix chopped peanuts directly into the dough). This cookie gets its unique shape from a pair of flat-edged tongs used to pinch the top of the dough in an angled manner that resembles the veins of a leaf. Special tongs called "*maamoul* tongs" are made for the purpose and available online. Similar tongs are called "pie crust (pastry) crimpers," but if you can't find them, you can use a pair of thin metal ice tongs or your fingers, though the lines will not be as thin or distinct.

Position racks in the top and bottom thirds of the oven and preheat the oven to 325°F (160°C/Gas Mark 3). Line two large baking sheets with parchment paper.

Spread the peanuts out on one of the baking sheets and bake, stirring occasionally, until lightly toasted and fragrant, 8–10 minutes.

Transfer the peanuts to a cutting board and let them cool completely. Reserve the baking sheet. In a food processor, combine the peanuts and white US granulated (UK caster) sugar and process until very finely ground. Scrape the filling into a bowl and set aside.

In a large bowl, whisk together the flour and salt. Add the ghee and use your hands to mix it into the flour until the mixture starts forming a crumbly dough. Add the water and continue mixing until a dough forms and there are no dry patches of flour remaining, kneading only as long as needed to form a smooth dough.

Using a 1-ounce (2-tablespoon) ice cream scoop, portion the dough and roll into balls. Flatten a ball in your hand into a disc and place 1 level teaspoon of the ground peanut filling in the center. Pull the edges of the dough disc up and over the filling to enclose it, meeting in the middle. Crimp the open seam shut with maamoul or pie (pastry) crimping tongs, leaving a ridge down the middle of the filled cookie (like the main vein down the middle of a leaf). Holding the filled leaf-shaped cookie seam-side up in the palm of your hand, use the tongs to pinch along each side of the cookie at a 45-degree angle to form lines that resemble the smaller veins of a leaf. Place the shaped dough on the prepared baking sheet and repeat filling and shaping to make more cookies. Space the cookies 1 inch (2.5 cm) apart on the baking sheets.

Bake until light golden brown all over and dry to the touch, 20–25 minutes, switching racks and rotating the baking sheets front to back halfway through.

Transfer the baking sheets to wire racks. Let the cookies cool on the pans for 1 minute, then transfer them to the racks to cool completely.

Lightly dust the cookies with powdered (icing) sugar before serving.

Southeast Asia, East Asia & Oceania

Peanut-Filled Shortbread Cookies

Ladder Biscuits

Preparation time: 45 minutes
Cooking time: 15 minutes
Makes: About 12 cookies

⅓ cup (65 g) white US granulated
  (UK caster) sugar
5 tablespoons (2½ oz/70 g)
  unsalted butter, softened
4 egg yolks
2 tablespoons almond flour
  (ground almonds)
2¼ teaspoons instant nonfat dry milk
1½ teaspoons anise seeds or fennel
  seeds, finely ground
1 cup (140 g) all-purpose (plain) flour
3 tablespoons vegetable oil

Timor-Leste sits at the eastern tip of a string of islands belonging to Indonesia, with one of its enclaves marooned from the main country in Indonesia. The Indonesian, and thus Dutch, influence of that country is noticeable since Timor-Leste was also occupied by Indonesia for almost a quarter of a century. Prior to that, the Southeast Asian nation was colonized and ruled by Portugal. Hence, many of its foods are products of those influences. One shining example is the Ladder Biscuit, a shortbread-like cookie similar in texture to the crumbly cookies traditionally found in Portugal, the Netherlands, and throughout Western Europe. The cookies are flavored with anise seeds and almond flour (ground almonds), though traditionally they are made with tropical almonds (*Terminalia catappa*)—smaller and milder in flavor than the common almonds (*Prunus amygdalus*) used in European baking. Since tropical almonds are difficult to source outside Asia, the more widely available common almonds are often used as a substitute.

Note: The cookie gets its distinct shape from a pair of flat-edged tongs used to pinch the top of the dough in an overlapping chevron pattern to create the "steps" of a ladder. Special tongs are made for this purpose, but they are difficult to source outside of the region. Instead, you can use a pair of thin metal ice tongs or the tips of two chopsticks laid parallel with the top of the dough, so they pinch a wide swath of it. The cookies are then baked until the design sets in, creating crunchy ridges on the top.

Position racks in the top and bottom thirds of the oven and preheat the oven to 350°F (180°C/Gas Mark 4). Line two large baking sheets with parchment paper.

In a large bowl, with a hand mixer, beat the sugar and butter on medium speed until fluffy and pale, about 2 minutes. Reduce the mixer speed to low and add the egg yolks, beating until well combined. Add the almond flour (ground almonds), milk powder, and ground anise seeds and beat until incorporated. Add the flour and oil and beat once more until evenly combined. The dough is intentionally oily.

Transfer the dough to a clean work surface (do not flour it), then roll out the dough with a rolling pin to ½ inch (13 mm) thick. Cut the dough into rectangular strips that are ¾ × 2¾ inches (2 × 7 cm). Using an offset spatula or table knife, lift the strips off the work surface and transfer them to the prepared baking sheets; because the dough is oily, they should not stick.

Using tongs (see headnote) or two chopsticks laid on their sides and positioned at a 45-degree angle to the long side of one strip, pinch about ⅛ inch (3 mm) of dough along one side and then switch to the other side, spacing the pinches equally so they create a neat chevron pattern along the length of the strip. Repeat with the remaining dough strips.

Bake until golden brown and oil is bubbling along the edges of the cookies, 12–15 minutes, switching racks and rotating the baking sheets front to back halfway through.

Transfer the baking sheets to wire racks and let the cookies cool completely on the pans to allow them to reabsorb the oil before serving.

Butter Cookie Spirals

Rosketti / Roskette

Preparation time: 25 minutes
Cooking time: 20 minutes
Makes: About 12 cookies

1 cup (140 g) cornstarch (cornflour)
⅔ cup (95 g) all-purpose (plain) flour
1 teaspoon baking powder
½ teaspoon fine sea salt
6 tablespoons (3 oz/85 g) unsalted
  butter, softened
⅓ cup (65 g) white US granulated
  (UK caster) sugar
1 teaspoon pure vanilla extract
1 egg

Though Guam, an island in the Pacific Ocean fifteen hundred miles south-southeast of Japan, is a territory of the United States, it was colonized by Spain and remained under its control for over two hundred years. That legacy manifests itself in the island's cuisine. These cookies are miniature versions of *rosca de reyes*, the famous holiday breads served throughout Epiphany in Spain and its former colonies. Sometimes they're shaped like discs imprinted with fork tines, but often, and in keeping with the native word for their shape, are formed as coils.

The native populations of Guam, called the Chamorro, make this cookie, a variant of simple butter cookies or Spanish shortbreads (recipe, page 97). The cookies are made primarily with cornstarch (cornflour), another signifier of the Spanish and Mesoamerican influence over the island's culture. Because they use so much cornstarch, like many Latin American countries' cookies, the weight measurement is important since measuring cornstarch by volume can be more delicate than when measuring wheat flour.

Position racks in the top and bottom thirds of the oven and preheat the oven to 350°F (180°C/Gas Mark 4). Line two large baking sheets with parchment paper.

In a medium bowl, whisk together the cornstarch (cornflour), all-purpose (plain) flour, baking powder, and salt.

In a large bowl, with a hand mixer, combine the butter, sugar, and vanilla and beat on medium speed until light and fluffy, 2–3 minutes. Add the egg and beat until incorporated and smooth. Add the dry ingredients and stir until a dough forms and there are no dry patches of flour remaining.

Scrape the dough onto a lightly floured work surface and form into a large cylinder. Using a knife, cut off pieces of dough, weighing each one to ensure that it is about 1½ ounces (42 g). Shape each piece into a rope 3 inches (7.5 cm) long, then spiral the rope around itself to form a snail or coil shape. Arrange the dough coils on the prepared baking sheets, spaced 2 inches (5 cm) apart.

Bake until light golden brown on the bottom and dry to the touch in the center, 15–18 minutes, switching racks and rotating the baking sheets front to back halfway through.

Transfer the baking sheets to wire racks. Let the cookies cool on the pans for 1 minute, then transfer them to the racks to cool completely.

Fried Honey Cookies

Yakgwa

Preparation time: 1 hour 30 minutes,
 plus 1 hour resting time, chilling time,
 overnight soaking, and drying time
Cooking time: 30 minutes
Makes: About 12 cookies

For the syrup:
1½ cups (505 g) brown rice syrup
¾ cup (250 g) light corn syrup
1 cup (8 fl oz/250 ml) water
2 inches (5 cm) fresh ginger, peeled
 and thinly sliced

For the dough:
2 tablespoons vegetable oil,
 plus more for deep-frying
 2 tablespoons for the dough
1⅓ cups (185 g) all-purpose
 (plain) flour
¼ cup (35 g) glutinous (sweet)
 rice flour
½ teaspoon ground cinnamon
½ teaspoon fine sea salt
2 tablespoons toasted sesame oil
⅓ cup (115 g) honey
¼ cup (2 fl oz/60 ml) rice wine or soju

These cookies belong to a group of confections in Korean culture called *hangwa*, a general term for many small desserts and sweets. The dough is made by rubbing sesame oil into flour and then sweetening it with honey, from which the cookies take their name. They are then stamped into a mold, deep-fried, and soaked in a syrup for hours or days. The original cookies—some accounts have them dating back to the tenth century—were most likely soaked in even more honey because it was a luxury ingredient the royals and aristocrats of the time could afford. Modern recipes, however, tend to make the soaking syrup with a mix of brown rice syrup and corn syrup because of the amount needed to soak the cookies.

The mold to create these fried honey cookies is commonly available in Korea and online, but in case you don't want to buy a special tool for them, they are also commonly shaped into simple diamonds. Soaking the hot cookies in cooled syrup allows them to soak in as much of the syrup as possible, contributing to their chewy but soft texture. The fresh ginger infused into the soaking syrup—and the rice wine in the dough—both help to cut through the sugars to keep the cookies from tasting overwhelmingly sweet.

Make the syrup: In a medium saucepan, combine the brown rice syrup, corn syrup, water, and ginger. Clip a candy/deep-fry thermometer to the side of the pan and place over high heat. Bring the mixture to a boil, then reduce the heat to maintain a steady simmer and cook the syrup, stirring occasionally, until the thermometer reads 220°F (105°C). Remove the pan from the heat and let the syrup cool completely; wash and dry the thermometer and reserve.

Make the dough: In a large bowl, whisk together the all-purpose (plain) flour, glutinous rice flour, cinnamon, and salt. Drizzle the sesame oil and the 2 tablespoons vegetable oil over the flour and use your hands to rub the flour and oil together until it creates a consistent mealy texture in the flour. Place a coarse sieve over another bowl and pour the flour-and-oil mixture into the sieve. Using a spoon or your hands, stir the flour to pass it through the sieve; this will take a little while, but it helps to create a uniform and lump-free dough.

In a small bowl, stir together the honey and rice wine until the honey dissolves. Pour the honey syrup into the sieved flour mixture and stir with a fork until it comes together into a solid dough, lightly kneading only as much as needed to no longer see any dry patches of flour in the bowl. Shape the dough into a ball and wrap in plastic wrap (cling film); let rest at room temperature for 1 hour.

Place the dough on a lightly floured work surface. Using a lightly floured rolling pin, roll out the dough to ¼ inch (6 mm) thick. Using a knife or pizza cutter, cut the dough crosswise into strips 1 inch (2.5 cm) wide, then cut the strips diagonally every 1½ inches (4 cm) to create diamonds. Using a toothpick, stab the underside of each diamond three or four times; this helps the cookies from puffing too much while frying. (Alternatively, portion the dough into 1-ounce/28 g balls and press each ball into a mooncake mold/cookie stamp with the flower insert, stabbing the dough with the toothpick while it's still in the mold. Carefully tap the mold to release the stamped dough round.) Place the cookies on a parchment paper-lined baking sheet and refrigerate for 30 minutes or up to overnight.

Line a large baking sheet with paper towels. Line a second baking sheet with parchment paper and place a wire rack on top of the paper. Pour 2 inches (5 cm) oil into a medium saucepan. Attach the candy/deep-fry thermometer to the side of the pan. Set the pan of cooled syrup near the stove. Heat the oil in the saucepan until it reaches 250°F (121°C) on the thermometer. Maintaining the oil temperature and working in batches of 5 or 6 cookies, place the cookies in the oil and let them fry until they float to the surface of the oil. Then increase the heat under the pan to raise the oil temperature to 325°F (163°C) and continue frying the cookies, flipping them occasionally to ensure they're evenly colored, until completely deep golden brown all over, about 5 minutes.

Using tongs or chopsticks, remove the cookies from the oil and transfer to the paper towels to drain for 1 minute. Remove the pan of oil from the heat and let it cool back down to 250°F (121°C) for frying the next batch. While the fried cookies are still hot, place them in the cooled syrup, turning to coat; let the cookies stay in the syrup while you fry the remaining cookies in the same manner, letting the oil cool down between the batches.

Once all the cookies are in the syrup, stir them gently to ensure they're evenly coated and then cover the pan and let the cookies soak in the syrup overnight or for 1 day. The next day, use tongs or chopsticks to lift each cookie from the syrup, allowing the excess to drain back into the pan, and transfer it to the wire rack set over the baking sheet. Allow all the cookies to drain and dry completely on the outside before serving.

CHINA

Chinese Walnut Cookies
Hup Toh Soh

Preparation time: 1 hour
Cooking time: 30 minutes
Makes: About 24 cookies

⅔ cup (80 g) walnuts
1½ cups (210 g) all-purpose (plain) flour
1½ teaspoons baking powder
¾ teaspoon fine sea salt
¼ teaspoon baking soda (bicarbonate of soda)
1 stick (4 oz/115 g) plus 2 tablespoons (30 g) unsalted butter, softened
½ cup (100 g) white US granulated (UK caster) sugar
2 teaspoons toasted sesame oil
2 egg yolks
Egg wash: 1 egg yolk beaten with 1 teaspoon water
Black sesame seeds, for sprinkling

These crunchy walnut cookies are a staple gift for Chinese New Year. Traditional recipes seem to contain no walnuts at all but reference the walnut in the way the shaped ball of dough looked once flattened. The cookies were often made with rendered pork lard and decorated with black sesame seeds.

Most modern recipes include walnuts to give the cookie a stronger tie to its namesake nut and because they taste great. This recipe swaps the lard for butter for a better taste, and it adds a bit of toasted sesame oil to accent the toasted walnuts and tie in the flavor with the traditional sprinkling of black sesame seeds. Other popular variations include peanuts and cashews; if you want to make the cookies with those nuts, simply swap in the same amount of them for the walnuts.

Position racks in the top and bottom thirds of the oven and preheat the oven to 350°F (180°C/Gas Mark 4). Line two large baking sheets with parchment paper.

Spread the walnuts out in a single layer on one of the baking sheets and bake until lightly toasted and fragrant, 6–8 minutes.

Transfer the nuts to a cutting board and let cool completely. Reserve the baking sheet. Using a food processor, process the walnuts until very finely ground.

In a medium bowl, whisk together the flour, baking powder, salt, and baking soda (bicarb).

In a large bowl, with a hand mixer, combine the butter, sugar, sesame oil, and egg yolks and beat on medium speed until light and fluffy, 2–3 minutes. Add the flour mixture and walnuts and stir until a dough forms and there are no dry patches of flour remaining.

Using a ½-ounce (1-tablespoon) ice cream scoop, portion the dough and roll into balls. Arrange them on the prepared baking sheets, spaced at least 2 inches (5 cm) apart. Using the pad of your thumb, lightly press down on each dough ball to make a depression. Lightly brush the top of each cookie with some of the egg wash and sprinkle the center with a pinch of sesame seeds.

Bake until golden brown and dry to the touch in the center, 15–20 minutes, switching racks and rotating the baking sheets front to back halfway through.

Transfer the baking sheets to wire racks. Let the cookies cool on the pans for 1 minute, then transfer them to the racks to cool completely.

Okinawan Brown Sugar Shortbread
Chinsuko

Preparation time: 20 minutes
Cooking time: 25 minutes
Makes: About 12 cookies

¾ cup (170 g) cold-rendered
  leaf lard, softened
¾ cup (160 g) packed kokuto
  (Okinawan brown sugar) or light
  or dark brown sugar
¾ teaspoon fine sea salt
1½ cups (210 g) all-purpose
  (plain) flour

Many modern cookies in Japan are bought in stores rather than baked in home kitchens. And both homemade and store-bought cookies tend to be based heavily on French and European styles of cookies, like *langues-de-chat* (recipe, page 259) or *sablés* (recipe, page 258) that are flavored with en vogue baking ingredients like matcha or black sesame. *Chinsuko*, though, are tiny shortbread cookies that are unique to Japan, particularly the island of Okinawa. The cookies bear a stronger resemblance to Spanish *polvorones* (recipe, page 97) or Portuguese *areias de Cascais* (recipe, page 96) than anything else. This makes sense because the southern Japanese islands were an important trading point for the Iberian Peninsula countries during the sixteenth century.

The basic mix is lard, wheat flour, and brown sugar, most likely *kokuto*, the raw cane sugar similar to *piloncillo* made in Okinawa. This recipe adds salt to enhance the flavor, though otherwise keeps the traditional mix of ingredients intact.

Position racks in the top and bottom thirds of the oven and preheat the oven to 325°F (160°C/Gas Mark 3). Line two large baking sheets with parchment paper.

Set a large heatproof bowl over a pan of simmering water. Add the lard and melt it completely. Remove the bowl from the pan and add the brown sugar and salt, stirring until evenly moistened and mostly dissolved. Add the flour and stir with a fork until it comes together into a solid dough, lightly kneading only as much as needed to no longer see any dry patches of flour in the bowl.

Shape the dough into a ball. Place it on a lightly floured work surface, then using a lightly floured rolling pin, roll out the dough to ½ inch (13 mm) thick. Using a knife or pizza cutter, preferably with a scalloped or fluted edge, cut the dough crosswise into strips 1 inch (2.5 cm) wide, then cut the strips into 3-inch (7.5 cm) lengths. Arrange the lengths on the prepared baking sheets, spaced 1 inch (2.5 cm) apart.

Bake until the edges of the cookies are golden brown and the cookies are dry to the touch in the center, 20–25 minutes, switching racks and rotating the baking sheets front to back halfway through.

Transfer the baking sheets to wire racks. Let the cookies cool on the pans for 1 minute, then transfer them to the racks to cool completely.

Samoan Coconut Cookies

Masi Samoa

Preparation time: 30 minutes
Cooking time: 30 minutes
Makes: About 72 cookies

3 cups (420 g) all-purpose (plain) flour
1 tablespoon baking powder
1 teaspoon fine sea salt
1 stick (4 oz/115 g) unsalted butter,
  softened
⅔ cup (130 g) white US granulated
  (UK caster) sugar
2 eggs
¾ cup (6 fl oz/175 ml) canned
  unsweetened full-fat coconut milk
1 teaspoon pure vanilla extract

The island nation of Samoa is rich in coconut palm trees and the products made from it, like oil or cream, are one of its chief exports. The meat from those coconuts is heavily used throughout their cooking, so it's no surprise that one of the most popular cookies on the island is made with it. Unlike many coconut cookies that utilize the dried shredded (desiccated) version, *masi*—Samoan for "biscuits"—are made with the milk of freshly grated coconut.

When making these cookies at home, canned unsweetened coconut milk is more convenient and works just as well. They are a softer style of biscuit thanks to the large amount of coconut milk and eggs, but they are typically baked longer than other similar cookies to dry them out a little bit and create a crumbly break. They also do not taste strongly of coconut, so if that is something you're after, add 1 teaspoon coconut extract along with the vanilla in the recipe. While the cookies are traditionally cut into rectangles/tiles, you can cut them into rounds or use any shape of cutter.

Position racks in the top and bottom thirds of the oven and preheat the oven to 350°F (180°C/Gas Mark 4). Line two large baking sheets with parchment paper.

In a medium bowl, whisk together the flour, baking powder, and salt.

In a large bowl, with a hand mixer, beat the butter and sugar on medium speed until light and fluffy, 2–3 minutes. Add the eggs, one at a time, and beat until incorporated and smooth. Pour in the coconut milk and vanilla and beat on low speed until smooth. Add the dry ingredients and stir until a dough forms and there are no dry patches of flour remaining.

Scrape the dough onto a lightly floured work surface. Using a rolling pin, roll out the dough to ¼ inch (6 mm) thick. Using a pizza cutter or a long knife, cut the dough lengthwise into strips 1½ inches (4 cm) wide, then cut the strips crosswise every 2 inches (5 cm) to produce rectangles. Reroll the dough to cut out more cookies. Arrange the dough rectangles on the prepared baking sheets, spaced 1 inch (2.5 cm) apart.

Bake until light golden brown at the edges and on the bottom and dry to the touch in the center, 25–30 minutes, switching racks and rotating the baking sheets front to back halfway through.

Transfer the baking sheets to wire racks. Let the cookies cool on the pans for 1 minute, then transfer them to the racks to cool completely.

sub-saharan africa

As in Southeast Asia, cookies in Sub-Saharan Africa are largely vestiges of colonialism, for example, in South Africa with the Dutch influence of sugar and spices. France also had influences on the treats of its former colonies Mauritius and Senegal, while other crumbly cookies of East and West Africa adhere to modern classical combinations based on local starches and ingredients. Store-bought and packaged cookies dominate in much of this part of Africa.

Peanut-Topped Sugar Cookies

Cinq Centimes

Preparation time: 15 minutes,
  plus cooling time
Cooking time: 20 minutes
Makes: About 18 cookies

2 cups (280 g) all-purpose (plain) flour
½ teaspoon baking soda
  (bicarbonate of soda)
½ teaspoon fine sea salt
1½ sticks (6 oz/170 g) unsalted
  butter, softened
1 cup (200 g) white US granulated
  (UK caster) sugar
1 egg
1 teaspoon pure vanilla extract
½ cup (130 g) natural peanut butter
½ cup (75 g) salted roasted peanuts,
  roughly chopped

These Senegalese street-snack cookies are named for their similarity to the French five-centime coin, though the cookies are most likely bigger than they used to be. The original treatment for these cookies may have been to take store-bought cookies—most likely French *sablés* (recipe, page 258)—and top them with a schmear of peanut butter and a sprinkling of chopped peanuts, but this recipe makes the treats fully from scratch. They use natural peanut butter (no salt, sugar, or hydrogenation), since that will best approximate what's used in Senegal.

Position racks in the top and bottom thirds of the oven and preheat the oven to 350°F (180°C/Gas Mark 4). Line two large baking sheets with parchment paper.

In a medium bowl, whisk together the flour, baking soda (bicarb), and salt.

In a large bowl, with a hand mixer, beat the butter and sugar on medium speed until light and fluffy, 2–3 minutes. Add the egg and vanilla and beat until smooth. Add the dry ingredients and stir until a dough forms and there are no dry patches of flour remaining.

Using a 1-ounce (2-tablespoon) ice cream scoop, portion the dough and roll into 1-inch (2.5 cm) balls. Arrange them on the prepared baking sheets, spaced 2 inches (5 cm) apart. Flatten them with the palm of your hand as you go.

Bake until light golden brown and dry to the touch in the center, 20–22 minutes, switching racks and rotating the baking sheets front to back halfway through.

Transfer the baking sheets to wire racks. Let the cookies cool on the pans for 1 minute, then transfer them to the racks to cool completely.

Spread about 1 heaping teaspoon peanut butter to within ¼ inch (6 mm) of the edge over the top of each cookie and sprinkle with chopped peanuts before serving.

Peanut-Topped Sugar Cookies

Coconut and Tapioca Biscuits
Ayigbe

Preparation time: 25 minutes
Cooking time: 20 minutes
Makes: About 18 cookies

2½ cups (350 g) tapioca starch
¼ cup (50 g) plus 2 tablespoons white
  US granulated (UK caster) sugar
½ teaspoon fine sea salt
¾ cup (6 fl oz/175 ml) canned
  unsweetened full-fat coconut milk

These sweet street snacks are a specialty of the town of Agbozume in the coastal region of Volta in Ghana. Tapioca, the fine powdery starch that comes from ground yuca (cassava) root, is mixed with fresh coconut milk, sugar, and salt and then formed into a dough that's baked and sold in markets. The cookies are typically baked in groups of six with their sides touching and stamped with a special press that creates a radiator-like shape on top of the cookies. Many homemade recipes omit the stamping and flatten the cookies by hand.

Unlike Haitian *bonbon amidon* (recipe, page 149), which uses cassava flour, the ground flour from the whole yuca root, these *ayigbe* use tapioca, which is the starch that comes out of the ground flour when washed in water. It gives the cookies an extremely light and fine texture akin to a wafer-like cracker more than a dense, crumbly cookie.

Position racks in the top and bottom thirds of the oven and preheat the oven to 350°F (180°C/Gas Mark 4). Line two large baking sheets with parchment paper.

In a large bowl, whisk together the tapioca starch, sugar, and salt. Add the coconut milk and stir until a dough forms and there are no dry patches of flour remaining. Knead the dough lightly into a ball.

Using a ½-ounce (1-tablespoon) ice cream scoop, portion the dough and roll into balls. Place a ball on a baking sheet and flatten it into a 1½- to 2-inch (4 to 5 cm) round with your fingers. Repeat with the remaining dough balls, spacing the dough balls close enough to the others that when you flatten them, the rounds just touch each other.

Bake until barely light golden brown on the bottom and dry to the touch all over, 18–20 minutes, switching racks and rotating the baking sheets front to back halfway through.

Transfer the baking sheets to wire racks. Let the cookies cool on the pans for 1 minute, then transfer them to the racks to cool completely.

Gari Biscuits

Preparation time: 25 minutes
Cooking time: 20 minutes
Makes: About 30 cookies

1½ cups (210 g) all-purpose
(plain) flour
1 cup (130 g) cassava flour
¾ cup (150 g) white US granulated
(UK caster) sugar
1½ teaspoons baking powder
½ teaspoon fine sea salt
½ teaspoon freshly grated
nutmeg (optional)
1 stick (4 oz/115 g) unsalted butter, cut
into ½-inch (13 mm) cubes, chilled
¼ cup (2 fl oz/60 ml) plus 2
tablespoons whole milk
1 egg, lightly beaten

The cassava (yuca) root is an important staple of the cuisine of Ghana and most of West Africa, so it's no surprise that it makes its way into a cookie from that region. *Gari* is the name for cassava in Ghana, and its ground flour is used in these buttery, tender biscuits. Most likely influenced by the baking traditions of Portugal and the UK, these cookies include wheat flour and egg, as well.

Unlike *ayigbe* (recipe, opposite), which use the starch from the root—tapioca—*gari* biscuits, use ground cassava flour, sometimes labeled as manioc; that is what you'll want to use here. Some old recipes used finely ground fresh yuca (cassava) root, though most now use the dry flour and sometimes mix in coconut (for flavor or to approximate the texture of cassava flour) or both. Nutmeg is also in some recipes but not in others, so it's listed as optional in this recipe.

Position racks in the top and bottom thirds of the oven and preheat the oven to 350°F (180°C/Gas Mark 4). Line two large baking sheets with parchment paper.

In a medium bowl, whisk together the flour, cassava flour, sugar, baking powder, salt, and nutmeg (if using). Add the butter and use your hands to rub the butter into the dry ingredients until it breaks down and the mixture is the texture of couscous. Add the milk and egg and stir until a dough forms and there are no dry patches of flour remaining.

Using a 1-ounce (2-tablespoon) ice cream scoop, portion the dough and roll into 1-inch (2.5 cm) balls. Arrange them on the prepared baking sheets, spaced 2 inches (5 cm) apart. Flatten them with the palm of your hand as you go. Using the tines of a fork, prick each round of dough on top three times.

Bake until light golden brown at the edges and dry to the touch in the center, 18–20 minutes, switching racks and rotating the baking sheets front to back halfway through.

Transfer the baking sheets to wire racks. Let the cookies cool on the pans for 1 minute, then transfer them to the racks to cool completely.

Nigerian Coconut Macaroon Balls

Shuku-Shuku

Preparation time: 45 minutes
Cooking time: 15 minutes
Makes: About 18 cookies

2 cups (200 g) finely grated coconut,
  fresh or thawed frozen
½ cup (65 g) powdered (icing)
  sugar, sifted
½ teaspoon fine sea salt
½ teaspoon pure vanilla
  extract (optional)
4 eggs yolks
½ cup (70 g) all-purpose (plain) flour

Nigeria's coconut macaroon uses only egg yolks instead of egg whites, which help to enrich the cookies with a golden hue. Also, instead of mixing flour into the dough—or leaving it out altogether—the dough for these *shuku-shuku* is formed into balls then *rolled* in flour (or breadcrumbs in some recipes). The flour creates a barrier to the sticky-sweet coconut mixture inside, helping the cookies maintain their ball shape and keeping them dry.

These cookies are sometimes referred to as "coconut candy" and the name *shuku-shuku* is also used to describe a coconut milk-based caramel candy, but these treats are cookies in the tradition of macaroons. Modern recipes use finely ground dried coconut for convenience, but older recipes sometimes call for freshly grated coconut, so this recipe uses the fresh coconut (which you can find frozen in many grocery stores) to provide a chewier and more tender consistency.

Position racks in the top and bottom thirds of the oven and preheat the oven to 350°F (180°C/Gas Mark 4). Line two large baking sheets with parchment paper.

In a medium bowl, combine the coconut, sugar, salt, vanilla (if using), and egg yolks and stir until evenly combined into a stiff dough.

Spread the flour on a plate. Using a ½-ounce (1-tablespoon) ice cream scoop, portion and roll into ½-inch (13 mm) balls. Roll each ball in the flour, shaking off any excess, then arrange on the prepared baking sheets, spaced 1 inch (2.5 cm) apart.

Bake until light golden brown and dry to the touch all over, about 15 minutes, switching racks and rotating the baking sheets front to back halfway through.

Transfer the baking sheets to wire racks and let the cookies cool completely on the pans.

Sesame Seed Butter Cookies

Ka'ak

Preparation time: 10 minutes
Cooking time: 25 minutes
Makes: About 18 cookies

2 tablespoons sesame seeds
2 cups (280 g) all-purpose (plain) flour
2 tablespoons white US granulated
  (UK caster) sugar
1 teaspoon baking powder
½ teaspoon fine sea salt
¾ cup (150 g) ghee or clarified butter,
  melted and cooled
¼ cup (65 g) full-fat yogurt
1 teaspoon pure vanilla extract
1 teaspoon ground cardamom
Powdered (icing) sugar, for coating

These cookies share the same name as the Egyptian version (recipe, page 50) because they are essentially the same cookie. The countries of Sudan and South Sudan sit directly south of Egypt and have been influenced by the country for centuries, particularly in cuisine. Whereas the Egyptian original is a relatively simple cookie, this Sudanese version adds toasted sesame seeds. Sometimes cardamom and/or anise seeds are added, too, giving a heady fragrance.

Ghee, a fermented clarified butter, and yogurt are also typically included in the mix, which provide a pleasant tang and softer texture than the usual pan-Middle Eastern *ka'ak*. These Sudanese cookies, though, aren't typically very sweet. Very little, if any sugar is added to the dough because the outsides are heavily dusted in powdered (icing) sugar, providing all the sweetness these treats need.

- -

Position racks in the top and bottom thirds of the oven and preheat the oven to 325°F (160°C/Gas Mark 3). Line two large baking sheets with parchment paper.

Spread the sesame seeds out on one of the baking sheets and roast in the oven until fragrant and lightly browned, about 6 minutes.

Transfer the sesame seeds to a medium bowl and let the seeds cool. Reserve the baking sheet. Add the flour, white US granulated (UK caster) sugar, baking powder, and salt to the sesame seeds and whisk to combine.

In a large bowl, whisk together the melted ghee, yogurt, vanilla, and cardamom. Add the dry ingredients and stir with a fork until it comes together into a solid dough, lightly kneading only as much as needed to no longer see any dry patches of flour in the bowl.

Shape the dough into a ball and place it on a lightly floured work surface. Using a lightly floured rolling pin, roll out the dough to ½ inch (13 mm) thick. Using a 2-inch (5 cm) round cutter, cut out rounds of dough. Reroll scraps to cut out more cookies. Arrange them on the prepared baking sheets, spaced 1 inch (2.5 cm) apart.

Bake until the edges and bottoms of the cookies are golden brown and the cookies are dry to the touch in the center, 18–20 minutes, switching racks and rotating the baking sheets front to back halfway through.

Transfer the baking sheets to wire racks. Let the cookies cool on the pans for 1 minute, then transfer them to the racks to cool completely.

Coat the cookies liberally with powdered (icing) sugar before serving.

Piped Cardamom Butter Cookies

Buskut / Buskud Ciida

Preparation time: 30 minutes
Cooking time: 15 minutes
Makes: About 24 cookies

2 cups (280 g) all-purpose (plain) flour
1½ teaspoons ground cardamom
½ teaspoon baking powder
¾ teaspoon fine sea salt
1 cup (200 g) white US granulated
  (UK caster) sugar
1½ sticks (6 oz/170 g) unsalted butter,
  softened
½ teaspoon pure vanilla extract
1 egg

These cookies—one of many styles collectively called *buskut* or biscuit"—
are a popular treat in Somalia and often made to celebrate the holiday
Eid. Typically, they are piped into a wreath or ring shape using a cookie
press. Another very popular variation is called *buskut dha dheer* or "long
biscuit," using the same dough piped through a ridged, flat disc, to create
corrugated planks that bake up crisp and are often used to sandwich fruit
preserves. Somalia's colonization by Italy and that country's influence on its
cuisine, is also likely an influence via the Italian *paste di meliga* (recipe,
page 124).

Ground cardamom is also usually the chief spice in these cookies,
showing the influence of Somalia's position on the horn of Africa
as an important point along the spice trade. While many recipes use
neutral oil as the fat, some modern ones use butter, which contributes
a better flavor to complement the fragrant cardamom.

Position racks in the top and bottom thirds of the oven and preheat the
oven to 350°F (180°C/Gas Mark 4). Set out two large baking sheets and
leave them unlined.

In a medium bowl, whisk together the flour, cardamom, baking powder,
and salt.

In a large bowl, with a hand mixer, beat the sugar and butter on medium
speed until light and fluffy, 2–3 minutes. Add the vanilla and egg and beat
until smooth. Add the dry ingredients and stir until a dough forms and there
are no dry patches of flour remaining.

Working in batches, scrape the dough into a cookie press/gun fitted
with a wreath or flower disc and press shapes 1 inch (2.5 cm) apart
on the baking sheets. If making the "long biscuit" shape, use the ridged
line disc, sometimes called the "biscuit" disc, to pipe 3-inch (7.5 cm)
lengths of dough, arranging them 1 inch (2.5 cm) apart on the baking sheets.

Bake until very lightly golden brown on the bottom and dry to the touch
all over, 12–15 minutes, switching racks and rotating the baking sheets front
to back halfway through.

Transfer the baking sheets to wire racks. Let the cookies cool on the
pans for 1 minute, then transfer them to the racks to cool completely.

Crunchies

Preparation time: 20 minutes
Cooking time: 45 minutes
Makes: 18 cookies

2 cups (190 g) rolled oats
1 cup (140 g) all-purpose (plain) flour
1 cup (100 g) unsweetened shredded
  (desiccated) coconut
1 teaspoon ground cinnamon
¾ teaspoon fine sea salt
½ teaspoon ground ginger
1½ sticks (6 oz/170 g) unsalted butter
¾ cup (170 g) packed light brown
  sugar
2 tablespoons British golden syrup
  or honey
1 teaspoon baking soda (bicarbonate
  of soda)

Even though South African cuisine has many influences from indigenous, Southeast Asian, and Dutch populations that have combined their traditions there over the centuries, these beloved bar cookies can pretty clearly be attributed to the influence of their inclusion in the British Commonwealth. The cookie bars, known as "crunchies," are dominated by oats and made with baking soda (bicarb) stirred into a mix of butter and golden syrup. They are like Australia and New Zealand's ANZAC Biscuits (recipe, page 283), which are also similar to English Melting Moments (recipe, page 280).

Instead of forming the dough into drop cookies, it is pressed into a rectangular pan, baked, and then cut into neat squares. Golden syrup—a British inverse syrup that tastes of butterscotch and for which there is no good substitute—is traditional in these cookies; however, many modern recipes use honey instead. Either one works here.

Preheat the oven to 325°F (160°C/Gas Mark 3). Line a 9 × 13-inch (23 × 33 cm) metal baking pan with parchment paper.

In a large bowl, whisk together the oats, flour, coconut, cinnamon, salt, and ginger.

In a medium saucepan, melt the butter, sugar, and golden syrup over medium-high heat, stirring until the mixture begins to bubble at the edges. Remove the pan from the heat and whisk in the baking soda (bicarb); it will bubble up. Pour the foaming mixture into the bowl with the dry ingredients and stir until it forms a dough and there are no dry patches of flour in the bowl.

Scrape the dough into the prepared baking pan and flatten into an even layer.

Bake until the cookie slab is deep golden brown all over, 35–40 minutes, rotating the pan front to back halfway through.

Transfer the pan to a wire rack and let the cookie slab rest for 10 minutes.

Place the wire rack upside down over the baking pan and flip them together, pulling on the parchment paper if needed to guide the slab out of the pan. Peel off and discard the paper. Flip the slab upright onto a cutting board and while still warm, cut it into a grid 3 down and 6 across to yield 18 cookies. Let the squares cool completely to firm up before serving.

South African Gingerbread Cookies
Soetkoekies

Preparation time: 45 minutes,
  plus chilling time
Cooking time: 15 minutes
Makes: About 30 cookies

2½ cups (350 g) all-purpose
  (plain) flour
1 teaspoon baking powder
2 teaspoons freshly grated nutmeg
1 teaspoon ground cinnamon
1 teaspoon ground ginger
½ teaspoon ground cloves
1 teaspoon fine sea salt
1¼ cups (250 g) white US granulated
  (UK caster) sugar
1 stick (4 oz/115 g) unsalted
  butter, softened
¼ cup (55 g) cold-rendered
  leaf lard, softened
2 eggs
¼ cup (2 fl oz/60 ml) dessert
  wine (see headnote) or grape
  must syrup/molasses

Descended from the Dutch tradition of *speculaas* (recipe, page 232) and *taai taai* (see page 232), these gingerbread-style cookies are a simple butter cookie spiced predominantly with nutmeg, but also cinnamon, ginger, and cloves. The name translates roughly as "sweet cookies" and there are unspiced versions that go by that name, too.

Older recipes use a 50/50 mix of butter and lard, though modern versions stick to all butter. In lieu of molasses or a caramelized sugar syrup, a sweet dessert wine is used, usually a South African fortified or sherry style; Italian moscato or Marsala also works. This is most likely a modern convenience concession to using a local grape must syrup called *moskonfyt*, which appears in old recipes and can be used here if you can find it. In either case, the light color of these gingerbread cookies sets them apart from their deeper-brown European counterparts.

Position racks in the top and bottom thirds of the oven and preheat the oven to 350°F (180°C/Gas Mark 4). Line two large baking sheets with parchment paper.

In a medium bowl, whisk together the flour, baking powder, nutmeg, cinnamon, ginger, cloves and salt.

In a large bowl, with a hand mixer, combine the sugar, butter, and lard and beat on medium speed until light and fluffy, 2–3 minutes. Add the eggs, one at a time, beating until smooth after each addition. Stir in the wine. Add the dry ingredients and stir until a dough forms and there are no dry patches of flour remaining. Scrape the dough onto a clean work surface and shape into a disc. Wrap in plastic wrap (cling film) and refrigerate for 1 hour or up to 2 days.

Unwrap the dough and transfer it to a lightly floured work surface. Using a lightly floured rolling pin, roll out the dough to ¼ inch (6 mm) thick. Using a 2-inch (5 cm) round or any shape cutter of similar size, cut out shapes of dough. Reroll the scraps to cut out more cookies. Arrange them on the prepared baking sheets, spaced 1 inch (2.5 cm) apart.

Bake until the edges of the cookies are light golden brown and the cookies are dry to the touch in the center, 10–12 minutes, switching racks and rotating the baking sheets front to back halfway through.

Transfer the baking sheets to wire racks. Let the cookies cool on the pans for 1 minute, then transfer them to the racks to cool completely.

Pink Jam-Filled Cookie Sandwiches

Napolitaines

Preparation time: 40 minutes, plus
  chilling, cooling, and setting time
Cooking time: 20 minutes
Makes: About 30 cookie sandwiches

1½ sticks (6 oz/170 g) unsalted
  butter, softened
¾ teaspoon fine sea salt
1¾ cups (245 g) all-purpose
  (plain) flour
¼ cup (80 g) thick-set raspberry
  or strawberry preserves
1½ cups (205 g) powdered
  (icing) sugar, sifted
2 tablespoons water
1 teaspoon pure vanilla extract
1 teaspoon fresh lemon juice
Pink gel food coloring

These crumbly butter cookie sandwiches from Mauritius are a standout because of the bright pink icing that coats the whole cookie. The Dutch, British, and French have all influenced the cuisine of Mauritius over periods of colonization, but French food culture had the biggest influence. That is apparent in these tiny cookie sandwiches made of two *sablé*-like cookies (recipe, page 258). Their name points to the treats possibly being a cookie version of the French mille-feuille, or Napoleon pastry, which consists of two or more layers of puff pastry sandwiched with custard and then topped with a powdered (icing) sugar icing.

The cookies here are made with just flour and butter (this recipe adds salt to enhance the cookie's flavor) rubbed together until they form a smooth dough. There is no sugar in the actual cookie because the cookies get sandwiched with a thick fruit preserve—often raspberry or strawberry, but numerous variations exist—before being coated with the characteristic pink icing. Warming the icing dissolves the sugar fully, allowing it to set smooth and shiny around the cookies.

Position racks in the top and bottom thirds of the oven and preheat the oven to 325°F (160°C/Gas Mark 3). Line two large baking sheets with parchment paper.

Place the butter in a large bowl and sprinkle evenly with the salt. Add the flour and use your hands to rub the flour and butter together over and over until they become a soft, pliable dough. Scrape the dough onto a clean work surface and flatten into a disc 1 inch (13 mm) thick. Wrap the disc in plastic wrap (cling film) and refrigerate the dough for 1 hour or up to 2 days.

Unwrap the dough and transfer it to a lightly floured work surface. Using a lightly floured rolling pin, roll out the dough to ¼ inch (6 mm) thick. Using a 1½-inch (4 cm) round cutter, cut out rounds of dough. Reroll the scraps to cut out more cookies. Arrange them on the prepared baking sheets, spaced 1 inch (2.5 cm) apart.

Bake until the edges of the cookies are light golden brown and the cookies are dry to the touch in the center, about 20 minutes, switching racks and rotating the baking sheets front to back halfway through.

Transfer the baking sheets to wire racks. Let the cookies cool on the pans for 1 minute, then transfer them to the racks to cool completely.

Flip half the cookies over and spread about 1 teaspoon of the jam over each. Top with another cookie to create a cookie sandwich. Place the rack of cookies over a sheet of parchment paper or a baking sheet.

In a small heatproof bowl, combine the sugar, water, vanilla, and lemon juice and stir until it forms a stiff paste. Stir in a few drops of the food coloring until the paste is uniformly colored. Place the bowl over a pan of simmering water to warm the paste, stirring until it loosens to a pourable, smooth icing. (Alternatively, microwave the paste in 15-second bursts until smooth.)

Pour a spoonful of the icing over each cookie sandwich so it covers the top, letting all the excess drip over the sides. Scrape up any icing that falls below the rack and reheat if needed to coat the rest of the cookies. Let the cookies stand until the icing hardens before serving.

Pink Jam-Filled Cookie Sandwiches

Bibliography

Books

100 Resep Kue Kering Klasik. Indonesia: Gramedia Pustaka Utama, 2013.

1000 Ricette della Cucina Italiana. Italy: Rizzoli, 2010.

Abed, Sina. *Afghan Desserts Made Simple*. (n.p.): Dog Ear Publishing, 2010.

Abood, Maureen. *Rose Water and Orange Blossoms: Fresh & Classic Recipes from My Lebanese Kitchen*. United States: Running Press, 2015.

Adamson, Melitta Weiss, and Segan, Francine, eds. *Entertaining from Ancient Rome to the Super Bowl: An Encyclopedia*. United States: Greenwood, 2008.

Aggarwal, Uma. *America's Favorite Recipes the Melting Pot Cuisine: Part III*. United States: AuthorHouse, 2016.

———. *Incredible Taste of Indian Vegetarian Cuisine*. India: Allied Publishers, 2016.

Ajo, Salma. *Melodies Under the Palms: Memories from the Iraq I Used to Know*. United States: AuthorHouse, 2016.

Albala, Ken. *Food Cultures of the World Encyclopedia*. Volume 2. United States: Greenwood, 2011.

Algar, Ayla Esen. *The Complete Book of Turkish Cooking*. United Kingdom: Routledge, 2013.

Algerian Cookbook: Authentic Algerian Cooking with Simple and Easy Algerian Recipes. 2nd ed. United States: BookSumo Press, 2019.

Ali-Karamali, Sumbul. *Growing Up Muslim: Understanding the Beliefs and Practices of Islam*. United States: Ember, 2013.

Allen, Beth. *Good Housekeeping: Great Home Cooking: 300 Traditional Recipes*. United States: Hearst, 2011.

Allen, Darina. *Irish Traditional Cooking*. United Kingdom: Kyle Books, 2018.

Altpeter, Gabriele. *Homemade German Plätzchen: And Other Christmas Cookies*. Germany: SomePublisher, 2014.

America's Test Kitchen. *The Perfect Cookie: Your Ultimate Guide to Foolproof Cookies, Brownies & Bars*. United States: America's Test Kitchen, 2017.

———. *Tasting Italy: A Culinary Journey*. United States: National Geographic Society, 2018.

———. *Desserts Illustrated: The Ultimate Guide to All Things Sweet*. United States: America's Test Kitchen, 2022.

Anton, Speranța. *Rețete culinare și Sfaturi Pentru Sănătate*. Romania: Polirom, 2015.

Asselle, Maria Grazia, and Yarvin, Brian. *Cucina Piemontese: Cooking from Italy's Piedmont*. United States: Hippocrene Books, 2005.

Assil, Reem. *Arabiyya: Recipes from the Life of an Arab in Diaspora*. United States: Ten Speed Press, 2022.

Atassi, Anas. *Sumac: Recipes and Stories from Syria*. Australia: Murdoch Books, 2021.

Aurell, Brontë. *ScandiKitchen: Fika and Hygge: Comforting Cakes and Bakes from Scandinavia with Love*. United Kingdom: Ryland Peters & Small, 2018.

Aus der Kombüse: Rezepte der Piratenpartei. Germany: Neobooks, 2012.

Auschwitz-Birkenau Memorial Foundation. *Honey Cake and Latkes: Recipes from the Old World by the Auschwitz-Birkenau Survivors*. United States: Melcher Media, 2022.

Ávila Granados, Jesús. *El Libro de la Repostería Tradicional*. Spain: Robinbook, Ediciones S.L., 2004.

Ayubi, Durkhanai. *Parwana: Recipes and Stories from an Afghan Kitchen*. Australia: Murdoch Books, 2020.

Baggett, Nancy. *Simply Sensational Cookies*. United Kingdom: Houghton Mifflin Harcourt, 2012.

Bajada, Simon. *Baltic: New and Old Recipes from Estonia, Latvia and Lithuania*. United States: Hardie Grant Books, 2019.

Barros, Luiza Medeiros Monteiro. *Brazilian Recipes*. Germany: BookRix, 2017.

Batmanglij, Najmieh. *Food of Life: Ancient Persian and Modern Iranian Cooking and Ceremonies*. United States: Mage Publishers, 1986.

———. *Cooking in Iran: Regional Recipes & Kitchen Secrets*. United States: Mage Publishers, 2018.

Baugh, Ingeborg Hydle et al. *Gudrun's Kitchen: Recipes from a Norwegian Family*. United States: Wisconsin Historical Society Press, 2012.

Beard, James. *James Beard's American Cookery*. United States: Little, Brown, 1972.

Benjamin, Beverley A. *Four Generations Cookbook*. Canada: FriesenPress, 2016.

Beranbaum, Rose Levy. *The Cookie Bible*. United States: Houghton Mifflin Harcourt, 2022.

Bertinet, Richard. *Pastry: A Master Class for Everyone, in 150 Photos and 50 Recipes*. United States: Chronicle Books, 2013.

Better Homes and Gardens. *New Cook Book*. United States: Meredith Books, 2006.

Betty Crocker. *Betty Crocker's Cooky Book*. General Mills, facsimile 1963 edition. United States: Hungry Minds, 2002.

Biscotti: Per la festa, a Colazione o All'ora del The il Biscotto è come un Sorriso. Italy: Script edizione, 2012.

Bissett, Wina. *Wina Bissett's Simply Indonesian: 100% Freshly Homemade with Love*. Indonesia: Gramedia Pustaka Utama, 2015.

Björk Jónsdóttir, Nina, and Magnus, Edda. *How to Live Icelandic*. United Kingdom: White Lion Publishing, 2021.

Bladholm, Linda. *Latin & Caribbean Grocery Stores Demystified: A Food Lover's Guide to the Best Ingredients in the Traditional Foods of Mexico, Peru, Chile, Argentina, Brazil, Venezuela, Colombia, and the Caribbean Islands Including Cuba, Puerto Rico, & Jamaica*. United States: Renaissance Books, 2015.

———. *The Indian Grocery Store Demystified: A Food Lover's Guide to All the Best Ingredients in the Traditional Foods of India, Pakistan, and Bangladesh*. United States: St. Martin's Press, 2016.

Blasi, Marlena de. *A Taste of Southern Italy: Delicious Recipes and a Dash of Culture*. United States: Ballantine Books, 2009.

Bloom, Carole. *Cookies for Dummies*. Germany: Wiley, 2011.

Bodic, Slavka. *The Ultimate Croatian Cookbook: 111 Dishes from Croatia to Cook Right Now*. (n.p.): Self-Published, 2021.

———. *The Ultimate Venezuelan Cookbook: 111 Dishes from Venezuela to Cook Right Now*. (n.p): Self-Published, 2021.

Boermans, Mary-Anne. *Great British Bakes: Forgotten Treasures for Modern Bakers*. United Kingdom: Square Peg, 2013.

Boga, Yasa. *Kue-Kue Indonesia*. Indonesia: Gramedia Pustaka Utama, 1997.

Book of Tasty and Healthy Food. United States: SkyPeak Publishing, 2012.

Borromeo, Lillian Mercado-Lising. *Atching Lillian's Heirloom Recipes: Romancing the Past Through Traditional Calutung Capampangan*. Philippines: Center for Kapampangan Studies, Holy Angel University, 2011.

Boudet, Sébastien. *The French Baker: Authentic Recipes for Traditional Breads, Desserts, and Dinners*. United States: Skyhorse Publishing, 2013.

Bouley, David, Lohninger, Mario, and Clark, Melissa. *East of Paris: The New Cuisines of Austria and the Danube*. United States: Ecco Press, 2003.

Boven, Yvvette van. *Home Baked: More Than 150 Recipes for Sweet and Savory Goodies*. United States: Harry N. Abrams, 2015.

Bowler, Gerry. *The World Encyclopedia of Christmas*. Canada: McClelland & Stewart, 2012.

Braun, Emil. *The Baker's Book: A Practical Handbook of the Baking Industry in All Countries*. United States: Emil Braun, 1901.

Braun, Jakob. *Die Nürnberger Lebkuchen: Praktische Anleitung zur Herstellung aller Sorten Lebkuchen nach Nürnberger Art*. (n.p.): UNIKUM, 2015.

Bremzen, Anya von, and Welchman, John. *Please to the Table: The Russian Cookbook*. United States: Workman Publishing, 1990.

Bretherton, Caroline. *Illustrated Step-by-Step Baking*. United Kingdom: Dorling Kindersley, 2011.

Brizova, Joza. *The Czechoslovak Cookbook*. United States: Clarkson Potter/Ten Speed, 1965.

Brodmann, Baron Chris. *Der Baron Bäckt*. Germany: epubli, 2015.

Broek, Rutger van den. *Koekjesbijbel: Rutger Bakt van Amandelkrullen tot Zeeuwse Speculaas*. Netherlands: Carrera, 2018.

Brones, Anna, and Kindvall, Johanna. *Fika: The Art of The Swedish Coffee Break, with Recipes for Pastries, Breads, and Other Treats*. United States: Ten Speed Press, 2015.

Broomfield, Andrea. *Food and Cooking in Victorian England: A History*. United Kingdom: Praeger Publishers, 2007.

Brown, Catherine. *Classic Scots Cookery*. United Kingdom: Angel's Share, 2011.

Brugge, Tini, and Vos, Gert. *Hemelse Spijzen: Een Jaarkrans van Recepten en hun Diepere Betekenis*. Belgium: Lannoo, 2004.

Bryant, Barbara; Fentress, Betsy; and Balslev, Lynda. *Almonds: Recipes, History, Culture*. United States: Gibbs Smith, 2014.

Bucheli, Jeannette. *Hilf Dir Selbst: Traditionelle Hausmittel und ihre Anwendung*. (n.p.): Appenzeller Verlag, 2014.

Buchhofer, Alexander. *Handbuch der Berner Kochkurse für Frauen und Töchter*. Switzerland: Michel & Büchler, 1894.

Byrd, Melanie, and Dunn, John P., eds. *Cooking Through History: A Worldwide Encyclopedia of Food with Menus and Recipes*. United States: Greenwood, 2020.

Byrn, Anne. *American Cookie: The Snaps, Drops, Jumbles, Tea Cakes, Bars & Brownies That We Have Loved for Generations*. United States: Rodale Books, 2018.

Byron, May. *Pot-Luck*. United Kingdom: Hodder and Stoughton, 1926.

Caggiano, Biba. *Modern Italian Cooking*. United States: Simon & Schuster, 1991.

Caldesi, Katie, and Caldesi, Giancarlo. *The Italian Cookery Course*. United Kingdom: Kyle Books, 2022.

Capasso, Lydia, and Esposito, Giovanna. *Gli Aristopiatti: Storie e Ricette della Cucina Aristocratica Italiana*. Italy: Guido Tommasi Editore, 2022.

Capatti, Alberto, and Montanari, Massimo. *Italian Cuisine: A Cultural History*. United States: Columbia University Press, 2003.

Carrara, Damiano, and Carrara, Massimiliano. *Dolce Italia: Authentic Italian Baking*. United Kingdom: Lulu Publishing Services, 2016.

Cartin, Patricia. *A Taste of Latin America: Culinary Traditions and Classic Recipes from Argentina, Brazil, Chile, Colombia, Costa Rica, Cuba, Mexico, Peru, Puerto Rico & Venezuela*. United States: Charlesbridge, 2017.

Casarini, Massimo. *I Quaderni del Loggione: La Collana di chi, a Tavola, ci si Mette d'Impegno*. Italy: Damster Edizioni, 2013.

Castella, Krystina. *A World of Cake: 150 Recipes for Sweet Traditions from Cultures Near and Far*. United States: Storey Publishing, 2012.

Chalk, Leila. *The Lost Chef: Hajro Dizdar and the Art of Bosnian Cooking*. (n.p.): Self-Published, 2020.

Chang, Danielle. *Lucky Rice: Stories and Recipes from Night Markets, Feasts, and Family Tables*. United States: Clarkson Potter, 2016.

Cho, Kristina. *Mooncakes and Milk Bread: Sweet and Savory Recipes Inspired by Chinese Bakeries*. United States: Harper Celebrate, 2021.

Choueiry, Ramzi. *The Arabian Cookbook: Traditional Arab Cuisine with a Modern Twist*. United Kingdom: Skyhorse Publishing, 2012.

Christmas in Switzerland. United Kingdom: World Book, 1995.

Chu, Anita, and Romanski, Caroline. *Field Guide to Cookies: How to Identify and Bake Virtually Every Cookie Imaginable*. United States: Quirk Books, 2015.

Clark, Letitia. *La Vita è Dolce: Italian-Inspired Desserts*. United Kingdom: Hardie Grant London, 2021.

Conferencia: Journal de l'Université des Annales. France: l'Université des Annales, 1922.

Corbin, Pam. *Cakes: River Cottage Handbook No.8*. United Kingdom: Bloomsbury Publishing, 2018.

Cordero-Fernando, Gilda. *The Culinary Culture of the Philippines*. Philippines: Bancom Audiovision, 1976.

Cortney, Bryce. *Aunt Lulu: Book One*. United Kingdom: Austin Macauley Publishers, 2023.

Costantino, Rosetta. *Southern Italian Desserts: Rediscovering the Sweet Traditions of Calabria, Campania, Basilicata, Puglia, and Sicily*. United States: Ten Speed Press, 2013.

Cowan, Cathal, and Sexton, Regina. *Ireland's Traditional Foods: An Exploration of Irish Local and Typical Foods and Drinks*. Ireland: Teagasc, The National Food Centre, 1997.

Coxall, Malcolm. *Traditional Baking Recipes of Spain.* Spain: Cornelio Books, 2018.

Crawford, Elisabeth Antoine. *Flavors of Friuli: A Culinary Journey through Northeastern Italy.* United States: Equilibrio, 2010.

Cumo, Christopher. *Foods that Changed History: How Foods Shaped Civilization from the Ancient World to the Present.* United States: ABC-CLIO, 2015.

D'Acampo, Gino. *Gino's Hidden Italy: How to Cook Like a True Italian.* United Kingdom: Hodder & Stoughton, 2016.

Dagdeviren, Musa. *The Turkish Cookbook.* United Kingdom: Phaidon Press, 2019.

Dahl, Felicity, and Dahl, Roald. *Roald Dahl's Cookbook.* United Kingdom: Penguin, 1996.

Dalal, Tarla. *Mithai.* India: Sanjay and Company, 1999.

Dalmia, Ritu. *Italian Khana.* India: Ebury Press, 2012.

Davey, William John, and MacKinnon, Richard P. *Dictionary of Cape Breton English.* Canada: University of Toronto Press, 2016.

Davidson, Alan, ed. *Food in Motion: The Migration of Foodstuffs and Cookery Techniques.* Oxford Symposium 1983: Proceedings. United Kingdom: Prospect Books, 1983.

———. *The Oxford Companion to Food.* Edited by Tom Jaine. 3rd ed. United Kingdom: Oxford University Press, 2014.

Davis, Hillary. *French Desserts.* United States: Gibbs Smith, 2016.

de Villiers, S. J. A. *Cook and Enjoy It.* (n.p.): Central News Agency, 1969.

Del Conte, Anna. *Classic Italian Recipes: 75 Signature Dishes.* United Kingdom: Hamlyn, 2012.

Delcart, André. *Winterfeesten en Gebak: Mythen, Folklore en Tradities.* Belgium: Cyclus, 2007.

Den Dooven, K. Camille. *The Hotel and Restaurant Dessert Book.* United States: C.H. Simonds Company, 1927.

Der Haroutunian, Arto. *Sweets & Desserts from the Middle East.* United Kingdom: Grub Street, 2014.

Dickie, John. *Delizia! The Epic History of the Italians and Their Food.* United Kingdom: Atria Books, 2008.

Dimayuga, Angela, and Mishan, Ligaya. *Filipinx: Heritage Recipes from the Diaspora.* United States: Abrams, 2021.

Diner, Hasia R., and Cinotto, Simone. *Global Jewish Foodways: A History.* United States: University of Nebraska Press, 2018.

Domenico, Roy P. *The Regions of Italy: A Reference Guide to History and Culture.* United Kingdom: Greenwood Press, 2002.

Duff, Julie. *Cakes: Regional & Traditional.* United Kingdom: Grub Street, 2015.

Duguid, Naomi. *Taste of Persia: A Cook's Travels Through Armenia, Azerbaijan, Georgia, Iran, and Kurdistan.* United States: Artisan, 2016.

Duncan, Heather. *Scottish Pride: 101 Reasons to be Proud of Your Scottish Heritage.* United Kingdom: Citadel Press, 2004.

Dusoulier, Clotilde. *Tasting Paris: 100 Recipes to Eat Like a Local.* United States: Clarkson Potter, 2018.

Eckhardt, Robyn. *Istanbul and Beyond: Exploring the Diverse Cuisines of Turkey.* United States: Houghton Mifflin Harcourt, 2017.

Edwards, Anastasia. *Biscuits and Cookies: A Global History.* United States: Reaktion Books, 2019.

Egerton, John with Egerton, Ann. *Southern Food: At Home, on the Road, in History.* United States: University of North Carolina Press, 1987.

Eldaief, Dyna. *The Taste of Egypt: Home Cooking from The Middle East.* Egypt: American University in Cairo Press, 2016.

Ellen, Roy, ed. *Modern Crises and Traditional Strategies: Local Ecological Knowledge in Island Southeast Asia.* United States: Berghahn Books, 2007.

Elliott, Mark. *Belgium & Luxembourg.* 8th ed. Ireland: Lonely Planet, 2022.

Elsasser, Marie. *Ausführliches Kochbuch für die Einfache und Feine Jüdische Küche 3759 Rezepten.* Germany: J. Kauffmann Verlag, 1921.

Esposito, Mary Ann. *Ciao Italia Family Classics: More Than 200 Treasured Recipes from Three Generations of Italian Cooks.* United States: St. Martin's Press, 2011.

Exodus Travels. *A Taste of Adventure.* United Kingdom: Ebury Press, 2012.

Farmer, Fannie Merritt. *The Boston Cooking-School Cook Book.* United States: Little, Brown, 1912.

Fauzi, Dayang Fawzia Abang. *Biskut & Kuih dari Sarawak.* Malaysia: Utusan Publications, 2008.

Favish, Melody. *Swedish Cakes and Cookies.* United States: Skyhorse Publishing, 2011.

Fenix, Michaela. *Country Cooking: Philippine Regional Cuisines.* Philippines: Anvil Publishing, 2017.

Fercher, Dietmar, and Karrer Andrea. *Austrian Desserts and Pastries: Over 100 Classic Recipes.* United States: Skyhorse Publishing, 2014.

Field, Carol. *The Italian Baker: The Classic Tastes of the Italian Countryside—Its Breads, Pizza, Focaccia, Cakes, Pastries, and Cookies.* Rev. ed. United States: Ten Speed Press, 2011.

Fieldhouse, Paul. *Food, Feasts, and Faith: An Encyclopedia of Food Culture in World Religions.* 2 vols. United States: ABC-CLIO, 2017.

Flores, Joseluis with Maye, Laura Zimmerman. *Dulce: Desserts in the Latin American Tradition.* United States: Rizzoli, 2010.

Franklin, Liz. *The Cookie Jar: Over 90 Scrumptious Recipes for Home-Baked Treats.* United Kingdom: Ryland Peters & Small, 2021.

Friberg, Bo. *The Professional Pastry Chef: Fundamentals of Baking and Pastry.* 4th ed. United Kingdom: Wiley, 2002.

Fuller, John; Renold, Edward; and Foskett, David. *The Chef's Compendium of Professional Recipes.* United Kingdom: Routledge, 2012.

G., Cristina *Cele mai Populare Retete ale Bunicii Învatate de la Mama: Mâncaruri si Sarate de Odinioara.* (n.p.): Self-Published, 2018.

Gambescia, Carla with Stein, Michael. *La Dolce Vita University: An Unconventional Guide to Italian Culture from A to Z.* United States: Travelers' Tales, 2018.

Gapultos, Marvin. *The Adobo Road Cookbook: A Filipino Food Journey.* United States: Tuttle Publishing, 2013.

Garten, Ina. *Cooking for Jeffrey: A Barefoot Contessa Cookbook.* United States: Clarkson Potter, 2016.

Gastronomia Estense: Le Ricette Mese per Mese. Italy: Tiemme Edizioni Digitali, 2020.

Gaudio, Giovanni. *Slow and Fresh: Recipes from Northern Italy.* (n.p.): Outfox Digital Publishing, 2014.

Geha, Joseph. *Kitchen Arabic: How My Family Came to America and the Recipes We Brought with Us.* United States: University of Georgia Press, 2023.

Georgescu, Irina. *Tava: Eastern European Baking and Desserts from Romania and Beyond.* United Kingdom: Hardie Grant Books, 2022.

Gilbert, Fabiola Cabeza de Baca. *The Good Life: New Mexico Traditions and Food.* United States: The Museum of New Mexico Press, 1949.

Giles, Pamela. *Brilliant Biscuits: Fun-to-decorate Biscuits for All Occasions.* United Kingdom: Little, Brown Book Group, 2012.

Ginsberg, Stanley, and Berg, Norman. *Inside the Jewish Bakery: Recipes and Memories from the Golden Age of Jewish Baking.* United States: Camino Books, 2011.

Glass, Victoria. *Deliciously Vintage Baking & Desserts: 60 Nostalgic Recipes That Will Make You Feel Like a Kid Again.* United Kingdom: Ryland Peters & Small, 2023.

Goldstein, Darra. *A Taste of Russia: A Cookbook of Russian Hospitality.* United States: Russian Life Books, 1985.

———. *Fire and Ice: Classic Nordic Cooking.* United States: Ten Speed Press, 2015.

———, ed. *The Oxford Companion to Sugar and Sweets.* United Kingdom: Oxford University Press, 2015.

———. *Beyond the North Wind: Russia in Recipes and Lore.* United States: Ten Speed Press, 2020.

Good Housekeeping Magazine. *Good Housekeeping's Book of Cookies.* United States: Consolidated Book Publishers, 1958.

Good Housekeeping. United States: C.W. Bryan, 1891.

Gore Browne, Miranda. *Biscuit.* United Kingdom: Ebury Press, 2012.

Gottfried, Pamela Jay. *Found in Translation: Common Words of Uncommon Wisdom.* United Kingdom: Lulu.com, 2010.

Gourmet Magazine. *The Gourmet Cookie Book: The Single Best Recipe from Each Year 1941–2009.* United States: Houghton Mifflin Harcourt, 2010.

Graves, Carwyn. *Welsh Food Stories.* United Kingdom: Calon, 2022.

Green, Jonathan. *Scottish Miscellany: Everything You Always Wanted to Know About Scotland the Brave.* United States: Skyhorse Publishing, 2010.

Greene, Gloria Kaufer. *The Jewish Holiday Cookbook: An International Collection of Recipes and Customs.* United States: Times Books, 1985.

Greenspan, Dorie. *Paris Sweets: Great Desserts from the City's Best Pastry Shops.* United States: Broadway Books, 2002.

———. *Baking Chez Moi: Recipes from My Paris Home to Your Home Anywhere.* United States: Houghton Mifflin Harcourt, 2014.

Guaiti, Daniela. *La Grande Cucina Regionale Italiana: Piemonte.* Italy: Gribaudo, 2010.

Guide to Italy and Sicily: With 19 Maps and 36 Plans. United Kingdom: Macmillan and Company, 1911.

Guinaudeau, Madame. *Traditional Moroccan Cooking: Recipes from Fez.* Translated by J. E. Harris. United Kingdom: Serif Books, 2015.

Guy, Sarah. *Europe's Best Bakeries: Over 130 of the Finest Bakeries, Cafés and Patisseries Across Great Britain and the Continent.* United Kingdom: September Publishing, 2019.

Hage, Salma. *Middle Eastern Sweets: Desserts, Pastries, Creams & Treats.* United Kingdom: Phaidon Press, 2021.

Hahn, Mary. *Illustriertes Kochbuch.* (n.p.): Outlook Verlag, 2022.

Hamm, Birgit, and Schmidt, Linn. *Grandma's German Cookbook.* United Kingdom: Dorling Kindersley, 2012.

Harlé, Eva. *Biscuits de Noël.* New ed. (n.p.): Hachette Pratique, 2020.

Harris, Andy, and Loftus, David. *Eat Istanbul: A Journey to the Heart of Turkish Cuisine.* United Kingdom: Quadrille Publishing, 2015.

Harris, Jessica B. *The Africa Cookbook: Tastes of a Continent.* United Kingdom: Simon & Schuster, 1998.

Hassani, Nadia. *Spoonfuls of Germany: Culinary Delights of the German Regions in 170 Recipes.* United States: Hippocrene Books, 2004.

Heatter, Maida. *Maida Heatter's Book of Great Desserts.* United States: Andrews McMeel Publishing, 1974.

———. *Maida Heatter's Cookies.* United States: Andrews McMeel Publishing, 1997.

Heberle, Marianna Olszewska. *Polish Cooking.* Updated ed. United States: HP Books, 2005.

Helou, Anissa. *Sweet Middle East: Classic Recipes, from Baklava to Fig Ice Cream.* United States: Chronicle Books, 2015.

———. *Feast: Food of the Islamic World.* United States: Ecco Press, 2018.

Herman, Heidi and Herman, Íeda Jónasdottir. *Homestyle Icelandic Cooking for American Kitchens.* (n.p.): Hekla Publishing, 2017.

Hersh, June. *Iconic New York Jewish Food: A History and Guide with Recipes.* United States: The History Press, 2023.

Hewitson, Carolyn. *Festivals.* United Kingdom: Taylor & Francis, 2013.

Hibben, Sheila. *The National Cookbook: A Kitchen Americana.* United States: Harpers & Brothers, 1932.

Hickey, Margaret. *Ireland's Green Larder: The Definitive History of Irish Food and Drink.* United Kingdom: Unbound, 2019.

Hidayat, Koko. *Crescent Cookies: Variasi Kue Kering Putri Salju.* Indonesia: Gramedia Pustaka Utama, 2007.

Hill, Patti. *The Queen of Sleepy Eye.* United States: B&H Publishing Group, 2008.

Hoffman, Emily Israel with Each, Molly. *A Blending of Bittersweet Memories.* United States: Lulu.com, 2011.

Holder, Geoff. *The Little Book of Scotland.* United Kingdom: The History Press, 2014.

Hollywood, Paul. *Paul Hollywood's British Baking.* United Kingdom: Bloomsbury Publishing, 2014.

Hornby, Jane. *Good Food: Teatime Treats.* United Kingdom: BBC Books, 2011.

Hung, Betty. *French Pastry 101: Learn the Art of Classic Baking with 60 Beginner-Friendly Recipes.* United States: Page Street Publishing, 2018.

Idowu, K. E. *Auntie Kate's Cookery Book.* United Kingdom: Macmillan Education, 1982.

Iori Galluzzi, M. A.; Iori, I.; and Jannotta, M., *La Cucina Ferrarese: Storia e Ricette.* Italy: Tarka, 2015.

Jacob, Jeanne, and Ashkenazi, Michael. *The World Cookbook: The Greatest Recipes from Around the Globe.* 2nd ed. United States: Greenwood, 2014.

Jacobs, Lauraine, ed. *A Treasury of New Zealand Baking.* New Zealand: Random House New Zealand, 2009.

Jaisinghani, Anita. *Masala: Recipes from India, the Land of Spices.* United States: Ten Speed Press, 2022.

Jamil, Rouhi. *Damas, Palmyre, Baalbek.* Lebanon: Librairie Universelle, 1941.

Janvier, Thomas Allibone. *The Uncle of an Angel and Other Stories*. United States: Harper, 1891.

Jaramillo, Cleofas M. *The Genuine New Mexico Tasty Recipes*. United States: Ancient City Press, 1981.

Jenkins, Sara, and Fox, Mindy. *Olives and Oranges: Recipes and Flavor Secrets from Italy, Spain, Cyprus, and Beyond*. United States: Houghton Mifflin Harcourt, 2008.

Jenner, Gail L. *Sourdough Biscuits and Pioneer Pies: The Old West Baking Book*. United States: TwoDot, 2017.

Johnson, Margaret M. *Irish Puddings, Tarts, Crumbles, and Fools: 80 Glorious Desserts*. United States: Chronicle Books, 2013.

Jones, Judith, and Jones, Evan. *The Book of New New England Cookery*. United States: University Press of New England, 1987.

Jones, S. *Simple Spanish Cookery*. United States: Peter Pauper Press, 2012.

Joyce, Sarah. *Un Pizzico di Joy*. Italy: Rizzoli, 2023.

Jurcă, Gheorghe. *Paște, Murgule, Iarbă Verde: Roman*. (n.p): Clusium, 2006.

Kärner, Karin Annus. *Estonian Tastes and Traditions*. United States: Hippocrene Books, 2005.

Kassis, Reem. *The Palestinian Table*. United Kingdom: Phaidon Press, 2017.

Kenedy, Jacob. *Bocca: Cookbook*. Germany: Bloomsbury Publishing, 2018.

Kennedy, Diana. *Nothing Fancy: Recipes and Recollections of Soul-Satisfying Food*. United States: University of Texas Press, 2018.

Kerper, Barrie. *Paris: The Collected Traveler— An Inspired Companion Guide*. United States: Vintage, 2011.

Kharzeeva, Anna. *The Soviet Diet Cookbook: Exploring Life, Culture, and History One Recipe at a Time*. Russia: LitRes 2021.

Khayat, Marie Karam, and Keatinge, Margaret Clark. *Food from the Arab World*. Lebanon: Khayats, 1970.

King, Niloufer Ichaporia. *My Bombay Kitchen: Traditional and Modern Parsi Home Cooking*. United States: University of California Press, 2007.

Klesta, Karolina, and Klesta, Patryk. *Polish Cakes & Desserts*. (n.p.): Polish Foodies, 2022.

Koehler, Jeff. *Morocco: A Culinary Journey with Recipes from the Spice-Scented Markets of Marrakech to the Date-Filled Oasis of Zagora*. United States: Chronicle Books, 2012.

Koenig, Leah. *Little Book of Jewish Sweets*. United States: Chronicle Books, 2019.

Kolektiv Jíme Zdravě. *Jíme zdravě o Vánocích: užijte si tradiční české Vánoce zdravě a přitom chutně*. Czech Republic: Verdon Capite, 2021.

Kostioukovitch, Elena. *Why Italians Love to Talk About Food*. Translated by Anne Milano Appel. United States: Farrar, Straus and Giroux, 2009.

Kristensen, Evald Tang. *Danske Börnerim, Remser og Lege: Udelukkende Efter Folkemunde*. Denmark: J. Zeuner, 1896.

L'Italia dei Dolci. Italy: Touring, 2004.

La cucina classica studii pratici, ragionati e dimostrativi della scuola francese applicata in servizio alla russa per Urbano Dubois ed Emilio Bernard. Italy: A spese d'una societa dei cuochi milanesi, 1878.

Larousse Gastronomique: The World's Greatest Culinary Encyclopedia. Rev. and updated ed. United States: Clarkson Potter, 2022.

Lennert, Joachim. *Culinary Guidebook: Germany*. Germany: Hueber, 2003.

Leventhal, Michael. *Babka, Boulou, & Blintzes: Jewish Chocolate Recipes from Around the World*. United Kingdom: Green Bean Books, 2021.

Levy, Brian. *Good & Sweet: A New Way to Bake with Naturally Sweet Ingredients*. United States: Avery, 2022.

Lindholm, Leila. *Sweet and Savory Swedish Baking*. United States: Skyhorse Publishing, 2009.

Lloyd Evans, Dyfed. *The Big Book of Christmas Recipes*. (n.p.): Nemeton, 2011.

Lonely Planet's Ultimate Eatlist. Ireland: Lonely Planet, 2018.

Long, Lucy M. *Ethnic American Food Today: A Cultural Encyclopedia*. United States: Rowman & Littlefield, 2015.

Lukins, Sheila. *All Around the World Cookbook*. United States: Workman Publishing, 1994.

———. *USA. Cookbook*. United States: Workman Publishing, 1997.

MacLeod, Coinneach. *The Hebridean Baker: Recipes and Wee Stories from the Scottish Islands*. (n.p.): Sourcebooks, 2022.

Magny, Olivier. *Stuff Parisians Like: Discovering the Quoi in the Je Ne Sais Quoi*. United States: Berkley Books, 2011.

Malgieri, Nick. *Cookies Unlimited*. United States: William Morrow, 2000.

———. *How to Bake: The Complete Guide to Perfect Cakes, Cookies, Pies, Tarts, Breads, Pizzas, Muffins, Sweet, and Savory*. United States: Dover Publications, 2018.

Malouf, Greg, and Malouf, Lucy. *Suqar: Desserts & Sweets from the Modern Middle East*. Australia: Hardie Grant, 2018.

Manekshaw, Bhicoo J. *Parsi Food and Customs*. United Kingdom: Penguin Books, 1996.

Marchetti, Domenica. *Ciao Biscotti: Sweet and Savory Recipes Celebrating Italy's Favorite Cookie*. United States: Chronicle Books, 2015.

Mariani, John F. *The Encyclopedia of American Food and Drink*. United States: Bloomsbury USA, 2014.

Marks, Copeland. *The Varied Kitchens of India: Cuisines of the Anglo-Indians of Calcutta, Bengalis, Jews of Calcutta, Kashmiris, Parsis, and Tibetans of Darjeeling*. (n.p.): M. Evans, 1991.

Marks, Gil. *Encyclopedia of Jewish Food*. United States: Houghton Mifflin Harcourt, 2010.

Martha Stewart Living Magazine. *Martha Stewart's Cookies: The Very Best Treats to Bake and to Share*. United States: Clarkson Potter, 2008.

Martin, Denise. *A Taste Back in Time: Recipes and True Stories of Family, Friends, Faith, and Food*. United Kingdom: AuthorHouse, 2014.

Maryam, Umm. *A Kitchen in Algeria: Classical and Contemporary Algerian Recipes*. United States: BookSumo, 2016.

Mason, Laura. *Sweets and Candy: A Global History*. United States: Reaktion Books, 2018.

Massoud, Shahir. *Eat, Habibi, Eat!: Fresh Recipes for Modern Egyptian Cooking*. Canada: Appetite by Random House, 2021.

Mathiot, Ginette. *The Art of French Baking*. United Kingdom: Phaidon Press, 2011.

Maynard, Kitty, and Maynard, Lucian. *Best Recipes from American Country Inns and Bed and Breakfasts: More Than 1,500 Mouthwatering Recipes from 340 of America's Favorite Inns*. United States: Rutledge Hill Press, 2004.

McCausland-Gallo, Patricia. *Secrets of Colombian Cooking*. United States: Hippocrene Books, 2004.

McGinn, Clark. *The Ultimate Guide to Being Scottish*. United Kingdom: Luath Press, 2013.

McMahon, Jp. *The Irish Cookbook*. United Kingdom: Phaidon Press, 2020.

Meggett, Emily. *Gullah Geechee Home Cooking: Recipes from the Matriarch of Edisto Island*. United States: Abrams, 2022.

Mehdawy, Magda, and Hussein, Amr. *The Pharaoh's Kitchen: Recipes from Ancient Egypt's Enduring Food Traditions*. Egypt: American University in Cairo Press, 2010.

Merceron, Julien. *À la Mère de Famille: Recipes from the Beloved Parisian Confectioner*. United States: Chronicle Books, 2016.

Meyer, Arthur L. *Baking Across America*. United States: University of Texas Press, 1998.

Mims, Ben. *Sweet & Southern: Classic Desserts with a Twist*. United States: Rizzoli, 2014.

Miralpeix, Assumpta. *Aquí hi ha Teca: Receptes de Cuina Catalana amb Història*. Spain: Rosa dels Vents, 2006.

Modesto, Maria de Lourdes. *Coisas Que Eu Sei*. Portugal: Oficina do Livro, 2021.

Morales, Bonnie Frumkin and Prichep, Deena. *Kachka: A Return to Russian Cooking*. United States: Flatiron Books, 2017.

Morse, Kitty. *Cooking at the Kasbah: Recipes from My Moroccan Kitchen*. United States: Chronicle Books, 1998.

Mountford, Meaghan. *Cookie Sensations: Creative Designs for Every Occasion*. United States: Rutledge Hill Press, 2007.

Muir, Jean. *Scotland: Celebrations & Soul Food*. United Kingdom: Matador, 2015.

Murphy, Jess, and Cluskey, Eoin. *The United Nations of Cookies*. (n.p.): Nine Bean Rows Books, 2022.

Myhre, Helen, and Vold, Mona. *Farm Recipes and Food Secrets from the Norske Nook*. United States: University of Wisconsin Press, 2001.

Nagy, Angéla F. *A Család Szakácskönyve*. Hungary: Kossuth Kiadó, 2018.

Nasrallah, Nawal. *Annals of the Caliphs' Kitchens: Ibn Sayyār Al-Warrāq's Tenth-Century Baghdadi Cookbook*. Netherlands: Brill, 2007.

———. *Treasure Trove of Benefits and Variety at the Table: A Fourteenth-Century Egyptian Cookbook*. Netherlands: Brill, 2017.

Natale in Tavola: Dolci e Dessert. Italy: De Agostini, 2012.

Nathan, Joan. *Jewish Cooking in America: A Cookbook*. United Kingdom: Knopf Publishing Group, 1998.

Natschke-Hofmann, Andrea. *Köstlich Backen für Kalte Tage: Rezepte für Kuchen, Gebäck und Mehr*. (n.p.): Thorbecke, 2021.

Neapolitan Express. I Dolci. (n.p.): Rogiosi, 2017.

Necchio, Valeria. *Veneto: Recipes from an Italian Country Kitchen*. United Kingdom: Guardian Faber, 2017.

Nederlanden, Elisabet der. *Holiday Cookies: Showstopping Recipes to Sweeten the Season*. United States: Ten Speed Press, 2017.

New Larousse Gastronomique. United Kingdom: Hamlyn, 2018.

Newhouse, Alana. *The 100 Most Jewish Foods: A Highly Debatable List*. United States: Artisan, 2019.

Newman, Yasmin. *7000 Islands: A Food Portrait of the Philippines*. United Kingdom: Hardie Grant Books, 2013.

Newton-Gamble, Ivy. *A Sweet Taste of Africa: Sail into a New Recipe Voyage*. United States: AG Publishers, 2008.

Nguyen, Andrea. *Into the Vietnamese Kitchen: Treasured Foodways, Modern Flavors*. United States: Ten Speed Press, 2006.

Niekerk, Brenda van. *How to Make Polvorones and Shortbread: Delicious Cookies*. United States: Lulu.com, 2013.

Nilsson, Magnus. *The Nordic Baking Book*. United Kingdom: Phaidon Press, 2018.

Nordin, Norzailina. *Kompilasi Hidangan Biskut*. Malaysia: Alaf 21, 2008.

Oetker, Dr. *1000: Die Besten Backrezepte*. Germany: Dr. Oetker Verlag, 2013.

———. *Das Große Weihnachtsbuch: Kochen, Backen und Geniessen*. Germany: Dr. Oetker Verlag, 2013.

Ojakangas, Beatrice. *The Great Scandinavian Baking Book*. United States: University of Minnesota Press, 1988.

Oliver, Jamie. *Jamie Oliver's Great Britain*. United Kingdom: Hachette Books, 2012.

Olizon-Chikiamco, Norma. *Filipino Cakes and Desserts*. Hong Kong: Periplus Editions, 2013.

Olson, Robin. L. *The Cookie Party Cookbook: The Ultimate Guide to Hosting a Cookie Exchange*. United States: St. Martin's Griffin, 2010.

Orellana, Sif. *Krudtugler og Kanelsnegle*. Denmark: Gyldendal, 2004.

Oria, Josephine Caminos. *Dulce de Leche: Recipes, Stories, & Sweet Traditions*. United States: Burgess Lea Press, 2017.

Oshoe, Padden Choedak. *The Nepal Cookbook*. India: Motilal Banarsidass, 2003.

Osseo-Asare, Fran, and Baëta, Barbara. *The Ghana Cookbook*. United States: Hippocrene Books, 2015.

Ottolenghi, Yotam, and Goh, Helen. *Sweet: Desserts from London's Ottolenghi*. United States: Ten Speed Press, 2017.

Ottolenghi, Yotam, and Tamimi, Sami. *Jerusalem*. United Kingdom: Ebury Press, 2012.

Papp, Katalin. *Nagyi Ünnepi Ételei*. Hungary: Kossuth Kiadó, 2012.

Parla, Katie, and Gill, Kristina. *Tasting Rome: Fresh Flavors and Forgotten Recipes from an Ancient City*. United States: Clarkson Potter, 2016.

Pateman, Robert; Elliott, Mark; and Nevins, Debbie. *Belgium*. 3rd ed. United States: Cavendish Square, 2016.

Patent, Greg. *A Baker's Odyssey: Celebrating Time-Honored Recipes from America's Rich Immigrant Heritage*. United Kingdom: John Wiley & Sons, 2007.

Pathmanathan, Sai. *Chews Your Own Tasty Adventure*. United Kingdom: Faber & Faber, 2023.

Patten, Marguerite. *Marguerite Patten's Best British Dishes*. United Kingdom: Grub Street, 2008.

Paul, Gertrude. *The Everyday Cake Book: A Recipe for Every Day of the Year Including February 29th*. United States: Moffat, Yard and Co, 1921.

Pavelle, Scott, and Pavelle, Kate. *Heritage Cookies of the Old and New World: Black and White Edition*. (n.p.): Independently Published, 2020.

Pawson, John, and Bell, Annie. *Living and Eating*. United Kingdom: Ebury Press, 2014.

Payard, François with Boyle, Tish. *Payard Desserts*. United States: Houghton Mifflin Harcourt, 2013.

Pepper, Lucy, and Pedroso, Célia. *Manger Comme un Portugais: Le Guide Essentiel sur la Cuisine Portugaise*. Portugal: Lua de Papel, 2017.

Pérez, Dionisio. *Guía del Buen Comer Español*. Spain: Editorial Maxtor, 2005.

Perini, Giacomo. *Schweizerzuckerbäcker: Oder, Genaue Unterweisung zur Anfertigung Aller in der Konditorer Vorkommenden Arbeiten*. Germany: B.F. Voigt, 1893.

Perrin, Emilie. *Biscuits et Petits Gâteaux*. (n.p.): Hachette Pratique, 2013.

Peyk, Charlotte. *Scandinavian Baking Without Eggs*. United States: Books on Demand, 2011.

Pezone, Alba. *In Cucina: Mes Plus Belles Recettes Italiennes*. (n.p.): Hachette Pratique, 2017.

Piazzesi, Paolo, ed. *The Delights of Good Italian Cooking*. Italy: Bonechi, 2007.

Pipe, Jim. *Ireland: A Very Peculiar History*. United Kingdom: The Salariya Book Company, 2011.

Polistico, Edgie. *Philippine Food, Cooking, & Dining Dictionary*. Philippines: Anvil Publishing, 2017.

Polzine, Michelle. *Baking at the 20th Century Cafe: Iconic European Desserts from Linzer Torte to Honey Cake*. United States: Artisan Books, 2020.

Potts, Olivia. *Butter: A Celebration*. United Kingdom: Headline, 2022.

Presilla, Maricel E. *Gran Cocina Latina: The Food of Latin America*. United States: W. W. Norton, 2012.

Rago, Rossella. *Cooking with Nonna: A Year of Italian Holidays: 130 Classic Holiday Recipes from Italian Grandmothers*. United States: Race Point Publishing, 2018.

Rainier, A. *Great German Recipes*. (n.p.): Lulu.com, 2012.

Ramamurthy, Ramya. *Branded in History: Fresh Marketing Lessons from Vintage Brands*. India: Hachette India, 2021.

Ramazani, Nesta. *Persian Cooking: A Table of Exotic Delights*. United States: Ibex Publishers, 2014.

Ramirez, Grace. *La Latina: A Cook's Journey Through Latin America*. New Zealand: Penguin Random House New Zealand, 2015.

Recipes to Treasure, Le Village Historique Acadien De La Nouvelle Écosse.

Rees, Huw, and Kilcoyne, Sian. *Wales on This Day: 366 Facts You Probably Didn't Know*. United Kingdom: Calon, 2022.

Restino, Susan. *Mrs. Restino's Country Kitchen*. United States: Shelter Publications, 1976.

Rihtman-Auguštin, Dunja. *Christmas in Croatia*. (n.p.): Golden Marketing, 1997.

Riley, Gillian. *The Oxford Companion to Italian Food*. United States: Oxford University Press, 2007.

Rinsky, Glenn, and Rinsky, Laura Halpin. *The Pastry Chef's Companion: A Comprehensive Resource Guide for the Baking and Pastry Professional*. United Kingdom: Wiley, 2008.

Riolo, Amy. *Arabian Delights: Recipes & Princely Entertaining Ideas from the Arabian Peninsula*. United States: Capital Books, 2008.

Robertson, Debora. *Notes from a Small Kitchen Island: Recipes and Stories from the Heart of the Home*. United Kingdom: Michael Joseph, 2022.

Roddy, Rachel. *My Kitchen in Rome: Recipes and Notes on Italian Cooking*. United States: Grand Central Life & Style, 2016.

Roden, Claudia. *The Book of Jewish Food: An Odyssey from Samarkand to New York*. United States: Knopf Publishing Group, 1996.

———. *The New Book of Middle Eastern Food*. United States: Knopf Publishing Group, 2008.

Rodgers, Rick. *Kaffeehaus: Exquisite Desserts from the Classic Cafés of Vienna, Budapest, and Prague*. United States: Echo Point Books, 2020.

Rombauer, Irma S.; Becker, Marion Rombauer; and Becker, Ethan. *Joy of Cooking*. United States: Scribner, 2002.

Rose, Peter G. *Delicious December: How the Dutch Brought Us Santa, Presents, and Treats: A Holiday Cookbook*. United States: State University of New York Press, 2014.

Rosenstein, Marc. *Turning Points in Jewish History*. United States: Jewish Publication Society, 2018.

Ross, Ruth Isabel. *The Little Irish Baking Book*. United States: St. Martin's Press, 1996.

Roufs, Timothy G., and Roufs, Kathleen Smyth. *Sweet Treats Around the World: An Encyclopedia of Food and Culture*. United States: ABC-CLIO, 2014.

Rough Guides, *The Rough Guide to New Zealand*. United States: Rough Guides, 2016.

Rountree, Kathryn. *Crafting Contemporary Pagan Identities in a Catholic Society*. United Kingdom: Routledge, 2016.

Ruggirello, A. M. *From Dill to Dracula: A Romanian Food & Folklore Cookbook*. (n.p.): Cardboard Monet Publishing, 2020.

Russell, Matthew, ed. *The Irish Monthly: A Magazine of General Literature*. Ireland: McGlashan & Gill, 1891.

Russell, Mona L. *Egypt*. United States: ABC-CLIO, 2013.

Saberi, Helen. *Afghan Food & Cookery*. United States: Hippocrene Books, 2000.

———. *Teatimes: A World Tour*. United States: Reaktion Books, 2018.

Sacerdoti, Daniela. *Margherita's Recipes: Free Recipes from Daniela Sacerdoti's Bestselling Novel, Set Me Free*. United Kingdom: Black & White Publishing, 2015.

Sanchez, Maria Bruscino. *Sweet Maria's Big Baking Bible: 300 Classic Cookies, Cakes, and Desserts from an Italian-American Bakery*. United States: St. Martin's Press, 2008.

Sandler, Bea. *The African Cookbook*. United States: Carol Publishing Group, 1993.

Santini, Aldo. *La Cucina Fiorentina: Storia e Ricette*. Italy: Tarka, 2014.

Sartoni, Monica Cesari. *Italy Dish by Dish: A Comprehensive Guide to Eating in Italy*. Translated by Susan Simon. United Kingdom: Little Bookroom, 2011.

Sassetti, João. *A Minha Filha vai Casar: As Receitas de Nossa Casa*. Portugal: Princípia Editora, 2018.

Sax, Richard. *Classic Home Desserts: A Treasury of Heirloom and Contemporary Recipes from Around the World*. United States: Houghton Mifflin Harcourt, 1999.

Scaravella, Jody with Petrini, Elisa. *Nonna's House: Cooking and Reminiscing with the Italian Grandmothers of Enoteca Maria*. United States: Atria Books, 2015.

Schael, Graciela. *La Cocina de Casilda: Dulces y Bocadillos de la Venezuela de Ayer*. Venezuela: El Nacional, 2005.

Scharfstein, Sol. *Understanding Jewish Holidays and Customs: Historical and Contemporary*. United States: Ktav Publishing House, 1999.

Schrandt, Dawn Marie. *Just Me Cookin in Germany*. United States: iUniverse, 2001.

Schuegraf, Ernst. *Cooking with the Saints: An Illustrated Treasury of Authentic Recipes, Old and Modern*. United States: Ignatius Press, 2001.

Schuhbeck, Alfons. *The German Cookbook*. United Kingdom: Phaidon Press, 2018.

Schuler, Elizabeth. *German Cookery*. United States: Clarkson Potter, 1955.

Schwartz, Arthur. *Arthur Schwartz's Jewish Home Cooking: Yiddish Recipes Revisited*. United States: Ten Speed Press, 2008.

Schwenger, Hans-Peter, and Wieland, Barbara. *Frankfurter Bethmännchen*. Germany: LöwenStern Verlag, 2019.

Sciama, Lidia D. *A Venetian Island: Environment, History, and Change in Burano*. Germany: Berghahn Books, 2003.

Scicolone, Michele. *1,000 Italian Recipes*. United States: Houghton Mifflin Harcourt, 2011.

Scott, Astrid Karlsen. *Authentic Norwegian Cooking: Traditional Scandinavian Cooking Made Easy*. United States: Skyhorse Publishing, 2015.

Scully, Terence, trans. *The Opera of Bartolomeo Scappi (1570): L'arte et Prudenza d'un Maestro Cuoco (The Art and Craft of a Master Cook)*. Canada: University of Toronto Press, 2011.

Segan, Francine. *Dolci: Italy's Sweets*. United States: Abrams, 2011.

Segnit, Niki. *The Flavor Thesaurus: A Compendium of Pairings, Recipes, and Ideas for the Creative Cook*. United States: Bloomsbury USA, 2012.

———. *Lateral Cooking*. United States: Bloomsbury Publishing, 2019.

Sekandari, Nafisa. *Afghan Cuisine: A Collection of Family Recipes*. 2nd ed. United States: Avagana Publishing, 2010.

Sember, Brette. *Cookie: A Love Story*. (n.p.): Sember Resources, 2012.

Sen, Colleen Taylor; Bhattacharyya, Sourish; and Saberi, Helen, eds. *The Bloomsbury Handbook of Indian Cuisine*. United Kingdom: Bloomsbury Academic, 2023.

Shafia, Louisa. *The New Persian Kitchen*. United States: Ten Speed Press, 2013.

Shedden, Flora. *Aran: Recipes and Stories from a Bakery in the Heart of Scotland*. United Kingdom: Hardie Grant, 2019.

Sheen, Barbara. *Foods of Egypt*. United States: Greenhaven Publishing, 2010.

———. *Foods of Poland*. United States: Greenhaven Publishing, 2011.

Sheraton, Mimi. *The German Cookbook: A Complete Guide to Mastering Authentic German Cooking*. United Kingdom: Random House, 2010.

———. *1,000 Foods to Eat Before You Die: A Food Lover's Life List*. United States: Workman Publishing, 2015.

Shipley, John. *Secret Shrewsbury*. United Kingdom: Amberley Publishing, 2019.

Sickha, Julie. *Kochbuch: Speisen wie zu Kaisers Zeiten*. Germany: Books on Demand, 2016.

Sidek, Norani. *Roti, kek, Pastri*. Malaysia: Utusan Publications, 1999.

Sigmundsdóttir, Alda. *The Little Book of the Icelanders at Christmas*. United Kingdom: Little Books Publishing, 2022.

Silverthorne, Elizabeth. *Christmas in Texas*. United States: Texas A&M University Press, 1994.

Silverton, Nancy with Molina, Matt, and Carreño, Carolynn. *The Mozza Cookbook: Recipes from Los Angeles's Favorite Italian Restaurant and Pizzeria*. United States: Knopf Publishing Group, 2011.

Simeti, Mary Taylor. *Sicilian Food: Recipes from Italy's Abundant Isle*. United States: Grub Street, 2009.

Simmons, Shirin. *A Treasury of Persian Cuisine*. United Kingdom: Stamford House Publishing, 2007.

Sinclair, Holly. *The Cookie Tray*. (n.p.): Self-published, 2012.

Sinclair, Pat. *Scandinavian Classic Baking*. United States: Pelican Publishing, 2011.

Sirvani, Muhammed bin Mahmûd. *15. Yüzyıl Osmanlı Mutfağı*. Edited by Mustafa Argunşah and Müjgân Çakır. Turkey: Gökkubbe, 2005.

Smith, Andrew F. *The Oxford Encyclopedia of Food and Drink in America*. Volume 2. United States: Oxford University Press, 2004.

———. *The Oxford Companion to American Food and Drink*. United Kingdom: Oxford University Press, 2007.

Spicer, Dorothy Gladys. *Festivals of Western Europe*. United States: Library of Alexandria, 1958.

Stanton, W. R., and Flach, M., eds. *SAGO: The Equatorial Swamp as a Natural Resource*. Netherlands: Springer Netherlands, 2012.

Steves, Rick, and Griffith, Valerie. *Rick Steves' European Christmas*. United States: Avalon Publishing, 2011.

Sunset. United States: Passenger Department, Southern Pacific Company, 1953.

Talati, Farokh. *Parsi: From Persia to Bombay: Recipes & Tales from the Ancient Culture*. United Kingdom: Bloomsbury Absolute, 2022.

Thakrar, Shamil; Thakrar, Kavi; and Nasir, Naved. *Dishoom: From Bombay with Love*. United Kingdom: Bloomsbury Publishing, 2019.

Thangarajah, Rani, and Eliezer, Nesa. *Recipes of the Jaffna Tamils: Odiyal Kool, Kurakkan Puttu, and All That*. India: Orient Longman, 2003.

The Great American Cookie Cookbook. United States: Publications International, 2001.

The King Arthur Baking Company. *The Essential Cookie Companion*. United States: Countryman Press, 2021.

Thompson, Jordan E. *Recipes for Refugees: Afghanistan*. (n.p.): Self-Published, 2021.

Thomson, Emma. *Flanders: Northern Belgium*. United Kingdom: Bradt Travel Guides, 2012.

Thorisson, Mimi. *Old World Italian: Recipes and Secrets from our Travels in Italy*. United States: Clarkson Potter, 2020.

Thorne, John, and Thorne, Matt Lewis. *Pot on the Fire: Further Confessions of a Renegade Cook*. United States: North Point Press, 2011.

Thornton, Arthur R. *Art's Old Canadian Recipes*. United States: Tate Publishing, 2009.

Tingginehe, Rosmin M., and Simanjuntak, Tiurma PT. *Ulat Sagu Papua: Budaya dan Risetnya*. Indonesia: Penerbit NEM, 2021.

Tipton-Martin, Toni. *Jubilee: Recipes from Two Centuries of African American Cooking*. United States: Clarkson Potter, 2019.

Tolstrup, C. *Mit Persiske Køkken: Et Bord af Fristelser*. Denmark: Books on Demand, 2022.

Toussaint, Carlos V. *Agenda Para Familia*. Mexico: Tipografía de Las Escuelas Salesianas, 1898.

Triwald, Gabriele. *Neue Prager Köchin: Kochbuch, Bestehend aus 719 Recepten für die Schmackhaftesten Speisen, Getränke, Früchte und Delicatessen*. Czechia: Hynek, 1876.

Trotter, Christopher; Yates, Annette; and Campbell, Georgina. *Traditional Cooking of the British Isles: 360 Classic Regional Dishes with 1500 Beautiful Photographs*. United Kingdom: Lorenz Books, 2018.

Truchelut, Jean Michel, and Zeiher, Pierre Paul. *The Pastry Chef Handbook: La Patisserie de Reference*. United States: BPI Editions, 2022.

Twena, Pamela Grau. *The Sephardic Table: The Vibrant Cooking of the Mediterranean Jews*. United States: Houghton Mifflin Harcourt, 1998.

Tye, Diane. *Baking as Biography: A Life Story in Recipes*. Canada: McGill-Queen's University Press, 2010.

Ultimate Food Journeys: The World's Best Dishes and Where to Eat Them. United Kingdom: Dorling Kindersley, 2011.

Unković, Barbara. *The Adriatic Kitchen: Recipes Inspired by the Abundance of Seasonal Ingredients Flourishing on the Croatian Island of Korčula*. United Kingdom: Exisle Publishing, 2017.

Valldejuli, Carmen Aboy. *Puerto Rican Cookery*. United States: Pelican Publishing, 1983.

Ved, Sonal. *Tiffin: 500 Authentic Recipes Celebrating India's Regional Cuisine*. United States: Black Dog and Leventhal, 2018.

Velásquez, Mariana. *Colombiana: A Rediscovery of Recipes & Rituals from the Soul of Colombia*. United States: Harper, 2021.

Vieira, Edite. *The Taste of Portugal: A Voyage of Gastronomic Discovery Combined with Recipes, History, and Folklore*. United Kingdom: Grub Street, 2013.

Vitz, Evelyn Birge. *A Continual Feast: A Cookbook to Celebrate the Joys of Family & Faith throughout the Christian Year*. United States: Ignatius Press, 2016.

Waerebeek, Ruth van with Robbins, Maria. *Everybody Eats Well in Belgium Cookbook*. United States: Workman Publishing, 1996.

———. *The Taste of Belgium*. United Kingdom: Grub Street, 2014.

Wakefield, Ruth Graves. *Toll House: Tried and True Recipes*. United States: M. Barrows, 1940.

Walker, Harlan, ed. *Feasting and Fasting*. Oxford Symposium on Food & Cookery, 1990: Proceedings. United Kingdom: Prospect Books, 1991.

Watson, Anne L. *Baking with Cookie Molds*. (n.p.): Shepard Publications, 2021.

Webb, Lois Sinaiko. *Multicultural Cookbook of Life-cycle Celebrations*. United Kingdom: Oryx Press, 2000.

Weiss, Luisa. *Classic German Baking: The Very Best Recipes for Traditional Favorites, from Pfeffernüsse to Streuselkuchen*. United States: Ten Speed Press, 2016.

Whelan, Christine Sahadi. *Flavors of the Sun: The Sahadi's Guide to Understanding, Buying, and Using Middle Eastern Ingredients*. United States: Chronicle Books, 2021.

Wifstrand, Selma, ed. *Favorite Swedish Recipes*. United States: Dover Publications, 1975.

Willi, Ernst. *Lust am Kochen für Gäste*. Germany: epubli, 2017.

Williams, Victoria. *Celebrating Life Customs Around the World: From Baby Showers to Funerals*, 3 vols. United States: ABC-CLIO, 2016.

Wilson, Dede. *A Baker's Field Guide to Christmas Cookies*. United States: Harvard Common Press, 2011.

Wolfert, Paula. *The Food of Morocco*. United Kingdom: Bloomsbury Publishing, 2012.

Wolff, Otto. *The Wurst!: The Very Best of German Food*. Germany: Smith Street Books, 2017.

Wolter, A., and Teubner, C. *Backvergnügen wie Noch Nie*. Germany: Gräfe und Unzer, 2012.

Wong, Cecily, and Thuras, Dylan. *Gastro Obscura: A Food Adventurer's Guide*. United States: Workman Publishing, 2021.

Ysewijn, Regula. *The British Baking Book: The History of British Baking, Savory and Sweet*. United States: Weldon Owen, 2020.

———. *Dark Rye and Honey Cake: Festival Baking from Belgium, the Heart of the Low Countries*. United States: Weldon Owen, 2020.

Zahara, Rita. *Malay Heritage Cooking*. Singapore: Marshall Cavendish International (Asia), 2012.

Zak, Zuza. *Amber & Rye: A Baltic Food Journey: Estonia - Latvia - Lithuania*. United States: Interlink Books, 2021.

Zereshki, Nasreen Z. *Recipes from My Persian Kitchen*. United States: Lulu Publishing, 2015.

Articles and Essays

Arab Observer, Vols 133–157. (National Publications House, 1963).

Keystone Folklore, Vols 22–24. (University of Virginia, 1978).

Nasrallah, Nawal. "The Iraqi Cookie, Kleicha, and the Search for Identity." *Repast* 24, no. 4, 2008: 4–7.

Nickerson, Jane. "News of Food: One-Bowl Method of Mixing Cookies Cuts Time for Task to Two Minutes." *New York Times*, November 17, 1947.

The Windsor Magazine. (1905). United Kingdom: Ward, Lock and Bowden, Limited.

Websites

196flavors.com/besitos-de-coco/
1000.menu/cooking/19570-sochniki-s-tvorogom-klassicheskie-po-gostu-v-duxovke
adamantkitchen.com/drommer-norwegian-browned-butter-cookies/
adventzagreb.hr/flavors-of-the-zagreb-advent/paprenjaci-peppery-gingerbread-cookies
afghancultureunveiled.com/humaira-ghilzai/afghancooking/2009/12/delicate-afghan-butter-cookies.html
afrifoodnetwork.com/recipes/snack-recipes/cinq-centimes/
ah.nl/allerhande/recept/R-R668470/friese-dumkes
ahappyhomeinholland.com/dutch-almond-cookie-recipe/
aheadofthyme.com/2017/03/nan-e-nokhodchi-persian-chickpea-cookies/
airmalta.com/en/blog/malta/eat-like-a-local-kwarezimal-recipe
alberteldar.is/2013/12/17/bessastadakokur/
allnigerianrecipes.com/desserts/nigerian-shuku-shuku/
alltastesgerman.com/german-spritz-cookies/
allyskitchen.com/persian-walnut-cookies-naan-e-gerdooi/
almostbananas.net/medovniky-slovak-spiced-honey-cookies/
almostnordic.com/bastogne-cookies/
amaltesemouthful.com/figolli-special-maltese-easter-tradition/
americandreamcakes.com/wp-content/uploads/2017/11/adc-recipe-co.pdf
amourdecuisine.fr/article-arayeche-ou-larayeche.html
anamariabrogui.com.br/receita/biscoitinho-de-amido-de-milho-sequilhos-e777
anamericaninrome.com/2016/10/fave-dei-morti-italian-cookies-for-the-day-of-the-dead/
appulia.net/ricette/mustazzoli-salentini-la-ricetta-originale/
apronandwhisk.com/figolli-maltese-easter-treat/
arrisje.com/gevulde-koeken-almond-paste-cookie/
asiancook.eu/indonesian/jajanan/12-crispy-sweet-rolls
asif.org/recipes/hadji-bada-iraqi-coconut-cookies/
atasteofthepast.wordpress.com/tag/shrewsbury-cake/
atlasobscura.com/foods/persian-nane-nokhodchi-nowruz
atozworldfood.com/estonia/snacks/ruiskatut-rye-cookies.html
audreysika.wordpress.com/2019/11/04/ayigbe-biscuit/
austria.info/en/things-to-do/food-and-drink/recipes/linzer-cookies
azoreangreenbean.com/2021/07/28/biscoitos/
backenmitchristina.at/rezepte/eisenbahner/
bakeafter.com/recipe/dessert/aveiro-crispy-cookies-raivas-de-aveiro/
bakefromscratch.com/jam-filled-kolaczki/
bakinginfashion.com/2020/12/28/ilusad-piparkoogid-estonian-gingerbread-cookies/
bakinglikeachef.com/biscoito-de-maizena-cornstarch-cookies/
bakkenderwijs.nl/recepten/koekjes/speculaasbrokken-recept/
bakkenmetmarian.be/recepten/antwerpse-handjes/?lid=5175
balkanlunchbox.com/three-four-ingredient-walnut-bites/
barefootinjandals.com/senegal-cinq-centimes/
bbc.co.uk/food/recipes/melting_moments_59381
belliesenroute.com/blog-backend/tag/Food+culture
bepbanhtiny.com/cach-lam-banh-nai-heo-1618/
beptruong.edu.vn/day-lam-banh/bep-truong-ban-banh/cookies-hanh-nhan
betumiblog.blogspot.com/2012/03/celebrate-with-cassava-cookies-gari.html
biscuitpeople.com/magazine/post/Sequilhos-Enjoy-your-coffee-with-Brazilian-gluten-free-biscuits?utm_source=web&utm_medium=web&utm_campaign=web-search
bitemykitchen.co/recipe/walnut-meringue-crescents-orasnice/
blessmyfoodbypayal.com/eggless-atta-biscuits-jaggery-whole-wheat-jaggery-cookies-atta-gud-biscuits-atta-jaggery-cookies/

bohmbakes.com/2020/12/06/paprenjak-paprenjaci-traditional-croatian-honey-and-black-pepper-biscuits
bonappetit.com/recipe/nan-e-berenji
bostonglobe.com/lifestyle/travel/2018/10/04/joe-froggers-marblehead-taste-tradition/9FJiAj2OCxEADfP7IYhy4I/story.html
budapestcookingclass.com/hungarian-walnut-cookies-hokifli-recipe/
byandreajanssen.com/traditional-dutch-pepernoten/
caaleyrebon.fr/2020/10/04/croquants-aux-amandes-vraie-recette/
cahidesultan.com/2022/02/16/portakalli-patlak-kurabiye/
cake2take.lt/product/sausainiai-su-aguonomis/
cakies.nl/recept/jan-hagel-koekjes/
cakieshq.com/recipe/traditional-dutch-pepernoten-peppernuts/
canadianliving.com/food/baking-and-desserts/recipe/lassy-mogs
carolinescooking.com/kleicha-iraqi-date-cookies/
chasingthedonkey.com/croatian-cooking-how-to-make-croatian-paprenjaci-black-pepper-cookies/
chefindisguise.com/2016/10/07/palestinian-date-cookies-kaak-bi-ajwa/
chefspencil.com/recipe/spanish-polvorones/
cherchelloise.over-blog.com/article-l-arayeche-111042575.html
cheznermine.com/2020/01/04/rosewater-pistachio-ghorayebah/
christmas-cookies.com/recipes/cookie-iron-waffle-cookies/goro/
chutodnaty.sk/zazvorniky/
cinnamonshtick.com/kichel-jewish-bow-tie-cookies/
cleobuttera.com/middle-eastern/fabulous-kahk-eid-cookies/
cnn.com/travel/article/ostie-piene-puglia/index.html
cocina-familiar.com/almidoncitos-receta-venezolana.html
colombia.com/gastronomia/recetas-colombianas/cucas-r248
comedera.com/prepara-unos-deliciosos-besitos-de-coco-venezolanos/
cookiecompanion.com/ghanakatha-cookie-from-sri-lanka/?lang=en
cookimia.com/almidoncitos/
cooking.nytimes.com/recipes/1013393-piparkakut
cookingcounty.com/qurabiya-cookie-recipe/
cookipedia.co.uk/recipes_wiki/%C5%A0trambesk%C3%A9_u%C5%A1i_(%C5%A0tramberk_wafer)
cooklikeczechs.com/gingerbread-cookies-with-icing/
cooknenjoy.com/casadinho-de-goiabada/
cookslovak.com/2017/12/05/crispy-ginger-cakes-or-zazvorniky/
cookwithmanali.com/atta-biscuits/
cooky.vn/cong-thuc/banh-tai-heo-chien-gion-23080
courierpostonline.com/story/life/2018/12/17/ancient-italian-pizzelle-cookie-still-popular-christmas-anytime/2027780002/
craftscrumbs.com/recipes/kanom-thong-muan/
croatianfood.eu/honey-cookies/
croatianfood.eu/medenjaci/
croatiaweek.com/traditional-croatian-recipes-paprenjak-biscuit/
crosbys.com/pubnico-soft-molasses-cookies/
cucchiaio.it/ricetta/ricetta-papassini-ittiri/
cucinaamoremio.it/recipe/casadinhos-de-goiabada/
cucineditalia.com/en/story-befana-recipe-for-befanini-biscuits/
culinea.nl/recepten/friese-dumkes-bakken/
culture-crunch.com/2021/02/17/cujuelle-de-calenzana/
culy.nl/recepten/jan-hagel-koekjes/
curiouscuisiniere.com/chinese-mung-bean-almond-cookies/
czechgastronomy.com/stramberk-ears/
davidlebovitz.com/canistrelli-anise-cookies-french-corsica-corsican/
davidwalbert.com/dw/2012/12/12/a-brief-history-of-the-sugar-cookie/
daylambanh.edu.vn/banh-lo-tai-heo
deliciousitaly.com/abruzzo-food/ferratelle-of-abruzzo
deliciousmagazine.co.uk/recipes/ottijiet-maltese-spice-biscuits/
delintia.com/en/kulche-birinjee/
denmark-getaway.com/finnish-shortbread.html
destination-abruzzo.com/post/the-most-popular-cookies-in-abruzzo-pizzelle-aka-ferratelle-or-neole
directoalpaladar.com/postres/panellets-receta
discovermessina.com/buccellati-cookies-recipe-sicilian-delicacy/
dolcidifranci.com/recipes/ramedinapoli

domacica.com.hr/skoljkice-punjene-pekmezom/
dulcear.com/blog/almidoncitos-venezolanos
dulciurifeldefel.ro/fursecuri-cu-stafide/
eastmeetskitchen.com/videos/recipes/thai-flower
  -shortbread-cookies-khanom-kleeb-lum-duen/
eatperu.com/cocadas
eatprato.it/it/i-prodotti/le-ricette-della-tradizione/
  zuccherini-di-vernio/
e-borghi.com/en/traditional-cooking/947/
  recipe-the-ferratelle-from-abruzzo.html
edmondscooking.co.nz/recipes/slices-fudge-and
  -sweets-2/ginger-crunch/
egyptindependent.com/kahk-cookies-history/
egypttoday.com/Article/4/115438/Learn-Egyptian
  -Kahk%E2%80%99s-recipe
elizabethskitchendiary.co.uk/medovniky-slovak
  -spiced-honey-cookies/
emikodavies.com/a-batch-of-soft-tuscan-cookies/
en.unesco.org/silkroad/content/did-you-know-spread
  -islam-southeast-asia-through-trade-routes
encasacookingspace.com/quince-thumbprint-cookies/
epicurious.com/recipes/food/views/spoon-
  cookies-233297
estoniancuisine.com/2018/08/31/mayonnaise-cookies
  -majoneesikupsised/
etelkalauz.hu/nero-teasutemeny-recept/
facebook.com/177484972292717/posts/afghan-
  kolche-khetayee-cookie-made-by-marzia-rplz-like
  -share-recipe-2-cups-regul/1568300486544485/
facebook.com/photo/?fbid=2120995841451660&
  set=a.1745613488989899
facebook.com/watch/?v=1305076090009155
facebook.com/watch/?v=316103587064521
facebook.com/watch/?v=514474936302111
farmersalmanac.com/the-history-of-jan-hagels-23330
feastinthemiddleeast.com/2019/12/18/the-cookie
  -that-soothes-your-tummy-middle-eastern-sesame
  -anise-cookies/
finland.fi/christmas/christmas-cookbook/#coo
fivesensespalate.com/polvorosas-venezuelan
  -crumbly-cookies/
food52.com/recipes/19499-ischler-the-emperor
  -of-cookies
foodandwine.com/recipes/cantucci-di-prato
foodbycountry.com/Germany-to-Japan/Ghana.html
foodofegypt.com/08/01/butter-cookies-ghorayeba/
foodsofengland.co.uk/meltingmoments.htm
foodtimeline.org/foodcookies.html#biscochitos
fullystuffedgeek.nl/rock-sugar-cookies/
gastronomiaevinhos.pt/bolinhos-de-gema/
germanfoods.org/recipes/spritz-cookies-traditional
  -german-christmas-cookies/
giallozafferano.com/moltoono/puto-seko-the
  -filipino-gluten-free-cookies/
gimmesomeoven.com/panellets-recipe/
globalkitchentravels.com/
  savboro-sri-lankan-sago-coconut-cookies/
godt.no/oppskrifter/bakst/julekaker/8345/
  syv-slag-sirupsnipper
gourmandiseassia.fr/boussou-la-tmessou/
gourmetcubicle.com/blog/marias-hungarian
  -snow-crescents-hkifli
greatbritishrecipes.com/melting-moments-biscuits/
gutekueche.at/klassische-linzer-augen-rezept-3718
hanielas.com/slovak-ginger-cookieszazvorniky/
hildaskitchenblog.com/recipe/assyrian-holiday
  -cookies-kileche-kleicha/
hispanickitchen.com/2011/06/01/pepitas-quince
  -jam-thumbprint-cookies/
healthline.com/nutrition/durum-wheat-vs-whole-wheat
helvetickitchen.com/recipes/2015/12/14/brunslibears
hort.purdue.edu/newcrop/morton/cashew_apple.html
hot-thai-kitchen.com/kanom-ping/
huruharada.blogspot.com/2013/12/resep-kue
  -putri-salju-paling-mudah.html
icecook.blogspot.com/2006/12/half-moon-cookies
  -hlfmnar.html
icelandfoodcentre.com/lakkristoppar-icelandic
  -meringue-cookies/
ijzerkoekjes.nl/recept.html
imperialbaking.be/nl/recepten/antwerpse-handjes
imturning60help.blogspot.com/2010/12/anna-sultanas
  -biskuttini-tar-rahal.html
indianexpress.com/article/lifestyle/food-wine/
  heres-how-you-can-make-bakery-style-karachi
  -biscuits-at-home-recipe-inside-7777761/
inspiracie.sk/recept/medovniky
inspirationsforall.com/en/tula-pryanik-recipe/
internationaldessertsblog.com/danish-brunkager
  -danish-brown-cookies/
iranpress.com/content/62089/traditional-cookie
  -tabriz-registered-national-heritage-list

irishtimes.com/life-and-style/food-and-drink/a
  -crunchy-crumbly-oat-cookie-cures-all-ills-1.3531989
isgeschiedenis.nl/nieuws/recept-voor-oud-hollandse
  -pepernoten
it.julskitchen.com/dolci/biscotti/zuccherini-di-vernio
it.paperblog.com/biskuttini-tar-rahal-i-village
  -biscuits-maltesi-2130404/
jewishfoodsociety.org/recipes/boulou-orange-blossom
  -cookies-with-seeds-and-nuts
jonasim.wordpress.com/2014/12/10/siropskokur-syrup
  -cookies/
jpost.com/diaspora/jew-cookies-a-dutch-dessert
  -staple-are-getting-a-new-name-659874
kampvuurkok.nl/vlaardingse-ijzerkoekjes/
kawalingpinoyrecipe.com/bread_and_pastries/
  puto_seko.htm
khal.com/posts/bhawanibee1234/gnanakatha-sri
  -lankan-nanakatha-recipe-sri-lankan-sugar
  -cookies-cookies/
khalifabakers.pk/
kingarthurbaking.com/recipes/thong-muan-recipe
kisekiya2.wordpress.com/
kiwibaker.com/kruidnoten/
koekjesbakken.com/antwerpse-handjes.html
kompas.com/food/read/2021/04/13/093100175/
  resep-sagu-keju-lumer-di-mulut-kue-kering-klasik
  -untuk-jualan
koogikontor.ee/2015/02/johvikakreemiga
  -kondenspiimakupsised.html
kotanyi.com/en/recipe/eisenbahner-cookies/
kristinholt.com/archives/13991
kristinsoley.com/2017/12/26/halfmanar.html
krumkaker.wordpress.com/2020/12/23/
  bordstabelbakkels-norwegian-table-stacking
  -cookies/
kuhinjazaposlenezene.com/bakine-sapice/
laboiteny.com/blogs/recipes/persian-rice-cookies
  -nan-e-berenji
labsalliebe.com/en/shirini-keshmeshi-persian-raisin
  -cookies-for-norouz/
lacucinaitaliana.com/italian-food/how-to-cook/
  spooky-italian-fave-dei-morti-cookies-for-halloween
ladyspatula.com/recipes/anise-date-rings
latimes.com/recipe/boulou
lauralaurentiu.ro/retete-culinare/prajituri-torturi/
  biscuiti-spritati-de-casa-cu-unt-sau-untura-si
  -smantana-dulce.html
laurasbakery.nl/gevulde-koeken/
leidbeiningastod.is/uppskriftasafn/item/
  moemmukoekur
letsteacheurope-erasmus.site/calabrian-mostaccioli
  -the-secret-recipe-between-history-and-traditions/
lezzet.com.tr/yemek-tarifleri/tatli-tarifleri/
  meyveli-tatlilar/portakalli-kurabiye-324199
lifanjota.com/2022/12/halfmanar.html
lindaben.is/recipes/engifer-smakokur-fylltar
  -med-salt-karamellu-smjorkremi/
littlesunnykitchen.com/aniseed-biscuits/
livinganordiclife.com/post/sirupsnipper
lkcuisine.blogspot.com/
luberon.fr/tourisme/produits-terroir/actu
  +recette-du-croquant+186.html
luciapaula.com/quince-paste-thumbprint-cookies
  -argentinian-pepas/
madensverden.dk/pleskner-gammel-original-opskrift/
maizena.com.br/receitas/sequilhos-saudades.html
makan.ch/recipe/kuih-makmur-peanut-cookies/
mamasguiderecipes.com/2017/04/29/puto-seko/
mangiamagna.com/mostaccioli/
marblehead.org/sites/g/files/vyhlif4661/f/uploads/
  joe_frogger_cookies.pdf
mariliisilover.com/2011/10/majoneesikupsised/
marthastewart.com/1050361/ischlers
masterclass.com/articles/langues-de-chat-recipe
matprat.no/oppskrifter/tradisjon/bordstabelbakkels/
mealsbymavis.com/shuku-shuku-nigerian-coconut
  -macaroons/
medievalcookery.com/helewyse/biscotti.html
meikepeters.com/blog/ottijiet-maltese-tea-time
  -cookies-with-sesame-seeds-cloves-and-aniseed
melissas.com/blogs/dessert/soetkoekies-spice-cookies
mesdelicesbymyriam.com/boussou-la-tmessou
  -patisserie-algerienne/
miljuschka.nl/oud-hollandse-traditionele-pepernoten/
milkmaid.lk/en/sweet-treats/milkmaid-gnanakatha
mills.no/melange/oppskrift/tjukksnipp/
minjina-kuhinjica.com/desert/kolachi/orasnice
  -video/
mirchitales.com/nan-khatai-khalifa-style-cardamom
  -flavored-shortbread-biscuits/
mommyshomecooking.com/venezuelan-polvorosas
  -cookies/

mondomulia.com/2018/11/28/mostaccioli-biscuits/
moroccan-food.com/moroccan-krichlat.php
mountainguides.is/blog/festive-treats-of-iceland
mundodeportivo.com/uncomo/comida/receta/
  como-hacer-panellets-de-pinones-2922.html
mydanishkitchen.com/2014/11/17/bordstabler-
  norwegian-cookies/
mycolombianrecipes.com/panderos-colombian
  -yuca-starch-cookies/
myhappykitchen.nl/bakken/surinaamse
  -gommakoekjes/
myhungrytraveler.com/cuisines/african-cuisine/
  coconut-balls/
myportuguesekitchen.com/2015/04/orange-and
  -vanilla-biscoitos.html
myvintagecooking.com/classic-gingerbread-cookie
  -recipe-paraisten-piparkakut/
nami-nami.blogspot.com/2005/08/mayonnaise
  -cookies.html
nami-nami.ee/retsept/3715/recipe
  .php?q=detail&pID=515
nazarethboroughpa.com/geninfo_history.html
nefisyemektarifleri.com/nefis-portakalli-kurabiye
  -pastane-usulu/
newarab.com/features/delectable-eid-cookies-rooted
  -deeply-egyptian-culture
newengland.com/food/desserts/hermit-cookies/
newfoundland.ws/lassy-mogs-recipe/
newmexico.org/things-to-do/cuisine/recipes/
  biscochitos
newmexicomagazine.org/blog/post/new-mexico-state
  -cookie-bizcochitos-recipe/
nonnabox.com/authentic-italian-pizzelle-recipe/
nordicfoodliving.com/danish-brown-cookies
  -brunkager/
northwildkitchen.com/norwegian-berlinerkranser
norway-hei.com/goro.html
norwegianamerican.com/krumkaker-the-1000-year
  -old-cookie/
nosalty.hu/recept/nero-teasutemeny-aranylekvartol
npfamilyrecipes.com/pig-ear-cookie-recipe
  -banh-tai-heo/
npr.org/sections/thesalt/2017/07/06/535605352/
  this-soviet-era-cookie-is-filled-with-sweetness-
  amid-scarcity
nutsnsquirrels.wordpress.com/tag/kletskoppen/
nytimes.com/2021/12/13/world/asia/india-eggs
  -hindu-nationalism.html
nzhistory.govt.nz/media/photo/edmonds-cookbook
oanhskitchen.nl/bastogne-koeken/
olgainthekitchen.com/walnut-shaped-cookies/
olgasflavorfactory.com/recipes/favorites/
  russian-walnut-shaped-cookies-oreshki/
oliviascuisine.com/dulce-de-leche-sandwich-cookies/
oppskrift.dagbladet.no/oppskrift/snipper
orangeblossomwater.net/index.php/2010/11/24/
  bousou-la-tmssou/
orientalwebshop.nl/en/banh-tai-heo-pig-s-ear
  -vietnamese-cookies
ourcookbooks.com/recipe/3329891/icelandic-ginger
  -snaps-pepparkakor.html
overetengesproken.nl/jan-hagel-koekjes/
pakistaneats.com/recipes/zeera-biscuits-cumin
  -biscuits/
persianmama.com/ghorabieh/
perudelights.com/cocadas-coconut-macaroons
  -filled-with-manjarblanco-and-nutella/
peruenvideos.com/make-cocadas-recipe-sweet
  -old-lima/
phaidon.com/res/recipe-card-broas-de-mel-e
  -amendoa.pdf
picniconabroom.com/leckerli
pilipinasrecipes.com/arrowroot-cookie-uraro
  -recipe/
pinoyinoz.blogspot.com/2013/12/arrowroot-uraro
  -cookies.html
polishhousewife.com/kolaczki/
portugueserecipes.ca/recipe/1088/1/madeira-broas
  -de-mel-recipe
pressreader.com/uae/the-national-news/
  20210514/281938840801096
quatresaisonsaujardin.com/croquants-aux-amandes/
quericavida.com/recipes/venezuelan
  -almidoncitos/9f8bd05c-f3d1-4e65-a945
  -9085099d1212
rainbowcooking.co.nz/recipes/old-fashioned
  -south-african-spice-biscuits-soetkoekies
rasakama.wordpress.com/2015/05/19/
  gnyanakatha-sri-lankan-traditional-cookies/
rbth.com/russian-kitchen/326182-tula
  -pryanik-honey-bread
receitasdatiaceu.com/receita/bolinhos-de-gemas/

receitasdeculinaria.tv/receita-do-doce-de-gema/

receitasemenus.net/areias-de-cascais/

recepti.index.hr/recept/620-hurmasice
-tradicionalna-turska-slastica

receptidee.nl/recipe/kletskoppen/

recetasderechupete.com/almendrados-de-allariz
-postre-tradicional-gallego/10205/

recetasgratis.net/receta-de-besitos-de-coco-74246
.html

recetatipica.net/cuca-cookies/

recetavenezolana.com/polvorosas/

recipe.school/en/recipe/casadinho/

recipeland.com/recipe/v/homemade-sago-biscuits-51217

recipereminiscing.wordpress.com/easy-christmas
-cookies/

recipeswitholiveoil.com/mostaccioli-cookies/

reciprocalrecipes.com.au/neapolitan-mostaccioli/

resepi.my/resepi-biskut-arab-susu/

resepichenom.com/resepi/biskut-suji-arab/show

resepisenang.com/2019/03/resepi-biskut-gajus
-sedap-senang.html

resepkoki.id/resep/resep-kue-semprong/

retetelemihaelei.com/fursecuri-cu-stafide/

rezelkealoha.com/puto-seko-seco-recipe-with
-three-ingredients/

ricette.giallozafferano.it/Papassini-sardi.html

roamingtaste.com/marens-kornflexkokur
-icelandic-chocolate-cornflake-cookies/#tasty
-recipes-22942-jump-target

royale.nl/nl/actueel/item/17-speculaas-vs-speculoos

ruralea.com/broas-de-mel-da-madeira/

russianrecipebook.com/sochniki/

rutgerbakt.nl/koek-recepten/fryske-dumkes
-bakken-recept/

saboreiaavida.nestle.pt/cozinhar/receita/
broas-de-mel

saboresdenati.blogspot.com/2020/12/panderos
-pandeitos-polvorosas-navidad-en-Colombia.html

saltyginger.com/soetkoekies/

sasina-kuhinja.com/videorecepti/bozicne-skoljkice
-sa-pekmezom-od-sljiva

saveur.com/article/Recipes/Almond-Cream-Tartlets/

savoringitaly.com/cuccidati-sicilian-fig-cookies/

savoriurbane.com/cornulete-fragede-cu-gem
-sau-magiun/

savourous.com/recipe-view/ayigbe-glutenfree-cassava
-coconut-cookie/

savourydays.com/banh-quy-dua-hanh-nhan-almond
-coconut-cookies/

sbs.com.au/food/recipes/maltese-easter-biscuits
-figolli

scandikitchen.co.uk/koldskaal/

scattidigusto.it/ricette/papassini-ricetta-tradizionale
-del-dolce-della-sardegna/

scroll.in/article/811296/a-sri-lankan-eid-time-to
-connect-with-ones-spirituality-family-and-friends

senegalsoul.blogspot.com/2012/01/cinq-centimes
-cookies-senegal.html

senseandedibility.com/mantecaditos-almond
-butter-cookies/

seriouseats.com/dulce-de-leche-recipe

shesimmers.com/2009/04/kleeb-lamduan-thai
-shortbread-cookies

shokolaadine.blogspot.com/2013/12/
kondenspiimakupsised.html

sicilianicreativiincucina.it/le-rame-di-napoli-ricetta
-siciliana/?lang=en

simplelivingrecipes.com/pt/sequilhos-de-leite
-condensado/

sinfullyspicy.com/2022/06/21/eggless-tutti-frutti
-karachi-biscuits/

singaporeanmalaysianrecipes.com/kuih-makmur
-kuih-raya/

skandibaking.com/finsk-brod-danish-shortbread
-cookies/

slovakcooking.com/2010/recipes/decorated
-honey-cookies-medovniky/

slurrp.com/article/from-nankhatai-to-shrewsbury
-the-story-of-indian-biscuits-1646303792575

smithsonianmag.com/arts-culture/croissant
-really-french-180955130/

solipapar.wordpress.com/2017/12/12/paprenjaci
-croatian-christmas-pepper-cookies/

soulfood.nl/surinaamse-maizenakoekjes
-gomma-koekjes

sousou-kitchen.com/krichlat-achoura/

southernliving.com/gingersnap-cookies-6836010

southpacificengagement.com/2013/04/17/tea-cookies
-present-kleeb-lamduan-thai-style-cookies

spanishsabores.com/polvorones-recipe/

spicingyourlife.com/ischler-cookies-are-from
-austria/

spoonfulpassion.com/cheese-sago-cookies-sagu-keju/

steirische-spezialitaeten.at/rezepte/linzer-augen.html

stvarukusa.mondo.rs/Deserti/Ostalo/a19636/
Starinski-recept-za-ORASNICE-Sitni-kolacici
-od-oraha-koji-se-tope-u-ustima.html

suhkrusai.net/kupsised/kondenspiimakupsised/

sundaybaker.co/breskvice-croatian-peach-cookies/

sustainmycookinghabit.com/traditional-croatian
-skoljkice-shell-cookies/

swedishspoon.com/dreams/

sweetysalado.com/en/2018/04/galletas-cucas
-colombian-gingerbread/

swissmilk.ch/de/rezepte-kochideen/rezepte/
SM2017_DIVE_14/chraebeli/

tabletmag.com/recipes/bow-tie-kichel

tarladalal.com/atta-biscuits-eggless-whole
-wheat-biscuit-42266r

tasteofmaroc.com/krichlate-recipe/

tasteofnusa.com/nastar/

tastingtable.com/1245022/ricciarelli-tuscan
-almond-cookies-recipe/

teajourney.pub/recipe/middle-eastern-kahk/

teoskitchen.ro/2015/10/cornulete-cu-gem.html

thaicuisinerecipe.blogspot.com/2007/03/
khanom-phing.html

thebalkanhostess.com/breskvice-peach-cookies/

thebigsweettooth.com/ghorayeba

thecookiedoughdiaries.com/biscoito-de-maizena/

thecroatiankitchen.com/2019/12/05/croatian
-honey-cookies-medenjaci/

theczechguidetocooking.wordpress.com/2015/12/06/
honey-gingerbread-cookies-pernicky/

thedomesticatedfeminist.wordpress.com/2012/12/24/
christmas-cookies-paprenjaci-and-medenjaci/

theduchezkitchen.com/soetkoekies-recipe/

thedutchtable.com/2013/01/friese-dumkes.html

theenglishkitchen.co/2021/02/english-melting
-moments.html

theitalianbkr.com/canestrelli-biscuits/

thejc.com/lifestyle/recipes/recipe-hadji-bada-1.68476

thejuggernaut.com/eggetarianism-india-eggs
-vegetarianism#

thekitchenwitchblog.com/2017/01/01/icelandic
-lakkris-toppar/

thelittleepicurean.com/2021/09/filipino-polvoron
.html

thelocalpalate.com/recipes/traditional-moravian
-cookies/

thematbakh.com/date-cookies-recipe-kaak
-asawer/#recipe

themondaybox.com/bosnian-butter-cookies-sape/

themoscowtimes.com/2020/12/11/people-who
-ordered-nemtsov-murder-found-putin-says
-a72337

thepetitecook.com/mostaccioli-cookies/

thequirinokitchen.com/pan-de-san-nicolas-filipino
-heritage-cookie-that-heals/

thesimple-sweetlife.com/norwegian-almond-cookies
-kransekakestenger/

thesouthafrican.com/lifestyle/food/recipes/
old-fashioned-soetkoekies-cookies-like-gran
-used-to-make/

thespruceeats.com/gingerbread-cookies-czech
-pernik-na-figurky-1135701

thesweetbalance.net/recipes/holiday-season/
traditional-maltese-kwarezimal/

thisismadeiraisland.com/honey-biscuits/

timesofindia.indiatimes.com/life-style/food-news/
from-nankhatai-to-punes-shrewsbury-cookies
-from-across-india-that-are-a-worth-try/
photostory/92704222.cms?picid=92704232

timesofisrael.com/israeli-chefs-take-hamantaschen
-to-a-whole-new-level/

timesofoman.com/article/52939-oman-dining-bake
-your-own-cookies

tine.no/oppskrifter/kaker/vafler-og-smakaker/
bordstabel-bordstabelbakkels

tishineh.com/touritem/323/Qurabiya-(-Ghorabiye-)

travelpotpourri.net/2016/12/10/
gingerbread-lebkuchen-pfefferkuchen-medovniky/

tresbohemes.com/2015/12/12-days-of-christmas
-cookies-day-one/

true-north-kitchen.com/krumkake/

twosisterslivinglife.com/eisenbahner-railroad
-cookies-a-folksy-austrian-christmas-cookie-recipe/

unicornsinthekitchen.com/persian-coconut-cookies
-shrini-nargili/

uniqop.com/ghorabiye-recipe/

untoldrecipesbynosheen.com/khalifa-nankhatai
-pakistani-cardamom-shortbread-cookies/

varecha.pravda.sk/diskusie/medovniky-alebo
-perniky-/5557-forum.html

vatel.pt/en/raivas-portuguese-cinnamon-cookies/

veggiedesserts.com/icelandic-pepper-cookies
-piparkokur/

vikendovepeceni.cz/2022/12/masarykovo-cukrovi/

visitsweden.com/what-to-do/food-drink/recipes/
chokladsnittar-chocolate-slices-cookie-recipe/

visittuscany.com/en/recipes/befanini/

washingtonpost.com/recipes/tunisian-bulo/

wbur.org/radioboston/2022/11/22/marblehead
-molasses-joe-froggger-cookie-north-shore-past

weekendbakery.com/posts/my-favourite-dutch
-cookies/

whatscookingamerica.net/cookie/biscoitos-de
-maizena.htm

whatson.is/whats-ons-christmas-recipes/

whattocooktoday.com/chinese-new-year-kue-putri
-salju-snow-white-cookies.html

whenfetametolive.com/un-kurabiye-turkish-flour
-cookies/

willflyforfood.net/food-in-egypt/

womensweeklyfood.com.au/recipes/kueh-makmur
-14362

wongnai.com/recipes/khanom-kleeb-lamduan-thai
-shortbread-cookies

worldrecipes.eu/lt/traskus-aviziniai-sausainiai-su
-aguonomis-ir-soda

yourfriendinreykjavik.com/icelandic-gingersnaps
-piparkokur/

youtube.com/watch?v=3FrDNL2rT-I

youtube.com/watch?v=4Z68XPfiHV8

youtube.com/watch?v=6bdIXTb4MX0

youtube.com/watch?v=bwx-J3MUx30

youtube.com/watch?v=CVs0HbqGvn0

youtube.com/watch?v=D93OG-uKz18

youtube.com/watch?v=fm0dvvdmiJo

youtube.com/watch?v=gjbMI5J1nMo

youtube.com/watch?v=HWIQHHBIyes

youtube.com/watch?v=IBoZZFC8iKk

youtube.com/watch?v=JEI5vt43bxU

youtube.com/watch?v=-kEgn0pYxXk

youtube.com/watch?v=Ovksuh16c0E

youtube.com/watch?v=oZilHI-ZFFA

youtube.com/watch?v=pF307z_8_PA

youtube.com/watch?v=TAmHBOoiAbc

youtube.com/watch?v=Uuqp5m_-H2c

youtube.com/watch?v=Uw--aTbUUUU

youtube.com/watch?v=v2CHEh-Ahaw

youtube.com/watch?v=VVXs5HW5srw

youtube.com/watch?v=vxt9gR8FJ9g

youtube.com/watch?v=xno21eaZT_E

youtube.com/watch?v=Y6Wl1ZnZokU

youtube.com/watch?v=YpQyvEdiUK4

yumlyfood.com/galletas-cucas

yummy-iceland.blogspot.com/2016/01/einfaldar
-piparkokur.html

yummy.ph/news-trends/sannikulas-cookie
-spampanga-aching-lillian-borromeo
-a00261-20190730-lfrm

zawadee.com/blogs/blog/a-taste-of-africa-shuku
-shuku-nigerian-coconut-balls

zserbo.com/breads-buns-biscuits/ischler-cookies
-as-we-like-it-in-hungary/

zsuzsaisinthekitchen.blogspot.com/2012/06/
nero-cookies-nero-teasutemeny.html

Index

Acknowledgments

Putting a book of this size together was quite the undertaking, but the hours, days, weeks, and months it allowed me to hang out in the library, endlessly picking books and culling through probably thousands of recipes was heaven for this research nerd.

Thank you to Emily Takoudes for giving me the opportunity to write such an exciting book on a subject I've unwittingly devoted most of my career to. Working with you and the team at Phaidon on this book has been nothing short of ideal. It's been refreshing and relaxing to work with such talented and eager creatives.

My unending gratitude to Project Editor Clare Churly who made the whole process of fine-tuning the book a dream come true. Our long-distance chats from Los Angeles to London put me at ease and were always a refreshing respite in the months of reading text and approving images. Thank you again so much for all your hard work and patient dedication in working with me.

Writing a book of this size is no small feat, but testing all the recipes is even bigger. My eternal gratitude to all the testers who happily provided me with valuable feedback and spent their own money on ingredients and their own personal time in making these cookies to be sure they work out well for all of you readers. Aaron Neishlos, Abby Zeiser, Alexis Rorabaugh, Alisson Xavier, Aliza Ali, Allyson Barkhurst, Amanda Berrill, Amy Lehpamer, Andrea Feldmar, Angela Abrantes Fischer, Anjean Vanden Bosch, Ariste Sallas-Brookwell, Beau Eder, Beth Carter, Beth Macinko, Bethany Lynum Ahrens, Betsy Beros, Brendan Sanchez, Camila Loret Demolar, Claire Wazana Meredith, Clara Parkes, Daniela Bustamante, Daniela Gorny, Danielle Pathmanathan, Deborah Benaim, Deirdre Synan, Doris Petersen, Elizabeth Joya, Elizabeth King, Ellen Gray, Emily Adsit, Emily Brandon, Emily Reid, Eric Chow, Evan Ruiz, Farideh Sadeghin, Federico Villalobos, Georgia Cowan, Georgia Geen, Grant Torre, Gwen Krosnick, Haroon Adalat, Heather Platt, Jack Van Amburg, Jack Volpi, Jackie Finch, Jade Cuevas, Jake Stavis, James Turnbull, Jamie Gancman, Jana Fay Ragsdale, Janet McKracken, Janine Hills, Jared McKenzie, Jennifer Gjurashaj, Jessica Chan, Jessica Hitt, Jessica Maxwell, Jessica & Marilla Keck, Jill Michnick, Joey Sammut, Jonathan Parks-Ramage, Jordan Abrams, J.T. Friedman, Justin Castells, Justin Hetzel, Karen Tremewan Carbone, Katharine Torrisi, Kathryn DeVinney, Katie Collins, Keisha Davis, Kelcie Pegher, Kelsey Cosby, Kento Saisho, Kevin Bender, Kris Roberts, Kristina McDavid, Lainey Manos, Landon Miller, Laura Nelson, Laura Ryan, Lauren Cona, Lauren Richards, Liliana, Vera, and Eleanor Ontiveros, Linda Hosmer Spain, Lindsay Popperson, Lisa Futterman, Liz Levin, Liz Sheldon, Lizzie Upton, Lovejoy, Lukas Volger, Madison Alig, Marcella Schneiderman, Maria Romano, Mary Kate Metivier, Matthew Piercy, Meaghan Sands, Megan Cornell Rega, Melissa Baker, Melissa Gaman, Michelle Long, Mick Côté, Miriam Mintz, Mitchell Fraser, M. Moore, Mollie Hudson, Molly Georgakis, Molly Weisman, Monica Baisch, Nicky Berger, Nidia Barcia, Paige David, Phebe Gibson, Philip Dwelle, Pippa Spindel, Rachel Jrade, Rachel Zarrell, Rodney Collins, Romina Ruiz, Ron Boehmer, Rosie Leonetti, Roxanne Miller, Ruby Sniderman, Ryan Willison, Sameer Khan, Sam Fischman, Sara Fay, Sarah Carter, Sarah Mergeanian, Scott Andreas, Scott Williams, Shelby Castells, Shira Toister, Shivani Rustagi, Simone Hudson, Sophie Zuckerman, Steve Viksjo, Steven Soundara, Suju Vijayan, Suzannah Longman, Sydney and LeAnn Chaparro, Sylara Marie, Taneka Rabas, Tara Anderson, Tizoc Brenes, Tom Natan, Tori Noriega, Tori Partridge, Trinh Nguyen, Trish Connelly, Vilma C., Zoe Komarin, and Zoe Maya—thank you!

And last but not least, my partner J. who put up with many of my so-called "hermit" days where I holed up in my library cave late into the night and on weekends to get work done while I was in a particular groove. You are my favorite recipe taster, and I value your opinion on these cookies and everything else I make the most. You get all the marbled Snickerdoodles for life. I love you always.

Recipe Notes

Sugar is white US granulated sugar (UK caster sugar), unless otherwise specified.

Turbinado sugar is sold as demerara sugar in the UK; just note that in the US demerara is a darker sugar and is not the same as the UK demerara.

Eggs are US size large (UK size medium) unless otherwise specified.

Butter is unsalted US butter, which is 80% butterfat, unless specified as European-style butter.

Nuts are whole, shelled, and raw unless otherwise specified.

Seeds are whole, hulled, and raw unless otherwise specified.

Individual fruits, such as apples, are assumed to be medium, unless otherwise specified, and should be peeled and/or washed unless otherwise specified.

Where neutral oil is specified, use vegetable, canola (rapeseed), grapeseed, sunflower, or corn oil.

Metric, imperial, and cup measurements are used in this book. Follow one set of measurements throughout, not a mixture, as they are not interchangeable.

All tablespoon and teaspoon measurements given are level, not heaping, unless otherwise specified. 1 teaspoon = 5 ml; 1 tablespoon = 15 ml. Australian standard tablespoons are 20 ml, so Australian readers are advised to use 3 teaspoons in place of 1 tablespoon when measuring small quantities.

When no quantity is specified for oils for deep-frying, use the depth of oil specified in the recipe to determine how much you will need. As a general guideline, to get a depth of 1 inch (2.5 cm) of oil in a 10-inch (25 cm) pot you will need 4 cups (32 fl oz/950 ml).

When deep-frying, heat the oil to the temperature specified, or until a cube of bread browns in 30 seconds.

Cooking and preparation times are for guidance only. If using a convection (fan) oven, follow the manufacturer's instructions concerning oven temperatures.

Unless otherwise specified, the position of the oven rack is in the center of the oven.

Batch cooking: When you are baking multiple batches of cookies, be sure that the baking sheets are cooled before you use them again. And reline with fresh parchment paper.

When sterilizing jars for preserves, wash the jars in clean, hot water and rinse thoroughly. Preheat the oven to 275°F (140°C/Gas Mark 1). Place the jars on a baking sheet and place in the oven to dry.

Exercise a high level of caution when following recipes involving any potentially hazardous activity including the use of high temperatures and open flames and when deep-frying. In particular, when deep-frying, add food carefully to avoid splashing, wear long sleeves, and never leave the pan unattended.

Phaidon Press Limited
2 Cooperage Yard
London E15 2QR

Phaidon Press Inc.
111 Broadway
New York, NY 10006

phaidon.com

First published 2024
© 2024 Phaidon Press Limited

ISBN 978 1 83866 886 0

A CIP catalogue record for this book is
available from the British Library and the
Library of Congress.

Commissioning Editor: Emily Takoudes
Project Editor: Clare Churly
Senior Production Controller: Andie Trainer
Cover Design: Julia Hasting
Interior Design: Hans Stofregen
Artworking: Cantina

Photography: Simon Bajada

Printed in China

Publisher's Acknowledgments
Phaidon would like to thank Vanessa Bird,
Julia Hasting, João Mota, Jo Murray, Kate Slate,
Ellie Smith, Tracey Smith, Caroline Stearns,
and Phoebe Stephenson.

About the Author

Ben Mims is a cookbook author, food writer and editor, and radio and video host. He has been nominated for a James Beard award.

Born in Mississippi, he was raised there with his mother, grandmother, and aunts who were expert bakers and always surrounded him with tins of all sorts of cookies. This love of baking led him to go to culinary school at the French Culinary Institute in New York City after graduating college. He lived in San Francisco as a pastry chef and in New York as a food editor at *Food & Wine* and *Saveur*, test kitchen director at *Lucky Peach*, and recipe developer at *Food Network Magazine* and Buzzfeed's Tasty, where he developed original recipes for three of their cookbooks. In Los Angeles, he was the cooking columnist for the *Los Angeles Times*.

His first cookbook was *Sweet & Southern: Classic Desserts with a Twist* (2014), followed by the *Short Stacks edition Coconut* (2017), and *Air Fry Every Day* (2018).

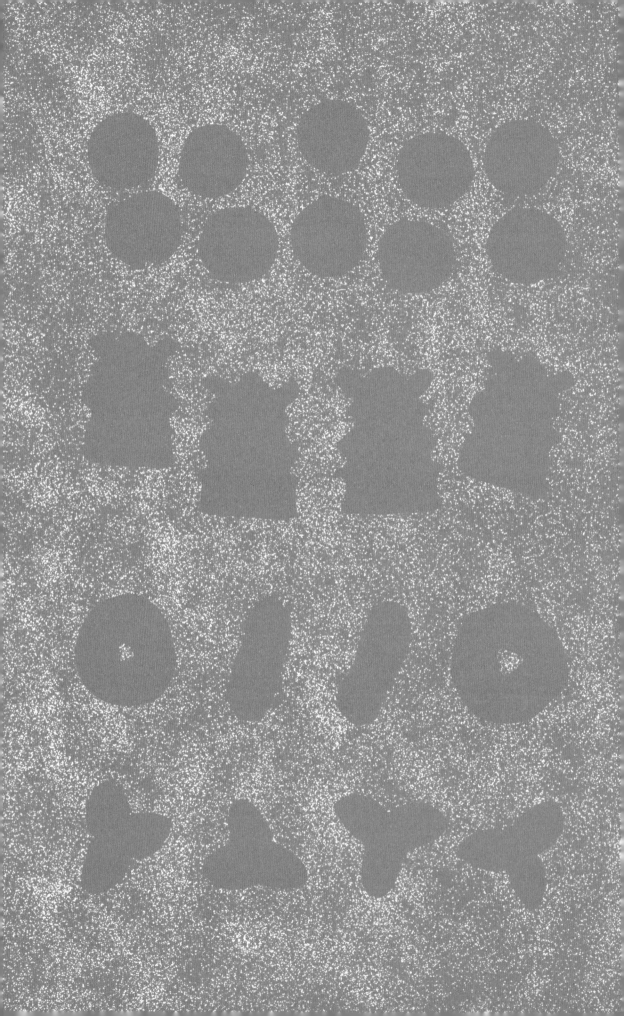